*f*P

Also by Robert A. Slayton

Back of the Yards: The Making of a Local Democracy

*New Homeless and Old: Community and the
Skid Row Hotel* (with Charles Hoch)

EMPIRE STATESMAN

The Rise and Redemption of
AL SMITH

Robert A. Slayton

The Free Press

NEW YORK   LONDON   TORONTO   SYDNEY   SINGAPORE

*f*P
The Free Press
A Division of Simon & Schuster, Inc.
1230 Avenue of the Americas
New York, NY 10020

Designed by Brady McNamara
Manufactured in the United States of America

10 9 8 7 6 5 4 3 2 1

Library of Congress Cataloging-in-Publication Data
Slayton, Robert A.
Empire statesman : the rise and redemption of Al Smith / Robert A. Slayton.
p. cm
Includes bibliographical references (p.) and index.
1. Smith, Alfred Emanuel, 1873–1944.   2. Presidential candidates—United
States—Biography.   3. Governors–New York (State)—Biography.   4. United
States—Politics and government—1901–1953.   5. Presidents—United
States—Election—1928.   6. New York (State)—Politics and government—1865–1950.
7. Irish Americans—United States–Biography   8. Catholics—United States—Biography.
I. Title.
E748.S63 S57 2001   974.7´04´092—dc21
[B]   00-060011
ISBN 0-684-86302-2

For Rita LaVerde Slayton

My Companion Through Life, My Partner, My Love

Contents

PART III: 1928

PART IV: FINALE

Oklahoma City, September 20, 1928

ON THE NIGHT of September 19, 1928, Al Smith's train crossed the Oklahoma state line, and they burned crosses in the fields.

Smith was in the middle of a campaign to win the presidency of what he considered to be the greatest country in the world. He based his appeal on the principle, as he had so often put it, that what mattered was "the record." He had been elected governor of New York an unprecedented four times, and then transformed the government of the nation's largest industrial state. Smith had expected to discuss his positions on such matters as health and welfare, education and housing.

But that did not happen. The public focused instead on the fact that he was the first Roman Catholic nominee of a major political party, that he grew up as a second-generation Irish immigrant in the tenement districts of New York City. In every fiber of his being, Al Smith personified the new American, and he had always defended the people who shared that mantle. This year, however, he was not looking for entry into a country club or a corporation, seeking instead the biggest prize of all: a title and position that had always been reserved for Protestants of the old stock.

Thus, Smith presented an unprecedented challenge to the nation; as a result he got drowned in a sea of hate, facing the dirtiest campaign in American presidential history. Parents were told that if a Catholic was elected, all Protestant marriages would be annulled, immediately rendering their children illegitimate. In Daytona Beach, Florida, the school board agreed to give each child a card to bring home to their parents. It read: "We must prevent the election of Alfred E. Smith to the Presidency. If he is chosen President, you will not be allowed to have or read a Bible." Pictures of the construction of the Lincoln Tunnel were passed out around the country, with captions explaining that it was a secret passageway to bring the pope from Rome to Washington. After Smith had won the Democratic nomination, William Lloyd Clark, affiliated with the Klan publication *Railsplitter,* mailed out thousands of postcards reading, "We now face the darkest hour in American history. In a convention ruled by political Romanism [the] anti-Christ has won." Widely circulated cartoons showed Smith on his knees, kissing the ring of a papal delegate, captioned " . . . And he asks the American people to elect him president."[1]

Bigots attacked Smith from every direction. The governor had emerged as the leading opponent of prohibition in American politics, so naturally they claimed that he was a drunk. Southerners called his thick, gravely voice "whiskey breath," proclaiming that he must have gotten it from drinking too much. People claimed that they had seen Smith intoxicated, that they knew, for example, a lady who had danced with him at a ball "when he was so heavily under the influence of liquor that she had to hold him up to keep him from falling." One man wrote to John W. Davis, the 1924 Democratic nominee, that in his town, "there are just two places of business . . . that have Mr. Smith's pictures in their show windows. And both are POOL ROOMS and known as BOOT LEGGERS HEADQUARTERS." Snobs and gossips even attacked Smith's wife, Katie, claiming she was too uncouth to be first lady.[2]

Above all, they denigrated Al's people—the immigrant, urban citizens that he had been raised among and whom he represented. M. K. Troxell wrote to the *Baltimore Sun* on September 18, 1928, that "very little is being said about his [Smith's] proposal to abolish the quota restrictions from the immigration law, but all intelligent people know that such a policy would mean unloosing on us a horde of immigrants from such races as have already been proved hardest to assimilate. It is plain that the object of this is to increase the foreign vote in the cities, which can be depended on to vote for liquor and be easily controlled by machines." William Allen White, the prominent Kansas newspaper editor, argued that "the whole Puritan civilization which has built a sturdy, orderly nation is threatened by Smith"; the New York governor was "a representative of the saloon, prostitution and gambling," of "a group who have back of them only physical appetite and no regard for law or reform." Bishop Edwin Mouzon of the Methodist church wrote in *Christian Advocate* that "the nomination of Smith . . . signalized the uprise of the unassimilated elements in our great cities against the ideals of our American fathers." The conclusion, the bishop felt, was simple: "Smith himself is utterly un-American."[3]

By late September 1928, in Oklahoma, Al Smith had had enough. The Ku Klux Klan had been extremely active there, with statewide membership estimated as high as one hundred thousand, the fifth highest in the nation, while the women did even better: their Klan affiliate was the largest in the country. The Grand Dragon of the state, N. Clay Jewett, was vice president of the University of Oklahoma, and as Kenneth Jackson, a leading historian of the urban Klan observed, "in Oklahoma City . . . the county attorney, a district judge, the mayor, and the sheriff, were among those with sheets in their closets."[4]

And this was no sewing club. Oklahoma City Klan No. 1 had a "whipping squad" to "take care of . . . these little matters in our neighborhood." In Tulsa, three masked men pulled John Smitherman, who had the double penalty of being black and successful, out of his home and beat him with a pistol when he tried to resist. Driven to a hillside, he faced a dozen men who accused him of registering Negroes to vote in the Democratic primary, and of being discourteous to a white woman. It was not clear which of the charges was worse, but the punishment was severe: they flailed him with a blacksnake whip, used a pocket knife to cut off his ear, and then tried to make him eat the body part while they slammed his ravaged back with the butt of the whip. He was left with a warning to leave town; demonstrating shocking courage, he stayed.[5]

Thus, opposition to Smith was widespread in Oklahoma, normally part of the solid Democratic South. Former senator Robert Owen declared that he would not support a "Tammany candidate" and bolted the party. The leading papers in the capital city chose not to endorse a candidate that year, but took a swipe at Smith anyway; their editorials read, "Principle, not party, is the important factor in the presidential campaign in 1928. . . . The *Daily Oklahoman* and the *Oklahoma City Times* will not join the Republican Party, but neither are they going to join a liquor movement."[6]

That was from the political establishment; others were even less reticent. Wade Loofbourrow wrote James Tolbert, head of the state's Smith for President Club, "I have been surprised to learn what a great number of Protestants and especially Masons are against Smith because of his religion." Dr. Mordecai Ham, pastor of the largest Baptist congregation in Oklahoma City, preached, "If you vote for Al Smith you're voting against Christ and you'll all be damned." A young woman in the pews, speaking in the other voice of Oklahoma, rose and said, "Hard on me, Dr. Ham; I came here to hear the gospel preached and I'm afraid I'll have to go to another church, perhaps to a Catholic church."[7]

Smith knew about all this from a variety of sources, and it bothered him deeply. In March, Belle Moskowitz, Smith's head of publicity and long-time confidante, sent James Tolbert a private memo listing her boss's appointments as governor that showed how many Protestants he had placed in high office. Any charges of favoring Catholics, she told him, were "part of the propaganda which has come to us from every part of the country. It is part of the established method of the Anti-Saloon League and the Ku Klux Klan . . . to raise religious prejudices to prevent the governor's nomination."[8]

Smith's reactions are particularly evident in the margins of a letter he had seen on the way to Oklahoma City. This was a cliché-ridden appeal for the governor's defeat from the Grand Dragon of the Arkansas chapter of the Klan to one of his state's delegates to the Democratic National Convention. In the right-hand margins of his copy, Smith scribbled brief versions of the ideals he believed in, like "Spirit of America" and, as a good Democrat, "Spirit of Jefferson." Around them, using the thick-pointed pencil he preferred, he wrote out criticisms of the Klan: "ignorant of history and traditions" and "breeding hatred." At the bottom, finally, there were two entries: "Our Divine Lord" and "No Greater Mockery = Burning †"[9]

Then, as Smith's train churned over the prairie, crossing from Kansas into the Sooner State at Enid, he saw the burning cross. At first, the candidate tried to laugh it off; turning to his oldest and most trusted adviser, Joseph Proskauer, a Jew, he asked, "Joe, how did they know you were on this train?"[10]

But inside he was livid. Upon reaching Oklahoma City, he spent most of the day rewriting the speech he would give that evening. Years later, in his autobiography, Smith explained, "I felt deep in my heart that I would be a coward and probably unfit for the presidency if I were to permit it [the bigotry] to go further unchallenged."[11]

By nightfall, the whole city and beyond had focused on Al Smith's upcoming speech. Railroads had offered special excursion fares so that people could come to see him from all over the region, families traveling from as far away as Texas and Arkansas. Tickets to the Stockyards Coliseum were small cardboard rectangles featuring the usual images and symbols: a drawing of the candidate, an American eagle in the background, and a bespangled Shield of the Republic. Twenty-five thousand had been printed, and by midafternoon there were few to be had.[12]

By seven o'clock the place was packed. Every seat was taken, and fights broke out for the rights to standing room. There were thirty thousand inside the coliseum itself, with another three thousand people in a nearby park, listening to huge loudspeakers. Beyond that, thirty-five radio stations, part of the National Broadcasting System, were ready to transmit Smith's remarks to millions more across the country.[13]

As the starting time of 7:30 P.M. came and went, the crowd entertained itself by cheering, waving hats and handkerchiefs and banners (there seemed to be a delegation from every county in Oklahoma, and plenty from neighboring states as well), and by singing "The Sidewalks of New York," Al's theme song. Finally, at 8:20 Scott Ferris, a former congressman, called the meeting to order, though Smith had still not arrived. Ferris introduced Governor Henry Johnston of Oklahoma, who began his speech of welcome. Then, at 8:30 P.M., just as Johnston bellowed "Smith is no ordinary man . . .," the candidate arrived, coming in from stage left, waving his brown derby to the crowd in broad strokes. A standing ovation lasted several minutes as Smith stood at the podium, feeling the crowd's roar roll over him, while he smiled and stretched out the famous chapeau in recognition and thanks. Dressed in a dark suit without vest (the coliseum was broiling), Smith adjusted the microphone and began.

He opened with the usual greetings and recognition of dignitaries, referring to the state as "Oklahomer" to a sprinkling of laughter. Soon Smith got down to business, telling the audience that he would discuss matters in an "open, frank way," that tonight he would "drag out into the open what has been whispered to you."[14]

Smith began mildly, with an attack on the turncoat Senator Owen. He then spent quite a while describing his record—what he had done to make New York State a better place to live in and how he had reformed the government there. He talked about the kind of charges made against him and rebutted them, telling, for example, how they always claimed he appointed only Catholics, citing instead the vast numbers of Protestants and Jews he had placed in high office.

But when he got to Tammany, to the argument that he would introduce machine politics to the White House, his mood changed. He had faced these charges before, he said, and as a result he knew "that the cry of Tammany Hall is nothing more or less than a red herring." Before he had ignored this problem, but now "it has grown to such a proportion that [it] compels me to let the country know that . . . I know what's behind it." Simply put, "It's nothing more or less than my religion."

Back in New York, Smith's aides were petrified. There had been word that there might be stink bombs in the auditorium, or far worse. Herbert Lehman, Smith's finance chairman, recalled that he had not been informed of the change in speeches, and was shocked at what was now being discussed. Although the *New York Times* reported a boisterous but generous audience in Oklahoma City, Anne Smith Cadigan, Smith's granddaughter, remembered her mother telling her about what it was like to listen that night on the radio, about the "cat calls, booing. . . . My mother said it was a mean-spirited crowd." Over at her uncle's house, Arthur Smith (the governor's second oldest boy) and his wife Anne also stayed by the radio, worried, as their son later described it, because "they expected a bullet, they expected to hear a gun go off."

Al Smith explained his objective that night: bigotry "is dangerous for the future life of the Republic, and the best way to kill anything un-American is to drag it out into the open, because anything un-American cannot live in the sunlight." He began to speak about the letter he had read from the Arkansas Grand Dragon, telling his audience how the Klansman had asked a delegate not to vote for him "on the grounds of upholding American ideals and institutions as established by our forefathers." He questioned how "any man or any group . . . gathered together in what they call the K.K.K., that professes to be 100 per cent American," could "forget the great principle that Jefferson stood for, the equality of man." He reminded them "that our forefathers in their wisdom, foreseeing probably such a sight as we look at today, wrote into the fundamental law of the country that at no time was religion to be regarded as qualification for office."

Smith was reaching a crescendo now. His voice went down several octaves, the tone solemn. People cried openly as he asked them all to "think of a man breathing the spirit of hatred against millions of his fellow citizens, proclaiming himself to be an American." This was ridiculous, it was immoral, and it violated everything the country stood for. Using language his audience would understand, Smith declared in ringing words, "There is no greater mockery in this world today than the burning of the Cross . . . by these people who are spreading this propaganda . . . while the Christ that they are supposed to adore, love and venerate . . . taught the holy, sacred writ of brotherly love." Referring to the Grand Dragon, Al concluded, "So much for him."

Smith's closing was potent: "Let me make myself perfectly clear. I do not want any Catholic to vote for me . . . because I am a Catholic." "If any Catholic," he explained, "believes that the welfare, the well-being, the prosperity . . . of the United States is best conserved and best promoted by Mr. Hoover, let him vote for Mr. Hoover."

"But, on the other hand," Al Smith continued, "I have the right to say that any citizen of this country that believes I can promote its welfare, that I am capable of steering the ship of state safely through the next four years, and votes against me because of my religion, he is not a real, pure, genuine American." To conclude, he made a simple request: "Let us debate it on the level . . . bring it out in the open, have the record consulted and the platforms scrutinized." If that happened, come what may in November, he would be satisfied with the result.

In the end, there remained a great deal of doubt about whether or not the speech accomplished very much. People of goodwill argue that the best way to kill bigotry is to treat it as they did bacteria in the old days: expose it to the light of the sun. But Al Smith that year faced the first truly great hate campaign in modern American history, a milestone no one could be proud of. One speech could never turn a tidal wave of slander and ignorance, and Smith would suffer a crushing defeat on Election Day.

But that misses the point. In Oklahoma City Al Smith's destiny caught up with him. His words there, his ideas, are what made him an important part of

American history. Although he enjoyed a long career, with many ups and downs on the public stage, his greatest contribution was his attempt to create a more democratic American society. America in the twenties was a nation torn apart, split between an older, rural society and the modern, urban age. In a period of intolerance and ignorance, marked by the Ku Klux Klan and the Scopes trial, no other politician at this high a level did more to demand that the new generation of immigrants be included as Americans. Today this is called "pluralism," and it is a standard part of our credo. This victory came about in large part because Al Smith, more than any other national politician of his day, bucked the conflicts of the time and defended the idea of an inclusionary society.

PART I

COMING OF AGE

Chapter 1

The Sidewalks of New York

LIKE ALL GOOD New York stories, this one begins with a neighborhood. For Al Smith was part and parcel of one small piece of New York City, a world that shaped him, providing values and viewpoints that guided him throughout his life.

When Al Smith entered this world on December 30, 1873, he joined a booming metropolis. New York City (at that time just Manhattan and the Bronx) had a population of 942,292, according to the 1870 census, with another 396,000 next door in Brooklyn. Forty-four percent of the residents had been born in foreign places, and 83 percent were first- or second-generation immigrants.[1]

This mosaic was made up of hundreds of local tiles. Al's was the old Fourth Ward district, running roughly from Canal Street and Old Broadway (now East Broadway) on the north, to Park Row on the west, down to Chambers Street in the south, with the East River forming the eastern edge. There were 23,748 people in the ward, of whom 13,292 (or more than half) were foreign born. In all likelihood, both of these figures represented undercounts, given most immigrants' fear of national authorities carried over from the old country, fears often reinforced by the inspectors on Ellis Island.[2]

The Fourth Ward became the stuff of legends, in part because it was such an archetypical urban district for the poor and the newcomer; conditions there symbolized the rest of the city. In 1867 city officials reported that there were 500 tenements in the ward, the majority of them—300—in "bad sanitary condition," 150 of which had no sewer facilities whatsoever. Over seven families lived in each of these low, small buildings, with an average of 35 persons per structure, fourth highest of the city's twenty-two wards. Another 346 people in the ward lived in cellars; Stephen Crane, in his "Bowery Tales," told what it was like to enter "a dark region where, from a careening building, a dozen gruesome doorways gave up loads of babies to the streets and the gutter. . . . Long streamers of

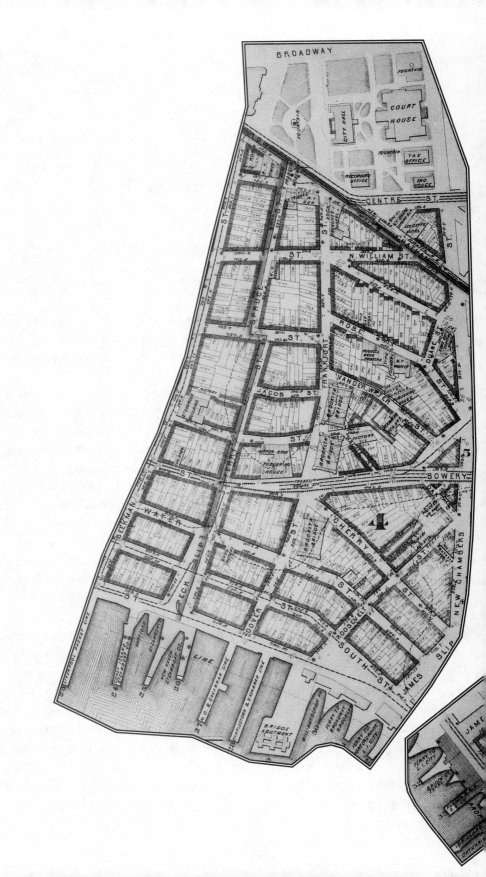

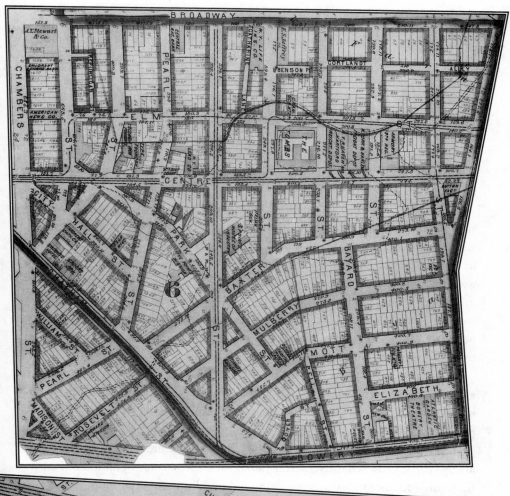

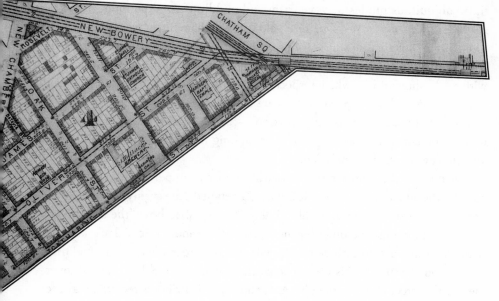

garments fluttered from fire-escapes. . . . Formidable women, with uncombed hair and disordered dress, gossiped while leaning on railings, or screamed in frantic quarrels. . . . The building quivered and creaked from the weight of humanity stamping about in its bowels." As recently as the early twentieth century, Al Smith claimed in his memoirs, there was a section in his district called the Lung Block, because so many people there died from tuberculosis. Helen Graff, an aged parishioner who attended St. James Church with the future governor, could remember tenements with toilets out in the hallways, buildings with no hot water, no electricity.[3]

The center of the district was Chatham Square, into which flowed, altogether, six different streets. Its two main thoroughfares, however, were the Bowery and Chatham Street. Of course, by then, "Bowery," from the Dutch word *bouwerji*, or "farm," had become an ironic misnomer. In the 1870s any hint of vegetation was gone, and it had become a major commercial boulevard, famous for creating the first urban subculture of the Bowery B'hoys and their G'hals. The B'hoys, wearing long-sleeved jackets, slicked-back hair, parading around with a pronounced rolling strut to their walk, were nativist toughs who gave the city a distinctive accent and a strong attitude it has never lost.

The avenue's southern neighbor was Chatham Street, which Alvin Harlow, author of the travelogue *Old Bowery Days,* claimed "for dirt, tawdriness, cheating, swindling, and thievery . . . was far worse" than the Bowery. *Harper's Magazine* described Chatham as "a street of varying width, irregular direction, and no great length, destitute of all pretensions to beauty, architectural or otherwise, always dirty, crowded, busy." And James McCabe, author of another one of those ubiquitous guides to voyeurism and middle-class slumming, the 1872 *Lights and Shadows of New York Life,* said that Chatham Street was "narrow and dirty," its inhabitants "low class foreigners." "Near the lower end," he reported, "are one or two good restaurants . . . but the remainder of the street is taken up with establishments into which respectable buyers do not care to venture. Cheap lodging houses abound, pawnbrokers are numerous, several fence stores are to be found here, and some twenty or twenty-five cellars are occupied as dance houses and concert saloons." "These are among the lowest and vilest of their kind in New York," he concluded.[4]

But despite the features that brought horror to upper-class visitors, the neighborhood had its charms. McCabe also detailed "the carnival of the Bowery," which was held on Saturday nights. He described how "the downtown stores, the factories, and other business places close about five o'clock, and the street is thronged at an early hour. Crowds are going to market, but the majority are bent on pleasure." This was no debauch: "As soon as the darkness falls over the city the street blazes with light. Away up towards Prince Street you may see the flashy sign of Tony Pastor's Opera House, while from below Canal Street the Old Bowery Theatre stands white and glittering in the glare of gas and transparencies. . . . The Atlantic Garden stands by the side of the older theatre, rivaling it in brilliancy and attractiveness." There were "scores of restaurants, with tempting bills of fare and prices astonishingly low," while "the lamps of the street vendors dot the side-walk at intervals, and the many colored lights of the street cars stretch away as far as the eye can reach." The Bowery was in effect a Broadway for the poor.[5]

So for a boy growing up at this time, the city was a place of wonders. There had long been horsecar lines, with dimly lit cars that made a pickpocket's job easy, and straw on the floors in the winter. But by 1868 the first elevated line opened, pulled along by huffing, puffing steam engines, and in 1878, when Al was only five years old, the Third Avenue El began service between Chatham Square and South Ferry. Smith's district also blazed with various new forms of illumination, tenement dwellers watching as gas lights lit up the night, to be replaced by the even brighter incandescent bulbs. Most of these were put up not by the city but by shopkeepers; in 1884 there were already 218 arc lights in front of stores and amusement parlors. "No tailor is so poor, no gimcrack store so impecunious that it cannot afford one," wrote one observer.[6]

Stores provided not only a fantasy land of goods and services, but also much of the pizzazz, the zip that made cities such alluring places to go to, such exciting places to live in, even in a neighborhood like the Fourth Ward. At 222 Bowery, for example, at Arnold's Cider Mill, a Saint Bernard dog, walking on a treadmill, ground the apples; the sanitary implications were horrifying, but it was a fabulous sight. The proprietor of the London and Liverpool Clothing Company, at the corner of Hester and Bowery, was another showman; when this Englishman found out that he was losing the Irish trade because of his nationality, he imported three or four Irish constables from the Emerald Isle to entice their countrymen into the store. Long before mimes appeared in Central Park, he had live mannequins in the window, sometimes just standing, sometimes strolling leisurely around the display space, sometimes gesturing (twirling the mustache was a favorite), sometimes revolving as they stood on a turntable. When this attraction lost its luster there appeared optical marvels like the woman cut in half, and even a live bear. As the writer Alvin Harlow noted, "The Bowery . . . ate it up."[7]

Above all, what fascinated everyone, what they all remembered, were the amusement arcades. Gaudy, exciting, they captured the imagination and lit up the city.

Foremost of these were the dime museums—not just one or two, but scores of them along the main streets of this district. Every single one had managed somehow to assemble the greatest collection of amazing artifacts the world had ever seen, brought exclusively to the Bowery from the far corners of the earth (especially darkest Africa, the jungles of Brazil, and the Himalayan slopes), with no expense spared—or at least so the hawkers said, at the top of their leathery lungs. No museum could survive without a mermaid in a glass case, although, sadly, no one had yet managed to snare a live one. In addition, they all had to have a midget, a bearded lady, and a fat person. Some galleries had two-headed calves and four-legged chickens, while others featured artifacts like crusaders' swords or ancient Roman spears. All of these places made sure, of course, that no customer got close enough to see the glue or the stitches that held these wonders together. Decades later, Al Smith wrote in his autobiography that he had gone to the Dime Museum "so often" that "at a moment's notice, I could have taken the place of the announcer as he described the mysteries of the India-rubber man; Jojo, the dog-faced boy; Professor Coffey, the skeleton dude, the sword swallower, the tattooed man and the snake charmer."[8]

Beyond that there were a myriad of places of live entertainment. The largest of these, like Tony Pastor's, featured first-rate plays and vaudeville acts, but there were also a vast number of smaller joints, where the entertainment was sometimes surprisingly good. Irving Berlin served his apprenticeship at "Nigger Mike" Salter's place on Pell Street, after which he sang at the Chatham Club while carrying a towel on one arm and a beer tray in the other. Al and Harry Jolson got their start in New York at the Gaiety Museum, and Harry also served as a singing waiter, this time at Callahan's Dance Hall and Saloon at Chatham Square and Doyers Street.[9]

But the biggest attraction of them all, the center of this world, was the riverfront. This was the economic heart of the district, as well as its largest shop, and for children it was the greatest playground in the world. At that time New York was one of the world's greatest ports; the harbor was filled with boats and adventure, as tall-masted ships arrived and departed for all parts of the region and the globe. On any given day you could see fishing boats arrive from New England, shiny and laden down with cod; sloops filled with bricks coming from yards way up the Hudson to serve the booming housing market; and barges filled to overflowing with flour or potatoes.[10]

And there was the world-class commerce as well. In 1890 over 80 percent of the coffee Americans drank came over the railings of the South Street docks, where longshoremen unloaded endless jute bags of beans, each one weighing 160 pounds. In his autobiography, Al Smith remembered, "the foot of Market Street was where the tea ships landed. There, day and night—by candlelight at night—the men would be leading horses up and down the dock and pulling up chests of tea from China and India out of the holds of ships." Below that were the docks that served ships arriving from Europe, and after that came the piers for the West Indian trade, vessels laden with exotic fruits (at least to tenement-bound New Yorkers) and other goods from the islands in the Caribbean. These tall ships would dock at the piers, their prows extending way out over the street like some kind of honor guard at an oversized military wedding.[11]

For children, this was a fantastic place to be. On one of those beautiful sun-filled days that occasionally breaks out even in New York, residents and passers-by could sit on the docks and enjoy the warmth while they watched the seaport lurch ahead in its daily routine. Long before reformers came up with the idea of "jungle gyms" (known as "monkey bars" in New York City), kids on the East Side went down to the docks and climbed all over the riggings of these ships. Near the end of his life, many years later, Al Smith still remembered that network of cables and ropes, claiming that the port "afforded a very good gymnasium—just as good as they have today." Al's daughter Emily wrote that she remembered "hearing Father tell how he and his companions performed their boyish gymnastics on the thin, long bowsprits that thrust themselves out over the cobblestones and busy trucks of South Street." And what must it have felt like, in an age before elevators, when Trinity Church was still the tallest building in the city, for a lad to sit on the deck of a ship, looking out at eye level to second-story windows, feeling for all the world like a giant from a fairy tale?[12]

If Al learned to love the magic of cities in his youth, he also learned about the variety of the American peoples. Down the block from Al's boyhood home was a Jewish cemetery, associated with Temple Shearith Israel, the oldest synagogue in America, founded in 1654. Jewish leaders acquired the land in 1682, and the first body was interred a year later. During the Revolutionary War the site was fortified as part of the city's defenses, and mixed in with the *landsmen* were eighteen soldiers and patriots who died in that conflict. The cemetery was around the corner from Al's church, a few hundred feet from his school.[13]

The most numerous group were the Irish; the bulk of the 200,000 to 400,000 immigrants that landed in New York City every year between the late 1840s and early 1850s were victims of the potato famine. By 1855 Irish immigrants made up 28 percent of the city's total population, and five years later the New York Irish made up 13 percent of all Irish in the United States, making it the Hibernian center of the country. Up until 1886, an Irish flag was hung from city hall every St. Patrick's Day.[14]

The Irish transformed Al Smith's neighborhood. By the time of the 1855 New York State census, the Fourth Ward was one of the most Gaelic in the city, with Irish immigrants (not including their American-born children) making up 46 percent of the ward's population. This was the second highest of any district in the city, and one of only three that reached 40 percent. By this time the immigrants had begun to cluster according to the county of their homeland, with people from Kerry concentrating in the Fourth Ward.[15]

Al thought of himself as simply Irish, just like the neighborhood, but for both the district and the man, this was only part of the truth. By 1855, for example, 4 percent of the population was German. As early as 1845, 310 people who had migrated from France lived there, and 62 came from Mexico or South America. Ten years later a more extensive study turned up 7 people from Belgium, 44 from Holland, 118 Swiss, 114 Poles, 84 Italians, and 35 Spaniards. They were joined by 73 Swedes, 56 Danes, and 70 Canadians. Any Irish immigrant had to deal with the fact that her neighbors included 41 people from the West Indies, 36 Asians, 5 former residents of Turkey or Greece (inconveniently lumped together in the tabulations), and 2 Africans.[16]

The Asians were particularly important, because they were about to form a neighborhood of their own just north of Smith's East Side District. The first Chinese nationals to arrive in this area of New York were sailors and merchants, most of them transients, but by 1850 a small enclave had formed. In a short time this grew considerably, as racial hatred in the western United States drove Chinese workers out of the railroad and mining industries to jobs on the New York docks and the neighborhood adjoining them. By the 1870s there were more than two thousand Chinese next door.[17]

Many accounts celebrated this cultural richness. A newspaper article described how the corner of Oliver and Cherry streets had nurtured a miniature industry around the bathhouse located there. "About two dozen small shops sell or rent soap and towels," the paper reported, telling how "in Yiddish, Greek, Italian and English," they hawked their wares. And that was just the start: "The polyglot signs are only one indication of a war being fought in a forest of hyphens. Chinamen eating chili con carne, Italians eating chop suey, Irishmen talking Yiddish are mild symptoms of the mixture of races" in that immigrant district.[18]

William McAdoo, the police commissioner of New York City from 1904 to 1905, saw and understood much of the ward's diversity. McAdoo appreciated the sheer variety of the citizens under his protection, and provided the city with statistical data as to the number of people on the Lower East Side from Scotland, Russia, Japan, Slavonia, and every other country he could list. McAdoo maintained that "the East Side is no less moral than the other sides, but the conditions are different. . . . In no one section of the city are there more devoted families, more affectionate and self-serving fathers and mothers, more virtuous and religious households than right in the heart of the most congested portions of what are called the slums of New York."[19]

⮤

Al Smith's family certainly fit the commissioner's description, and it was typical in another fashion as well: despite what he believed, Al's roots were as complex as America's, or at least as varied as the typology of the Fourth Ward. Humor and gossip in the streets later claimed that Smith was hiding the fact that his real name was "Schmidt" or that his enlarged proboscis was a genetic reminder of Hebraic origins. None of this was true; but then again, he was not purely Irish either.[20]

When Al wrote his autobiography, *Up to Now,* he devoted a grand total of two paragraphs to his mother's family. If this seems minimal, he said even less about his father's background, beginning and ending with the statement, "I do not remember ever hearing him tell where his parents came from." Al's most beloved child, his daughter Emily, told interviewers that while she had "made some inquiries . . . as to the racial . . . mixture of her family," she had never heard or discovered any definitive evidence. Her own best guess was that her father's grandparents represented four different ethnic strains. Throughout the 1928 campaign, while Smith was proud to champion the immigrant, he also downplayed his own diverse origins; at one point George Van Namee, his campaign manager at the convention, suddenly realized that neither he nor any of the correspondents had any idea what the "E" in Alfred E. Smith stood for. Van Namee asked New York mayor Jimmy Walker, a delegate and long, close friend of the governor, but he did not have the answer either. Only the candidate could reveal that it stood for "Emanuel."[21]

What did this mean? His grandson Walter recounted that as far as his grandfather was concerned, "he was 100% Irish. . . . If someone said, well, 'this is the greatest Irishman that ever lived' . . . he'd never correct them." Even during the tense 1928 campaign, Smith claimed that his two "ancestral locales" (as the *New York Times* put it) were New York and Ireland, telling reporters about his mother's Irish roots, about the fact that his father was born in New York City, and that beyond that he could not recall ever "hearing his father discuss his forbearers." Over and over, Smith was referred to as the leading Irish-American politician of his era, in fact of any period of American history prior to the arrival of John Fitzgerald Kennedy.[22]

But was this true? Thanks to the research of Frances Perkins, a lifelong Smith ally and America's first female cabinet member, the more complicated story is revealed. Alfred's paternal grandfather, Emanuel Smith, was Italian, a resident of Genoa. Born in either 1808 or 1813,[23] Emanuel emigrated to America in 1825 and denounced his citizenship from the Kingdom of Sardinia on April 9, 1844. Was Emanuel's last name really Smith, an unlikely moniker for an Italian immigrant? If not, was this close to the original, a bastardized form made up, as was so often the case, by immigration inspectors who were not exactly fluent linguists; or did Emanuel adopt this simple-sounding name as part of his American identity?[24]

We do not know the answers to these questions, nor do we know what he did for a living. Records cite his occupation as "mariner," but given that Emanuel was only twelve or seventeen years of age when he came over, was that really his occupation, or was it possible that he simply earned his passage by working as some sort of cabin boy? Eventually he married Magdalena Colby ("possibly Kolbe"), born in Germany in 1816, coming to the United States in 1837. Peter Mulvihill, Al's maternal uncle, described her as a "blonde German woman" who cleaned the firehouse where he worked.[25]

Their first child, Alfred, was born on November 20, 1839, and baptized on the first of December, indicating that both parents were good Catholics. His sponsors had French and Italian names, Joseph Jaraud and Rosanna Brutus. Two years later a daughter was born, Teresa; she was baptized at St. James Roman Catholic Church, with English- and German-sounding sponsors.

Alfred received only a little education at a church school. He served for many years in the Liberty Hose Company, one of the boisterous volunteer fire teams that served as both social club and political recruiter; and enlisted in the army during the Civil War. His first wife was a Miss Donnelly of Brooklyn, who gave him a daughter, and then passed from the earth. The child was raised by a grandmother, and eventually Alfred remarried; it was his second wife, Catherine, who bore him a son that he would name after himself.[26]

By this time Alfred Smith, Sr., the governor's father, had become a teamster, someone who ran a carting company. According to the 1855 census, this was the seventh most common job classification in New York City, and one that attracted a lot of immigrants (58 percent of its practitioners were foreign born). These men had to be expert horsemen, able to work long hours at hard tasks, but prone, as a result, to overwork and a variety of illnesses.[27]

Within this world Alfred did well for himself. By 1855 most teamsters were already working for larger companies, but Smith maintained his own shop. His was a small establishment, with two vehicles and a few teams of horses, the whole enterprise bringing around fifteen dollars a week for a great deal of hard labor. Al's recollections were always limited by the fact that his father left for work at 6:00 A.M. or daybreak, whichever was earlier, and he rarely returned before night fell. Exhausted, he would clean up, eat the evening meal, and retire.[28]

The senior Smith was an expert swimmer and a grand storyteller, a proud man who valued friends above all. Over and over he repeated, "A man who can't do a friend a favor is not a man," a sentiment carried out on many evenings when he brought companions home for dinner unannounced. Not surprisingly for an immigrant businessman and former fireman, he was also an active, albeit minor, member of the local branch of Tammany Hall—the city's preeminent political organization—and good friends with Tom Foley, the district's leader.[29]

On his mother's side, however, Al's roots were as green as the Emerald Isle itself. His maternal grandmother, Maria Mulvihill, was the daughter of Peter and Mary Marsh, Protestant residents of Westmeath County, near Dublin. Peter was a barrister in the courts, a member of the professional class, with an estate named—appropriately if immodestly— "Marshland," in the village of Moate.[30]

It was natural that a family of this substance would raise Maria as a lady, providing her with a classical education. She became a young woman who was known for the quality and beauty of her needlepoint and embroidery, as well as for her generous approach to learning; in the New World, for example, she often wrote letters for neighbors in her elegant handwriting.[31]

Maria had one other characteristic, however, that would shape her future family tree: an extremely strong will. This meant that when she met and fell in love with Thomas Mulvihill, nothing would keep them apart. Not the fact that he was a tailor and below her station; and not that he was a Roman Catholic. She responded to the second difference simply, by converting to his religion. But either of these taboos was more than enough reason to emigrate to America. Maria married Thomas; got pregnant and gave birth to their first child; and came to America, in that order.[32]

It was not an easy trip, nor an easy landing. They traveled in 1841 on a clipper ship of the Black Ball line, a rough passage that took sixty days, with Maria clutching an infant that was scarcely one month old at the time they set out on their journey. When they landed at South Street, at the foot of Beekman Place, they had nowhere to go, no contacts, in all likelihood with no possibility that they could ever return safely to Ireland. So they picked up their baggage and began to walk. Three blocks later, they saw a sign offering rooms for rent in a house on the corner of Dover and Water streets. The lower floor was the home of a family of German immigrants named Dannerman, but a flat on the third floor stood open, so the Mulvihills moved in, or as the older generation used to say, they "took the rent." Most of the rest of their life was spent in that apartment.[33]

Within a few days Thomas secured employment with a tailoring firm that had just opened its shop on nearby Catherine Street, a company called Brooks Brothers. Thomas worked there all his life as a skilled employee earning a reasonable wage, enabling him to afford a decent-sized family of six children, one of the younger daughters being named Catherine.[34]

Al's mother, from the first, inherited the troubles of the Irish. Later accounts described Catherine as a pious, severe-looking woman; Frances Perkins said that Al had "a beautiful mother," but portrayed her as "spare, broad-shouldered, big-boned," with a full nose, high cheekbones, and big forehead, appearing like a character out of the "Great Mothers of the Gracci."[35]

She did not say much in public, but it was Catherine Mulvihill Smith who provided Al with his set of values, his moral compass. Everyone remembered that she had, as her granddaughter Emily recounted, a "very strong character"; or as Perkins explained, Al's mother had "none of the easy-going Irish in her. She wasn't that kind. She was a strong-minded, strong-charactered person." She never raised her voice, nor lowered her standards for how people should act (Joseph Proskauer called her "a soft-voiced, pious Catholic"), and as a result she became the major influence on Al's moral sensibility, teaching him about the church, about discipline, and above all else, about integrity. Catherine, quietly, persistently, with her bright eyes and erect posture, was the one who taught Al that if "your honor was tarnished, you never had any strength. *Honor* was the strong thing." Years later, whenever the governor entered a room where his mother was present, he would always kneel by her chair to receive her blessing before proceeding with any business.[36]

Alfred, Sr., would have run across Catherine in a number of places. By the early 1870s they were both parishioners at St. James, and his horses were stabled over on Dover Street, just down the block from the Mulvihills. In an age when families used to spend their free time out on the stoop, it is quite possible that the cartman saw this young woman several times a day, on his way to and from work at least, if not in the course of his deliveries throughout the neighborhood. Their courtship took about a year. On August 7, 1872, they wed, and on December 30, 1873, a son, Alfred was born.[37]

⋘

But was he Irish? Father Arthur Smith, the governor's grandson, remembered Mamie, Al's younger sister, and described her as "swarthy . . . she looked like an Italian," much as her father did. Mamie recalled hearing her father comment, when Irish-American politics was hotly discussed, "Thank God I haven't got a bit of Irish in me, I've got no Irish in my blood." When neighbors criticized the Italians who were moving in and "spoiling the neighborhood," Alfred, Sr., got mad, defending his kinsmen, declaring that they were fine folk, well fit to be Americans.[38]

Thus, if we ask the question, was Al Smith Irish, as a matter of ancestry, the answer is: only partially. But in America, particularly in an age bubbling with new immigrants, heritage is only partially derived from birth; it is also the product of experience and memory, community and upbringing. Al did not know his hard-working father all that well, and Alfred, Sr., did not speak much about his parents (Al was not lying when he later said he did not know about this side of the family). His mother raised him, shaped his views and his values, giving him roots and his Irish identity.

William Griffin, in *The Book of Irish Americans,* argued that "anyone . . . with two, three or even four nationalities among his ancestry is free to identify with whichever . . . he prefers," and Al's selection was clear. This son of Alfred Smith and Catherine Mulvihill, Griffen concluded, became "Irish because he himself chose to be Irish." In the long run, that remained the most important fact regarding Alfred E. Smith's ethnicity.[39]

Al remained uncomfortable with the rest of his ancestry simply because he did not know much about it, and no adult wants to reconsider an identity so solidly forged. But Al Smith's origins meant that from the earliest age he had to contest with ethnicity and the city, with neighborhood and with family. From his first years, he became wedded to the themes, the issues, and the problems that would shape his adult life and his role on the great stage of American politics.

Chapter 2

Neighborhood

MORE THAN ANY OTHER monument, the Brooklyn Bridge is a reminder of what a unique and complex place New York was in the late nineteenth century. At either end of the bridge's soaring roadway stood a magnificent city, the great metropoli of Gotham and of Brooklyn, each, by itself, among America's most populous urban centers.

But if the bridge celebrated a merger of cities, it also highlighted their separation—the parochial sense that divided New Yorkers into residents of boroughs, sections, and, ultimately, dense neighborhoods that, more than anything else, provided residents with their understanding of how the world works. Brooklyn and New York may have merged in commerce, but they never did in culture, and each district's population has maintained a distinct identity, separated by accents, attitudes, and for part of the twentieth century, competing baseball clubs.

Despite this, residents in the late 1800s still understood that the bridge was a truly remarkable structure. Mary Shapiro, one of the many writers to tackle the subject, told how, more than a century after the bridge opened, it was "difficult to imagine the impact that the completion of the Brooklyn Bridge had. . . . For its time, it was an engineering achievement of almost miraculous proportions." This vision commanded everyone's attention, but especially those living in the close vicinity; Shapiro noted how "its long sweep of steel, etching a gentle arch across the sky, created a futuristic backdrop for nineteenth-century New York." Something titanic, something spectacular, had been added to the city, but especially to Al Smith's neighborhood.[1]

Al often said that "the Brooklyn Bridge and I grew up together," and he was right. The apartment he grew up in, at 174 South Street, sat right across from where the bridge gradually hurled itself across the river, so Al watched the whole thing from the front room windows of his family's railroad flat. In 1922 he recounted for reporters what a hold it had on his imagination, how he had "spent a lot of time . . . superintending the job in my boyhood." Decades later, he could still maintain, "I have never lost the sense of admiration and envy I felt toward the men who swarmed like flies stringing the cables and putting in the roadways as the Bridge slowly took shape." By the time he was a young man, the bridge had become part of the Irish-American community's folklore, the popular song, "Danny by My Side," opening with the line, "The Brooklyn Bridge on Sunday is known as lover's lane." In 1933, at a gala ceremony marking the fiftieth anniversary of the opening of the bridge, Smith got up in the main ballroom of the Hotel St. George and sang that tune from memory.[2]

Before the opening, Al's father had obtained part-time employment as a guard keeping people from venturing onto the edifice. But he was determined that his son should always have the right to say that he had walked across the bridge before it was actually built, so Alfred granted himself permission to take his nine-year-old son across the span. There was no roadbed, only a rope-and-plank walkway stretched across the East River, making this, overall, a rather exciting and novel idea. For some reason he chose a winter's morning, and with his mother sitting at home ("saying ten rosaries all the time," Mamie recalled), father and son walked hand in hand across the swinging catwalk, returning home safe and sound, to Catherine's relief.[3]

When Al stopped looking up and started looking around, his vision captured the other side of the bridge's significance—that despite living in a city that opened up in every way possible to the rest of the world, he was embedded in a separate, cloistered neighborhood, referred to by locals as the Fourth Ward.

Al Smith grew up in a tight community, a place where people gave and received affection, allegiances, and values. According to the standard version, residents were hard-working folk from every possible background the world could provide, and the section was reasonably safe and stable. Robert Moses, Smith's parks commissioner, in a memorial for his boss explained that "within a radius of five miles Alfred E. Smith could see . . . Neapolitans who brought into Little Italy the colors and passions of the Mediterranean; refugees from the knout in Russia, sturdy Germans of the turnverein saengerfest, pre-Nazi variety; old Americans being elbowed aside by new Irishmen who understood the art of reconciling nationalities before the League of Nations and Dumbarton Oaks were thought of." Overall, it was a model working-class environment. The reality, however, was that the neighborhood was *a lot* more diverse than this benign image depicted, in ways that went far beyond concerns over ethnicity.[4]

Take, for example, the matter of race. It was a far shorter walk from Smith's house to Chinatown, than it was to the legendary docks he talked so much about.

Yet he spent relatively little time in the Asian district, and the influence on the man and his subsequent political career appears, at first sight, to have been negligible. The only mention Al ever made of the area or its residents was when his daughter Emily got married in 1926 in the governor's mansion, when he was overjoyed to see Louis Fook, the so-called mayor of Chinatown, whom he greeted warmly as a neighbor.

This trifling incident was more important for what it omitted than for what it displayed. For if Al Smith took little notice of his next-door brethren, other than on ceremonial occasions, it also meant that he had sidestepped a world of racial hostility. Al seems to have ignored—or not even noticed—that Fook was also a member of the On Leong Tong, and served as peacemaker in battles between that society and the Hip Sing Tong. Fook's predecessor as "mayor" had been Tom Lee, who died of old age in 1918. Lee wore a chain-mail vest for protection, and rivals once dropped a flagpole from a roof, narrowly missing the "mayor's" head. Another time a bullet shattered the alarm clock next to his bed; in all probability the round had been aimed at a more delicate apparatus. How did Al and his neighbors feel about all this, or that Lee was married to a German woman and had two sons by her? Did they share the opinions of police commissioner McAdoo that "Chinese wives"—whites married to men of Chinese birth or descent—were "the most wretched, degraded and utterly vile lot of white women and girls that could be found anywhere"? They must have heard about the trial of Quimbo Appo, a Chinese-born tea seller who was accused of murdering his Irish-American wife, Catherine Fitzpatrick. The papers said that drink had created within him "an insatiable craving for blood," and when enraged, he slit his wife's throat. The truth—that he had killed his landlady when she tried to stop a fight between the two spouses—may in fact have been even more horrible to local residents, since this actually took place at 47 Oliver Street, around the corner from St. James where Al went to school and attended church.[5]

Another problem that vastly complicates our view of Al's neighborhood is the Bowery, which began at Chatham Square, about half a block from St. James. Every account of New York—except those featuring Smith, where this issue is ignored—highlights this section as the home for the city's underground culture. Daniel Czitrom, for example, an historian of Tammany Hall and urban street-political culture, wrote how, "after 1850 the Fourth Ward . . . eclipsed . . . the Five Points as the section of New York most associated with poverty, crime, and vice;" he titled his article on Smith's beloved section, "The Wickedest Ward in New York." Charles Stelzle, a German-American minister and labor activist born and raised on the East Side, corroborated Czitrom's account when he wrote, decades earlier, that this section was "synonymous with depravity."[6]

Numerous forms of vice gave this district its well-earned reputation. This was the home of one of the city's largest collections of cheap lodging houses—not surprising, given the floating population of sailors. With this trade came other services, such as pawnshops; more than half of the city's pawnbrokers did business south of Fourteenth Street, and the first establishment to be devoted exclusively to this trade opened at 25 Chatham Street. Tattoo parlors, whose clientele included transient sailors and other rough trade, were also common; the second tattoo parlor in New York was opened in 1875, two years after Al was born, at 11 Chatham Square.[7]

Far worse were the saloons. In 1898 the New York City Police Department reported that there were ninety-nine places of amusement along the Bowery, most of them saloons with entertainment; only fourteen of these, the police believed, could be classified as respectable. In many of these dives, whiskey cost only three cents, and this elixir was piped through a hose right into the glass. No guarantee, however, that it would not cause blindness, and that was a shame, because then the imbiber would have missed the sights at Geoghegan's Bar. Waiters at this fine establishment were described as "gorilla-like," and for five dollars apiece they would cease waiting on customers—on the spot—and two of them would go over to the house prize-fighting ring and engage in a bare-knuckle bout. Patrons could also catch many of the beggars from the area who stopped off there, and watch as blind men discovered vision, cripples walked again, and the one-armed man rediscovered his lost limb. If that was not excitement enough, hardy souls could always meander down to the Hole in the Wall on Water Street, near Dover. Run by Gallus Mag, a large woman of English descent, the proprietress was hardly the custodian of the queen's manners; Mag's trademark was her ability to bite the ears off rowdy customers, and she displayed these anatomical trophies in a pickle jar up on the back bar.[8]

A lot of the saloons in Al Smith's district were not nearly this flamboyant, but rather dark, dingy places. In the early twentieth century the Committee of Fourteen, an anti-vice group, sent investigators into the area and found places like the Seaman's Hotel at 2 Front Street. Their agent "found the back room and the toilet in a dirty rotten condition, also nothing but drunks in the barroom." An official who checked a bar at 21 Chatham Square noted that the premises "appear to be disorderly and catering to prostitutes. A cabaret show is in progress on the second floor behind tightly drawn curtains, unescorted women are admitted to the same and premises are largely patronized by pimps, young toughs, corner loafers, gangmen and cheap sports."[9]

With the bars came prostitutes, lots of them. Timothy Gilfoyle's research on New York prostitution shows that this district not only had one of the city's largest vice populations, but that its practitioners were among the poorest in the metropolitan area. In 1857, Walt Whitman wrote that "the hardest houses [of prostitution] of all are those in Cherry, Water and Walnut Streets," all on the waterfront section, where Smith played as a child and only blocks away from where his own children grew up. Here, writes Gilfoyle, "the prostitutes are generally drunkards. . . . You see the women half exposed at the cellar door as you pass." A decade later the reformer Matthew Hale Smith claimed that the whores of Water Street were "the lowest and most debased of their class. . . . Crime and vice has done its worst with them." Gilfoyle's maps show that prostitution was still quite active in this area through the first decades of the twentieth century.[10]

There was even cocaine in Al Smith's beloved neighborhood. The pastor of St. James in 1908, James Curry, actually became "one of the first men in the city," according to the *New York Times,* "to become interested in this evil." Following his denunciations of the drug, the Department of Health began an investigation that uncovered numerous "sniff parties" going on in the area.[11]

One of the highlights of the district, furthermore, was blood sports, epitomized by Kit Burns's Sportsman's Hall, known for its dog-fighting and rat-killing contests. Burns was a heavy-set man with a face scarred by smallpox. As a child, he explained to a reporter from the *New York Daily Tribune,* he had always been "passionately fond of dogs, and dogs were fond of him."[12]

Burns showed his fondness in a rather strange fashion, by having them fight in the rat pit. Patrons entering his saloon, en route to the fighting arena, passed the bar, on each side of which rested a stuffed dog. One was Jack, who had dispatched one hundred rats in six minutes and forty seconds, thus setting a new American record and achieving his taxidermic immortality. His opposite mate, Hunky, won his laurels by "going out game," that is, killing his opponent before dying of wounds, the sign of a fighting spirit.

There were four major attractions at Sportsman's Hall: rat killing by a weasel, rat killing by a dog, rat killing by a man, and dog fighting. The third of these, which involved a male human catching rats with his bare hands and then tearing off their heads with a quick bite, was considered a little rough even for this crowd.

Even after reform movements closed Kit Burns's place, tough clubs remained. Jimmy Durante, a contemporary of the governor who remembered playing piano at parties given by Al Smith's mother, described the "best places" by noting that " 'Best' is just comparative. Those joints were as tough as the steak off a ten-year-old cow. Some were worse than others, but they were all pretty bad." He noted that "the Chatham Club . . . was the hardest, noisiest club" in the area: "Real gangsters hung out there, and they weren't the snow-sniffing, stab-in-the-back kind either. What they could do with the knuckles and blackjack was a crime."[13]

Finally, this was one of the city's centers for homosexual activity, another matter not talked about in the biographies, but a very real part of life in the Fourth Ward. The waterfront and the Bowery, with their high population of adult males, their transiency, and their cheap boardinghouses, became by the turn of the century some of the leading rendezvous spots for New York's homosexual population. Historian George Chauncey notes that straight New Yorkers in this section "encountered [gays] frequently in the . . . streets, parks, and beaches, where they seemed to be an almost ubiquitous presence." Jimmy Durante remembered that "the first place I worked in was a Bowery joint for the boys with five finger-marks on the hip. You know, the la-de-la lads who are that way about each other. I was only fourteen."[14]

Al Smith was about the same age at that time, and yet he seemed to have escaped all of these tensions, these influences. For the neighborhood that shaped Al Smith had another side, one that did shape the boy's outlook and career in far, far more important ways.

⤙

By the time Al was born, the Fourth Ward may have been poor and ethnic, but it was hardly a ghetto, a place where one group was clustered in segregation; instead it sustained an amazing degree of heterogeneity. Everyone who has ever lived in a city knows that this can easily lead to conflict—everything from shouts across an alley, to bloody fistfights over sacred turf, to full-scale riots that can gut a neighborhood like a passing firestorm.

But in Al's section there is no evidence that this happened. Human nature dictates that some arguments had to have occurred—over who would use the clothesline, or whose voice was too loud—but these disputes were private and low key, invisible in that no one ever records such outbursts for posterity. What is notable, therefore, in the Fourth Ward was the absence of the larger battles of consequence, the ones that involved ethnic, racial, or other social tensions.

In fact, there is not even evidence that they noticed the fleshpots. Many of Al's neighbors claimed they had no problems with the brothels and saloons up the street; Bernard Pisani, for example, said that there was no contact between Oliver Street and the Bowery; as a result, he felt "no danger." When Helen Graff was fifteen and sixteen years old, she thought nothing of going to dances and coming home at midnight, climbing up to a fifth-floor walkup unescorted. She said, "We had no fear"; her only recollection of the haunts of the Bowery, a separate neighborhood, was "they were very kind to kids, you know." People of different ethnicities all lived side by side, she noted, and got along "very well . . . we never saw any animosity," as long as the rules were obeyed, such as prohibitions on intermarriage; adults "didn't like it," for example, if an Irishman married an Italian girl. Hugh Carey, only the second Roman Catholic governor of New York, when asked about the region just above Chatham Square, said, "In those days it was entertainment and clubs and so forth . . . it was good entertainment . . . there was a lot of talent on the Bowery." The system of small communities, in other words, enabled people to see only what they wanted to see.[15]

But if that seems unusual, it was in fact typical of many other urban working-class communities, albeit in an early stage of their development. The first people to live in these areas, immigrants and laborers, as they moved into and huddled in the tenements, sought relief from the dangers and strangeness all around them: the chaos of the booming city; the horrors of unregulated capitalism; the shock of the new, a newness that seemed to shift mass and shape almost momentarily. These tough, frightened souls sought as their foremost goal some kind of security, and they found it in a small community that provided neighbors whom they could depend on and trust. This unit, these people, would be the most important resources in trying to survive, and then, maybe, possibly, even prosper.

And the quest for closeness, for finding people to share life's traumas and raptures with, was terribly heightened by the density, the forced intimacy of the city. If living next door in a thin-walled tenement meant occasionally getting on a neighbor's nerves, it also meant a shared bond. Tenants annoyed the family next door with fights or celebrations, but it meant that now everyone was part of these emotional events. All had the same poor facilities, the same toilet in the hallway, the same landlord that they trembled before on rent day, then cursed every time the water went out or the boiler broke down. Down the block residents talked to other people in the same boat; the geographic tightness produced knowledge neighbors could count on, facts that enabled the locals to sort the good from the bad.

This system, however, could not extend very far. This was a world defined in small portions, a universe encompassed by a few city blocks. Safety was based on face-to-face recognition, a familiarity with each individual's personality and character. Al wrote in his autobiography, "When I was growing up everybody . . . knew his neighbors—not only people who were immediate neighbors but everybody in the neighborhood," pointing out that "my father, my mother, my sister, my wife, all five of my children and I, were all born within five blocks of one another." This was a source of pride that he was part of a strong, dependable community, rather than a sign of parochialism. Throughout his life, he remained "Al"; not "Alfred," but "Al," someone you knew in a friendly way, someone you were at home with, someone—in this world—you could have confidence in.[16]

But what about the other people, the people outside one's circle of reliability and caring? They were different, so how could they be trusted? In a later stage of development in many urban areas, the answer would be violence, the anger being drawn from the nationalistic politics of Europe, from religious bigotries of all sorts, from competition over jobs or housing, or from just about anything; it is all too easy to just hate.

But in the very early stages of these communities, not just in New York but in Chicago and in other cities across the country, it did not necessarily work that way, because sometimes prejudices had not yet developed. Nationalism and its associated hatreds, for example, did not always come over on the boats that left from Naples and Bremen; how could peasants identify with a modern state when Italy did not exist as a united land until 1866, Germany until 1871? Poland became a nation only in 1919, for the first time since it was carved up by the imperial powers in 1793, more than a century prior, and way beyond the memory of anyone still alive. The peasants coming over in those terrible steerage conditions identified with a village, or maybe even a province; nationalism, with all its awesome power, would have to be taught to later generations.[17]

But even if they had not yet learned the hates and fears that would cause so much bloodshed, residents still had to deal with people who were very, very different. This meant that in order to keep some sort of peace, as well as to maintain their sanity, urban residents developed a system of deliberate ignorance and avoidance. People remained on their side of the tracks, among their own, and tended to their affairs. Those who lived outside were ignored. Although they were also in a sense neighbors, they were not part of the neighborhood, this little segment, and thus not a part of the circle of contacts it was safe to deal with. They were not necessarily bad, merely different and unknown, and hence not included in the system of close bonds and understandings. People looked past and beyond them, and went about their business. Most important of all to Al's upbringing, in this neighborhood, residents also let them go about theirs as well.

The best example of this outlook is the way that Europeans in the Fourth Ward related to the Chinese community that developed north of Chatham Square, a block from St. James. This was a different racial group from the myriad of European peoples, separated not only by language and culture but by the far more formidable barriers of religion and, above all, skin color. Next only to African-Americans, these were the ultimate outsiders, to be rejected and even, at certain times and places, driven out.

But in the Fourth Ward this never happened. There is no record of racial warfare, but there is plenty of evidence that the offspring of European immigrants turned a blind eye to their neighbors next door, despite their very real prejudices. During the 1863 draft riots, for example, when hatred ran wild in the streets, local

residents refused to march into Chinatown, and they actually attacked a provoca-
teur who tried to argue that Asians should be fought just like the blacks. Later, in
1884, William Assing became the first Chinese-American policeman in New
York, assigned to this district, and had no problems arresting whites.[18]

Other accounts corroborate this attitude. Dr. Bernard Pisani's father was a
doctor in the area; Bernard, in fact, grew up several houses down from what
later became the Smith homestead at 25 Oliver Street.[19] As a boy, he had heard
about the dungeons in Chinatown, and his father would mention that the Chinese ate rats. But he also noted that "more than a good third" of his father's
patients were Chinese and that they were free to walk around his neighborhood,
just as he felt free to walk through their section. Similarly, Helen Graff, a lifelong resident of the neighborhood who was born in the first years of the twentieth century, said that although few Chinese lived in the area, none ever went to
St. James that she could remember (she was quite emphatic on this), but that she
often went to eat at restaurants in Chinatown and had no fear at all of going to
that neighborhood. In other words, an entirely different religious and, even
more astounding, racial group did not disturb her at all. Because she had a way
of handling the situation, she felt at ease when she crossed the color line.[20]

Thus, the result of the social rules of the small, local community was that no
one had to deal with places and peoples outside their sphere. Instead, they
removed these others from the urban landscape, maintaining relatively little
contact, except in such formalized public events as the exchange of goods and
services. This system in turn minimized hostility between segments. Although
no one expected to depend on the others the same way, neither did anyone
always feel a need to confront them, especially when they were separated by
such urban boundaries as a street or a park or a square.

In Al Smith's youth, this attitude, approach to diversity and pluralism was
reinforced by a major demographic trend. If this system had developed in the
early days of the Fourth Ward, by the time young Alfred arrived on the scene the
population in this section had already stabilized, lessening the likelihood of conflict and bolstering the established system of tolerance. In 1875—two years after
Al was born—the ward had 20,828 residents; 52 percent of them had been born
outside the United States. But by 1890 the population had actually diminished—
the ward was down to 17,809 inhabitants—and only 47 percent had been born
overseas.[21]

Thus, during the era of Al's childhood, the ward became more settled as the
pace of change slowed down. Despite images of the Lower East Side and of
Manhattan as thriving nests of new immigrants scuttling about, the reality was
that even by this time, newcomers were fighting to get out of those cramped
quarters and move to the outer boroughs. If in 1900 the city's core island held 62
percent of New York's foreign-born population, by 1920 this had gone down to

47 percent. Over these same years, however, Brooklyn increased its share from 28 percent to 33 percent, while the Bronx emerged as the new home for immigrants, its percentage of the foreign-born population in New York City almost tripling, from 4.8 percent to 13.2 percent.[22]

As Al grew up, in other words, his neighbors were calming down as the local scene settled into place. This meant that Al Smith was only exposed to a single, increasingly coherent social outlook throughout most of his life, but especially during the years he was trying to make sense out of things.

〜

The social structure of these tiny, separated communities helps us better understand the small town outlook which would pervade Al Smith's future career. Clearly he was parochial and provincial, but in the opposite sense of how these words are usually used. In common parlance, they mean something nasty, a belief that everything outside a narrow vision, a small circle, is foreign and bad.

But Al was the opposite. The fundamental values of his world, the beliefs at the core of Al's approach to anyone and everything—even a presidential race—could be summed up in the simple concept of tolerance. Al grew up in a society whose motto was "live and let live." Go about your own business, ignore what was different or unpleasant, and accept that those on the other side of the street would do what they needed to do as well. Prejudices existed, but did not in any way serve as the pretext for antagonism or violence. Add to that the fact that Catherine shielded her son (whom everyone described as a smiling child) from whatever dark conversations occurred, and the result was that Al Smith emerged from the Fourth Ward with one of the most comprehensive visions of ethnic and racial tolerance of any politician in the first half of the twentieth century. It made him the perfect figure to become the leading spokesperson for the vast numbers of newcomers to American society who were arriving on the boats every day and congregating in the nation's cities.

The downside of this outlook was that Al Smith grew up a rather trusting soul, most of all when it came to anything beyond the ken of his local experience. John O'Brian, a Republican lawyer active in New York State politics, maintained that Smith "hated shams. . . . He was a forthright, honest man;" while the *New York Evening World* reported that "The greatest charm about Al Smith lies in his complete lack of affectation and his 100 per cent frankness." Frances Perkins once observed that her boss, governor and presidential candidate Al Smith, was always on the surface, had little in the way of guile and deceit; as she put it, he "had very few reserves." She felt this stemmed from the world of his segmented neighborhood and the amazing familiarity and trust it engendered: "Everybody was poor, everybody knew what you paid for rent, everybody knew how much your father earned and when he died how much your mother had. . . . You couldn't keep up appearances and nobody did. . . . There were no pretenses." As a result, "friendship meant total friendship. You didn't say 'school friend' or 'neighborhood friend' or 'dancing school friend.' . . . A friend was a friend."[23]

☙

If there was one thing Smith believed in, trusted above all else, it was America. Unfortunately, his sources for knowledge on this topic were limited, since it was that same local community that provided education, both formal and informal. And for Al Smith, this meant above all, St. James Roman Catholic Church.

St. James was not only Al Smith's school and parish, it was also the most important institution in the community, one that was shaped by, and in turn helped develop the local environment. An uptown relocation of a parish church built on Ann Street, one-half mile south, St. James's predecessor had been founded by a Cuban-American priest, a symbol of the parish's diversity. The new building was dedicated on September 18, 1836; High Mass took place in the basement, and the Very Rev. Dr. John Power of St. Peter's Church delivered the sermon.

Despite the pleasant ceremony, in those days it still took courage to be a Catholic, even in New York City; this was a nativist era, with self-described patriots attacking immigrants on the grounds of their "inferior" religion and heritage. When Francis Patrick, author of an anti-Catholic tract, arrived in New York in September 1836, the *New York Herald* admonished "Our Protestant brethren" to "buy liberally" his work: "It will describe scenes far more voluptuous than any yet published. All ye pious married ladies in the city prepare and buy; put down popery—put it down for God's sake." Three days later the paper's editors reminded readers that, "Blood or race is everything—locality or birth nothing. The blood of man and woman is as mysterious as the breed of blood horses." People with the "Anglo-Saxon blood . . . vindicate wherever they go—under whatever clime—their claims to superiority of . . . mind, intellect, and moral power." The paper concluded, "Let the breed be pure."[24]

The group that these nativists were most concerned about was the Irish, despite the fact that the Famine migration was still more than a decade away. But the Irish were already numerous enough and self-conscious enough that in 1836 several of them established a new nationalist association, affiliated with a similar group overseas. A charter was arranged that year, but not until 1851 did they start to call themselves publicly by their official name: the Ancient Order of Hibernians. The founding meeting was held at St. James, and a century and a half later, in 1986, when the archdiocese tried to tear down this church, the Hibernians stepped in to save the place where their American branch had originated.[25]

St. James was now predominantly Irish, with strong links to a growing immigrant tradition. The first pastor was the Reverend Andrew Byrne, whom the church history described as "six foot two, ruddy as a farmer, with a powerful magnificent voice, but with manners and disposition as mild as a woman's or child's." Father Byrne was succeeded by Father John Maginnis, and then by Father John Smith, who purchased a rectory for the church on the next block over, at 23 Oliver Street. Father Smith was also pastor when the first of the famine boats came in. The winter of 1847 was a bad one, and seventeen thousand Irish died aboard ship as they tried to make it to the American shores. As these death boats arrived, Father Smith and Father Mark Murphy, his assistant, went down to the holds to administer last rites to those who required them. Father Murphy caught ship's fever and died, and although Father Smith was able to assist him with the final rituals of the church, he too gave in five days later, passing from the earth on February 16, 1848.[26]

His successor was Father Patrick McKenna, a priest who invented novel ways to expand the parish. In 1854 he bought a building that had ministered to seamen, the Mariner's Temple on Roosevelt near Cherry Street, to turn it into a school. At a cost of $30,000, this was a major undertaking for the fledgling parish, and Father McKenna was determined to see that it got started on the right foot. On the next Sunday after the purchase, following High Mass, the good father suddenly locked all the doors, which seemed like the perfect moment to begin collections, as he personally went from pew to pew for donations. Church records, hardly an impartial source, claimed that "the pastor's plan was appreciated" and that "the people good naturedly responded." Whether they were actually so pleasant is a likely subject for skepticism, but the reality is they did donate $7,000 that afternoon, an enormous sum.[27]

St. James was a typical urban church, small and overcrowded, by the time young Al became a congregant. The original altar was made of stone brought over from Caen, France, and covered a large area, at least fifty feet. Upstairs there would eventually be an organ, and there was always a large basement, which would later play a prominent role in Al Smith's life when it was used as a theater. By 1878 the congregation had reached twenty-five thousand, far too large for a building this small, and this figure did not include a floating population of three thousand Catholic sailors. Masses must have been frequent and crowded.[28]

Years later, Emily Smith Warner, Al's favorite daughter, remembered that "the Church naturally formed . . . the heart and center of the parish, and in that compact neighborhood it was an intimate part of our daily lives." Above all, this was embodied by Father John Kean, who became pastor in 1879 and was a dominant influence in Al Smith's life.[29]

With his narrow, wide-set eyes and thinning hair, Father Kean appeared omniscient, constantly looking in on the classrooms, observing the children at play on the street, inserting his presence into every aspect of neighborhood life. At 9 P.M. sharp, he thrust his head out the window and ordered—not request-ed—all children indoors; Mamie recalled that no one dreamed of disobeying. When a nearby saloon keeper engaged in the unheard-of practice of serving women, Father Kean started a long-term and ultimately successful campaign to put him out of business.[30]

Father Kean was also instrumental in creating the organizational life of the parish, the myriad services and organizations that St. James provided for its community. By 1878, for example, there was a Society of the Sacred Heart ("to honor the love of our Divine Lord to man"); a Society of the Living Rosary; a Holy Name Society (with three hundred members by 1886); a St. Vincent DePaul Society; the St. James Rifle Corps ("which took part in all public cele-brations," Al later explained); the Longshoreman's Protective Society; plus a Young Men's and Young Woman's Sodality. The last group hinted at the size and scope of the roles women played in the church. In 1886, for the parish's fifti-eth anniversary, the pastor wanted to organize a street fair; he called for lady volunteers, and no fewer than 250 showed up. As a result, "immediately, not only our parish, but the city was invaded by this small army, equipped with book and pencil, persuasive tongue and beseeching eyes." Other accounts spoke of their powers of "persuasion and argument" and that they appeared to be "as reg-ular and well ordered as a regiment of soldiers."[31]

Above all, the church provided services for the children of the parish. By 1878 there were approximately 1,450 young people attending classes at St. James— 650 boys taught by the Christian Brothers and another 800 girls by the Sisters of Charity. This institution had a fine reputation. One historical critic of Al Smith still referred to it as "one of the best grammar schools in the city," and by the late 1870s over fifty of its students had gone on to become teachers in the public schools. For other graduates, particularly the young men who were perceived as breadwinners, the priests took it upon themselves to go out into the neighbor-hood and round up better jobs for them, as office boys, for example. In addition to the school, in 1882 Father Kean built an orphanage for 200 children (opened on Christmas Day) and an industrial school to feed and teach orphans and homeless children.[32]

In that neighborhood, Alfred and Catherine Smith would enroll their son Al at St. James, although the timing was not nearly as automatic as it would become later; records show that Al began classes in 1880, several months prior to his sev-enth birthday. The school he walked into was four stories tall, with lofty, narrow windows that were rounded at the top, cathedral style. Classrooms were big rooms filled with seats, with high ceilings—over ten feet tall—to fit the elongated church windows. There was, of course, no elevator, so the school remained always a walkup, with narrow, steep stairwells.[33]

Al became a part of this place; as long as he was at St. James, he served not only as a student but as an altar boy. His curriculum included rhetoric, ancient and modern history of the world, U.S. history, elocution, grammar, literature, and various branches of mathematics; as late as 1872 the school still taught surveying as a required subject. Given that the Christian Brothers' teaching style stressed memorization, the pupils, not surprisingly, excelled in precision drill. In 1892, for example, the girls of St. James School formed a living flag during that year's Columbian parade, the first time anything like this had ever been performed in New York City. There was also, however, a social conscience. As late as 1933, Al recalled that as a youth he had been made to read a poem by Thomas Hood entitled, "The Song of the Shirt," an open attack on the exploitation of women by sweatshop operators.[34]

But Al's education left him crippled in one critical way that would later devastate him as a politician, when combined with the social values he got from the neighborhood: everything he learned, both at St. James and outside, reinforced an incredibly naive sense of America. His school books, for example, fostered a simplistic belief in a simple, beneficent nation. It is virtually impossible to determine exactly which textbooks Al Smith used during his years of formal education,[35] but it is easy to determine which volumes were the standards, the best sellers, and thus most likely to have been purchased by Father Kean. All of these primers were devoted to sentimental patriotism, with an emphasis on great men. A typical volume was William Swinton's *First Lessons in Our Country's History*, one of the most popular texts of the era. The author explained to his young readers that, "the greatest *character* of the war of Independence was Washington. This meant that he was great in every way, not only as a soldier, but as a statesman and a man. . . . Washington was perfectly *unselfish* because he was perfectly *patriotic*."[36]

Aside from texts like this, Al did not read much; throughout his life one of his standard lines was that the only book he had ever read was *The Life and Battles of John L. Sullivan* (in fact, his reading in later life was considerably wider, his correspondence including numerous thank-you letters to authors). Published in 1883 by Richard Fox Publications, the slim volume had many of the same characteristics as the magazine that Fox had founded and made famous, the *Police Gazette*. Like that tabloid, *Life and Battles* was filled with adolescent male fantasies, particularly those surrounding the noble hero that was its subject, the first celebrity boxing champ in America. We know, furthermore, from sources such as Jim Farley that the young man did idolize Sullivan and followed his bouts religiously, so it is likely that, in fact, Al did read this volume.[37]

The Life and Battles of John L. Sullivan had a number of lessons for a lad seeking guidance on the meaning of America. While most of the book is a straightforward account of Sullivan's fight career, on page five it notes that Sullivan's "boyhood training was in the ball field, where the admirable system of exercise afforded by the national pastime developed his young muscles and brought him early to that perfection of manly vigor that has made him such a wonder to the world." In addition, "He has enjoyed all the advantages of a Boston education, where the standard is high." The sense here is of the New World as a kind of working-class utopia, where healthy, well-educated adolescents flourish, to the marvel of the rest of the planet. By page twenty-two we see the results of all this training in the wonderland of America: Sullivan was "the very picture of robust health and manly beauty, and made a beau ideal of a prize fighter." In addition, the author suggested, everyone would benefit from this bountiful environment: on the inside back cover was an ad for another Richard Fox publication, *The Lives and Battles of Famous Black Pugilists,* with a picture of an heroic African-American fighter on the cover.[38]

And this was not the only information Al received; popular culture provided another form of education. As a young man, for example, Al attended the Buffalo Bill Cody Wild West Show, with its images of heroic cowboys and the romantic, nationalistic drama of the so-called taming of the West. In the 1893 program Cody depicted himself as the archetypical American, the true product of a proud nation. All of the country's traits were on display as patrons read how "young, sturdy, a remarkable specimen of manly beauty, with the brain to conceive and the nerve to execute, Buffalo Bill par excellence is the exemplar of the strong and unique traits that characterize a true American."[39]

There was little hope that the young man would supplement these images with more subtle data, for Al Smith was hardly a well-traveled gentleman; as late as 1922, when he was about to be elected governor for a second term, Smith told the *New York Evening World* that for months at a stretch he rarely got above Canal Street, only a few blocks away. Not only did Al grow up in this area, in other words, he refused to follow the usual pattern of success that meant moving out, and uptown as well. Instead, he stayed in the Fourth Ward with his family, not leaving until he was over fifty years old.

This parochialism, combined with his nationalistic education, meant that early on, Al Smith developed a positive, simplistic view of America. He repeatedly told crowds that while the Declaration of Independence was "the most remarkable state paper in all the history of the world," the document itself "did nothing." Rather, "it was a strong, vigorous American spirit behind it that made it effective."

Walter Lippmann said that Smith "believes in the soundness of the established order and the honesty of its ideals," while Will Rogers observed that Al Smith was "the most sentimental prominent man I ever met. He glories in the past."[40]

But Al Smith took these beliefs and combined them with his understanding of human nature as practiced in the old neighborhood, to come up with a unique concept of American politics. The American people were basically tolerant and good, just like the folks on the Lower East Side. As a result, Al thought the system he knew so well was universal, and practiced all over this great land. He was convinced, therefore, that he truly understood the American people and, furthermore, that they could be trusted implicitly when it came to politics and values. This is what he must have meant when, in 1922, he told the *New York Evening World*, "I've met a lot of people from all over the country outside New York and I've found them fundamentally the same kind of people I was raised with,"[41] a remarkable statement indeed.

Above all, this is why he adopted "Let's Look at the Record" as the slogan for his professional career. One of the chief consequences of his upbringing was that Smith believed that, with the terribly complicating issue of diversity minimized, all that was left was each man and woman's actions—"the record," in other words. As an adult, Al always expected that his achievements, his resumé, would be the most significant issue in any campaign, that factors like bigotry were so minimal as to be irrelevant in public life. Years later, describing life in the neighborhood, Al's daughter told interviewers that prejudice "never came into our lives at all until [Al] ran for governor. For eleven years he ran for the [New York] Assembly and . . . we didn't know anything about such prejudices, not until the first campaign for governor in 1918."[42]

But Al's naiveté about America projected this belief onto an immense framework. To Smith, all of the differences of ethnicity and regionalism and race and religion in the nation would mean nothing, because they would be handled just the same way these factors were handled in the Fourth Ward. Just like in the neighborhood, the people of New York State, and then America, would look at each candidate fairly and choose the best man or woman based on what he or she had done, not whom he or she was. As late as October 1, 1928, deep into a presidential campaign that was exposing him to another part of the American character, he told a crowd in Rochester, "I took personal pleasure and personal delight in looking into the countenances of so many fellow American citizens, and whether they were on the far northwestern plains or in the central part of the west, they look just like our own neighbors here in New York."[43] The world of the Fourth Ward taught him that as a child, and he would carry it with him for a long time to come.

Chapter 3

The F.F.M. Man

OF ALL THE STORIES told by Al Smith, his favorite anecdote dated from 1911. Serving in the state legislature, he was involved in a floor debate with three upstate Republican representatives: Ed Merritt, Fred Hammond, and Jesse Phillips. As the discussion grew heated, an assemblyman from Buffalo, Gott-fried Wende, asked the privilege of interrupting.[1]

Wende's addition to the proceedings, breathed with the air of a town crier announcing the results of a critical battle, was the declaration, "Mr. Speaker, I have just heard that Cornell won the boat race." Merritt was the first to reply: "That doesn't mean anything to me. I'm a Yale man." Hammond then chipped in, "It doesn't mean anything to me. I'm a Harvard man." Finally, Phillips added, "It doesn't mean anything to me, I'm a U. of M. man."

If the speakers thought that they were humiliating Al Smith, bringing him up short with their pedigrees, they most definitely underestimated the man's quick-ness of wit. Al simply turned and said, "It doesn't mean anything to me . . . I am an F.F.M. man." At that a Tammany assemblyman yelled out, "What is that, Al?" and Smith answered, "Fulton Fish Market. Let's proceed with the debate."

Al loved this tale because it was in so many ways a metaphor for his coming-of-age years. During this period he received a variety of forms of schooling (some of it from jobs on the docks and in the F.F.M.); acquired the ability to deliver a quick and telling line; and eventually learned responsibility and even fell in love.

❦

At St. James school, we do not have any of little Al's grades, but secondary accounts indicate that he was an average scholar at best. At the same time, how-ever, there is also clear evidence that he was already beginning to shine in his command of the language. At an early age Al was more willing than any other student to bound from his seat and look up words in the big dictionary that they had on display, and he could soon floor his fellow pupils with his advanced vocabulary. This quality came to the attention of the priests, and when he was twelve years old Al got chosen to be St. James's junior representative at a competition for elocution involving all the local parochial schools. The contest was held at the De LaSalle Institute, on Second Street near Second Avenue; Catherine dressed young Alfred and his sister in their Sunday best and took the children to the hall herself. Daniel Donovan was the senior speaker from St. James, while his partner, the product of a classical education, delivered a lofty recitation entitled, "On the Death of Robespierre." The two boys swept the event, and Al received the silver medal, a triangle hanging from a small silver bar inscribed "Alfred E. Smith for Elocution." As a result of this success, he was asked to give the commencement address for the graduating class of 1886. Al delivered a reading entitled the "Miseries of Traveling," a safe subject for the locals.[2]

Besides this, he learned religion; every day Al attended a class entitled Christian Doctrine. This, of course, implies that the priests raised Al as a doctrinaire Catholic, but the truth was nothing like that. Instead, historian Robert Ernst explained how, in places like St. James, "The Church imparted dignity. It was a symbol of strength with which the individual identified himself and the means of salvation, offering escape from the poverty . . . of the present world"; religion, in other words, was not a set of laws, but an approach to life. Frances Perkins remarked that Al Smith "didn't know theology—he never knew theology of the Roman Catholic Church, and I don't think he cared much about it. He knew religion, and that was all that he needed. And he took it . . . simply and naturally." Grandson Walter remembered that Al was never a "philosopher" about his religion, he "never flaunted" it, but that it was always there; while another grandson, Father Arthur Smith, told how Al "would die rather than miss Mass on Sunday," but that was as far as it went, never engaging in heavy-handed discussions about religion. His grandfather, Father Arthur recalled, "didn't talk about his religion, but he lived it."[3]

Al got on well with the priests, and they had an enormous influence on him. Years later he described Father Kean as "a powerful and magnetic personality. . . . I felt his teaching and example as an influence in my own life such as only a well-beloved and respected teacher rouses in a growing boy."[4]

☙

Outside school, the young man now developed a hobby: Al Smith became, in his youth, a passionate, devoted lover of animals, a rather unusual preoccupation given his surroundings. This was hardly farm country, where a boy could grow up amidst a wide variety of creatures; Al lived in the city, a place where there were only strays and rodents, where the barn was replaced by a cramped tene-ment with no room to spare. So where did he learn to love animals so much?

The answer has to do with ocean voyages, back in the days of sailing ships. These were long, lonely excursions, where the number of companions was inherently limited and inevitably boring. Sailors quickly acquired pets at every port they called at, as a way of fighting off boredom and monotony.

When they got home, however, the dog, cat, or possibly more exotic creature quickly became excess baggage. Smith wrote that "hardly a sailor's boarding house along the waterfront . . . was without a private menagerie." In a short time, many of these animals that had been so captivating, such a source of enter-tainment aboard ship, became a nuisance, and when a young boy came along who loved the cute little creature, the owner quickly asked if he would like a new pet. It was the sailors, in other words, along with the dogs that ran all over the neighborhood, that introduced young Al to the wonders of the animal kingdom.

And the boy turned out to be a quick study, quite the enthusiast. At one time the attic at 174 South Street contained four dogs, a parrot (the perennial sailor's companion), a monkey, and one "West Indian goat"; it is not clear if the pedigree added to the goat's desirability, but Al always maintained that his pets were "all living in peace and harmony," up "in the garret of the South Street House." This was just the beginning, however; Al then decided that he would start collecting canines. In one of the milder examples of this avocation, he and a group of like-minded companions rounded up seven dogs; at this point it occurred to them that their parents might frown on this howling assortment of mutts, so they stored the pack surreptitiously in the shed of a warehouse on Front Street. Eventually Al had twelve dogs stashed upstairs, along with the goat, various birds, and some cats. His mother's patience was truly remarkable (how the decorous, proper Catherine Smith tolerated this is unknown, although sainthood cannot be ruled out), but eventually reason prevailed, and a menagerie was built at the back of his father's stable. But the seed had been planted, and Al never lost his love of pets of all sizes and shapes, but above all, dogs.[5]

After the canines *et al.* were gone, Al found other uses for the attic. He began to organize the boys in the neighborhood and brought them up there to put on amateur theatricals, complete with scenery and songs. The stage may have been tiny, but the standards were high; Al's sister always remembered the time she tried out for a particular part, and Al dismissed her summarily, without a word, because he felt her acting was not up to snuff. Once again, Catherine earned her place in heaven when she traipsed downstairs to apologize to the neighbors for the noise.[6]

Aside from such diversions, there was one activity more than any other that fascinated Al, that spoke to the inevitability of entering the adult world. The sound of firebells remained one of the most exciting events in the daily life of this neighborhood, and most of the boys abandoned whatever they were doing to chase the source of that clamor. Even better, Al's uncle, Peter Mulvihill, was a fireman at Engine Company 32 over on John Street, so all in all, this seemed like the most glamorous job in the universe.[7]

Al did everything he could to become a junior league fireman, later reminiscing that he "practically lived in that engine house during my recreation hours, after school." This meant that he could clean up the engines, polish brass fittings, check on the equipment, and do other chores to help his heroes. Above all, what brought him to the attention of the august Captain John Binns was his personality. Little Al could sing and dance, tell stories, and give recitations like no other child in the neighborhood.[8]

Anyone with that kind of talent had to be rewarded, and Al's prize was a grand one indeed. He became, in essence, the mascot of Company 32. They taught him the code—how the number of bells indicated which part of the district fire had broken out in. If Al was on station when the alarm went off, his duty was to grab the battered metal coffee can and the basket that was kept stocked with sandwiches. The lad would stand aside as three horses launched the old engine out into the street, and then Al would close the doors behind them. Running to the spot the bells had indicated, it was then his task to keep the coffee and the sandwiches constantly replenished, till he became a familiar to many of the local storekeepers. If the blaze was extinguished quickly and they returned before bedtime, Al received the ultimate gift: he would ride on the engine, the envy of every other boy in the neighborhood. It was a good life, and a possible career in the making.[9]

And then all of this came to an end. In 1885, when Al was eleven, his father's health began to fail. At first, he felt too weak to lift the heavy loads into the back of his wagon, so Alfred, Sr., hired a man to do the heavy work and began taking jobs as night watchman. The situation, and his constitution, worsened, and first one horse, then the other, and finally the wagon itself were all sold. Other changes had to be made too, as the family moved around the neighborhood, first to 316 Pearl Street, then to 12 Dover. Al started to deliver a variety of newspapers, including Henry George's *Leader,* which his parents enjoyed reading. He earned two dollars a week, and also sneaked them a free copy of George's paper. His initial capital was only twenty cents.[10]

By Election Day 1886, the father could barely move and had been confined to his bed for months. Somehow he roused himself to walk to the polling booth several doors away, managing to make it down the two flights of steps only with the support of a friend and Tammany official, Henry Campbell. Alfred, Sr., cast his ballot and returned to his doorstep, but could go no further. He sank onto the front steps and sat there until Catherine came down with some cushions to prop him up. After a long rest, she and Campbell lifted him into a chair, then carried the sick man up the stairs to his home. A few days after that, on November 11, Alfred Emanuel Smith, Sr., died.[11]

The father's passing left the family devastated. He had never made enough money to accumulate much in the way of a financial reserve, and the long illness, the doctor's bills, and the medicines, combined with the reality of everyday expenses, meant that no money was left. So poor were the Smiths by this point that the money for the funeral had to be raised among Alfred's many friends. Al wrote in his autobiography of his father's death, "His long illness and almost complete disability for months . . . left us in very straitened circumstances." At the time, he noted, "I was just one month short of thirteen years old."[12]

On the evening of his father's funeral, Al and his family returned to the place he described as a "cold and cheerless . . . little flat." On the way back from the cemetery, his sister recounted, Al told his mother, "I'm here. I can take care of you." At the apartment, he made a fire in the kitchen stove and according to at least one account, cooked dinner for the family.[13]

But bills did not wait for grief, and the state had terrible remedies for families that could not take care of their children. In those times there was the very real possibility that officials would come and remove the little ones, sending them to the bleakness of an orphanage, an unthinkable prospect for Catherine Smith. Delay served no purpose, so that very night, the widow took steps to earn an income; prior to her marriage she had been employed as an umbrella maker, not surprisingly, given that the city's district for this industry was nearby, on Pearl Street. Taking Al in tow, she looked up her old forelady, who lived just a few blocks away, asked for her job back, and received it. In addition, Catherine agreed to bring home "nightwork," the old-fashioned term that meant she would do piece work in the evenings to add a few more pennies to the pay envelope. Al held onto his paper route, but that was all; her goal, besides meeting expenses, was to see that her children managed to finish school, the hope that Al and Mamie would each receive a grammar school diploma.[14]

This lasted for a year, until, her health failing from the terrible hours and working conditions, Catherine was forced to seek an alternative. In that neighborhood, people stayed within the web of the small, tight circle when they needed help, but the resources, the flexibility of those tiny portions of humanity were at times formidable. In this case, it was the landlady of the building they lived in, at 12 Dover Street, who came through in the pinch. The building had a small candy and grocery store in the basement, and the owner offered the meager furnishings and stock if Catherine took over the rent. The deal set, Mamie helped out after school as Al peddled his papers, while his shift behind the counter began after the dinner meal and continued to closing.[15]

Not everything that happened at this point was hardship. The big adventure of that stage of Al's life came during the winter of 1887–1888. The season had seemed just about over as March 1888 began mildly, with temperatures on Saturday, March 10, going up to the mid-fifties. But a storm was on its way, a monster of a storm, and it slammed into the metropolis on Monday morning. Hurricane-class gusts as high as eighty-four miles an hour shattered New York on a day when even the average wind speed was thirty-five miles per hour, with snow piling up everywhere. Eyewitness accounts described people fighting for one-and-a-half hours just to cross a single street. By that night the temperature dropped to one below zero, and the mean for Tuesday, March 13, was nine degrees, the lowest since record keeping began in 1869. One historian observed that this event, which went down in the books as the famous blizzard of 1888, was "a legitimate full-fledged hurricane. It drove sleet with a force sufficient to draw blood upon hitting unprotected skin. And it came with sudden devastating force against a city that was totally unprepared for it." Before it was all over, two hundred people died.[16]

Al's big worry, however, concerned dogs, no great surprise. In the small back storage room behind the store, Catherine allowed Al to keep one—just one—pet. At this time it was Gertrude, a scotch terrier who had just given birth to four puppies. The proud owner explained, "I was not very much concerned with the inconvenience of our customers or the fear of the perishable quality of the merchandise," but rather of how he was going to get food and warmth to the canines trapped by the storm. Eventually Al decided to launch a relief mission and dug a tunnel to that basement doorway.[17]

Gertrude's safety taken care of, the waterfront beckoned to the young man. The East River froze solid, an unprecedented event, so wily entrepreneurs established ladders, charging five cents to get anyone safely onto the ice so that you could walk across to Brooklyn. Al and his friends "beat the ladder game" by simply sliding down the same pier, then strolled over to Brooklyn and back, a rather terrific outing.[18]

But that was Al's last great excitement before the noose of real life drew much closer around the Smith family. Catherine's health was deteriorating, and Al had to make a decision. His mother later disclosed to Frances Perkins how her son "stood up and took whatever came and carried his burden and always could think of a way to solve the family problems, even when he was a little boy. I had to rely on him." Sometime in the spring of 1888, a month or two before his graduation from grade school, Al quit to find full-time work. He would never return to a formal classroom.[19]

This event, momentous at the time, eventually grew and became part of the

Alfred E. Smith legend for both allies and foes. For his friends, it was a prime example of Al's Horatio Alger life story, a triumph that he could go so far without any diploma, and thus a source of pride. To his enemies it was another sign that the brash Irishman from the East Side of New York had no couth, no class, and obviously no education. They would remind him of this over and over, throughout his long career.

Neither description is totally accurate, since what happened to Al was not all that unusual. This was years before the mass of Americans received much education, and in truth, the average citizen in 1880 had fewer than four years of schooling, while Al almost completed the eighth grade. At that time there were only two high schools in New York City.[20]

At the same time, while it is clear that Smith never dodged this responsible act, his lack of a degree, even the most basic, always haunted and embarrassed him. Belle Moskowitz wrote the reformer Lillian Wald how her boss had "a great reverence for teachers and a tremendous respect for education. He appreciates what was, as he puts it, 'denied him' by circumstances." When he talked to Frances Perkins about his failure to ever go back and finish his education he would sigh; in his autobiography he wrote simply, yet with incredible stiffness and formality, about what must have been at least a rough decision: "The pressure upon the family treasury was so great that it was necessary for me to branch out and find greater earning capacity. I left school before graduation." This was not something he was proud of, so he did not talk about it in later years.[21]

In his search for employment, Al first turned to the industry he had grown up with, carting. It was a natural choice, and there must have been plenty of his father's contacts to draw on.

The result was a position with William J. Redmond as a truck chaser. This was an era before telephones were commonplace, and the most common form of communication was still messenger. Al's job was to dash hither and yon along the waterfront he knew so well, until he found specific drivers; he then delivered the details of their next pickup or delivery, carrying back any information they had for the boss. The salary was three dollars a week; Al always brought his complete pay envelope back to his mother.[22]

It was a job, but not a very well paying one; he soon went to Clarkson and Ford, an oil company. Al was now assistant shipping clerk and general all-around gopher (*handy boy* was the term used back then), making eight dollars a week, and still tied to the neighborhood; the firm stood on Front Street near Peck Slip. To make a little extra money at night he also began to use his voice, announcing the results of fights as they came off the ticker tape, including the 1892 bout in which James Corbett beat his idol, John L. Sullivan.[23]

That year he moved again, taking a position with John Feeney & Company, a commission house that dealt in fish in one of the city's leading wholesale emporiums. Al Smith had now become the F.F.M. man.

The Fulton Fish Market is part of the lore of Gotham. In 1816 the Common Council of the City of New York decided to honor Robert Fulton, who had died the year previous, by naming a street for him. This was part of the Beekman Estate, which in 1807 assigned the city the block bounded by Fulton, South, Beekman and Front streets for a public market. The city built its first building there in 1821, and vendors, dealing in produce of all kinds, flourished on this site.

By 1830, however, the fish dealers, set up on the second floor of this early structure, were doing so well they sought to expand into a building of their own. According to the major report done at the time, this move came with the endorsement of their downstairs neighbors, who told the investigating commission that the "water and other nuisances from the fish market descend into the stores below," causing problems. Then, as now, fish was a smelly business.

In response to these concerns, work began on a market building that would be dedicated to the trade. Over the next decades, several different structures became obsolete and were replaced, until in 1883 a new Fulton Fish Market opened, described by its leading chronicler as "a dark-red brick-and-iron fortress, with whimsical stone animal carvings, no doubt intended to relieve the general air of gloom." This sported overbearing gables, plus three tall cupolas, which sprouted from the roof.[24]

The reason the fishmongers needed a building of this size was the scale of their operations. By 1880 the dollar value of New York State's commercial fishing industry, concentrated in its biggest city, was the third largest in the nation. It was also fourth in terms of capital invested and fifth in the number of persons employed, ranking just below commercial giants Maryland and Massachusetts. Boats arrived at the Fulton Fish Market from New England, from up the Hudson River, from Long Island and New Jersey and the Connecticut shore, all trying to sell their catch in the town with the nation's biggest population and, hence, biggest appetite.[25]

Al's title with Feeney & Co. was assistant bookkeeper, which had absolutely nothing to do with his actual duties. In reality, he was once again an all-purpose helper, rolling in barrels, packing the carcasses in ice, selling, cleaning, wrapping fish of all kinds.[26]

The aspect of his work that Smith later made famous involved a mildly unscrupulous means of manipulating the marketplace. Fish wholesalers knew that their commodity was very, very perishable (seafood spoils rapidly). As a result, prices fluctuated quickly and dramatically, or as Richard Lord, who also worked as information officer for the F.F.M. explained, they can rise or fall "within the minute." A successful dealer had to be able to calculate and recalculate a number of factors quickly, a world of subtle nuances that changed so rapidly that Lord commented that true expertise "has to be in your blood."[27]

Of these factors, the most important was the size of the day's catch, which, because of supply and demand, would be the major influence on prices and availability of product. Advance knowledge of this dimension would be a powerful aid in setting the best price to guarantee both maximum profit and sales.

Al Smith became a key player in obtaining this knowledge at the best advantage. Jim Farley, Al's friend and a leading Democratic Party honcho, later said that Al caught his boss's eye because "when tempers flared, Al Smith could win by skillful use of his tongue what others had to settle with their fists." According to Farley, John Feeney told Al, "If you don't have the biggest mouth in the Market, you've sure got the loudest," and then set about making use of this particular talent.[28]

Feeney handed young Al a brass telescope and told him to go up to the roof every morning. Al's job was to watch the Buttermilk Channel (between Governor's Island and Brooklyn, one of the main routes by which the fishing fleets arrived at the market) for the return of the schooners. As soon as he could see clearly enough, the young man was to note how high or low the boats rode in the water—a prime indicator of the size of the catch—and call down this information to his superiors. While this method did not allow for subtle descriptions, it did provide Feeney with advance notice of a glut or a shortage, so that he could peg his prices accordingly.[29]

This business required a long day. Al started at four every morning and worked until four in the afternoon, except for Friday, when he began at 3 A.M. The pay was $12.00, a big increase from what he had been making in his last job. Mamie was making another $6.50 a week addressing envelopes, so at least the wolf was no longer clawing at the Smiths' door. In addition, the job entitled him to take home all the produce he wanted, and Al made full use of it, the family practically living on a fish diet. Al always claimed that he had a recurring nightmare of those years, that a large fish was constantly pursuing him, seeking revenge for all of its relatives that he had consumed. Later, as a politician in Albany, he explained that "If all the fish I handled were put into the capitol building they would pry the roof off, bulge out the windows, cover the lawn, and cascade down State Street . . . in a stream fifteen feet deep. I speak the fish language."[30]

But Al's portrayal of this work was a bit disingenuous and, although he never realized it, disguised the real significance of this experience. According to the standard depictions, Al's stint at the F.F.M. indicated his experience with rough industrial work at the city's core. The tasks were brutal, simple-minded, and long, and it was here that he learned about the modern working world.

A walk through the Fulton Fish Market, however, shows how inaccurate this image was, how different the work there remains from the mass production factories or western mines of the late nineteenth century. Jobs in the market may be long and hard and physical, but they are far from repetitious. Things are constantly changing, and new tasks crop up frequently. In addition there is the mercurial fact of dealing with the public, which is anything but predictable.

Furthermore, most of the jobs require a fair amount of skill. The standard tools of the market, then and now, are the hand-held hook and the small hatchet-pick. The latter are carried slung over the shoulder, and both are very sharp. Despite the presence of these implements and the slickness of wet surfaces everywhere, the injury rates remain negligible. As a means of gauging how remarkable a feat this was, the market's record should be compared to that of another industry where workers also carried honed blades and where the floor underneath was also constantly wet and slimy: the meatpacking industry. Upton Sinclair's *The Jungle* depicted record-high accident rates, and meatpacking still suffers one of the highest accident rates of any industry in the country.

Above all, the F.F.M. is a small, intimate world, where many of the firms are still family owned and have been in the same hands for years, and even generations. Turnover is limited, and community is strong, making it the antithesis of anonymous industrial labor. In the market, a man earns his reputation and has to live with it: one fishmonger, asked to explain relationships in this tiny world, stared grimly out to sea, then grunted with finality, "Nobody forgives or forgets."

Ironically, therefore, while the real story of the F.F.M. belies Smith's tough working-class image, it instead helps explain why Al eventually became such a fervent reformer. Years later, when he discovered modern industrial life, when Al Smith led the inquiry into the Triangle Shirtwaist fire, he truly and sincerely was shocked by what he saw. At that time, investigators like Frances Perkins took him up to attics and down to cellars and had Smith look in the faces of children as they trundled into the factories at six in the morning. Al thought he knew factory work, but he did not, and so was outraged when he had to confront the real thing; in later years his dismay, his surprise, his anger were real, as were his responses to terrible industrial conditions.

⤙

Al was now becoming a dapper, somewhat stylish young man. The best photos we have of him from this period show a lanky, somewhat gawky youth with a thin, narrow face and big ears, dressed in the dapper fashions of the Bowery. One of the girls from the neighborhood later described Al's costume to a reporter, commenting on what a fashion plate he was, how "he used to wear fancy vests, a red necktie and tight trousers."[31]

Around this time his fancy turned to bicycling. Baseball had not yet triumphed as the great urban sport it would become in the next century, and two-wheel locomotion was the big craze of the 1880s and 1890s. A thriving industry in rentals sprang up in the Wall Street area, where there was asphalt pavement instead of cobblestones. After the day's trading had ended, on a pleasant summer's eve, citizens of every class could be seen out in front of the Sub-Treasury Building, learning how to ride.[32]

Al learned how to stay on top of this wobbly vehicle, though not without mishaps, including the time he somehow bounced over the curb, crossed the sidewalk, and then, totally out of control, rode down three steps through the open door of an all-night telegraph office. Once he had mastered the device, however, longer excursions were possible, across the Brooklyn Bridge and out into the fields of Long Island. In time, he even became a member of the Century Club, whose sole standard of admission was riding one hundred miles in a single day. This honor Smith attained on a Sunday morning, when a friendly group left lower Manhattan at nine in the morning and cycled to Far Rockaway. They stopped, went swimming, had their afternoon meal, and pedaled back home. Al became so well known that a local paper depicted him atop his mechanical steed, with the caption, "Alfred E. Smith: The Coasting King." Catherine clipped the drawing and accompanying article and pasted it into a scrapbook she had been making for him, using the empty pages of one of her husband's blank Wells Fargo receipt books.[33]

The big love of his life, however, and the youthful hobby that most influenced his later career, was acting. Theater was always a vibrant force in the neighborhood, given that this section included the rialto of entertainment that was the Bowery. At Niblo's Garden on Prince Street, Al had entered the world of the footlights for the first time, when, as a young boy, he watched Kit Chanfran perform in *The Arkansas Traveler*. There were a plethora of playhouses and performers close at hand, and Al grew up with such stars as Weber and Fields and Harrigan and Hart.[34]

It was St. James Church, however, that actually got him involved in performing. In its desire to create a strong and supportive environment for all members of the community, the church had started the St. James Literary Union for young people. At first they met in a house at 49 Henry Street that the rectory had bought for them in 1877, but in time their focus became the stage in the church basement. Changing their name to the St. James Players, the group became a major bulwark of the church, producing an enormous range of entertainment for the local residents, as well as being a superb fund raiser.[35]

The St. James basement sat eight-hundred patrons, more than most theaters at the time; contemporaries of Al who saw him on that platform remembered that "the stage was wide and deep and the footlights conspicuous." Each play had only a brief run, so sometimes the group shifted to a legitimate hall to continue performing; one of the St. James Players' most popular productions, Dion Boucicault's *The Shaughraun,* enjoyed three runs of two weeks apiece in the basement and was such a smash hit that the group then produced it for two nights at the London Theatre on the Bowery. Many performers even made the transition to actual employment by joining the chorus in professional productions; they became supernumerary players—"supes," to use the patois of dramaturgy. Al managed to get hired—at a dollar a night—at the Windsor Theatre as a Roman legionnaire in the epic *The Fall of Rome,* and became a Russian peasant for what must have been an equally grandiose adventure, *Siberia.*[36]

Starting around the age of eighteen, Al became a stalwart of the St. James troupe; as he put it, he was "dead stuck on acting." We have few reviews of his work; his daughter Emily caught a revival performance when she was fifteen years old, and as she delicately put it, her "judgment . . . was not entirely objective." "Certainly," she explained, "I found it impossible not to see that it was really Father . . . upon the stage." There are, however, some indications that Al's talents, while real, were not all that he wanted them to be: while there is no question that he was one of the leading members of the group, he also quickly evolved into a character actor, specializing in villains.[37]

The St. James Players were known as one of the best amateur groups in the city, but there were still some rocky moments, both on stage and in the community. One performer had only a loose sense of dialogue, Al remembered, and did not grasp entirely the subtle, yet relevant difference between speech parts and italicized stage directions in the script. No threat to John Barrymore, the young man took the boards and bellowed to the audience, "Ha-ha! My time has come! Grabs knife and cuts rope!" Al remarked that there was "a pleasant surprise awaiting him when he came behind the scenes."[38]

Frivolity like this, of course, came from the loose informality of players and audience. Emily commented, in an observation that included scores of small urban playhouses all over the country, that there "was much neighborhood intimacy in the basement of the church." One night Al was playing the villain again, this time Jem Dalton in *The Ticket-of-Leave Man.* A typical turn-of-the-century potboiler, the play called on Al to struggle with Hawkshaw the detective, a predecessor of Sherlock Holmes. But while he was building up to this epic fight, a group of young boys squirreled their way down the aisles until they were literally perched in the footlights. Suddenly Hawkshaw, ever stalwart, knocked the pistol from Dalton's hand and forced him to the ground, defeating the knave;

Jem (or Al) was on his knees helpless. A suitable denouement should have followed, but unfortunately for the lead, he was not as well known to the locals as Al Smith was. One of the boys picked up the prop gun and put it in Dalton (Smith)'s hand, yelling, "Here you are, Al." The audience roared, and even Al had a hard time keeping a straight face.[39]

Most of the characters in these plays were, at best, two-dimensional with an occasional background of simple patriotism, thus reinforcing Al's naiveté. In one, *The Mighty Dollar,* he declaimed, "Why, this is the most wonderful country on the face of the earth, sir. We excel all the rest of creation in everything, sir, either natural or artificial. We have the longest nights and the brightest days, the highest mountains and the biggest rivers . . . the biggest cities and the biggest buildings."[40]

If there was one play that was typical of Smith's youthful acting career, it was Dion Boucicault's *The Shaughraun.* Boucicault, long since forgotten, was one of the most popular playwrights of the nineteenth century, authoring or adapting over 150 plays in a career that stretched from 1838 to 1890. Quantity does not, however, guarantee quality, and few of these were memorable. Instead, the playwright was particularly "shrewd," as one scholar of Victorian theater put it, "at anticipating the unsophisticated tastes of the popular audiences of the nineteenth century." Boucicault "devoted a vigorous lifetime to giving the people what he believed they wanted—an extravaganza of melodramatic parts, comic characters and music-hall entertainment." Within this genre he reigned supreme, or as another critic drily remarked, "It is as the best melodramatist of the third quarter of the nineteenth century that Boucicault most deserves to be remembered."[41]

With *The Shaughraun,* Boucicault "realized the peak of his talent." Though set in Ireland (Boucicault traveled constantly between the British Isles and Broadway), the play opened in New York at Wallack's Theater on November 14, 1874, and a year later at the Drury Lane Theater in London. Phenomenally successful, it earned half a million dollars in the United States alone.[42]

The story is classic melodrama. Arte O'Neal is a lovely colleen betrothed to the noble hero, Robert Ffolliott. Cory Kinchella, the evil villain, covets two things: Arte's person and Robert's land. Wandering around in the background is the Shaughraun, a kind of tramp, a wise, funny, Irish storyteller, who interjects an element of farce and makes light with the audience, offering both comments and explanations as to what is happening onstage. There are numerous twists and diversions—at one point Kinchella turns Robert over to the hated British—but in the end good triumphs and evil is vanquished. Kinchella—Al's character—always lost out.

But for all the ups and downs of Al's theatrical career, it had a lasting effect on the young man, since in truth, the theater taught Al Smith how to be a superb politician. It gave him, for example, a fantastic memory. In later years as governor and presidential candidate, Smith dazzled observers by his ability to look at a pile of data, then walk out to an audience and quote facts and figures without looking at a single note card. His standard method of speechwriting was to take an envelope, jot down a series of notes on the outside, place inside a batch of newspaper clippings numbered in corresponding fashion, and head out to the podium. He was also capable of dictating a speech from scratch, repeating it once or twice aloud, and having it memorized.

At least equally important, his years on the stage turned Al into a great orator. Plays like *The Mighty Dollar* and *The Shaughraun* may not have been Shakespeare, but the humorous content did require a sense of timing. The latter piece involved a number of asides, where the performer turned to the audience and talked directly to them. A tricky business, it demanded a delicate sense of rhythm and cadence, which Al mastered nicely. Theater also teaches the delicacy of language—how different words and sounds convey a message better than others—and above all, it teaches how to tell a story. In later years, Al Smith became an expert at explaining complex governmental issues vividly to vast popular audiences using folksy examples, inserted at just the right places, emphasized with the hand gestures and body movements of a trained thespian; if Al Smith told a joke to make a larger point, everyone got it. In his autobiography, Al remarked, "For innocent pastime, for recreation, for knowledge, for training the memory, and for giving a person a certain degree of confidence, there is no better amusement than amateur theatricals."[43]

By the time he was in his twenties, Al was becoming fairly well known as an amateur talent. At St. James, his performance as Bardwell Slote in *The Mighty Dollar*, even though it was not the hero's role, got him top notice in a local paper. Silver Jubilee Celebrations for the St. James Union and for Father Kean's ordination, in 1896 and 1899, respectively, both featured Alfred E. Smith as the keynote speaker.[44]

Al's notoriety as an actor started to spread. He appeared in *The Confederate Spy* at the Lexington Opera House on Fifty-eighth Street between Lexington and Third avenues, and gave the main oration at the annual gala of the Leo Catholic Club of Fordham, up in the pastures of the Bronx. Another speech was delivered in East Orange, New Jersey, to the Christ Church Men's Club, and the St. James Players rendered *The Mighty Dollar* at the Catholic Summer School that met along Lake Champlain, 350 miles from Chatham Square and the Bowery.

All of this reinforced Al's natural self-confidence, a trait that Catherine had nourished in him. One old resident of the neighborhood told Frances Perkins how Al was a regular at dances and parties, but that one time they were planning a picnic and had forgotten to invite him. Just then he happened to walk by and joined the discussion. "You haven't been asked to go," one of the young ladies reminded him, and he replied, "Oh, you'll ask me . . . you won't be able to get along without the talent."[45]

This success stood in marked contrast to the rest of his life, however. He was still living in a proud but hardly middle-class part of town, and after four years at the Fulton Fish Market he decided to take a better position, as a shipping clerk for the Davidson Steam Pump Works in Brooklyn. There was not much to the job, checking steam pipes and fittings that the company manufactured; as his daughter Emily put it, "Outside of the increase in pay that this new job brought, there was little else about it that attracted Father." He had minimal education, and there seemed little chance of ever getting ahead, of getting out of the neighborhood and bettering himself, of even living a happy and fulfilled life. On that last score, however, his luck would soon change.[46]

⌖

The mission seemed simple enough. Al had a buddy, John Heaviside, who, as the son of one of the policemen in the neighborhood, was a pretty well-known fellow. He lived a couple of blocks over, on Catherine Street, so there was plenty of opportunity for the two men to come into regular contact.[47]

No one remembered the exact date, but sometime in 1894 John had some papers, dealing with the family plot at Calvary Cemetery, that had to be signed by his aunt who lived up in the Bronx. In those days the Bronx was a *long, long* way off, so it seemed natural that he asked Al along for company. The two young men set off on their journey, taking the elevated steam railway as far as 129th Street and Third Avenue, where that early form of the New York rapid system ended. After that they took a horsecar; and for the final leg of the trip, hoofed it to a house at 3681 Third Avenue, on the corner of 170th Street.

Many things about that trip must have impressed Al: the open spaces, the lush greenery. But all that paled in comparison to the sight of one Katie Dunn. Catherine Dunn was the daughter of Simon Dunn and Emily Josephine Heaviside, both immigrants from Ireland. Her father was a ship's chandler, running a store that outfitted sailing ships, and by the time she reached the age of ten they could afford to move from Cherry Street to the relatively luxurious and suburban Bronx. Simon must have acquired a sizable nest egg, since sometime after the move the family lost two sons, a third moved away, and even Simon himself passed on, yet there is no evidence of hard times for the Dunns. Instead, Katie was sent to St. Joseph's Academy for Young Ladies, a Catholic finishing school where the nuns taught her not only book work but how to be a lady—subjects like embroidery and china painting.[48]

In later years and after five children, Katie acquired a matronly appearance. The best picture we have of her prior to her marriage, however, a cameo portrait, shows this young woman as a love-struck Al Smith must have seen her, and she was a knockout. Although the image is faded and cracking, it is still possible to see how delicate and beautiful she was, with big, enchanting eyes and soft, pale features, topped by ringlets of dark, curly hair.[49]

Katie never revealed what she thought of this outgoing young man who was suddenly on her doorstep, but it is clear that for Al, it was, to use an old-fashioned cliché that seems so appropriate to the period and to what happened, love at first sight. We have absolutely no evidence of Al's ever having taken out anyone else, yet he would pursue this lass with patience and dedication. They would become, to use more modern terminology, partners for life.[50]

But this proposition was much easier said than done, especially given the distances. The Bronx was considered a wilderness, "so far north that it might have been in Canada," as one author put it. Edward Flynn, a local resident who grew up to become political boss of that borough, recounted that in his youth, "the Bronx still retained a great deal of its rural or small-town atmosphere"; by the time of the 1890 census, around the time Al first met Katie, only 88,908 people lived there, compared to 1.44 million in Manhattan.[51]

So it is not surprising that the courtship got off to a slow start. After their initial meeting, they did not see each other again for several months. Al made *repeated* inquiries to her cousin Johnnie as to whether there were possibly more papers that needed to be taken up to the Bronx, until finally they agreed to make a trip *sans* documents. Occasionally the Dunns traveled back to the old neighborhood to see Katie's uncle the policeman, which allowed for additional visits. Eventually (after a year or two, Al reported in his autobiography), Al was taking the trip up to the Bronx by himself.

The courtship of Katie Dunn followed the patterns of an earlier age. The proper amusements for a rollicking evening were to sit around the piano while Katie played and have the whole family sing old, sentimental ballads, as well as more modern vaudeville and show tunes. Sometimes Al would swing her around the parlor or do a recitation. There is no evidence that anything less chaste, less innocent ever occurred, but there is plenty of testimony that they enjoyed these sessions enormously, bolstered by the fact that Al and Katie were still entertaining themselves like this when they died.[52]

The inevitable trip back and forth, however, remained a long one. Sometimes Al, in an act that predated one of the most standard experiences of tired subway riders, would be lulled to sleep by the rocking of the cars and doze. In a later age that practice would carry certain dangers with it, and so it was in the 1890s: Al had his umbrella stolen. When his mother gave him a new one, he adopted the strategy of tying some twine between the bumbershoot and his suspenders, so that he could enjoy his slumbers without undue loss. But clearly something had to be done.[53]

Al had taken his time in the courtship, but he also had to overcome some resistance. The Dunns knew his family, knew the old neighborhood, and that provided a comfort level, but they had some concerns as well. Al had only a fair job, and above all, there was that theater thing. This was an age eons before Hollywood showered money on superstars, and an actor was someone involved in a transient and unsavory business. No daughter of Emily Josephine Dunn was going to forsake her reputation by hitching up with that kind of young man. Quietly, firmly, Al renounced career ambitions for the theater, a rather modest sacrifice in all likelihood, and removed that obstacle.

☙

All of this courting—the singing in the parlor, the trips to the dances—was done in the slow, exquisite ballet that was so common to that era. Al and Katie fell in love, but it took them six years of occasional visits, of weekends alone and apart, of having umbrellas snatched, before they were wed.

It was the bride's prerogative to pick the church, so on May 6, 1900, the couple celebrated their love and a new century by walking down the aisle of St. Augustine's Church at Franklin Avenue and 167th Street, one of the oldest in the Bronx. Officiating, however, was none other than Father John Kean, by now having served more than twenty years as pastor of St. James. Distinguished elder churchmen like that did not often travel outside their parish, and it was a sign of the affection and esteem that Kean held for Al that he agreed to handle the ceremony.[54]

There was no money for an elaborate honeymoon—Niagara Falls must have seemed an impossibly long way off—so Al rented a small apartment near Bath Beach in Brooklyn where they could spend the summer enjoying the sea breezes and taking an occasional swim. Al commuted from the office, and when autumn beckoned, they moved back to the old neighborhood; it seemed natural to both of them, and Al simply felt, as he commented, that he had "brought her back to the ward she was born in," back to a place that they both understood and felt secure in.[55]

Their first apartment was at 83 Madison Street, just down the block from St. James. The street was narrow, and as Al or Katie looked out the front windows they could see into apartments just across the way. Thus, their married life, their family life, began amidst the intense intimacy of the city. In a reasonable time, on January 26, 1901, their first son was born, and carrying on a family tradition, the father named him Alfred E. Smith, but added a "Junior" this time. With the new addition more space was needed, so Al and Katie and Alfred, Jr. moved a few doors over to a place at 79 Madison Street, where Emily arrived. The next stop was 9 Peck Slip, and a daughter they named Catherine, after Al's mother; eventually two other children, Arthur and Walter, rounded out the family. Al now had a family; it was time to start a career.[56]

Chapter 4

"The Hall"

NEW YORKERS ARE KNOWN for their accent, but also for their unique vocabulary, and on the South-East Side of Manhattan, everybody knew what it meant when you said, "The Hall." You were not talking about Tony Pastor's joint or some place that served beer, but rather, the venerable institution known as Tammany Hall.

Tammany was named for Tamanend, grand chief of the Lenni-Lenape branch of the Delawares, a tribe of Native Americans who lived in southeastern Pennsylvania and Delaware and spoke Algonquin. Their cousins, a subtribe called the Canarsie, had even sold Brooklyn to the Dutch.[1]

The great chief became part of colonial America's history in the 1770s, when revolution was in the air. All symbols were political in those days, so when a group of young men in Philadelphia formed a patriotic society similar to the Sons of Liberty, they decided to name it after an indigenous hero. They founded the Sons of Saint Tammany, though sainthood was far from their goal; this was a quintessentially political society active in the cause of independence, and similar organizations using the name of Tammany eventually arose in eight of the thirteen colonies, including New York.

After the war, many of these organizations disbanded, but the members remained active democrats opposed to more aristocratic organizations like the Society of Cincinnati in New York City, whose membership was limited to elites like George Washington and Alexander Hamilton. Soon a group, consisting mostly of artisans and workingmen but with some wealthier citizens who feared the return of aristocracy, began meeting, starting on January 25, 1786, in Barden's Tavern in lower Manhattan. By March 1789 they were sufficiently organized to issue an appeal, including the statement that "it has become apparent that our independence, so recently and so dearly obtained by our fathers and our brothers . . . is in danger of being . . . disturbed." As a result, "In order . . . to counteract the machinations of those slaves and agents of foreign despots," a new organization, "founded on the basis of American liberty as the rallying point of freemen, is indispensably necessary." The members adopted a constitution in April, which spoke of "the indissoluble bonds of patriotic friendship"; and on May 12, 1789, there was the first glorious meeting of the new Society of Saint Tammany, an event filled with the kinds of political speeches that were so common in that post-Revolutionary era. This included the reading of the Declaration of Independence in its entirety, thus starting a yearly tradition that lasted well past the time when Al Smith joined, and even led, the Hall. Initiation fees ranged from two to eight dollars, based on ability to pay, and dues were twenty-four cents a quarter.

At first, Tammany excluded anyone who was not a native-born citizen, and also Catholics. But the club was actively involved in local politics, and pragmatism ruled. In 1809 they endorsed their first Irish Catholic, and by the end of the next decade sons of Erin were prominent throughout the society.[2]

In time, Tammany adopted a reasonably elaborate organization, mostly drawing on Indian symbols; the Hall was referred to as the "wigwam"; Tammany members were called "braves"; and the board of directors consisted of thirteen "sachems," or chiefs, headed by the grand sachem. There were also a secretary, a treasurer, a sagamore (master of ceremonies), and a doorkeeper, who was given the unfathomable title of wiskinsky; no one has ever revealed its Indian origins, if such exist. The Society of Saint Tammany had several full-time halls until 1812, when it took over a red brick, mansard roofed structure on Park Row and Frankfort Street, right in the heart of Al's future neighborhood. That lasted until July 4, 1868, when they opened the headquarters that Al would know throughout most of his career, at 145 East Fourteenth Street between Irving Place and Third Avenue, the longest-lasting and most famous of all the Tammany Halls.[3]

Although Tammany was active in American politics throughout the early nineteenth century, supporting, for example, candidates like Thomas Jefferson and Martin Van Buren, it really blossomed during the Gilded Age after the Civil War, for two primary reasons. First, there was a dramatic need for an organization to run the city. New York was absolutely booming, the population jumping from 942,000 in 1870 to 1.2 million in 1880; in one decade, in other words, it had added a population larger than that of most cities in America. Business was exploding at a rapid pace, and the port handled 70 percent of the nation's imports.[4]

The city's government could not keep pace, and so business turned to the political machine as an alternative. The city council may be stymied, the clerk's office might not know what to do, but anyone could get anything by paying off the boss. No one had developed rules, for example, to govern the conditions under which someone could construct a steam railroad down Third Avenue, so the system became paralyzed. Entrepreneurs, moving at terrific speed and ignoring any concerns of public welfare, wanted to build *now,* and only Tammany Hall, it seemed, could make that possible. The machine saw to it that the city still functioned, although not always in everyone's best interest. Weak government made for a strong machine.

Coupled with this was the change in voting blocs that transformed municipal politics. Immigrants dominated the New York political scene in the Gilded Age, particularly the large body of famine Irish, but also a sizable wave of Germans. These people were poor, adjusting to the rules of America, but also the rules of unrestrained urban capitalism. They had few friends outside their fellow immigrants. If you got in trouble, if you were just simply hungry, there was no welfare system, and the charities, run by downtown elites, were condescending and intrusive.

In stepped the machine. If your son got picked up by the cops, they sent a lawyer to court. If you were cold, a load of coal arrived. If your house burned down (at a time when insurance was rare), the first person on the scene was the ward leader. The list was endless, and included even such simple acts of status and recognition as attending a wedding or a funeral. And the most amazing thing was that all the ward leader wanted in return was one little, tiny act; once a year you were expected to go to the polls and vote for these people who had done so much for you. It seemed like the smallest of gestures, and the least you could do. Who cared if in the meantime they looted the city treasury and built structures like the Tweed Courthouse, originally budgeted at $250,000 but after graft and corruption took hold, costing taxpayers more than $13 million?

The goal of this system was to turn out the vote, and Tammany had a pretty fair track record in this regard. In the presidential election of 1888, for example, 62 percent of southerners went to the polls, while in the nonsouthern states the figure went up to 73 percent. Tammany made them all look like slackers, however, by getting 86 percent of all eligible males—over the age of twenty-one years, native-born or naturalized citizen—to cast a ballot. By 1900 the South had engaged in a successful effort to disenfranchise poor whites and throw blacks out of the system altogether, so their tally dropped to a dismal 29 percent, while the rest of the country had slipped slightly, to 65 percent. Tammany was undaunted, and stayed with the 86 percent figure. Most of their voters were also reliable; in some assembly districts in the Tammany stronghold regions, particularly in lower Manhattan, Democratic candidates racked up margins of 80 to 90 percent of the vote.[5]

The most important by-product of the Hall and its subheadquarters was the best social service organization in the city. Boss Tweed founded this system, giving each ward leader a thousand dollars for coal for the poor during the winter of 1870–1871 and donating another fifty thousand dollars just to the Fourth Ward, the district Alfred and Catherine Smith lived in. Between 1852 and 1869, the New York State legislature passed appropriations for private charities that totaled just over $2 million. When Tweed took power, he saw to it that between 1869 and 1871 alone they donated $2,225,000.[6]

A fair amount of this money went for lavish feedbags put on by most of the Tammany bosses. Account after account describe enormous dinners, with thousands of people sitting down to a meal; and boat rides, employing massive excursion liners to take everyone in the district to some pleasure spot, where dinner was served. Helen Graff remembered the later, simpler versions, when Tammany used to take the people of the neighborhood every year to a picnic at Battery Park, serving up sandwiches, cookies, and fruit. Reformers with full bellies decried this corruption of the democratic process, but Tammany officials knew that there was nothing more important to these people than food, so they gave it away for free, and in large amounts.[7]

At the local, intimate level of the neighborhood, Tammany established several kinds of headquarters. Although the average leader drank very little, many of them owned saloons; the old joke used to go that the quickest way to break up a meeting of the Tammany executive committee was to poke your head in the room and scream, "Your tavern is on fire." One writer, Harry Roskolenko, remarked that "every corner . . . had saloons. . . . And every corner was a political island."[8]

In addition, every assembly district (the jurisdiction that succeeded wards) had a club, a political central where politicians and paupers got together to transact business, and also to spend time in each other's company. Politicos could meet with the public, or sit and share a cup of coffee with cronies, passing an afternoon or evening. The leading student of these institutions called them "the ganglia of politics," places where decisions were made, relief was distributed, and pageants were put on. Everything from entertainment to education went on in these clubs, and they became so important that an observer claimed, "They rival the churches in their ritual and, by the combination of . . . these activities, they fill the gaps in our economic, social, and political structure." Decades after he had graduated out of one of these clubs, Al remembered how irrelevant it was that the city "may offer a thousand and one different attractions, amusements and educational opportunities," because "the local political club is . . . a natural center for everyone in the neighborhood." Helen Graff recalled that the Tammany club in her district had a bowling alley for men in the basement and a card room for ladies that was also used for meetings; she could even recall going to dances there. Politics in those days was, for many New Yorkers, their leading form of entertainment, the voluntary association they most preferred.[9]

❧

By the turn of the century, Tammany was confronting its greatest challenge— the changing tides of immigration. Over a half-century and more, they had learned how to appeal to the Irish and the Germans, but now they had to shift gears, ignore their own prejudices at times, and reach out to Italians and Jews, Poles and Greeks. On the Lower East Side, an area including the Second, Fourth, and Eighth Assembly Districts, 42 percent of the population in 1910 was born in Russia, and 15 percent was second-generation Russian. Another 19 percent came from the old Austria-Hungarian Empire, the vast majority of these also Jews from the Pale of Settlement. Italians and their children made up 8 percent of the area. Only 1.03 percent of the residents of this area had been born in Ireland, and only 1.50 percent had Irish parents. James Hooey, one of the great Tammany leaders, once told an audience that in the old days, life was "comparatively simple." But now, he explained, there were "whole districts made up of Jews, Italians, Poles, Czechs, Greeks and negroes, all with their own conflicting interests, their own prejudices and racial peculiarities, all seeking to be satisfied and not ignored." Thus, "the problems of the political leader have multiplied in numbers and . . . complexities."[10]

Tammany leaders responded as best they could, some better than others. While the leadership ranks remained mostly Irish, the smart ones reached out to the new groups of voters, bosses like John Ahearn, who got the firemen—almost all Irish—to wash down the walls of the synagogues in his district every year at Rosh Hashanah. Big Tim Sullivan, who owned the Third Assembly District on the Bowery, just north of Al's area, once dealt with some Irish punks who were harassing Orthodox Jews. Big Tim, never a piker, had his police (a blissfully accurate term) raid the toughs' hangout, saw to it that the landlord evicted them, and then took over the space himself and turned it into his clubhouse. Another Tammany headquarters displayed out front as many flags as there were nationalities in the Assembly District, which meant that there were banners for the Irish, Italians, French, Russians, Syrians, Chinese, and Swedes, among others.[11]

❧

The dominant Tammany chieftain south of Fourteenth Street in the late nineteenth century was that same Timothy Sullivan, known universally as "Big Tim," an archetype of the local political boss. One reporter called his district "the most perfectly organized and the strongest in New York."[12]

Big Tim got the nickname fairly, as a hefty child. Born in 1863 in a tenement, his father was a laborer who died leaving a widow and six children; Timothy was only four at the time. His mother tried to keep him in school, but there was not a lot of money for extras. One bad winter he arrived for classes with his cold, blue toes poking through the front of his broken shoes. The teacher, a Miss Murphy, took him aside and made inquiries. When she discovered the nature of the problem—that the family just could not afford any more—she gave the boy a note and sent him to the one place that everyone knew took care of the poor. Tim emerged from the local Tammany clubhouse wearing a pair of new shoes, the first he had ever owned in his life. In return, as an adult with power and resources, Big Tim saw to it that the district gave away five to ten thousand pairs of brogans every winter.[13]

Big Tim became known for that kind of generosity. His banquets were legion, feeding five thousand men at a time, the kitchens serving up ten thousand pounds of turkey, two hundred gallons of coffee, five thousand pies; at the end each diner received a pipe and a sack of tobacco. Even his enemies estimated that Tim spent more than twenty-five thousand dollars a year to feed, shelter, and provide for the people of his district, and he was often seen at dawn taking bands of unemployed men down to the docks to arrange for jobs. Tim explained, "I never ask a man about his past; I feed him, not because he is good, but because he needs food." He felt that "there ain't much to it to be a leader. It's just plenty of work, keep your temper . . . and don't put on any airs, because God and the people hate a chesty man."[14]

Outside the neighborhood, Big Tim was known for something else, for, alas, the lad was not exactly a saint. As the boss of the Bowery district, it was his job to protect (and collect from) all the brothels, all the hop houses and bad booze joints, all the bare-knuckle boxing rings in the area, plus assorted gambling dens, clubhouses for thieves and gangsters, and any other places that the law did not favor. Blue-ribbon investigating committees found that "the criminals of New York naturally gravitate" to Big Tim's turf, and that his political workers sometimes helped out and ran gambling dens or whorehouses. Big Tim himself never denied the fact that he was a millionaire, notwithstanding the fact that his salary was only $1,500 a year.[15]

But Tim did have his moments. Like most Tammany leaders, he never drank or smoked, although he suffered from a powerful gambling addiction. Unlike his peers, he did enjoy literature, and loved Victor Hugo's *Les Misérables*. He could even assist the reform movement, albeit for his own reasons. When local thugs turned the district into a shooting gallery, Tim was instrumental in having the state legislature pass a bill that made it illegal to carry a concealed firearm; in his honor, it became known as the Sullivan Act, one of the most important laws of its kind in America. Of course, it was also extremely helpful whenever Tim wanted to deal with a gangland opponent, since all he had to do now was alert the cops and have them find the real (or planted) firearm.[16]

In the long run, however, all this power could not protect him from misfortune. Sullivan developed mental illness and was committed to a sanitarium in Westchester County. One night he kept his guards up by playing cards with them, and then, while they dozed, took his leave. A manhunt turned up nothing for two weeks, until someone realized that a body they had found in the Bronx, run over by a freight train, was not that of a tramp, as they had believed, but was actually Big Tim. Eight priests presided over his funeral, and twenty-five thousand people followed the casket to the cemetery.[17]

The man who replaced Big Tim as the great leader throughout the South-East side of Manhattan was Al Smith's political mentor. Tom Foley was not born in Ireland, as some accounts have it, but in a place almost as far from Manhattan: Brooklyn. As in so many working-class families, the father died when the children were little. Tom was thirteen and broad of back, so he left school and got work as, among other things, a blacksmith's assistant. In time, he relocated to the Fourth Ward, opening a saloon at Water Street and James Slip, all the way down by the docks. Foley was warmhearted and generous, maintaining an upstairs room filled with at least a dozen beds, so that every night a score or more of the neighborhood's derelicts (and potential voters) received free room and board. Soon he was an election district captain in the Second Assembly District (the successor to the Fourth Ward), and a rising star.[18]

It was not clear whose firmament he was appearing in, however. The boss of the Second Assembly District was Paddy Divver, one of the greatest thorns in Tim Sullivan's tough hide. Divver was notoriously independent of Sullivan, protected, he believed, by his close relationship with Richard Croker, the grand sachem of Tammany himself, Boss Tweed's successor once removed (Honest John Kelly had followed Tweed; Croker then replaced Kelly). Foley, on the other hand, had lined himself up with the Sullivan organization, and in 1901 he took on Divver for the district leadership, prompting one of the epic battles of New York politics. Polite commentators noted that each side used whatever tools were at their disposal; the reality was the most brutal warfare possible. Thugs beat up voters, men cast ballots several times a day, the names of the dead were used at the polling booths. When it was all over, Foley was the victor, and now one of the most powerful men in the area. Later, when Big Tim passed to instability and then death, Foley became the big boss of lower Manhattan.[19]

Tom Foley quickly established himself as a presence in Smith's neighborhood, in part because he was always on call at one of his saloons, but mostly because he was constantly checking the district from his home at 15 Oliver Street. Bernard Pisani remembered how Foley would "walk briskly . . . you knew he was someone who was important"; and Helen Graff recalled "a big, heavy-set man," whom she thought was "absolutely marvelous . . . he was so good to the poor." "There was nobody," she believed, "like Tom Foley."[20]

Tom Foley continued the best traditions Tim Sullivan had established and left behind the worst. In 1911, for example, he took what the *Tammany Times* claimed was "every man, woman and child" in his district—forty thousand of them—up to Sulzer's River Park and Casino in Harlem for a grand picnic. Over the course of the day, residents watched a vaudeville show and free movies, then downed torrents of vittles, including twenty-five thousand ham sandwiches, thirty-five thousand cakes and pies, one ton each of ice cream and popcorn, all washed down by ten thousand bottles of soda and five thousand gallons of lemonade and orange juice. The *New York Evening Telegram* described a similar event, detailing how "Chatham Square was crowded . . . with thousands of mothers with their children, who embarked on board long rows of surface cars" which took them to Tom Foley's picnic. "The youngsters were excited," the paper reported, "with the prospects of more than enough of good things to eat, toys, horns, and new caps, while their elders . . . were pleased with the only glimpse of green trees . . . enjoyed this summer." Everything was in abundance, as "express and delivery wagons descended upon the park with 'goodies' for the children. Rooms were filled with candy. Cake was there by the hundred-weight. Toys by the ton filled a room." It was easy to see why, years later, New York's Foley Square was named for this benefactor.[21]

But Foley also looked to the political organization of the district, taking care of things at both the top and the bottom of the pecking order. He opened a saloon on Centre Street, opposite the Criminal Courts Building, which introduced the first circular bar in New York City and became a prime watering hole for lawyers and politicians. Certain house rules always stood: no women would be admitted, for example, and a bartender should never charge a customer for drinks or cigars served to the owner. In its day it served as a great place to cut a deal or ask a favor.[22]

More important in the long run, Foley set up his district office as a school for budding young politicians, making it one of the best farm teams in the business. He established a headquarters by taking over Paddy Divver's old Downtown Tammany Club at 59 Madison Street, a high-ceilinged two-story brick and stone building with an ornate front entrance. Any man who became a Foley worker there had to submit to intensive discipline, one reporter describing it as "a kind of political West Point." The key virtues were loyalty and hard work, for both the organization and for constituents; two of Al Smith's biographers wrote that in Foley's organization you did what you were told "with the precision of the army. To do anything else was to have a swelled head, and a swelled head was political death." As one example, you never lied as to what you could or would do, but if you agreed to do a favor, you followed through, no matter what. This was called "taking a contract," and it was a solemn oath; Al Smith used the term all of his life to denote any agreement to perform a service. Regulars had to show up at the Downtown Club at least four or five nights a week to listen to the complaints and problems of the people in the neighborhood, and then to take contracts to help them.[23]

Tammany was no democracy, but leaders like Foley saw to it that the average family—people like the Smiths—was involved in politics to an extent with few parallels in American history. In these neighborhoods, everyone talked about politics, and elections became grand extravaganzas. Every boulevard became the scene of an orgy of bonfires, and that evening the cops were under strict orders not to harass the little urchins of the street whom they usually loved to roust.

Torchlight parades were the standard in all of these neighborhoods, with legions of men carrying kerosene burners or gas-soaked rags on the end of poles as much as four or five feet long. On this grand night, shopkeepers closed their doors—in part because no one would go out shopping, in part for fear of damage. One chronicler reported that "merchants had to hide everything moveable and inflammable, even their wagons, to save them . . . and despite their efforts, an occasional one was sacrificed, along with window stands, news stands, packing cases, pushcarts, signs, even store porches." Residents fired pistols, rifles, and shotguns to celebrate, and the political clubs sometimes wheeled cannon out to thunder a salvo. On numerous occasions trolleys and streetcars had to stop because their path was blocked by a bonfire, or even worse, because the conductor found himself staring down the barrel of a howitzer.[24]

From an early age Al was involved in this culture. His father was a stalwart Tammany supporter and used to earn extra money hauling the boxes of blank paper ballots to the polling centers, while the son earned a few pennies per thousand to fold their contents. Al shimmied up trees and lampposts to watch the demonstrations that lit up the district, and his earliest political memory was of the Democratic and Republican parades in the 1884 presidential campaign, when he had not yet reached the age of eleven years. Of course, like every other man, woman, and child in the area, he knew people like Tom Foley, having gone to the big man's picnics and outings.[25]

As a young man, it was almost inevitable that Al began to make political friends in the neighborhood. From childhood he had hung around Foley's saloon, a wonderland of comings and goings, and Foley frequently distributed coins to the kids in the neighborhood; most of the time it was a penny, which as Al mentioned, "in those days . . . looked big," and when the boss flashed a nickel "you thought it was Sunday." By the time he was twenty years old or so, Al was taking minor contracts, to deliver a message, for example, or to check up on an old person who was in trouble and may have needed help of some kind.[26]

He also made the acquaintance of Henry Campbell, who owned a lucrative wholesale and retail grocery business, as well as a number of pieces of real estate. Campbell was typical of Tammany's shadow politicians; he held no elected or appointed office, yet was knee-deep in politics, and even sat on the executive committee of the Hall. As was common in those days, he created a political club of his own, a hangout for the young men who wanted to enter this field, called the Seymour Club.

Al enjoyed strong memories of Campbell. The grocer had been around when Smith's father had taken sick, and even paid many of the doctor's bills. As Al's interest in politics grew, he joined the Seymour Club, soon becoming secretary. More important, he was a stand-out member of the crowd, always reciting or singing or dancing or telling a story, a master of conviviality; one fellow remembered that Smith kept them "roarin' by the hour." Campbell, a bachelor, took what Al remembered as "a fatherly interest" in the young man and frequently had him over for dinner at his house on Madison Street, which, like everything else in that dense setting, was just down the block.[27]

In 1894 Al entered electoral politics as a participant for the first time in his life, notwithstanding the fact that he was not yet twenty-one, not yet a voter. Back then, Paddy Divver still ran the Second Assembly District; Foley was in charge of one of the smaller election districts nestled within this realm, but he had already affiliated with Tim Sullivan.

The issue that year involved a congressional seat in Sullivan's territory, whose current tenant was the Honorable Timothy Campbell (no relative of Henry). Richard Croker sent word to Big Tim that Campbell should be bumped from the ticket, replaced by Henry Miner, the owner of a number of entertainment spots in the area, including Miner's Bowery Theater. The reasons for this move are lost to the mists of time and pettiness; Miner told the press that he had an agreement with Campbell that they would trade off taking turns in Washington, a fairly typical arrangement for accommodating many players; but with Croker, there was always the possibility that this was the payoff for large donations.[28]

Fueling the fire locally was the oxygen of snobbery. Miner lived way uptown, on Madison *Avenue* (an entirely different world from Madison *Street*). He had just made a glamorous marriage, to the actress Annie O'Neill, and the word was that he wanted to enter Washington society the easy way, by buying a congressional seat. Residents felt outrage, not so much against the notion of corruption, but because they believed that Miner was an arriviste, someone who had moved on and now felt he could treat them as pawns.[29]

All this controversy brought Smith to a meeting at Tim Campbell's political headquarters, the Oriental Club. The sitting congressman branded Miner a carpetbagger, decried the violation of home rule, and spoke against boss control.[30]

Miner, supported by Croker's apparatus, won the Democratic nomination, but Campbell launched his own candidacy on an independent ticket and attracted support from Tom Foley, Henry Campbell, Big Tim Sullivan, and for the first time, one Alfred E. Smith. The contest was a rough one, and though there is no record of Al's ever engaging in fisticuffs, he did use his oratorical talents over and over to support Campbell and denounce Croker and Miner.[31]

Campbell lost, but Smith's career thrived. The fight had brought him much closer to Tom Foley, and the local boss began to take him under his wing, eventually as a protégé. Al became a part of the Foley organization, and the scrapbook his mother had started began to feature more and more items of a political nature. Often they did not even mention her son directly, and thus indicated the growing importance of politics in the household. Included for example, were a copy of William Jennings Bryan's "Cross of Gold" speech, an 1895 map of the city divided into Tammany and anti-Tammany districts, and articles clipped from the local papers giving election results. At the same time, Foley took more and more of an interest in Al's activities, buying a box when the St. James Players put on a performance of *Incog* at the Central Opera House.[32]

In time, Smith and Foley became extremely close, both as political allies and personal friends; the best testimony to this was how Foley's passing in 1925 shook Al to the core. His official statement from the governor's office included the testimonial, "My personal and political welfare were as much concern to him as though I were his own son," but far more telling was the personal correspondence he exchanged with the grieving widow. Al wrote her that "it took quite sometime" for him "to recover from the shock," and that he had received hundreds of letters and telegrams from all over the country; dutifully, he avowed, "I have answered them all." Bessie Foley replied with enormous feeling, opening her letter, "I can only address myself to you, dear Al, as the one true friend of my heart." She explained, "I shall not attempt to thank you for your unswerving loyalty and fidelity to Tom these long years. . . . I can only think and thank God for all his mercies to me, chief among them being your wonderful friendship for my Tom." At the funeral, according to the *New York Times*, Al's body "shook with sobs" as he bent over the casket, and "his face was wet with tears." As they left the cemetery, Al remarked, "Tom, next to my mother, was the best friend I had in the world." In the realm of Irish culture, there could be no higher compliment.[33]

Though Tim Campbell had lost that 1904 race, the citywide ticket rode to victory, and Al got a small share of the spoils. On January 15, 1895, he received his first political appointment, as a process server in the office of the Commissioner of Jurors. The pay was only eight hundred dollars a year, a little more than sixty dollars a month, but it was better than what he got in the factories, where the standard was ten or twelve dollars a week. Besides, it was a lot more interesting, enabling him to travel all over the city and see things and meet everyone from "the small storekeeper . . . to the broker and banker on Wall Street," as Smith later reminisced. Not all of the duties were that enjoyable; Al noted that "the subpoena server in the offices of a busy business man was about as welcome as a safety-razor manufacturer would be at a barbers' convention." He worked hard at it, however, and soon got a promotion to investigator, checking up on people who had claimed exemption from jury duty. In one case he had to look into a stockbroker who had submitted a doctor's note testifying that his patient was deaf. Suspicious, Al put his acting skills to work and showed up at the man's office pretending to be a potential customer suffering from a bad cold, and thus unable to speak above a whisper. Amazingly enough, the broker was still able to take the order, and Smith gave him the bad news.[34]

Al remained active in Foley's organization and was becoming known as one of its rising members. A clipping in the Wells Fargo scrapbook described him as a "leader" of the Foley forces, but also noted that they were willing to use the entire variety of his talents; he was entered into a cycling race against an opponent from the other side of the political fence. Far more important, it was in 1901 that Foley challenged Divver for control of the entire Assembly district, and then won it. Al was extremely active, a "strong influence," as Foley put it, helping his mentor rack up a margin of better than three to one.[35]

The new boss moved carefully, and for the local seat in the New York State Assembly he chose a bright young man named Joseph Bourke. In those days the entire Assembly stood for reelection every year, so Bourke won in 1901 and then again in 1902, a somewhat forgone conclusion in that district if you were Tom Foley's man.

But being a Foley man meant a lot more than standing up once a year and giving speeches. It also meant a lot of work, constant work, on behalf of constituents. By 1903 Bourke was getting haughty, and his absence at the Downtown Tammany Club became more conspicuous than his presence. Foley decided to drop him and go with someone else.[36]

As soon as this choice bit of news entered the neighborhood pipeline, Henry Campbell was in Foley's office. No one ever recorded the conversation, so we will never know if the sell was easy or hard. The results were clear, however; Alfred E. Smith would receive the nomination for State Assembly.[37]

Al was no politician yet, just a working stiff in the halls of municipal justice. Campbell walked over from his meeting, about a ten-minute jaunt, barged into the office of the Commissioner of Jurors, and told Smith that Tom Foley would nominate him for the office at the district convention that evening. Few people had telephones in those days, so Al divided up the responsibility for announcing the good news, running home to tell Katie and the kids, sending a friend across to Brooklyn to inform his mother.[38]

For all the excitement, it was not automatic that Al would accept the nomination. The Commissioner of Jurors, former Judge Thomas Allison, took Al aside and warned him against taking this step. Without much education, Al would be ineffective in those chambers. Besides, assemblymen were the most minor players in the political machine, held in substantially less awe or esteem than a good precinct captain; in the Tammany scheme of things they were nothing more than flunkies who were supposed to vote when and how they were ordered.[39]

Al would accept none of this; for the young man from the F.F.M., it seemed that he was finally on his way. He accepted the nod, knowing that the convention would follow Foley's orders to the last iota. After that, the process involved an amazing number of precise steps, all conducted within blocks of each other, making it a study of formality in miniature. Al had to go home from work and clean up, while passing along to the appropriate parties the place where he would meet a delegation from the convention. He greeted them at the St. James Union, his theatrical club on Oliver Street, and after they had informed Al of the convention's decision, the group would walk around the corner to the district hall at 48 Madison Street, a triumphal march of less than one block, where Smith would deliver an acceptance address to the assembled throng. Complicating all of this was the fact that Al still had a limited wardrobe and his winter suit remained in mothballs. The candidate, therefore, spent the exciting moments prior to notification standing in his kitchen, dressed in his wife's apron, vigorously pressing the coat and pants of his only appropriate summer outfit.

But to Al it was just glorious. Over a quarter-century later, all he could remember was how he "was received in the convention hall with loud acclaim. . . . All the delegates were men who had known me for a great many years." He gave his first address of the campaign, though, he recalled, "it wasn't much of a speech."[40]

He got better, although he really did not have to. Foley's endorsement in that neighborhood was only slightly less compelling than the Second Coming of The Lord. But nobody liked a slacker, so Al went all out. Posters and pictures cropped up in the windows of storefronts and apartments everywhere. The campaign was conducted from the back of a truck, and Al's theatrically trained lungs carried his message far, a block or more without loudspeakers, notwithstanding the clanging of the streetcars in the background. An article cited him as "a very pleasing talker and convincing in argument, which, with his personal magnetism, has made him very popular among his people." George LeBrun, who was organizing Italian-Americans in this district that year, characterized Smith as the kind of campaigner "with who you wanted to be friends right away."[41]

Everyone in the neighborhood knew him by then, even a local fellow named Eddie Cantor. In his memoirs, Cantor wrote that Smith "was a ward heeler and a do-gooder, the first I'd ever known, the nearest thing to a knight in shining armor that ever showed up around Catherine, Oliver, Madison, Monroe or Henry streets." Al was "a young, good-looking guy in a jaunty straw hat, and he was our hero." Cantor described one of Al's campaign methods, how he would "gather up all the boys hanging around Catherine Street" and take them to Bassler's saloon. He would then line them all up at the bar and place his order. Cantor explained: "If you were wearing short pants he'd order 'sarsaparilla,' another short pants, 'another sarsaparilla,' he'd come to a boy in long pants, 'one beer.' What a guy. Everybody in the neighborhood loved him." The future star of stage and screen got so carried away he even took to the stump, telling voters why they had to vote for his man: "Most of my audience were crazy about Al. How could I miss?"*

The people of the district not only loved Al Smith, they voted for him. Early on Election Day his mother and his sister Mamie came over from Brooklyn to watch the day's events and stayed until the polls had closed and the votes were tallied. There were four candidates in the race: a representative of the Prohibition party, a rather lost cause in that world, who managed to amass the sum total of 5 votes; a Socialist, who got 106 votes; and Paul Kaminsky, the Republican, who wound up with 1,472. Al had nothing to worry about, as he raked in 4,942 ballots, or 75.7 percent of all votes cast.[43]

The day after the election his name was mentioned for the first time in the *New York Times*, although Al may not have noticed the single line in the midst of all the election results. Far more important, his friends took care of him. Judge Allison checked the statute books and discovered a godsend, that he could con-

---

*The next year Cantor was not so wise in his choice of candidates. He campaigned for Morris Hilquit, a Socialist, and a bunch of Tammany boys gave him a "D.A.," a "dental assist," knocking loose some teeth. Not all of Foley's protégés were nice guys like Al.[42]

tinue to work his old job up to the day he took the oath for his new one. With no other source of income, Al continued to serve subpoenas, "up to and including December 31." Henry Campbell wanted to make sure Al's days at the emergency ironing board were over, so he took the conquering hero down to Brooks Brothers and bought him two new suits. All that remained was to wait for the new year, kiss Katie and the children goodbye, and take the train up to Albany.[44]

Chapter 5

Albany

THE NEW YORK State Capitol Building is immense, but also something of a Grand Guignol masterpiece. What should have been a simple building became, courtesy of changing administrations and rules of patronage, a thirty-year project that cost far more than anyone had ever bargained for, making it, in fact, the most expensive building in North America at the time it opened in 1897. There was no great dome on the top, one of only ten state capitols to omit this, but there was just about everything else. Because four different architects had had a hand in its design, the ground floor was Romanesque, followed by two stories done in the mode of the Italian Renaissance, followed by another Romanesque floor, topped by dormers and turrets out of the French Renaissance. William Kennedy, the great Albany writer, claimed that "the Capitol is, in all respects, a presence beyond human scale."[1]

Typical was the Great Western Staircase, an incredible structure 77 by 70 feet in dimension, and 119 feet high, or close to that of a modern twelve-story building. It was nicknamed the "Million Dollar Staircase," but that was too modest; it actually cost $1.5 million.[2]

Designers chose to build in Corsehill Sandstone, imported from Scotland, because it was soft when first quarried and then hardened after exposure to air, following which good rubbing imparted a high polish. A battalion of stonecutters—536—were hired, most of them immigrants from Scotland and Europe, and told to start carving right away. At first, these men had clear directions: all the governors of the state up to that time, for example, had to be etched into the tops of the columns. After that, every major figure of the time appeared, including Lincoln and many of the victorious generals from the Civil War. Reformers could not be overlooked, so there were images of Harriet Beecher Stowe, Frederick Douglass, and Susan B. Anthony. Nor could inventors, so they included Robert Fulton. There was even a poets' corner, featuring the faces of Walt

Whitman, Henry Wadsworth Longfellow, and James Whitcomb Riley, among others. And when the designers ran out of celebrities from every walk of life, they gave the cutters a free hand. In the end, when Al Smith arrived in Albany in January 1904, he confronted a staircase that included a thousand faces that have never been identified, all of them either relatives of the men doing the work (there are many children's visages among the alcoves), or else products of these immigrant artists' creativity.[3]

The room he entered seemed even more fabulous. The Assembly Chamber was gigantic and richly ornate. The floor plan stretched 90 feet in each direction, almost as big as the 113- by 80-foot hall the U.S. Senate meets in. Holding the chamber upright were four immense pillars of highly polished granite, 4 feet in diameter, while overhead hung numerous chandeliers, made of brass and alabaster. The largest of these, over the center of the room, weighed four thousand pounds.[4]

All around was a blaze of color, so that a state report a century later could declare that the room had "an almost Moorish character." Everything was done up, all the ornamentation, in red, gold, and ultramarine, while members sat in mahogany armchairs finished in red leather. Huge drapes, described as "sumptuous in fabric and large and noble in detail," covered rows of windows (of both clear and stained glass), while twenty-four bronze poles, each graced by a triple tier of etched glass globes for gas lighting, helped illuminate the floor. In a place like this, it was easy to be overwhelmed, even if you were not undereducated and far from home.[5]

On Al's first day on the job he trudged up to the capitol, and then climbed the enormous two-story staircase to reach the lobby because he did not know there was an elevator. Being in the minority party and a freshman, Al received seat number 142 in the back; only eight other assemblymen were farther from the center, more inconsequential than him.

When the Assembly got down to business, Al's prospects did not improve. We think of machine politics as an urban, bureaucratic phenomenon, but in fact the machine style dominated both parties and most regions at the time. In New York State, the Republicans ruled.

Their empire was lavish. In those days the Assembly and Senate had much greater power in relationship to the executive branch than they would enjoy in a later era. Members not only chose the U.S. senators, they appointed many of the governor's administrators, controlled the budget, and exercised ruthless control over all of the state's municipal entities, which had little in the way of home rule. Republicans dominated both houses, the Assembly courtesy of an antiquated system that gave upstate areas, lavish in space but sparse in citizenry, the majority of districts. As late as the turn of the century, people in these rural sections could remember voting for Lincoln in 1860, and they had voted Republican in every election since then too. In time this produced, under the leadership of Boss Tom Platt, an anti–New York City bloc, as voters elected a group of patricians terrified of the urban, immigrant, industrial proletariat of the nation's largest metropolis.[6]

As strong as this system was, it got cemented in the 1890s, just before Al arrived on the scene, with the Reverend Charles Parkhurst's exposé of vice and corruption in New York City. Parkhurst's revelations in 1892 led to a legislative investigation, known as the Lexow Commission (after Clarence Lexow, its sponsor). Hearings and eventually prosecutions demonstrated the link between police and vice lords, all facilitated by many of the Tammany Hall regulars.[7]

This was one of the first of the great New York City corruption investigations (though hardly the last), but the timing was particularly bad for Tammany Hall. New York State had a system mandating that every twenty years, a constitutional convention review and revise the fundamental document of its government, which was to occur just as Lexow started his campaign.

Thus, in the midst of the hoopla and headlines, the convention began its deliberations, and upstate Republicans used the opportunity to carve out a system of apportionment that stripped the cities of as many districts as possible, denying representation to new generations of urban immigrants. Each county, for example, was guaranteed one seat in the Assembly (not the Senate) regardless of the size of its population, and no two counties divided by a river could command more than half the seats in the legislature, even if their population justified it. Strangely, only New York and Kings counties, otherwise known as Manhattan and Brooklyn, fit this description. By the time the upstaters were finished, New York City, with the majority of the state's residents, had 67 of 150 seats in the Assembly and 25 of 56 seats in the Senate. The day the system was passed, Charles Lincoln, a prominent Republican delegate, told his son, "I believe we made sure today that in my lifetime, and probably yours as well, the city will never control the Legislature." At no time between 1904 and 1910, Al's early years in the Assembly, did the Republicans command fewer than 94 seats in that body.[8]

☙

Life was not hard for a member of the Assembly. The session began on the first Wednesday in January and lasted until April, or May 1 at the latest, a total of only four months out of the year. The weekly schedule consisted of an evening session on Monday, reconvening during normal hours on Tuesday, Wednesday, and Thursday; there was also a Friday meeting, but it was sparsely attended until the closing weeks, when the crush of business required longer meetings. Rare was the Saturday conference, and members who were not from the local area would traditionally board a train late Friday afternoon, returning the following Monday.[9]

This short cycle was feasible only because of the tight control of the Assembly's business by the leadership. In both chambers, but especially in the Assembly, the Committee on Rules dictated what happened during each session. Consisting of the Speaker, the chair of the Committee on Ways and Means, two other important committee chairs (chosen by the Speaker), and two minority members, this body had the power to discharge all other committees, and also enjoyed sole responsibility for choosing which bills would be brought to the floor for a vote.[10]

Anyone who was not privy to this exclusive circle was rendered powerless in a vast variety of ways. For an individual member to get a bill passed, he traditionally had to have it appear before, and get passed by, the appropriate committee before it could be considered by the body as a whole. Committee action, however, was totally at the whim of the chair. This dignitary decided when the meetings would take place, who should be notified, what matters would be considered, and which ones delayed or ignored. If by some fluke a member's bill was actually passed through, it then had to go before the Committee on Rules, and finally to the Speaker of the Assembly. Tucked within this worthy's desk were two drawers, referred to as "grave yard No. 1" and "grave yard No. 2." A few rare bills emerged from the former, but as one observer described it, a bill buried in the latter receptacle "had no chance of resurrection." Most bills, therefore, came in a torrent at the end of the session, under the tutelage of the Speaker and his associates. Even worse, some of these items were "strike bills," which were introduced solely to extort money from the party or industry whose interests would be adversely affected by the legislation; utilities and banks were considered particularly good targets. The coterie that pulled off these scams, a group including both Republicans and Democrats (proving greed knows no party), was known as the "Black Horse Cavalry."[11]

Thus, a legislator did not need a great amount of brains, skill, knowledge, or innovation. During one debate, a member was so enraged by the speech of his colleague across the aisle that he fired a law book at him, missing the speaker but knocking off the hat of a lady observer who happened to be on the floor. And while the Republican bosses controlled their members with an iron hand, the Tammany leadership did the same to their people as well. Democratic members, most of them from New York City, were expected to stand as they were told, speak as they were told, and above all, vote where and when and how they were told to by their bosses down on Fourteenth Street. They made fifteen hundred dollars a year for this work, with lots of time off to earn extra money. Frances Perkins remembered that there was a room in the corridor connecting the two chambers, called the Assembly lunchroom. Small and not terribly clean, it contained a short counter without stools and a few tables. Members could order sandwiches, pie, or coffee, eat their food there, or more commonly take it back to their desk, where they dined without the luxury of forks or spoons. Watching this, Perkins came to the conclusion that the Assembly was "an interesting and sometimes revolting spectacle."[12]

Al became part of this "spectacle" at his first session, the one that opened on January 13, 1904. It was not a positive experience. Leadership assigned him to the committees on banks and on public lands and forestry; he understood little about the first and less about the second. As he later remarked, "I knew nothing about banking laws and had never been in a bank except to serve a jury notice, and I had never seen a forest." The first bill he ever heard on the floor was "An act to Amend Section 161 of the Banking Law, in regard to the number of directors of trust companies necessary to form a quorum," which, mercifully for Al, was referred to committee—albeit, unfortunately, his own committee on banks. Sixteen more bills were introduced by four other members, all of which got remanded to the appropriate committee for consideration or destruction.[13]

Those early years in Albany were hard for Al. He was thirty-one years old, of medium build, but with a boyish face that did nothing to inspire respect or esteem. Speaker Frederick Nixon ignored him, and the two did not even meet until three days before the end of the session. When Governor Benjamin Odell threw a ball for the legislature, Al wore one of the dress suits that Henry Campbell had purchased for him at Brooks Brothers, but found himself in a cattle-car-like receiving line, one that saw to it that he was ushered in, allowed to shake hands with the governor and his wife, and escorted out, all within three minutes.[14]

In the Assembly, Al did as he was told, voting the Tammany line. Bill after bill came before him, using the language and concepts of law and budgets, disciplines he was totally unfamiliar with. He could not tell which document was a strike bill and which bill was for real, which legislation was a matter of debate and which was a forgone conclusion. "A Comptroller's report," he remarked in a speech years later, "just looked exactly to me like the figures on the window of a Greek restaurant." New York's leading reformer, Lawrence Veiller, told interviewers that in those years Smith was "in every way an out and out sordid Tammany man who never had shown any indication to do anything other than to obey orders that he received from the machine." Former governor Hugh Carey explained that Smith was "expected to be one of the boys, go along and hit the cuspidor with a cigar butt and just be one of the jolly fellows from downtown who took their orders from . . . the bosses." Al was not required to do anything noteworthy; no one expected it of him.[15]

Of course, that was just how it was supposed to work. Political machines, whether they are in New York, Chicago, Pittsburgh, or Albany, all share certain rules. One is that the local scene is the most important—what political scientist Milton Rakove called the "almost single-minded concentration on the retention of power" at the citywide level. As a result, he explained, "the machine subordinates power and perquisites at all other levels of the American political and governmental system—county, state and national . . . to the machine's interest in the city."[16]

In this pecking order, assemblymen were considered the lowest of the low. One writer claimed that "the average legislator . . . drifts through the session in a mental fog, not infrequently thickened by liquor. . . . During the closing hours . . . he votes, parrot-like, as he is told." James Bryce, in his famous work *The American Commonwealth,* noted that "nothing is more remarkable about these state legislators than their timidity. No one seems to think of having an opinion of his own."[17]

Al fit this mold and was, at first, no great addition to the legislature. Tom Foley had told him, just before he left, "Don't speak until you have something to say. Men who talk just for the pleasure of it do not get very far," and Al took this to heart. In his first two years in the Assembly he did not make one speech, and introduced only six bills, none of them of particularly staggering importance, out of a total of 4,451 that the Assembly entertained. When Al finally did address the body, furthermore, he indicated that he should have paid closer attention to Foley's advice. What makes this inaugural speech even vaguely important was not the rhetoric but the fact that it came about because Al was voting against the wishes of Tammany. Unfortunately, young Al had not yet developed the ability to articulate these ideals, so instead he resorted to feeble ethnic humor to excuse his vote. "Mr. Speaker," he declared, "I want to tell a story about two Scotchmen. . . . Said Sandy to Andy . . . 'why do you drink whuskey?' Answered Andy: 'For medicinal reasons'; 'but Sandy, why do you drink whuskey?' 'Because I like it,' replied Sandy. That's why I'm voting for this bill, Mr. Speaker—because I like it."[18]

Back home at the Downtown Tammany Club, things were going a lot better. Al had been trained well by Foley, and he spent most of his time attending to the people of his district, handling everything from employment to personal disputes. The job of assemblyman took on Solomon-like overtones when a constituent asked Al whether or not he should pay a dentist's bill, given that the false teeth made for his wife did not fit. The answer is unrecorded, but these kinds of disputes, at least, made some kind of sense to Al.[19]

It also worked for his constituents, who gladly returned him to office. Al never ignored the campaigns, and electioneering was big and bold and fun. He spoke in Battery Park, and he spoke in the streets and in the markets. If the candidate could not show up, surrogates took over, much as Al himself had done in earlier campaigns. Samuel Dickstein, for example, who wound up becoming a judge and a U.S. congressman, was a law student in 1906, and got up on "soap boxes . . . on the streets and the sidewalks of the East Side" to give speeches about Al Smith. The Democratic organization chipped in, buying tickets to every ball and sports event in the district; taking out ads in the programs of dozens of organizations, churches, and clubs; sponsoring parades; and setting up bonfires.[20]

As an assemblyman, Al had to stand for reelection every year. In 1904 his margin slipped, from 76 percent down to 69 percent, but this was still a very safe district. For the next eleven years and elections, Al's lowest vote total would be 61 percent (in 1912), his highest an astronomical 83 percent (in 1906).[21]

These victories entitled Al to some modest rewards, and he needed them. Although his salary had grown considerably, so had his expenses; he now had to maintain living quarters in Albany and travel back and forth every week as well. More Smith children had arrived, and the family moved to larger quarters to accommodate them. Assembly rules entitled him to draw $70 a week until only $250 remained, which would not be paid out until the session ended. Long before then, Al was usually broke.[22]

Worst of all, Al was still a yes man, and his ego had reached a low ebb. He lived in a small hotel called the Tub, down the hill from the Capitol building. On the floor of the Assembly, his job consisted of "reading amendments to laws that I had never heard of before. In fact, I never knew there was so much law." After a year of this nothing seemed to change: "My second year was as much of a blank to me, so far as knowledge of what was going on in the legislature was concerned, as my first one had been." Emily Warner, his daughter, remembered that he used to sum up this period, his lack of imprint on the Assembly, by stating simply, "Nobody knew me!"[23]

One night he and Tommy Cosgrove, another Tammany assemblyman, lugged a stack of bills back to one of their hotel rooms; Al remembered, "We spent an hour looking over those things beginning 'be it resolved,' and then we went for a walk along the river." As they walked along, Al told his colleague,

"Tommy . . . we're in the wrong place. Whoever thought we were Assembly-men?" When Cosgrove agreed, Al lamented that he could "tell a haddock from a hake by the color of his eye," but he could not "tell a bill from a bale of hay."[24]

In the summer of 1905, after Al's second term in the Assembly had ended, he met with Tom Foley for breakfast at Holtz's Restaurant on Broadway at Franklin Street, and told the old man he wanted out. Tammany had just won the mayoralty, and Foley had available a choice spot, Superintendent of Buildings for the City of New York. Al requested the job, on the grounds that he had become "fairly well convinced that the position of member of Assembly was a little bit too much for me." But Foley convinced Al to think it over and give legislative politics another chance. After considering the matter for several more weeks, Al Smith agreed to try the Assembly for one more year.[25]

It was a fateful choice. Some people, and most legislators, can accept obscurity in return for job security and perks. Others cannot stand it, and Smith was among them. Down deep, Al believed in himself, believed that he could make it. His mother gave him some of that self-confidence, and the rest of it came from the neighborhood, where he was liked by one and all and seemed the heartiest of fellows. As a talented speaker and showman, he was used to moving people to his way of thinking, and it irked him when not only did this technique not work, but nobody even listened to him.

So Al Smith decided he would be somebody, and would do it in politics, and his life changed dramatically as a result of that decision. Al began to read every bill from start to finish. When he did not understand a term, he looked it up. If the bill was an amendment to existing law, he went to the New York State Code and examined the original legislation, figuring out how and why it was to be altered, an endless process of cross-reference and then cross-cross-reference. Night after night, he haunted the New York State Library, a grand, two-storied cavern that took up the top floors of the Capitol's west side. As he sat at the wooden desks, surrounded by the drawers of the card catalogue and by shelves of books, and with two upper balconies crammed with volumes looking down on him, he began to learn how the legislature worked. When the library closed, he went back to his tiny room and continued to read, continued to check and cross-check. Back on the floor, if he could not understand a member's speech, he paid the clerks for transcripts, and took the printed words back to his quarters, along with every bill introduced, every bill passed, to read them all, every last one. He even tackled the monster of monsters, the annual appropriations bill, hundreds of pages and thousands of items, a document one author claimed was "as complicated as an income tax return filed by John D. Rockefeller . . . and as difficult to understand as a railway time-table in Russia." It took years to learn the system, but he did it, and with his actor's talents, most of these details were committed to memory. For the first time, Al Smith was surprising everyone, even himself, exceeding theirs, and even his own expectations.[26]

He also began getting some badly needed help from a source that looked on him as an ally, not as a fool. In his second term, Al had made the acquaintance of a young German-American who had just joined the Assembly from another Tammany district, this one farther uptown. His name was Robert Wagner, and the two became fast friends, even rooming together. Wagner was quieter than Al, slower in speech, but had a law degree, and both men benefited from the other's presence, as Al helped with the gift of gab, and Wagner explained how to read the plethora of bills in front of them. Thus, even before the time Al began his regimen, Wagner was fortifying his friend's confidence by showing him that he could accomplish this task.[27]

Al's first big break came from a most unusual source. James Wadsworth, Jr., seemed about the least likely candidate to take a hankering to the assemblyman from the Bowery. If Al could not tell exactly where his father was from, Wadsworth knew just when his first ancestors came to the New World; he had descended from William Wadsworth, one of the first selectmen to arrive at the Massachusetts Bay Colony in 1634. Later ancestors included a general who fought in the Revolutionary War; this particular gentleman then traveled to the Genesee Valley in New York State, where he acquired holdings so vast that one could ride for twenty-eight miles without leaving the estate. The family soon became active in local politics, bolting the Democratic Party over the slavery issue and remaining forever after in the Republican camp. James's father, known throughout the Valley as the "Boss," served in local and state offices, then went to Washington to represent his district in the U.S. House of Representatives. The son attended Yale, where he majored in history, but was mostly obsessed by a new sport sweeping the campus, known as "baseball." Elihu Root, one of the truly grand old men of the Republican Party, scholar, statesman, and aristocrat, declared that Wadsworth "is endowed by nature with a clear strong mind . . . and decision of character. He was born into an intimate family tradition of loyalty and devotion to American principles. . . . He is honest, sincere, and has perfect courage." And in November 1904 he was elected to the state assembly.[28]

In later years Wadsworth would become the model of elite, business-oriented conservatism, but in those early days he was something of a reformer. Unlike some of his peers, James was not hostile to the needs of city dwellers, nor did he dismiss the men of Tammany out of hand. He championed a bill, for example, that made it legal to play baseball on Sunday, recognizing that country clubs were open that day and that the rich played golf and tennis on the Christian sabbath, so why not let the poor have their entertainments? In one speech on the floor, he claimed that he would rather see a lad "trying to stretch a three-bagger into a home run" than to have him spend that time "near the back door of some saloon."[29]

And, for reasons neither of them ever explained very well, he developed a friendship with Al Smith. Some friendships are like that; they depend more on chemistry than on obvious factors. The two shared a straightforward honesty and also had some doubts about the fairness of the existing system. James enjoyed Al's company, the songs and imitations and little jests that Al delivered to help the day pass along. Emily Warner described them as "intimate, intimate friends."[30]

Even more, however, he saw something in the young man that was worthwhile. In his memoirs, Wadsworth claimed that by the time he arrived on the scene, Al "was attracting attention not only because of his wit and natural ability at making friends, but because he was talking sense." At least for Wadsworth, Smith's "harsh voice and . . . violations of the rules of grammar were forgiven and forgotten. Slowly but surely [Al] gained respect on both sides of the aisle."[31]

In a short while, Wadsworth became a very good friend to have, indeed. Members from both parties were becoming angry at Speaker Nixon's rigid and ruthless control, and they even began comparing him to the notorious Joseph Cannon, Speaker of the U.S. House of Representatives and the archetype of despotism in that era. Reformers looked on in dismay as assemblymen flouted honest laws, like the provision that banned members from accepting free railroad passes, one of the most common forms of bribery at that time. Instead, the Pullman Company lobbyist, openly and in view of all, stood on the floor and wrote out passes, filling in the name of a representative's closest relative "and one." Men like Wadsworth were disgusted.[32]

When Speaker Nixon died suddenly on October 5, 1905, at the age of forty-five, the young turks plotted a revolt. They received assistance from many sources, not the least of which was Theodore Roosevelt, a former governor and now president. Teddy was anything but demure; he knew New York State politics and he wanted them cleaned up. All of these parties decided on the shockingly young—twenty-eight years old—James Wadsworth, in part because his integrity was so unquestionable. So in January of 1906 the former Yale first baseman became Speaker of the Assembly.

Wadsworth fought many battles and had many duties, but one of the first and most important matters he had to attend to was the assignment of committee positions. There were over four hundred slots to be distributed to 150 candidates, each man getting two or three committees. Precedent and seniority ruled, and when in doubt, the party leaders reigned. Of course, the Speaker retained the right to name anyone he chose, and Wadsworth was no fool and a reformer to boot, so he shifted around some of the key posts. When it came to the opposition, however, he "followed the usual custom, with one exception, of accepting the recommendations of the Democratic leadership."[33]

That exception was Smith. If Wadsworth had perceived the budding talent that was there, Al's party bosses had remained blind, passing the Bowery man over in favor of more stalwart Tammany honchos. As Wadsworth put it, his colleague had "been buried," assigned to committees that had little to do and rarely met. The new Speaker, "resented this wretched treatment of Al."[34]

Thus, when the Democratic leaders showed up with their list and Wadsworth saw that Al remained in committee purgatory, he damned custom and rebelled. "Now gentlemen," he told them, "I can't stand for this. Now listen, you mustn't *treat* this man this way. *You know you mustn't.*" There was some protest over these accusations ("rather mild," the Speaker thought), and then Wadsworth "altered the list so as to put Al on a really important committee."[35]

Wadsworth did not just pick an important committee, he gave Al a whopper—the most controversial, most activist committee in the Assembly that year. Back in 1905 the *New York World* had done an exposé on a struggle to control the Equitable Insurance Company, with clear implications that officers were engaged in vast and far-reaching financial improprieties. In response to the public hue and cry, the governor appointed a special commission to investigate the life insurance business, headed by the reformer Charles Evans Hughes, who would go on to become one of the greatest governors in New York State history. Hughes had uncovered an abattoir of corruption and nepotism—items like loans that violated state law being made to favored parties and millions spent to buy legislation, accounted for under the quaint heading "legal expenses." Hughes had just turned in his final report, and now it was time for the legislature to debate and then act. And Wadsworth had assigned Al to the Assembly's Insurance Committee.[36]

In time, the committee passed out bills that transformed the insurance industry in the state that was the nation's financial hub, banning stock speculation with investors' money, mandating standard procedures, outlawing donations to politicians. Al played only a minor role in all this, but for the first time he was in the center of things, he was learning at the core, rather than from the margins. It would be rare, after this, for him to be out of the spotlight for long.[37]

Al began to sponsor bills of his own, fifteen in the 1906 session. Few amounted to much, but it was a start. Smith became the proud sponsor of a bill to change "the forest, fish and game law as to sale of wall-eyed and yellow pike," as a good F.F.M. man. He fought to have air brakes installed on every car of every train, and introduced a measure that allowed any justice of the peace who had practiced for five years to be admitted to the bar without the customary education. Whereas in their 1905 report the staunchly Republican, reformist Citizens

Union described him as "Inconspicuous," by 1906 he had become "Intelligent and active; somewhat above average of machine man." That year he had his first nonelection write-up in the *New York Times,* gaining a sub-headline when he gave a speech to endorse a bill taxing the property of nonresidents who owned estates in New York. The address bristled with facts and numbers and statistics, delivered in a folksy manner. Al was starting to develop a style all his own—a combination of hard data, rigidly controlled, and old Irish storytelling.[38]

Year by year, Al's role in the legislature grew. By the 1907 session, he was a recognized player, and accordingly got appointed to several of the committees dealing with utility regulation, a hot topic at that time, including those covering electricity and gas and water supply. Far more important, he became a member of the Committee on the Affairs of Cities and a special committee looking into revisions of the New York City charter. For the first time in his career, Al began to get assigned to bodies that were tackling issues he cared and knew something about.[39]

Al introduced twenty bills that year, none of which passed. He began to champion the cause of controlling the sale and distribution of narcotic drugs, and within the next few years he took on the issue of cigarettes. As the result of his efforts, the legislature banned the sale of cocaine without a doctor's prescription, and he also fought for a bill to make the manufacture and sale of cigarettes illegal in the state. That year the Citizens Union described him as "active and aggressive; one of the best Democratic representatives from New York City."[40]

One of the bills that did not pass signaled Al's new ethnic politics. The Sons of Columbus, an Italian-American organization in his district, decided that their countrymen deserved some recognition and put together a bill to honor the greatest Italian explorer, which would set aside a special day to celebrate Christopher Columbus. They took the measure to Al and asked him to present it to the legislature. Modest in scope, it made clear that no businesses or courts would be closed, which would prove a fatal flaw, and Al spoke on its behalf. Both houses approved the legislation, but Governor Hughes vetoed it on the grounds that it did not create a real holiday, since there was no interruption of day-to-day life. Later on Smith would reintroduce the measure and see that it was passed, but something much larger was occurring than the inauguration of a new ethnic pageant. Al was beginning to take on the role of champion of urban immigrants, a spokesman who claimed that they too had the right to be a part of American society in every way, in this case by adding to its list of rituals.[41]

One other event of that period had unusual long-term consequences for Al Smith. On the night of Tuesday, March 28, 1911, the Democrats caucused in the Assembly Chamber until very late, breaking up at 1:00 A.M. Several newsmen, along with the clerks, remained behind to finish their work, and at 2:15 A.M., one of the staff came running in to announce that the Assembly Library, Al's home through those long work-filled evenings, was on fire. According to Louis Howe, one of the reporters sitting there, a few buckets of water could have doused the blaze at that early stage, but none could be found. No alarms existed either, so the night watchman ran downstairs to call for help.[42]

This would not be the last time that Al would deal with the issue of fire safety, but that night at four in the morning, the phone in his room at the Hotel Ten Eyck rang, and a voice on the other end told him the Capitol was burning. His first reaction was that this was a practical joke, but as he went to the window he could see the red skyline. The old fire buff roared into action, dressing as quickly as possible, running up the hill to see what was going on.

What he saw when he arrived was disheartening. Before firemen could smother the inferno, it damaged both chambers. The floor of the Assembly was a lake, prompting one member to joke that they should stock it with fish. Many offices had been ruined, and the Million Dollar Staircase looked like a waterfall at one point.

But the greatest destruction by far was in the State Library. Billed as the greatest library disaster of the era, the fire had consumed 450,000 books and 270,000 manuscripts, many of the latter priceless and irreplaceable. Although scholars then and later legitimately fretted over the loss of colonial documents, ironically, it was Al Smith's legacy that suffered the most damage. As the shelves gave way, the oldest records, parchments from the Dutch and British periods, were buried at the bottom under layers of more recent materials, and the flames never reached them. The latest materials, those chronicling Al's apprentice days in the Assembly, were on the top, and burned to cinders.

Al by now was refining his natural talents to command the legislature through wit and humor. The *Herald*, a Republican paper, claimed that "as a story teller [Smith] has no rival in Albany. . . . It is nothing for him to tell dialect stories for three straight hours and to keep his listeners in paroxysms of laughter." One of the devices he created to win over upstate legislators was a regular series of corned beef and cabbage dinners he sponsored every Thursday night during the legislative session. Gathering in four or five men he wanted to get to know, Al took them down to the restaurant at Keeler's Hotel. The menu at these soirees invariably consisted of corned beef and cabbage, boiled potatoes, dark, fresh rye bread, and steins of imported beer. For hours after the dishes had been cleared, he would regale colleagues with stories and songs, jokes and tales, while all the other diners craned their heads to listen to the best entertainment the house had ever enjoyed. Al never brought up politics, never pressured or lobbied any of the members. What he was doing was far more subtle: he was demystifying himself and New York City, showing that someone with a thick accent and a Bowery address could still be a hale fellow, could be a person others enjoyed being around, and maybe even respect. Across dozens of evenings, Al Smith performed the critical, admirable service of proving to upstaters that the new crowd just might be all right. This paid dividends in the Assembly, with even greater rewards when Al ran for governor, and many politicians from rural districts came to his support.[43]

Sometimes, however, Al could not resist temptation, and the humor became more barbed, more insightful. On one occasion back in the Assembly Chamber he was championing the first workmen's compensation bill in the state's history, when a rival member from across the aisle, Jay Pratt of Oneida County, rose and asked if he could pose a question. The Speaker agreed, so Pratt turned to Smith and said, "Mr. Tammany leader [Pratt always addressed Democrats as "Tammany leaders"], what good is the Workmen's Compensation Act to the three-hundred-and-fifty thousand men out of work . . .?" This was a red herring; whatever the merits of the proposal were, it would only apply to those already employed.[44]

Al spoke without hesitation. "Mr. Speaker," he replied, "I was walking down Park Row one night and a man came up and hit me on the shoulder and said, 'Hello, Al. Which would you rather be, a hammock full of white door knobs, a cellar full of stepladders, or a piece of dry ice?' I said I would rather be a fish, because no matter how thick plate glass is, you can always break it with a hammer."

Pratt sprang to his feet; the indications are that he was angry, and it would have been a miracle if he had not been thoroughly confused: "I don't get the point of the gentleman's remark," he snapped.

Al looked at the man calmly and remarked, "There is just as much point to my answer as there is to your question." The debate continued without any further interruption.

At the same time, Assemblyman Smith was putting in as much time as possible in his home district, meeting his constituents in Foley's Downtown Tammany Club, which was becoming Al's favorite political hangout. When the Assembly was in session he appeared on the weekend, but after that he showed up six nights out of seven, holding office hours "just the same as a doctor . . . and I had a line of patients there night after night." Increasingly, he made sure that interpreters were there to help him understand, and then handle, the needs of his diverse constituency.[45]

As he still lived down the block, residents saw that he was not the kind who moved uptown after he made it, or as Al deliciously explained, he was not someone who "cooks his corned beef and cabbage in the basement so the neighbors won't smell it." Harry Roskolenko, who was no fan of the Tammany system, called Al "a much-loved politician, able to convince any number of East Side Jews that he was as much for them as the socialists were." In 1910 the Citizens Union asked him why he had not campaigned more vigorously, why he sent out no literature, and Al could proudly respond, "I did not send any documents of any kind to the voters of my district during my recent campaign. It is unnecessary as they know me personally and my increased majority is an indication of their confidence in me."[46]

He began to develop a routine. When the Assembly was in session, every Monday afternoon he left for Albany, returning late Friday afternoon. After the train pulled in to Grand Central Station, Al would head over to the Knickerbocker Hotel where he met Katie and the two children old enough to enjoy a night out, Alfred, Jr., and Emily. Arriving at about six or six-thirty, Al took everybody out to dinner at the Knickerbocker's dining room, followed by a vaudeville show, especially the latest at the Palace Theater in Times Square. The dinner, by the way, caused numerous heartaches for the children, who had not inherited the famous Smith affection for fish. But this was always a Friday repast, and the good Catholic Smith family would never eat meat. Emily wrote that she and her older brother would scrutinize the lavish menu, filled with dishes so near and yet so out of reach, and wind up ordering eggs.[47]

By now, things were getting crowded for the family Smith. Al had found a spot at 28 Oliver Street, which, given the geography of status in that area, was a big step up. Oliver Street, which Al would make famous, really was nicer than the surrounding lanes; many of the houses were neat brick homes, with stoops made up of half a dozen steps, rising only two or three stories above that level, with a small foyer. Just around the corner, on Henry Street, you could see the difference; here the tenements were all four or five stories tall, with no stoop, just an entrance into a narrow, dark hallway. Since Foley kept an office on Oliver Street and a judge and a congressman lived there as well, after Al moved in it became known as Politician's Row. Dr. Bernard Pisani grew up there and recalled "a very delightful" block: "People were friendly. . . . They knew their neighbors. . . . It was peaceful," and "you played on the street," with stickball and roller skating common.[48]

But it soon got crowded at 28 Oliver, a five-room, third-floor walkup that had the family ensconced in the top railroad flat. The ceilings were low, and space was so tight that Al slept on a couch in the living room. That would not do, so in

1909 the family moved to 25 Oliver Street, across the street. Since this was such a short hop, Al called out all of the local militia: the boys of the Downtown Tammany Club took care of most of the work; a member of the Street Cleaning Department carried over the two heavy items (a stove and the icebox); and the small boys on the block managed the little items. With such an elaborate crew, the entire job took only two hours from start to finish.[49]

This house became the closest Al Smith ever had to an ancestral manse, and it is now an historic site. He and Katie spent more time here than at any other of their residences, and they raised their family there, as well as in the governor's mansion in Albany. The building was a red-brick townhouse, with three floors, a basement, and high ceilings, so everybody could stretch out; this included the Smith's fifth and last child, Walter, who arrived in December, just months after the move, and thus helped them inaugurate the new quarters.

There was also—no coincidence—plenty of room for the pets. The Smiths always had at least two dogs, but in 1911 the menagerie got more complicated. The family was spending the summer out at Far Rockaway, and some friend, knowing Al's fondness for animals, gave them a present of two goats and a carriage for hauling children. Goats are not usually considered the quintessential urban pet, but Al rose to the occasion (he wrote in his memoirs, "I suppose I was just as insistent as the children that we keep them"). Coming up with the perfect solution, the new zookeeper of Oliver Street had workmen build a door through the back fence that enclosed the family yard, which also happened to adjoin a stable on Madison Street. That provided, in Al's words, "a private stall for the goats with a rear entrance into the yard of the . . . house." The goats then proceeded to become the most popular attraction for all the children in the neighborhood, who made sure that the animals put in time and a half hauling them around, "and they worked on Sunday as well."

By 1909 Al was a recognized leader in the Assembly, one of the two or three most powerful Democrats there. The *New York Times* began to refer to Smith as the spokesman for Tammany Hall, and the *Tribune* called him the "Bowery statesman. . . . easily the strong man in the Democratic ranks in the Assembly." Al started to take control, making it a habit to create a list of meaningless and nonsensical bills (from both parties) and then exposing and ridiculing these examples of junk legislation. One Republican politician, Lemuel Quigg, told his son that Smith was "the most dangerous man in the state to tangle with because he knew more about state government and its actual operation than any other man."[50]

Smith began to carry the burdens of leadership. Most of the work of the chamber was done by a few veterans who drew up the key measures that kept the

Assembly and the state running and the bills that made necessary changes to the statute code. Al was putting in what Hugh Carey called "the backbreaking work" of preparing legislation—of deciding what would be tackled and what ignored, and by whom. He knew that for most of the members, their only contact with the mammoth appropriations bill was that they favored it for shaving paper in the morning, useful for plugging up nicks and scratches because the paper was so soft and there was so much of it. Smith was reading this bill, understanding it, critiquing it, then influencing its priorities and its budget from the floor. Al began to complain that the Assembly was composed of 150 members: 3 doing the work and the other 147 interfering with them.[51]

Smith would reach new positions of power, in part because of his own skills, but also as a result of forces way beyond his control. By 1910, reform fever seemed to be boiling up both in the country as a whole and in New York State. Nationally, ex-president Theodore Roosevelt was rebelling against the conservatism of his successor, William Howard Taft, in a way that few public figures could ignore, given Teddy's natural tendency for the dramatic and loud. In New York State, Republican legislative leaders had for too long blocked reform, even by their own governors—people like Charles Evans Hughes—and the citizenry was starting to get fed up.

What brought these simmering sentiments to a boil was the act of a courageous state senator, Benn Conger, a Republican of deep integrity. Conger openly accused Jotham Allds, president pro tem and majority leader of the upper house, of accepting money from bridge companies to influence his vote in state appropriations. Conger also claimed that these interests had donated heavily to the Republican war chest in New York, in hopes of other favorable treatment.[52]

Allds of course denied all charges. Unfortunately for him, Hiram Moe, a representative of the bridge interests, admitted in public that he had given the legislator five thousand dollars over several months' time. The Senate brought Allds up on charges and found him guilty of bribery; he would have then been expelled but had already resigned. In a sad moment for the public trust, Conger also took this step, although, as one commentator remarked, this was "much to the delight of his Republican colleagues."

The cat was out of the bag now, with larger investigations underway. These inquiries turned up the fact that ten of the leading Republicans in the state had been illegally taking public funds and then privately using them to speculate on the stock market, racking up enormous profits.

The public was outraged. Democrats swept the 1910 elections, bringing their

first governor in seventeen years to the executive office and claiming both houses of the legislature. Al rode this wave, pulling off the second highest majority of
any district in New York City. When the counting was over, the Democrats had
86 seats out of 150 in the Assembly and 29 out of 50 in the Senate.

The Tammany leadership used the opportunity to clean house. Out went
Thomas Grady, minority leader in the Senate, a man of great speeches but also
an alcoholic. He was replaced by the smart, fire-brand reformer Robert Wagner, who became the youngest president pro tempore of the Senate in the state's
history.

Over in the lower chamber, the bosses wisely accepted Daniel Frisbie, an
independent Democrat, as Speaker, but made sure that one of their own had a
key place in the seats of power. In party caucuses they named Al Smith as Majority Leader, but also saw to it, in an unprecedented move, that he became the
chairman of the all-powerful Ways and Means Committee, the body that controlled the flow of legislation to the entire Assembly.[53]

Smith immediately set out to run a tight ship. He scrutinized the $50 million
in expenditures, noting that it was balanced by only $37 million in income. To
close this gap Smith wrote to all the department heads, close to two hundred of
them, asking each to cut 10 percent of their expenditures. Over and over, he
checked figures; if a department needed a certain number of clerks or engineers
or staffers, Smith asked why. What do these people do, he queried, why are they
needed? In the end he managed to pare $15 million dollars from the expense side
of the ledger.[54]

He was equally tough on his colleagues. On one occasion when a controversial bill came to the floor, everyone ducked, deciding it would be a good time to
check out the home district. Al ordered all the Tammany men under his direct
control to return to Albany, or he would see that they never ran for office again.
Regarding the upstate Democrats, he instructed the Sergeant-at-Arms to round
them up and haul them in, in handcuffs if that was required. None of these
threats had to be carried out, but none of them were ever necessary again,
either.[55]

Al Smith tried, in essence, to prove that he was as good as anyone else, that
the people he represented could produce a leader as honest, as fair as any other
group. When rebellious antimachine Democrats, led by a young aristocrat
named Franklin Roosevelt, tried to buck Tammany rule, Al instructed them how
to fight by the rules, regardless of the impact this might have on Tammany.
Franklin remembered that "we stayed out, and won the fight; and incidentally,
we won, also, the definite knowledge that Smith would play square with friend
and foe alike."[56]

This attitude even stretched across the aisle. Al's opposite number that year was Edwin Merritt, who found himself in the overcrowded capitol without an office, notwithstanding his position as minority leader. Al had a lavish space now, so he invited Merritt to take over one corner of this space, even though his colleague had been involved in the incident that led to the F.F.M. remark.

Merritt declined, however, on the grounds that this arrangement might embarrass Smith. Al told him, "Nothing is going to be done here except the state's business; there is nothing going to be said that you can't hear; we can disagree later." Merritt softened, and moved in. Over the next few years Merritt showed Al something of the towns and villages of rural new York, while Smith took him to the tenement districts and taught Merritt about the problems these people faced. In 1914, when Merritt died, Smith spoke at his funeral, describing how he had developed for the deceased "as strong an affection as it was possible for one man to have for another not of his own relationship."[57]

Meanwhile, lots of work had to be done. In that session Al personally introduced seventy-two bills. Some of this was of epic importance, such as the culmination of the successful fight he had been leading for several years to get New York to enact a Workmen's Compensation Law. When that bill passed in 1910, with Al leading the fight, New York became the first state in the union to enact this reform, one that set the stage for later federal insurance programs covering old age, unemployment, and health.[58]

But above all, Al's training and instincts—his common sense and his belief in decency—led him to become something of a reformer in those days. He supported administrative reform and efficiency because the system of state government was so new to him. Since he had to learn everything, nothing was familiar, nothing was sacred. His lack of legal training also helped, because he had never learned the benefits of procedure, and thus could cut to the core of what was substantive and separate it from what was ceremonial.

His interest in social reform, on the other hand, came from an expanding sense, not only of right and wrong, but of whom he represented, and the importance of this role. By 1911, when he was majority leader, the U.S. Immigration Commission found in one 10,000-student New York City school district, three-quarters had been born overseas into any one of twenty-eight national and ethnic groups, including Moravians, Finns, Syrians, Magyars, Slovaks and Lithuanians. These were Al's constituents, and he knew that they had needs and problems.[59]

Eventually these concerns brought him to the attention of the elite reform movement. Frances Perkins came to see him in 1910 as a representative of the New York Consumers League, lobbying for a bill limiting the working hours of women and children to fifty-four a week. On her way up to the capitol for the first time, she tagged along with Joseph Hammett, Albany representative of the

Citizens Union. Looking over the railing of the visitors' gallery onto the floor of the Assembly, they saw members engaged in various conversations, but only one man was bowed in study. Frances asked the name of that chap, and Hammett pointed out Alfred E. Smith, a diligent and knowledgeable assemblyman, although, he acknowledged, "It's a pity he's a Tammany man." Undeterred by that epithet, the young woman asked to meet him, and after she had been introduced and vouched for, asked his view on the bill she was advocating. Al responded, straightforward and with crisp knowledge, "Jackson's got the bill. It's still in committee and not moving very fast. Better ask for a hearing." He then left and returned to his desk.[60]

They would meet again and again, planning changes in the way government took care of its citizens. Perkins told interviewers that she had to "go at him piecemeal . . . "; he had "no preconceived philosophy . . . but if you could prove to him that the girl's back ached, that she was tired, that she didn't have enough to eat . . . then it seemed only humane." By that year the Citizens Union, fighting for a general pension plan for state employees, could report in *The Searchlight*, its regular bulletin, that Majority Leader Smith had expressed support ("he was greatly impressed") with their platform.[61]

Smith's newfound status as a reformer was incredible, considering the fact that all the while Al remained a "Tammany Man"; he could engage in these activities only after he had obtained permission from the head of Tammany Hall. No such leader had ever shown the slightest interest in these matters before, but then again, the Hall had never seen a man like the one Al Smith now served under. In a long lineage of bosses, Charles Francis Murphy was by far the most outstanding leader Tammany Hall would ever produce.

Murphy came from good immigrant stock, both his parents emigrating from Ireland. Born in 1858 in a tenement in the Gas House area on the East Side of New York around Fourteenth Street, he became a horsecar driver, but spent most of his time on a local baseball team, the Senators, where the short, stocky man played catcher. The Senators served as the athletic outlet of a social club, the Sylvans, which Murphy had organized; by now he was becoming widely known in the community as something of a leader, and soon turned this to profit by opening a saloon. In time, this became a hangout not only for his teammates, but for many of the other young men in the area who enjoyed the male comradeship, as well as the five cent charge for a schooner of beer and a bowl of soup. Politics was a natural follow-up, and by 1892 Murphy had become a district leader, one of the royal peers of the Tammany clan; five years after that, he received an appointment as dock commissioner, the only position he ever held with the City of New York.[62]

Murphy started to rise in the ranks for several reasons. Above all, he was a superb organizer; one commentator explained that on Election Day, anyone in the district who was known to be a Democrat (that meant most of the voters) and had not cast his ballot by 3 P.M., received a written notice requesting his presence at the voting booth, forthwith. Murphy also took the traditional Tammany practice of community support to new heights, donating considerable sums to churches and charities; the minister of St. George's Episcopal Church told his congregants one Sunday that the world would be a better place if all political leaders were like Charlie Murphy. In addition, Murphy maintained a puritanical stance against vice, unlike many of his peers. The boss had little to do with women, marrying late, and no one ever dreamed of delivering an off-color joke in his presence. After the Lexow Commission report, Murphy was more than willing to help in the cleanup of the sex trade, and thus could support candidates riding the wave of popular outrage.[63]

Problems mounted, however, as the machine stumbled on with petty, thuggish leaders at its helm. By 1902 Tammany faced a major decline in its influence, and with the hounds circling, Richard Croker, the Boss, decided to protect his greater interest—and his hide—by adjourning to his estate in England on a somewhat permanent basis. In a short while, the sachems picked Murphy as his successor.

Murphy proceeded to turn Tammany Hall around, showing remarkable skill in organizing the voters, cleaning up the machine, and, especially, picking the right candidate for the right slot. He consolidated his authority, holding court at either his office on Fourteenth Street or his favorite restaurant, Delmonico's, where he dined in the Scarlet Room while courtiers came to call. This chamber received its title because of the lavish red rugs and upholstery, augmented by rich mahogany furniture. Seated in a heavy armchair behind a huge table that rested on legs carved as tiger claws, Murphy epitomized the title "Boss."[64]

Murphy held on to the reins of power because he had a sharp mind and a quiet tongue. A good listener, he could grasp the essence of a situation and plan a campaign without letting on that he had heard a thing. A writer from the *Literary Digest,* after watching Murphy in action, claimed that the leader talked in "short, jerky, low sentences, which seldom are over twelve words in length. Frequently a full minute will elapse between one sentence and the next." At the same time, Murphy would be shooting off endless questions, functioning as "an insatiable interrogator. When he asks someone's advice he keeps him talking all the time, and yet the man who is being interrogated does not seem to realize how much he has been talking." The impact that all this was having on Murphy's own think-ing, however, was never revealed, as he liked the boys to think "he had some-thing in reserve." On one occasion, when asked why Tammany had lost an election, Murphy replied, "We didn't get enough votes." It was not for nothing that he has come down in history as the "Silent Boss."[65]

By the time Al Smith was reaching for power in the Assembly, Murphy was the great boss—*his* boss. No one, for example, ever called the Silent One "Char-lie"; it was always "Mister Murphy" or "Commissioner." And Mister Murphy expected Al, like anyone else in the Hall, to follow his orders to the letter. In example after example, when measures hostile to Tammany's interest reached the floor, Al showed that he remained, as the civic leader Robert Binkerd described it, "a member of his organization in harness." When the great reform governor, Charles Evans Hughes, for example, tried to pass a direct primary system, Republican and Democratic bosses lined up to defeat this measure, which would have challenged their authority so fundamentally; in the Assembly, Al Smith followed Murphy's orders and joined the effort to defeat this step toward more direct democracy. The list of Murphy's commands became a long one, as Al worked to defeat a public service commission, a bill destroying race-track gambling in New York, or else brought to fruition a land grab for Tam-many. John Lord O'Brian, a reformer who saw many of his projects go up in smoke as Al carried out Murphy's orders, remarked that "whenever there was a party issue, or anything resembling a party issue up, [Al] adhered to the line."[66]

What made Murphy remarkable, however, what made him, in the words of Bronx boss Ed Flynn, "the best Leader Tammany Hall ever had and one of the wisest political overlords New York ever had," was the amazing fact that Mur-phy saw that there was more to politics than graft and power.[67]

Murphy's vision of politics, in fact, was considerably more complex than that of the Tammany leaders who preceded or followed him. These men had all been and would continue after Murphy to be dullards, bulls who took a firm, unyield-ing line when it came to their interests. Murphy, on the other hand, displayed a remarkable subtlety. While he cherished the use of patronage at lower ranks, Murphy understood that to hold those positions he needed to elect the top of the ticket, even if the candidates were not Tammany disciples. And he could no longer do that with hacks or buffoons, men who proved that they were less than able, and would thus repel the voters, no matter what miracles the district lead-ers performed. Thus, in many elections, Murphy supported candidates who looked favorably on the Hall but had no long history of machine control; instead, many of them came from business and elite backgrounds and were entering politics for the first time. In his first big election as boss, in 1903, Mur-phy chose Republican reformers Charles Fornes and Edward Grout to run for the number two and three slots on the ticket, respectively—President of the Board of Aldermen and Controller. For mayor, he managed to concoct George McClellan as a candidate. McClellan, son of the Civil War general, was wealthy, polished, a member of the elite, and not particularly strong of character. For years to come, with figures like these at the front of the ticket, Tammany rolled on to the greatest winning streak in its history.[68]

Murphy also showed some other remarkable tendencies. He readily accepted that experts, not hacks, were required in positions covering areas like public health and education. While graft from contractors continued at a steady clip, he proceeded to cut Tammany's connections to the underworld—especially prostitution, which he abhorred—but also gambling and payoffs from the police, the latter of which had caused the deleterious Lexow investigations. Murphy, unlike any other boss, felt that such doings were immoral, and he also had the savvy to recognize that paying off cops was bad business in the long run. No other leader of Tammany Hall, from Tweed to the fall of the machine in the mid-twentieth century, ever had the brains to reach that same conclusion.[69]

The first time he called together the district leaders, Murphy made it clear what the new system was like. He told them point-blank that graft from prostitution should be considered a thing of the past. Any district leader continuing this practice would be broken. In fact, he noted that in their ranks that night sat one man of whom he planned to make an example. They all knew that this referred to Martin Engel, an important district leader who profited from one of the worst red-light districts in the city. Shortly thereafter, Engel received a visit from Florry Sullivan, Big Tim's *larger* relative, well over six feet tall, and, as one writer put it, "a mighty man with his hands." Engel was henceforth thrown out of office, figuratively and literally, following which Florry and his boys (not the police) began to shut down the rows of brothels by entering each establishment and expelling the proprietor by sheer force. Soon the neighborhood achieved what one reporter referred to as a state of "moral purification."[70]

But what really threw the reformers for a loop, and what earned Murphy his place in history, was that he began to support a host of reform legislation. Murphy gave his okay, and the boys in Albany and in city hall passed stronger tenement laws and a scholarship program for poor children of the slums. Workmen's compensation became a reality because Murphy went along, and he backed efforts to pass new laws regulating safety, hours, and wages, to the point that during his reign, and with his okay, New York became one of the leading states in dealing with the abuses of rampant industrialization. Frances Perkins felt that this legislation "marked a change in American political attitudes and policies" that "can scarcely be overrated," calling it "a turning point." But none of this would have passed without Murphy's agreement and consent, prompting one leading historian of reform movements to argue that "surely, Murphy played a vital role as one of the baby-sitters who helped rear this fragile child of the twentieth century to lusty adolescence, if not to manhood."[71]

Murphy's endorsement of progressive thinking had an enormous impact on Al Smith. As Al became a reformer, he found that he enjoyed the support of his party, that he did not have to work as an independent when he fought for the good. Murphy now told him to fly with his better instincts, to use his skills to fight larger battles, for larger issues. In 1913, those instincts would be put to a terrible test.

Chapter 6

The Triangle Shirtwaist Fire

THE ASCHE BUILDING takes up the northeast corner of Greene Street and Washington Place, placing the bustle of its upstairs factories only one block from the green tranquility of Washington Square Park. In 1911 Triangle Shirtwaist was on the top three floors of this tan, grimy ten-story brick building, square and squat in its architecture and decorations, a building that was not particularly ugly, beautiful, or remarkable in any way.

Today there is a plaque on that building. It reads, "On this site 146 workers lost their lives in the Triangle Shirtwaist Company Fire on March 25, 1911. Out of their martyrdom came new concepts of social responsibility and labor legislation that have helped make America's working conditions the finest in the world."

The last line is debatable, but it is beyond question that labor and safety conditions in New York, and in all cities across America, were transformed in the wave of reform legislation that followed the fire. And in the middle of it was Assemblyman Alfred E. Smith. If, during his apprenticeship in the legislature, Smith had learned about the nuts and bolts of the political system, what he lacked was a cause, a rationale for using that expertise. The Triangle Fire would provide that and more, as it would fundamentally alter how he viewed the very role of government in American life.

❧

Before that horrible day in March, the Triangle Shirtwaist Company was as typical, as unassuming, as the building that housed it. New York had become, by the turn of the century, the premier center of women's garment manufacturing in the United States, the city's shops turning out between two-thirds and three-quarters of all the clothes made for women in this country. The industry, which would later move to the west Thirties, and eventually offshore, in those days clustered its factories in the district south of Fourteenth Street, so Triangle was right in the center of things. Even the shop floor was typical, with long rows of sewing machines stretching from one end to the other; on the ninth floor the tables abutted the back wall, so that in an emergency, workers would have to walk as much as seventy-five feet before they could reach an aisle and even start to head toward an exit. Each station contained a sewing machine and a little bit of space to work in; beneath this sat a box filled with wispy threads of lint; above this rested a small container to catch the machine's oil drippings, a lethally flammable combination. There were 575 women operators on the actual shop floors, the eighth and ninth levels of the building.[1]

But Triangle would never again be typical after 4:40 P.M. on a Saturday afternoon in March, when a fire broke out in a rag bin. No one has ever determined how it started, whether from a spark or a cigarette (smoking was banned in the factory), but it hardly matters. Within seconds, the flimsy fabrics and paper patterns in the shop, the oil, the wooden tables, everything was a roaring blaze. Women fought to save their lives, only to discover the horrors of the new industrial order. Yes, there was a fire hose, but it was cracked and rotten and had no water pressure. Yes, there was a staircase, but practicality dictated that its door must open in, instead of toward the outside, thus blocking the entrance as women pushed forward, trying to escape the inferno. Yes, there was a back entrance, but it was chained shut, to make sure that no one would steal a garment or take an unauthorized break. Yes, there was a fire escape; but no code covered its construction, so it gave way as soon as a few frightened bodies crowded onto it. No, no one had ever conducted a fire drill, because it took time, and time was money. Terror grew as the survivors crowded into the one small elevator car, measuring only five by six feet, the operator making frantic trips to save as many as he could. All the rest were trapped inside the burning factory.[2]

The scenes of horror grew worse as the fire rose. James McCadeen, a worker in a nearby building, "saw a girl come to the edge of the roof and stand for a minute. Her hair was in flames. I couldn't look any more." That anonymous victim was joined by many more, who made the impossible choice between being burned alive or jumping to their deaths. Some of them, facing an alleyway, plunged onto a spiked wrought-iron fence and were impaled. Others, plummeting all the way down, built so much speed that they cracked giant holes through a pavement embedded with glass circles for decorative purposes, plunging into the subway below. One woman jumped into the Fire Department's most modern piece of equipment, a fourteen-foot net; she hit with a force equivalent to sixteen tons of pressure, wrecking the device and dying as she hit the concrete. On the last trip down in the elevator, the women heard thuds as their colleagues reached the same horrific conclusion, and leapt to their deaths down that long shaft rather than be consumed by the flames.³

The whole thing did not take very long, less than half an hour. Afterward, while the coroner of the City of New York—hardly a stranger to death—stood there and sobbed, Fire Chief Edward Croker walked down the aisles, viewing bodies that had been incinerated down to bare bones, gaping at the skeletons slumped over the sewing machines. A *New York Times* reporter came upon a headless and charred trunk on the sidewalk and inquired of a nearby policeman if it was a man or a woman. The grizzled veteran, who claimed he had worked other New York calamities but they were nothing like this, responded, "It's human, that's all you can tell." By the time they got through counting the bodies, 146 souls had perished. Triangle had become the worst industrial fire in New York's history, a record it still grimly holds.

Existing facilities could never handle this kind of catastrophe, so officials took over the long, covered pier at Twenty-Sixth street and converted it into a makeshift morgue. As the attendants prepared the dead to meet the living, a crowd of several thousand formed, absolutely frantic to determine whether or not one of their loved ones had perished. Every time a newsman left this facility to post his story, a *Times* reporter said, "a hundred faces were turned up to him imploringly, and a hundred anguished voices begged of him tidings of those within. Had he seen a little girl with black hair and dark-brown cheeks? Had he seen a tall, thin man with stooped shoulders?" Over and over, ambulances and hearses arrived from the fire scene, bringing new loads of bodies as the crowd expressed its fear in passionate calls and moans. Hands pulled at the tailgates, desperate for some information, no matter how grisly, and in one case tore off blankets to reveal two bodies that were still somehow holding each other, an embrace outlasting death. Cries in Yiddish and Italian meanwhile flew to the heavens. Of the 126 women and 20 men who lost their lives, most were of immigrant stock; the average age was nineteen. Finally, at midnight, policemen started to let the first of the family members in, in groups of twenty, and the horrible process of identifying the victims began. The first one to enter was a tiny woman with a shawl over her head. One-third of the way down the long aisle of bodies, she stopped in front of coffin number 15 and crying, fell to her knees. The long night had just begun.⁴

In other parts of the city, trauma turned to outrage. Soon there were protests; speakers at public meetings called for investigations, while unions and socialist journals implored the workers to support the trades union movement. Assemblyman Smith, whose district included many of the grieving families, told the *New York Herald* that the fire codes were deficient, that the "laws are most certainly inadequate and we must revise them at once." Even artists got involved; John Sloan noted in his journal on March 26, "After breakfast I got a cartoon idea . . . re the frightful fire of last evening." The design included a black triangle, each side marked, respectively, "Rents," "Interest," "Death." On one side stood skeletal death, on the other a bloated capitalist; inside rested the burned body of a girl.[5]

The day after the fire, in the offices of the Women's Trade Union League, a Committee on Safety, consisting of many of the city's leading citizens, began operation. Financed by a $10,000 grant by philanthropist R. Fulton Cutting, the first chair was Henry Stimson, who soon left to become secretary of war, followed by the financier Henry Morgenthau, Sr. Other members included representatives of the women's movement like Mary Dreier and social work leaders such as Frances Perkins and Henry Moskowitz.[6]

This activity culminated on Sunday, April 2. The Trade Union League had rented the Metropolitan Opera House for a meeting at 3:00 P.M., and a large crowd turned out, representing all segments of angry New York. In the gallery sat workers and their families, while downstairs the Fifth Avenue crowd dominated.[7]

Numerous speakers talked to the assemblage. Rabbi Stephen Wise, the best-known Jewish religious leader in the country, declared, "We have laws, that in a crisis we find are no laws and we have enforcement that when the hour of trial comes we find is no enforcement. Let us lift up the industrial standards until they will bear inspection."

In the end, the meeting called for a resolution asking that the city create a Bureau of Fire Prevention, a basic measure that did not exist at this time. As the motion passed, voices clearly expressed dissent, anger at the mildness of it all. The event hovered on the brink of disorder when a lone voice brought a hush to the crowd.

The tone was quiet yet strong, much like the speaker. Tiny Rose Schneiderman, a leader of the women's union that had fought Triangle just recently and failed, gave one of the most moving speeches in American working-class history. "I would be a traitor to those poor, burned bodies," she explained, "if I were to come here and talk good fellowship. We have tried you good people of the public—and we have found you wanting." Rose knew what conditions her friends and coworkers faced: "The old Inquisition had its rack and its thumbscrews and its instruments of torture with iron teeth. We know what these things are today: the iron teeth are our necessities, the thumbscrews are the high-powered and swift machinery close to which we must work, and the rack is here in the firetrap structures that destroy us." "Every week," she said, "I must learn of the untimely death of one of my sister workers. Every year thousands of us are maimed. The life of women and men is so cheap and property is so sacred." "I can't talk fellowship to you who are gathered here," she concluded, "too much blood has been spilled."

Rose Schneiderman sat down to initial silence; her impact, however, was enormous, as that speech now shaped the subsequent debate. Life in the industrial city no longer made sense, she had shown, no longer fostered life. Representative democracy had to respond to these horrors, had to overtake them and bring them under control, or other alternatives would be sought. In response, the Committee on Safety found its representatives traveling to Albany, laying before the state's chief executive a petition to take action. Governor John Dix admitted that he sympathized with the delegation and its aims, but suggested that they meet instead with the Democratic leaders of the two branches of the legislature: Robert Wagner in the Senate and Al Smith in the Assembly.[8]

The reformers wound up in Smith's office first. He knew of the fire, of course, and had paid his respects at the homes of several of his constituents who had lost family members in the conflagration.

As a first step, Al began instructing his guests how to go about changing government; he was still operating at this point more as a master practitioner of politics, rather than as a passionate advocate. They had originally conceived of a blue-ribbon commission, made up of all the best people, irreproachable in its integrity and funded from the executive budget or from private donations.

Smith patiently explained the flaws behind this scheme. Rich people, he responded, were "always very busy, and you can't get their attention for very long." Instead, it would be far wiser to create a committee of the legislature, a committee including, and led by, the same kind of people who would eventually have to pass any improvements to the state code. "It isn't the finest people who have the most influence in the legislature," he argued. "The members there are just like anyone else—they think their own work is the best. If you want to get anything done, ladies and gentlemen, I advise you to ask for a legislative commission."

The idea took, and on June 30, 1911, Governor Dix signed the bill creating the Factory Investigating Commission (FIC). It enjoyed full powers to subpoena witnesses and records, employ staff as it saw fit, appoint officers, and adopt its own rules. At the same time, however, the state limited the powers of this extraordinary body by appropriating the negligible sum of only ten thousand dollars for the first year; members appointed from the legislature, for example, received only their travel expenses. They also restricted the commission's purview to first- and second-class cities, of which there were only nine in the state.[9]

But the potential remained. The framers of the legislation managed to extend the range of the commission's concerns far beyond simple fire safety to the broader issue of industrial conditions. The initial agenda (which would later be stretched much further) included fire hazards, unsanitary working conditions, occupational illnesses, factory inspection, tenement sweatshops, and the status of existing laws and enforcement. Other states had taken on part of this mandate: an Illinois commission had investigated diseases, and a Massachusetts body examined liability concerns. The broader scope of this commission, however, meant that New York had become the first state in the country to launch a general investigation into the conditions of industrial work.[10]

The group convened on August 17, 1911, and elected Robert Wagner as chairman and Alfred E. Smith as vice chairman. Shortly after that, the commission began its regular schedule of hearings and meetings. In the first year alone, they held twenty-two public meetings in cities such as Buffalo, Rochester, Syracuse, Schenectady, and Troy, interviewed 222 witnesses publicly, and took 3,489 pages of testimony. This traveling road show of reform would come into a city, advance notices declaring that its purposes were "strictly non-partisan" and "non-sensational," and then, with a staff member leading the witnesses through their paces, public hearings would instruct both members and the public about the realities of industrial life. Sessions began at 9:30 in the morning sharp and often lasted well into the evening.[11]

At first the commission concentrated on fire safety issues. The problem, they discovered, was not that owners violated the safety codes but rather that the codes were far too lax to protect workers' safety. The Asche Building, for example, was considered a model of fireproofing, and in one sense it was: the building remained relatively undamaged, while all inside perished. H. J. F. Porter, not only their fire expert but a former vice president of the Vernet Lamp Company in Pittsburgh, testified to great effect how small measures like better escape routes and fire drills made a huge difference.[12]

But while members debated and prepared remedial legislation to deal with fire safety, their focus quickly shifted to larger concerns of industrial working conditions. The scope of their investigation led them to confront some of the most wretched work environments in the nation's history. Laundry workers waded through standing water, coated with the remains from soiled table linen and personal garments. Candy factory employees had to slosh through the sticky slime that overflowed from huge vats. In some factories, toilets had no seats; in others they only flushed once a day. One mill owner simply provided a barrel in the basement, notwithstanding the fact that he was a member of the local board of health.[13]

Investigators found that some jobs were frightfully dangerous. Workers handling lead, for example, received no warnings, had no facilities to wash their hands before they ate, and became poisoned at an early age. Their highest wage remained fourteen dollars a week, denying the claim that high risk brought high compensation.[14]

Worst of all were the conditions under which women and children labored. Investigators roamed through the tenements, finding sweatshops where women worked by street light to save the cost of gas, unaffordable on their slim wages. Children cried from exhaustion, their parents' only response to urge the small fingers on, paste another petal on the artificial flower, in the rush to earn a few pennies more for bread. Their older brothers and sisters no longer expressed their rage and toiled on, listless, their eyes dulled. Adults working in these tenement conditions earned as little as one and a half cents an hour, and entire families sometimes earned only two dollars for an endless day's efforts. One group of women crocheted slippers and, by working from dawn through night, finished a dozen pairs every two days. For this effort they earned forty cents. In some places, adults and youths stricken with tuberculosis worked on children's clothing, on dolls, and on foodstuffs, transmitting their germs to multitudes of customers.[15]

The commission reached the bottom when it began to investigate conditions of women and especially children in the state's canning industry. One reporter took a job in such a factory to write an exposé on child labor for *Good Housekeeping* and discovered that "everyone of those tiny children is sick and tired. Exhaustion saps the puny strength, fatigue and undernourishment destroy the energy needed for . . . life. . . . Working like little automatons sit the Italian children, their swollen fingers split from the constant breaking of beans and tied up in filthy bits of rag." The Factory Investigating Commission's study of over thirteen hundred children employed in this industry found that most were less than fourteen years old, with some of the tykes as young as three years, picking and sorting fruits and vegetables. Their workday began at four in the morning, ending as late as ten at night.[16]

And this was still better than what their mothers suffered. These factories existed close to the orchards and the fields, providing shacks for workers to live, but also guaranteeing that with a minimum journey to work, the maximum time could be spent on the job. As a result, during canning season an 80-hour or 100-hour week was standard, but one woman actually managed 119¾ hours in a seven-day week, the rough equivalent of three modern forty-hour jobs. Working at this schedule, she enjoyed a grand total of 48¼ hours every seven days to sleep, eat, and enjoy the natural bliss of the countryside around her. When investigators asked one child how long he had been working at the job of rolling cigarettes, his reply became a masterpiece of modern anomie. "Ever since I was," he answered.[17]

As Wagner and Smith worked with the reformers, the commission built a remarkable body of data on industrial conditions. Nothing in their work was haphazard, nothing was casual, everything had to be based on detailed, exhaustive studies. When the commission tackled the bakery industry, they looked at five hundred establishments in New York City alone, and administered physical examinations to eight hundred workers. They learned that employees were afflicted with body lice, venereal disease, and oozing sores, that 35 percent had respiratory diseases, how workers spit in the dough or used it to dry their hands. No one could contradict them in their claims. In their quest for exactitude, FIC specialists even contacted Frederick Winslow Taylor, the father of time-motion studies, and asked his help in determining how much value a worker added to the product.[18]

Smith and Wagner were always part of this work. Their investigators made it a point that the commission principals saw everything, smelled everything, felt everything. In one candy factory, Frances Perkins wanted to show how bad the fire escape was, so Al volunteered to take the tour. Going to an upstairs room, he had to walk up three steps to a window. Barring that were three steampipes, but slim Al managed to pass this obstacle and get to the outside. Looking down, he saw Perkins clearly enough, but there was no ladder. The owner later explained that he had removed it because hoodlums had used it to break in and steal sweets.[19]

Al also led the inquiry as the New York commissioner of labor testified that he had no comprehensive list of the state's factories. Voicing the amazement of the group, it was Smith who asked the question, How do inspectors know where to go? and Smith who again had to digest the answer: "We have to guess it or learn by experience. . . . The inspectors get around about once in every two years, and if they find a new factory or building, they write up a report on it."[20]

Al Smith became the stalwart of the commission, showing the same bulldog tenacity he had displayed when he mastered the legislator's art. But this was different; now Smith was using that particular personality trait on behalf of social reform. He corresponded regularly with leading figures in the field, and whenever he was in New York, spent as much as three days a week in the lead attorney's office on lower Broadway. Throughout it all he tried to function much as he had in the Assembly, helping lead them to sense by using a little humor, a little insight. In one particularly tense moment, for example, one member, Robert Dowling, was fighting against a recommendation for new fire safety codes; looking at Fire Department figures on the number of people who had died in fires, he argued that this represented only "an infinitesimal proportion of the population."[21]

An opposing member, Mary Dreier, flared as she protested the obvious, that the statistics he had discussed "were men and women. They were human souls!

It was a hundred percent for them!" It was Al, however, who cemented the victory (and made everyone laugh) by chiding the original speaker, who happened to be a coreligionist, "Good Catholic doctrine, Robert!"

At the same time he fought off pressure. Murphy now stood behind him, but the more conservative elements of the business community did not. At one point, a flashy young realtor named Charles Noyes drove his bright yellow Stutz automobile to 25 Oliver Street to confront Al about some hostile testimony. Standing on his doorstep, Al started by telling Noyes that his fancy car was ruining the assemblyman's good reputation in the neighborhood. "If you've got anything to say to me," he continued, "you come down before the Commission and say it. Don't try and approach me in any private or secret way. This is where I live. Goodbye."[22]

Al was getting angry about a lot of things by then, since his work on the Triangle investigation meant that for the first time he had to confront industrialization directly. Frances Perkins told how one time in Auburn, she took Smith and Dreier to a rope factory, both of the committee members showing up at 6:45 P.M. to see the women file in, and both present at 7:00 A.M. to watch them leave. This dutiful band of social investigators then decided to follow one of these workers home, and actually went up and knocked on that tired lady's door. She invited them in and offered coffee, prompting Al to tell her that they should be waiting on her instead, and then all three watched as children appeared and the family tried to make sense of their day's existence. Conversation followed with the adults as to what they had and what they dreamed of and why the gap was so large. Perkins recalled that the woman did not put it in terms of anger or dialectics, but in language that Al understood in his heart, how she had grown up in a world where parents and children knew each other, but in her own family they never seemed to be able to get any time together, and even the common meal was an impossibility. After that, if anyone tried to dispute Al over the issue of night work for women, he would respond passionately, "You can't tell me. I've seen these women. I've seen their faces. I've seen them."[23]

Al's anger became a positive force for change, as he championed a host of bills through the legislature. In the process he became responsible for many features of modern life that Americans now take for granted.

The legislature responded to their colleagues and passed bill after bill. By the time they got done, fire drills and sprinklers became required features in all factories, and the labor code had been transformed. Women could not be forced to work for four weeks after a pregnancy; clean facilities for washing, eating, and toilet functions were now mandatory, and the commissioner of labor gained the power to label as "unclean" any product coming from a manufactory where there was evidence of contagious disease. Children under fourteen could no longer work in cannery sheds or tenements, and regulations now covered the hours of women in those canning horrors, as well as limiting night work for females. Factories had to provide seats with backs for women workers, instead of keeping them on their feet all day long.[24]

Eventually the commission produced thirty-two bills, most of which passed the state legislature, while the city enacted another thirty ordinances. By the end, New York had amply earned a reputation as one of the nation's leading reformers in the regulation of manufactories, along with such pioneering states as Illinois and Massachusetts. In 1920, for example, Pennsylvania employed fifty-three factory inspectors, Michigan had nineteen, South Carolina only three; New York State, on the other hand, brandished a force of 123 inspectors to make sure its workplaces met the code of laws. After the 1913 legislature retired, the New York Federation of Labor announced that no other body "in . . . history . . . surpassed the session of 1913 in the passage of so many or so important remedial measures for wage-earners of New York State."[25]

The federation paid tribute to Smith and Wagner in this declaration, an honor well deserved. Each man took on the job of getting the bills through their respective houses of the legislature, no easy task. When they tried to pass the most obvious of bills, one limiting the hours of workers in the canning factories so that they were guaranteed one day off a week, the industry launched a major lobbying effort, complaining that such regulations could not be followed during harvest season. Al rebutted with a speech on the floor of the assembly chamber, commenting, "If these distinguished champions of women and children were to rewrite the Divine Law, I have no doubt they would change it to read, 'Remember the Sabbath day, to keep it holy—except in the canneries.'" The bill carried.[26]

By the time they had finished, a miracle had occurred; the work that Al Smith and Bob Wagner performed between 1911 and 1915 changed the way we lived. Walk into any restaurant, any movie theater, any school or office, and the commission's work is obvious. The Triangle investigators, for example, found that doors that opened inward were disastrous, as humans frenzied by a fire always push forward, creating so much pressure that the person in front could never pull the door toward them. At the same time, it became clear that a successful exit could never depend on turning a metal doorknob; this was a feat of manual dexterity at best difficult for a scared individual, at worst impossible if the hardware became red hot.

Today doors must egress to the outside, and there is always a panic bar that can be slammed with a foot or a shoulder. The commission required that all doors and windows leading to fire escapes be marked with crimson paint, although their original concept called for "a clearly painted sign marked 'exit' in letters not less than eight inches in height . . . and in addition, a red light shall be placed over all such exits." Today's version is the bright red exit sign we see everywhere, disturbing the decor of a restaurant, marring the darkness of a motion picture auditorium. Fire drills, another measure that every school child and office worker knows and makes fun of, were also mandated for the first time.[27]

Some of the measures of fire safety were less public but equally important. At the top of the list of changes, sprinklers became mandatory in factories. Another one of the first reforms, passed in 1911, took the responsibility for fire prevention in New York City, divided between a host of bureaus and departments, and concentrated it instead in a new and powerful Bureau of Fire Prevention. For the first time the Fire Department had exclusive control over this critical area, instead of sharing it with entities like the Bureau of Buildings and the Department of Water Supply, and the fire commissioner could demand an inspection of any building, or even have it vacated without the sanction of higher authority. This codified bureau—standard practice now—was the first of its kind in the country. By 1912, the initial year of operation, the bureau had conducted 132,601 inspections of New York buildings and had 128 sprinkler systems installed, a measure that in all likelihood would have saved the lives of the Triangle victims.[28]

Al Smith had now joined a crusade that in time would redefine the role of government in American life. In many ways he became part of the Progressive movement, that controversial collection of reformers who sought to tame the excesses of society by using scientific investigations to provide answers, then enacting these in new and powerful regulations. This burst of exuberant energy opened the door to a whole new generation of political activists, especially women and patricians (like Teddy Roosevelt) who, during the Gilded Age, would have been repelled by the sordidness of government.

But below this level, something larger was occurring to the New York assemblyman: he was developing new, fundamental values. Throughout his life, Al remained a reticent Irishman when it came to his deeper instincts, and it was few and far between the times when he let these emotions out, when he pulled back the curtain and let them dance before the crowd. In part because of this, Al Smith never became a political philosopher, and he was never gifted with the skills of a great writer.

Instead, he simply understood, on the deepest possible level, what human decency was all about. When pro-business conservatives advocated an idea, drawn from some of the founding fathers, that government was intrusive and its reach must be minimized, he became suspicious, not because of his mind but because of his heart. He had seen the bodies, the live ones and the dead ones, crippled by a kind of industrialization no one had ever planned for or knew how to handle, and he knew that it could hurt people.

So without really thinking it through, without consulting the scholars or the lawyers, Al Smith was now fighting for a program based on a very different vision: that government was the voice of the citizenry, the larger embodiment of common values, a progressive force to protect us from our own worst members. This would be realized much more fully during the New Deal of the thirties, but back in the teens, Al Smith and others were already starting down that path.

For Al Smith, his work on the Factory Investigating Commission opened up enormous new vistas, both literally and in terms of his career. For the first time in his life, he traveled across the broad regions of New York State, seeing how farmers and villagers, small businessmen and large landholders lived. His career blossomed as well, a fact ably supported by an examination of the Assembly Members' books, large accounting ledgers, giving a full recital of each member's accomplishments for the session. As late as 1910 Al was responsible for only twenty bills, but by 1911, as he began to shepherd the Triangle reforms through the legislative process, he introduced seventy-three bills, forty-seven of which became law. In addition, he now came into regular contact with many of the state's leading reformers, men and women who praised him for his contributions to the state's well-being. And at the same time, his vision grew; he realized that power and success lay outside the local scene. Al Smith now understood that solutions to the problems he cared about could originate from somewhere other than the Assembly District, at the state and even the national level. It was time to move up, move on to new leadership roles in new arenas.[29]

Chapter 7

Leadership

BY 1913 AL SMITH had begun espousing the three major beliefs that would become the cornerstones of his political career. The first and strongest was his commitment to the urban immigrant. To that special vision, he added industrial reform, the sense that decency and responsibility must become part of the way the nation conducted its business, to be regulated by the government. Finally, there was his interest in administrative management, a commitment to achieving the other two goals as efficiently as possible.

With this ideological battery, Smith stood poised to become a major statewide figure, even chief executive. That kind of triumph, however, was hardly preordained, so instead, the story of his rise to prominence became a zigzag sequence of triumphs and defeats.

The first happy accident that propelled him on his way came in 1912. At the top of the national political ladder, the main player was the greatest personality of his age, the incomparable Theodore Roosevelt. Having become fed up with William Howard Taft, who sided with the stand-pat conservatives rather than the liberal reform elements of the Republican Party, Teddy did the unthinkable and bolted. Gathering around him the great change makers of America, he formed the Progressive, or Bull Moose, Party, telling their convention, "We stand at Armageddon and We Battle for the Lord."

Whether the Lord listened in is debatable, but it is easy to trace what the American electorate thought of all this. Viewing a Republican Party split down the middle, they turned instead to the scholarly Woodrow Wilson, and for the first time in thirty years, a Democrat sat in the Oval Office.

As the United States went, so too did New York. Democrats rode the coat-tails of a triumphant presidential campaign and seized not only the governorship, but both houses of the legislature as well. When the Assembly convened on January 1, 1913, there were one hundred Democrats and forty-two Republicans, almost an exact reversal from the tally just a year earlier.

By this time Smith had become his party's leader in the Assembly; they had even nominated him for Speaker back in January 1912, a quixotic gesture given the party lineup at that time. Nevertheless, it was still a sign of his new status, and the elite New York City Committee of Fourteen wrote to congratulate Al, telling him he deserved the honor, especially "if ability is to be recognized."[1]

So when the first meeting of the 1913 session opened with its new membership, it was clear who would be chosen as the new Speaker of the Assembly. The vote followed along strict party lines, as it always did, and Alfred E. Smith emerged to command the body he had almost left in disgust less than a decade before.

There was history here. Al Smith became the first man from Tammany New York, the first son of Irish immigrants, the first representative of the urban masses, ever to reach this level of power, facts that everyone was aware of.[2] Al himself felt that his career had reached its summit, and his daughter Emily wrote that as he took his place in the spotlight, she realized that something had changed, that now Al was "more than just my father."[3]

On the day he took office, Smith stood there, facing not only his peers but his mother, his wife, his five children, and accepted the gavel that symbolized his authority. In a brief address, he told the majority that they had to pay special attention to the power that had suddenly descended on them. If it was true that "the people in no uncertain terms gave to our party the control of the affairs of this state," then "it is our duty to show the keenest possible sense of that responsibility."[4]

Bouncing between his seat on the Assembly floor and the podium, Al controlled the session. Assembly records indicate that he was the absolute master of procedure, and even opposing reporters commented on the efficiency of his system. The *New York Times* complained that Al sounded like "a barker at Coney Island," with his "hoarse, raucous voice." They did not like the fact that he ate at his desk and, even worse, spoke with food in his mouth, but the paper did recognize that bills moved through the Assembly at a record pace. As the *Knickerbocker Press* put it, "Speaker Smith is running the Assembly and nobody else. He is conducting it on a business basis."[5]

Smith tried hard to keep focused on the people's business. The latest round of recommendations from the FIC had to be defended and passed, and reformers were now sending him messages asking his support for their favorite bills. He soon, however, had to turn those talents to a nasty bit of business that would consume most of his brief time as Speaker.[6]

In 1912 Tammany had nominated for governor William Sulzer, a former assemblyman who was known to be a trustworthy member of the organization. Put more bluntly, Sulzer was a hack.[7]

Once he became governor, however, Sulzer began to change his tune, and declared independence. In particular, he started to champion the direct primary, placing him in complete opposition to Charlie Murphy and the sachems, who had no desire to lose their right to name the party's candidates. In time this conflict escalated to all-out war, with Sulzer railing against the "party lash," cutting off patronage appointments, and freezing out favored contractors from lucrative projects.[8]

Murphy retaliated by probing Sulzer's career, digging for any dirt he could find. In time, he got the legislature to appoint a special investigative committee to this end, a body which discovered that Sulzer had misrepresented the source of his campaign funds during the 1912 gubernatorial campaign, which was illegal, if not terribly so.

Although the charges were slight, Sulzer appears, over the decades, as a less than stable personality. He refused to release evidence that supported his case, evaded questions, and turned instead to loud and hysterical attacks on Murphy and the Tammany machine. This led to further inquiries, some of which turned up an even more damaging revelation, that he had used campaign funds to speculate on stocks, a very, very serious charge.

By this time Sulzer could find few defenders anywhere, and Murphy smelled blood in the water. Revenge was going to be devastating and total. Thus, on Murphy's orders, the Assembly called for an almost unprecedented move, the impeachment of a sitting governor.

The motion passed, and suddenly Al was in the hot seat. Instead of using his speakership to lead the fight for reform, he was now in charge of the most sordid, raucous proceedings imaginable. All at once, his entire standing changed, as he no longer acted as leader, but reverted instead to minion, a stooge following Murphy's commands.

There was little to commend the work of which he was now such a fundamental part. As the wheels of party rancor flowed under Smith's benign supervision, the Assembly voted to impeach, and after a brief debate adopted eight articles to be presented to the Senate, which would sit as a jury. Months later that body convicted Sulzer on three of these counts, then voted overwhelmingly to remove him from office.

None of this reflected well on Al Smith, and it is hard to imagine that he enjoyed any part of the affair. Samuel Gompers felt disgust "to see that some of the men with whom I had the honor of being associated in the [Factory Investigating] Commission . . . have been worked up, or are working themselves up in a frenzied effort to 'get' the governor," and cut off all contact with Robert Wagner, who led the Tammany charge in the Senate. Al had to confront the fact that among the donations that Sulzer failed to report was a check from Abram Elkus, who had been his beloved counsel during the Triangle work. Newspaper accounts claimed that Al tried to get Murphy to "let the whole matter drop," to no avail. In his autobiography, Al glossed over the whole event in a few paragraphs, innocuously commenting that the "session of 1913 was the longest and stormiest."[9]

One other aspect of the affair remains relevant in light of future events. Sulzer sought friends in unusual places, and reached an agreement with the publisher William Randolph Hearst, an alliance of the eccentric with the outlandish. Hearst hired private detectives to follow Smith, Wagner, and other Tammany leaders in an effort to catch them in the middle of some illegal practice. Nothing turned up, but that never stopped the Hearst press from reporting in huge headlines the chicanery of Tammany, in contrast, this time, to Sulzer's innocence. Smith and Hearst began to prowl one another like angry boxers, a mere hint of the combat that would flare in later years.[10]

But all of this had a terrible effect on Tammany's fortunes. The public reacted to Murphy's heavy-handed methods with revulsion, and concluded that the charges against Sulzer, confirmed or not, were now immaterial, that the real issue was who ran the state. The *Syracuse Journal* asked its readers, "Which do you prefer—Sulzer, who has grievously sinned before he became governor, but who has been assailing vice in Tammany's capital ever since that time, or Murphy in absolute control of the government?" Even the staid *Nation* felt that "the man in the street believes the worst of Sulzer, but supports him against Murphy."[11]

On top of all this arose one of those juicy little escapades that always seemed to crop up when Tammany needed it least. In July 1913, only a few months after the impeachment, thugs gunned down a professional gambler named Herman Rosenthal on a Manhattan street in broad daylight. That in itself made for a banner headline, but the fact that seven policemen happened to be in the immediate vicinity, and that they all assumed the posture of statues as the murderers fled, turned this into a joke. An investigation by Charles Whitman—then New York county district attorney and later governor and Al's opponent—turned up the interesting fact that Rosenthal had a silent business partner: police captain Charles Becker, who demanded huge payoffs in return for police protection. When Rosenthal threatened to blow the deal by squealing, Becker had agreed to the assassination.[12]

Once again, New York reeled under the vision of police in cahoots with, and even exceeding, the worst elements of the underworld, bringing into question the whole structure of the city's government. This was not the image Tammany hoped to project, right after it flexed its muscles to the point of dismissing a governor when he did not act according to their whims.

Voters responded, and in November 1913, the Democrats lost all they had gained the year before. Republicans retook the governor's mansion and both houses of the legislature. Although his party would dutifully nominate Al for Speaker, Smith went back to being minority leader. He remained, however, a powerful figure, a member of both the Ways and Means and the Rules Committees, the two bodies that controlled the flow of legislation.

At least Al could now go back to work. When the Republicans tried to amend the workmen's compensation bill so that insurance companies could delay payments, Smith cried out in what the *Times* claimed was "his most acrimonious speech of the session," "Who wants the bill? Do the manufacturers want it? No! Does the workingman want it? No? . . . Then what other interested party is there? The casualty company? That's who you are working for." At the end of his speech he told his colleagues, "You . . . have ruined the compensation law. You have gone the limit for the casualty companies. The people's case is lost." He would continue in this role throughout the legislative session of 1914.[13]

By this time Al had also acquired a mannerism that would become a trademark for the rest of his life. On top of his head invariably rested a derby, usually pushed back over the right ear, juxtaposed against the cigar clenched in the left side of his mouth. At one time a friendly member of the judiciary opined that this appearance was unseemly for a legislative leader, that "this isn't the Bowery." Legend has it that Al Smith answered back, in a voice that boomed through the halls of the legislature, that wearing the hat any other way gave him a headache and that he would not put on airs for anyone. It seems unlikely that the claim of vapors is true, given the number of photographs we have of Al wearing hats in the proper manner, but nevertheless he became associated not just with the derby, but a brown one at that, his most famous campaign symbol.[14]

⌒

By now Al knew to make the best of his opportunities whenever they came along. And in 1915, everything Al had trained for those long years in the legislature, all the skill and knowledge he had acquired so laboriously, got projected onto a larger stage. For the first time, he would be noticed by people and places that had little to do with the Fourth Ward or Tammany Hall or even the Assembly floor.

The event was a constitutional convention, which New York State was supposed to hold every twenty years or so, although the last one had taken place in 1894. After the 1912 election, the Democrats seized what they thought would be their sterling opportunity, and called for an early convention. Republicans fought back and delayed things until the state government changed hands again. In 1915 the long-awaited event was about to begin.[15]

This was no small matter. New York truly was the Empire State in those days, and any changes there would most likely be copied widely. Combined with the fact that New York City remained the nation's press capital, it meant that the whole country watched what was going on, as reporters and specialists cranked out endless pieces of description and commentary.

The convention was naturally a Republican-dominated body, reflecting the state's gerrymandered districts; out of 160 delegates, the breakout included 116 Republicans and only 52 Democrats. So at the earliest sessions delegates chose as their chair Elihu Root, one of the most distinguished political figures in America. Root enjoyed a remarkable record at that time, having served as secretary of war during the McKinley and Roosevelt administrations, during which time he created the modern army general staff system and wrote the constitution for the Philippine Islands. From there he became secretary of state and also headed the Republican National Committee during the 1904 presidential campaign. His work as president of the Carnegie Endowment for International Peace and as negotiator on the Open Door Agreement with Japan led to his winning the Nobel Peace Prize in 1912. In addition, they all knew that he had been one of the floor leaders at the previous convention in 1894, and hoped that some of that experience might come in handy. And Root, notwithstanding his work for world peace, had come to be considered the embodiment of traditional conservatism in America, fighting hard, for example, for William Howard Taft in 1912.

Root surrounded himself with a group of peers, people like George Wickersham and Henry Stimson. The former had served as President Taft's attorney general, while the latter replaced Root as secretary of war in the Roosevelt administration. This old guard, known as the "Federal Crowd," would surprise members from both sides of the aisle with their independence and, above all, would find themselves working with and praising the efforts of Alfred Emanuel Smith. Given their impeccable credentials, it was these approbations, more than anything else, that turned the event into a triumph for Al.[16]

The convention opened on April 6 with Root firmly in charge. Every day from then until they adjourned on September 9, he would appear formally dressed in a cutaway coat at ten in the morning, two in the afternoon, and eight in the evening, to call delegates to order at each session. On one morning when the minister failed to show up, he even delivered the opening prayer.[17]

The Al Smith of 1903 would have been a lightweight in this crowd. Among the delegates that Al would be challenging were men like John Hill Morgan, Yale class of '96 and a trustee of the Brooklyn Public Library. But this was 1915, not 1903; now the Citizens Union endorsed Smith's candidacy for a delegate's slot, and when he walked into the Assembly Chamber to take the oath, the Albany crowd that had come to know him so well delivered a roaring ovation.[18]

More important, he arrived with something besides his friends' approval and applause. Al was still a hard worker; prior to the first meeting, he asked Jonah Goldstein, a young lawyer who had supported him through several Assembly campaigns, if he could dig up the official record of the 1894 convention. Jonah (whom Al alone referred to as "Jonny") came through with the real goods, the complete record in several volumes. Just as he had done with appropriations bills, Al sat down and read it cover to cover.[19]

Thus, he showed up at the first meeting well armed with precedents. Sitting in front were Root, Wickersham, and Judge Morgan O'Brien, leader of the Democratic forces. At issue was how they were going to organize the convention, and the three disagreed. Al stood up and offered a solution, suggesting that they set it up the same way it had been done back in 1894. Root and some of his colleagues turned, asking sharply, "What do you know about the last Constitutional Convention? We were here, you weren't." Al then picked up one of the volumes, calmly turned to the relevant page, and answered, "Let's look at the record." According to at least one account, that was the first time he publicly used the famous phrase that became his catch line.

⤜

The convention began on a Sunday, and by Tuesday Al was demonstrating how well he had mastered procedures, as he instructed the body on minute and intricate matters. Root appointed Smith to Committees on the Organization and the Powers of the Legislature, and also to the Committee on Industrial Interests and Relations; he did not, however, place Al on the obvious and crucial Committee on Cities. Smith, in turn, quickly gained a reputation as a fierce but knowledgeable debater; one Republican delegate explained why his colleagues should not dream of taking a particular action without first taking account of the opposition: "If you think you can," he warned them, "you don't know my Brother Wagner and my Brother Smith."[20]

Beyond advocacy, Al Smith's work in the 1915 New York State Constitutional Convention is critically important to an understanding of his record as a public speaker. Smith never penned the *bon mot,* but was instead capable of riveting audiences with clear language, a command of the facts, and a gentle sense of humor. Little of this shines through on the printed page, and there are few records of his style in debate. There are no transcripts of the contests in the Assembly during his years there, or of his later gubernatorial bouts with the legislature. Thus, the exact, word-by-word record of the 1915 Constitutional Convention remains the only account of what Smith was like in heated argument.

A fine example came in the debate over literacy tests for voters, clearly an attack on his immigrant constituents. Al's lengthy comments demonstrated his enormous range, how he could move from high eloquence to simple humor, and then, if necessary, improvise a conclusion. Early on, he is angry and articulate, telling his colleagues, "I do not know any better food for the Socialists and the Anarchists . . . than to be able to point to the fact that a man owning property . . . upholding the government, is refused a voice in the management of that government through the ballot, simply because he cannot speak English." Al pointed out that a Socialist had even been elected to the U.S. Congress from a New York district, but he remained in isolation, adding, "the reason it took them so many years to elect one" was that their natural constituency had been taught "that all men are equal in this state, that they have the same opportunity and the same chance with their neighbor." Smith then shifted seamlessly to a funny story, about a Socialist from Schenectady who came to the Assembly. When "he found that the debate was open, free and unrestricted," that a majority vote always carried, well then, a miracle happened: that fiery radical "went immediately down to the Ten Eyck barber shop and got a hair-cut."

Just then, Al ran out of time, but not story; William Barnes, Republican leader and his archenemy, suddenly interrupted to note that Smith had exceeded his limit by five minutes. Al never wavered, but instead turned to the bench. "Mr. Chairman," he asked, "I wish the gentleman from Albany had let me get out of the barber shop, I don't like to finish there," breaking up the entire convention. The chair could not resist, and ruled that "the gentleman from Albany will allow the gentleman from New York time enough to get out of the barber shop."[21]

It was not just humor that Al used to argue his points, but his knowledge of state business and almost total recall. At one point, chairman Root asked for a report on the legislative history of public service corporation regulation, and Al accepted the assignment. Root inquired as to how long it would take Smith to compile the data and be ready to address the body, but Al replied that he could speak extemporaneously, and then floored everyone by delivering a two-hour address, sans notes, filled with facts and figures. He finished to an ovation. On another occasion Al claimed that emergency bills—local improvements at high prices passed at the end of the session—remained one of the prime methods of logrolling and wasting money. An opponent challenged him, claiming that only one such bill had been passed in the last Assembly session, that the practice was less common than Al had suggested. Without a blink, Smith corrected him, stating that in fact seventeen such bills had been approved. When Root questioned this, Al simply rattled off the details for all seventeen, describing for each one the sponsor, the amount, and what the state was overcharged for.[22]

In time, Root and the other leaders began to depend on Smith's talents, using him to defeat measures they opposed. One such case involved William Barnes, who had emerged as the leader of the forces of reaction; chairing the committee on the legislature and its organization, at one point he had rebutted advocates of fair apportionment by pounding on the desk and shouting, "I don't believe in the rule of the majority."[23]

Barnes submitted a powerful amendment to the constitution, that the legislature be banned from passing any bill that granted "to any class of individuals any privilege or immunity not granted equally to all members of the state." It was clear what his intent was: to roll back all progressive legislation that assisted women, children, or any other group in society that was not universal. Barnes shiftily argued that his amendment had been designed to safeguard "the ideal of equality from the principle of privilege," that he merely was opposing "class legislation," but most members recognized this for what it truly represented: the broadest and most significant challenge to the reforms that had made New York such a national leader in caring for its citizens. With this change, the courts would have to throw out such measures as workmen's compensation, widows' pensions, and child labor laws.[24]

Barnes's proposal was too much for all but the most hard-core conservatives, and the Federal Group led the charge against it. But Root and Wickersham were shrewd old war horses, and they knew they needed an eloquent spokesman who could reply with knowledge and heartfelt passion. They chose Al Smith, and when the debate came, Wickersham gave his younger colleague twenty minutes of his own time. Al added this extra portion to his normal allowance and spoke with the emotion and clarity Wickersham had bet on. He declared that the constitution should not be perceived as some kind of divine force, but rather as a working document to benefit the people of the state. "The great curse in poverty," Smith contended, "lies in the utter hopelessness that goes with it. Having that in mind, may I ask you, is it wise, is it prudent . . . to reduce the basic law to the same sharp level of the caveman's claw, the law of the sharpest tooth . . . and the greediest jaw?" Barnes's proposal went down to defeat.[25]

One of his convention statements in particular had a powerful effect on his political career, and indeed, fostered an entire school of Smith historiography. At one point in the convention, over a debate on home rule, Smith blurted out, "I would sooner be a lamp-post on Park Row than the Governor of California."[26]

This horrible line haunted Smith for the rest of his life, and remains the most oft-used piece of evidence for historians trying to prove his parochialness, and thus his lack of fitness for national office. But while some ill will and local pride may be evident, the full context renders the comment fairly innocuous.

During the debate to give New York City greater home rule powers, Smith had been preceded by a condescending upstate scholar-statesman, who took up much of the convention's time by reciting a lengthy, pedantic argument that the constitutional relationship between New York State and New York City was identical to that between the United States and the colony of the Philippines. Al became livid at this demeaning analogy and lost control, telling the convention that he did not enjoy finding out that his home town would "receive that kind of home rule . . . that Washington was satisfied to give to the Philippines, a half-civilized bunch of half-dressed men that we got by accident." In a later time, that remark would have rightfully caused him more trouble, but he went on, enraged, declaring, "A man will stand a certain amount of injury, but he will always resent insult to the last degree." At that point a Republican interrupted him to argue that California—which "is not the Philippines, but a very progressive American state"—had similar laws governing its municipalities, and Al exploded with the ill-tempered line about the Golden State, a reflection of Smith's passion more than his parochialism about the rest of America.[27]

When the convention concluded, it had to present its final product, a revised constitution, to the state's voters, and there it ran into trouble. The greatest shortcoming stemmed from the delegates' refusal to install majority rule, instead maintaining a pattern of unequal representation in both the Assembly and the Senate. This failure was so galling, so blatant, that even Al, after all his hard work, found that he had to vote against it, one of twenty-eight Democrats and five Republicans who took this step. In his closing statement to the convention, delegate Smith praised much of the work, but lamented that his city had "a right to expect something better. . . . That we have been discriminated against by the up-State there can be no question." He felt that the members, in all fairness, needed to find out "what the wishes of the majority are, no matter what the majority is, or what its political faith may be"; until that was done, he would have to vote in the negative. Ten years later, Smith told a reunion of delegates, "No man that lives in New York City could stand for that section of the Constitution."[28]

Other problems beset the proposed document; in particular, the framers committed a terrible mistake by placing the entire measure on a single ballot line, rather than having the people vote on each of the various sections. Al campaigned against it, and the bill went down to a defeat so overwhelming—910,000 to 400,000—that *The New Republic* remarked that its few supporters "were not only beaten, they were contemptuously dismissed."[29]

Although the constitution of 1915 was never adopted, the convention that produced it had an enormous effect on Al Smith. As learned men debated the form of state government, Al devoted a great deal of thought to what kinds of changes were necessary to create a sound and functioning state administrative system. Members talked about the idea of an executive budget, of consolidating the multitudinous branches of government into a system of departments to eliminate duplication and control spending, of creating the first cabinet in the state's history. Al listened, and when he became governor, made these same measures the centerpieces of his successful effort to transform the state and turn himself into the most important governor in New York's history.

Above all, Al emerged a political star. Praise came from every quarter, Ogden Reid, publisher of the arch-Republican *New York Tribune,* calling him "a true leader, a genuine compeller of men, a man of wit and force." Lawrence Tanzer, the head of the Citizens Union, stated that Al "displayed a practical knowledge of the workings of state government not rivalled by anyone else," and Beverly Robinson, a Harvard graduate and Republican delegate, observed Smith had "one of the greatest powers of clear statement of any man I ever listened to."[30]

Best of all were the remarks by Root and Wickersham. Neither made it a habit to compliment Democrats, let alone those produced by Tammany Hall. But Wickersham said that Al was "the most useful man in the convention" and regretted that the Tammanyite had never become a lawyer, for he would have readily offered Al a job in his firm at a starting salary of twenty-five thousand dollars a year; Murphy, upon hearing this, replied, "But if Al Smith were a lawyer, he wouldn't be Al Smith."

Smith's relationship with Elihu Root flourished as well. During the convention Root began to consult Al with some regularity, and even joined him on some unusual issues, including reapportionment and opposition to the literacy test. When it was all over, Root told everyone, "Of all the men in the convention, Al Smith was the best informed on the business of New York State." In 1926 Al said that the convention was "a great opportunity for me, a great opportunity. I made everything I could out of it."[31]

⌁

Smith had grown far above his Tammany roots without renouncing them. Yet there was increasing tension between his goals and the Hall's interests, stemming not so much from social issues like New America versus Old as over which rewards suited this up-and-comer. Al may have dreamed of being a statewide leader, but to Charlie Murphy, the youngster had earned more than anything else the right to a cushy job with a big salary and lots of patronage control.

Thus, in August, at the middle of the constitutional convention, a delegate named Mark Eisner stepped off the floor to take a call. He walked back in, requested that he be allowed to make an announcement, and intoned, "Gentlemen of the convention. . . . The Tammany Hall executive committee just met down in New York and they have nominated Al Smith for Sheriff." Eisner sat down, and the convention gave Al a round of applause.[32]

Smith's fellow delegates had good reason to cheer. In those days, the job of sheriff no longer required anyone to carry a gun or a badge, and the police had long since taken over the task of rounding up criminals. Instead, the sheriff served as an instrument of the court, whose chief duty was to collect money and property from failed businesses and deadbeat fathers. The sheriff received a base stipend of twelve thousand dollars, a substantial increase from Al's current fifteen hundred dollars a year. Better yet, the office operated primarily on a fee basis, its chief official receiving half of everything he collected. Altogether, the standard estimate was that this office holder brought home fifty to sixty thousand dollars a year. The system seemed so prone to corruption that after Al finished his term, the city changed the compensation back to a regular paycheck.[33]

Using the Tammany system of accounting, the position also brought with it power, in this case the right to appoint a number of offices that were exempt from civil service, and thus could become prime fodder for greasing the machine. Some of these were so important that Ed Flynn, boss of the Bronx, commented that whoever was in charge of the sheriff's spot "would pretty nearly decide control of the county organization." Murphy wanted someone he could trust in that kind of position.[34]

But there were other voices, other factors that had to be considered. Tom Foley urged Al to turn it down, arguing that everybody in the neighborhood would know about his new-found riches and ask to share in the benefits. The real increase in Smith's income, therefore, might be whittled down in this manner to as little as ten thousand dollars over the two years, unless, as Foley quaintly put it, "you want to give them all the marble heart." Newspaper accounts also indicate that Al strongly preferred the more exciting post of borough president of Manhattan.[35]

But Boss Murphy still ran the show, so for two years Al would be sheriff. He won endorsements handily, with accolades not just from regular Tammany supporters but from the downtown crowd as well. Even the Citizens Union, which, prior to 1915, had never had the slightest inclination to praise a Tammany candidate, backed Smith, explaining, "As to his qualification for this office there can be no question. . . . The Union is [not] unmindful of his political connection," but nevertheless felt that, "his service to the State in the Constitutional Convention . . . entitles him to special consideration."[36]

This was a big bombshell for that era, its ricochets pinging all over the city; when had the goo-goos (good government types) ever endorsed a Tammany stalwart? An editorial in the *New York World* argued that "the Citizens Union endorsing a Tammany candidate is a spectacle sufficiently rare," that it merited attention even when juxtaposed to news from the flaming battlefields of World War I. Others, however, seemed far more displeased than surprised; Henry Stoddard, a heavyweight in reform circles, refused to submit his standard contribution since he was now convinced that "every dollar expended in a campaign that includes the election of 'Al' Smith, the Tammany candidate for sheriff, is a dollar expended against the best interest of the community. . . . How your organization could be lured into forgetfulness is beyond me." Of course, Tammany had another way of looking at this, one honcho making the amazing statement to the *New York Press*, "That Citizens Union crowd is getting to be almost human. . . . Wish they had more votes."[37]

But Al could count on other kinds of support as well. Young Eddie Cantor campaigned for Smith, who saw to it that the singer received a free—and badly needed—overcoat as payment. Tammany's braves hooted it up for Al, but the most elaborate event occurred when Al's neighborhood put on an "Old Home Night" to boost his campaign. Traffic shut down for blocks around Oliver Street, and local residents decorated tenements with Japanese lanterns and whatever light fixtures they could manage. Women prepared lavish amounts of food, while the men handled the bar and fireworks.

The event quickly became the community's exclusive extravaganza. Tom Foley and the other politicians tried to chip in, but were turned down; Foley lamented that no one had ever done anything like this when he had run for sheriff, and residents told him, "You're not Al Smith." Three bands competed for attention with free outdoor movies; it is not clear who won. Various ethnic groups put on performances, and folk dances were especially common, although the *New York Times* primly noted, "Modern dances will not be barred." In front of 25 Oliver Street admirers hung an immense painting of the candidate—bordered in red, white, and blue lights—and Al and Katie and the children faced an endless line of well-wishers. Only at one point did the crowd hush, when word flowed that ancient Mrs. Whalen, who had seen Al come into the world and now wanted to express her support, was being wheeled up to see him. Otherwise the tenor of the evening was best captured by the repeated times Smith tried to tell everyone how much he loved being there, and each time the crowd interrupted by yelling, "Hurrah for the next sheriff."[38]

By late October Wall Street bookies were giving odds of six to five that Al would become sheriff by a margin of 50,000 votes. They were close: Smith actually beat Bowers by 120,000 to 72,000. Samples of different groups indicated that Irish voters cast over 70 percent of their markers for him, while Italian districts tallied between 52 percent and 63 percent and Jewish districts registered anywhere from 29 percent to 52 percent.[39]

It had been a great victory, but the office did not mean much to Al. During the campaign the candidate boldly announced that while he did not know much about being sheriff, if elected, by January 1 he would know more than the Republican incumbent, and by January 15, "I will know all about it." He was right.[40]

Al took care of his Tammany obligations with patronage appointments, but still cleaned up the office as best he could and tried to avoid the favoritism that seemed to go with positions like this. Employees brought the filing systems up to date and savings occurred; in his first year in office Al Smith decreased expenditures by 3.3 percent and increased revenues by 30 percent. When the pastor of St. James asked Al to use his influence to get some fire department citations squashed, Smith refused, drawing on his Triangle experience to explain that children might die if the violations were not corrected. And when the good father remarked that there was no money to pay for those improvements, Al immediately organized and starred in a benefit performance of his old favorite, *The Shaughran,* the cast including a young state senator named Jimmy Walker, who played the hero—this time.[41]

But other than moments like that, Al was bored. Around the same time that he was elected, the proposed state constitution went down to defeat, and Al wrote to a reporter friend, "I would like to be back in the legislature myself." By 1917 he at least had the national emergency to interest him, explaining, "If it had not been for the war and the time I put in selling Liberty bonds . . . and seeing the boys off, I would have had nothing to do." His duties included ridiculous items like swearing in ten thousand special deputies for potential home defense, fortunately a rather unlikely scenario.[42]

Instead of worrying about how to defend the shores of lower Manhattan from German invasion, Al tried hard not to lose touch with politics, and prepared himself for future campaigns. He still read and studied every bill that went through the legislature, making sure that nothing escaped him; and remained on the lookout for the good line, the good speech, clipping editorials on "The Living Lincoln" and "The Italian People," pasting them on bond paper, and filing them carefully in envelopes.[43]

⟿

After two years, Al's finances were in much stronger condition; the family had bought its first car, for example, although Al would never learn how to drive. But he wanted out, and up.

Not that Tammany was opposed to the move. Al Smith represented the next generation of vote getters, and the sachems knew it. As early as 1915 the press reported rumors that Al would be the next candidate for mayor, in 1917. As late as July of that year, the *New York Times*, discussing reports on whom Murphy favored, told its readers, "It is altogether likely that Sheriff Alfred E. Smith would be his selection." But it did not turn out that way.[44]

Instead, Tammany turned for its mayoral candidate to a relative nonentity named John Francis Hylan. Murphy had bowed to the influence of publisher William Randolph Hearst and to John McCooey, the formidable boss of Brooklyn; both had favored Hylan, a total mediocrity. Still, he had fought against the lords of the subway, the business tycoons who gave bad service for high fares, which just happened to be a favorite issue of Hearst as well. He had also served as county judge in Kings County, which made him so close to McCooey that the *Times* called Hylan's election "a personal triumph" for the Brooklyn boss.[45]

This did not mean Murphy planned to ignore Al Smith. Al's prize was to run for president of the Board of Aldermen, technically the second most important office in New York, although an extremely distant second. But far more important, this move placed Al as the number two man on the ticket, letting the party use his services in the campaign and play off his popularity, exposing him to the widest possible audience.

In a short while, Al became just about the only politician to take the election seriously, as Hylan declined a vigorous campaign, and incumbent mayor John Purroy Mitchel grandly self-destructed by accusing the Democrats of treasonous sympathy with Germany because German immigrant voters tended to favor Tammany. Smith remained in earnest and campaigned all over the city, going to parts of the five boroughs that he had never seen before.

His most famous moment came in a public debate with Robert Adamson, his opposite number on the Mitchel ticket. Adamson proved as inept as the man he hoped to serve under, when he condescendingly asked Smith what qualifications Al could possibly have to make him fit to become president of the Board of Aldermen. Calmly, with the quiet that precedes thunder, Smith began his answer: "My qualifications are twelve years a member of the New York legislature and four years Democratic floor leader." Then came the torrent: "I was for one year Speaker of the Assembly. I was for six years on its cities committee, which revised the New York charter." On and on it went, gaining momentum, as Al detailed every iota of his vast experience, how he had prepared the state budget, how he cochaired the Triangle committee, the role he played in the constitutional convention. After finishing the litany, he dealt Adamsom the final blow: "If there is any man in the city with the same legislative experience," Smith declared, "let him speak. I will be glad to surrender my nomination to him, and go back to Fulton Market."[46]

Of course, the Hylan ticket won easily, but Smith was even more bored in his new job, once again, a position far below his talents. Further complicating the matter was the fact that Smith and Hylan did not particularly like one another, since the former regarded the latter—quite accurately—as nothing more than a Hearst mouthpiece, and a rather inarticulate one at that. During the entire term (Al presided over only a small part of this), the board passed 863 bills, of which the Citizens Union pronounced, almost all were "routine." Only five measures, they felt, "would arouse any degree of interest in the average citizen," and even these were hardly barn-burners, their list including a ticket speculator ordinance and two laws that dealt with the care of sidewalks. After that it went downhill.

Al's time would come soon, however. On election night, 1917, the crowd at Tammany Hall cheered, "Hurrah for 'Al' Smith! Three cheers for the next governor of New York!" Although William Randolph Hearst had magnanimously offered himself for the position of governor in 1918, saying that he would be willing to sacrifice and take on the burden of becoming chief executive of the largest state in the union, Murphy had no desire to see the publisher's ambitions enthroned in Albany. Instead, he maneuvered to have Smith nominated, and in the end, even Hearst came on board, as Al agreed to issue a statement supporting municipal ownership of public utilities, one of the newspaperman's pet issues. Upstate Democrats, on the other hand, asked only for someone who could make a good showing in their districts; Smith, who had already achieved statewide fame as a leader with integrity from both the Triangle investigation and the constitutional convention, fit these qualifications as well.[47]

It was a campaign marked by powerful issues. For the first time, Al confronted the national debate over prohibition, an issue that would plague him long after the enactment of the Eighteenth Amendment. In New York, the Anti-Saloon League worked hard to get this constitutional addition passed, and as part of the effort, researched the background of many local politicians. When

William Anderson, head of the New York State organization, had his lawyer go up to Albany and check on Smith's legislative record, his investigator "came back with the most deadly lot of stuff I have ever seen assembled against any legislator." Anderson then took this material and went up to a meeting of the Methodist Conference covering the western part of the state; later he reported, "I just read the record, damning so far as the liquor question was concerned. It almost paralyzed the Methodists—they were so shocked." In one published statement, Anderson claimed that if Smith won, prohibition lost, and American soldiers in France would then indulge in a "liquor orgy." Al talked about the "personal abuse and many false statements" he had to suffer that year, how the arguments were so hysterical and had strayed so far from "the record." In time, it became clear that he was developing a thin skin when it came to this topic and this sort of attack, which would later affect his governorship as well as his bid for the presidency.[48]

Women's votes also mattered that year, a new feature on the political landscape. In 1917 New York joined the list of states that granted women a long overdue right to the ballot, so 1918 became the first gubernatorial election where their votes factored into a statewide race. Murphy responded as shrewdly as ever, naming one woman to the executive board for every male district leader, a total of thirty-two new members. Some ladies supported Smith because of his progressive record, but others—particularly members of the Women's Christian Temperance Union (WCTU)—opposed him because of his positions on temperance and on account of his religion. This would not be the last time a Smith campaign caused dilemmas for women, nor was it the final round between Al and the formidable coalition of the Anti-Saloon League and the WCTU.[49]

As if that was not enough, the state, the country, even the world, was in the midst of the worst influenza outbreak in modern history, with tens of millions dead around the globe. Political rallies were scarcely attended, as voters prudently avoided public places where they could contract disease. In some localities the police banned all meetings, even church services, but a few Republican officials took advantage of the calamity for political gains. In Hornell, New York, for example, two days before Smith was due to speak, health authorities issued an edict against the assembly because of the possibility of contagion; somehow this fear did not carry over to schools, houses of worship, or amusement parks, all of which remained open. But in the end, politics gave way to legitimate fears, and both Smith and Charles Whitman, his Republican opponent and the incumbent governor, canceled most of their speaking appearances.[50]

Al did what he could to reach voters. Courting labor, he told unions that their members should be commended for their patriotic war work. He also enjoyed endorsements, from the Non-Partisan League; from President Woodrow Wilson, who received him at the White House for a fifteen-minute talk; from the *New York Times,* which called him the "best-equipped man nominated for Governor of New York"; from Hearst's *New York Journal,* which commanded readers, "You Will Vote to Re-Elect Al Smith"; and from an assistant secretary of the navy, Franklin Roosevelt, who praised Smith as a national leader.[51]

Then something happened—something out of the ordinary—that would influence the rest of his political career. Abram Elkus, a prominent attorney who had headed the staff of the Factory Investigating Committee, started a Citizen's Committee for Smith; this would augment the regular campaign organization and create a vehicle whereby independents and Republicans could back Elkus's favorite candidate. But Belle Moskowitz, a leading woman reformer with vast experience in the field of industrial policy and youth programs, approached Elkus (on the advice of Frances Perkins) and inquired why he was ignoring independent *women* voters. The attorney replied that she had brought up an important point and suggested she take the contract, should organize the group herself. Moskowitz had only three weeks to do the job, but came through superbly. Although this was the first time she delivered for Al Smith's career, her service in this cause would continue until her death more than fourteen years later.[52]

Moskowitz met Al Smith for the first time at the Lyceum Theatre, walking in on a session of his hard-boiled campaign committee. She soon set up a series of meetings with the newest bloc of voters in the state, the first of which was billed as "by and for women." By his second appearance, Smith was already moving off course, condescending to the ladies, not presenting the issues, so much so that comments started to surface that Al was "wrong on the woman subject." Smith was used to dealing with smart, professional women on a one-to-one basis, people like Frances Perkins and Mary Dreier on the Factory Investigating Committee, but he had never thought about how to address them as a bloc of voters, so older gender concepts had taken over by default.[53]

His third and final speech of this kind, however, before the Women's University Club, turned the tide. Al wanted to present only brief remarks, shake a few hands, and let Bob Wagner, who would also appear, make the primary address of the afternoon. But Moskowitz explained to him that he could talk to these women just as he did to any professional audience and that he should be honest and knowledgeable about the state's business. Slowly Al came around, and when he asked her what he should speak to the women about, Mrs. M instantly produced a sheet that listed his positions on most of the issues that he had built his career on over the past fifteen years, including women's working conditions, health, and fire safety. Smith got up and delivered what Moskowitz felt was the best speech of the campaign, with trademark honesty and his remarkable command of the facts. At the end, he declared, "You see, I know what it is to run a great state. You can check up on me, for if I do wrong it will not be a case of ignorance but of willful intent." Over and over again in his career, Al would follow this remarkable woman's sage advice, until as her granddaughter and biographer, Elisabeth Israels Perry, made clear, "the political relationship between Belle Moskowitz and Al Smith . . . would blossom" from just a working relationship into what was truly a "partnership."[54]

The final excitement in this close race came four days before voters went to the polls. Al's campaign by then had centered on the claim that Governor Whitman had emasculated the Public Service Commission, which regulated utilities like subways, instead of making it the champion of integrity and safety that it should have been.

In New York City on Friday, November 1, the Brotherhood of Locomotive Engineers began a strike against the Brooklyn Rapid Transit Line (BRT), to protest twenty-nine members who had been fired for joining the union. The BRT hired scabs to replace them, and one of these, Edward Luciano, was running a train even though he had received only two and a half hours of training instead of the usual twenty days. Tired, barely recovered from the dreaded flu, he was in no shape to drive when the dispatcher, short of men, asked him to take out one more train. That run began at 6:00 P.M., and shortly after, Luciano ran through a number of crucial switches; the train, now traveling as fast as seventy miles an hour, derailed and slammed into a concrete wall, killing and maiming many of the people inside. Making matters even worse, this last-minute addition had had to use older wooden cars, which popped open as if they were made out of wet tissue paper. Some passengers died as they flew against the sides of the tunnel; others wound up on the tracks, decapitated or else having limbs shorn off as succeeding cars sliced right over them. Even as the train ground to a halt, it wound up mashing some of those who had somehow survived being thrown against the embankment, until all that was left, in the words of an historian of transit, was "a shapeless mass of human flesh, wood splinters, and metal fragments."[55]

To this day, the wreck on November 1, which cost the lives of at least ninety-three people, remains the worst disaster in the history of this nation's mass transit. And if Edward Luciano displayed ineptitude, the company was even more at fault for assigning him—without nearly sufficient training and in spite of health problems—to the trip in the first place.[56]

Al had been scheduled to speak at the Brooklyn Academy of Music, and he seized the moment. He referred to his lengthy experience in both industrial safety and state legislation, and charged Whitman with dereliction of duty, of packing the Public Service Commission so that it could not do its job and protect people from accidents like this. His anger growing, Al rhetorically asked, "What has Governor Whitman to say about all this. . . . What does he propose to do for the people of the State?"[57]

Smith later remembered Election Day as "the longest . . . of my life up to that time." Al's mother, who had vehemently opposed women's suffrage, could not be kept from the polls when her own son vied for the governor's chair. At 8:00 P.M. Smith joined Elkus and the Citizens Committee in the Hotel Biltmore, and they began to settle in for a night in front of the ticker tape, the fastest means of receiving election returns in those days. Early results from the city precincts showed Al in the lead by a substantial margin, but soon the upstate votes came flooding in. Emily Smith recalled with dismay, "Father's early lead began to melt away. At first I could hardly believe that the trend against him would continue, but it did. . . . There was nothing I could do, but in my youthful desperation I made a solemn promise that if Father were elected I would not eat a piece of candy for five years," adding significantly, "I was fond of candy."[58]

The adults took stronger measures, since by dawn the race was still in doubt, with votes not yet tallied in several upstate counties. The margin had grown paper-thin, and reports started to filter in from Democratic leaders that chicanery might take place in Republican strongholds. Al gathered together his key men, people like Bob Wagner and Jimmy Walker, and arranged to leave at once with them for his upstate headquarters in Syracuse. The candidate showered and changed clothes, and with his sleepy crew caught an 8:30 A.M. train from Grand Central. Within hours they had arrived and were checking that the ballot boxes were secure.[59]

In the end, Smith won the election, 1,009,936 votes to 995,094, a margin of less than 15,000. Far more important was the source of his victory: Smith lost the area outside Manhattan and Brooklyn by 132,000 votes, but he carried the two boroughs by 186,000, Manhattan alone giving him a lead of 105,000 ballots.[60]

Thus, Al Smith had begun his larger political career on the same note that it would follow as long as he ran for elected office. Immigrants and city dwellers recognized that he was someone in higher politics who stood up for them, accepted them as equals, and above all, who gave them respectability. As a token of their affection, they turned out solidly to thank this politician who offered so much. In New York City, Italians supported him by figures as high as 79 percent, while the Irish gave him 80 percent, the Germans 70 percent, and the Jews 50 percent (several points higher than they had ever given a Democratic candidate for governor). Upstate, the figures for ethnic voters in various cities showed the same trend. In Utica 62 percent of the Italians voted for Smith, as did 69 percent of the Poles; in Buffalo the Irish turned in astronomical numbers, granting him over 85 percent of their ballots. Tom Foley summed up this feeling when he wrote to James Farley, "I do feel pleased . . . to think one of our own people is elected governor." Al had made good, not only for himself, but for all those he represented in American society.[61]

PART II

GOVERNOR

Chapter 8

The New Governor

THERE WAS A PART of Al that always believed he would wind up in the governor's mansion. Way back in 1904, when he was still a discouraged assemblyman, he had sent his mother a postcard of the executive residence and wrote on the back, "Dear Mother: This is a picture of the governor's residence. I am going to work hard and stick to the ideals you taught me and someday—maybe—I'll occupy this house."[1]

Tradition had it that the sitting governor invited his successor to come up ahead of time so that they could discuss the transition, but Charles Whitman refrained from making any acknowledgment of Smith. Al, Katie, and the children actually left for Albany not knowing exactly where they were supposed to go when they got there. Fortunately, a reception committee met the Smith family and took them up the hill to see their new home.[2]

All except Alfred, Jr., that is. There was no way his father was going to travel without at least some representative of the animal kingdom and they had taken along, of all the pets possible, Caesar, a great dane of enormous proportions. Al, Jr., now volunteered to walk him up to the mansion, although it is doubtful he was the one in charge.

Thus, by the time Al had walked through the front door and was shaking hands with Governor Whitman and his aides, up bounded boy and oversized dog, both rebelling against being cooped up on the long train ride. In a flash, the pooch was free and, overjoyed to see his master, jumping up and down. Al calmly brought Caesar under control, then drily joked to Whitman, "Don't be frightened, Governor. It's only the Tammany tiger come to take possession of the governor's mansion."

Al's inauguration would occur days later, on January 1. The formal ceremonies began at 12:30 in the afternoon; Smith stood at the Speaker's table in the Assembly Chamber, flanked by his wife, his mother, and his five children. Katie wore a blue velvet gown, embroidered with sapphire and crystal beads, overly accessorized (as she was wont to do), with a jeweled Spanish comb and a fan of white ostrich plumes. Al's speech was startlingly brief—only two pages—in which he thanked all the relevant parties and spoke mostly of the war that had ended only a few months before, and the work that had to be done for returning veterans. When asked how he felt about the occasion, he commented jocularly, "This is the finest birthday present I have ever received."[3]

It was more than a pleasing gift, however. Al had redeemed his heritage and become the first from his community of urban immigrants to make it this far in politics. A little over a year later, he told the Democratic State Convention in Albany that when he had arrived in January 1919, "I came here with one thing in mind, and that was that I either demonstrate to the people of this State that you can take a plain, everyday Democrat from Park Row, and he can be Governor of this State, or else by God, I will lie in the gutter." For Al Smith and his constituents throughout the state—and soon the nation—the governorship represented an entire people's coming of age.[4]

Al Smith's first term as governor was an apprenticeship. It was a time to forge the supporting team he would carry with him throughout his political career, while tackling the issues of the day and learning the ropes of statewide politics, rather than achieving lasting change in state government.

The most pressing issue was the aftermath of war and the return of millions of soldiers and sailors. For most mayors and governors, the end of the war meant an excuse for speeches and parades, a time to show the flag and review a victorious army. Logic dictated that this would be most true in New York, because the city's port was the primary point of arrival for troops returning from Europe. But only a few politicians and administrators, such as the head of the Veterans' Administration, admitted in public that parades up and down Fifth Avenue were not nearly enough of a response. The whole nation would face an enormous shift in employment and housing, in addition to a host of lesser problems. And few, other than the new head of the State of New York, seemed to be paying any attention to this.

Al's insight came at least in part from a remarkable inner circle of close advisers. There were three of them, and they came to have a critical influence on the development of his political career.

The first was Joseph Proskauer. Proskauer descended from Austrian and German Jews who had settled in Mobile, Alabama, before the Civil War. Born in 1877, Joseph grew up in this very southern small town and in fact, remained a partisan of the South throughout his life; the memories of the War Between the States "were personal and specific," as Proskauer later put it.[5]

Mobile, however, hardly fit the description of an inbred southern city. Although the population had capped at thirty thousand, its identity as a gulf port meant that it had experienced much conflict and many masters; five flags, residents claimed, had flown from the city mast, including those of Spain, France, England, the Confederate States, and the United States itself. As a result there developed an atmosphere of tolerance, a culture similar to that of New Orleans, infused with Latin and especially French and Catholic influences.[6]

Proskauer quickly demonstrated that he had the makings of a prodigy; at age fifteen he graduated from a local academy, and decided to seek acceptance at one of the most prestigious schools in the nation. In 1892, Columbia College in New York City (not yet a university) admitted the young man, and Joseph boarded the train for a whole new world.[7]

Columbia at that time was a far cry from what it would later become; the entire campus fit into the block between Forty-Ninth and Fiftieth streets, Park to Madison avenues, and almost all of the undergraduate students came from the local area. As a practicing, devout Jew as well as a southerner, Proskauer experienced what it was like, as he later wrote, to be a "stranger in a strange land. . . . I felt myself alien"—to the point that he considered himself a "novelty" to many of his classmates. Loneliness resulted, but eventually Joseph's skill at academics, his forcefulness in debate, his articles in the school's publications (including the editorship of the *Columbia Literary Monthly*), all won out, and he gained a great deal of acceptance.[8]

Proskauer continued at Columbia for seven years, matriculating through the law school as well as the undergraduate program. Along the way he confronted anti-Semitism both at school, when the brand new Columbia University Club refused to admit him; and in the workaday world, when most firms bypassed a young Jewish lawyer. Slowly, from the jobs that came his way, Proskauer achieved increasing success before the bar; eventually this led him to the firm of James, Schell, and Elkus, which would soon become Elkus, Gleason, and Proskauer. After that, he quickly rose through the ranks, and eventually became one of the preeminent jurists in New York and the United States, serving in time on the New York State Court of Appeals, as well as earning the presidency of the New York County Lawyers Association and the vice presidency of the Association of the Bar of the City of New York.[9]

Despite his intellect and achievements, Proskauer was hardly a beloved individual. On the bench, he demanded an incredibly high standard from the lawyers appearing before him, believing that they had to learn every nuance of every case, even displaying knowledge of the business their client was engaged in before they could argue effectively before him. Given that the judge did not suffer fools "at all," as his grandson put it, he would actually in some cases step in and take over the case from a lawyer if the poor man was not performing up to his standards. For many barristers, therefore, it became a "painful, painful experience" to try a case in his court, and grandson Anthony Smith recalled discovering, as he became an adult, how "you could very often see some of the tightening of the face from fellow lawyers when his name was mentioned. . . . There were a fair number of people who detested him."[10]

Strange that this gruff intellect fell in love with Al Smith. Proskauer had danced around Smith's orbit from the other side of the ballroom for many years, participating in various reform crusades to clean up Tammany Hall, appropriate activity for an upper-class Republican. But when he joined the Elkus firm much of that began to change, as he became exposed to the other side of the Hall—its ability to help the people of the city. After 1911 his proximity to Elkus, the chief attorney of the Factory Investigating Commission, brought him into close contact with Smith, and Proskauer's work with the Citizens Union also provided a more balanced assessment of the crusading legislator from the immigrant East Side.[11]

There were personal factors as well. Proskauer knew firsthand the trials of the outsider trying hard to do good, and recognized Smith's skill and strength, his intelligence and his capacity for growth and leadership. There was also the shared vision of government as a caring force. Above all, Proskauer became taken with Smith's open personality, by the fact, as his grandson recalled, "that Al Smith kept his word, did what he said he could do, and did it in a very above board and honest way."[12]

But in the long run, all of this fails to explain their closeness, as real friendships depend more than anything else on sheer chemistry. Ruth Proskauer Smith, the judge's daughter, said that there were not many people her father looked up to, but that Al Smith "was really an idol to him," the only person, in fact, that he felt this way about; even the judge himself, hardly given to sentimental niceties, told interviewers that he and Smith were "as close as two men could be."[13]

By 1918 Proskauer was one of Smith's campaign managers; far more important, by that time he had emerged as one of the new governor's two key advisers. Proskauer took on the role of *eminence grise*, Smith's intellectual adviser, helping him decide matters of grand design, of political philosophy and policy. The judge would help Al frame large arguments, providing direction and even elegant language when necessary.

Proskauer was complemented beautifully by Belle Moskowitz, who had also descended from the older wave of Jewish immigrants, her parents arriving from East Prussia in 1869. Belle Lindner was born in 1877 and grew up in Harlem, then a mixed residential neighborhood for immigrants who had moved out of the Lower East Side. From early in life, she showed an interest in social and political activism and by the time she had reached the age of youthful maturity, was working in settlement houses. Her focus became young women, and as such she participated in, and even led, many of the city's foremost campaigns to deal with various forms of vice, becoming particularly well known for her efforts to license dance halls. She quickly developed a remarkable style—the ability to combine earnest idealism with a knack for creating concrete measures to actually solve problems; all of this tempered by a very real sensitivity to the needs of the people on whose behalf she labored.[14]

Belle Moskowitz knew of Al's work with the Factory Commission, of course, but there was little contact between them—not surprising, given that she thoroughly opposed the Hall. But in 1918, she was attracted to Smith's progressive record and his integrity, and accordingly joined his campaign. After that, she stayed on; at first, her primary function was to guide Al into the world of women thinkers and doers, reminding him of how important these people could be to him as he fought to improve New York State.

But from this humble beginning, the two quickly developed a remarkable bond. Mrs. M, as Al and others usually referred to her, became the person in charge of Al's practical side, making sure that his day-to-day business got done, and got done right. Formally, her only post came after 1923, when Al appointed her publicity director of the Democratic State Committee (a job that she created to keep that body functioning between elections), but long before that it was clear she had really become his strong right hand. Belle Moskowitz was the person who not only wrote the press releases, but also edited the speeches, dug up the information, and squirreled out who was available and who *should* be available when it came to making an appointment. At times, she even introduced major, brilliant new policies; Al always listened.

But if the governor paid attention, others were skeptical. Given the era, this became a pioneering relationship for women in politics. Moskowitz always understood how delicate her role was, and sought to find ways to develop her power within the Smith administration most effectively, without alienating male traditionalists who would never cede authority to a woman.

The result, according to her granddaughter and biographer, the historian Elisabeth Israels Perry, was that Belle Moskowitz, much like Eleanor Roosevelt and Frances Perkins, chose to advance a series of ideological goals, rather than a personal career. She adopted an attitude that Perry insightfully labeled "feminine," as opposed to "feminist," politics, whereby she presented herself as a vision of true womanhood—a mother and a housewife and a secretary—while also pursuing her very real policy initiatives. So effective was this role that even David Edelstein, judge of the U.S. District Court of Southern Manhattan and an acquaintance of Governor Smith, referred to her as "the quintessential secretary."[15]

The reality was far different. Many observers noted the woman sitting in the corner, frequently doing her knitting, and soon noticed that the governor would tend to ask, "What do you think, Mrs. M?" The shrewder ones finally realized that he always asked that question, and started to take notice.[16]

Moskowitz's influence was unparalleled. She would write genteel, lady-like notes to politicians all over the state, that still made clear just how sharp the administration was, like the letter she sent to Rockland County Democratic boss Jim Farley to congratulate him on his 1927 election victory. She flattered by opening, "you certainly were 100 per cent," but then delivered a button-hole-specific analysis, remarking, for example, "It is interesting to see what a big vote there was on the grade crossing amendment in the rural counties." During the 1928 campaign, when she announced that John Raskob would be the new chair of the Democratic National Committee, one of the reporters told her, in front of his colleagues from all over the country, "It is you who should have been made National Chairman"; adding, after Mrs. M issued her characteristic denial, "I mean it." Henry Pringle, hardly a Smith supporter, but a leading national journalist who knew all the players, observed, "And every other newspaperman in the room was of like opinion."[17]

Smith and this unique woman developed an enormously deep friendship, based on respect and affection. Al understood how smart she really was (even Proskauer, not one to lavish praise, claimed she "was one of the most brilliant women I ever knew"); and also her commitment to ideals (her husband, Henry, wrote that she maintained a "relentless hatred of evil—personal or civic" all of her life). Moskowitz, in return, became a pit bull when it came to Al's interests, reducing all who voted against her candidate with the condescending remark, "They just were not educated up to him." When she died in 1933 Al told the press, "She had the greatest brain of anybody I ever knew," and in private wrote to Walter Lippmann, "She was so intelligent, so devoted, so loyal. . . . I will miss her very much."[18]

It was Moskowitz who introduced Al to the third member of the triumvirate, Robert Moses. The son of German Jews, Moses matriculated at Yale, went to Oxford, and earned his Ph.D. from Columbia University. Interested in reform, he had begun working for the Bureau of Municipal Research when he caught the eye of Mrs. M, who went everywhere and knew everybody. When she began to set up a Reconstruction Commission, one of the major activities of Smith's first term, she tapped the bright young researcher to help her run this body.[19]

In a short time, Moses became the man who implemented Smith's decisions, who did the hard research, who wrote the bills that made Smith's and Proskauer's and Moskowitz's visions reality. Long after he achieved status as far more than an apprentice, Moses continued as Al's doer—the fellow who handled the technical details. By 1924 the governor placed him in charge of the state's parks system, and Moses quickly assumed a lot more authority than anyone had planned.

This was the start of a well-earned reputation for arrogance (even Proskauer found him "abrasive"), as the rising star had the habit of insulting people all over the place. Moses, for example, took it upon himself to write the Director of the Budget to tell this official how the state's accounts should *really* be handled. He was so wrapped up in his own importance that he blithely assumed that he and the director were "sufficiently good friends so that you would rather have me tell you this pointblank. . . ." But, Joseph Wilson, who had held his position for eleven years, thundered back that Moses's letter was chiefly "illuminating in so far as it reflects your entire ignorance of the details that go into making a budget."[20]

Al, meanwhile, stuck with Moses because he was sincerely fond of his protégé, but also because Moses got things done. Former governor Hugh Carey described Moses as an "extraordinary drafter" of legislation, a man who "liked the artistry of . . . using the great powers and leverage of the state."[21]

Moses responded to this affection and support by granting Smith unique devotion. The future powerbroker understood Smith's loyalty to him (which he later described as "fathomless"), and also the fact that Smith alone had plucked him out of the ranks and given him his start in what became a fabulous career. In later years he commented that "all that I know that's of any practical value about the basic things in politics," came from Smith; "without him I would have been just another academic researcher." Most telling of all, however, Moses worked under every chief executive of the state of New York from Al Smith to Nelson Rockefeller but addressed only Smith as "Governor."[22]

Joseph Proskauer, Belle Moskowitz, and Robert Moses were more than Al's kitchen cabinet, they were his intimates and friends and the source of many of his ideas. It was Moskowitz, for example, who thought up the most important initiative of Smith's first administration.

Mrs. M got together with her friend, Frances Perkins, and came up with a brilliant piece of insight. The country was about to go through a major transformation. New York, with its concentration of industry, would be especially hard hit, but nobody seemed to be doing anything about it.

She argued instead that Smith should set up a committee to create a comprehensive plan for the transition from war to peace; it would cover every aspect of the state's concerns—from housing to education, from the Americanization of immigrants to the state's tax system. She began to refer to it as a "Reconstruction Commission." No other governor, no other administrator, had come up with this kind of plan. Even Woodrow Wilson, by then exhausted in spirit and obsessed with the peace treaty, declared that all readjustment problems should be handled by "spirited businessmen and self-reliant laborers," with no comprehensive government role.[23]

Moskowitz pitched the idea to Smith, explaining how reorganizing state government could bring back the old federal crowd from the 1915 constitutional convention, placing several strong Republicans in his corner. With an incredibly canny ear to what a later generation would call sound bytes, she explained that while Al's predecessor, Charles Whitman, had been known as a war governor, Al Smith would be labeled the "reconstruction governor."[24]

Al was astute enough to recognize just how smart her idea was, and by their next meeting, Mrs. M had not only come up with a list of names, but she also had found out whether they would serve on the commission. The selection was impressive, with thirty-six members representing fields such as agriculture, labor, business, and even child welfare. Twenty-three lived in New York City; five were women. Abram Elkus would head it, but included in the roster were luminaries of the age: leaders such as Bernard Baruch, financier and chair of the Federal War Industries Board; Charles Steinmetz, inventor and head of the General Electric Company; Felix Adler, founder of the Society for Ethical Culture; and George Foster Peabody, director of the Federal Reserve Bank in New York. Moskowitz, of course, became Executive Secretary, and she brought Moses in to be chief of staff.[25]

Republicans in the legislature refused to fund it, but the Commission consisted of some very rich individuals. Moskowitz managed to raise $44,000 to keep the work going, although at one point some of the young staffers did not get paid for six weeks. Working with various members, she saw to it that the commission divided its work load by setting up a series of committees, thirteen in all, covering topics such as housing and unemployment, labor issues and business readjustment, health and education, and, especially, reorganization of state government.[26]

The last of these was Al's special concern. The years spent in the Assembly learning the ins and outs of New York State's complex and unwieldy system taught Smith just how clumsy and wasteful this structure was. In 1915 he had codified these ideas, and the knowledge became for him a blueprint to transform the state. Moses prepared a report that heralded a new era, recommending that over a hundred state bureaus be consolidated into a series of departments organized into a cabinet; that the state adopt a central, executive budget; that the governor's term be extended from two to four years; and that a cumbersome ballot should be shortened. In time, this entire list would be incorporated into the structure of New York State government, most of it during Smith's terms as governor.

One of the other important branches of the commission was the Committee on Education, which dealt with the issue of Americanizing immigrants, and thus redeemed part of the promise that Al had made when he went to Albany. Any discussion that shied away from strident patriotism, furthermore, would be an act of the greatest courage, given the wave of jingoism that had swept the nation with the coming of war, and the terrible Red Scare that followed.

Under the leadership of Felix Adler, the committee recommended a program of widespread education, stressing instruction in English, especially for young people. At the same time, it eschewed condescending or punitive measures, arguing that the best way to make any new resident an American was to involve that individual in democracy itself. They argued that this was a spirit that had to be achieved not just intellectually, but in the heart as well, and that the best way to teach this was by doing: "To become a democrat," the committee's report declared, "one must practice democracy." The commission went even further, and advocated that this principle had to carry over into every aspect of immigrants' lives, even arguing that union work, "participation in the government of the industry to which the worker belongs," would be a "most important step." In addition, they recommended that lectures and debates on American values should be delivered in native tongues—that the use of these languages, "instead of being forbidden, should be allowed and even encouraged." These ideas were among the most progressive of the time on this subject, and became guideposts to reformers across the country on this emotional yet critical topic. The fact that they appeared at the height of the postwar hysteria, when all dissent from a narrow vision of what the word *American* meant was considered bolshevist treason, only highlighted the courage and importance of their work.[27]

In the long run, the commission was more important for what it proposed than what it enacted. A first-term governor, hamstrung by an opposing legislature, could set into law few of these proposals. Its importance, therefore, lay in the quality of ideas presented—many of which would form the basis for Governor Smith's future, successful programs—and in its status as one of the first examples of comprehensive planning in the history of the state.

But the Reconstruction Commission was only one of the ways Al tried to do a good job as governor. In the best Tammany tradition, he decided he would have to meet the people face to face on a regular basis. Al announced, accordingly, that he would set up offices at city hall in New York City, at the mayor's building in Syracuse, and at an appropriate facility in Buffalo, and in each of these sites he would hold open hours for the public to come and discuss whatever they cared to bring to his attention. With all the good intentions in the world, Governor Smith set up weekend sessions to meet his constituents, dreaming that he would encounter the poor mother whose boy sat in prison, someone who had a need and a right to see him, but instead, as Frances Perkins quipped, "He invited all hands to come and see him. . . . The misfortune was that all hands did." Some of his callers ("apparently intelligent," Al commented) seemed to believe that the governor had the ability to reverse court decisions rendered from any level or jurisdiction. One contingent (Smith called it "a small army") even felt compelled by their good natures to offer their services to the state for any position that offered a minimum salary of two thousand dollars a year or more.[28]

Al soon cancelled these sessions, but he worked hard in other ways to respond to his constituents. Shortly after taking office, he asked Frances Perkins to pay a visit. After she had been ushered into his office and the chitchat taken care of, Smith offered her a post as one of the members of the Industrial Commission of the State of New York. This body, the state's department of labor in essence, enjoyed enormous prestige all over the nation, and stood in the middle of the industrial turbulence that marked that era. No woman in New York history had ever been appointed to a position anywhere near that high. The notion was breathtaking, literally; Perkins said his suggestion left her speechless. She took the job, nevertheless.[29]

Al also had to confront issues concerning the state's police powers, and one of these decisions had a powerful impact on his family as well. When Smith took office, the notion of a New York constabulary was a relatively new one; the bill establishing the state police had passed by only one vote in 1917, and Al did not see much use for this force. He was also worried that they might be used as strikebreakers, as had, in fact, occurred in other states. In his inaugural address, Smith declared that he planned to abolish the unit, and as a result was soon visited by George Chandler, its commanding officer. Chandler delivered an eloquent rebuttal, describing the many services they provided to the rural sections of the state, insisting on their integrity, and he convinced Smith of the troopers' worth. Al accepted these arguments, and the force remained. Troopers soon began to assist in various aspects of state government, including work in the governor's mansion, which meant a great deal of contact with the first family. One of these young men—John Warner, a protégé of Chandler's—seemed to spend more time there than any other, and it was not until years later that Al realized that his decision on state policy had enabled his daughter Emily to meet her future husband, and for Al to acquire a son-in-law.[30]

The use of force, however, was not the only way Al confronted the issue of the state's power and how it should be wielded. One of the most significant aspects of the immediate postwar era was a terrible hysteria over subversives—the Red Scare of 1919 and 1920. At the national level, Attorney General A. Mitchell Palmer tried to ride the movement to the White House, and thus had the Justice Department engage in a series of raids whose publicity was matched only by their illegality and stunning lack of results.

In New York State, the legislature established the Joint Legislative Committee to Investigate Seditious Activities, which became known as the Lusk Committee after its chair, Senator Clayton Lusk of Cortland County. Lusk and his task force had engaged in a series of sensationalistic raids to seize documents from groups they felt had been plotting to overthrow the U.S. government, a list that included seventy-three branches of the Communist Party; the headquarters of the Industrial Workers of the World; the Russian Soviet Bureau; and the Rand School of Social Science, a lyceum for adults run by the Socialist Party.[31]

At first Al went along with this sentiment—not surprisingly, given his simplistic view of American values and the American people. In a speech at Cornell University on June 20, 1919, he told the audience that knowledge and democracy had to be used to stop Bolshevism, but if that failed, radicals would be forced to make a choice between "education or the nightstick." A month earlier, he had signed a bill making it a misdemeanor to display a red flag at any rally or parade dedicated to "the furtherance of any political, social, or economic principle, doctrine or propaganda."[32]

But Al was just as easily outraged when self-proclaimed guardians of liberty defied his vision of democracy. In the 1919 Assembly elections, voters responded to many of the postwar difficulties of economic distress and nationalistic bigotry by electing five members of the Socialist Party. No one denied that they had each received a majority of the ballots in their district, but at the first meeting of the lower chamber, Speaker Thaddeus Sweet summoned them all up to his platform, then delivered a blistering attack, including the charge that they had been "elected on a platform that is absolutely inimical to the best interests" of the state and the nation. What made the diatribe even more remarkable was that it convicted them for advocating positions such as supporting the communist revolution in Russia, the overthrow of the U.S. government, and opposition to American entry into the war. But while all of these had been stressed by some Socialist orator, somewhere, sometime, none of the five had ever issued a single one of these declarations.

Thus, when the legislature voted to disbar them, pending an investigation into the legitimacy of their holding office, the resolution bluntly stated that they had been condemned, "not in their individual capacity, but in their capacity as members of the Socialist Party of America." Only six members of the legislature voted against the sanction, including two Democrats from the Bronx. Tammany assemblyman Louis Cuvillier, on the other hand, felt that "if these men are found guilty, they ought to be taken out and shot."[33]

It was too much for Smith; less than a week later, he issued a dramatic, unequivocal statement. The governor began by stating that he was "unalterably opposed to the fundamental principles of the Socialist Party;" nevertheless, it was "inconceivable" to him "that a minority party duly constituted and legally organized, should be deprived of its right to expression. . . ." Instead, he pointed out, "faith in American democracy is confirmed not only by its results, but by its methods . . . of free expression;" these, indeed, were our foremost "safeguards against revolution." To discard the methods of representative government," he concluded, "leads to the misdeeds of the very extremists we denounce—and serves to increase the number of the enemies of orderly free government."[34]

Smith began delivering a series of speeches all over the state, advocating a position similar to that of his Reconstruction Commission. He argued that you could not "stop disorder and discontent . . . by defeating legislation" or by throwing duly elected representatives out of the Assembly; for democracy to succeed, it had to be impartial and all inclusive. In this sentiment he was soon joined by such bodies as the Bar Association of the City of New York, which formed a committee of men such as Joseph Proskauer and former governor Charles Evans Hughes to oppose the legislative edict; and the *New York World*, whose editor set up a "Representative Government Fund" to raise money to help the Socialists retain their seats.[35]

Despite this support, posterity nevertheless shows that this was a moment of supreme courage on the part of Al Smith, a time when he grew and changed. Smith stood, if not alone, at least somewhat isolated against a national tide of political bigotry—in elections, in the movies, in newspapers, and, above all, in an unprecedented use of government force against citizens whose only crime was their political affiliation. In 1920, taking a stand against this tidal wave very possibly meant political suicide. Smith's decision indicated that he had stood up for something he believed in, gambling his political career against his values more than ever before.

In New York, meanwhile, the Assembly had become obsessed with this madness. Ignoring most of their regular business, members devoted the unprecedented equivalent of twenty-four days to debating the sanctions against their erstwhile colleagues. On Friday, April 1, 1920, after an all-night session, legislators voted overwhelmingly to expel the five Socialists—three of them rejected by a count of 116 to 28, the other two by 104 to 40. Members split not so much along party lines but on a rural-urban axis, with most of the dissenting votes coming from New York City delegates, regardless of affiliation.[36]

This vote forced Governor Smith into a hard decision. According to New York State law, it became illegal to call a new election to fill vacancies after April 1, unless the proposal was part of a special session convened by the governor. Legislators thought they had taken themselves, and Al, off the hook, by delaying up until the deadline itself, figuring that any politically savvy governor would just sidestep the issue and ignore a petition by the Socialist Party, putting everything off to the next session.[37]

Faced with this situation, Al convened a meeting of his top advisers, twelve in all, to discuss what he should do. Many agreed with the strategy of avoiding conflict, but Belle Moskowitz, the only woman at the meeting, argued vigorously that fair play and democracy demanded that he call a new election.[38]

Moskowitz later claimed that Al took her aside a few days later to let her know he had just called for a special session, but the reality was that he waited four months to take this step. The state had been faced with a postwar housing shortage of unprecedented proportions, and with the legislature hung up on debating the legitimacy of socialism, nothing had been done. So on August 12 he called for an Extraordinary Session to deal with housing, and used this opportunity to issue proclamations for special elections in the five districts in September. All five Socialists ran again successfully, and the assembly threw out only three this time; the other two, however, made sure their victory was ratified, then resigned. Democracy lost once again, but at least Al had taken a tough stand on a difficult issue, and could rightfully take credit for mantaining his integrity, at potentially high cost.[39]

The legislature, meanwhile, guided by the Judiciary and the Lusk Committees, came up with a package of bills designed to cleave seditiousness from the life of New York State. These measures proposed the creation of a new state police agency to prosecute radical activity, the recertification of teachers on the basis of a loyalty test, and increased Americanization classes for factory workers and immigrants; it also gave the appellate court the right to strike any party from the ballot if deemed subversive, and mandated the licensing of private schools on the basis of their ability to uphold American values. This last measure had been specifically designed to deal with the dreaded Rand School, an institution one legislative patriot described as being filled with "moral perverts and social defectives."[40]

The governor vetoed all these bills, asking Proskauer to prepare drafts of his messages. These statements, modified by Al, became some of Smith's foremost pronouncements on civil liberties in the course of his long political career; he decried, for example, "the existence of a bureau of secret police," because he understood and shared "the traditional abhorrence of a free people to all kinds of spies." Regarding the call for loyalty tests for educators, Smith argued that such a measure "deprives teachers of their right to freedom of thought," and "it limits the teaching staff to those only who lack the courage or the mind to exercise their legal right to just criticism of existing institutions. The bill confers upon the Commissioner of Education a power of interference that strikes at the foundations of democracy." Similarly, he branded the bill to license academies "vicious," proclaiming that "the safety of this government . . . rests upon the reasoned . . . loyalty of its people. It does not need for its defense a system of intellectual tyranny which . . . must of necessity crush truth as well."[41]

Arguing that democracy must come from the bottom up, Smith and Proskauer denounced the bill to ban unpopular political parties. "Law, in a democracy," they declared, "means the protection of the rights and liberties of the minority. . . . It is a confession of the weakness of our own faith in the righteousness of our cause, when we attempt to suppress by law those who do not agree with us." Because of his faith in democracy, Smith could never approve a law that conferred upon judges, "learned though they may be, but nevertheless human, the power to disfranchise any body of our citizens."[42]

These statements became important, in part because whenever a person stands up for principles they reveal something of what she or he believes in. Smith never took the radical threat all that seriously and never joined the jingoist movement, for several reasons. He had dealt with the Socialists in his ward and in the Assembly, and knew that they were not all that terrifying. In one of the speeches attacking the expulsion, Smith claimed that there were two kinds of radicals: those who used violence and those who tried to change the government by lawful means. Socialists, he felt, belonged in the latter category, and therefore they were "all right."[43]

Far more important, Al Smith saw through the facade of the Red Scare to its nasty nativist core. In his second annual message to the legislature in January 1920, Governor Smith denounced Bolshevism, but also made it clear that he would never confuse that group with the vast numbers of immigrants "who have helped to build up our great nation by self-respecting labor and their citizenship." He mentioned that many of their sons had paid the ultimate price recently on European fields, and then launched into a deeply personal statement. Speaking from the heart, Smith explained, "I express myself thus feelingly because I know them. I have lived among them. Many of them have been my friends and neighbors." He made clear that much of the discontent of these citizens resulted from the "homesickness of men and women who do not yet feel at home in their new surroundings," but also from the "exploitation of their helplessness and ignorance." This kind of anger, Al felt, "every red-blooded man respects."[44]

But above all, Al was not worried about the Socialists and could support them fully and with a free conscience because he completely believed that in the long run, democracy and fair play always triumphed in America. When one supporter of the Lusk bills proclaimed that he was opposed to radical propaganda, Smith replied, "So am I, but I think the way to combat it is to appeal to the common sense of our people." This was the Al Smith of the old Fourth Ward, looking out on a world where people sooner or later treated each other with decency, his vision of the great commonwealth of the United States untarnished by the events swirling around him, just as his boyhood had ignored the seamier sights of the Bowery.[45]

So in 1920, Smith rightly blamed most of his troubles on the legislature. At the close of the 1919 session he told them that their work had now become part of the history books, "and it does not contribute a bright page." The next year, after they had failed to pass any of the measures Al advocated, he commented that their lack of accomplishment "adds no luster to our history." He complained that the majority had shown an "utter disregard . . . for what meant progress and welfare," and that their attitude "constitutes a formidable challenge to democratic representative government. Getting the legislature to back reform, Al thought, would be the toughest fight of his young gubernatorial career. He had not reckoned on a certain publisher of the yellow press.[46]

Chapter 9

Picking Fights

AL SMITH TRIED to turn his first term as governor into a success, fighting
for improvements and to build a record he hoped would lead to reelection.
Instead, he became consumed in a foul political battle, and had to suffer political
defeat, before he could come back and truly establish himself as the governor of
New York State. Along the way, he and the newspaper magnate William Randolph Hearst became arch-enemies, a fight that would last throughout Smith's
lifetime; ironically, the first and most brutal round revolved around the most
basic and innocuous of commodities.

It is difficult, in our modern era, to understand what a concern the milk supply
was to Al Smith's generation. Having no such thing as formula, or any other
industrially prepared substitute, most citizens considered milk one of the most
important and nutritious foods available, a vital commodity for everyone from
infants and children, through healthy adults, to ailing old-timers.

Unfortunately, neither the supply nor the quality of milk matched this kind of
demand. Few standards existed, and even as late as the post–Civil War period,
New York City's milk came largely from local stables whose cows were regularly fed swill, a by-product of the distillery industry. As a result, their milk was
low in butterfat, so producers regularly added chalk or magnesia to make it look
more substantive.[1]

In the late 1860s the state and the city passed a series of laws to improve the
condition of milk, but huge gaps remained. As late as 1897 New York City
refused to mandate that all milk be pasteurized, and did not adopt this basic measure until 1914, condemning generations of children to the possibility of tainted
nourishment. By the time Al entered the governor's office, it was still possible to
buy milk at a variety of grades and prices, but most of it was sold as loose milk, or

liquid that had not been separated by quality and grade and was instead dispensed out of large vats. Supervision of such a commodity, of course, was far harder than it was for products centrally produced and sorted in modern factories.[2]

Further complicating matters—and raising the price for the poor—was the matter of supply. By 1920 New York City residents alone drank 2 million quarts of milk a day: production was controlled mostly by the Dairymen's League, a combination of farmers; while distribution was handled by the Milk Conference Board, a distributors' organization. Much of this latter business was run by a few industrial giants, but officials of these firms, companies like Borden's and Nestle's, explained in public testimony that business practices dictated that milk could most profitably be turned into manufactured products such as condensed milk. Thus, almost 55 percent of the milk produced in New York State was denied to the customer as standard, fluid milk, and instead became bulk products, most of which went overseas. New York City, which should have had cheap milk because of its proximity to a vast rural hinterland, instead paid some of the highest prices in the country, figures that were steadily rising as well; between 1916 and 1918, for example, grade A milk rose from 13 to 18.6 cents per quart, a jump of 43 percent.[3]

Despite public outcry, there was little that the governor—any governor—could do to change this situation. In 1917 the legislature had passed a law creating a Council of Markets to deal with the agricultural side of the state's business; this was patterned after the state Board of Regents which supervised education, and became an attempt to try and remove partisan politics from this sector of the economy. The council had sole and full responsibility for regulating producers, distributors, and retailers of agricultural-based goods; and exercised this through two departments—one of Agriculture, the other of Foods and Markets.

But that same law removed all power over this issue from the governor. Council members received their appointments for ten-year terms from a joint vote by both houses of the legislature and could only be removed by a vote of the Senate. The council then appointed the heads of the two major departments, plus their respective counsels and executive secretaries. One of the investigating bodies that looked into the milk situation reported back to Governor Smith that he had "no power" to appoint or remove members of the council or staffers in the departments, that he could not add new bureaus or alter the salary of any official, so that all in all, he could not "control in any way the administration" of the state's apparatus for regulating its agricultural products.[4]

The long-festering problem blew into a major crisis on January 1, 1919, the same day Al took the governor's oath, when the Dairymen's League struck and refused to ship any more milk to New York City because of the low prices set by the Milk Conference Board. They took this action without prior notice, so none of the relevant authorities had been able to create stockpiles to tide over schools, hospitals or any other facilities, and the amount of milk entering the city dropped by 45 percent. At the city's milk stations, for example, a municipal charity set up to provide inexpensive milk to the poor, instead of the twenty thousand quarts sold a day, only nine thousand were available.[5]

Newly elected governor Al Smith did what he could, not only to deal with the strike (which lasted about two weeks), but also to correct the problems with the state agencies in this area. In his first message to the legislature on January 1, he declared that the high cost of milk represented a "public menace" and announced that he would appoint a commission representing all parties—producers, distributors, and consumers—to find a solution, a fairly typical means of tackling a problem in that era.[6]

For the new governor, however, this was just a start, although the road always led to frustration. Smith called on the legislature to repeal the law that exempted associations of farmers and dairymen from the state's public health and antitrust laws; the Republican legislative leadership told him privately that they would not accept this. Then he tried to use persuasion and public pressure on the Department of Foods and Markets to get it to start an investigation of its own; this also led nowhere. A few months later, he called for a change in the law establishing the Council of Markets, advocating that it be replaced by a single, strong commissioner of agriculture, with the power to centralize and strengthen the state's role in this complex and ornery business; Al tried to rally the state's agricultural societies behind this, but the Republicans, representing the corporate farming interest, saw to it that the bill was never reported from committee. Still fighting, the governor created his own organization to carry on an outside investigation, the Fair Price Milk Committee, consisting of leading citizens appointed by Smith and by the mayor of the City of New York. Although much information might accrue from their work, the commission was still only advisory, so Al finally employed the Morland Act, which permitted the governor to appoint an independent investigator to look into any branch of the state government, whether it reported to him or not, and set George Gordon Battle as an independent force to look into the Council of Markets.

Battle, finding the agency rife with incompetence, recommended that the senior commissioner be removed and that the entire setup be changed, commenting that the council "has proved itself a wholly useless failure and there is no justification for continuing its existence." Al could only act in impotence once more, sending this report as well to an unsympathetic legislature. Meanwhile, Smith's thinking had progressed dramatically, to the point that he concluded that milk should be declared a public necessity, and thus regulated in the same way the state dealt with utilities.[7]

Al Smith was not the only one thinking about milk, and thus, into this strange mixture was added the oddest player of them all. William Randolph Hearst entered New York when he bought the *Journal* and the *American,* turning them into the leading competitors with Joseph Pulitzer's *World* for the right to titillate and champion the city's poorer newspaper readers. He first crossed swords with Al back in 1907, when Tom Foley ran for sheriff and Hearst put up one of his own men for the position. By then Hearst had increasingly become a presence in New York politics, twice getting himself elected to the U.S. House of Representatives from a Manhattan district, and in 1905 running for mayor on the ticket of the Municipal Ownership League, calling for, among other things, a city takeover of the subway system. In 1917 he tried for Tammany's mayoral nod, but a group of regulars, including Foley and Smith, beat him down. Still, the Hearst papers backed Al in his 1917 race for the Board of Aldermen, and again when he ran for governor the next year, especially after Smith issued a statement in favor of city ownership. During the campaign Al even brought his children up to the Hearst residence on Riverside Drive to play with the publisher's offspring.[8]

After that, things started to go sour; it is not totally clear why this happened, but given the remarkable shifts and twists that Hearst would undertake throughout his career, such an understanding may well be beyond the realm of reason. Clearly Al did not pay much attention to him after moving to the governor's mansion; Al's daughter Emily, for example, believed that Hearst got angry when Al would not appoint him to the welcoming committee to greet returning servicemen. Of course, given that Hearst had adamantly opposed the war and was considered by many to be a traitor, Al's denial seemed plausible to everyone else. But then, when Al refused to appoint a Hearst attorney to the state supreme court, the newspaper syndicate began to attack the Smith nominee instead as a "tool of the interests," because he had been an attorney for the New York Central Railroad.[9]

Soon there was more. During the milk wars, Hearst had gotten as much mileage as possible from the crisis, printing photographs of dying, emaciated children that purportedly were taken on New York's Lower East Side, but most likely were shots of the victims of the Armenian starvation. Then, in May 1919, Hearst decided that he had found the person responsible for this tragedy, and that man was Al Smith.[10]

The attacks after that were rather fabulous. Many papers, including Pulitzer's *New York World,* had presented images showing a child being starved by the milk trust, but Hearst made it personal. "Governor Smith is whimpering and whining," his editorials roared, "but babies in New York are dying for lack of milk." Cartoons showed Al climbing over the tombstones of dead children who had had no milk as he made his way to the governor's chair, while articles claimed he was responsible "for the starving and dying children . . . for the multiplication of the little mounds in the graveyards and the added death dollars in the Milk Trust's treasury." The basic premise hammered home again and again was that Smith's pleas of helplessness were phony—that he had proved himself willing and able to make miracles happen when it came to the needs of big business but was less responsive to the needs of the poor. The words were bad enough: "when a . . . mother with a starving child appeals for relief . . . the Governor is perfectly helpless . . . but when a corporation asks him . . . off comes his coat and the thing is done," but the cartoons were worse. Artists always depicted Al as an elitist tool of the business class, clad in top hat and tails, lying to the public while he made deals to carry out the will of his masters. On at least one occasion, the papers carried an interview with a health official who blasted the governor's handling of the milk situation, notwithstanding the fact that the entire account had been written by an Hearst reporter back in his office at the newspaper.[11]

Many individuals—Al's kind of folk—believed the papers, so Hearst's lies carried weight. One man who wrote to Governor Smith admitted that Hearst may be an "Anarchist, but he has one good thing he exposes you grafters," and asked Smith rhetorically, "What the hell you care about the Public?" The writer then compared Al to "that *Judas W. Wilson* he has sold the whole world to England to tyranny and so has you done sold the Public to the Milk Trust but you get your reward. . . . The other guy is deing allready and so you'll get it too." One letter that claimed, "You went against our poor . . . by . . . raising our milk and food," was signed, "Mother with 3 childrens."[12]

That was too much for Al. Politics was one thing, but Hearst had crossed the line of decency with an olympic broad jump. On October 18, 1919, at a speech before the Woman's Democratic League, Smith hurled the gauntlet. Claiming that during the war, "every small municipality in a radius of fifty miles . . . was burning his newspapers because they had in their minds that he was not loyal," Al then reminded them, "I have been loyal; I have lived among my people and they have respect . . . and confidence in me." Hearst, on the other hand, "has been loyal to no one, not even to his own." The crowd of over three thousand ate it up, giving the governor a screaming, standing ovation; one woman yelled out that Hearst was the most dangerous man in America, while other women chorused, "Right! Right!"[13]

Al then launched his showstopper: a blue-ribbon Citizens' Committee was renting Carnegie Hall for a debate; Hearst could have half the tickets so that the galleries would remain balanced, but Smith was going to have his day, and the whole city would hear him. The big bout was set for October 29.

The publisher declined the invitation, of course, but in as nasty a manner as possible. His reply began that he was "surprised that Boss Murphy did not send the invitation," since as far as he was concerned, "it was Tammany that hired Carnegie Hall." Hearst had no intention of ever meeting the governor, "publicly or privately, politically or socially," and had neither "time nor inclination to debate with every public plunderer or faithless public servant." More likely, he must have realized that with his soprano, almost falsetto voice, and his hunched-over speaking stance, Hearst would have stood little chance against Smith.[14]

Nevertheless, Al showed up on the night of October 29 ready to go. Despite the briefness of the host's introduction, Al fidgeted in his seat until it was his turn to speak, then delivered what would become the most passionate speech of his entire life, though hardly his most thoughtful.[15]

With his very first words, Al displayed his intensity, asking the crowd for "their absolute silence and attention." He mentioned the obvious missing presence by crowing, "Of course, I am alone" (a voice called out, "He hasn't the nerve to face you, Al"), and used the strongest invectives of his political career; for a brief moment, Al spoke in the language of the schoolyard, of his childhood, of his anger. His opponent (whom Al did not mention by name until much later in the speech) "has not got a drop of good, clean red blood in his whole body," Al bellowed, "And I know the color of his liver, and it is whiter, if that could be, than the driven snow." Notwithstanding his earlier appeal for silence, the crowd broke into a roar of applause, punctuated by the incessant waving of small American flags.[16]

Al then launched into a lengthy refutation of Hearst's charges, taking them apart one by one. Several accounts of that night claim that Smith's face grew red, that he appeared livid as the sweat poured off him. The transcript, however, reveals that he remained in control most of the time, the old actor from St. James taking center stage as he masterfully carried his audience along as he rang the changes on Hearst's treachery. Using mannerisms he had learned in *The Mighty Dollar*, Smith employed dazzling asides, keeping up the tension as he described an intricate legal puzzle and suddenly interjecting stage directions, telling the galleries, for example, "ten days after that—watch the circumstantial case, and follow me along with it now, while I put it all together and show you the motive . . . ," emphasizing with hand gestures, making sure they remained spell-bound, that his triumph was complete.[17]

Al walked away that night tired and victorious, although the results were less conclusive. He had made a powerful and bitter enemy who would influence his life for many years to come, while the real issue, the lack of quality milk, remained unresolved. But the political realities had boxed him in—despite everything he tried the legislature remained unyielding—so in the end, it is hard to see what else Al could have done but defend his integrity with all his heart and skill.

⟋

Making enemies in politics was easy, but in the coming days Al would need all the friends he could find. The year 1920 brought a presidential election, and Al came from not only the largest state, but one with a sizable Democratic voting bloc. As early as April, politicians began working to place Al in nomination at the San Francisco convention; few thought he had any real chance of getting the nod, and instead perceived this as an appreciation of a favorite son.

In public, Al treated this groundswell as a joke. As the Republican convention finished and all eyes turned toward the Democrats, Governor Smith played golf with Boss Murphy at the latter's summer home in French Lick, Indiana. He had not yet read the Republican platform, he told the boys in the press, and to emphasize this nonchalance, Smith and Murphy engaged in a leapfrog game for the newsreel cameras, in what must have been a rather remarkable sight.[18]

Other people, however, had very different ideas. Early in 1920 Belle Moskowitz contacted Edward Bernays, one of the founders of American public relations, and asked him to submit a plan for a presidential publicity campaign, "to interpret Governor Smith and his work to the public of New York State and the country." Bernays's outline included all the major media outlets, and covered the complete range of the governor's speeches and personal appearances, but it was never acted on.[19]

The Democratic convention of 1920, moreover, seemed remarkably dispirited, the party anchored to the millstone of Woodrow Wilson's failed genius, to his visionary internationalism. Many of the delegates sensed how completely the public had become alienated from this program. When the convention managers unveiled a giant oil portrait of the still-sitting president and some delegates began a pro-Wilson demonstration, the New York State delegation split into two camps and engaged in a fistfight.

For Al, however, it was a great event. Party leaders had arranged to have his name placed in nomination by no less a figure than Bourke Cockran himself, a personage now long forgotten, but who remains one of the greatest American orators, a voice that could only be compared, according to some accounts, to that of William Jennings Bryan.[20]

In his speech, Cockran painted Al's life in classic American strokes, telling the crowd, "I nominate here today the man whose career savors more of a page from a romance than a mere biographical narrative . . . a man who has risen from a peddler's wagon . . . to the Governor's chair."[21]

But Cockran also affirmed who Al was, what his roots were, and, above all, whom he represented and stood for. He pointed out that Al had "never lost a friend and never ceased to make new ones. . . . All of them, from his playmates on the sidewalks of the East Side to the statesmen he has moved among as Governor, call him 'Al Smith.'" This might seem like an insult to some, but as Cockran explained, his candidate was "the only man who could be called by such a diminutive without in any way debasing the dignity of so high an office." The reason for this success was clear: "Al Smith is in no way different from us, and that is why we love him."[22]

Cockran concluded on a ringing note. He told the crowd, "We offer him to you as president of the United States. We will accept no compromise in the convention. If you take him we will give you the state of New York and if you reject him, we will take him back and run him for governor!" This brought the audience to its feet. Starting with the New York and then the Illinois delegations, a demonstration for the East Side candidate began in earnest, one of the few at this lackluster convention, with delegates pouring into the aisles.[23]

At that moment, something happened that would stick with Al for the rest of his life. Tammany had naturally brought along its own band, and now it burst into life. The man in charge was Joe Humphries, and before he left New York, he threw in his bag the songs and scores of all the old Harrigan and Hart vaudeville tunes, such standbys as "Little Annie Rooney" or "A Bicycle Built for Two," plus long-forgotten triumphs like "Paddy Duffy's Cart," "Never Take the Horseshoe from the Door," and "Dad's Dinner Pail." The band began to play tunes from this old-fashioned medley; everyone got a big kick out of this and began to sing, even a hard-boiled newspaperman from Baltimore named H. L. Mencken. Mencken described how one delegate grabbed a "lady politico and began to prance up the aisle," to be joined by crowds of others, swinging in time to the music.[24]

Of all the songs, however, it was the first tune that stuck. This one was not a Harrigan and Hart piece at all, but a ditty composed by another pair of vaudeville virtuosos, Lawlor and Blake. "The Sidewalks of New York" began with the refrain,

> *East Side, West Side, all around the town*
> *The tots sang Ring-a-Rosie,*
> *London Bridge is falling down*
> *Boys and girls together,*
> *Me and Mamie O'Rourke*
> *Trip the light fantastic*
> *On the sidewalks of New York.*

If ever a song sounded like Al Smith, sounded like the world he came from and remained a part of, this was it. The ballad became his theme song. After the 1928 presidential campaign, Al wrote, "It seems to me that every second tune I hear is that . . . melody."[25]

The fact was, however, Al did not actually hear that song the first time it was played on his behalf. Standards of political modesty being what they were in those days, he left the stage as soon as Cockran took the platform, leaving Katie to sit there and glow with pride as the orator spoke to a packed house. Years later, Al implied in his autobiography that the only thing he remembered about the convention had to do, inevitably, with pets and animals: how he snuck out to buy cowboy saddles for the ponies Arthur and Walter rode back at the governor's mansion. But the *New York Times* reported that after the nomination, "the Governor . . . is as pleased as a boy with a new toy," and to every note of congratulations he only responded, "Wonderful! Wonderful!"[26]

The convention was soon over. Delegates, knowing that they had little chance of party victory that year, could find no stalwart champion and turned instead to a relative unknown, James Cox of Ohio, who dutifully lost that November by a wide margin.

But when Al came back home, he had a real campaign to run: his second bid for the governorship. Quickly he recognized this as a difficult race, with times turned against the Democrats. His opponent that year was Nathan Miller, a corporate attorney (he had once been general counsel for U.S. Steel) and former judge, who had been described as having "the habits of mind and social approach of an appeals judge of the McKinley era."[27]

Smith tried to run on "the record," campaigning about the needs of New York State, about what he had achieved, and about what he planned to do in the future. In his acceptance speech before the state convention, Al trumpeted, "We are not entering this campaign on the defensive." Instead, he stood atop "a clear-cut progressive record, and I challenge my opponents to find fault with it." The fact remained, however, that much of Al's gubernatorial career at this point consisted of advocacy, not accomplishments.[28]

Despite this, Miller chose to play it a different way, attacking everything having to do with the Democratic party *except* Al Smith's record. Mostly, Miller talked about the Wilson administration—how it had betrayed the Americans at the peace table, the Irish when it failed to attain a free Ireland, the Germans when it declared war on the fatherland, and the Italians for having gained so little for them at Versailles. To all of these groups, Miller asked if they could afford to have more Democrats in office.[29]

Smith chose Joseph Proskauer to be his campaign manager, a request that surprised the judge, even though he acquiesced. Al explained that Tammany would take care of the working people in the wards, but he needed Proskauer to go after the independent vote, which, as Proskauer noted, Smith "thought he deserved and . . . he believed would elect him." Al's closest adviser came through, setting up the Independent Citizens' Committee for Smith to rally the city's elite reform groups around his candidate.[30]

That year, Al even courted the enemy, speaking out in favor of municipal ownership of subways. Sure enough, shortly before the election, William Randolph Hearst turned his powerful news organs, the *Journal* and the *American,* away from a third-party candidate, and had them exhort readers to vote for Governor Smith, notwithstanding the extreme charges they had made earlier. Just before the election, in fact, the *Journal* issued the command: "YOU WILL VOTE TO RE-ELECT AL SMITH."[31]

Even this support was not enough, and for the first time in seventeen years, Al Smith lost an election. Returns showed, nevertheless, that he was a formidable vote getter. By any measure, 1920 was a Republican year at the polls, when Warren Harding demolished James Cox by a margin of 16 million to 9 million votes. The national Democratic ticket also ran poorly in New York State, but still, it was these returns that made Al look so good: Cox lost New York by 1.2 million votes, while Smith lost by only 74,000, which mean that Al Smith beat the national ticket by over 1 million votes in his home state. In New York City, Cox got 40 percent of the vote, local Assembly candidates (who had even less to do with national politics and had the fullest support of the machine) got 55 percent, while Al walked away with an astounding 71 percent of the ballots.[32]

Others noticed this as well. Robert Lansing, Wilson's secretary of state throughout most of the war years, sent congratulations on what he felt was a "splendid showing . . . a tremendous triumph and a tribute to you as a faithful servant and a man." The aging reform leader, William Church Osborne, telegraphed Al that, "even in defeat, you came closer to swimming up Niagara Falls than any man I had ever seen." And Bourke Cockran, remembering the joy of a few months prior, told *his* candidate that he was "the most formidable asset remaining to the Democratic Party . . . the party of which you are the chief ornament."[33]

The Smith family had to move out of the mansion and back to 25 Oliver Street, which for all its past glories now seemed much more cramped. Far more important, for the first time since 1903, Al had to earn a living at something other than politics.

Al Smith was about to become a businessman, and the line of work he chose seemed like a logical one. Early in 1920 two wheeler-dealers, George Getz and James Riordan, had organized the massive United States Trucking Company to control the hauling business in New York City, and offered the job of chairman and chief operating officer to the soon ex-governor.[34]

For Al, the people and the position seemed just right. Riordan had begun his career as a working stiff just like him, starting out by driving a truck for a living. Getz had something even better going for him: he loved animals and kept a private zoo behind his home, just as Al would do in Albany. Beyond personalities, there was poignant nostalgia here; by taking the position, Al Smith would be returning—triumphantly—to the old family business his father had worked so hard at.[35]

But Alfred, Sr., had barely made ends meet as a teamster. His son was now accepting a position that paid fifty thousand dollars a year, putting him in charge of two thousand employees, twenty-five hundred horses, two thousand horse-drawn and three hundred motor-driven trucks, plus innumerable depots all over the city.[36]

Al took the firm by storm, and succeeded in accomplishing goals that he could only dream about when it came to state government. He totally reorganized and rationalized the operation, making sure that every trucker carried a full load, and that no deliveryman ever had to make a return trip empty. These efforts paid off; expenses dropped enormously as Al got rid of wasteful equipment and facilities, from $5.7 million to $3.4 million, a slashing of more than 40 percent within three years. In 1922, for the first time, the company posted a modest profit of $208,179.[37]

Through Riordan and other connections, Al also began to become part of a small circle of elite business friends—a sociable gathering of fellows who used to sit around and gab or go out for a game of golf together. One of the leaders of this gang was William F. Kenny, whom Al had originally played with when the two were just wee lads—Kenny's father, Thomas, had been a local battalion chief for the New York City Fire Department down in Smith's neighborhood—but had gone on to fabulous wealth as a contractor. Riordan was no slouch, either; he followed a successful business career by speculating in the market during the boom years before and during the war. Other regular members of the group included Tim Mara, a prosperous stockbroker and owner of the New York Giants football team; and William Todd, who had made his money in the shipbuilding business.[38]

Kenny, a short, stocky, bulldog-faced man, provided their hangout. A staunch believer in Tammany, he turned one of his penthouses into the Tiger Room. Located at 44 East Twenty-third Street, now 304 Park Avenue South, this was a massive affair. The layout was huge, covering about a quarter of a block; a ballroom took up the first of two floors, with a twelve-foot-high arched ceiling and a gigantic fireplace at one end of the room, all decorated with dark wood paneling. On the floor above that, reached by a private elevator, were the rooms the men used for their get-togethers—cozy places with lots of wood on the doors and moldings, lighted in part by small, ornate windows, some with stained glass. The biggest room displayed an immense tiger-skin rug, complete with skull and fangs.[39]

During this period Al Smith was never far from the public eye, serving as founding board member of the Port Authority of New York and New Jersey and testifying at hearings before the New York State legislature, where he mesmerized the audience by reducing piles of data to the pitiful story of how Mr. Potato got to market cold and friendless and rumpled because of the current conditions. Smith wrote letters of recommendation for woman's advocate Marion Dickerman; gave speeches at the unveiling of a statue of a doughboy in Greenwich Village; and kept the faith when he told the annual meeting of United Hebrew Charities that Jews and Roman Catholics (both of whom he referred to as "our people") personified family life in New York, with their devotion to children and their low rates of divorce. He even took part in a Boy Scout fishing contest. No one caught anything, until Al danced out with a wooden minnow dangling on the end of his line; pointing to the tiny carving, he declared, "It's a gefilte fish," a line urban immigrants adored. By 1921 the ex-governor was receiving so many invitations to dinners that he had to adopt a policy of declining all of them.[40]

It was a familiar antagonist, however, who pushed Al Smith back into the political fray. By 1922 the man pushing hardest—and most successfully—for that year's Democratic gubernatorial nomination was William Randolph Hearst.

For all his quirkiness, Hearst was a strong candidate. No one could shrug off the amazing weight of his New York papers, written for and to the working people of the city. This power had enabled the publisher to even elect his own mayor, John Hylan, whose immense perquisites—all the patronage and contracts—would be used to further the Hearst quest for higher office.[41]

Al tried hard to stay out, despite his animosity toward Hearst. He enjoyed the world of business, and for the first time could plan financially for his family's future. In April he adamantly told reporters, after leaving a meeting with Tammany boss Murphy, that his mind was made up, that he would stay in the trucking business, and had no desire or intention of seeking the nomination.[42]

But that meeting became only one of a series, as all parties pressured Al to support their particular cause. Murphy actually tried to have it both ways; he came up with what he felt was a dream solution of running Hearst for governor and Smith for U.S. Senate on the same ticket. Tammany leaders pushed this fantasy to Smith on the grounds that Hearst would contribute uncountable sums of money to the party, and that bygones should be bygones in the name of party regularity. Smith in turn reacted as he would have to a fatal rash. According to the *New York World*, when Brooklyn boss John McCooey came to plead the case for joining the ticket, Al snarled, "I'm damned if I will. . . . Do you think I haven't any self-respect," and swore to "lick Hearst . . . if it is the last act of my life."[43]

It was a visit from Norman Mack, Democratic boss of Buffalo, however, that did the trick. Mack told Smith, bluntly and in no lost phrases, that either the East Sider declared soon for the gubernatorial nomination, or that the delegates from the state's second largest city would soon be solidly pledged to Hearst. Al was back in the race.[44]

Al chose as his vessel for the big announcement a former assistant secretary of the navy under Woodrow Wilson, Franklin Delano Roosevelt. Roosevelt had been an up-and-comer in the party, running for vice president in 1920, when polio struck him down. He was now well on the way to recovery, and represented a patrician tradition, as well as the farming regions where Smith could always use more support.

Thus, there occurred what immediately became known as the "Al" and "Frank" exchange. On August 13, 1922, in a public letter addressed, "Dear Al," Roosevelt stated, "I have been in touch with men and women voters from almost every upstate county and there is no question that the rank and file of Democrats want you to run." He flattered Al, telling him, "Many candidates . . . are strong by virtue of promises of what they will some day do. You are strong by virtue of what you have done," and pointed out that Al's support had come not only from Democrats, but from "literally hundreds of thousands of Republicans and independent men and women who knew that you had given this state an honest, clean and economical government." And now there was a crisis, so that in "every county the chief topic of conversation is: 'Will Al Smith accept if he is nominated?'" It was time to decide.[45]

A few days later, in the second, equally public phase of this political Gaston-and-Alphonse routine, Smith wrote "Dear Frank," telling Roosevelt that he appreciated the "kindly sentiments," how they compelled him "to talk to you from my heart." Following statements about his desire to remain in the business world, Smith finally admitted, "I have been so honored by my party that even the members of my family would be dissatisfied if I did not answer the call. . . . I feel I would be ungrateful if I were to say that I would be unwilling to assume the leadership," if it was to be thrust upon him at the state convention. The game had now officially begun.

It quickly became clear that Al had the nomination for the asking, but complications arose when Murphy came up with what seemed a reasonable compromise with the publisher's forces: What about nominating Hearst for U.S. senator? The position was prestigious, and no one, downstate or upstate, minded the idea of sending the man hundreds of miles away to Washington, where he would be involved in everybody's business but that of the state of New York.

No one minded, that is, except Al Smith. Delegations pleaded with him, to no avail; if Hearst was on the ticket, Al was off. The last and saddest of these visits came from Bourke Cockran, there on Murphy's orders. Short and stout, a few years away from death, Cockran appeared at Smith's suite on the eighth floor of the Onondaga Hotel, where the potential candidate sat up in bed. The old man used all of his skills, the fire and the lightning, the appeals to party loyalty, every arrow in a lifetime's quiver of words and gestures, as Al sat there, according to Jim Farley, with a "black scowl" on his face. When it was all over, Al exploded, rehashing all the old wounds. On occasion, Cockran tried to interrupt, but Smith cut him off roughly, shouting, "I listened to what you had to say, now you listen to me." Defeated, Cockran finally thanked Al for his time, and they shook hands. The door closed behind him, then suddenly, briefly, reopened, as Cockran poked his head in and said, "I want you to distinctly understand that I did not come here of my own volition."[46]

Al held the course, helped in part by his aging mentor, Tom Foley, who at the height of the conflict stuck his head in the door, glared at Al and barked, "Stick!" Murphy had no choice, and compromised by taking Dr. Royal Copeland, health commissioner and Hearst ally, as senatorial candidate. Smith won nomination on the first ballot, and Hearst, mollified by Murphy's concession, had his papers endorse Smith, albeit as the lesser of two evils.[47]

It would not be a difficult election; when Al opened his headquarters at the Hotel Biltmore in New York City, he showed up carrying a bar of soap engraved with the words, "Vote for Alfred E. Smith for Governor," and laughed to reporters, "We are going to clean up in this campaign."[48]

A lot of the fun that year came from the ineptitude of Nathan Miller, an uninspired candidate from an uninspired state party. One observer at the Republican convention in Albany reported that there were "over a thousand . . . delegates . . . all very much alike in appearance and manner of speech. I never saw so many people together who were so much alike." Miller had fought against an amendment reorganizing state government along efficient lines, instituted a loyalty test for teachers, curbed free speech, and gutted the Department of Labor. In a campaign speech before the annual convention of the New York League of

Women Voters, he announced that there was "no proper place" for a league of women voters, and that organizations like this, which stood outside the two-party system, were "a menace to our free government and to representative government." He also attacked women for advocating measures like health care and pension systems, since these would remove what he called "the stimulus which is necessary for human progress." The next day, the convention voted to formally condemn him, notwithstanding the fact that 81 percent of the delegates had listed their party affiliation as Republican.[49]

Smith, on the other hand, did everything right. With Proskauer as his campaign manager again, he lined up elite support right away, to the point that Walter Arndt, secretary of the Citizens Union, could write Al about "the regard in which you are held by thousands of Republican and Independent voters." Gauging accurately where his strengths and weaknesses lay, Smith, now emerging as one of New York's greatest campaigners, dedicated three-quarters of the few remaining weeks to the upstate regions that needed the most work, followed by a rousing conclusion in New York City, where he could end the campaign on a roaring high note of triumph.[50]

By the final stretch Al was flying, in great form. In the last days of the campaign he reached out to everyone in the state, throwing his umbrella of inclusive Americanism over all of New York's peoples when he spoke at Liberty Hall in Harlem before a predominantly black crowd of eight thousand (by comparison, Radio City Music Hall seats only five thousand). "You know where I stand," Smith trumpeted, "For two years in Albany I stood for the rank and file of the people." This meant the folks in the audience too, it was clear, and they celebrated *their* candidate, and a movement from Republicanism to Democracy, with a series of torchlight parades.[51]

Just before the election, the *Times* reported that things looked close, while betting in the financial district ran even money or eleven to ten in Miller's favor. Proskauer optimistically projected a statewide margin of 200,000 votes for his candidate, but then, he was supposed to do things like that.[52]

But the people of New York held the trump card, and they showed how they felt about Al by voting for him in dazzling numbers. Smith took the state with 55.7 percent, the highest he would ever score in five races for governor. He beat Miller by a margin, not of 200,000 as Proskauer had predicted, but of an astonishing 386,000 ballots. Smith's total of 1.4 million votes was the largest given to any gubernatorial candidate in the history of the state up to that time, and the entire Democratic statewide ticket also won. For the first time in years Democrats controlled the Senate, although the Assembly, because of the gerrymandered districts, remained immune to that year's onslaught.[53]

Far more important, the election placed Al at the head of a much larger movement. Jews, the one group of immigrants most resistant to Tammany's charms, voted for Al by incredible margins, some of the districts on the Lower East Side giving him as much as 75 percent of their vote.[54]

There were larger implications to all this as well. Nationwide, the 1920 U.S. Census showed that for the first time in the history of the United States, more than half of the population lived in cities. For all of these people, busy both adjusting to America and reshaping it with their own hard work and local culture, Al Smith would be the one they looked to as their spokesman.[55]

Even Smith knew that something was different this time around. After his victory back at the state convention, the *New York World* commented that Al Smith had become not only the party's nominee, but also its undisputed state leader, a post he had never held before. On election night, when Smith walked into Tammany Hall, he seemed to be in a mild state of shock. The papers described him as having his hat somewhat askew on the side of his head, with a long-forgotten cigar clamped into the corner of his mouth. To all the congratulations he could only dazedly reply, "Wonderful, wonderful"; one account stating that he had never expected such a big majority, that "his manner was that of one who felt that the bigger the vote the greater the obligation he had to the people of the state."[56]

Al's stunned demeanor was appropriate. The 1918 victory had made him governor, one of many, soon off the stage. This second term, coming on a wave of electoral abundance, showed that he was now a power, and here to stay for quite a while; Al had arrived. Dimly, with gathering consciousness in the months and years to come, Smith began to recognize that he was now the most important politician in the state.

Chapter 10

Winning Administrative Reform

JANUARY 1, 1923, was a lousy day for an inaugural parade, but to the people of New York State, it really did not matter. Al and his family had arrived in Albany four days prior, amidst what the *New York Times* described as a "young blizzard," to the cheers of what seemed like everyone in Albany. Inaugural morning itself dawned cold and wet; a torrential rain was coming down, mounds of snow were beginning to melt, and everyone had to march through ankle-deep, chilling slush. By the time the band and military honor guard had struggled to the reviewing platform, Al took one look at the drenched and bedraggled soldiers and cancelled all military ceremonies, moving everything indoors.[1]

Despite the weather, no one in the capital could recall ever having seen or heard a welcome like this before; one correspondent, categorizing the day as a "deeply democratic event," compared it to Andrew Jackson's inauguration in 1829. Demand for tickets far exceeded the thirteen hundred seats in the Assembly Chamber where Al would take his oath, and Albany radio station WGY began its broadcasting history by sending out Smith's address as the first sounds it would transmit, a harbinger of the way new forms of media would eventually change politics and campaigning for American politicians.

As Al Smith walked into the Assembly Chamber where he had come of age as a politician, a police band entertained the crowd with tunes like "Rosie O'Grady" and, inevitably, "The Sidewalks of New York." The music stopped as his party entered, and a steady roar began; some voices managed to carry over the din, and then the crowd picked up a call that somebody was "all right." A shout from the gallery—"Who's all right?"—received a chorus of answers, as everyone boisterously replied, "Al Smith."

Smith stood in contrast to the joyous throng. Reporters noted that his visage was deadly solemn, "as though his mood ... had been impelled by some feeling deeper than pride and satisfaction over public acclaim." Al was about to get a chance to become one of the great governors, one of the important men in the history of the state, to move from politician to statesman, and the significance of his role weighed heavily on Smith.

His speech was brief, with no ringing call to action. It was notably filled with "thank yous"—the commendation to outgoing Governor Miller was effusive—but still redolent with power. Smith's voice was that of authority, the sound of one who has commanded and knows how to get things done, who now intends to win more battles than ever before. "I am mindful of the responsibilities that are placed upon me when I take up the reins of government. I know exactly what it means," Al told them, the sound of experience resounding: "I have been through it, not alone as the Executive," but also having watched other governors struggle and fail.[2]

When the ceremonies dimmed, the magnitude of the endeavor sank in. Al Smith understood that he governed a state first among many. By the early years of the twentieth century, the Empire State—a regal term, but legitimate then—led the nation in two-thirds of every major industry the country had. The dollar value of its manufactures exceeded the economy of every nation in the world except colossi like Great Britain, France, and Germany, the great powers of the world. By 1925 the state's population was over 11 million, of whom 5.9 million, or 63 percent, lived in New York City. Of the total, 9.7 million, or 87 percent, were citizens, the rest legal aliens (this was according to the census; the secretary of labor also estimated that in the year of Al's inauguration, 850,000 persons had entered the country "clandestinely").[3]

The whole state seemed to boom out of control in that era. Between 1880 and 1910, Rochester and Syracuse doubled in population, Buffalo tripled, Yonkers quadrupled, and Schenectady quintupled. This meant change, rapid change that had to be tamed so it would benefit the people and not harm them. By 1928, for example, the state would have 10,209 miles of roads for cars on state and county highways (only 3,303 were paved with concrete), compared to 8,400 miles of railroads.

Roads, however, were but a single problem of the many that Al Smith would tackle in a long career as governor, one in which he acquired a reputation as a well-known liberal. While it remains true that he excelled in dealing with social issues, that kind of notoriety takes attention away from what was truly his greatest accomplishment in all his years in Albany. It is not as exciting to talk about budgets and reorganization as it is to highlight hospitals or schools, but in truth, Al Smith was first and foremost, in the historian Paula Eldot's perfect term, an "administrative reformer." This kind of issue seemed incredibly dull, but for Al Smith it was vital, and his foremost cause. His ideals in this fight, and the techniques he then used to win these reforms, became the epic story of Smith's governorship.[4]

By now, having lived so long under the system of government that Al Smith created, it is hard for any New Yorker to imagine just how backward the state's machinery remained when he took over the governor's chair for his second term. New York functioned under a constitution that had been little changed since 1846, when it was adopted in a Jacksonian era that distrusted strong central government of any kind. But by gutting the governor's office, New York wound up with a system that may have restrained the possibilities of dictatorial control, but also wreaked havoc on any attempt at effective government.[5]

Under the rules that prevailed in 1922, the governor served a term of two years, barely enough time to learn the rudiments of the job before it was campaign season again. Even more frustrating, he had little control over the administrative branch of government, as the heads of many of his departments were elected by the voters on independent ballot lines. Not just officials like lieutenant governor, but the comptroller, the secretary of state, the state engineer, the canal commissioner, and the prison inspector all earned their sinecure from the voters, and thus frequently came from a different party than the governor, buttressing their sense of independence (not to mention how this confused the voters, few of whom could differentiate between the candidates for, say, state engineer). And then, just to make absolutely sure that the citizenry would be thoroughly bewildered, most of these officials did not serve concurrent terms with the governor. Even worse, many others were appointed by the legislators, often for segments longer than the governor's two-year span, further fragmenting all sense of authority whatsoever. Finally, over the course of years, the legislature had also added many new boards and commissions, most dealing with local problems and none anchored into the central administration.

By the time Al got there, the situation had reached the level of madness, on a scale only an inmate of an asylum could feel affection toward. Below the level of governor, for example, there were 189 department heads, commission chairs, and functionaries, all of equal status, of whom only a handful actually reported to the governor. These officials could be appointed by sixteen different procedures—few of them involving the state's chief executive—and were removable by any one of seven different methods. No cabinet system, no consolidation into comprehensive departments, no concept of an executive branch gave order to this chaos, so one develops instead, a sense of fascination and wonder that government could function at all.[6]

Al fought this nightmare with all his heart, but it was large and goofy enough that he had lots of fun doing it, as he pointed out the excesses it fostered. There was, for example, the Department of Military and Naval Affairs, a rather unusual organization, one might say, for a *state* government, but its main responsibility was running the local militias and handling the state's military-related affairs and responsibilities.

It did not, however, have any control over—in fact, anything whatsoever to do with—the Monument Commission of Miles' Irish Brigade, the Adjutant General's Office, the Armory Commission, the New York State Monuments Commission, state expenditures for veterans of the Civil War and of the Spanish-American War (handled by two separate bodies, of course), and most sadly of all, even over the Naval Militia, not withstanding its own title. All these other bodies were separate and independent; they remained totally unrelated—administratively, if not functionally—to what should have been the parent department, or to the governor's office, or in fact, to anything beyond their own little bailiwick.[7]

Consider, for a moment, the overlap between the Department of Public Works, the Highway Department, and the State Engineer's Office, each of which enjoyed sizable staffs, offices with drafting tables, blueprints, all the accoutrements of professional work. But one does not feel so bad when one realizes that, after all, this was only a small part of the ten different engineering departments the state maintained, all separate entities, naturally. Along the same lines, the state constitution included a superintendent of prisons, who could only be removed by the Senate, not the governor. Over the years the legislature compounded this failure of accountability by adding a Commission of Prisons that had nothing to do with the superintendent's office, and then established a Board of Parole, which was totally different from the Commission on Probation, as any fool could see.[8]

The most dangerous element of this system, however, was its financing. While different sources of revenue were tallied by separate agencies that had nothing to do with one another, with no central accounting system, each of the 189 functionaries, plus one forlorn governor, submitted his or her own budget and authorization requests directly to the legislature, bypassing the executive branch entirely. Under this masterpiece of local chaos, which made feudalism seem simple by comparison, these endless appeals for appropriations went to the budget secretaries of each chamber, who then forwarded them to the respective finance committees. This gave these last two bodies enormous powers to set salaries against a governor's wishes, for example, or to fund one of the endless commissions. While technically dozens of people seemed to be involved, in truth, only a handful of key players, plus some clerks, really did the work and had any idea of what was going on.[9]

And clearly, no one was in charge of all this, least of all the governor. That was too bad, given that he had the highest profile in the state, and everyone assumed he had the authority, blaming him for any and all mistakes. But the 1919 budget, which took up 640 pages, covered salaries for twenty thousand state employees, allocated $6½ million dollars in new construction, and had taken the legislature six months to draw up, arrived at the governor's office on March 31, and was due back, with all vetoes, changes, and recommendations, within ten days.[10]

Al hated this system, and had long ago become the foremost tinkerer in Albany, someone who always tried to make the wheels spin a little faster. Frances Perkins remarked how she "never knew anyone who was so interested in the form and pattern of government, and how to do it . . . on how things are done, on how much it costs, on where the money comes from, on how the money is spent." What made Smith remarkable was that he rose above this sense of details to a broader vision, as he fought to remake the state's structure.[11]

Al had a unique and pioneering sense of what government should be—one that has remained valid through the ages. He came from an era of polar choices: elite reformers who would handle the budget with integrity and honesty, but often ignored the needs of many of their constituents; or machine bosses, who approached the city's coffers as a starving man would a Roman bacchanal, but assiduously made sure that the poor and working classes were cared for.

Al Smith pursued a third vision, and eventually realized it. In this version, administrative reform became the servant of social justice, because it permitted more money to be spent on the poor and fostered support for a fair and effective government. Al concentrated on both the purpose behind an expenditure as well as the amount, and was more than willing to spend on human needs, as long as the fund was administered with integrity. In Schenectady in 1923, Governor Smith told his audience that reorganization of government was the most important goal he could accomplish, not because it saved money or was orderly, but because the state, "in its present dislocated, disorganized and scattered form," could not "render the services it should, nor even be brought in harmony with the needs and desires of the people." As long as this held true, Al believed, the citizenry would be willing to support all kinds of expenditures, because they knew that they were getting their money's worth. In his autobiography, Smith wrote, "It is a mistake to think that the people approve of reduced appropriations when in the process of reducing them the state or any of its activities are to suffer. What the people want is an honest accounting for every dollar appropriated. They want every dollar of public money to bring a dollar's worth of service to the state." By 1924 Smith had implemented the largest tax cut in the state's history—a 25 percent reduction—while still rapidly increasing spending on social services. Al would do things the right way, but he would never balance the budget on the backs of the poor.[12]

❧

Al was no johnny-come-lately to the world of administrative reform, having championed it as far back as his stint in the legislature and during the constitutional convention of 1915. Far more important, however, was the work of the Taxation and Retrenchment Committee of the Reconstruction Commission of 1919. Smith had brought to it his top staffers Moskowitz and Moses, and working with their boss, the three of them came up with the four key proposals that would eventually make New York a modern administrative venture: combining the 189 state offices into a cabinet-level series of departments; reducing the number of state officials elected by the public to a total of three, otherwise known as the "short ballot"; creating an executive budget system, which let the governor draw up the budget first, then having the legislature vote on it; and lengthening the governor's term to four years. It is testimony to their work that all of this eventually became law, and is now the commonly accepted structure of the state. It is testimony to Smith, however, that he managed to get passed three out of these four fundamental changes. Thomas Dewey, twice Republican candidate for president but also governor of the Empire State, stated, "We are indebted to Governor Alfred E. Smith more than any other man for the modern framework of government."[13]

Smith had actually gotten part of this agenda passed during his first term, back in 1920, but like everything else in New York politics, it was a complicated venture. New York State law required that changes of this magnitude—constitutional amendments—had to pass two legislatures not having the same Senate, and then be approved by the people. In 1920 Smith introduced the appropriate bills, and with his support, they passed. But by the end of the year he was out of a job.[14]

Governor Miller supported the idea behind reorganization, but with little enthusiasm. Some of this might have been political calculation; it was a known fact, for example, that the commissions, appointed by the Republican legislature, were a prime source for patronage, as each body had its own secretary, and these positions were not covered by civil service. As Al put it, "The men that are creating them have the secretary in mind ahead of time." In 1921, under Miller, the legislature decided to reject the reorganization amendments.[15]

But by 1923 Al was back. His mandate from the voters clear, he managed to get the legislature to approve the reorganization package in 1923, and then again in 1925. After that, in the fall, voters listened as Smith told them that "failure to pass these amendments . . . will constitute a serious menace to the public welfare," and also "menaces the future of good government in this State"; and then approved his plan by a 60 percent margin.[16]

Anyone who thinks that this would end the story, the people having spoken, would not have lasted long in the labyrinth-like arena of New York State politics. Fortunately Al Smith was made of sterner stuff.

The legislature had added one kicker to the process: that after everything passed, there would then have to be a commission to draw up the specific laws that would actually write the amendments into the constitution. This seemed a bit cumbersome, but it remained a last chance to try to gum up the process.

At first the task of appointing the commission went reasonably well, with a certain amount of courtesy on both sides. Everyone, however, realized that the crucial appointment was that of chair, since this person would head the executive committee that did most of the work.[17]

The Republicans picked H. Edmund Machold, a rather unusual choice. A former Speaker of the Assembly, Machold was one of the leaders of the "Black Horse Cavalry," the oldest of the very, very old guard who wanted to retain all prerogatives, all sinecures, all power for the legislature in its existing form. Machold had referred to reorganization, which his colleagues were now suggesting he head, as "ill-advised and ill-considered," and thought that the executive budget in particular was "revolutionary and dangerous."[18]

Smith responded with a move that surprised everyone. Reaching back to *his* old guard, the elite, progressive Republicans whom he had fought side by side with during the 1915 constitutional convention, Al put up as his man Charles Evans Hughes: former governor of the state, Republican candidate for president in 1916 against Woodrow Wilson, a man of impeccable pedigrees and, not inconsequentially, a long-time advocate of reform, whom everyone agreed was a superb choice.

Hughes won the chair, brought back a favorable report, and the legislature finally passed the appropriate bills in 1926 and 1927. Smith had triumphed, and as a result, produced a total transformation of state government. No longer would canal commissioners or engineers have to run for office; the ballot had been reduced to four slots, those of governor, lieutenant governor, comptroller, and attorney general. A horde of agencies would either be eliminated altogether, or else merged into a series of departments, which in turn created the governor's cabinet. Each of these departments, furthermore, now had to submit an itemized budget request by October 15. The governor's staff would make revisions and compile a comprehensive budget to the legislature, to be delivered no later than February 1; until then, no appropriations bill could be passed. After that, the legislature could revise, reject, or accept any of the items, or add new ones. Only on the matter of the four-year term of office did Al come up short, but the common sense of this measure guaranteed that it would also be put into effect in time. The *New Republic* said that reorganization "simplifies and economizes the administrative organization of the state. . . . The new instrument of government is remarkable for what it achieves, but it is equally remarkable for what it omits."; Warren Moscow, dean of Albany reporters, wrote how "those with longer memories and better perspective know that Smith, more than any other one man, set the tone for the government in New York State, and that politicians of both parties still run on his record." Al had changed New York forever, and done it in the face of a hostile legislature.[19]

But that hostility meant that Al's victory had to be as much political as administrative. Thus, the successful fight for these bills revealed Al's ideals, but even more, what a virtuoso politician he really was, the remarkable bag of skills and tricks he could conjure up in order to achieve what no other governor—even those with majorities in the legislature—had ever managed to do.

Republican assemblyman Eberly Hutchinson, chair of that chamber's Ways and Means Committee, once complained that "the governor is a hypnotist. He has hypnotized both the newspapers and the general public. He waves his hand and says shut your eyes or open your eyes. The people do as he bids them. If he says black is white they say black must be white because Governor Smith says so." Hutchinson's remarks were clearly an exaggeration from an exasperated man on the losing side of debate, but they accurately reflected Smith's enormous political skill, his ability to get the job done and to reach out to the average citizen.[20]

Al understood what every good advocate knows: that in order to win, you must constantly remain in the public eye. Smith's speeches, statements, and addresses hit over and over on the same basic issues he wanted to win on more than anything else—matters like reorganization and water power. The public uproar never faded, and sooner or later the legislature would have to respond.

In order to do this, Smith pioneered in using several techniques to get his point across. He recognized, for example, the importance of the governor's annual statement and his closing address as a means of both reaching out to ambivalent legislators, as well as getting his views aired in the press. In January 1923, he broke precedent—which was to have the clerk read the annual message to a dozing army of bored politicians—and instead showed up in person to read it himself. The *New York Times* commented that the old practice required a reading that was "lackadaisical" and "somnolent," where not only was "all emphasis lacking, but important passages are frequently slurred, if not actually omitted, in order to save time." The sage of the St. James Players would have none of this, and thus eliminated the usual exodus from the floor, as legislators stuck around to hear what Al Smith had to say, as he laid out his program in dramatic and compelling terms.[21]

After that the real arm twisting began. Smith had the legislators' respect because he was one of them and because he knew how they operated, courtesy of his long years as their colleague. He would begin nicely, calling various leaders from both legislative chambers to his office and then locking the doors and rolling up his sleeves; "I am one of the easiest men to sit down with . . .," he said, besides being "well supplied with good cigars." That way, they could "sit down and talk it all out and let us get some place." If that did not work, Smith resorted to cajolery, common sense, and, on those rare occasions that he lost his temper, blunt invectives. When Senator Charles Hewitt remained numbingly intransigent during one meeting, Al finally blew up and told him, "Charlie, your friends here ought to send you to the Brunswick-Walker Company to have your head melted down for billiard balls."[22]

Above all, though, Al's success was the product of his speechmaking. Smith became a great man in politics in an age when talking directly to audiences was still the standard, and he used this as his foremost tool for swaying the electorate. In order to win reorganization, for example, Al barnstormed the state, appealing to voters directly, telling them, in an unprecedented move, "drop a line to your Senator and Assemblyman and ask them to give these matters their personal and careful attention and not to take for granted what the leaders of the party tell them."[23]

And then there was his style—a combination of homespun storytelling and wry humor. Al Smith merged Belle Moskowitz's encyclopedic knowledge of local politics with what one biographer called his "ability to translate his experience of life into political programs that . . . appealed to voters," his talent for carrying audiences along with him. Addressing a hearing of the State Water Power Commission, for example, Smith started by addressing Republican congressman Ogden Mills's claim that Al's support for public control made him "comparable with Lenine (sic), Trotsky or some Socialist or Communist." Then, in what must have been a stage-whispered aside, Al pontificated, "The comments in Albany upon the Congressman's senseless tirade were anything but complimentary to him." In truth, however, these remarks did not trouble Al, since, as he immediately pointed out, "if there exists . . . a Socialist Party on the question of water power, it contains . . . three well known members" who all supported his position. The first was Charles Evans Hughes; followed by former governor Nathan Miller (Al felt that "if Governor Hughes and myself are Socialists, Nathan L. Miller has the right to claim the leadership of our party"); and, finally, "knocking on the door for admission to the Socialist Water Power Party" that famous left-winger Owen Young, chairman of the General Electric Company.[24]

But it was not just the words; it was the performance. Al on the stump was a sight to behold. Blessed with an actor's memory, his standard preparation for a speech was to take a series of number 9 envelopes (a little smaller than nine by four inches) and sit down, sometimes for hours, with the various clippings and documents he felt were relevant to his talk. After pondering the material, Al would then take the top envelope and, using a thick-tipped pencil stub, scrawl a list of points he wished to make, in numerical order. Behind this, he would stack the other envelopes, each numbered correspondingly, and insert the clippings he wished to use into each one. That was it, all he needed; the remarkable mind and the thespian's instincts would take care of the rest.[25]

As Al stepped out into the spotlight, the audience saw a man about five feet, eight inches, although he looked taller when he sat down because of his long body frame and extended neck. Still a swimmer and golfer, the governor had a solid chest, and he wore his blond hair parted in the middle, according to the fashion of the times. His face had an oval shape, with clear, pink skin, blue eyes, teeth that were less than perfect, and a massive beak. Although he would still sport the brown derby as his trademark, otherwise the clothes had matured along with the man, to formal dark suits. And even after most men had switched to a belt and short underwear (including Smith's later rival, Herbert Hoover), Al still stuck with the old standbys of suspenders and long johns.[26]

Then he began to speak, and all this was transformed; "vitality goes out from him in a flood," one critic commented. His face would get red and Al would sweat—*perspire* is far too timid a term—as he drove every point home. The stage was his to command, and he used every single inch, running, dancing across it as he pulled the audience along with him to understand the mysteries of government and politics. Al would bend and stoop, getting everyone to crawl into the recesses of the state treasury and discover what his opponents had hidden there; or else stand and gesture—his favorites were a fist crashing into the podium, or the finger pointed in grim accusation. When Joe Proskauer's daughter Ruth wanted to campaign for Smith up at Radcliffe in 1928 and she feared she had no flair for speaking, Al told her, "You just make this gesture (creating a fist and shaking it in the air) and you'll be all right."[27]

And when passion failed, there was always wit and laughter. Hugh Carey called this gift "mirthology," the ability to use humor to keep one's senses and score a point; and Raymond Moley observed that Al Smith was always a better story teller than even Franklin Roosevelt. While the latter's "love of a joke was boisterous," FDR nevertheless became "corny and repetitious when he tried to be funny." Smith's humor, instead, "was spontaneous, infectious, and exceedingly funny." During the constitutional convention, for example, he had joined the debate on a literacy test for voters, supporters of this measure claiming that only those who could read and write should be allowed the franchise. The sage of Oliver Street, clearly opposed, pointed out that there were plenty of residents up at Sing Sing who could not only sign their names, but had found their way in there because of their talent at signing other people's names. As governor, Smith on the campaign stump was sovereign when it came to dealing with hecklers, such as the time one chap yelled out, "Tell 'em all you know Al, it won't take very long," and Al rebutted, "I'll tell 'em all we both know, and it won't take any longer."[28]

Smith also made speeches memorable because of his distinctive voice. Al spoke in a tone that may best be described as "gravelly." Less kindly observers claimed that "to compare his voice to anything liquid short of Niagara is an unwarranted metaphor," or that it was like the "gruff bark of an Irish setter." The ultimate metaphor came from Gene Fowler, stage reporter and chronicler of Jimmy Walker, who wrote that when Al sang "The Sidewalks of New York," "the bullfrogs had met their master."[29]

Equally famous was his accent, a classic rendering of that American dialect usually referred to as Noow Yawkese. Al enjoyed, for example, talking about "woik" on the "raddio" (the latter was a term he used all his life and made famous). As life went on everything got "betta" for a "poisun," particularly one engaged in public "soivice."

But contemporaries also realized that verbal foibles aside, Smith had mastered the instrument that was his speaking voice. The governor could command a room as if he had a gavel in his throat, one commentator observed, and another claimed that when he spoke, it was "like a thunderclap in a boiler factory," shutting everything down. Beyond power, Al's trumpet knew how to coast through the entire scale of notes, how to use inflections and tones, as legislators and reporters sat there stunned when he ended each sentence of a speech with a rising snap that cracked like a whip across their mind. And the same skill could be used softly too. H. V. Kaltenborn, possessor of one of the all-time great radio voices, related that every year, Al would give a talk at the Brace Memorial Newsboys Home. Kaltenborn understood that he and the other eminent guests were "just fillers-in who were barely tolerated by the hungry boys." Al, on the other hand, "knew just how to win and hold this young audience. Instinctively he said just the right things in the right way."[30]

The result of all these skills was an unparalleled ability to communicate ideas to an audience, to persuade and cajole and educate, to create a political force to get administrative reform passed. Judge Simon Rifkind remembered attending,

as a young attorney, a Smith lecture down at the old Academy of Music on Fourteenth Street. "Never before nor since have I heard a public speaker enthrall his
audience" to that extent, and with "an analysis of the budget" no less. Smith had
"an extraordinary skill in communicating with his listeners, whatever the subject
was. . . . He had them sitting on their seats," even though he was "discussing the
budget, if you can believe that. He had me enthralled, everybody. We were waiting for, what is he going to reveal next?" Walter Lippmann wrote that "When Al
Smith was governor of New York, he bridged this chasm [educating people for
the tasks of government] as no one before or since has bridged it."[31]

Being a man of the people had other political advantages as well. Publishers
and editors, especially from the upstate papers, wrote editorials against him, but
Al got along fine with the reporters, so his arguments still managed to reach the
public. Back when he was sheriff, one of Al's deputies had ejected a reporter who
had gotten boisterous when Smith did not emerge promptly to take questions. Al
ran over to the newspaper office and pleaded with an editor that the journalist
could print anything he wanted, even that "Al Smith's crazy," but that he must
understand that Smith was not "kicking reporters *out* of my office. I want 'em
there." As governor, he cracked jokes with reporters, helped them when they
were in trouble or short a few bucks, and even visited fellows in the hospital. In
return, journalists kept his confidences and allowed him to recall any slips that
that grizzled voice may have uttered.[32]

Still another enormous asset in Smith's political wares was his stunning reputation for integrity, earned the hard way. Al's appointments to senior positions
were scrupulous, passing most tests for diversity and quality, even using the
standards of a later, more enlightened age. By 1928, when he left the governor's
mansion, analysts found that appointments to the top twenty-five departmental
or divisional leadership positions included fourteen Democrats, eight Republicans, and three independents. Broken down by religion—the hot-button issue of
his era—there were eleven Catholics and fourteen Protestants. To the 156
offices below this level, Smith chose 72 Republicans against 58 Democrats, the
rest independent or undesignated. Only 33 were Catholic, compared to 105
Protestants, 11 Jews, and 17 others. Less than 40 percent of his appointments
came from New York City, even though it contained more than half the state's
population; and 14.4 percent were women. During the 1928 election, Lillian
Wald wrote to friends how she had met priests in the Vatican who claimed that
they did not want Smith elected, because if he was, no Catholic would ever be
appointed to anything in the federal government.[33]

The centerpiece, the kind of poster boy of integrity in the Smith regime, was
Colonel Frederick Stuart Greene, Smith's commissioner of highways. Few posts
controlled more contracts or jobs, but Smith picked a man of noted accomplish-

ments and honesty. Greene was, of all things, a Virginian (the rough equivalent of a Martian to parochial New Yorkers), a graduate of the Virginia Military Institute who earned his rank building roads in France for the American Expeditionary Force. Greene was also a registered Republican, at least at the time of his appointment. Al put him in the job as early as 1919, but Greene had been released by Nathan Miller. To his credit, Al brought him back as soon as he returned to the executive office, and to any party cronies who complained, Al replied, "Of course he is a _____ in May, but think of what an angel he is in November."[34] (There are a number of versions of what the blanked-out noun was, none credible.)

And finally, there was one other characteristic. Because of this repertoire, Al Smith was generally remembered as a gravel-voiced, hard-working executive who kept the people's interests foremost. But in the long run, it was more than just charisma that enabled Al Smith to win his battles to reform the government of New York State; it was intelligence. Jonah Goldstein, lawyer and New York politician, said that Al would read a law the same way the rest of us would "read a detective story." As sheriff, Smith was able to enter any dispute and quote page and paragraph of his statement of duties to support whatever action he planned to take, just as later, when governor, he over and over displayed his line-by-line knowledge of the state constitution as he fought for reform.[35]

All of this knowledge brings into question one of the great myths of Al Smith, that he was a stranger to books. Everyone believed this, not surprisingly, since even Al repeated it, probably because he never wanted anyone to believe he was putting on airs. The journalist Frank Kent stated what became the classic report when he wrote that Smith "does not read books. . . . Novels and essays, history and poetry do not attract him." Al corroborated this on many occasions, writing to Herbert Bayard Swope, publisher of the *World,* "You know I am not much of a reader," or telling reporters, "Don't try to make any kind of a scholar out of me. . . . I'm sorry, but it can't be done."[36]

Al's denials were consistent with the neighborhood-kid-made-good image, but could not bear scrutiny. They do not vie, for example, with the governor who devoured government reports; Kent quoted friends who said that Smith "eats documents up." Smith also came out of a world where the newspaper was the most important and most exciting source of information, and by all accounts he was insatiable in his appetite for them. Ed Flynn, the great boss of the Bronx, wrote in his memoirs that he knew that Smith had never read a book, but claimed that the governor "read every newspaper in the State of New York."[37]

And there are even indications that Al Smith tackled, on occasion, full-length books. On one of the rare moments when he let down his guard, Al wrote an acquaintance, "I read with deep interest the manuscript which you forwarded, touching on many important subjects," and in 1927 corresponded with Joe Tumulty, Woodrow Wilson's old campaign manager, that he had received a book about Wilson and the prohibition movement, and "when things cool down here a bit I will get a chance to read it."[38]

So with humor, showmanship, and finally intellect, Al Smith had taken on old issues and met with brilliant success; in New York, Al had fundamentally reformed the government of the state, establishing the modern system we have grown accustomed to. Emily, Al's most political and insightful offspring, wrote that her father never hesitated to rank his accomplishments as governor, and always felt the reorganization of state government "stood first."[39]

Even more amazing, and establishing a model for all times, he achieved administrative reform without losing his humanity. Walter Lippmann described Al Smith as "what a conservative ought to be . . . if he knew his business." As Smith told one audience, "I know how to cut . . . down . . . the expenses of the state. I can do it. But I want somebody to pick out for me what activity of the State must suffer when I do it. I will certainly never do it at the expense of the helpless and defenseless who cannot come back at me." Al had reinvented the machinery of government. Next he would transform the role it played in the lives of all the state's peoples.[40]

Chapter 11

Forging a New America

AL SMITH WAS NO philosopher, but his words and deeds provide clues as to
how he perceived the role of the state in American society in the first part of
the twentieth century, an era marked by enormous changes. Al took citizenship
seriously, and he simply believed in a government that had basic, fundamental
obligations to human decency, and that no individual, no group, should be excluded from that shelter; long before other politicians, he understood the importance
of mutual tolerance, of diversity, of a society incorporating various ethnicities,
races, and genders. He fought for this last vision, not because of political oppor-
tunism, but because he sincerely felt that that was what America was about.

Al Smith's basic notion of government was that it remained an extension of the
community, an entity to which we ceded a few rights—especially the right to be
hurt—in return for safety based on consensus, power derived from the consent of
the governed. He had learned this lesson in those early encounters with a terrible
form of industrialization unfettered by rules of humanity or even fundamental
decency, following only an out-of-control marketplace that even many businessmen found to be too turbulent. Smith was no radical by any means; he supported
business and wanted it to thrive. But he believed that it had to be bound by the
rules of the community and that government was the means to convert common
beliefs and values into limits on human greed. In speeches, he argued that "the
State is a living force. . . . It must have the ability to clothe itself with human
understanding of the daily, living needs of those whom it is created to serve." He
would note how, "too many people are prone to the idea that health is the concern
of the individual. I believe it to be the business of the State because the State itself
cannot be healthier than its people." With these words and ideas, he began to create the forerunner of the New Deal, introducing the modern form of liberal government. Indeed, Norman Thomas, longtime leader of the Socialist Party, said of
Al, "As governor I thought him much better than Roosevelt." Al did this two
ways: by extending the government's reach into areas never before considered, in

order to safeguard the citizenry's well-being; and by extending rights and recognition to groups previously excluded from the mainstream of New York's politics. In both efforts he foreshadowed national trends, and by pioneering in creating an inclusionary society became a leading progressive.[1]

Typical was Smith's support for education. As the result of his own deprivation, the governor believed deeply in the importance of the classroom. Only someone with this perspective could write that the state could postpone or delay a number of obligations without much injury to its welfare, "but the process of education must always be kept at one hundred per cent of efficiency . . . because time lost cannot be regained by the children who are injured by the state's failure to make adequate provision for their education." Al's noble goal required only two things—"money and nerve"—and the governor had the latter and would arrange for the former.[2]

Under Governor Smith, spending on education skyrocketed. In the 1918–1919 fiscal year, New York State contributed over $7 million to local governments for schools and related activities. By the 1926–1927 budget year, Smith had increased this figure to over $70 million, tenfold in eight years, a change educators could only dream of in later eras. High school enrollment doubled, and the state created a long-overdue network of rural school systems. Compensation for teachers rose dramatically, starting to become a wage that reflected the complexity of their work: between 1918 and 1926 average salaries doubled, from $1,023 to $2,046.[3]

Public health received similar attention to that Smith afforded education. Conditions in state hospitals were terrible: between 1904 and 1923 the number of patients had increased by eighteen thousand while new construction provided only six thousand additional beds. Brooklyn State Hospital housed 1,177 patients in a facility designed to barely handle 637; at Kings Park Hospital for the mentally ill, the patients were kept confined during the summer months because there were not enough attendants to watch them if they went outside.[4]

Two weeks after Al's inauguration, however, the Manhattan State Hospital burned down. The overcrowded building, a wooden structure dating back to 1853, took twenty-five lives with it—inmates and employees—and focused attention on the condition of the state's medical facilities.[5]

Smith saw beyond the immediate tragedy, and decided to use this opportunity to change how the state financed all major social projects, not just hospitals. In the past, these had been provided for out of existing revenues and in a piecemeal fashion, which stalled most large efforts. Advocates claimed that this was simply a means of controlling spending, a pay-as-you-go approach. Al understood the limits of this method claiming that under the existing system, you did not pay and you did not go. Instead, he suggested floating bond issues, expressly targeting specific items that required long-range, expensive funding.

One of his first proposed bond issues was $50 million for medical buildings of all sorts, including facilities for tuberculosis victims, the mentally ill, crippled children, and epileptics. To support these efforts, Al and Belle Moskowitz—one of the countrys' great innovators in public relations advocacy—created a blue-ribbon Citizens' Committee to lead the fight. This body produced a handbook 115 pages chock full of data, and had five thousand copies made up to equip speakers all over the state. Under their aegis, half a million leaflets got printed and distributed, plus seventy-five thousand posters calling for a yes vote, which the transit companies agreed to post for free on all buses, subways, trolleys, and ferries in New York City; Boy Scouts posted them up on telephone poles. Dr. Franklin Williams, director of the National Committee for Mental Hygiene, remarked that "whether one read his newspaper, or took a ride in the subway, or opened his mail, the Bond Issue was there. The only place I didn't find it was when I took my bottle of milk in the morning from the doorstep." The bond measure passed.[6]

Governor Smith similarly sought long-term financial solutions to deal with housing, but with less success. Ever since his first term and the postwar housing shortage, Smith understood the desperate need for new residential construction. Between 1914 and 1924 average rents in New York City had gone up by 67 percent. At the same time, average weekly factory earnings had gone down, from $28.93 in October 1920 to $27.40 in 1924. New construction in Manhattan in 1919 was only 144 apartment units, compared to 4,077 in 1917, so that by 1921 the vacancy rate in New York City apartments was an unbelievable 0.15 percent (the federal government defines a tight housing market as having a 6.0 percent vacancy rate or less).[7]

Smith remained too much of a conservative to believe that government should build its own housing; for him the problem was how to spur private industry to increase construction. That did not mean, however, that he was willing to let the marketplace function without intervention; for too many years he had seen where that approach led. As Al put it, "There is no legislation that will make houses grow on empty lots," but "home, everyone must have."[8]

Because of this limited vision, Smith attacked only two secondary problems which had contributed to the housing shortage: the difficulty of acquiring large plots of land; and the interest rates on capital (which in turn affected rents). Al and his advisers proposed the creation of a state housing board and a state housing bank, which would work in tandem. The board would first consider proposals from a newly formed category of limited dividend corporations; upon approval, it would ask the bank to draw on the credit and powers of the state and issue low-rate tax-exempt bonds, as well as condemning the property and taking possession.[9]

This plan, passed in 1926, had modest goals and produced modest results. The grim reality, then and later, was that low-income people really could not afford rents that made even limited dividend projects feasible, and that some mechanism would have to be created to have the state directly take on this burden. It would, in fact, require a more progressive decade to enact a different concept of public housing. But in the context of the twenties, the New York bill remained the only one of its kind in the nation; the *Emporia Gazette* (Kansas) complained that Smith's plan "goes further than either [Theodore] Roosevelt or LaFollette ever went in state control of an industry."[10]

The parks of Smith's administration would also become famous, but here it was Robert Moses, soon to become both the greatest user and abuser of land space in the history of New York City, who would lead the way. When Moses broached his grand schemes, Smith told his young aide that he was trying to sell New York a fur overcoat when what it really needed was red flannel underwear—that a few small parks would do the trick. But Moses piled Smith into a touring car and took him for long rides all through the natural scenery of a complex and varied state, and especially, to the beautiful shorelines of Long Island. Al caught from Moses the vision of parklands, places where working people could go to escape the city and enjoy the breezes.[11]

Smith responded with his usual combination of administrative reform and expansion of the state's welfare function, all wrapped in a concern for the average citizen. He created a State Council of Parks, with Moses as chairman, to consolidate work in this area and do regional planning, and appointed to it the grand old Republican patricians who had been fighting this battle for decades.

He then acquired the land via a $15 million bond issue approved by the citizenry in 1924; this enabled the state to create the magnificent Bear Mountain Park along the Hudson River and buy seven thousand acres on Long Island to build a network of fifteen parks, as opposed to the one that existed there in 1923. Local millionaires opposed his plan and confronted the governor in his office, prompting a famous line that summed up Smith's approach to his job and his constituency. When one of their stalwarts, Horace Havemeyer, claimed that the new parks meant that his town, East Islip, might be "overrun with rabble from the city," the mood became ice, as Al's eyes flashed. "Rabble?" he bellowed, "That's *me* you're talking about." Havemeyer tried desperately to change the tone with a feeble joke, "Why, where's a poor millionaire to go nowadays if he wants to be alone?" Al told the rich man to try the Harlem River Hospital, an institution for the mentally insane, and signed the appropriation.[12]

And while Governor Smith often initiated changes in how the state operated, sometimes he had to respond as technology created new challenges. Al grew up, for example, in a world where lighting came from gas fixtures, and transportation meant the two wheels of a bicycle or the four legs of a horse; by the time he started his second term in 1923, however, both electricity and cars had become commonplace.

Electricity was a major change. In 1907 only 8 percent of American homes were wired; by 1920 half had achieved this status. If this meant great national achievement, there were ominous overtones as well—concerns over robber barons and monopolies. Small power companies seemed to have a tendency to vanish in this era, swallowed up by giant trusts, and between 1919 and 1927, thirty-seven hundred utility companies disappeared nationwide. Instead, by 1929, sixteen utility holding companies controlled over 90 percent of America's electrical power capacity.[13]

For Al Smith, electric power was no boring discussion of engineering; he saw the utility question as being not about watts and ohms but over a basic issue of democracy. Once again, he raised the question of how the state would ensure that each citizen got a fair shake in the allocation of what was now one of the necessities of life. In his 1924 annual message, the governor began this debate by warning that if the state's water power potential were turned over solely to private interests, "monopoly may be created more powerful and more sinister than any which this country has known before."[14]

Smith wanted to set up a joint public corporation, similar to the Port Authority of New York and New Jersey, to develop the state's resources. This body would build and then operate the actual facilities under the great rivers and dams, and run lines to local utilities; these entities could then buy their power from the state at lower rates, enabling them to reduce the price they charged customers. In this notion, Smith echoed the concepts of many western governors and legislators who also had to confront this issue; but New York, which contained such magnificent potential sites as Niagara Falls, was one of the few northeastern states that also created a progressive plan to deal with this issue, and by so doing, helped to lay the groundwork for future projects like the New Deal's Tennessee Valley Authority.[15]

Another opportunity and challenge created by technology was the motorcar. During Al's years as governor, the state—and all of American society—underwent a revolution of historic proportions as it entered the age of the automobile; in 1916 there were already 134,000 motor vehicles licensed in New York, but by 1922 the figure was over 1 million, a growth of 650 percent in nine years that showed no signs of ebbing. Sadly, by the later date there were already 1,715 fatalities in auto accidents, and people started talking about problems deadly familiar to later generations, such as driving under the influence of alcohol or narcotic drugs.[16]

By 1923 Governor Smith had gotten passed the basic structure of regulation that still exists today—the general motor vehicle law that requires every automobile operator to have a driver's license. The next year he created the modern bureaucracy to administer this law, starting with a motor vehicle commissioner and various other officers, giving them the power to revoke licenses and setting in place the system that would eventually be summed up by the dreaded initials, DMV. And to keep the traffic flowing, by 1928 appropriations for roads had increased fivefold over what they were when Smith entered office. A system of three thousand miles of new highway had been constructed.[17]

Houses and parks and cars were all important, but in the long run Al Smith never lost sight that his job was about using government to help the people of New York. In an era when American politics—American life—was being transformed by the long-overdue initiation of new groups into the body politic, there was an even greater way that Al could be of service to the men and women whom he had always seen as his primary constituency: by becoming their foremost spokesperson and champion. Over and over, he told audiences, "The flag stands for equal opportunity. It left open the gateway of opportunity irrespective of race, creed, or color." Al used to explain that "the country is just as dependent upon the city as the city is dependent upon the country." It was not the immigrant tenement dweller who was besmirching the American shores but rather the nativist bigot, whom he branded as "unpatriotic and unAmerican." And he did this at a time when America was closing the doors to newcomers with particularly biased legislation like the Immigration Acts of 1921 and 1924, when it was potential suicide for any politician with national ambitions to say such things.[18]

Those concerns did not deter Al Smith. In a decade of forgettable presidents, he was the immigrants' hero. Nathan Glazer and Daniel Patrick Moynihan wrote that "Al Smith came close to being for the people of the Lower East Side of America" what Lincoln and Jackson had been for the men and women of the frontier—the one individual who opened up the doors of America to them.[19]

If Al was the hero and ideal of all the immigrants, it was because he was able to see their needs as individuals and make specific efforts to meet them. In Smith's day, Jews had come to New York in unprecedented numbers. As a youngster on the Bowery, he had grown up around them and then defended them as neighbors; Eddie Cantor recalled that when "tough, heavy-set men of the alleys . . . would throw a rock at an old peddler merely because he had a beard . . . Al Smith would come to the old man's aid and put his arm around him like a brother." "It was the downright, simple heroics of the thing," Cantor explained, "that struck the slum boys with wonder." Later, the *Jewish Daily News* complimented him on his support for a bill asking President Woodrow Wilson to veto an anti-immigration measure. They reported that "certain Assemblymen from up-state had intended to speak against the resolution, but Alfred E. Smith . . . delivered such a fiery charge in favor of the resolution that the opponents lost courage to carry out their intentions." What an *Irisher mensch!* What a hero![20]

Later, as Smith assumed the roles of state and even national leader, his ties to the Jewish community grew. He understood deeply that they shared the same antagonists—that the bigots who despised Jews were not likely to invite Al

Smith in for a cup of tea either. Former governor Hugh Carey used to tell the story of how Al once joined an elite country club to play golf, and showed up with Judge Mitchell May; May happened to be Jewish. They were about to tee off when club officials took Al aside and quietly explained, "Governor, this is a restricted club, we don't have Jewish members." Just as simply, the governor informed *them*, "I don't know if you have Jewish members or not, but Mitchell May and I are playing, or this place will be a state park in a month." They played through, and the club changed its policy.[21]

There was also the very obvious fact that Al had surrounded himself with Jews. Of his three key advisers—Joseph Proskauer, Belle Moskowitz, and Robert Moses—all were, in fact, members of this religious/ethnic group. This in itself drove the old Irish pols of Tammany Hall batty, and they composed a vengeful ditty that ended with the nasty refrain, "And now the brains of Tammany Hall . . . are Moskie and Proskie and Mo-ses."

What made this even worse was that the one ethnic group, ironically, that Smith did not fight so diligently for was the Irish. The fact was, for all of the governor's Gaelic pride and his personal identity as a son of the Emerald Isle, Al's Irish ethnicity was primarily sentimental and did not extend to the politics of Ireland.

Al attended, of course, the post-World War I meetings calling for Ireland's freedom from Great Britain, and even headed an organization to raise funds for impoverished Irish women and children. But the emphasis remained on relief, and the speeches were somewhat lightweight, with none of the revolutionary rhetoric that marked this debate. When Irish political leader Eamon de Valera came to the United States in 1920, Al met him in the capital and served lunch in the governor's mansion, but the mayor of Albany gave the official public reception. Similarly, when Irish leaders called on Smith to commute the sentence of Jim Larkin, a revolutionary spokesperson as well as Industrial Workers of the World official who had been convicted for preaching, rather than practicing, ideals labeled as "anarchy," Al refused to discuss any notion of Irish patriotism. Several months later, he did in fact commute Larkin's sentence to term served, but that was because Larkin's crime was one of freedom of speech, because Larkin had been a model prisoner, and above all, because of the dissent by several judges of the court of appeals, including one by Benjamin Cardozo.[22]

Al Smith refused, in other words, to ever consider his heritage as a force for separating people, refused to engage in what later generations would call race baiting. This stood out in sharp contrast to the ethnic demagogues of this era, men like James Michael Curley of Boston, who built most of his career by attacking the descendants of England in every speech he gave to the descendants of Ireland. Al, on the other hand, had his secretary correct the statement that he planned to speak on behalf of the Irish Republican Army's efforts against Britain; "the people . . . who gave out this statement to the newspapers," George Van Namee made clear, "had no authority from the governor to do so."[23]

Thus, Al's Irish identity, no matter how strong, remained cultural and nostalgic rather than political or nationalistic. The records of the American-Irish Historical Society in New York City, for example, whose motto reads, "That The World May Know," indicate very little contact with the state's leading Irishman; Smith did not even join until 1930. This vision was in turn tempered by the fact that Al truly considered himself to be an Irish-*American;* when speakers would claim that the Irish made America, Al replied with total sincerity that this was false, because of "the undeniable fact that this country was presented to civilization by God Himself."

Because Al's ethnic identity was warm and fuzzy he also tended toward stereotypes. Paul O'Dwyer, one of New York's great reformers and a true student of his own heritage (late in life, he made sure that his law office offered academic journals of Irish history in the waiting room in addition to the usual magazines), noted that Smith had very little contact with people who were actually working to support the Irish freedom movement; Smith showed no interest, so as a result, "we didn't trust him." Even worse, O'Dwyer told about the time the YMCA asked him to speak at a St. Patrick's Day celebration. The caller from the Y remarked that St. Patrick must be just about the most famous Irishman ever. O'Dwyer, who knew his stuff, pointed out that St. Patrick was not really Irish, was originally a slave, and that he probably came from Brittany. Then the caller mentioned that at least they were serving a real Irish meal—corned beef and cabbage. O'Dwyer replied that this was not at all Irish, but merely working-class food, the cheapest meat and vegetables available, and that the Irish were just the poorest people around. And so it went for several more rounds. Word of the conversation got out, however, and when March 17 rolled around, Al Smith got up at the annual dinner of the Friendly Sons of St. Patrick to castigate "some young whippersnapper" who had the effrontery to say such foolish things and challenge Al's simple, treasured images.[24]

If the situation with the Irish was complicated, Al's relationship with nonimmigrant groups like African-Americans was even more complex, reflecting both ambiguities within Smith himself, and the tension of race relations in American society as a whole.

In the decades after the Civil War and emancipation, African-Americans in New York had, like their brethren across the United States, followed the party of Lincoln and of liberation, the Republicans. They joined in the crusades against Tammany Hall and supported reformers of all kinds. In 1898, however, Boss Richard Croker founded the United Colored Democracy, the first black Tammany club. He then chose Edward Lee, chief bellman at the Murray Hill Hotel, to head this branch of the Hall, and began to meet with Lee regularly.

There is no question that this was a legitimate effort on the part of Tammany leadership, at least in terms of their world and its value system. Jobs flowed in the standard way as soon as the voting strength of black citizens started to become organized and apparent. Their rewards were numerous and wide ranging, and the effort to gain employment for Tammany supporters even included putting pressure on contractors. African-Americans, in the era that Al came of age in New York politics, gained appointments as assistant corporation counsel and assistant district attorney, as well as the usual positions of janitors and elevator operators in public buildings. Ten blacks got taken on by the Docks Department, and another forty became streetsweepers. The construction of the New York subway system, whose builders were usually recipients of Tammany contracts, meant the employment of five hundred black Democratic Party stalwarts. Lee himself became a deputy in the sheriff's office.[25]

In 1915 the leadership of the United Colored Democracy shifted to Ferdinand Q. Morton. Morton, a graduate of Phillips Exeter Academy and Harvard University, became assistant district attorney heading up the Indictment Bureau, then gained appointment to the city's three-person Civil Service Commission with the formidable salary of $7,500. He served as the all-powerful political boss of Harlem from then until the 1930s, dispensing patronage and making sure that African-Americans represented black districts on the City Council and in the state legislative chambers as well.[26]

Morton and his organization delivered. Democratic mayoral candidate John Hylan received only 27 percent of the black vote in 1917, but got 70 percent four years later, about the same proportion of black votes Al Smith found in his camp in 1922. Even Marcus Garvey, head of the United Negro Improvement Association, found it worthwhile to align himself with Tammany's version of black democracy.[27]

As with Jews, Al's attitude toward blacks was formed in part by the influences of his neighborhood. Al's father used to talk about the great draft riot of 1863 and how, as a volunteer fireman, he had worked not only to douse the flames but also to calm and disperse violent crowds. On one occasion he cut down a black victim whom the mob had strung up, just in time to save his life, and then removed the man to safety. Another time he gathered in two blacks who were pursued by a mob that was stoning them, hid the men in barrels, then loaded them into his truck, and carried them over to Brooklyn on ferryboats. According to the account given by Al and his sister, Mamie, Alfred used to assert, "They are children of God . . . and they have a right to live."[28]

Smith's own childhood memories of blacks also reflected his belief that the local scene was hidebound, but fundamentally tolerant. Al used to tell the story about what happened when the local police station hired its first African-American patrolman. At first his fellow officers shunned him, but gradually this changed to respect and even friendship, while another black officer rose to the rank of Captain. This was Al's old notion of the good urban community that, in time, overcame its prejudice and gave in to the apparent qualities manifest in all human beings, regardless of their race, religion, or color.[29]

By the time Al became governor, however, things had changed a bit. Between 1920 and 1930 the black population of New York State had more than doubled, from 198,483 to 412,814; roughly 75 percent of that total lived in New York City.[30]

In office, Al Smith offered the black community the usual forms of recognition, viewing their veterans as they marched home from France, or greeting five thousand blacks attending the national meeting of the segregated branch of the United Order of Odd Fellows when they convened in New York City. Smith had no qualms about showing up at a large meeting in a Harlem church, and many of his long-standing issues for immigrants—such as a belief in volunteer organizations and his opposition to the literacy test—found a ready audience there. In 1922, after following torchlight processions up Seventh Avenue to Liberty Hall in Harlem, Smith told the crowd that if he were reelected to Albany, the executive office would be open to "any group of people and they shall receive every consideration that one man can give another." This was no more—but also no less—than he had offered any other group.[31]

But did he in fact make good on that offer? American history has often been a story where African-Americans remained in a unique position of promises made to all newcomers being broken in their case alone, of the long hard road that immigrants followed being closed just to them.

Smith's record was mixed. Although he continued to give out jobs at the lower levels, in an administration that assiduously appointed women as well as men, Jews as well as gentiles, there was no black appointment of any note. The black newspaper, the *Amsterdam News*, which remained Republican despite the shift of voters, saw many problems, and editorialized in 1926 that Al was "a cool, calculating politician who will let nothing stand between him and his desire to be named by his party for the presidency."[32]

This ambivalence stemmed, above all, from the fact that Smith was being pulled by several different instincts and influences. On the one hand, he knew just how explosive race was in American life—that this issue more than any other could cause riots and make—or destroy—a politician's career. This would become particularly true the closer he got to the bid for the presidency in 1928, running in a party that depended for its electoral base on a solid, racist South.

Countering this were several other factors. Many of his advisers had superior records on what later became known as civil rights, and Henry Moskowitz's positions on these issues were so advanced that he became one of the founding members of the National Association for the Advancement of Colored People.

At least as important, those who opposed black rights also opposed Al Smith and everything he stood for, in the nastiest way possible, and Al could never let that pass. Bishop James Cannon of the Methodist church, one of the country's leading prohibition advocates and a dedicated Smith hater, made it a point to survey New York saloons by going up to Harlem, reinforcing racial stereotypes. One of the most important findings of his trip (besides the availability of alcohol), was that blacks were extremely enthusiastic about Governor Smith, a reversal from their historic position as Republicans. Cannon blamed this on the fact that Smith supported alcohol, which blacks seemed to desire.[33]

Such calumny brought out the best in Al Smith. Writing to a prohibition leader, he discussed the Declaration of Independence, then added that this document "drew no color line and, certainly, it was intended to refer to all citizens whether born under the flag or whether brought under it by an oath of allegiance."[34]

Regarding race, in other words, Al Smith remained a typical, reasonably liberal politician of the time. His better instincts included African-Americans under his umbrella of American citizenship, but the incredible cost of such sentiments in an age of Jim Crowism made him refrain from pushing the matter too far.

Al's attempts to deal with inclusion, to forge a new America, had to confront issues of class as well as those of ethnicity and race. His earlier experiences in the Triangle Shirtwaist investigation led him to embrace the most fundamental principle of the labor movement, that human beings were more than an item in the ledger sheets of business. In several speeches, including his major annual messages, he asserted over and over that "the state should by statute declare that the labor of a human being is not a commodity or an article of commerce."[35]

Smith supported labor in two ways: First, he promoted measures that raised the standard of living of working men and women. But in addition, he made sure that their organizations, the labor unions, received a fair shake in the halls of government, something far from taken for granted in an era when Calvin Coolidge sat in the White House and the "American Plan" meant an antilabor open shop. Al instead fought to curb the scope of injunctions and refused to use the state police as strikebreakers, no matter how insistent manufacturers became. If violence erupted during a labor conflict, troopers would show up, but with strict instructions to do their duty in a fair and evenhanded manner.[36]

When necessary, his intervention could be a lot more dramatic than that. One of the most important industries in New York was the manufacturing of ladies' clothing, but it was also the most contentious. Composed of a myriad of small shops, difficult to organize either by workers' representatives or manufacturers' associations, this was the cutthroat business that gave America the term *sweatshop*.

As early as the first days of 1920, Governor Smith called representatives of both the Cloak and Suit Manufacturers Protective Association and the International Ladies Garment Workers Union (ILGWU) to his office to avert a strike, an effort so successful that Joseph Barondess, one of the founders of the ILGWU, telegraphed Smith, "You undertook to solve this perplexing problem and did the job well."[37]

The odds that any kind of peace would last were about as good as that skirt lengths would remain the same for more than one season. The two, in fact, were directly related, as cutthroat competition, the most horrible open market, drove conditions back to the bottom, and the workers to a renewed interest in strikes. By 1924 forty thousand workers prepared to shut down two thousand companies, and Smith appointed a commission to investigate and advise. The governor's reputation for integrity was enough to get the union to postpone the strike, and in time, the commission implemented unemployment insurance for clothing workers, as well as setting up a permanent bureau of research to keep track of conditions in the industry.[38]

But eventually, Smith's most important contribution to labor was a remarkable individual named Frances Perkins. She came out of the finest background possible: born in Boston, raised in Worcester as a Congregationalist, a graduate of Mount Holyoke College. Al first met her when she came to Albany in 1910 on behalf of the Consumers' League, lobbying for a bill to limit the hours of workingmen and children to fifty-four hours a week. A few years later, she became his chief investigator in the Triangle work, and the two developed a strong bond based on mutual respect. Perkins recognized Al for his good instincts regarding the people of the state and for his capacity for leadership, claiming that in many ways he was superior to Franklin Roosevelt. This was pretty fancy talk, given the fact that it was FDR who took the revolutionary step of appointing Perkins as his secretary of labor, the first woman cabinet member in U.S. history. Smith on the other hand, recognized just how smart and dedicated she was—a strong, honest woman he could trust with secrets and trust with his ideals. The old line used to go that when someone asked how Al Smith knew so much, insiders would tell him it was because he read a book. When the newcomer asked the title, the reply came, "He knew Frances Perkins and she was a book." People who worked with Perkins at the end of her life, at the School of Industrial Relations at Cornell University, remembered how she still talked of him with deep reverence and affection.[39]

Shortly after the 1918 election, while he was still technically head of New York City's Board of Aldermen, Al Smith wrote Frances Perkins to thank her for her support and added, "I get much satisfaction from the fact that I know I can call on you for help." When Smith took office that year, he found that the leading state organization that handled industrial matters was the Department of Labor, headed by a five-member Industrial Commission appointed by the governor. Shortly after the inauguration, he appointed Perkins to this body, and her hometown paper headlined, "Fanny Perkins, Former Worcester Girl Gets $8,000 Job and Starts a Rumpus."[40]

In truth, Perkins's job was actually to end any rumpus that might shut down part of the state's economy and put people out of work, rather than to start one. Al soon assigned her to handle a strike in Rome, New York; this was a small but potentially violent event, where one-sixth of the entire workforce was on the picket lines, battling a collection of copper companies for the eight-hour day and decent wages. Mostly Italian immigrants with limited English, these men had no organization and no strike fund, but had somehow managed to stay out peacefully for two months, until July 14, when they rioted and knifed a mill owner. The mayor called for the state police; Smith sent some troopers, and then asked Perkins to go as well.[41]

It is not clear if Al knew it, but he was sending this woman into a war zone. Because of the violence in town, which had now escalated to firearms, the conductor on the local train normally refused to stop in Rome, so Perkins made him pull up and open his doors just to let her off. She then flagged a taxi to go into town, but the driver insisted on lowering his convertible top and making her stand up on the seat cushions, so that everyone could see she was not a scab. At one point, a group of armed workers stopped them, and Perkins and the assistant who accompanied her made brief speeches about their identity and their mission. This was sufficient, and the strikers let them go on.

Perkins got all sides to talk to her; some of the strike leaders even revealed that their men had acquired dynamite and were not afraid to use it. But the owners still refused to negotiate with strikers in any fashion, so she came up with the idea of calling the governor and suggesting that he send the entire Industrial Commission down to hold hearings. Al liked the idea but did not know if he had the power to give that order to an independent body, so Frances quoted chapter and verse to convince him. Smith now made his move, pulling out the police and sending in investigators and arbitrators instead. Perkins had not mentioned the explosives in these conversations, and with state intervention of a different sort on the way, workers quietly threw their fireworks into a nearby canal. Faced with pressure and publicity, the manufacturers gave in to the strike demands.

But in fact, it was the team of Al and Frances that was the real dynamite. As early as 1920, under their tutelage, the New York State approach to labor enforcement was the envy of the nation. In that year forty-five states had factory inspection laws, but most of them were weakly enforced. Colorado and Connecticut each had only four inspectors, while Indiana employed five and Iowa had two. Even major industrial states like Michigan thought to hire only nineteen inspectors; Ohio used thirty-five of them, and Pennsylvania fifty-one. New

York, on the other hand, maintained the largest organization of its kind by far in the country, a task force of 123 inspectors.[42]

Workers appreciated Al for his efforts on their behalf, and he incorporated their needs and concerns into his plans as well. The very first piece of real estate he ever bought during his four terms as governor was for the Labor Department; in 1927 he told his cabinet that when he had started in the governor's mansion, "there wasn't an office building in the City of New York that would let the Labor Department into it; let the fellows coming in there with their heads and arms tied up and smelling of iodoform all over the place and the mob of people in and out." As a result of the sights and smells (iodoform, by the way, was a particularly smelly antiseptic dressing), "all the people in the rest of the offices were threatening to quit if the Labor Department wasn't put out." Al felt that workers had a right to state services, and if the only way for them to get these was by buying a building, then so be it.[43]

And the unions responded. As early as his 1915 bid for sheriff, Samuel Gompers and Rabbi Stephen Wise were already telling the *New York Morning Telegraph* that "labor should stand by Smith as a friend." As governor he enjoyed the endorsements of the State Federation of Labor and the four railroad unions every time he made the race.[44]

Al understood labor's fears as he understood his own, and met with success for the same reasons; theirs were the same problems he had confronted as a young man in the industrial city and later as a reforming legislator. But as governor, Al Smith also had to confront one of the most powerful social forces of the century, women's bid for equality, and here he had mixed instincts indeed.

In part, Al inherited his ideas on women from his Irish heritage and late-nineteenth-century upbringing. The world of the famine Irish that Al's mother was born into, and that she in turn imparted to her son, taught that strong women could be accepted, although not always appreciated, in all relationships involving gender. As Hasia Diner has pointed out in her pioneering study of Irish-American women, sisters, wives, and mothers were expected to hold the family together, to exercise and use responsibility to preserve the basic structure of the most fundamental unit of society. They could speak back to men—engage them in physical combat if necessary—and could pursue their own career and economic goals. Al's mother, widowed early on, had taken up the reins and seen to it that her family was always taken care of.[45]

Because of this background, Al accepted women in many positions of power, and according to historian Susan Ware, during this era, "One of the few places where women secured more than a token position in politics was the Democratic party in New York State," which included such leading figures as Eleanor Roosevelt, Molly Dewson, Caroline O'Day, Elinor Morgenthau, Nancy Cook, and Marion Dickerman. Frances Perkins told of the number of rich and socially established women Smith converted to the Democratic Party when they came to him to discuss some matter of social policy, such as child labor or shorter working hours for women. Obviously the governor agreed with their position, but there was much more; his total lack of cant meant that he treated them with honesty and sincerity, and hence, equality.[46]

But working against this was his Victorian sense that women were different, more fragile, and had to be protected. Some of this had its positive aspects; combined with his devotion to Katie, Al remained throughout his life a paragon of rectitude, and not even a hint of scandal has ever been attached to his name. Perkins described him as a "very correct man—very correct." She explained that he "had the highest standards of how ladies should be treated. The business of being chummy with ladies who came up to Albany . . . never crossed his mind. . . . He followed the strictest principles and there was none of this get-gay stuff that you see around." In a lifetime of working together, he never addressed Perkins by her first name.[47]

But that same propriety implied a sense that women were more delicate, and even had to be shielded from the coarseness of male behavior. Perkins told the story of the first time Al invited her to a business meeting; it was held at a restaurant in New York City, attended by a number of high level government officials, all of them male. When Al showed up, however, he had brought along Katie and his mother; after introducing them to Frances, Al took Perkins aside and explained, "There were to be ladies present tonight [Belle Moskowitz would also be there], so I asked my wife and mother to come." Al would never attempt to include women in such a setting without the proper chaperons.[48]

This ambivalence even affected Smith's relationship with Moskowitz. In his tribute to his senior aide after her death, Al argued that "women in politics sometimes make the mistake of not being themselves and imitating men. In Mrs. Belle Moskowitz the opposite was true." Even though she had one of the finest brains of anyone he knew, Smith maintained, "she was essentially a wife and a mother. . . . She demonstrated that participation by women in public life does not involve any of their essential feminine qualities."[49]

With Perkins, too, there was never any question of his respect for her talents; but while Smith truly wanted to get her a seat on the Industrial Commission, he could not accept her as the head of that organization, could not believe that a woman would act effectively in a position where she had to order male executives about.

Thus, Al hesitated for several years before he appointed her to commissioner, the top spot. When the position opened up in 1924, leading women reformers launched a major lobbying campaign to get Perkins named to the position. Florence Kelley of the National Consumers League wrote him, as did Mary Dreier, who had served with Al back on the Factory Investigating Commission. Dreier called Perkins an obvious choice. "It is needless to tell you of her qualifications," she said. "You know them as well as I and I feel sure that you too appreciate how eminently fitted she is for this position." She addressed the gender issue as well, arguing at first, "Frankly, I don't know any man as well qualified as is she," but then added, "I realize the fact that she is a woman is an obstacle but I also know that you have been willing to pioneer with courage when giving a place to a woman if she is qualified." Eleanor Roosevelt also wrote, and the pressure became so strong that Perkins became embarrassed, writing Al a hand-penned note that her recommenders had acted without her knowledge or consent, and suggesting that he ignore the petitions.

Despite Perkins's gentility, she truly was the best person to lead the commission in 1924, and the women who wrote to Smith were powerful and respected; some of them, like Dreier, were old friends whom he normally listened to. Nevertheless, he refused to make the appointment, and it was not until 1926 that Al Smith named Perkins to take over the Industrial Board. Three years later, when Al's successor as governor, Franklin Roosevelt, planned to name Perkins to his cabinet, Al objected, saying, "men will take advice from a woman, but it is hard for them to take orders from a woman."[50]

These contradictory instincts placed him squarely in the middle of a running dispute in feminist politics, one that persevered long after he left the scene and affected his standing with various advocacy factions. Many women reformers, then and, later, argued that women must be considered equal in all matters dealing with commerce, and, above all, equal under the system of laws that govern city, state, and nation. This was the position taken by advocates of women's suffrage, as well as other crusaders who argued that any qualification based on gender was illegal. Other feminists, however, back then and consistently over time, argued that women really were biologically different, and that they therefore were suited to different roles in society, and entitled to a different form of protection. Examples of these advocates ranged from Jane Addams, who argued that women must lead the peace movement, to those who fought for restricted conditions for women and children in the factory. These issues were so controversial in Al Smith's time that Nancy Cott, in her superb study of the women's movement, stated that "women's efforts in the 1910s and 1920s laid the groundwork and exposed the faultlines of modern feminism."[51]

In some ways, Al Smith fit perfectly in the camp of those who perceived women as different members of the human race and thus subject to a different set of laws. Back in his days in the legislature, his work on the Factory Investigating Commission made him a leader in improving working conditions for women and children, often by restricting their role in the workplace. Later as governor,

Smith signed a law that women elevator operators could not be required to work after ten o'clock at night and that their hours could not exceed fifty-four a week, stating, "The conservation of the health of women and minors who have to work is an important duty of the state." The next year he vetoed a bill removing restrictions preventing women from being employed at night in printing plants. He remarked at one point, "I believe in equality, but I cannot nurse a baby," and also argued that women had to be protected because they could not organize themselves into unions, in part because of discrimination by these organizations, but in part because their own goals were to raise a family.[52]

Decisions such as these were warmly received by some but not all of the feminists in that era. Women like Florence Kelley claimed that sex-based legislation was a necessity, that "so long as men cannot be mothers . . . legislation adequate for them can never be adequate for wage-earning women." Industrial reformer Alice Hamilton echoed Smith's concerns about conditions and the lack of organization when she argued on behalf of "the great inarticulate body of working women," who were "largely helpless," a group that had "very special needs which unaided they cannot attain," that "it would be a crime . . . to pass legislation which would not only make it impossible to better their lot . . . but would even deprive them of the small measure of protection they now enjoy."[53]

But this position entirely alienated Smith from the other group of feminists, who believed that women must be equal before the law. These advocates found their form of expression in the National Women's Party, headed by Alice Paul. They lobbied vigorously against any limitations on women's hours or conditions of employment, and in 1928 endorsed Herbert Hoover against Al Smith, because of the latter's positions on the rights and restrictions of women under state law.[54]

Their viewpoint was partially, but not entirely fair. Smith was never dogmatic on this, and championed and then signed a bill banning sexual discrimination in the salary schedules for public school teachers. In his message accompanying the bill's approval, Smith wrote bluntly, "I am unable to understand why a woman performing the same duties as a man should receive less compensation for her services"; he also saw to it that bills were passed banning such practices from the civil service code as well.[55]

These same kinds of paradoxes even occurred in Al's stance on the era's most crucial issue, women's suffrage. Al was, by nature, opposed to extending the vote to ladies. Hugh Carey explained that in the world Al Smith grew up in, voting was an honor, an exciting ritual; "the very entry into the system, of being able to cast a vote, of being counted . . . was a prize," one that should only go to the head of the household. Besides upholding male hegemony, this also maintained domestic tranquility, they argued, since husbands and wives could not fight over their choices.[56]

Lots of people agreed with these beliefs, most notably Catherine Mulvihill

Smith. Al's mother was "violently" opposed to women voting, and swore that if the issue ever came before the people, they would soundly defeat any such proposition. When the vote finally did come for women, she declared loudly that she would never exercise that particular franchise. Love for a son, of course, overrode all such notions, and when Al ran for governor shortly after, she was one of the first five people in her district to register. But her earlier views must have still influenced the future state chief executive, and even Al's daughter remarked that he never seemed to discuss this much around the house.[57]

At least as important, Tammany Hall stood four-square against women in politics as Al came of age within the organization, and mentors like Tom Foley and Charlie Murphy were outspoken in their resistance to this reform. By the time Al started rising in the ranks, Tammany men viewed suffragettes as a form of urban loon, and Al told how, back when he was serving subpoenas on his first Tammany job, he had to deliver a notice of jury duty to one of these creatures. She invited him in and then proceeded to read a formal lecture on women's rights, after which she informed him that he ought to tell everyone from the commissioner of jurors to the Supreme Court that she would not serve on any jury until women had achieved full rights of citizenship.[58]

But times were changing, and the old ward bosses were, more often than not, practical rather than ideological. In 1915, New York State had its first referendum on the women's suffrage amendment, a proposal to amend the state constitution, and it failed to carry the popular vote. Both New York City and the upstate districts voted in the negative, and it is likely that most of the Tammany sachems opposed it, although Murphy, already hedging his bets, allowed suffragettes to use the clubrooms for meetings.[59]

The next time the referendum appeared was in 1917, and by now Tammany saw the handwriting on the wall, and came out solidly for the rights of women. A large part of this was because of the work of the state's chapter of the Women's Suffrage Party (WSP). They had distributed 2.9 million pieces of literature in 1915; this time they would hand out 5.2 million leaflets and flyers, almost 2 million in Manhattan alone. They covered every major public event, and even made it a point to target all the standard forms of working-class recreation: baseball games, boxing matches, and amusement parks like Coney Island.[60]

Of particular concern to Tammany, the suffragettes also played a very smart game of ethnic politics, being sure to always use speakers who could address groups in their respective native tongues. Jewish areas, Tammany's perennial concern, were especially targeted, but in Irish districts they changed the banners from suffrage yellow (which might look like the hated color orange) to a beautiful shade of green. Mary Donnelley spoke in those areas, and there was a Polish band available for rallies held anywhere that *Polski* brethren might show up.[61]

In 1917, the referendum passed in the city, but failed in the upstate counties.

The five-borough margin was large enough, however, to carry the measure statewide, and New York became the first major industrial state to adopt suffrage. It was clear that urban, immigrant, working-class districts had put the measure over the top. Two years later, newly elected governor Alfred E. Smith, carried along by this bandwagon, called a special session of the legislature and asked it to ratify the Nineteenth Amendment to the U.S. Constitution. Smith claimed that women deserved the vote, and that affirmation of this right would make New York a model for the rest of the nation. Suffrage passed both houses of the legislature, with a unanimous vote on each occasion.[62]

The record, thus, remains mixed, and produces more good questions about Smith's positions than there are good answers. Which was he: a social or an egalitarian feminist? One who embraced the differences of gender, or someone who advocated equality before the law? And were these differences real, or did he merely pick his decisions to win political points? When it came to women's issues, even suffrage, why did Al Smith seem to straddle the fence so badly?

The answer goes to the core of our understanding of Smith as a leader and as a politician. If there was one thing Al Smith never was or would be, it was a theorist. He simply wanted to make life better for the people of the State of New York, including its women. Al could not believe it was moral to allow women to work 119 hours a week, a condition he found in the canning factories back in his legislative investigations, and he thought children should go to school and not have to work. On the other hand, his basic compass of fair play also meant he could not accept discrimination against women either, regarding salaries, for example, or over the right of a woman to hold a government job when she could do the work. If these two sentiments revealed a contradiction, so be it. Smith would let the academics and the uptown thinkers worry about that, and see what he could do to make working women's lives better.

In the long run, the result of all these efforts was that Al Smith became governor, not just of New York, but of a new America, a place different in some ways from the nation it had been in the past. There were new languages now, and women had a right at the table too, no longer relegated to child rearing and the home. As industrialization transformed not just the Empire State, but America and the world, government had to respond, expressing the cares and concerns of the community, creating new programs to protect those who had found disadvantage, rather than prosperity, in the new economic order. And if the results of Governor Smith's efforts to produce an inclusionary democracy were mixed, it remained one of the first prolonged attempts by any politician to manage the change at all, an effort that helped in part make Al Smith an American leader.

Chapter 12

Prohibition

It was Al Smith's misfortune to be governor at a time when America confronted its greatest attempt to ever control citizens' private habits, an experiment known as prohibition. A triumph of the small town over Gotham, the movement had been founded, to a large extent, on bias against immigrants and city dwellers. As a result, Al Smith, with more reluctance than is usually realized, wound up becoming the national symbol of opposition to this ban on liquor.

By the late nineteenth century, the major national group calling for an end to alcoholic beverages was the Women's Christian Temperance Union, founded in 1874. Frances Willard, who took over in 1879 and truly was responsible for placing this cause on the national stage, remains a rich and complex character, far beyond the stereotype created by characters like the psychopathic, hatchet-handling Carrie Nation. Willard brilliantly used the issue of drink to open the doors of public life to a gender that had been notoriously locked in the private realm. How could women not become part of politics, she argued, when the major victims of the drunkard were his wife and children, the hearth and home whose safety had been entrusted to women? Using this as the basis for her attacks, she argued over and over that women should—*must*—be permitted to discuss, advocate, and even determine policies regarding safety, economics, sanitation, and, in fact, every other aspect of modern society. Throughout her life, for example, she kept on her desk a portrait of Terence Powderly, head of the Knights of Labor, the largest labor organization in the country prior to the American Federation of Labor. It was even said that on occasional trips to Europe, she was seen taking a sip or two of champagne. Alcohol, in other words, was merely a vehicle for Frances Willard to pursue larger changes.[1]

By the turn of the century, not only were women accepted players in the debate over prohibition, they were seen as leaders and, even more, the stalwarts of the movement. In December 1922, when the Women's Democratic Club of New York held a luncheon to honor returning first lady Katie Smith, the lead speaker could still quip that she knew that she was addressing a "100 percent women's audience" because there were no hip flasks present. The line was good for a chuckle, but there was truth to it too.[2]

Over time, however, Willard's influence diminished, and the WCTU got taken over by middle-class women whose husbands were losing ground in an industrializing economy. It became an organization of resentment, lashing out against mysterious forces that were changing the country to the detriment, they thought, of their class and their race. On the heels of this shift, in 1895, the institution that would eventually carry most of the fight for prohibition, the Anti-Saloon League, held its first meeting. It was this group that would push the movement in a number of powerful new directions, to short-term victory and historic defeat.[3]

Within less than a decade after its founding, the Anti-Saloon League was a powerful force, having organized chapters in thirty-eight states; by 1908 the staff included 250 field workers and 150 stenographers and clerks. By then the league's national organ, the *American Issue,* had a paid subscription list of 300,000 supporters; its main printing plant could turn out 1 million copies of the *Issue* every month, with capacity left over for pamphlets, books, pledge cards, and other advocacy works. Between 1909 and 1923 the American Issue Publishing Company cranked out an unbelievable 157 million periodicals, plus another 245 million other pieces.[4]

Many of these were handed out in church; early on, the League cemented an alliance with some of America's Protestant denominations. The one that became the bulwark of the prohibition movement was the Methodist Episcopal church, the largest religious organization in the United States. Second only to the Methodists were the Southern Baptists, followed by the American Baptist Home Mission Society. Other champions included the Disciples of Christ, the United Brethren church, and the Congregationalists. These churches all became chief components of the prohibition drive, with ministers using their sermons to deliver political as well as moral messages, providing as well a grass-roots network for distributing all the various forms of prohibition literature. Nationwide estimates of the number of churches supporting the drive at its height went as high as sixty thousand.[5]

There is no question how effective the league was. By 1908 two-thirds of the land area of the country was totally dry. In 1897, for example, the California chapter of the league began its efforts, and within less than a decade, six counties had voted themselves totally dry, as had one hundred municipalities; another six counties were roughly two-thirds dry.[6]

In order to accomplish this, however, the league and its allies among the religious and the women's groups had adopted some extremely questionable methods. Alcohol was always referred to as a poison, even though in moderate quantities it is no more than a mild sedative. Prohibition-enforced textbooks taught young children horror stories, how "a cat or dog may be killed by causing it to drink a small quantity of alcohol. A boy once drank from a flask he had found, and died in a few hours." For those who dared to touch the forbidden substance, death came swiftly and in a most terrible manner. One schoolbook explained that "when alcohol is constantly used, it may slowly change the muscles of the heart into fat. Such a heart . . . is sometimes so soft that a finger could easily be pushed through its walls." Just in case Junior or Sally did not get the full message, "You can think of what would happen if it is made to work a little harder than usual. It is liable to stretch and stop beating and this would cause sudden death." And this may have been the best of all scenarios, since (the league claimed) anyone who persisted in drink was likely to suffer genetic diseases, both for themselves and for their posterity; it was clear, for example, that "the children of those who drink have weak minds or become crazy as they grow older."[7]

But the prohibition movement also incorporated another viewpoint into its basic political ideology, a distinct tone of bigotry. As immigration rose, the league made clear that alcoholism was a foreign import, and stressed the rise in consumption of beer and wine. One writer, for example, detailed how in 1850, the consumption of all alcoholic beverages in the United States was 4.08 gallons per inhabitant per year. By 1892 this had shot up to 17.04, a gigantic 400 percent increase. Yet at the same time consumption of whisky—the spirit taken by Americans—had sunk from 2.25 gallons to only 1.5 gallons per capita; the slack, of course, had been taken up by the radical increase in beer consumption, from 1.58 to 15.1 gallons per person. The immigrant's drink, in other words, was destroying America.[8]

Soon this linkage grew, until the prohibition movement's leading strategy was an apocalyptic vision of America's future. The fight to end the saloon, its advocates thundered, was not just about making the streets safer or even preserving homes and children. It was about American civilization, and whether it would remain pure or mongrel. One editor wrote, "The Anglo-Saxon stock is the best improved, hardiest and fittest . . . if we are to preserve this nation and the Anglo-Saxon type we must abolish" alcohol, a damnation limited to foreigners and the depraved of the cities. In time, this viewpoint took over, till it dominated the movement.[9]

This approach, however, guaranteed that eventually Al Smith would butt heads with prohibition advocates, whether he wanted that fight or not. If Smith stood for the new America, his own sense of right and wrong meant that he would have to take up this mantle. And the other side saw him coming a mile away, long before he recognized that this was his struggle. They knew instinctively what he represented, as the country's leading dry cleric, Bishop James Cannon, told the Methodist press: "Governor Smith wants the Italians, the Sicilians, the Poles and the Russian Jews. . . . We shut the door to them. But Smith says, 'Give me that kind of people.' He wants the kind of dirty people that you find today on the sidewalks of New York."[10]

By the second decade of the twentieth century, the prohibition forces had their sights set on the most powerful change of all; a constitutional amendment that would ban alcoholic beverages for all time. In 1917 Congress approved the Eighteenth Amendment, falling before a movement that depicted this as a wartime measure of the utmost patriotism. Banning booze meant that riflemen would fight sober and fire straighter; and while every man, woman, and child practiced "Meatless Mondays" and "Wheatless Wednesdays," to save food for the war effort, how could anyone even consider using grain to produce beer and whisky? It might be rough at first, but in the long run, everyone, especially the younger generation, would benefit from this national sacrifice. The House of Representatives passed the bill 282 to 128; the Senate vote was 65 to 20. Senator Henry Cabot Lodge of Massachusetts, an aristocrat who still knew a thing or two about Boston, questioned whether there existed anywhere in the world an army large enough to enforce prohibition. But as the numbers continued to pour in from the agricultural regions, the final outcome became inevitable, and in more than constitutional terms: prohibition would always be a triumph of the small towns and the rural districts over the industrialized regions of America. On the morning of January 16, 1919, at 10:32 A.M., the elected representatives of the sovereign jurisdiction of Nebraska voted to ratify the amendment, the thirty-sixth state out of forty-eight to take that action, thus overcoming the three-quarters hurdle necessary for ratification. In the state house at Lincoln, the vote had not even been close—thirty-one to one—and now prohibition was the law of the land.[11]

How would Al and his city respond? If history was a guide, not well. As early as 1810 pamphleteer Tench Cox noticed in New York the growth of a "peculiar taste for lively or foaming beer." Unfortunately for thirsty New Yorkers at this time, the standard brew process used English techniques, producing a beverage with little carbonation that spoiled easily in the summer.

In 1848 Ferdinand and Maximillian Schaefer made their all-important contribution to New York City history by introducing German lager. This was lighter and fizzier, but best of all, it could be served all year round. One paper noted that "New Yorkers ran mad after it, and nothing was spoken of or drunk but LAGER." A city that would eventually produce poets and writers galore could not refrain from composing verse, as local wags recited:

> *'Twas drank in "fader land" first,*
> *But now we drink it here,*
> *Then drink it boys! Drink freely!*
> *Three rounds for lager bier.*

According to the historian Richard Stott, by this time, "lager . . . became . . . something of a symbol of the . . . city's working class."

Notwithstanding this tradition, during Al Smith's first term as governor, New York became the forty-fourth state to adopt the prohibition amendment (obviously long after it had been ratified—this was a symbolic victory only). The vote reflected the same lineup of forces that had determined the national campaign; in the state Senate, all the Democrats opposed it, while the two like-minded Republicans came from Albany and Buffalo. Similarly, in the Assembly, Al's old chamber, the eleven Republicans who cast negative ballots all came from New York or the two cities just named, and half had backgrounds that were German, Jewish, or Irish. Almost all of the Democrats who voted the same way were also members of these ethnic groups.[12]

Al never put it in these words, but it is clear that he did not think much of the idea of prohibition. He had grown up in a world where the neighborhood tavern was a warm and friendly place—a part of the community that helped take care of local residents. As a young man, he learned to drink, but no more than anyone else; he was a light to moderate social drinker who enjoyed an occasional beer. Later, during the prohibition era, he began to serve cocktails—the tall, diluted highballs that so many sophisticates took up—and at the end of his years, like many elder statesmen, acquired a taste for champagne. Franklin Roosevelt, who crossed Al's path at many social gatherings, made clear that it was impossible even to consider that Smith "has ever been or would ever be a drunkard."[13]

All this meant that Al saw the new statute mostly as a foolish nuisance, and did not exactly obey the letter of the law. He also did not obey the spirit either. In fact, he did not obey it at all. Emily Smith Warner reported that while the executive mansion was dry during public functions, in private, beer was not an unusual drink, and at dinner parties among friends, wine and cocktails were served. Herbert Lehman told interviewers that Al had his own private stock of liquor on the second floor of the mansion in a "big central hall with red walls," that "we all knew that." Part of this cache came from establishments like the Biltmore Hotel, which had to publicly give away at least part of its treasury when prohibition came in, and of course passed some rare bottles along to one of its favorite residents, who just happened to be the governor.[14]

No one in Al's social world felt any different either: Joseph Proskauer, one of his closest advisers, a southerner and an advocate of states rights, was against prohibition and never obeyed it. It is also hard to imagine that the Tiger Club was dry. The Tammany newsletter accepted large paid notices from the California Vineyard Products Co.—out of Brooklyn, New York—whose entire ad read, in enormous type: "Zinfandel and Muscatel Wine Grape Juices."[15]

Al did not even try to keep these violations of law very secret, and sometimes his casualness got him in trouble. One time, for example, chatting with a newspaperman, Governor Smith waxed on about how he missed the time when a man could blow the foam off a good beer and put his "foot on the rail." The reporter went public with this off-the-cuff remark, and it became national news. In a letter to a dry senator, Al had to explain, "I have enough common sense and experience of life to understand that the saloon is and ought to be a defunct institution." His comment had been a facetious one, "intended for gentlemen with a sense of humor." He had misjudged his companion, "the only occasion in my public life on which I have ever known a newspaperman to violate the ethics of his profession."[16]

When the governor was not shooting himself in the foot, his friends were, further complicating Smith's political life. The journalist Oswald Garrison Villard wanted to write a friendly piece about Smith and alcohol, so he decided to mention that Al did drink, but by this act he should appear open and courageous, as opposed to the hypocrisy of so many other politicians who grabbed a glass with one hand and then signed a prohibition notice with the other. But in the course of the piece, which appeared in the *Nation* on November 30, 1927, under the powerful title "Presidential Possibilities: Al Smith," Villard told his readers he would answer the pressing question, "Does 'Al' drink and does he drink too much?" His answer seemed casual in tone, starting out, "Well, I am reliably informed . . ." and then the bombshell " . . . that he drinks every day, and the number of his cocktails and highballs is variously estimated at from four to eight."[17]

This meant little to Villard; his next, blithe, contradictory lines were, "It is positively denied that he is ever intoxicated, much gossip to the contrary notwithstanding. He is a Wet, and he lives up to it, and for that consistency he is to be praised."[18]

Everyone, of course, ignored that later part, and it instead became popular knowledge that Smith put away eight drinks at a sitting.[19] Villard was aghast, writing a friend, "I am very much outraged by the misuse of my words in regard to Governor Smith's drinking habits," protesting that he had only the most innocent of intentions. For the record, Walter, the youngest Smith boy, insisted that his father never had more than two drinks in any given evening, but damage had been done.[20]

And although Al did indulge both in fresh beer and bad politics, this image must also be tempered by the fact that he was much too conscientious a citizen, much too enamored of the glories of the U.S. Constitution, not to mention much too good a politician, to consider or advocate direct rebellion against the highest law of the land. In a letter to the righteously titled Self-Determination League of Liberty, Al gave a typical summary of how he perceived his duties as governor. He told Mr. D. Robertson Browne of that distinguished organization that he felt "satisfied that you will find that the public record of my whole career indicates that I have at all times stood not only for enforcement but strict enforcement." When the White House called a conference of governors to discuss giving teeth to the Volstead Act, Smith not only attended, he became one of the very few such officials to follow up and call a local conference of mayors, sheriffs, police commissioners, and district attorneys from throughout the state to confer with federal officials. As New York's chief executive, he would uphold the law with reasonable efficiency.[21]

Above all, however, though Al may have found prohibition to be a personally distasteful brew, he did not perceive it as a critical political issue, compared to the important social and administrative problems facing the state and its people. In his autobiography he commented that "it always seemed curious . . . that the men in and out of the legislature who interested themselves most in the suppression of the liquor traffic never took much interest in social legislation such as the Factory Code, workmen's compensation, pensions for widowed mothers, public health or parks." Emily Smith Warner told about how, at first, she could never remember her father "saying anything much about" prohibition.[22]

So in the first years of the Noble Experiment, Al went about his political business without worrying too much about liquor—legal, illegal, or otherwise. He never advocated direct repeal, eventually calling for a modification of the law to permit sale of light spirits such as beer and wine. If he got any signals from the public about this topic, it came in letters like the one from a writer who simply described herself as "a Poor Mother" down in the old Fourth Ward, a lady who complained, "They have taken away the Liberty of the poor people by taking away a glass of beer and Dad's old Dinner pail can't be filled anymore."[23]

At the same time, however, the opposing side began to take on the governor. William Anderson, state superintendent of the Anti-Saloon League in New York, bombarded Smith's office with declarations, like the missive that began, "Conditions in New York as respects to violation of the liquor law have become . . . a scandal," and continued to the apocalyptic conclusion, "It is impossible to sow the wind of liquor violation without reaping the whirlwind of anarchy generally." Anderson incessantly reminded Smith, "You are responsible as the chief executive officer of the state for enforcement of the law. . . . Any failure on your part now will make you a party to the de facto conspiracy to discredit prohibition." Overall, Al took the tirades in good humor, only occasionally striking back, such as the time large ads appeared in the Elmira papers declaring that Smith "wants the saloon back," and Al labeled these claims "unfair and ungenerous." Otherwise he did not consider this a serious matter.[24]

But in 1923 an event occurred that catapulted him to the front of the national debate, and shattered his ambivalence about prohibition forever.

The issue would involve enforcement. Prohibition began, of course, with the Eighteenth Amendment, which banned—the actual word was "prohibited," hence the term with which this measure was always associated—all and any manufacture, sale, or transportation of "intoxicating liquors." This meant, incidentally, that actual possession of such substances was not illegal; the Anti-Saloon League had caved in on this loophole early, as a way of making sure the amendment got through.

Nine months after ratification, Congress passed (over President Wilson's veto) the Volstead Act, which became the operating charter for prohibition. Minnesota representative Andrew Volstead's bill—the good people of his district ejected him four years later for his trouble—defined illegal substances as any beverage containing more than one-half of 1 percent alcohol, a limit too low for even near-beer. At the same time, the bill made sure that this and all other provisions would be weakly handled, by placing enforcement under the jurisdiction of the Bureau of Internal Revenue. Later generations would take it for granted that courageous prohibition officers were treasury agents, but back in the twenties, everyone knew that this meant only that the real police officers of the federal government—the agents of the U.S. Justice Department—had been told to keep their hands off.

Beneath this structure, however, prohibition advocates also expected states to erect their own statutes; their campaign was not just about a series of laws, but a national crusade to make the country stronger despite its weaker instincts. The legislature of New York State dutifully followed suit, and on March 4, 1921, passed the Mullin-Gage bill to provide state officials with authority in liquor cases, which was then signed by Governor Nathan Miller. Mullin-Gage provided not a dime to pay for these efforts, but it had been passed.[25]

Two years later, on May 4, 1923, the last day of the session, the legislature repealed the Mullin-Gage Act, cutting the deadline so tight that the final vote took place at two in the morning, and thus created one of the biggest crises of Al

Smith's career. If he signed the repeal, it meant that the largest state in the union had now gutted and cast out its prohibition law entirely, major national news. On the other hand, if he vetoed repeal—thus allowing the New York version of the Volstead Act to remain on the books—he would be loudly proclaimed a hypocrite, given his presumed habits and his early statements attacking prohibition, as limited as they were. Keep in mind, too, that by this time, Al and his advisers were looking toward the Democratic nomination in 1924; they knew that becoming the lightning rod for prohibition would add unnecessary controversy to this effort. For the first time in his life, Al discovered that booze really was a poisonous substance.

Smith had thirty days to make his decision, and as one journalist put it, Al "must have wished devoutly that it had been thirty years." Twice a day the Albany press corps pleaded, "How about the repealer?" And twice a day, the governor of the state—who knew a hot potato when it burned him—obtusely replied, "When I'm asked that . . . I always say, 'How old is Ann?'" In private, however, he told an aide, "They have me down and out."[26]

Al came under every possible pressure during those terrible four weeks, as the *New York World* editorialized, "Will Smith Wreck His Party?" Obviously the Anti-Saloon League demanded that he veto the repeal—that is, leave the Mullin-Gage enforcement act on the books. Wayne Wheeler himself, general counsel and chief troubleshooter of the national organization, sent Smith an extended brief, claiming that if New York repudiated prohibition, it "would savor of perfidy to her sister States." Such conduct, Wheeler declared, could not take place "without imperiling the whole constitutional system."[27]

Smith got it from the other side too. Charlie Murphy had been a saloonkeeper, and so to him, the issue was black and white. Al had to agree to the repeal. The two met for hours in the library of the old man's Long Island summer home, and sachems and retainers waiting outside claimed the argument was heated—quite shocking, given Murphy's trademark silence. According to these accounts, Al emerged grim faced, with no agreement reached between the governor and his mentor.[28]

There were other voices as well, some that Al Smith did not fully appreciate. A young up-and-comer named Franklin Roosevelt (no stranger to cocktails), wrote Smith, "I am mighty sorry for the extremely difficult position in which you have found yourself over this darned liquor question." The only way to handle it, Roosevelt urged, was to veto the act and leave the law on the books, then call a special session of the legislature and request a new law that would obligate state officers to deal with liquor offenses only when called upon to do so by federal personnel, and never to initiate such action themselves. This shrewd solution, a harbinger of the political skills the young man would later bring to the presidency, fell on deaf ears; Al saw Franklin in those days as very much a youngster, and this was work, if ever there was such, for the adults of his inner circle.[29]

Behind all the advice was Mullin-Gage's failure as public policy. Almost immediately upon its original passage, the courts began to fill with cases. It took only ten days for the DA's office in New York County to announce that it now had ten times as many cases as attorneys could handle, and the city chemist already had enough liquor samples to identify that his office needed a year to finish them all, with more arriving every day. In New York and Kings counties combined, a total of 19,908 arrests under the state law had resulted in the stunning legal victory of only twenty-two convictions in jury trials.[30]

With all of these factors to consider, Al called a public hearing, to be held on May 31 in the Assembly Chamber, the day before his decision came due. The room was packed, while still more petitioners clustered outside his office. WCTU members came out in force, listening as federal officials testified on the need for a state law enforcement presence, given that their own budget was so meager. One speaker claimed that it all boiled down to a choice between the Constitution and a cocktail, between "the Star Spangled Banner" and "The Sidewalks of New York," which probably did not do much to sway the governor. Throughout the five-hour session, Al held his tongue; he already knew what his answer would be by that time.[31]

Long before the hearing, Smith had begun preparing. In order to reach a decision, he brought in his two closest advisers, Proskauer and Moskowitz. The only other person present was daughter Emily, who had requested permission to join them, asking, "May I sit in the corner? I promise you I will not speak." Accounts differ as to whether Smith or Proskauer composed the first draft, but all agree that the governor spent considerable time revising, producing the final version.[32]

At 6:00 P.M. on June 1, 1923 (the day after the hearing), Smith called a press conference in the capital. As the newsmen watched, Al, sitting at his desk, affixed his solid, clear signature to the Mullin-Gage repeal bill, thus signing it into law and eliminating the New York State enforcement mechanism. At the same time, he released a long statement—over four-thousand words—detailing the rationale behind his decision. The governor made clear that he considered the Eighteenth Amendment the law of the land, and that there was no question in his mind that "after repeal there will still rest upon the peace officers of this State the sacred responsibility of sustaining the Volstead Act with as much force and as much vigor as they would enforce any State law or local ordinance." All the repeal did was to eliminate a system of double jeopardy; no one could any longer be tried in both state and federal courts for what was virtually the same offense.

Prosecutions of the Volstead Act would still occur at the usual rate, except that all such cases would be heard in the federal courts from then on.[33]

Analysts then and historians after spent a lot of time debating why Smith acted as he did. The cynics argued that Murphy pulled the strings and Smith danced the dance. Others pointed out that the decision reinforced the image of Smith as a good administrator; ideals aside, part of the debate about Mullin-Gage was over who would bear the cost of enforcement. There was also the argument that Smith took this position because he was an early advocate of state's rights—an argument that would also explain part of why he would later break with Franklin Roosevelt's New Deal, when the federal government grew enormously. All of these pieces provide part of the picture, but still miss what was at the core of Smith's decision.[34]

In his autobiography Al wrote simply, "I . . . determined in my own mind that I would have to resolve the question according to my own conscience;" most likely, that was what the Mullin-Gage repeal was really about. Al Smith, the governor-politician, had weighed all the angles, but in the end, made his decision as a human being. The fact was, he did not agree with prohibition, did not think it was a good law or one that had been enacted with respect for all the peoples of the republic, especially those he had increasingly come to stand for. Maybe Frank Roosevelt and the others had been right and smart with their suggestions, but the law was still bad. And for a man who had made his motto, "Let's look at the record," that was what counted in the long run. Throughout his life, Al never used the word *integrity* in connection with this decision, and if that word meant a planned, rational decision to stand up for what one believes in, he was right to refrain from its use. For in the long run, Al simply signed the Mullin-Gage repeal because he refused to be a hypocrite. On another occasion he told his secretary, George Van Namee, "I am satisfied that as long as I do what I believe to be right I won't have to worry. I am sure that any law that is good for the people is good for me too."[35]

But life was not one of Buffalo Bill's Wild West Shows, where the good guys smiled and virtue triumphed. Al expected a response, but never planned for a typhoon; how could anyone care that much about having a drink, when there were so many other pressing issues around?

The answer was, they could care a lot. Wayne Wheeler of the Anti-Saloon League passionately declared to a reporter from the *New York Times*, "The action of Governor Smith will stir the nation as did the shot on Fort Sumter. . . . Tammany dictated the signature along with the liquor interests," but in the long run, "enforcement would become stronger than ever. New York will stay in the

Union in spite of Governor Smith." The *Schenectady Union-Star* complained that "if the rummies get things to their liking, you are going to see such an orgy of lawbreaking, crime and violence that New York State will be a spectacle before the nation." A member of an upstate chapter of the Ku Klux Klan told a Buffalo paper that no matter what the governor did, this organization would make sure that the Eighteenth Amendment was enforced in their area.[36]

Significantly, it was not just radical drys who were taking notice. The *New York Times* gave Smith's Mullin-Gage decision a five-column headline and ran pages of comments by other governors and from the nation's press. Editors at *Red Book,* the official New York State legislative manual, printed the entire text of the repeal statement, the only time during Smith's eight years as governor they did anything like this.[37]

Responses started to arrive from all over America, indicating just how national an issue Smith's position had become. Harry Hartwell wrote from Mobile, Alabama, "You are a damn fine Governor and your friends should be distinctively proud of you. . . . I have a great admiration and respect for the man who in the conscientious discharge of his plain duty dares to stand alone." Frank Fletcher weighed in from Contra Costa County, California, "to express to you appreciation of your upright and patriotic stand," while R. E. Corkins of Cincinnati complimented the governor because "you had nerve enough" to sign the repeal "and did not let a lot of long-haired men and short-haired women dictate to you." Others felt, like George Bradshaw of Norfolk, Virginia, that "you have done an awful bad thing by signing the repeal . . . to please the wicked people who are selfish and want to have their own way, whose God is in their belly. . . . God is going to call you to account for it in the day of Judgement." On June 13, the *Outlook* published an editorial, "Governor Smith Burns His Bridges."[38]

Even worse was still to come. In his appeal to Smith, Franklin Roosevelt had written, "It is going to hurt you nationally a whole lot to sign the Repealer Bill. This information comes from people who like you a lot and admire you a lot, of most of whom you have never heard. Incidentally, they are quite powerful in national affairs." Franklin was referring, of course, to Al's plans for the 1924 Democratic nomination. Whatever his chances were before, now they would always be connected to prohibition, a movement as much about resentments as it was about alcohol; Smith had taken on these forces, furthermore, without having made a conscious, deliberate decision to do so.[39]

The *New York Times* now asked William Jennings Bryan—three times losing Democratic candidate for the presidency, a leading dry, and still a powerhouse in party affairs—how he felt about Smith's decision. Bryan, old and bellicose with only two years left to live, answered in emotional, divisive terms: "When the Governor of the largest State in the Union boldly raises the black flag and offers to lead the representatives of the outlawed liquor traffic in their assault upon the nation's honor and the people's welfare, he must expect resistance from the defenders of the home, the school, and the Church." Bryan issued a declaration of war: "If the wets expect to obtain control of the Democratic Party and make it the mouthpiece of the underworld, they must prepare for such a struggle as they never had before."[40]

Al quickly released a nasty, angry reply, arguing that Bryan had completely missed the point of the gubernatorial message; "Running true to form," Smith wrote, "he uses a thousand words in replying and says nothing." The fury rising, he mocked Bryan's "narrow reasoning power." Furthermore, this whole discussion was for naught, because he was not even a declared candidate for higher office, despite what Bryan alleged, but "when I have been, I have usually been selected by the people. . . . In Mr. Bryan's case a wise and discriminating electorate usually takes care to see that Mr. Bryan stays at home."[41]

Whether or not that last line made Al feel any better we have no way of knowing. But what was incredibly clear was that Al Smith had been propelled into the national spotlight on a battleground not of his own choosing, in a fight where he had displayed remarkably thin skin. With his decision on Mullin-Gage, Al had involuntarily declared himself the leading wet in America. He would now be forced to speak out constantly on this issue, and if his advocacy had been reluctant at first, it would in time become heartfelt, as he responded to the barbs that hurt so badly, that did not seem to be part of the fair play that he had learned in the Fourth Ward.[42]

When Smith had been mulling over whether to sign the repeal, Felix Frankfurter, then a professor at Harvard Law School, expressed his views to Henry Moskowitz, Belle's husband and a close friend of Al as well. The great jurist reminded Henry of his prior assurances "that your Governor is a great man," then added, "The test of his quality is now to be made. . . . This disposition of the Mullin-Gage repeal will show the mettle of the man." Frankfurter stressed that on this decision, Smith will be "damned if he does and damned if he doesn't," then significantly concluded, "If he vetoes the repeal, he will be damned for a comparatively brief time . . . if he signs it, he would be damned for good." Years later, Josephus Daniels, Democratic warhorse from Tennessee, wrote a friend that southerners were becoming weary of the charge that their opposition to Smith's presidential campaign stemmed from religious bigotry. "Nearly all of it," he complained with resignation, "is based upon his part in securing the repeal of the Mullin-Gage enforcement act and his attitude against prohibition."[43]

Chapter 13

The Sound of the Siren

As GOVERNOR OF THE largest state in the union—and thus ostensibly with a head start on the largest bloc of votes in the Electoral College—Al Smith automatically was a presidential contender. In an article appearing in the *World's Work* under the heading, "Governor Alfred E. Smith and the Presidency," an anonymous author argued, "Any man who can be elected Governor of New York State by a plurality approaching 400,000 . . . becomes a figure of national importance." The writer lauded Smith as "precisely the kind of person the American people like and even love," citing his large family, his devotion to an aged mother, his sincere friendliness, even "his emancipation from the rigid rules of grammar;" there was also praise for "his insistence in regarding government as primarily a human relationship and only secondarily a legal one." A national audience was now getting a glimpse of Al's grand vision of how a state should be run.[1]

Smith's fame was skyrocketing. The day after Al signed the Mullin-Gage repeal, Louis Knox of Albany sent a telegram that read, "I am seventy-two years old, a Republican, but hope to see you our next president." Grover Borders, a Democratic committeeman in East St. Louis, told Smith, "You may rest assured that the Democrats of this part of the State are behind you for the nomination for President of the United States." Jim Farley, the incredibly shrewd Rockland County boss who would become FDR's campaign manager, wrote the governor on June 23, 1923, "I am not a rabid optimist Al but I am telling you frankly that the sentiment is there and unless I miss my guess that the delegates lose their head completely you will cop the prize" at the Democratic convention in 1924. By July 1923, the *New York Times* reported that Wall Street touts were offering odds of one to twenty that Alfred E. Smith would be the next president of the United States, and had set up a pool of two thousand dollars to handle all comers.[2]

After the close of the 1923 legislative session, Al took off to visit Charlie Murphy at the boss's summer home in French Lick, Indiana. Usually this trip was part recreation, part homage, part strategy meeting. But that year Murphy gathered a conclave of party leaders to consider the path Smith should follow in the next year's national contest.

At French Lick, Al and Murphy met with representatives of northern and midwestern states who spoke enthusiastically about a Smith bid in 1924. Senator Kenneth McKellar of Tennessee dissented, warning that while southerners seemed fond of the self-made New Yorker, they could not accept his position on the far wet side of the prohibition issue. Al, still not understanding the impact of the Mullin-Gage decision, was surprised at this news.

The governor should have been a lot more concerned, for beneath prohibition lay something vile, something subterranean and vicious that nice Americans did not talk about in public, something that would have a lot to say about Al Smith. The twenties was the heyday of the Ku Klux Klan, a period when the hooded order controlled cities and states, governors and mayors, legislatures and town councils, all across America. These kinds of people saw Smith in only one light, and referred to him as the pope-loving governor of "Jew York."

Thus, any Smith bid for the presidency would have to contend with blind bigotry. Senator Tom Heflin of Alabama—who based his senatorial career on anti-Catholic hatred—told his audiences that when it came to the Klan, the message was simple: "God has raised up this great patriotic organization to unmask popery." Some fearmongers announced that the pope was planning a takeover of the entire Mississippi Valley, but Governor Sidney Catts of Florida, in a burst of local pride, claimed that it was really the Sunshine State His Holiness sought. Others claimed that Georgetown University—a Catholic school, of course—had arranged its cannons so that they aimed at the White House. Some people seriously suggested that nuns should be fingerprinted as a security precaution, and Senator Heflin, who never missed a trick when it came to Romanists, objected vehemently when President Coolidge hung red drapes in a White House reception room, because it looked like cardinals' trappings.[3]

And this was not a mere fringe element, not just local efforts by crazed bigots. America was in transition, deeply divided over what to do with the new land it was becoming. People were scared, and got nasty. At the First Presbyterian Church in the Borough of Queens—right in Al's back yard—the Reverend William MacDonald brought to his congregation a KKK spokesman known only as "the Human Dynamo." Dynamo dramatically entered from the back, along with thirteen other unmasked but robed klansmen, as the congregation sang "Stand Up for Jesus." Behind him marched a color guard with two American flags, while a third figure carried a "fiery" cross that used modern electricity in lieu of hellfire.[4]

Human Dynamo then told the crowd of five thousand that Al Smith "knows the history of Catholicism but not of America." The governor had tried to overturn the Eighteenth Amendment and had tried to subvert the U.S. Constitution, so he would be stopped cold: "There are 6,000,000 people in the United States who have pledged their lives that no son of the Pope of Rome will ever sit in the Presidential chair."

Al, however, did not concern himself with any of this, simply believing that America practiced politics according to the Fourth Ward's rule book. When H. L. Mencken wrote as early as 1923, a year before the convention, that "the day" Smith "was nominated the Methodist Ku Klux Klaners of every state south of the Potomac would begin building forts along the coast to repel the Pope," Al ignored him; it was just a cute line. Daughter Emily wrote of this period, "Experienced though Father was in politics, he did not have an adequate understanding of the enormous . . . power of the Ku Klux Klan." She added, "I have never thought of Father as a naive man, but insofar as his idea of the reason for the Klan's opposition to him was concerned, that word, in my opinion, was appropriate."[5]

By early 1924, Smith supporters began organizing campaigns in New York, Massachusetts, Pennsylvania, and Rhode Island, and the urban bosses started to look on Charlie Murphy's protégé as a winner. On April 15, Alfred E. Smith stood before the Democratic State Convention in Albany and accepted the resolution that made him a candidate for the Democratic nomination for president. Humbled, always honest to a fault, he began by giving a speech that discussed the pedestrian business of state government, and only later stopped abruptly: "I want to step out of my character as Governor and have a personal word with you," he told them. "I heard the resolution that you passed."

There is no newsreel of the moment, but it is easy to imagine the emotion in Al's voice, knowing who he was, knowing where he came from, as he said, "It would be a difficult task for any man to stand before an audience of this kind and be able adequately to express the appreciation he must feel" for the honor they had just bestowed upon him. As he stood there, knowing he had to stretch, to try and reach the next, penultimate level of politics, he promised he would always try and take the high road. Al had spoken bluntly, simply, frankly, as he usually did with the big issues.[6]

But after that moment of grace, Smith's campaign went through a period of emotional turmoil. At first, on a high note, Herbert Bayard Swope of the *New York World* put together a plan to bring the Democratic convention to Gotham for the first time since 1868. His coalition wedded Charlie Murphy to the local business community, and this group raised the monumental sum of $255,000, an amount that loomed large before the eyes of a debt-ridden national committee. So on January 15, they ignored contenders like Chicago or San Francisco, and announced that New York City would host the 1924 festivities, to be held in Madison Square Garden.[7]

Soon after, tragedy struck. Charlie Murphy died suddenly; he and Al had been meeting only days before, drawing up a plan for the upcoming battle, and now he was gone. Al was so shocked, the *New York Times* reported, that he literally "refused to take the news." Even later, when he agreed to meet with the press, his fragile composure fell apart. Twice during the interview Smith broke down and openly cried, telling newspapermen, "It's awful. . . . No one had a better friend," as he scrubbed his eyes with a handkerchief. The official statement by the governor's office bore the mark of Smith's pain; done in first person, it was deeply emotional. Al told the public, "It is difficult for me to gather my thoughts together. I am suffering the loss of a close personal friend," a man he felt "privileged to have known."[8]

But Murphy's passage had ramifications far beyond Smith's personal sorrow. Franklin Roosevelt used to say that "Murphy always made it a point to keep Al honest" when it came to Tammany's dealings, that he kept the old pros from involving the young man in their schemes. The shrewd old Tammany boss understood that his sharp, sincere protégé counted for something more than another deal; Murphy shared Al's vision that their world could finally gain its place in America.[9]

But Charlie Murphy added a lot more than vision to Al's efforts at higher office. Besides commanding clout at the highest levels, he served as an invaluable political adviser to Smith, someone a little more knowing and cynical when it came to national affairs. If Murphy had lived, he would have restrained Al's enthusiasms, his willingness to seek the simple right and wrong, to let his hurts carry him into hopeless battle. Now, instead, the old man was gone.

Belle Moskowitz and Joseph Proskauer moved in to fill the gap and manage upcoming events, and then added a different face to the team, that of Franklin Roosevelt.

They had not originated the idea. Several weeks prior to his death, Charlie Murphy had paid a call on an old enemy, since Roosevelt had at various times in his career made war on Tammany. Now, however, it was the moment for politics to make strange bedfellows; Murphy asked FDR, who had been assistant secretary of the navy under Woodrow Wilson and the 1920 Democratic candidate for vice president, to use his national contacts to begin gathering support for a Smith candidacy. Later accounts claim that this took Franklin by surprise, but the young aristocrat was always far more ambitious, far smarter, far more prepared than anyone in Smith's inner circle ever realized. According to FDR's own account, before the meeting had ended, he was lecturing Murphy on how many delegates they could expect to get and the likelihood of gaining the nomination that year (which Franklin thought was not very good at all).[10]

Moskowitz and Proskauer followed up, this time asking Roosevelt to become campaign manager, but in name only; they would do all the work. Franklin, figuring it was better than nothing—it at least got him on board an important political movement—accepted. To the inner circle, however, the move was window dressing, Roosevelt a mere figurehead. Even the erstwhile candidate barely called his new chair, offering just a brief phone conversation after the younger man's appointment. Instead, according to the *New York Times*, Al swept into the Prudence Building headquarters and "took charge of his own campaign." Franklin ignored their condescension, and established what was virtually a separate and autonomous nerve center in his New York residence, making statements, writing press releases, pitching Smith in ways that would appeal to different constituencies across the wide expanses of America. Above all, he sent out over a thousand letters, all signed personally, to delegates and influential persons from around the country, establishing one of the most formidable intelligence networks in American politics.[11]

The pieces now started to come together. *What Everybody Wants to Know About Al Smith*, a thirty-six-page pamphlet, became the leading campaign document of the Smith forces, who distributed it everywhere. Eddie Cantor, by then a great theatrical star appearing on Broadway in *Kid Boots*, offered to set up a Smith-for-President Theatrical League; FDR also contacted Irving Berlin, the leading songwriter of his generation, who enthusiastically composed a ditty with the less-than-catchy title, "We'll All Go Voting with Al." It would never replace "Sidewalks of New York."[12]

All kinds of celebrities got pulled onto the bandwagon. Commissioner of Highways Frederick Stuart Greene—an engineer, of all things—came up with a brilliant public relations ploy when he suggested, "it would be a good thing to get (don't laugh) Babe Ruth to write a letter to some New York paper to say he is for Smith—there are some millions of baseball fans who hang upon his word," and Roosevelt took up the idea. The Great Bambino wrote back, "Sure, I'm for Al Smith." He explained to Roosevelt, "There was one thing about your letter . . . that went across with me good and strong, that was the talk about the humble beginning of Governor Smith. . . . I wasn't fed with a gold spoon when I was a kid. No poor boy can go any too high in this world to suit me." For the rest of his life, Ruth would be a devout Smith supporter.[13]

Various constituencies began to line up. In Baltimore, an African-American journalist announced, "Governor Smith is the colored man's hope in America."

Blacks saw how Al had stood up for the new immigrant Americans, and dreamed that he might do the same for them. In New York City, the International Colored Unity League held a "Monster Rally" under the title, "All God's Chilluns Ain't Got Wings," where speakers endorsed Alfred E. Smith for president.[14]

Final arrangements began to be made. Herbert Lehman quietly agreed to become the financier, penciling significantly at the bottom of a note to FDR, "I shall be very glad to help in defraying the expenses of the Committee." Tickets to the convention itself at Madison Square Garden became difficult to get, and then impossible. By May 31 Norman Mack wrote Charles Evans Hughes about how hard it would be to obtain seats, and by June 14 Smith's secretary wrote one supplicant to explain how bad it was: "The Governor has only one box which seats six people, although there are seven in his family." George Van Namee told Anna Germain the problem was simply that there was "no way of sitting six million people in a building which only seats thirteen thousand."[15]

The Smith forces began to exude confidence, even cockiness. Al set up his personal living arrangements on the top floor of the Manhattan Club, right across from the Garden, at Twenty-Sixth Street and Madison Avenue. He boasted to reporters, "You can write the headline now, boys, 'Smith wins the nomination,'" arguing that his greatest strength was that "the real people of the country want to see me nominated." Norman Mack told a friend, "We have the Smith campaign going in good shape." Early "poll results" were also positive; in the days before advanced techniques had been developed, politicos would go to movie theaters to watch how crowds reacted to the newsreels. John Maley of Denver reported that President Coolidge (the Republican candidate that year) received no applause, while Smith's appearance on screen got a "tremendous" roar from the crowd. It was easy to ignore the fact that Franklin's files swelled with letters like the one from "An American-Democrat" that said, "The people are very much surprised at you—a Protestant and an Episcopalian—trying to have a Romanist elected President. It's a dangerous game you are playing. . . . We don't want and will not have a man for President, who has sworn allegiance to a Foreign head."[16]

As the big date approached, New York City, at the time the glittering centerpiece of America's nightlife, put on its best—and its worst—for Al and all his visitors. The Famous Players-Lasky Corporation, a movie syndicate, agreed to have Smith's photograph included in their ads in all the Sunday newspapers, which meant a circulation of 3 million, of which 650,000 went outside the city's limits. Smith banners and posters plastered walls, elevators, subways, even traffic signs. Cab drivers, engaging in a new form of rudeness, badgered their fares to vote for the local hero. At the Forty-Ninth Street Theatre, in the middle of *The*

Melody Man, Lew Fields turned to Daniel Gallagher (who played a character named "Al") to ask the innocent question, "Who is Alfred?" Before Gallagher could get his line out in response, not one but several members of the audience literally stood up and shouted, "Why Al Smith, of course, who is going to be nominated for president!" The entire play stopped in its tracks, while the audience cheered for several minutes. Fields had to step out of character and speak to the crowd on how much he loved dear old Al, and the show finally went on.[17]

At this point, Al's major competition and still the leading contender for the Democratic nomination was William Gibbs McAdoo. The tall, gaunt McAdoo had impeccable Democratic credentials: he was Woodrow Wilson's son-in-law and had served in that president's cabinet as secretary of the treasury; many considered him the last Democratic president's heir apparent. Since then he had been rallying support, especially in the southern and western states, but unfortunately, he also appeared on the fringes of the Teapot Dome scandal, which involved private companies' gaining access to government petroleum fields that had been set aside for the military as a national security reserve. McAdoo had done some unrelated legal work for Edward Doheny, one of the executives involved, and he was now tainted with the "oil brush" of the era's worst case of governmental corruption.

McAdoo appeared to the delegates as a study in contrasts. Born in Georgia two years into the Civil War, the young man grew up in a home that was decidedly Confederate in its sympathies. Attending law school, he wound up in New York City, serving as a corporate attorney, but also becoming involved in many reform causes, especially rights for women and workers.[18]

Above all, McAdoo had emerged as the candidate most in harmony with the KKK, and quietly counted on their votes. Most of the agreements were tacit, but because William Gibbs McAdoo had never in his life repudiated the KKK in any way, shape or form, to most Americans he became associated with them, and became known as the Klan candidate. James Cox, the 1920 Democratic candidate, attacked McAdoo because he "remained silent at the sponsorship of his campaign by the Ku Klux Klan. . . . The Klan was solidly behind him"; while George Foster Peabody wrote friends about "the feeling that the defeat of Mr. McAdoo was an essential thing to break down the fanatical power of the Ku Klux Klan." Thus, as the Democratic convention unwittingly set out to fight over the meaning of America, McAdoo served as the perfect opponent for Al Smith.[19]

Smith and McAdoo, along with thousands of delegates, alternates, policemen, vendors, and just plain spectators, finally began to square off as the convention opened on Tuesday, June 24. Tex Rickard, the impresario of this shindig, had decked Madison Square Garden in patriotic bunting, while inside, new galleries went up, increasing seating from thirteen thousand to twenty thousand. The press room alone had space for seven hundred reporters.[20]

From the first, one problem was the crew up in the stands, the political equivalent of baseball's bleacher bums. This year, Tammany had seen to it that the bulk of seats in this section would be filled by their loudest disciples, men and boys who shared the twin attributes of an aggressive personality and lungs like the bellows of a steel mill. Many got in by showing faked passes, or simply bulling their way past helpless ticket takers and even cops. The problem was that they were totally out of control. With Murphy gone and Al busy with the nomination, the Hall was in flux, and there was no one at the helm to call the shots or restrain boisterous members. In this kind of environment, the worst elements could have their own way.

So when the time came, the thugs in the galleries would need no prompting to cheer their friend Al Smith and razz everyone else with a gusto and crudeness unprecedented in American political history. A typical moment came in an early speech, when the speaker patriotically announced, "What this country needs is another Paul Revere." The hooligans thought he had said, "What this country needs is a good beer," and cheered loudly.[21]

Smith's first big night came on Thursday, June 26, when his name was to be placed in nomination. There were a number of candidates for this honor; Al had wanted Bourke Cockran to repeat the magic of 1920, but the old Irishman had died in 1923, so the job fell to Franklin Roosevelt. According to Joseph Proskauer, he was the one who suggested to the governor that Roosevelt should be tapped to deliver the nominating speech that year. Smith was hesitant, asking, "For God's sake, why?" but Proskauer replied, "Because you're a Bowery mick and he's a Protestant patrician and he'd take some of the curse off of you."[22]

Proskauer also wrote the speech that would propel FDR back onto the national scene, the famous "Happy Warrior" oration, its signature term drawn from a poem by Wordsworth. Roosevelt protested the flowery language, telling Proskauer that "you can't get across Wordsworth's poem to a gang of delegates," and wrote his own draft. Proskauer hated this new version, and after considerable haggling, suggested that a third party be called in to help decide. Herbert Bayard Swope, publisher of the *New York World* and a Smith supporter, got the nod and dutifully showed up in FDR's apartment that night. Both documents were anonymous; Swope read FDR's first and called it "rotten," then raved about Proskauer's draft. Roosevelt fought all night, until Proskauer pulled rank, telling him that he had authority from the governor to demand that either his speech be delivered, or they would find another spokesperson. In later years, Roosevelt did not acknowledge that he had used Proskauer's speech; Proskauer, in turn, never forgave FDR for this omission.[23]

By Thursday, the night the speech was to be delivered, the boys in the galleries wanted Al and no one but Al. Any attempt to introduce other issues or other candidates was hooted down with a vehemence that left Thomas Walsh, the convention chair, shaking with anger.[24]

Roosevelt had arrived earlier, moving up to the dais in his wheelchair out of the crowd's sight. Just before the big moment, he asked Joseph Guffey of Pennsylvania to go up to the podium and "shake it," test the fragile structure to make sure it would bear the full weight of the big man whose hour had come.[25]

Guffey told him that everything was fine, and Franklin Delano Roosevelt began his walk into the spotlight. Even this crowd, hardly a gentle force, came to a hush at the sight of such bravery. Roosevelt had been working on this moment for some time, devising a strategy where he would hide a crutch under his right arm, while on his left he would hold himself steady by gripping the extended arm of his son James. Then the massive chest and shoulders would swing back and forth, and propel the crippled body up to the pulpit. It took only six or eight steps—Louie Howe, Roosevelt's devoted aide, sat upstairs and growled, "Spunky damn Dutchman"—but by the end of the journey sweat covered Franklin's brow. Years later, Jim Roosevelt used to tell friends that his father gripped his arm so hard that he "bruised it up," he "burned it." But that night, Franklin's first act was to throw back his head and grin that unbelievable smile, a portent of his later political triumphs.[26]

Roosevelt began with a call for calm, saying that he expected "that the guests of this convention will render the same fair play to all candidates and their friends that we would expect in any other city," bringing down applause from friends and foes alike. He spoke to everyone there, to "you equally who come from the great cities of the East and the plains and hills of the West, from the slopes of the Pacific and from the homes and fields of the Southland." He asked them to pay attention to his candidate, a man who had transformed the politics of the nation's premier state and now stood poised to do the same for the rest of the country: "He has the rare power to express the great fundamental truths and ideals in homely language carrying conviction to the multitude." Franklin Roosevelt thundered that his candidate, *their* candidate, alone "has a power to strike at error and wrongdoing that makes his adversaries quail before him. He has a personality that carries to every hearer not only the sincerity but the righteousness of what he says." Then, at last, the capping line that would remain fixed to Al forever; Roosevelt's final, graceful proclamation, "He is the 'Happy Warrior' of the political battlefield . . . Alfred E. Smith."[27]

It does not ring well through the ages, but in 1924 these words made the crowd crazy; the foremost historian of this convention wrote, "The bedlam was indescribable." A half-dozen bands played simultaneously, but not necessarily the same song, as delegates marched through the aisles; just then, the doors popped open and an entire parade of Smith supporters from outside barged their way into the overpacked auditorium, pushing their banners and posters up the aisles as best they could. Worst of all, someone had had the brilliant idea to install up in the stands a bank of fire sirens. Big, incredibly loud fire sirens, giant electric screamers hooked up to cases of dry-cell batteries. Some unnamed functionary yelled, "All set," and lowered his arm as his army started their engines; the result was an electronic wail of apocalyptic proportions that drowned out frail human speech and unnerved most mortals.[28]

Franklin, meanwhile, shaking like a leaf and wringing wet, managed to make it back to his room; Marion Dickerman went up to see him and found the elated speechmaker sitting up in his bed. He held out his arms and exclaimed joyously, "I did it!" The next day Walter Lippmann, the dean of American journalists, wrote him, "I am utterly hard-boiled about speeches, but yours seemed to me perfect in temper and manner." It was "a moving and distinguished thing."[29]

The parades and the sirens eventually died down, but the troubles facing the Democratic party lingered. In hindsight, historians branded the Democratic convention of 1924 as one of the most egregious examples of the cultural wars that racked America during the 1920s. The issue that would bring it all out had to be the Klan.

The Klan held its peak position in American life that year, with as many as 2 million official members, plus legions of supporters. Immensely powerful, the organization controlled a number of governors and state legislatures and was the dominant force in many American cities, not just in the South but through the Midwest and the Pacific Northwest as well; the state with the largest Klan membership, for example, was Indiana.[30]

The Democratic Party tried to deal with this force but was polarized, just like the country itself. Behind the scenes, the platform committee grappled with a decision; just about everyone disliked the Klan, but how far should they go in condemning it? In particular, should the KKK be denounced by name; could they risk alienating the delegates with Klan sympathies, possibly splitting the party?

The debate in these sessions was angry and emotional. Proskauer recalled seeing William Jennings Bryan "on his knees praying to God Almighty to destroy the anti-Prohibitionists." Congressman Henry Hawes of Missouri, arguing that the very future of the party was at stake, pointed directly at Bryan and told the Great Commoner to his face that he had enjoyed the support of Catholics and Jews in his past campaigns for the presidency, and he now had to return that favor and stand by these people.[31]

The resolution that finally emerged was relatively mild, asking that the Bill of Rights be applied to all citizens, and denouncing "any efforts to arouse religious or racial dissension;" the Klan was not mentioned once. When this was read to the assembled convention on Saturday, June 28, therefore, it was followed by a minority report that tried to substitute blunt language: "We condemn political secret societies of all kinds" and would "pledge the Democratic Party to oppose any effort on the part of the Ku Klux Klan . . . to interfere with the religious liberty or political freedom of any citizen, or to limit the civic rights of any citizen or body of citizens because of religion, birthplace, or national origin."[32]

The debate on these proposals started Saturday night at 8:45 P.M., and the first speaker, Senator Robert Owen of Oklahoma, set the tone for the forces supporting the majority plank. He claimed that he did not like the Klan, but believed that many of its members were sincere individuals with noble motives; no one should condemn the whole group because of a few rotten apples. The next speaker, William Pattangall of Maine, brought cheers when he argued that as long as Catholics, Jews, and African-Americans were subject to a military draft, they should not be denied any of America's freedoms; he ended with the simple line, "I hate bigotry."[33]

Tumult broke out when Andrew Erwin of Georgia took the rostrum. Everyone expected this offspring of a Confederate officer to support the Klan, and hisses and catcalls began to foam out of the pro-Smith galleries. Within seconds, however—his whole speech was little over three minutes long—it became clear that he was condemning the Klan bitterly. Now delegates from the McAdoo-affiliated states began to heckle and shout, some of the members from southern districts shaking their fists and yelling for the speaker to step down. Erwin told the crowd that the Klan was not just a fraternal organization like the Rotary Club, that it had to be stopped. If the South could not do it alone, then the rest of the nation would have to help.[34]

After Erwin's brief, brave statement, it took poor Thomas Walsh a full ten minutes to restore order to that frantic crowd. Following a few other remarks, he introduced the final speaker of the evening, William Jennings Bryan. Three-time Democratic nominee for president and Woodrow Wilson's first secretary of state, Bryan had always led the agrarian wing within the party, but now represented fundamentalism in both politics and religion.

The Nebraskan began by speaking against the sentiment of the local forces, claiming that the controversy had only started because a small group had demanded the inclusion of three little words. Cut these out, and the minority version would go through easily. Everyone knew what the words were, but pausing for effect, Bryan recited, "Ku Klux Klan."

It was too much drama in the service of too little justice; the crowd blew up. Over and over they forced him to stop speaking with yells and roars, until Walsh had to step in to try to regain order. Bryan was exhausted—an old man who was managing only a couple of hours sleep during the entire convention—and in the end fell back on the faith of his fathers, speaking in their language of evangelical Christianity, impervious to the impact this may have had on Catholics or Jews, addressing all the delegates as "Christians," telling them to stop fighting among themselves and to come back together "in the name of the Son of God and savior of the world." It was a disaster.

Voting on the platform began at 11:35, amidst chaos. Fights broke out and only the presence of a thousand newly arrived New York City policemen prevented the assemblage from developing into a full-blown riot. Walsh finally announced what would become the official tally on the platform as 541 $\frac{3}{20}$ in favor of the minority plank, 542 $\frac{3}{20}$ against it. By a margin of only one vote out of 1,084 $\frac{6}{20}$ cast, the Democratic Party had failed to condemn the Ku Klux Klan by name.

❧

Balloting for party nominee finally began on Monday, June 30, which was supposed to have been the convention's last day. The first vote started with a line that the whole nation would hear on the radio, over and over, throughout the innumerable ballots to come: "Alabama casts twenty-four votes for Oscar Underwood of Alabama," delivered in that state's unmistakable drawl. The total number of delegates' votes was 1,098, and under the two-thirds rule the winning candidate had to gain not just a majority, but 732 of these ducats. At the end of the first roll call, McAdoo was in front with 431 ½, Smith followed with 241, and various favorite sons picked up the rest of the count. Over the next couple of ballots the lines held firm.[35]

On Tuesday little changed, except for a growing sense of frustration. By the end of the day, delegates had cast their ballots through thirty separate roll calls, and it now became clear that the convention was stalemated. McAdoo's figures declined slightly to 415 ½, and Smith's had gone up to 323 ½, but neither man was anywhere close to victory.

The meeting barely rolled into session on Wednesday, July 2. One hundred delegates had already gone home, and their alternates now took over these seats.

People began to become apprehensive about the upcoming Fourth of July weekend, the second of the convention, common sense, however, dictating that they would had to have made it home by then.

That afternoon at least they had some excitement. A voice from the floor called out, "Mr. Chairman . . . I desire to obtain unanimous consent to explain my vote." It was William Jennings Bryan again. Chairman Walsh, ignoring the delegates and galleries, ruled that there were no objections.

Bryan spoke for almost an hour, explaining why he thought McAdoo should receive the nomination. Again he was met with jeers and sirens from the galleries, which everyone associated with the governor of New York. Neither man benefited; Bryan was an old, pathetic man, while Smith seemed anarchy's candidate. Even Franklin Roosevelt snapped at one point during this debacle, sending a short, terse note that read, "Dear Siren Man: Cut out the siren! No more today."[36]

But by now everyone knew what the convention was really about. At the end, Bryan looked at the people in the galleries and told them, "You do not represent the future of the country." One supporter wrote the old man that his antagonists were "a bunch of Irish Catholics who want Smith put in so the Pope can run the country. Should the convention have been held in an American city, and not in the European outpost, the people would have had courtesy enough to listen." Another correspondent explained, "The Roman Catholic Church through its slave, Tammany Hall, controls New York City and even the public schools."[37]

And, even more, to members of the oldest elites, what was happening in New York City was a fundamental challenge to the civilization they presided over. Elizabeth Tilton came from the best New England stock, a true liberal who had fought for women's suffrage, the League of Nations, and the Child Labor Amendment. But she was also devoutly in favor of prohibition and supported race conservation, a synonym for anti-immigrant racism. In an unpublished manuscript, she wrote in trembling tones about those days, how the "women who came from the South grow white now when they recall the torrid heat and more torrid passion underneath." She cried openly over "the fight that was coming between two cultures, Old America of prairie, plantation and everlasting hill and the Other America of the Big Cities," remembering "the Puritans. . . . Here was the country they made, all fibre and the firm mind bent on setting up in politics their vision. . . . And now Tammany was bent on stealing the Vision. . . . Oh, those . . . women. My heart bled for them." For individuals like Tilton, Al Smith's America meant the end of their world.[38]

Bryan's dismal speech only caused both sides to harden their positions; for ballot after ballot the lines held. By Thursday, nothing had changed, other than the fact that the delegates had voted sixty-one times, beating the old Democratic record for the longest convention, set back in 1860 at fifty-seven ballots; the Republicans meanwhile had never gone more than thirty-six, in 1880. On Friday, July 4, McAdoo reached the highest figure he would ever attain, 530 votes on the sixty-ninth ballot; he was 19 short of a majority, 202 under the two-thirds margin that would clinch the nomination.

It had turned into a marathon. Will Rogers joked, "This thing has got to come to an end. New York invited you people here as guests, not to live." One state chairman told his delegation that they either had to pick another candidate or find a cheaper hotel. Rogers claimed that in years to come, children would ask, "Father, were you in the big war?" and their dad would reply, "No, son, but I went through the New York convention."[39]

For day after day, the balloting continued, beyond anyone's reckoning. By Wednesday, July 9, everybody had suffered enough; maids, chauffeurs, even shoeshine boys were turning down tickets. Finally, on the incredible one hundred third ballot—a record that will mercifully last forever—the convention picked a dark horse compromise candidate to whom no one had paid any attention before—John W. Davis, a Wall Street lawyer. In order to appease the agrarian forces, they then chose as his running mate Charles W. Bryan, William Jennings's brother. At least so they said. Jim Farley wrote in his private notes that the national leaders had also agreed that "as long as Bryan had messed the whole thing up so . . . a member of his family should be in on the beating and his brother Charlie was nominated for Vice-President."[40]

But there had to be one last disastrous episode before it was over. Right after Davis's nomination, Al had gone over to wish him well; in the meantime, on the floor, Norman Mack, the Buffalo boss, requested that the convention offer Smith, as governor of the host state, a chance to address them. No one objected to *anything* at that point, and the resolution passed. Word went out to Al to hurry over.[41]

The timing was terrible. Al was tired and hurt, aware that earlier during the convention twenty thousand people had attended a Klan rally in nearby New Jersey where they beat an effigy of him into a pulp. The sudden announcement meant that he had no time to think, no time to consult with calmer advisers.

The speech was the worst in his career, arrogant and mean-spirited. He had the gall to tell the delegates, "If you have been annoyed in any way by the various people with whom you have come in contact in their zeal to explain to you why in their opinion I am the greatest man in the world, overlook it." Smith further infuriated the audience with the declaration, "It is conceded that New York is the greatest city in the world, and that it is the very center and the very heart not only of this country but practically of all the world." He then added that "the record of progress" under his administration "cannot be equalled by any state of the Union." After that came a recitation of all that he had done in New York, without a line to heal the convention's bleeding wounds. When he finished by declaring, "I shall take off my coat and vest" to work for Davis, everyone was glad the speech and the convention were finally over.[42]

The 1924 Democratic convention in New York had brought important issues to the fore, but in the worst way possible. For many Americans, like the person who wrote, "If we do not have a test at this election, a Catholic, a Jew, or a colored man will not have a chance again," Al Smith had represented the good fight, as he and his forces stood before the most powerful politicians the Klan could muster and never backed down. But that triumph was masked by the city's ineptitude, drummed out by the sirens' screams. All that remained was anger, and a desire for revenge on the part of those who felt slighted by Smith and by his America.[43]

Chapter 14

Business as Usual

THE 1924 DEMOCRATIC CONVENTION was a troubling episode in what was otherwise a happy and successful period in Al Smith's life, a time when he became the dominant politician in New York State, an important player on the national scene, and, overall, enjoyed what in retrospect would be the best years of his life.

After the convention, Al still had work to do for the presidential ticket, but this also affected his status in New York, since he had been making the traditional noises about stepping down from the governorship after two successful terms. Smith had been sincere when he promised to support John W. Davis as the Democratic candidate, even although everyone else considered this a hopeless mission. New York had far and away the most votes in the Electoral College, and if Davis had even a ghost of a chance of winning, it would mean that he had to carry the Empire State; to do that, he had better have a sure-fire winner at the top of the state ticket. According to Al's autobiography, when he asked Davis "point-blank" how he could best support the party's national effort, Davis replied with equal bluntness, "Run for governor again."[1]

Al claimed that this was the only reason he changed his mind: "In an effort to help the national ticket," he wrote, "I consented to renomination." This seems unlikely, however. True, Al did support his candidate, but he also wanted to vindicate himself after the bitter convention, and above all, by then Alfred E. Smith was a warhorse. Politics was in his blood, and his nose started to twitch when he heard the sound of the guns. Did he have second thoughts about this race? Of course, but fighting against this was the terrible addiction of adrenaline, the eternal lure of the main stage.[2]

So despite some work on behalf of Davis, Al's 1924 gubernatorial campaign came together easily; Smith and his team were hardly novices by that point. Raymond Ingersoll, an independent Democrat who would later become borough president of Brooklyn, took over as campaign chair. Herbert Lehman would be official treasurer, partly as a way of ensuring his personal contributions. Behind the scenes, as always, was Mrs. Moskowitz managing the day-to-day details, while Jim Riordan handled the real money matters.[3]

But the decision that would have the most long-lasting effect on Al's future career was one of strategy. For all of Smith's skill as an extemporaneous speaker, he had been leaning for some time to the formal set-piece speech, an oration where he could highlight a specific issue clearly and firmly: "I had the idea," he said, "that one well-thought out speech gives the voters an infinitely more intelligent understanding of state issues" than a flurry of brief talks. Thus, in 1924 Al decided that he would give at most only one speech a day; there would be no whistle-stops—little of the back-of-the-railroad-car greetings and handshakings. Each address would be indoors, in one of the state's cities or major towns. And every one would be an important statement, concentrating on a single issue as forcefully as possible, and then pushing home the governor's proposed solution.[4]

This decision had consequences both then and later. In 1924, it meant that the campaign stressed the candidate's record even more than usual; politics was relatively clean that year. Much more important, however, this sparse approach became enshrined in Smith's mind as the model for any major campaign, even a presidential one.

His opponent in 1924 would be Theodore Roosevelt, Jr., son of the late president. Teddy, Jr., had served a term in the state Assembly, and from 1921 to 1924 toiled as assistant secretary of the navy, the post once held by his father.

Young Roosevelt was an interesting and unusual choice as gubernatorial candidate. An honorable man, he vehemently opposed the KKK, eliminating this as a factor. He also declared, "I have never been a 'Volstead' Prohibitionist," meaning he opposed hard liquor and the saloon, but also believed that "beer and light wines were not only permissible, but were necessary," in order to make the law workable. But above all, he was a novice in state politics, writing in late 1923 about how he "would have to spend real effort" to become familiar with the issues, since, as he honestly stated, "I am not thoroughly at home in the local situation."[5]

On the campaign trail, Al made mincemeat of Teddy, mostly because of the youngster's own missteps. Roosevelt had assigned himself a grueling schedule of three hundred campaign stops, in contrast to Smith's approach. This quickly tired the Republican candidate and he began to make blunders, the worst of which came during a speech before the students of Hamilton University. As part of his talk, Roosevelt congratulated them on having just won a big football game against Colgate University; unfortunately, Hamilton had been defeated, and an angry student in the audience shouted, "We lost." Tired, humiliated, not thinking, Theodore, Jr., turned to his aides and demanded, "Who told me that?" in earshot of everyone in the house, provoking widespread laughter. This was just too choice for Al to resist, and from then on, whenever he challenged Roosevelt, the speech would begin, "I wonder who told him that?" or "Who told Teddy that?", always in a delicious and dead-on imitation of his hapless opponent's voice.[6]

Smith's well-oiled campaign organization also set up a Committee on Misinformation to reply to Republican charges, one of the earliest examples of what would later be called a war room, another of Mrs. Moskowitz's innovations. When, for example, Roosevelt claimed that Smith had delayed building a number of new hospitals, the committee arranged a reply by Dr. S. S. Goldwater, superintendent of Mt. Sinai Hospital and the Rockefeller Institute's adviser on hospital construction. Goldwater told the press that Smith had not lost a minute in pushing the new buildings; rather, it was the Republican legislators who had been agonizing over plans and specifications.[7]

Al had other unique supporters as well, some of whose efforts would later take on historical significance. Moskowitz had thrown her support behind a new statewide women's Democratic organization. By the end of 1923, this group had arranged in fifty-four counties to have a woman co-chair elected by the party's entire membership (instead of being appointed by the leaders), and it organized thirty local Democratic Women's Clubs throughout the state.[8]

Their most important contribution, however, was to provide the opportunity for Eleanor Roosevelt to come into her own in politics; in the early years of her marriage, she had appeared as the proper wife of a rising politician. But after Franklin contracted polio, Eleanor had to move into the spotlight, at first hesitantly and as his representative, but increasingly as her own spokesperson. And her first real campaign, the event in which she truly began her political career as separate from Franklin's, was Smith's 1924 gubernatorial race.

An enthusiastic supporter of the governor, Mrs. Roosevelt had given one of the seconding speeches for Smith at the State Democratic Convention that year, and she now became the leading woman in his state campaign, next to Mrs. M. At headquarters, Roosevelt would pick up the phone and call long distance to some Democratic leader—male or female—and start explaining how that person should go about getting out the vote in his or her district; or she would contact friends Nancy Cook and Marion Dickerman, and they would jump in the car to pay calls on county chairmen about organizing women voters.[9]

Her most outrageous stunt, and a symbol of just how alive and vibrant she became in this campaign, was the Teapot Dome car. Teddy was hardly a criminal, but he had the misfortune of having worked for Harry Sinclair, another one of the scandal's villains. Eleanor came up with the incredible idea to take a Ford motorcar and build a giant working teapot on top, which spouted real steam. She and a number of the other women then drove it out to follow on Teddy's campaign train; after he would speak, the teapot auto—screaming, in essence, "oil" and "corruption"—would pull into the same little town or village. One or two of the ladies would address the crowd that naturally gathered to gaze and chuckle at the curiosity, while the other members of the party handed out pamphlets and literature. Eleanor later referred to this as a "rough stunt," and it was hardly her crowning moment as an advocate of fair play. But it was both clever and effective, and she would always assert that she came of age politically in the Smith campaign of 1924.[10]

Otherwise, Al's greatest accomplishment in an uneventful campaign came in a speech in Buffalo on October 18, 1924. On that night he reached unusual rhetorical highs, as he described to the audience a KKK christening, an image of a hooded Klansman holding the infant against his breast as a minister performed the church's ritual. Al saw this as blasphemy, "a disciple of the Christ of Love and Peace, breathing into the heart and soul of an infant child the spirit of hate and war." He explained how "the whole move is so out of line with the spirit of our free institutions, it is so out of tune with the history and purposes of this country, it is so abhorrent to intelligent, thinking Americans of all denominations, that it must in time fall to the ground of its own weight." Then the clincher, the lines that would stick in peoples' minds: "The Catholics of the country can stand it; the Jews can stand it; our citizens born under foreign skies can stand it; the Negro can stand it; but the United States of America cannot stand it."

Al Smith won that year by the closest margin of his four winning gubernatorial contests, beating Theodore Roosevelt, Jr., by fewer than 110,000 votes out of more than 3.35 million cast. These figures, however, disguise a singular victory: in those days, politicians had real coattails, and none were longer than those of a winning presidential candidate. Calvin Coolidge not only beat Davis profoundly, he swept New York State like a firestorm, carrying it by almost 870,000 votes; Smith should have been wiped out. Instead, he managed to beat the tidal wave: the last man in the state to pull this off—to get elected governor while the presidential candidate of the same party lost—had been David Bennet Hill back in 1892.[11]

The election was historic for another reason. Al now became only the fifth governor in the history of the state to win a third term; the last one to achieve that was William L. Marcy back in 1836. The Republican *New York Post* said that Smith's unprecedented reelection was "unquestionably a vote of confidence," while the *Times* extolled, "Again Governor Smith has demonstrated his unrivalled hold upon the affection and confidence of this city and State. . . . Nothing finer has been seen in the history of democratic institutions." On Election Day aides brought up from the state museum the very chair that De Witt Clinton had used when he reached a similar milestone back in the nineteenth century, and Al sat in this throne for the photographers. After that, it was back to work, business as usual.[12]

☙

Al's first task would be to settle again a score with his most persistent foe, William Randolph Hearst. In 1917, Hearst had finally managed to get one of his cronies elected mayor of New York City. John Francis Hylan had grown up in Brooklyn, and became a motorman on the local rapid transit lines. Both then and later, as he worked on a law degree, Hylan became friendly with John McCooey, the Brooklyn Democratic boss, and eventually came under the wing of publisher Hearst. Given his background in municipal railroads, Hylan soon adopted transit reform, Hearst's pet issue, as his own; subways in those days were the life blood of the city's working class, and Hylan would always fight to keep fares low. With the powerful press syndicate behind him, as well as Tammany support, Hylan served for four years, and was reelected in 1921.

As the 1925 mayoral race loomed, Al resolved to depose Hylan. Under the prodding of publisher Hearst, Hylan had made it a point to challenge Smith constantly, claiming the governor never did enough to guarantee good, cheap service of any kind to the people of New York.

These kinds of attacks, of course, were unwarranted, annoying, and short on logic and facts; not surprising, given that John Francis was not exactly the brightest pup in the litter. Robert Moses used to tell how he had assisted Hylan during one of Red Mike's campaigns for Gracie Mansion (the man's hair was bright crimson, by the way). That year, Hylan had one speech and one speech only, a stemwinder about the need for maintaining the five-cent fare. Over and over, in every section of every borough, Hylan used his speech until just about everyone in the city had heard it, while the local press (with the exception of the Hearst reporters) must have felt like they were being subjected to an exquisite form of torture. Hylan finally asked Moses to write him—wonder of wonders— a second speech. Bob worked diligently and composed a careful, articulate address, one that Hylan had enormous difficulty delivering. The denouement (so claimed Moses) came when the bamboozled and exhausted Hylan reached the last line, the simple, cliché-ridden, "I call for the spirit of 1776." Red Mike, at the end of his rope, gripped the platform, plunged ahead, and told the crowd, "I call for the spirit of one-seven-seven-six."[13]

If Al Smith went after Hylan now, it would actually be a fight for control of the Democratic Party in New York, just what Hearst wanted. With Murphy gone and weak leaders succeeding him at Tammany, there arose a clear opportunity to pick a new leader at the Hall. Hearst wanted it to be him (whether in person or via a crony); Smith, of course, would block this bid with his dying breath, if need be.

If Al was going to unseat Hearst's protégé, it would have to be done in the Democratic primary; in order to do that, he would need his own candidate. Smith offered the job—a tough one, but not exactly that of a giant killer—to several men, including Robert Wagner, but they all turned him down. Instead, he settled on the majority leader of the New York State Senate, one James J. Walker.[14]

Given his later antics, it is fair to say that Jimmy Walker has entered the stuff of urban legend. Slim, gorgeous, a Tin Pan Alley songwriter, bon vivant, and playboy, Walker would personify New York during a decade that roared with prosperity and booze. After law school and before entering politics, he had frequented the Broadway scene, often paying some down-on-his-luck songwriter a few bucks for the rights to a tune that struck his fancy, then publishing it under his own name. Most of these were sentimental ballads—There's Music in the Rustle of a Skirt" or "In the Valley Where My Sally Said Goodbye"—but in 1908 Jimmy's ear for a good tune paid off, and he actually composed his biggest hit: the less-than-timeless ballad, "Will You Love Me in December As You Do in May," nevertheless became a national sensation.[15]

Jimmy was glib and fast with a line—he once argued against censorship because, as he put it, "I have never yet heard of a girl being ruined by a book"— and looked the part of a fabulous Broadway "stagedoor johnny." He designed his own clothing, from dress suits to pajamas, and spent long hours successfully figuring out how to make a suit coat whose lapels would not break, even when the wearer leaned forward as Jimmy did while making a speech. What worried Jimmy most, however, was the fact that he had no hips whatsoever. This concerned him sufficiently that he had his suits designed with a secret system that attached his pants to the waistcoat by a series of disguised straps and buttons; this not only guaranteed that his trousers could not fall down, it also prevented any possible shirt line from showing between pants and vest, a terrible no-no for skinny Jimmy. Father Arthur Smith, Al's grandson, remarked that Jimmy Walker "would put you in mind of a Fred Astaire . . . dapper, very, very dapper."[16]

Al knew Jimmy from the old days; the youngster's father was a precinct official down in Greenwich Village on whom then Assemblyman Smith had occasionally called. Later, when Jimmy grew up and went to the state house, he and Al actually roomed together for a season or two, making something of an odd couple—the plainspoken, serious Smith contrasted with the flightier Walker. One night Al walked into his roommate's bedroom and saw Walker decked out in beautiful red and white striped pajamas, prompting him to comment that the senator looked like a peppermint stick. Walker returned the informality by referring to Smith as "Algie," a term he continued to use long after Al had reached the governor's mansion, and that must have driven Katie batty.[17]

But there were also features of the young man that appealed to Al Smith. Walker had a superb mind; stories abound of the senator's coming in late for meetings (usually after a night of partying), glancing at a bill, then minutes later delivering a first-rate speech that provided both a clear description of the measure itself and the reasons why it should be supported. Even Joseph Proskauer, always a stern critic, said of Walker, "There's no smarter man I ever knew." Jimmy also shared Al's deeply rooted commitment to the new people of the cities; one time, for example, the Senate was debating a bill to open more parks on Long Island; the arguments grew hotter and hotter, until Walker could not take it anymore. Shaking his fist at colleagues, he shouted, "These millionaires made their millions out of the poor despised kikes and wops of the tenements whom, through you, they are now seeking to shut out . . . from a day in the country."[18]

Even so, Smith had major reservations about Walker. If Walker's slovenly work habits repelled Al, the playboy antics were totally unacceptable. It was well known that Jimmy's marriage existed in name only and that he had had affairs with a variety of showgirls, eventually setting up house with Betty Compton. Father Arthur Smith, a grandson, claimed that Smith was "very bitter" about Walker's "breaking up his marriage," and throughout all the years Al and Katie never invited Jimmy and Betty to their home.[19]

Jimmy got word of Al's objections and began to put on one of the best performances of his life. He stopped becoming a fixture of Broadway after dark, began appearing with his wife on his arm, and even circulated word that he was on the wagon, the most outrageous sham of them all. When the two finally met at Al's beach house on Coney Island, Jimmy looked contrite and sober; Al even offered him a drink, and he refused. When the governor inquired how the playboy had accomplished such a remarkable transformation, Jimmy answered, with the seriousness of a man in sight of his goal, "We all grow up sometime." Al caved in totally (the second time Al offered him a snort, Jimmy replied, "Just a glass of soda water"), and accepted the young man as his candidate. When Proskauer, incredulous, asked, "Al you believed him?" the wide-eyed Smith replied, "Joe, the man swore to me on the memory of his sainted mother."[20]

Al began the campaign by marching with Walker right into Hylan's home ground of Brooklyn, leading a torchlight parade across the East River. Speaking at Prospect Hall, Smith said that the subway fare issue was a red herring, that Hylan was blindly subservient to someone he referred to as a "super-boss," and then asked the crowd the emotional, rhetorical question, "When I stood against the forces of racial and religious bigotry" at the recent convention, "where was the mayor? He was in secret conference with the Klan, with the representatives of the Klan." In a speech that filled five pages of text, Al mentioned Walker only once, for a total of two lines.[21]

This was not going to be a genteel bout. Hylan had claimed that Walker received his nomination from a mysterious "poolroom king;" he now said that Smith was a tool of the traction interests who wanted Hylan's defeat so that fares could go up. As evidence of this charge, of course, the mayor could only point out the irrelevant fact that Smith had once headed the U.S. Trucking Company. Hylan referred to Walker as nothing more than a "dummy" and commented in a Brooklyn speech that Smith had "taken three days laboriously to prepare a vulgar tirade that . . . any occupant of the alcoholic ward at Bellevue could have written in fifteen minutes in quite the same style, but with more evidence of education and intelligence."[22]

Smith responded in a letter released to the public several weeks before the primary, reiterating his depiction of Hylan as a puppet and denouncing the candidate's master: "Mr. Hearst has the nerve of a bengal tiger, to be loafing in the splendor of his palatial estate on the Pacific Coast and attempting to dictate the politics of the greatest city in the world." Hearst in fact, *was* in California, where he received reports that there was "absolutely no doubt . . . Mayor [Hylan] will get [the] regular Democratic nomination." While the *American* told its readers that Hylan was the Abraham Lincoln of New York City, Hearst saw to it that his candidate also revived the old charges that Al had sold out to both the "milk trust" and, this time, the "meat trust," the latter selling "putrid" food to the people of New York.[23]

On Election Day, in the most bitter primary fight in the history of the city, Jimmy Walker picked up 403,615 votes, beating Hylan by almost 100,000 ballots. A month and a half later, in November, Walker romped over his Republican opponent by the usual margins, 748,687 to 346,546. The night that Hylan lost, Hearst called his *New York American* to check the results; reporter Gene Fowler answered, "The people have spoken . . . but they needn't have been so loud."[24]

It was, above all, Al Smith's victory. The *New York Times* editorialized, "the name of Alfred Smith appeared on no ballot . . . but his was the chief influence. . . . it was he who freed the city of the frightful incubus of Mayor Hylan." The governor had now solidified his right to dictate to the state and city parties whenever he wanted, at a time when Tammany honchos made sure that only weak leaders followed Murphy. This definitive triumph also made headlines nationwide, the *Atlanta Constitution* calling him "the ablest . . . party leader

Al at age four at Coney Island. *Museum of the City of New York*.

Al and his mother. She gave Al his sense of integrity as well as his Irish heritage.
The private collection of Anne Smith Cadigan.

Alfred Emanuel Smith (Al's father) is on the right. He was a cartman in Lower Manhattan who worked long, hard hours and died when Al was still young. *Museum of the City of New York*.

Al as a young student at St. James, directly below the priest in the center. *Museum of the City of New York*.

The Smith home at 25 Oliver Street, where Al and Katie raised their children. This residence, more than any other, is associated with Al Smith, and it became a registered National Historic Landmark in 1973. *Museum of the City of New York.*

Above, right. Al as a young man. He was popular, but with little prospect of greatness. *Museum of the City of New York.*

Below. A photo from Al's theatrical days. Although he chose not to pursue acting, this hobby provided critical training for his future career, from learning how to transfix an audience to delivering a punchline. *Museum of the City of New York.*

Katie Mulvihill as Al Smith first saw her. Though she would grow matronly in later years, theirs was a lifelong romance. *Museum of the City of New York*.

Below. Al Smith being sworn in as sheriff. Though the job paid well, he was quickly bored and looked to bigger things. *The private collection of Anne Smith Cadigan*.

Al Smith with Charlie Murphy on the right. Murphy was the smartest boss Tammany Hall ever had and Smith's mentor. *The private collection of Anne Smith Cadigan*.

Al and Katie on vacation with family and friends; he is in the center, she is on the right. *Museum of the City of New York*.

The Smith family on the steps of 25 Oliver Street. Top row (l to r): Al, Jr., Emily; center: Al, Katie, Catherine; bottom: Walter, Arthur. *Museum of the City of New York*.

Portrait of the Governor. *Museum of the City of New York.*

Opposite, top. Al Smith's gubernatorial inauguration parade, 1919. He was the first representative of urban immigrants to reach this high a position. *Museum of the City of New York.*

Opposite, center. Al Smith with the sachems of Tammany Hall, 1929. Jimmy Walker is second from left in the front; in the center is John Voorhis, at age 100 the grand sachem. The man behind and to the left of Smith is George Olvany, Tammany's leader (albeit a weak one) after Charlie Murphy's death. *Museum of the City of New York.*

Opposite, bottom. Al taking the oath of office for his third term as governor, following the 1924 election. He was now the fifth man in the history of the state to achieve this milestone. Aides brought down the gubernatorial throne De Witt Clinton had used and Al sat in it for the occasion. *Museum of the City of New York.*

Governor Smith with Scouts. There were few duties he enjoyed more than occasions like this one. *The private collection of Anne Smith Cadigan.*

Al throwing out the very first ball in the history of Yankee Stadium, on opening day in 1923. Katie is next to him. *The private collection of Anne Smith Cadigan.*

Al Smith on the campaign trail in 1928. Not all the greetings were this pleasant. The Ku Klux Klan prepared receptions for him that included burning crosses. *Museum of the City of New York.*

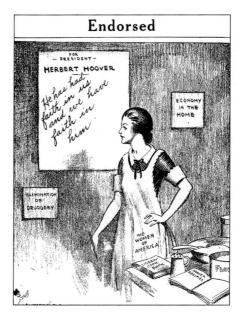

Herbert Hoover was in many ways the first candidate to appeal to women voters, because of his efforts to engage them on the home front during World War I. *Herbert Hoover Library.*

Al delivers a speech both to a live audience—which he preferred—and over the "raddio." *The private collection of Anne Smith Cadigan.*

One of the first celebrity sports endorsements in American political history: "Champions of Al Smith." *New York City Municipal Archives.*

Smith and the press in 1928. Joe Cohen, his press secretary, is the figure standing behind him with the open jacket. *Museum of the City of New York.*

Smith and the Cardinals on the steps of city hall in NYC in 1926; Al is in the center. He had absolutely no sense of the sorts of problems this photo would cause him. *The New York Times.*

Smith and Joe Robinson, U.S. senator from Arkansas, his running mate in 1928. Like so many things in the Democratic campaign, the choice was poorly thought out, more personal than practical. *Museum of the City of New York.*

Two products of Ku Klux Klan anti-Catholic propaganda that appeared during the 1928 presidential race. *New York State Library*.

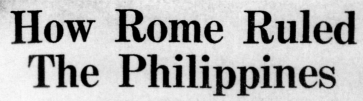

How Rome Ruled
The Philippines

PUBLISHED BY THE FELLOWSHIP FORUM

THE TRUE STORY OF THE IMMORALITY AND
DISHONESTY OF CATHOLIC FRIARS

For several cen...........friars of various Catholic
orders w............pines. They knew no law
.............heir own lust.
............astity as well as of pov-
............land, and the fruits of
............traged their daughters.
............four centuries kept the

THREE KEYS TO HELL
—OR—
Rum, Romanism and Ruin
By WM. LLOYD CLARK

AMERICA'S FOREMOST LECTURER AND WRITER UPON POLITICAL
ROMANISM, COMMERCIALIZED VICE AND THEIR ALLIED EVILS

Recommendations from Great Men

THIS book contains 500 large pages, 450 pages of text and 50 great cartoons. It is printed on high grade eggshell paper, and bound in flexible imitation leather with gold imprint on cover. It covers every phase of the BURNING QUESTION OF THE HOUR. It lifts the curtain and you behold the scarlet hag of the Tiber in all HER loathsome hideousness. In this fight against Political Romanism there is no North, no South, no East or West. All God-fearing patriots are banded together in one common cause to save America from the doom that fell on Spain, Portugal and Mexico.

HE'LL NEVER MAKE IT WITH THAT LOAD

"THE AL SMITHS! OH, MY DEAR!"

—and he asks the American people to elect him President.

Opposite and above. Hate material collected by the Smith campaign in 1928. *"The Al Smiths! Oh, my dear!" is courtesy the* New York World, *all else Rare Book and Manuscript Library, Columbia University.*

WILL IT LEAD TO THIS

The 4th Degree Oath of The
KNIGHTS of COLUMBUS

EXTRACTS FROM TH
ALLEGED OATH

ARE YOU INTERES

The AMERICAN
STANDARD

VOL. II. No. 9   NATIONAL SEMI-MONTHLY

Jewish Corruption in "Jazz"

Words of the "Popular" Songs, Written and Published by a Jewish Monopoly, Are Filled With Vulgar and Indecent Suggestions, Heightened With Idiotic, Sensuous "Music" of Jungle Type

Rome Suggests That Pope May Move Here
Coolidge Appointing Many Roman Catholics
New York Names a Square for Leif Ericson
Papal Terms Placed in Cross-Word Puzzles
Arabs Attack Balfour, Resisting Jews

Jesuit Hypnotism Uncovered

Rudyard Kipling Sees War Waged With Invisible Weapons—Protestants Attacked Mentally—Power of the Christ-Mind Is Destroying "Prince of the Power of the Air"

Five Cents a Copy   One Dollar a Year

More hate material collected by the Smith campaign in 1928. *Rare Book and Manuscript Library, Columbia University.*

Smith with draped flag. *The private collection of Anne Smith Cadigan.*

Smith with Franklin Roosevelt in 1929, as Roosevelt takes over as governor. The smiles would not last, as Al increasingly came to resent the younger politician. *Museum of the City of New York.*

Opposite, top. Opening day at the Empire State Building. Grandson Arthur is on the right; years later, he felt he should have had a better haircut for the occasion. *Museum of the City of New York.*

Opposite, center. Smith with Roosevelt on the Observation Deck on the 85th floor of the Empire State Building. Note how low the restraining wall is, the only protection against falling off the tallest building in the world. *Museum of the City of New York.*

Opposite, bottom. Smith in his office at the Empire State Building. He is sitting in the same chair he used in the New York State Assembly. A print of the Brooklyn Bridge is on the wall behind him. *Museum of the City of New York.*

Smith with King Prajadhipok of Siam; the king remarked that he had things like the Empire State Building in his country as well. When a shocked Smith inquired as to what he was talking about, the king replied that he, too, had white elephants. *Museum of the City of New York.*

Members of the Tiger Club (l. to r.): John Raskob, George Norton, Al Smith, William Kenny, and James Riordan, whose suicide would cause Smith terrible heartache. *The private collection of Anne Smith Cadigan.*

Katie and the kids. Top to bottom: Walter, Arthur, Catherine, Emily, Al, Jr. This is in order, youngest to oldest. *The private collection of Anne Smith Cadigan.*

Al and Katie step out on Easter Sunday, 1941. *Museum of the City of New York.*

Above and opposite. Al and his beloved animals at the Central Park Zoo; the hippo is named Rosie. *Museum of the City of New York.*

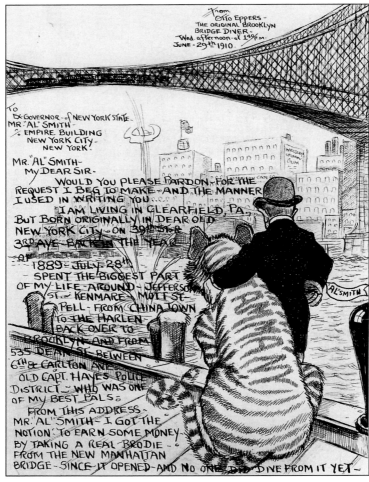

In 1935, Al received an envelope containing this amazing letter from Otto Eppers, who had once jumped off the Brooklyn Bridge, but now felt Al Smith was the only man who would help him. *New York State Library*.

New York's democracy has ever known," while the *Richmond News-Leader* said that he "emerges from the primaries much more powerful than he was in 1924."[25]

In these, Al's last years as governor, life was good in Albany. He kept his usual hectic schedule, but had developed the systems and personnel he needed to make it all work. Around him was a tried and true team of top government administrators—not just Proskauer and Moskowitz anymore. Smith pushed them and got the best out of them, but also cared deeply about their welfare. Mildred Graves Ryan, the daughter of Mark Graves, Al's director of the budget, remembered the terrible time when her younger brother contracted measles and died during a horrid, bleak winter. She recalled in particular what she referred to as "a miserable February night" when sleet was falling, "the hilly streets were a glare," and everybody stayed home. But in her household there was more, a sense of tragedy, of being "very alone and sad." Suddenly the front bell rang. Her father opened the door and saw to his amazement the governor of New York standing there. Mark Graves was shocked; he told Smith, "You shouldn't be out in this awful weather, especially when you have had such a . . . day with the legislature." Al gently put his arm around Graves's shoulder and told him, "Do you think I would let a friend spend such an evening alone?", ushered himself in and sat with the family for quite a while.[26]

Aside from moments like this, the governor's schedule was hectic, but underneath all was tranquil. When he left work at the end of a day in Albany, Smith returned to the executive mansion. Samuel Tilden, an austere bachelor, was the first governor to ever sleep there, and by the time Al and Katie moved in, it was filled with heavy, dark furniture, "dull and Victorian . . . just homey," according to Mildred Graves Ryan; Al and Katie made relatively few changes. Their apartment on the first floor consisted of a large bedroom, a separate boudoir, and their bath; at night they slept in a large mahogany four-poster bed in the middle of the room. Just off an alcove, they also installed a private altar where they could practice the rituals of their faith. On the second floor were some of the Smith children's rooms, plus spaces for adults who visited; over them, on the third floor, there was a nursery, ready to house any of the grandchildren, the favorite guests of all.[27]

Al and Katie had never experienced this kind of formal living before, and thus had no experience with directing a household staff. In general, therefore, they left the maids and butlers and housekeepers to their own duties, with relatively little supervision, ensuring an open, easygoing home where everyone called the governor "Al."[28]

Instead, the Smiths lived life on their own terms. Al got up at 8:30 in the morning, took a cold shower ("just as cold as it is possible," said one press account), then shaved himself. By 9:15 he was taking breakfast, two cups of coffee with orange juice and toast, plus an egg if a really busy day loomed ahead. Keeping him company throughout this were Katie, usually his daughter Emily, and a host of the day's newspapers. Al always read plenty of them, from all across the state. By ten in the morning, he had finished, and then went to the capitol, sometimes taking the official limo, sometimes strolling over on his own.[29]

At night, Al would be hungry (he frequently arrived as late as eleven or midnight); lunch had been a sandwich or skipped altogether, so he dined on lamb stew (his favorite) steaks or chops, spaghetti, or even sauerbraten. Fridays, of course, there was fish. Throughout it all Al chomped on a thick cigar; like most of the other politicians of his age, he rarely bought his own, feasting on the endless boxes that everyone he knew supplied him with.[30]

On those few nights when the governor got home early, there were a variety of forms of entertainment, most of them, but not all, drawn from the days when Al and Katie courted. The couple loved to sing together; or sometimes they engaged in a game of two-handed rummy, with Katie usually the winner. Eventually they adopted one of the marvels of the age, the motion picture, and had a projector installed in the mansion. A sheet would be stretched across the main room for the spectacle, with adults in chairs and children sitting on the stairs off to the side. A projectionist from one of the Albany theaters would come over to run the gizmo, and when all seemed in place, Al would yell out, "Are you ready, Professor?" Answered in the affirmative, the governor would then bark, "Lights," and the show would begin.[31]

But the greatest source of happiness in Al's life was his marriage. By this time Katie had become matronly in appearance, although some journalists claimed that in person she looked far more slender than she did in any of the news photos. Nevertheless, everyone thought of her as a wonderful, motherly figure, or as Al Smith IV delicately put it, "a large woman . . . physically and mentally as well."[32]

Katie saw her role as that of mother and housewife, not political adviser; even a neighbor could sense that she was a "very, very sweet . . . woman," with no sense of career. The state's future first lady told the *New York World* in 1915, "I never advise him about politics. . . . I leave all those things to him"; and a family friend observed that Katie seemed "very reticent and retiring." She "never interrupted, never embellished his stories or anything like that. He was center stage at all times."[33]

She remained, however, immensely proud of her husband. Katie loved to go to meetings and conventions, loved to see the adoration Al received, and could never stand to see him attacked. Family members and friends described how she would sit in a movie theater during newsreels and boo his opponents when they came on the screen (Al would nudge her and gently say, "Now stop that Katie"); or the time Al was attacked during a debate, and Katie just sat there and sobbed, how "the tears just rolled down her face."[34]

Above all, she loved him, as he did her. Hugh Carey said that Al Smith "adored" his wife, and the term that has filtered down among the family is simply, "There was a devotion to each other." And Al being Al, no one made any bones about this feeling, in public or otherwise. When Katie and Emily went to Europe in 1925, Al was waiting on the dock when they arrived back in New York. The *New York Times* wrote how, "The Governor kissed his wife dozens of times at the direction of . . . photographers. . . . Governor Smith was so glad to see his wife that he really did not require any prompting."[35]

Then there were the children. Foremost of these was Emily; she had the strongest character, was closest to her father, and might have become his heir apparent if she had been born a boy. None of the other youngsters was as interested in politics, and none was so often an observer in the executive office or on the campaign train. Frances Perkins claimed that Emily was the prize of the pack, with her father's brains and imagination, that Al "knew she was the best of the family." Family members remembered her as somewhat aloof, or as one put it, "more . . . distinguished," not as "fun loving" as the other children. Within the family circle, her nickname was "The Duchess," and they used to say that she and her husband were "friends of the Windsors."[36]

Emily's grandest moment in Albany came in 1926 when she got married. Her fiancé was John Warner, a captain in the state police. Warner came from an old family and had a bit of an English accent; it was a Smith family joke to imitate his upper-class voice, but they loved his charm and his dashing good looks. The massive ceremony (fifteen hundred people came, and Al commented that it was the biggest crowd since *Ben-Hur*) was one of Al and Katie's proudest moments; Warner had even converted to Catholicism for the marriage.[37]

Each of the children received attention from their parents. Katherine, the middle child, was quieter, more withdrawn than the others, so up at the pool table on the mansion's third floor, Al would try and draw her out to join the fun, to "get her spoked up," as Walter Smith, a grandchild, put it.[38]

But of all the children, Walter, the baby of the family, had the greatest time during the years Al held forth in Albany. "Wings," as Walter was called, did not approach his father's position with the greatest seriousness. It was Walter who most often invited the local children over to play basketball or baseball, and a number of former parishioners at the nearby cathedral remembered him as "a very nice, friendly fellow," or as "a good egg." On one fabled occasion (this was in 1925, when Wings was twelve), he was out playing baseball on a busy street next to the mansion. Local residents, knowing that cars could come zooming down the road at any minute, called the police to take action, and accordingly, two local constables soon arrived at the crime scene.

Most of the boys took to the hills, leaving Walter holding the bag. The cops asked his name and where he lived (Walter tried to be obscure, saying only, "In Eagle Street, I don't know the number"), and the officers said he would have to accompany them downtown. Walter replied in a quivering voice, "But I can't go to jail now. I'm going to New York . . . with my father." "Who is your father?" the police asked, and Walter promptly told them. Oh-oh. Switching tactics, they now tried to simply admonish the lad, one officer telling him, "I'm surprised to find you playing with such a gang of roughnecks. Don't you know you shouldn't play ball in the streets?" And now, finally, Walter's true colors came to the fore, turning this minor incident into the stuff of family legends. Walter "looked his indignation" and staring the cop in the face, announced, "Every one of these boys is just as good as I am, even if my father is the governor." He then added, "Well, I guess you'll have to arrest me just the same." The police then escorted the boy to the station and did their duty—sort of. He was not booked, and they agreed to make no entry in the police blotter after plea-bargaining reduced his sentence to an agreement to try to get the other boys to play ball somewhere other than on busy streets. As one of the two officers put it, in what must have been terrible honesty, "We felt sorry for him, of course, but we had to do it. I'm glad its over."[39]

Of all the children, however, it was Alfred, Jr., who caused his parents the most consternation. On October 16, 1924, as his father battled for reelection, the oldest Smith boy and Bertha Gott of Syracuse got married before a deputy city clerk in the Bronx, followed by the mandatory Catholic ceremony. None of this was done with the knowledge of their families; neither even knew of their future son- or daughter-in-law's existence. Al took it with the best grace possible, merrily acknowledging that "the boy went off in dime-novel fashion. . . . He's like a lover under Southern skies but he doesn't know it. . . . He's a young Lochinvar all right." Katie, on the other hand, was not quite so calm, almost fainting when she heard the news. But a year later, when Arthur announced that not only had he eloped at the same time Alfred had, but that he had hidden the marriage from his parents for all that time, Katie had learned to take such things at least a tad more casually.[40]

Governor Smith also had one other source of comfort in Albany; Al loved animals, and for better or worse, this always meant *lots* of animals. At one time or another (mostly at the same time) the zoo behind the executive quarters housed raccoons, bears, deer, monkeys, rabbits, pheasants, a red fox, barn owls, what Belle Moskowitz referred to as "some fat lambs," and a goat named Heliotrope (don't ask; nobody knows). The lambs, by the way—Ike and Mike— used to chase reporters around the grounds, and on one occasion when Katie was entertaining Democratic clubwomen, butted each guest as she emerged from her respective limousine (Al commented, "Who put Mike on the Reception Committee?"). Meanwhile, the Boy Scouts donated an elk, and from the creatures of the water, there were goldfish, turtles, and eventually an alligator, a gift, incidentally, from a New York City police detective (again, don't ask).[41]

On one particularly scary occasion, the bear in Al's zoo managed to open the gate, climb the rear wall, and somehow make it up the fire escape of the orphanage next door (obviously an ursus with city smarts and moxie). The little girls there knew all about the zoo—they were guests every Christmas at the mansion—so the bear did not faze them in the slightest; they actually thought it was kind of cute when he sat down on the floor and began to play with their toys, pushing them along the floor. One of these incredibly cool and collected damsels then got the bright idea that the bear might be hungry, and since all young children knew what bears liked to eat—they had read the stories, mind you—she went downstairs and asked the nun for a piece of bread with jelly for the visitor. Smiling indulgently, Sister played along with this obvious fantasy and served the food, but started to become a tad suspicious when, one by one, each of the twenty-five girls traipsed down with that same request. At this point, she decided, there would be no more bread, figuring half the stuff had wound up smeared on the walls. Not quite, she discovered when she went upstairs, and as one properly religious account put it, "Only the Grace of God kept the holy woman from collapsing on the spot," as she watched the happy bear, its muzzle coated with jam, grunt contentedly on the floor. Al immediately came over with some of his more burly gardeners and took the big boy home, which was not really a problem since the bear's belly was so full, fortunately only with bread and jam.[42]

And sometimes, just sometimes, Al's professional obligations and leisure enjoyments merged, and he wound up in the middle of historical events. As every diehard Bronx fan *knows*,[43] the single most important moment in American sports was when Yankee Stadium opened to the public. On that seminal day, it was Al Smith who threw out the first ball.

In 1922 contractors had begun work on Babe Ruth's future home, a massive steel and concrete edifice with the first triple-decker stands and the first electric scoreboard in baseball history, a structure that has been compared (at least by New York sportswriters) to the Roman Colosseum. The structure used twenty-three hundred tons of steel, a million feet of Pacific Coast fir, an identical number of brass screws to hold it all together, and was claimed to seat sixty thousand fans. All in all, it was fitting testimony to the power and wealth of the Empire State in the 1920s.[44]

Opening day, Wednesday, April 13, 1923, dawned chilly and springtime windy-cold, with most of the 74,217 paid attendees still wearing topcoats.[45] Outside a crowd estimated at 25,000 was somehow turned away peaceably; inside, according to the *New York Evening Telegram*, "everything smelled of . . . fresh paint, fresh plaster and fresh grass," a rare combination for Gotham, then and now. At 3:00 P.M. the Seventh Regiment's band, standing on the third base line, began to play the "Star-Spangled Banner," led by John Philip Sousa himself. A parade by all the players and attending dignitaries followed, after which there was an official ceremony wherein Babe Ruth was presented with a fancy case containing a big bat; one paper called this "a delicate hint to the slugger," one of the few occasions that particular adjective was ever applied to the Babe.[46]

Then came the big moment for Al. He picked up a shiny new baseball, tucked it between thumb and first finger, and threw a hard straight shot, smack square into the glove of catcher Wally Schang, the first ball ever to be pitched in Yankee Stadium. No one knows if the governor understood that, according to tradition, he was supposed to lob it wide by several feet; consciously or not, Al broke the mold once again. He then sat back and watched the Yankees do what they did so well in those beautiful, bountiful days, clobbering the opposing Boston Red Sox, 4–1. Ruth performed his own christening ceremony in the third inning, knocking a signature blast into the right field stands batting in three runs. Afterward, asked for a comment on the new stadium, he replied, "Some ball yard."[47]

As the 1926 state elections loomed, Al issued the usual protests, telling everyone that it was time to go back to private life and make some money for Katie and the children. Underneath that, of course, obligation and ambition dictated another course. By this time it was clear that Smith was the best vote getter the state Democratic Party had ever had; Felix Ray, in the *New Republic*, joked that Smith "can lose all right, but you couldn't call it a habit," while a cartoon depicted a distraught politician, labeled "N.Y. State G.O.P.," head down on a table and crying, clutching in his hand a paper with the headline, "Democrats to Draft Smith for 4th Term."[48]

The other reason to run, was Smith's own presidential ambitions. In order to be viable in 1928, he had to hold on to his power base, New York State. Without it he was nothing, but as long as he held on, it well might be his turn at the next national go-around.

The usual suspects gathered to manage what looked like an easy contest.

Besides Moskowitz and Proskauer, Herbert Lehman took over as chair of the Citizens' Committee for the Re-Election of Governor Alfred E. Smith, with Jim Riordan, Al's old friend from U.S. Trucking days, as treasurer. They managed to raise more than $160,000 for Smith's campaign, the big contributors including Colonel Jacob Ruppert of the Yankees, who was good for $1,000.[49]

The designated Republican casualty that year was Ogden Mills, a local congressman whom Herbert Hoover later chose as secretary of the treasury. Al figured that his opponent, another novice at state politics, would be easy pickings. He decided, therefore, to let Mills start first, then waited; as he told aides who complained of the delay, "I will start in my own good time. . . . His campaign will blow up before he gets through." Smith also expected that with Mills, a candidate from an old, distinguished family, "the campaign would be waged on a high plane, and based upon issues."[50]

Al could not have been more wrong on that last guess. Young Ogden did not have many issues that he could use against the governor; about their only real difference was that Mills felt that electric power facilities should be in solely private hands, as opposed to Smith's sense of a public-private venture. But instead of marching onto this high ground, Mills based his campaign on the contention that Smith was Tammany controlled, and then resurrected the old Hearst canard that Al had hoisted milk prices and killed babies. He told crowds, "Alfred E. Smith holds another office than that of Governor, one not elected but wielding tremendous political power. He is a director . . . of the Society of Tammany." Coached by Victor Watson, one of Hearst's longtime editors, Mills would claim that Governor Smith had used his corrupt ties to jerk up the cost of milk, dooming the children of the poor to destruction.[51]

Smith by now was accustomed to this kind of campaign and could give as well as he got. In Hornell, New York, he expressed his regret: "It has now become evident that the alliance between Hearst and Mills has resulted in degrading the Republican campaign to the usual Hearst level." Another time, he held up a cartoon that showed Mills in the foreground with a hulking shadow labeled "Hearst" standing behind him. Al pointed to the dark mass and thundered, "You know who that is! That is Hearst. Lowbrow, sinister looking creature that lurks behind the candidacy of Ogden Livingston Mills."[52]

That year, however, Al did not need the invectives, given his opponent's shockingly inept performance. Mills must have had a dunce for his campaign manager, because somebody okayed a newspaper ad that read, "Most of us are like Al; had to work or starve. Mills never had to work." Somehow, this was supposed to get the people of New York State to vote for Mills, but it is difficult to imagine how that was possible. Upon seeing this document, Al must have felt that all those Sundays going to Mass had finally paid off; he would begin his discourse on this statement with mock agreement, declaring, "I take no exception. . . . It is true," and then have a lot of fun at Mills's expense as he described his working-class origins and the benefits of a lifetime of hard work. Another time Mills's evil fairy godfather got him to declare, "If I am elected Governor, I will get along with the Legislature like a cooing dove." One wonders who came up with these gems, and Al could hardly contain himself when he gave a speech in reply, beginning with a request to look at some of the recent great leaders of the state, men like Theodore Roosevelt and Charles Evans Hughes, pointing out with wicked precision how neither of these men—indeed, any leader at all—could be considered a "dove." His own record of course, stood for itself: "It is known to everybody in the State . . . that I am no cooing dove, and what is more I never will be."[53]

Once again, women came out to campaign and vote. Democrats took the lead, but this year there was also a strong Mills Republican Business Women's Committee, a phenomenon Smith would encounter again, with much greater potency, in 1928. Eleanor Roosevelt led the Democratic effort once more, and felt strongly enough about the efficacy of her efforts to ask Al to write a letter of thanks to the women of the state for their work.[54]

Come November, Al Smith won, no surprise. He took 52.8 percent of the vote, beating Mills by almost 250,000 votes out of 3 million cast. Will Rogers quipped that the man who ran against Smith "ain't a candidate. He is just a victim."[55]

⤢

With his fourth victory, Alfred E. Smith, the son of a truckman, had entered the pantheon of New York governors. None of the greats—not Teddy Roosevelt nor Charles Evans Hughes—had pulled this one off, and the only other man in the twentieth century to match him would be Nelson Rockefeller. In the eighteenth and nineteenth centuries, George Clinton had managed to get elected seven times, but given the era (1777–1801), this was not necessarily by popular vote.

It was Al's last term, his last stand as governor. He would finish up many of his pet projects, especially his recasting of the state's administrative system. In 1928 he would leave Albany and the executive mansion, and the state would be a different and better place because of him.

Governor Alfred E. Smith's greatest concrete achievement was his reshaping of the state structure. When he first took office there was corruption and chaos, a system better designed for running a feudal kingdom than a modern unit of government. He fought for and won, not an equally arcane paradigm designed by accountants and academics, but a long-overdue imposition of common sense and efficiency; no one has ever done more to make New York State a functioning entity. And he did it without ever forgetting some other values—like mercy or justice—and without sacrificing the needs of the poor, the working class, or minorities.

Smith's other great achievement was to transform politics in the state, the same thing he did for the national scene. Because of who he was and what he stood for, Al Smith enticed countless immigrants to engage in the democratic process, to come out and vote. He made assimilation work in the best way, not by requiring anyone to give up their folkways, but by merely asking them to perform as citizens.

This altered the state's political equation. In Timothy Henderson's analysis of immigrant voting patterns in New York City, he found that in three Italian districts, comparing 1916 (the last gubernatorial election before Smith) with the events of 1924, the average Democratic tally grew from 45 percent to 73 percent, a complete turnaround. Four Jewish districts demonstrated the same conversion, shifting their Democratic support from 43 percent to a Smith-driven 73 percent. All of these people voted for their own—they loved Al Smith so much—but by so doing, they also became Americans.[56]

And in the end, Al Smith's greatest contribution was that he really was a leader. Not at first, not consciously or deliberately, Alfred E. Smith set out to reform our industrial age. Taking the reins of the greatest state in that era—a microcosm of the nation, filled with factories, farms, and the House of Morgan to boot—Smith set a course to ameliorate the abuses of capitalism at its worst, not its best. He never, ever sought to substitute another system for free enterprise—he was not so inclined and was never that philosophical—but instead simply tried to remove those aspects of the system that hurt us, that damaged human beings. But by so doing, he established his legacy, a model of good and fair government.

PART III

1928

Chapter 15

Opening Rounds

IN RETROSPECT, IT IS remarkable that Al Smith's 1928 nomination felt so inevitable. Opposition to a Roman Catholic, to a New Yorker, and to a wet was evident throughout the country and even within the Democratic Party; but by 1928 no one wanted a repeat of the 1924 disaster, and it seemed Smith's year, the moment when they had to give him a chance.

Al always protested that he would do nothing to seek the Democratic nomination again, but he knew it was his for the asking. His successful fight against Hylan had received national attention; followed by the stunning victory in the 1926 governor's race, Smith now had the reputation of a powerhouse politician. R. E. Powell, writing in the *Durham Morning News,* explained, "There has been quite an increase in Al Smith followers in North Carolina since the New York executive triumphed over Hearst and Hylan"; while *The Nation* reported, "That this will increase the talk of him as candidate for the Presidency is beyond question," calling his nomination, "both desirable and inevitable." As early as January 1925, the *New York Times* could report that the "Boom for Smith as President Grows," telling how the Albany executive office had received a flood of letters calling for Smith to stand up for his party in 1928.[1]

Soon it became a landslide, beyond control. Joe Tumulty, who had served as Woodrow Wilson's secretary, reported hearing from a Kansas politician that he had heard "considerable Al Smith talk" in the Sunflower State, and how in Texas, "it was the opinion of many . . . that you were the one man who could lead us out of the wilderness." Supporters organized a Southern Smith Bureau in Virginia in 1927, and Franklin Roosevelt claimed that the sentiment in Georgia, even among opponents, was that if Smith showed strength in the convention, "we might as well give him a run for his money."[2]

Al Smith's name stood for something in all these places, not just "Catholic" or "wet" but also integrity and honesty in government. In Denver, Julius

Aichele, John Maley, and Anna Hansen incorporated the first Smith for President Club in 1925, followed two years later by the Al Smith for President Association of the Rocky Mountains and the Pacific States, out of Ogden, Utah. The *San Francisco Bulletin* claimed that "not even his enemies deny that he has a kind heart and more than his share of common sense"; and in 1926 even the imperial Japanese government asked for a copy of Smith's plan for the "reorganization of the Administrative system."[3]

Nationwide, pundits began to develop the conventional wisdom that portrayed Al as a winner. Don Seitz, in *Outlook*, commented how Smith had been strong enough to deadlock the 1924 Democratic convention, but "he is much stronger now." The distinguished journalist and author Henry Pringle began as early as 1927 to speculate on the makeup of Smith's cabinet, telling readers breathlessly that Belle Moskowitz might become the first woman ever to be appointed to that body. Will Rogers, reaching out to a very broad, very American audience, sent a dispatch from Albany, "the official home of Al Smith, New York's hereditary Governor. Al likes the old place here, but I believe he could be persuaded to move." And an unknown columnist in the *Independent* tellingly observed, "When it comes to candidates, no honest Democrat can disregard the monosyllable, 'Al.'"[4]

It all seemed so fair, so logical, so reasonable that one's senses could be dulled to any other reality. Pierre Crabites, in London's *Fortnightly Review*, calculated that if Smith took the solid South, plus New York, New Jersey, Massachusetts, Connecticut, and Rhode Island, he had the election. Others could count too. Nicholas Murray Butler, president of Columbia University, a Republican but an old Smith supporter, wrote Claude Bowers in 1927 that "Smith will easily defeat any Republican who has thus far been prominently named," predicting that Al could carry not only the states named in the British piece, but also Maryland, Delaware, Missouri, and Illinois, which would have meant a sweeping national victory of substantial proportions.[5]

As the months passed, the praise became ever more personal. As early as November 1924, Al was hearing from Colonel Edward House, Woodrow Wilson's old political adviser, that he was "the one outstanding figure in this hour of Democratic defeat." Marion Fox, in the *Atlantic Monthly*, predicted with terrible assurance in 1927 how "few politicians of either party doubt that Governor Smith will be nominated by the Democrats."[6]

Even worse, down deep Al did not need the applause to know he had a winning formula. On the one hand, Smith felt fundamental empathy with the outsider, the citizen who remained less than 100 percent American. Yet at the same time, he also believed devoutly in traditional American values and images and could support ideals that seemed both noble and corny at the same time. Al assumed that because of this duality, he could bridge a critical gap between the old and the new Americas, the heartland of farmers and small towners, and the emerging urban vistas filled with immigrants. All this stemmed, of course, from his old innocence—his sense that the rules of the Fourth Ward prevailed everywhere, and thus he knew and understood how Americans played the game. On February 22, 1928, the *New York Times* could still report that "Governor Smith said he was convinced that there was no essential difference between the average man of a Middle Western mining town and the man he might meet anywhere on the Bowery." Smith's press conference also included the telling line, "If you are right you can convince them that a thing ought to be done."[7]

Al Smith should not have been nearly so sure of himself, and by a Texas mile, not a New York minute. Any Democratic strategy had to be based on controlling a solid South, and with a wet Catholic as nominee, that was anything but assured. George Fort Milton, editor of the *Chattanooga News,* editorialized that, "So far as I can see, Governor Smith is making no gains in the South." Dixon Merritt, a fellow Tennessean, went even further, asserting that "every Atlantic seaboard State south of Maryland is in the doubtful column" for the Democrats, if Smith became the nominee. The journalist quoted a North Carolina politician who argued, "Governor Smith is the greatest liability the Democratic Party ever had, and that's saying a great deal." In another piece, Merritt let the bile flow even more freely, opening with, "Beyond the practicalities of a pleasant smile, Alfred E. Smith knows nothing about statesmanship." After reciting objection after objection, the author ended with a salvo that hit home anywhere but under the Brooklyn Bridge, and would become accepted by both the public at that time and historians long after the election. Merritt claimed that Al was "a New Yorker, not in the broad but in the narrow sense of that term." He remained, in other words, "a Manhattanite; of that kith and kin and caste which, complacent in its egotistic self-sufficiency, regards Ninth Avenue as the Far West and the Jersey meadows as beyond the frontier." Then and later, it was an unfair charge; Al's ideals were always at their core universalistic. His accent, his religion, and his wet sympathies grated, but his platform and thinking cannot be said to have been hostile to the South's interests. In 1928, however, regionalism was still too powerful a force in American life to be overcome by arguments like these.[8]

Smith also stood at the apex for the national debate over prohibition. Carter Glass, senior senator from Virginia, announced to an audience at his state's distinguished university, "Any one is a fool who thinks the Eighteenth Amendment will be repealed in the next hundred years"; as a result of this reality, any party that endorsed a wet plank "will be annihilated." In an article entitled, "Could Smith Be Elected?" Glass was even more explicit: a candidate who advocated repeal "would . . . be badly beaten in Virginia and the South and the country."

Edwin Meredith of Iowa, a former secretary of agriculture and, like Glass, a Democrat, added, "To win in 1928 the Democratic Party needs the West. No wet can win the West."[9]

And there were other issues. What westerner or southerner would accept control from a leader of a New York political machine? George Fort Milton declared, "The public is not yet ready to install Tammany Hall in the White House." Then there was that terrible accent, as Al spoke on the "raddio." Milton pulled it all together in one, comprehensive, damning statement, when he disclosed, "The main Southern dislike of Smith's nomination stems from his dripping wet views, his Tammany origin, background and environment, and his general Manhattanite point of view, and I see no diminution at all of objections on these grounds."[10]

Of course, what no one on either side would talk about—except maybe the Klan as it geared up for the coming struggle—was religion, the biggest issue of them all by far. Will Rogers joked in 1926 that "Al Smith's the most popular man the Democrats have. . . . Some have suggested that he would be elected if he changed his religion and turned Protestant," but only fools and children laughed. On October 24, 1927, one year before the presidential ballot, Walter Lippmann could write Belle Moskowitz about what he saw developing across the country: "There is a very powerful whispering campaign already on foot," he told her; "What is your suggestion on the way to meet it?"[11]

The answer came as a negative: little if nothing would be done to fight intolerance. First of all, the signs were still piling up that 1928 would be a wonderful year for Al Smith. On August 2, 1927, standing in the Black Hills of North Dakota, Calvin Coolidge, in one of those cryptic statements that made the man's reputation, declared that he "did not choose to run for president in nineteen-twenty-eight," with no explanation offered, then or ever. Later historians will be tempted to ask, "So what?" but anyone studying the era closely knew the truth: that at that time, Calvin Coolidge was far and away the most popular politician in the United States and a sure bet for reelection. When he left, a gigantic gap opened up in American politics, and the presidential run became a horse race.[12]

Within weeks of Coolidge's totally unexpected declaration came the next stunner. On September 17, 1927, George Fort Milton's *Chattanooga News* published a letter from William Gibbs McAdoo, a reply to a query from Milton about what plans this party leader had for 1928. McAdoo talked about his party and the issues before the nation, and then announced, "I shall not . . . be a candidate for the Democratic Presidential nomination." The door stood totally wide open now.[13]

And all those objections in the South and the West? Norman Mack, Buffalo newspaper publisher and a member of Al's inner circle, wrote the governor twice in April 1927, informing Smith that when Senator Carraway of Arkansas said that 51 percent of all southerners stood against the New Yorker, "This, of course, is absolutely untrue and ridiculous, and I am amazed that the southern people have not resented it." Mack also told him that he had solid intelligence on that region, that "the religious issue . . . is dying out."[14]

On December 30, 1927, Al Smith celebrated his fifty-fourth birthday, in the governor's mansion. It was all done in typical Smith style, with a family dinner followed by what the press called "a moving picture entertainment in the drawing room." Only a few friends joined the children and Katie, but that night they saw a vision. When it came time to have dessert, the chef had created an enormous 150-pound birthday cake that took everyone's breath away; sugar and pastry, it was a model of the White House. The year of Al Smith, 1928, was only two days away.[15]

As late as September 1927, no official organization had been set up to work on a Smith nomination, so later that year, a group of New York Democratic leaders started to meet on their own at the Vanderbilt Hotel in Manhattan to begin informal planning. With the opening of the new year, Smith and his people took more overt steps, but still tried to keep it low-key. Throughout the winter and on into the spring, the man-who-might-be-a-candidate gave no interviews, made no great speeches, took no campaign tours to expose himself to the American people, and confined his actions to the daily grind of being governor.[16]

Others, however, took up the cudgels. In the Sooner State, for example, Judge James Tolbert organized a meeting at the Elks Club in Oklahoma City to discuss "Al Smith for President." *Collier's* became a prime supporter, casually assuring readers as early as January 14, "That Governor Smith will be the Democratic nominee seems to be assumed generally by politicians of both parties." And aides were already critiquing his public image, one of them chiding, "Cannot someone suggest to the Governor that when posing, he do so without a cigar and without too prominently showing his gold teeth?"[17]

The first thing the Smith forces had to do was win some primaries. This was a relatively new challenge; Wisconsin had passed the first law mandating that the electorate choose its delegates to the party conventions in 1905. By 1912 there were thirteen primaries, and by 1928 seventeen states selected 456 delegates to the Democratic meeting by popular ballot, rather than by rule of the party boss.[18]

On March 13, with frost still on the ground in some parts of the country, New

Hampshire announced with a bang that the race had begun. The winners that day were Al Smith, Herbert Hoover, and New Hampshire's continued reputation for holding the bellwether primary.[19]

State after state followed after that for the New York hero. By April 4, after primaries in Wisconsin, Maine, and New York, Al had 244 delegate votes already in the bag; in order to win, he needed two-thirds of the 1,100 delegate votes in the convention, or 733⅓.[20]

Finally, it was time to take action; coyness no longer seemed a useful or viable strategy. By April 15 Al's total had gone up to 264, more than a third of what he needed to claim victory. At the New York State Democratic Convention on April 17, former Lieutenant Governor George Lunn introduced a resolution that formally and officially put Al's brown, East Side derby squarely into the ring, a declaration seconded by Eleanor Roosevelt on behalf of women Democrats. Al was now on the move, literally as well as figuratively; at the time of the convention he and Katie were on tour in North Carolina. When they got to Asheville he gave his first speech ever to a southern audience, concluding with the line, "And before I leave I hope to meet yez-all personally." The crowd ate up his down-to-earth personality, the Republican *Herald-Tribune* testifying that "Carolinians tasted the salt in his character" and endorsed him.[21]

The last big prize of the convention season was California, residents in the land of sunshine and honey voting on May 1. Moskowitz was deeply worried, given that most of the dominant newspapers in the state belonged to William Randolph Hearst, Al's old demon enemy. Rising to the fight, she pulled out every trick in her abundant inventory, sending scads of information and literature (and seeing to it that much of it was printed locally on the West Coast), making sure, as she described it, that "even the movie-studios were ransacked for old-time New Yorkers entitled to vote in the primaries," an appeal to which "they responded with heart-warming enthusiasm." Herbert Lehman also showed up, bringing with him 200,000 pamphlets to be mailed to registered Democrats.[22]

Mrs. M hoped for a narrow victory: besides the Hearst papers, California was home to Smith's adversary from 1924, William Gibbs McAdoo, who had thrown his support behind Senator Thomas Walsh of Montana, and Los Angeles seemed a bastion of dry Protestants. But Election Day proved just how wrong she was, and foretold the importance of the Smith campaign in shaping politics in a changed America.

First, Al swept the Democratic precincts of the state, tallying more votes than his next two opponents, Senator Jim Reed of Missouri and Senator Walsh, *combined*. Even more important, however, Al Smith walked through the cities of

California like a triumphant Caesar. San Francisco threw him the keys to the town, a six-to-one margin over Reed; not a surprise, given that Al was wet, and the Babylon by the Bay lost its innocence at an early age.[23]

Less expected, however, were the results from the southern tier of cities. Los Angeles, a stronghold of McAdoo and Walsh, picked Smith over Reed by a three-to-two ratio, while San Diego also joined the statewide pattern, granting the governor more votes than the two senators could muster between them.

Al's remarkable victory was in part one of demographics. In 1920 America had crossed a divide, becoming an urban nation, as the census reported for the first time that 51 percent of the people lived in cities of some sort or another. These citizens were no longer on the other side, no longer a minority. And they all loved Al Smith. Later that year they would follow him into the Democratic Party, a move that Franklin Roosevelt would cement into one of the greatest shifts in the history of the nation's politics.

On May 2, the day after the California primary, James Cox, the Democratic candidate in 1920, sent Al a telegram; simple, chummy yet eloquent, it read: "Congratulations on California. It's in the air, old fellow." With California wrapped up and other states tumbling after it, Smith would go to the convention with more than half the delegates, his supporters claiming they could count on seven hundred votes on the first ballot alone. All those predictions of an easy victory had turned out to be right after all.[24]

The question remained, however: why had Al managed so neatly in 1928, when his attempt to be nominated just four years before had caused a donnybrook to break out in party ranks?

There are several reasonable answers. First, with McAdoo out of the race, there was no strong opponent, and Al galloped over a field of lesser figures. In addition, once the snowball had picked up speed and become an avalanche, it acquired its own compelling rationale. As the writer Samuel Blyth drily commented, "There is considerably more political nourishment in getting on the bandwagon than there is in standing by and making faces at it as it passes by." Above all, not to support Al that year might have meant political suicide for the Democrats. The *New York World* explained how, "The opposition to Smith has identified him so thoroughly with the principles of religious tolerance, personal liberty and social equality that a refusal to nominate him would be . . . a rejection of these principles. The shots aimed at Smith have hit the Democratic masses." Describing factors that party elders knew intuitively, the paper wrote, "The Democratic Party in its strategic strongholds is composed very largely of men and women whom the Klan casts out, the Anti-Saloon League berates, and the snobs look down upon"; as a result, they "can not reject Smith without rejecting millions of its constituents." Time and numbers, in other words, had caught up with the party and with the nation, and placed Al Smith into the driver's seat.[25]

⤨

It would be Al's year all the way, and that meant he had the right to make the big decisions, or at least to exercise veto power if he wanted to. One of the biggest of these was the choice of a site for the Democratic Party's national meeting.

Political conventions in those days were boisterous and important affairs. The primary system was just gearing up, so there was real suspense at the end, a sense that the amazing and unpredictable could occur as the nation learned at the last minute just whom the party faithful had chosen as their champion. Platform debates were important events as well, since there was still the quaint belief that a candidate might possibly stand for some set of ideas or principles, and that he might even remain beholden to those set down by his assembled party. In that kind of environment, the planks of a party platform mattered a lot, and the concepts, even the words, were worth fighting for. And finally, the convention would organize the national party structure for the next four years. Each candidate chose a chairman—actually his campaign manager—who would lead during the election season, then quietly wind the apparatus down for almost four years, to eventually revive it in order to begin making arrangements for the next big round.[26]

On January 12, 1928, the Democratic National Committee (DNC) convened in Washington to choose a site for their extravaganza. San Francisco, Cleveland, Miami, and Detroit all made strong bids, but behind the scenes a master entrepreneur was at work. Jesse Jones was not only one of Houston's most ardent sons, he was also publisher of its leading paper, the *Houston Chronicle*. And Jesse dearly wanted to improve the reputation of the place, get past its image as a frontier oil town filled with people who talked slow *and* funny, hicks who enjoyed bourbon, loud parties, and dung on their shoes, and not necessarily in that order. Jesse believed the best bet to put Houston on the map as a cosmopolitan entrepôt was to have the Democrats—the party of the South, after all—bring their convention to his hometown.

Early on, Jones figured the easiest way to pull this off was to use the oldest and most trusted means of all: money. Jesse called in the city fathers, entranced them with visions of the kind of business a national convention would bring and the promise of growth and expansion for the future, then delivered his marching orders. In order to approach the DNC he would need at least $200,000 as an opening bid, plus another $150,000 for a new convention hall that would seat twenty-five thousand people.[27]

Jesse got his money, all of it, and by the time he paid his little courtesy call in

Washington, he was able to produce, on the spot, a personal check for the full amount of his promise. We have no idea of exactly how the members of the DNC felt when they gazed upon their own private pirate's treasure; no one mentioned it in their memoirs. But it was an awful lot of money: the Republicans were already on record as accepting $125,000 from Kansas City to hold the convention there, so Jones's figure was fabulously extravagant in comparison. He had also calculated the number just right, providing a sum that would totally pay off all debts from the failed 1924 campaign and clear the Democrats' books for the new run, a thought as powerful in their minds as that of any working stiff that somehow, someday the mortgage really would be paid off and life would be on an even keel at last.[28]

Jones had a couple of other darts in his quiver. Over and over, he and his janissaries told anyone who would listen that picking Houston would be the best thing that ever happened to Al Smith, the most likely nominee, because the South would never bolt if the convention was held in their region. There was also a bit of prettifying going on, with Jones telling everyone what a garden spot Houston was, a description just a mite far of the truth. In his testimony before the selection committee, for example, Jones claimed, "Our climate in June is very comfortable," roughly as honest as referring to the Sahara as balmy.[29]

By late January, at the party's Jackson Day dinner, the deal had been cut. Al and his forces went along, with little in the way of argument or even leadership, as if things like this really did not matter that much.

It could have, however, at least symbolically. The last time the Democrats had met in a southern city was in 1860 in Charleston, when they split down the middle and presaged the Civil War. For the Smith forces, going back to that region in 1928 represented an olive branch, a way to heal some of the wounds from 1924 and to help bring the party together. But there seemed little consideration of these factors, pro or con, as they made their decision with scant deliberation.[30]

This casualness led to another strangely quick decision on a crucial matter: the choice of a running mate. Al's vice president would become part of his name, part of his political identity, and would also bring into the party's ranks a state, maybe even a region, but some bloc of voters. It was a crucial opportunity to surmount some of Al's handicaps.

But Al and his crew took this choice lightly, because, like so many other things in national politics, it was not part of their experience. In New York State there was no comparable position at that time, and Al had always been the only one to head an election ticket, a one-man show. So why should he think the vice-presidential choice would matter?

There was not much discussion in the press about who was in the running for the second slot on the Democratic list, a silence that reflected the lack of interest at party headquarters. What little analysis appeared argued that the choice should be dry to balance Smith's fluidity, and should come from either a doubtful border state or the heart of the farm belt. The two names offered to fit either of these scenarios were Senator Cordell Hull from Tennessee; and Gilbert Hitchcock, boss of Nebraska.[31]

The man who eventually got the job had none of these qualifications, but did share Smith's vision of America—for Al, the most important characteristic of all. Joseph Robinson, an Arkansas senator, was of English descent and a Methodist. Born in the hamlet of Lonoke, he graduated from the University of Arkansas and University of Virginia Law School, and immediately entered politics, running successfully for the state house of representatives the same year he passed the bar. He went on to serve in the nation's lower legislative house, ran successfully for governor, and then went back to Washington as senator, since 1923 occupying the highest position possible for a Democrat during the twenties, that of minority leader.[32]

It was one of Robinson's speeches in the Senate that brought him to Al Smith's attention. The leading anti-Catholic bigot in the Senate—indeed, in all of American politics—was Senator Tom Heflin of Alabama. Heflin earned the right to the title as early as 1921, when he first arrived on the floor of the nation's upper house and felt compelled to discuss immigration restriction. Speaking on May 2, he told the Senate about the "red anarchists and bolsheviki in the United States," how, "if I had my way about it, I would shut our immigration doors tightly for one year at least, and I would very rigidly restrict it for all time to come." The foreigners being let in, he argued, "are of no service whatever to our people. They constitute a menace and danger to us every day." He, on the other hand, stood for "the honor and glory of my flag and for the preservation and perpetuity of American institutions."[33]

In less formal settings he was even more candid, telling a Klan meeting in 1927—as Smith's star ascended—that the "Protestants of America are determined to keep Popery out of the White House." On a later occasion, being informed that U.S. battleships flew a flag bearing a Latin cross during religious services (there was no sectarian significance, it was merely to denote that the ship was engaged in devotional activity), Heflin attacked the display of the "Roman Catholic flag" on American warships, a claim the navy dismissed as nonsense. Heflin also liked to reveal that a Catholic employee in the Treasury Department had secretly engraved a rosary on the latest plates for the dollar bill.[34]

Then, early in 1928, the Hearst papers announced that they had evidence that the Mexican government was bribing several U.S. senators, including Tom Heflin. The investigation that followed proved that all charges were groundless, published only for their sensationalism (Hearst, like Heflin, was at least consistent in his record). But Heflin was in high dudgeon now, and on January 18 claimed the incident was all a sinister plot by Mexican Catholics against their most outspoken enemy, how the Pope was trying to involve the United States in a war with Mexico and Nicaragua. Above all, he used the occasion to attack Al Smith, telling senators that they should "bow their heads in shame" at the mere mention of the New Yorker's name, asking all Americans to "gird your loins for political battle. . . . The Roman Catholic edict has gone forth in secret articles, 'Al Smith is to be made President!' . . . They will lay the heavy hand of a Catholic state upon you and crush the life out of Protestantism in America." He then threatened to ask the Senate "to deport every man and woman who . . . owe double allegiance, first to Romanism and second to Americanism," and finally shouted, "Talk to me about Al Smith. . . . He will never be nominated with the deliberate judgement of the people of the United States."[35]

This was finally too much for the minority leader. Alone among his colleagues, Joseph Robinson stood up to respond, the very first time anyone had ever challenged Heflin in public on this issue. It is not clear if Robinson was more impassioned by such a blatant act of party disloyalty or by Heflin's horrid bigotry, but the accounts claim that he spoke as soon as Heflin sat down and that his face was florid. Holding nothing back, he told Heflin, "No man who is a Democrat in the finest sense of the word would ever proscribe another man because of that man's religion." Robinson spoke in clear and ringing tones, how "the glory of this Republic and the lustre of the flag . . . are locked up in the memory, the deeds, the achievements of American citizens, and no distinction has been made, or can be made, as to what religion they profess." Al could not have put it better himself.[36]

Accolades poured in from around the country to Robinson, many citizens echoing the remarks of W. G. Lewis, head of the Watts Commercial Club in Oklahoma, who wrote his Arkansas neighbor about his "able, and courageous defense of American Principles of Government and religious tolerance." Heflin, on the other hand, found himself denounced by every major paper in Alabama; the *Montgomery Advertiser* referred to him as "a callous and wretched demagogue." Will Rogers even quipped, "I am pleading with Alabama to please not exterminate all catholics, Republicans, jews, negroes . . . Al Smith . . . Mellon and Coolidge and the Pope. Of course, my plea will do no good, for Tom knows the intelligence of his constituency better than we do."[37]

It is hard not to be sympathetic with Smith's interest in Robinson. Yet, neither man's papers contain any correspondence between the two, and the first time the New York forces made contact was many months later, when a Smith official went down to Little Rock just before the Houston convention began; one account says that his offer came totally out of the blue, that the overtures were "astonishing" to the senator. Later, it was not until after the convention that Robinson even began to receive his marching orders, and even then it came from an oblique quarter, when Key Pittman, senator from Nevada, Democratic wheelhorse, and *not* a member of Al's inner circle, wrote the Arkansan about Smith's campaign strategy, and how "the burden of the agricultural problem will be placed on you."[38]

Thus, Robinson became vice-presidential nominee in a manner typical of the entire Smith presidential campaign. The senator had expressed his commitment to the issue that Smith stood for more than any other, and he could appeal to the South, and maybe to farmers, although in all fairness there were more qualified choices if these were the issues. He was also dry, which somehow was supposed to balance Al's wetness, an unlikely guess given how strongly that New York accent had become associated with bathtub gin. He was some of this, in other words, and some of that, but the key question seemed to be, did anybody really care? There is absolutely no record of discussion of other alternatives or of electoral strategies, any sense of how the Smith forces came to this decision. Nothing in the files indicates any prolonged debate, any concept of political calculation, of a strategy at work. Instead, just that terrible casualness, a quick and light response to Robinson's possibly heartfelt remarks. Like so many steps taken that year, this decision was sincere, but not necessarily smart.

Back in Houston, Jones and the city he loved were making good on their promises. A local architect delivered a design for a hall that looked, to one historian, like an "art-deco armory." Production was Texas-style; even though the city did not even own all the land when construction started, in an incredible forty-six days the structure had been completed.

It was no piker's effort, either. Three stories tall, made of Texas pine, the building covered several acres. Opposite the enormous platform was seating for over two thousand delegates and alternates, and when the raised seats behind and the galleries around the sides and the back got counted, the estimates were that seventeen thousand people could easily fit inside. This did not include the viewing mezzanine, which allowed two thousand visitors an hour to pass through, an accommodation for those who only wanted a glimpse of the proceedings.[39]

Others started making preparations as well. George Van Namee, the governor's secretary back in Albany and a member of the inner crowd, got the nod to become convention manager this critical year. Van Namee went to Houston early, taking over two large hotel banquet rooms and converting them into reception centers and offices, putting out the contents of a dozen boxes of literature that had been sent on ahead. George felt compelled to do everything he could to prevent a repeat of 1924, so he took a cue from his wife (he was a newlywed), who owned the prestigious Thorley Florists on Fifth Avenue. To everyone he could, George sent a lovely bouquet with a card that read, "Say it With Flowers," a gentle sentiment that presumably implied that air raid sirens might be banned this time around. Katie Smith, meanwhile, made up her mind to go, after being warned off by friends because of the terrible heat enveloping Houston by then. Even Al asked her to stay home, but this time she put her foot down; nothing was going to keep her from watching the greatest moment in the life of her beloved—and in her life as well—so she told him, "Listen, I'm going. I'm perfectly all right and I'm going to that convention if it's the last thing I ever do."[40]

In 1928 Houston had 265,000 people, a tad smaller than New York's seven million, but double the figure of ten years prior. It was a bustling little burb, and even though it was fifty miles from the Gulf of Mexico, the port of Houston managed to dock over twelve hundred ships from all over the world annually, exporting more than 2 million bales of cotton, the kind of figures that made any local Babbitt proud.[41]

All the cotton in the world, however, could not disguise the fact that Houston in the summer gets a tad warm. James Phelan, a Democratic leader from San Francisco, cursed the moment when his city lost and that Texas town garnered the laurels, writing, "The selection of Houston brings painfully to mind that the emblem of the party is the donkey. I understand that the heat and pests are intolerable." Throughout the convention the daytime temperature never peaked at less than one hundred degrees, a sizzle that could defy any fan, hand held or mechanical, pitted against it, causing one delegate to back out on the grounds that "Texas in June is the most horrible thought to me imaginable. . . . I cannot go to the convention. . . . The inferno of Southern Texas makes it out of the question." Reporters, comparing the Republican and Democratic sites, wrote that they would "fry in Kansas City and die in Houston." Keynote speaker Claude Bowers called it "the most deadening heat we had ever felt."[42]

Northerners soon adopted the local costume, men appearing in white linen suits and seersucker, women in light, colorful dresses with lots of flowers as decoration. As they all walked around, they quickly learned what it meant to be in an arriviste city of the New West. Delegates fought their way through crowds made up in equal measure of Yankees, cowboys on horseback, and the bands that seemed to appear on every block. Hotel elevators, even packed to the gills, could not come near to carrying this kind of traffic, and the *Times* quipped that at the Rice hostelry, the convention headquarters, "five cars were as good as none" when it came to getting to one's destination. One guest, who waited three hours at another emporium for an elevator to take him to his seventeenth-floor lodgings, finally lost patience, took out a gun, and fired four shots through the elevator door; nobody was hurt, of course, since the car was somewhere else, presumably the same place it had been for the last three hours.[43]

Walking around was like going to the sideshow of a small town carnival. Barkers sold live horned toads, packed in plaster boxes with perforated glass tops, as the perfect convention souvenirs. Inside the hall itself, protest broke out over the rule that delegates munching on hot dogs could be admitted, while those eating hamburgers were to be refused entry. No one ever explained this piece of hair splitting, but one dealer of the banned comestibles complained that "they are made of the same meat; the only difference is that hot dogs have pants on."[44]

The big question regarding hospitality, however, had to do with stronger items than snack meats. The Treasury Department had sent Alf Oftedal, deputy commissioner for prohibition enforcement, to Kansas City and Houston "to establish a dry zone around these cities" during their respective political conventions. Under his guidance, Houston police confiscated large quantities of beer and spirits for months before the arrival of the Democrats in June. And yet, veteran reporter Henry Pringle could still note that "proud citizens were filled with gratification that a convention was in session"; to express this feeling, "they invited the visitors to their homes, gave them the most comfortable chairs, and brought out their liquor. Scotch, rye, gin, and all the other proscribed beverages were available in large quantities." And just in case there were any fears concerning the quality of this largesse, "One's host was happy to recommend the honesty of his personal bootlegger and the purity of his stock."[45]

Of course, in such a diverse gathering there were also bound to be some cultural clashes. Local residents, having heard for years about the "braves of Tammany Hall," the thugs who supposedly roamed those fabled vestibules, half expected to see men wearing blankets and carrying tomahawks get off the train, or at least a bunch of Bowery Boy–style roughnecks, rather than just ordinary politicos. New Yawkers returned the favor by driving their hosts batty every time they mentioned the convention city's name; as everyone from Gotham knows, a major thoroughfare in lower Manhattan is Houston Street, pronounced "How-ston," and not "Use-ton." That little item must have grated hard on Texas ears, winning the governor few converts.[46]

Some peccadilloes, however, were far more serious. In the 1928 South, Jim Crow was at its horrific peak, and a Democratic convention in that part of the country meant a segregated, racist convention, unless one had a lot of courage. Just days before the convention opened its doors, Houstonians reminded each other, and the rest of the country, where they stood on the color line by lynching a wounded black man; seven barbarians forced their way into the Jefferson Davis Hospital, abducted their victim, and hung him outside the city limits. Southern papers callously joked that this was just an attempt on Houston's part to add a little local color to the convention.[47]

This was a town where blacks encountered segregated hotels, segregated public transportation, segregated everything, and even the convention got stained. Although the Colored Section was up front, just below, albeit to the side and behind, the right-hand speakers' platform, it was roped off by a chicken-wire cage, a demeaning and humiliating barrier. George Foster Peabody wrote to Franklin Roosevelt, "When one reads the story of the wire cage in . . . Houston . . . it makes me feel that it is almost impossible for me to ask a Negro to vote the Democratic ticket this year." Al was hardly a Jim Crower and Belle Moskowitz's husband, Henry, was one of the founders of the NAACP, but they permitted this outrage, either because, with so many other cultural strikes against Al, this was no time to raise the race issue; or else it was a case, once again, of that casualness that figured everything else was second in importance to the head of the ticket.[48]

The convention's organizers did modernize the proceedings in some ways. For the first time in history, sessions were timed to appeal to an audience of radio listeners, and the opening gavel came down, not on a balmy Texas morning, but at an evening hour when people around the country could tune in. Following custom, the outgoing chair of the Democratic National Committee, Clem Shaver of West Virginia, asked for nominations and elections of a temporary chair for the convention as well as other officers; all of these had been selected by the party apparatus beforehand, and all of them were duly ratified by the crowd without a murmur.[49]

The temporary chair was, in fact, the important position just then, because that individual delivered the keynote speech, the first stemwinder that might—it was prayed—set the tone of the convention and get the excitement going right away. Smith's forces had picked Claude Bowers, a distinguished journalist of Hoosier descent, who served on the editorial board of the *New York World* from 1923 to 1931. Will Rogers called him "a bear" and warned his readers, "You haven't heard the Republicans called anything till you hear this fellow—comedy, oratory, facts and sense." The outline of the speech, however, had been chewed over and approved months before, when Bowers attended a meeting of Smith leaders held at the Manhattan Club, with Franklin Roosevelt acting as host. The guest list included Joseph Proskauer, of course, but also Robert Wagner and George Olvany, Murphy's successor—albeit a weak one—as head of Tammany Hall. This assembled board gave their imprimatur to Bowers's plans, although the sailing would not always be that smooth.[50]

According to Bowers, a series of other small meetings followed to discuss drafts of his speech. The most distinctive of these came when he got a call from no less a personage than Al himself, who had just gotten in from Buffalo, and had a couple of hours before he had to go out again; he wanted to talk with his spokesman. Bowers did not exactly love the idea; as far as he was concerned, the speech was all done by then. So he arrived, in his own words, "thoroughly disgusted."[51]

Whatever his mood, Bowers confronted a veritable vision. Smith had just finished shaving and still wore soapsuds on his cheeks as he emerged from the bathroom. His attire consisted of woolen underwear (this was in June), a tight-fitting set of long johns that highlighted just how skinny Al's legs really were. Capping all this off was a cloak over his shoulders, and when the doorbell rang, as it incessantly did, Al would run to the door to refuse entrance, lapsing "into sort of a dog-trot," as "the robe would flow out behind him with his skinny legs out in front." All in all, Bowers recalled, totally disarmed, "it was something I wouldn't have missed for anything."

Smith had conned Bowers into coming by stating that he wished to discuss the statements on taxation; the reality was far more serious. Al felt deeply worried that there would be an attack on Tammany Hall at the convention, a proxy effort to get at the New York candidate. He wanted a preemptive strike, a defense of the New York institution.

Bowers stood there shocked. Linking Al to Tammany Hall in the first rounds was not a good idea, not a good idea at all. But Smith was mad now, doubling up his fists and preaching. Over the next few minutes he dictated exactly what should be said, laying out the words he wanted to hear so desperately from a national stage. Bowers would ignore every one of them.

But Al's diatribe was important because it revealed the ideals and innocence behind the casualness. This campaign was not about doing the day-to-day yeoman's work of running an organization geared to victory; anyone could do that, and, after all, it had come about so easily, so many times in New York State. What counted now was finally, totally, standing up for what was right on the biggest stage of them all, not turning your back on your roots. He had to let them know that corned beef and cabbage, ravioli and braciole, chicken soup and kreplach, all were as good as apple pie. The Smith board of strategy had already told Bowers quite clearly that he was not supposed to answer every charge, every claim made against the candidate, that he must be positive rather than defensive. Al's demons, who would haunt him far worse after this campaign, were already in charge, more than he ever realized.

Despite all that discussion, Bowers's speech turned out somewhat flat. Months after his meeting with Al, in Houston on the first night of the convention, it began to rain. Not a tepid rain, but a Democratic downpour. And Bowers, hoping to make a grandstand entrance, had decided to wait until the last minute to make his way from the hotel to the main hall.

This was, in retrospect, a bad idea. Everyone had already taken off from the hostelry, so there was only one man left in that large lobby space, and all the cabs had gone on to seek fares elsewhere. Bowers, of course, had no umbrella, and no one in the hotel had one to beg, borrow, or steal from. Finally, in desperation, he turned to his lone fellow guest for help, and the man walked outside and literally stopped a large car in the street, commandeering it to take Bowers to his speaker's podium. All seemed to finally be going well until the keynoter realized that the vehicle contained three priests, and he reeled at the prospect of headlines concerning the Catholic conspiracy that stood behind every move of the Smith candidacy. But necessity and the realization that no photographer would be outside in the rain prevailed, so he went on to his destination, and arrived unmolested.[52]

The hall was packed, and leaking. Bowers opened with a line that took no prisoners: "The American Democracy has mobilized today to wage a war of extermination against privilege and pillage." Over and over, he hit on this theme of grass-roots democracy, borrowing from the principles of advertising to strike a message home by sheer repetition, declaring, "We stand for the restoration of the government to the people who built it by their bravery and cemented it with their blood." He told his audience about "the little gilded group that now owns and controls the government," a cabal that "can pour a golden stream into the slush fund and make no impression on the fortunes they have legislated into their coffers."[53]

It was strong stuff, but also problematic. Although there was no question that attacking the role of money in politics seemed justified just a few years after the Teapot Dome scandal, the speech remains distinctive for its lack of new ideas. Bowers delivered page after page of excoriating, and possibly justifiable, attack on the Republican big money forces, but failed to offer any hint of what the Democrats proposed to do instead, other than restore "the common man" to power. Commentators claimed it was divisive, and Lewis Gannett described Bowers's talk as "a strained shriek."[54]

Despite this beginning, the convention was officially on, and it was all about

Al. Newsboys sold papers by yelling the magic name, and cowboy singers, wearing chaps and sombreros, crooned odes to a man named Smith. Everyone walking into the Rice Hotel passed beneath a banner reading, "Texas for Al Smith," and it seemed so right and true at that moment.[55]

Katie was in her element. Al called her every night from Albany, for she was the one on the scene this time. Her emotions were beyond words, a heady broth drawn from two parts pride in her beloved life's mate, one part exhilaration at having her family reach such a pinnacle, and one part delight at having the spotlight focused on her for once. After it was all over, she told a woman reporter, "No matter what happens in November, Houston was the thrill of my life. To see those thousands going wild about Al was—well, I just can't put it into words. It was my hour."[56]

Other folks in Houston also felt deeply about what was going on, but were not so positive. Dry women called for a "season of prayer" to save the Democratic Party from the prospect of a drunkard standard-bearer. A large crowd attended a mass meeting down at Richey's Tabernacle, where the main topic seemed to be declarations that God would block Al Smith's attempt "to steal the United States from the Christian people."[57]

Nominating speeches began on the second day, June 27, and continued through to the 28th. There were so many—not only a seemingly endless number of paeans to Smith, but also speeches for favorite son candidates and for vice-presidential contenders—that Will Rogers quipped about Al, "If his seconders all vote for him he will walk in" (Rogers also noted, "This is Thursday," so "the elevators in the hotels are going up today").[58]

The one that counted, of course, was the official nominating speech delivered by Franklin Roosevelt. This was actually the third time he had spoken up for Al, making it kind of a habit; as usual, he prepared thoroughly. While Proskauer again crafted the initial draft, existing archives at the Roosevelt Library demonstrate that there were at least a half-dozen versions, and Franklin redid the last paragraph again and again. Roosevelt was moving onto new ground here, deliberately creating the first talk ever designed to be read over the electric tones of a wireless, telling Walter Lippmann he looked on this as a "definite experiment . . . of writing and delivering . . . wholly for the benefit of the radio audience." The final touches were not applied until the day he left for Houston, and besides releasing it to the press, he had a special version made up for the podium, consisting of cardboard sheets with clear markings of "heavy" and "low" to indicate points of emphasis.[59]

Fifteen thousand people saw him that night, and 15 million listened in at home. He began in that wonderful patrician voice, its sateen texture glistening with confidence and goodwill. If this was the third time he had stood before a convention on behalf of Al Smith, "The Faith which I held," he informed them,

"I still hold." The difference was that this time, "the whole country has now learned the measure of his greatness."[60]

The big man from Dutchess County laid it out, enunciating the qualities that every leader most possess, then demonstrating at length how Alfred E. Smith had achieved so much in each of these roles that he now personified every one of them. Franklin rolled through the words, letting the phrases and tones master each and every listener seducing and entrapping them. Finishing his recital of Al's record, the speaker climbed, subtly and strongly but without straining, to his conclusion: Smith was more than a politician; rather, he was "a pathfinder, a blazer of the trail to the high road." In the person of Al Smith, Roosevelt intoned, "We offer one who has the will to win—who not only deserves success but commands it. Victory is his habit—the happy warrior—Alfred E. Smith."

There was a huge parade now, of course, but this time the New Yorkers had learned their lessons. Nothing—and the managers had made clear that they meant *nothing*—was to remind people in any way of the noise and the coarseness of 1924. Generously, the Empire State delegation stood back and allowed other contingents to lead the march that now bellowed down the aisles; if there were any disturbances, they would not have a Lower East Side accent.[61]

But this was small potatoes, and the parades seemed to lack spontaneity, not surprising, given that everyone knew what was going to happen that year. What they had not expected, however, was the quality of Roosevelt's speech. After that talk, Will Durant described him as "the finest type of man that has appeared at either convention," depicting "a figure tall and proud, even in suffering; a face of classic profile." The speech itself had been "impassioned but restrained; it is not shouted, it is quietly read . . . this is a civilized man. . . . For a moment we are lifted up." Al gratefully sent along a "Dear Frank" missive, "This must be right because it brought tears in the Mansion when you spoke it"; and even the *Chicago Tribune,* the most bitterly partisan large-city GOP paper around, gave Roosevelt its ultimate compliment when it called him "the only Republican in the Democratic Party." Durant made the telling comment, "Nothing better could be said for the Governor of New York than that Franklin Roosevelt loves him."[62]

The next order of business was the platform. Crafted by Senator Key Pittman of Nevada and by Judge Proskauer, it gave every appearance of being a courageous and exceptionally progressive document. The opening page, for example, included the statement, "Government must function not to centralize our wealth but to preserve equal opportunity," a continuation of the notes Claude Bowers had sung during his opening address. The Democrats declared openly that "labor is not a commodity," and called for collective bargaining as a cornerstone of industrial relations. They believed in "equality of women with men in all political and governmental matters," and would clearly favor "an equal wage for equal service." There was even a statement about the need for free speech on the radio airwaves. The convention supported this fine, solid document, and passed it unanimously with relatively little discussion.[63]

But beneath this apparent harmony, much deeper waters roiled. The problem was prohibition. Senator Carter Glass of Virginia had scripted a masterpiece of compromise, a statement that called for enforcement of the Constitution and nothing else. Lots and lots of barn doors were left open—like the one that allowed for repeal of the Eighteenth Amendment—but everyone, he argued, would have to agree that the law should be obeyed in the meantime, and all parties would be satisfied.[64]

Glass was dead wrong about that, even though his wording carried the floor ("this convention pledges the party and its nominees to an honest effort to enforce the Eighteenth Amendment"). Drys took this as too weak for words and became highly suspicious of what was *really* behind the platform—a fear that would be confirmed in a matter of hours after the voting had concluded.[65]

Even worse were the objections from Smith. If he had initially been a reluctant convert to the cause of prohibition repeal, back in 1923 when he agonized over the Mullin-Gage bill, by now he was an ardent champion. He had seen too much of the hypocrisy of the drys, too much of their bigotry toward Catholics and immigrants and everyone else who was not like them but was a lot like Al Smith. By 1928 the barbs had turned a rash into a wound, and this year, Al was determined to run an honest show.

Thus, during early discussions about the platform, it was Al who objected to the prohibition plank. The Volstead Act was unenforceable, he complained to his advisers, and everyone in the country knew it; he was not going to lie to the American people. As late as the evening the convention ratified the platform, Al told his daughter Emily, "That isn't on the level. . . . It doesn't *say* anything. It only dodges and ducks." All that, however, remained behind the scenes, fights resting in an incubator to hatch in a day or so.[66]

On the night of Thursday, June 28, 1928, the Democratic convention met to choose its candidate for the presidency of the United States of America. In those days etiquette required that top contenders stay home from any convention that might nominate them, so back in Albany, a new radio had been installed in the executive mansion. Al and the family sat glued, listening in every night until after midnight, sometimes going to bed as late as 4:00 A.M. This was the first time in history that a major party's meeting had been broadcast coast to coast on a radio network, and everyone commented that Houston was coming in so clear, it was like the convention was taking place right there in the parlor.[67]

Even now, as he was about to achieve a legendary goal, Smith refused to become a hypocrite, even at the cost of political gaffes that could have been catastrophic. The night Claude Bowers delivered his speech, for example, Al invited the reporters and photographers in to share the moment with him, and the flash boys began to set up their cameras. The governor meanwhile called for a bucket of ice, and soon an entire setup, including glasses and several bottles of whisky, was on the low table right in front of Smith as he sat on the sofa. With no apparent self-consciousness whatsoever, he proceeded to mix himself a highball, and then made up drinks for his guests, his friends. Technically, this was not illegal; the booze was pre-Volstead. And Al was just being himself. But neither of those facts would have stopped this from being the bombshell photo of the campaign, the governor taking a drink to celebrate the start of his convention. And no one, least of all Al, seemed to be aware of the possibilities. At last, someone finally had the enormous good sense to pull the table out of sight, and no member of the press ever squealed.[68]

Now, on the big night, Al had gathered his family and close friends around him. Outside, jamming the streets, on the lawn and even up onto the porch, a crowd waited, unable to hear and trying to get their cues from the actions of those inside the mansion. Cigar in hand, Al leaned over the radio as the roll call began that would put him on the road to a possible presidency. The opening words seemed to bode ill: "Mr. Chairman, Alabama casts one vote for Smith, eight votes for George and six votes for Hull." But Al had expected this, and Arizona came next, delivering all six of its ballots; the trend soon became clear.[69]

When the roll finally ended, Al Smith had 724⅔ votes, a resounding majority, but 10 fewer than were needed under the two-thirds rule. Former Ohio senator Atlee Pomerene promptly rose to announce, "Mr. Chairman . . . I request that Ohio's entire forty-five votes be recorded in favor of Al Smith," and other delegations followed, cementing the spirit of party loyalty. At the end of this revised first ballot, Al had 849⅔ votes and the nomination.[70]

Back in the executive mansion, Smith took off his glasses, his hand quivering a little, and told everyone, "My heart is where my palate ought to be." His eyes were moist. Belle Moskowitz turned to Robert Moses and proudly told him, "Bob, it's over." Well-wishers crowded around, and as Al regained his composure, he began to relax and lose the calm, restrained countenance he had maintained all that week, looking now more like a boy who was just happy that it was his birthday. Al walked out to the balcony, and the cheers tumbled into a roar, a clamor that went on and on for several minutes before the governor could thank the crowd and go back inside.[71]

In Houston, Katie sat high up in her official box, holding back tears, her delicate handkerchief rolled into a ball, clutched tight in her hand. People from all over came to congratulate her, and she could not keep the moisture from coming now. Busy with well-wishers, she ignored all the journalists, until one reporter, Emma Bugbee of the *New York Tribune,* got two policemen to lift her till she was on eye level with Mrs. Smith, and could talk to her woman to woman. Sweet, lovely Katie came totally undone, crying as she told Bugbee, "This is the happiest moment of my life, to find that others appreciate the Governor as I do. I want to thank you all." Just before then, locals had handed up Sam (as in Houston), a very young, very Democratic Texas donkey, and Katie just sat there, cradling the animal in her lap like a baby.[72]

Not everyone was celebrating. Even in the revised vote, Alabama, Florida, Georgia, Missouri, North and South Carolina, Texas, and Virginia had refused to endorse Smith, and the delegations from Kansas, Mississippi, and Oklahoma split their votes. The South, supposedly the bedrock of the party, refused to bolt but also refused to endorse; as one historian put it, Al had won the nomination but not the party. Cone Johnson, a Texas delegate, wrote later about his experiences, telling a friend, "I sat by the central aisle while the parade passed following Smith's nomination and the faces I saw in that . . . procession were not American faces. I wondered where were the Americans."[73]

And then came the bombshell. At 1:40 P.M. the next day, Senator Pat Harrison of Mississippi, presiding chair at this late moment, called the convention to order so he could read a telegram from their candidate. It began calmly enough, thanking them, declaring, "I accept the call of my party," pledging that he would stand by the platform.[74]

But when Harrison had first seen the telegram he had blurted, "My God. . . . This will cause a riot," then delayed releasing it until the hall was empty. It was the last section that had caused his reaction, the part that said that while Al would always uphold the law, it was "well known that I believe that there should be fundamental changes in . . . national prohibition." While this could only be done by the people themselves, he went on, "I feel it to be the duty of the chosen leader of the people to point the way which, in my opinion, leads to a sane, sensible solution of a condition which . . . is entirely unsatisfactory to the great mass of our people."[75]

In Houston, Harrison finished reading, but with that statement out in the open, the storm broke. To drys and southerners, Smith had now announced that he was the sworn enemy. Within hours, Bishop Cannon of the Methodist church and the Anti-Saloon League announced that he would hold a conference in July to defeat Smith and work for dry candidates only. Alice David of Oklahoma lamented, "It will be a long time in the memory of the people who live today, before the millions of good fathers and mothers in the Democratic Party, who fought relentlessly to outlaw the liquor traffic, will forget the action of the party at Houston, Texas." There, "Hearts were trampled without mercy when this convention chose a sopping wet to disgrace the leadership of the party." And worst of all, "This man lost no time in writing, 'I have not changed my views on the liquor question.'"[76]

There are various theories as to why the telegram went out, and which of Smith's aides was behind the decision. Claude Bowers reported that Moskowitz had insisted on it, but most analysis pointed to Walter Lippmann, columnist for the *New York World* and close friend of the governor. Franklin Roosevelt wrote in 1930 that "it was the *World* which literally drove Al Smith into sending that fool telegram." And Lippmann did, in fact, write to Mrs. M on June 25, "Things are going so well at Houston that we must take full advantage of the excellent spirit which is developing. I have given a lot of thought to the telegram which the Governor proposes to send when he is notified of his nomination. The part dealing with prohibition seems to me fine."[77]

Lippmann's letter, however, points to the truth of the matter—that it was, in fact, Smith's idea. The roots of the Houston telegram were nourished back in 1923, when Al vetoed Mullin-Gage because he thought it was the honest thing to do. But even more, they had been planted back in his childhood, when he learned that the American people were good and that if told the truth, they would rise to the occasion. Will Rogers had said that the prohibition plank was a farce—it looked as if it was "wet on week days and dry on Sunday"—and Al Smith would not run for president on a facade.[78]

In a few days, the candidate would compound this controversy with another. Al had to pick the new permanent chairman of the national committee, a figure who would represent the party at least as much as, if not more than, the vice-presidential candidate. He was supposed to be in charge of the entire campaign and would hold the seat until 1932 and the next election. Al chose John Jacob Raskob.

This was an unusual selection, to put it mildly, since Raskob was neither a politician nor a Democrat. Born in Lockport, New York, to an Alsatian cigar-maker father and an Irish mother, Raskob, like Smith, would become a self-made man. Finishing course work at a local business school, John rose no higher than a $7.50 a week salary as a stenographer, and cast about for more.[79]

A friend had gone out to Lorian, Ohio, and Raskob sent him a letter, asking about opportunities. Word came back that they were good, and the owner of the local streetcar line needed a secretary. John sent his application, and then negotiated a huge raise as a condition of employment, hiking his income to $1,000 a year. His new boss's name was Pierre Du Pont.[80]

That was in 1900, and it was a very good time to be working for the Du Ponts.

Two years later, Pierre joined with his cousins Coleman and Alfred to gain control over the real family business, a thriving munitions operation back in Delaware. Raskob rode along with them, going all the way; by 1915 he was a director, treasurer, and member of the Executive and Finance committees of the board of E. I. Du Pont de Nemours and Company.[81]

John returned the favor by helping the Du Ponts make lots of money—lots and lots and lots of money. In 1913 Raskob became interested in the auto business, his attention focusing on a small corporation run by a man named Durant. Henry Ford and his flivvers clearly dominated the market, but there might be room for a competitor or two. The secretary invested some of his own money, and got Pierre to buy some shares too. After World War I broke out, the Du Ponts found they had sizable profits to let loose, and they bought a controlling interest in the car company; by 1917 they owned the General Motors Corporation. Overall, during the war years, they had purchased $50 million worth of stock, and by the time Al Smith had won the nomination, the value of this commodity was up to $800 million—in 1928 currency. If that was not enough, in 1919 Raskob had also come up with the idea that it might help sales by allowing buyers to purchase a car on an installment plan rather than asking for the full price up front, as was standard back then. That year he created the GM Acceptance Corporation, the first system to allow people to buy an automobile on time, and within eight years 60 percent of all vehicles in the United States were sold that way, many of them carrying GM logos.[82]

By the late twenties, Raskob was a figure to be reckoned with, a man worth an estimated $100 million who sat on the board of companies that employed over 300,000 people; this meant that over a million Americans ate bread with the wages he controlled. A Republican who had voted for Coolidge in 1924, in *Who's Who* he listed his occupation simply as "capitalist." He had held no active position in politics before 1928, but was already on record as a dedicated opponent of prohibition, which he referred to as a "damnable affliction." In his personal life, Raskob remained a devout Catholic; his donations to the church totaled over a million dollars, and Pope Pius XI had responded by making him a Knight of the Order of Saint Gregory the Great, as well as a private chamberlain in the papal household. Raskob was already a charter member of the Knights of Malta, American Division.[83]

Lots of people claimed, in later years, to have introduced Raskob to Al Smith. A nightclub star and friend of the governor, Eddie Dowling, said that as early as 1919, the millionaire had come backstage after a show, and the two men got to talking about the milk scandal Hearst was foisting on the governor. Raskob expressed fierce support for Smith, so Eddie made the introduction. Ed Flynn, boss of the Bronx, wrote in his memoirs that he had been the matchmaker, and other authors cited William Kenny, who brought Raskob into the circles of his Tiger Club. Frances Perkins, on the other hand, thought it was Mrs. M who made the arrangements, on the grounds that a rich Catholic might turn out to be a good contributor in any one of the Smith campaigns.[84]

Regardless of who performed the introductions, both Smith and Raskob were stalwarts of the Tiger Club, and by 1928 they had become good friends. Raskob was spending a lot of time in the governor's mansion, and Al was inviting him to various events, chatting about their common interest in various Catholic activities and institutions.[85]

But despite all this, a super-rich, wet, Republican-voting political neophyte was hardly well positioned to manage the Democrats. When Raskob accepted the job he delivered a brief speech that began, "I am not a politician and have never been affiliated with any party, nationally or locally." The committee also released a letter from Raskob that called prohibition "a complete failure"; and in an even more bizarre twist, criticized *both* parties for waffling on the issue.[86]

From every corner and every angle, criticism of the appointment bellowed forth. Picking a Catholic for this kind of office was a problematic strategy, producing claims that only members of Al's church would serve with him in Washington. Willmoore Kendall of Vinita, Oklahoma, wrote Franklin Roosevelt that if Smith "means to surround himself exclusively with Catholic advisers, that is a further reason why many of us will be forced to desert the party standard." Add to that Raskob's untrammeled advocacy of repeal, and the result was an ad taken out in the *Progressive Age* of Scottsboro, Alabama. The text read in part, "AL SMITH could not find in the Solid South . . . or the West, or the east, even one solitary, single Democrat, he thought could be TRUSTED TO LEAD the Democratic forces!" Instead, "He took as superior to all Democrats John J. RASKOB, A WET, REPUBLICAN CATHOLIC to teach me how to say my Democratic political prayers." In other quarters, liberals quaked when Raskob made statements like, "more business in government and less government in business"; labor leaders began to consider the merits of the Socialist Party; and fundamentalist Christian populists asked if Smith stood for "Rum, Romanism and Motors." Walter Lippmann called Raskob an "innocent lamb," and Carter Glass wrote a fellow senator, "I think no more deliberate or greater insult was ever offered a national political party than the appointment of this man to the chairmanship."[87]

Once again, the decision was Smith's; Bernard Baruch wrote Al on July 3, "I am sorry I could not help you with the question of a campaign manager, but I had the impression that on that matter your mind was definitely closed and so I did not . . . discuss it with you." Smith himself made the final selection at 3:00 A.M. on the date of the announcement, after a prolonged meeting in Al's suite at the Biltmore. Everyone else—Belle Moskowitz, Joe Proskauer, Frank Roosevelt, even vice-presidential nominee Robinson—was against the choice of Raskob.[88]

Al had a number of reasons for his decision, of course. He expected Raskob to contribute a small fortune to the campaign (which indeed happened); he also wanted a businessman, in that great decade of prosperity, to give the Democrats more respectability. Supposedly at that late night meeting he raised the example of 1924, when the people of New York State had elected him governor by a solid margin but voted for Coolidge for president. "The only way I dope it out," Al told his advisers, was "that a whole lot of people who were willing to elect a Democratic Governor were afraid, for business reasons, of a Democratic administration in Washington. Jake Raskob will change all that. He's our best bet." Once again, there was that same pattern, of Al's making a decision that was intensely personal, sure that the American people would see its truth.[89]

Thus, in the end, the convention revealed both Al Smith's naiveté and his great appeal. In a telling moment, when everyone in the executive office in Albany was under incredible strain, an old policeman from the East Side of New York showed up with a hard-luck story. Seemingly ignorant of the great events going on, with everybody keyed up for the Houston news, the white-haired chap told his tale again and again, filled with circular reasoning, repeating the same events over and over. Everybody got annoyed except for the governor, who listened all the way through, and then put in a call to fix things up. Later, on the day after the nomination, when every dignitary in Albany came to call, Al went outside onto the veranda and made a few remarks to the crowd. As he stood at the railing after his talk, there, pushing through the crowd, emerged a row of faces—the street urchins of this city thrusting out their tiny grubby hands in congratulations—and Al responded far more generously than he did that day to any of the bigshots. As one observer put it, "He goes big with kids of all ages."

That same reporter also offered one of the best descriptions of Smith that anyone ever penned. The governor was "the freckle-faced small boy who shoots the biggest marble. Who doesn't have to wear an overcoat when *you* have to. Who swims harder and bikes farther and runs to a fire faster than you can. Who is everything you'd give your shirt to be, especially if you have only one shirt." From the perspective of Albany, that should have summed it up.[90]

~

Al made it official at 7:00 P.M. on August 22, 1928, when he delivered his acceptance speech from the podium of the Assembly Chamber in Albany. Outside it was raining, but inside Al glowed. Behind him, on his right, sat Joe Robinson and, closest in of all, John Raskob. Microphones would carry his voice, accent and all, to an astounding 111 radio stations nationwide. Key Pittman of Nevada, on behalf of the national Democratic Party, notified Al that he was the nominee; Pittman's declaration of an already obvious fact covered three formal pages of text, as was the custom in those days. Al now stood before the crowd, before America, and looked out across a room where, as he began to explain, "I learned the principles, the purposes and the functions of government," and where he also discovered that "the greatest privilege" anyone could have was to serve a nation "which has reared him and raised him from obscurity to be a contender for the highest office in the gift of its people." Then, on page following page, twenty in all, he laid out his position on every issue that he thought would matter in the two and a half months to come. But the opening paragraph had said it all, who he was and why he was there, on that day and in that place and time.[91]

The race of his life was now on.

Chapter 16

Taking On America

THE ELECTION OF 1928 was seminal, the defining event of a critical decade. In the 1920s America was changing from a society based on Victorian values—belief in progress, subordination to authority, reliance on community—to one that embraced modernism, with its pessimistic, cynical individualism.

One of the most fundamental transitions our culture ever had to go through, it stemmed from events and inventions that often shook, not just American, but Western society. In World War I, for example, men marched against machine guns, following orders, and died in numbers that still stagger the imagination: on June 1, 1916, the first day of the Battle of the Somme, the British Army suffered fifty-seven thousand casualties, nineteen thousand of these dead, a record that still stands, notwithstanding the next conflict's firepower. Soldiers, and then civilians, began to question established authority, the structure of society.

After the war, Americans had to confront other great engines of change. Most of these were consumer goods that offered so much pleasure, but also posed fundamental challenges to the traditional modes of life; they tantalized while threatening community. People across the country started listening to the radio, which brought sweet music at every hour of the day, but also new political ideas and pop culture that seemed harsh and discordant. Movies offered vast horizons to folks hidebound in local settings, but presented other lifestyles, other ideals. The auto gave mobility undreamed of before, but meant that teens were no longer protected by the scrutiny of village elders; one judge referred to this invention as nothing more than a brothel on wheels.

Running desperately to make sense of these basic shifts, Americans became a people both exhilarated by change and very, very scared. Event after event reminded them of what they had lost, restoking fears and bitterness: the Scopes trial (which resulted in the creation of Bob Jones University as a fundamentalist bastion), Sacco and Vanzetti, the debate over immigration restriction.

It was all too much, so in the end, many people felt there was nothing left to believe in other than the small world they knew intimately, with its carefully developed, almost intuitive, secure, and assuring social order and regulations. In the twenties, trying to deal with modernity, America drew back into a world of tiny social clusters, places, and settings that were the only things left that could give comfort and provide trust.

The best example of this was the Ku Klux Klan. The name derived from the Greek term *kuklos,* which means circle; it made clear who was inside, part of the group, and who was outside. The bigots, of course, defined the former as white, native-born Protestants only, the latter as the people Al Smith represented and more. But far beyond the Klan, this concept of the tightly defined cluster giving security, ease, and power remained a defining characteristic for all Americans in the twenties, and not just the hooded haters.

Take the case of H. L. Mencken, one of the most *bon* of all the *bon vivants* America produced in the twenties. Mencken loved that decade, because it gave him so much to make fun of, an activity he both adored and excelled in as has no other American, before or since. He referred to his countrymen as "homo boobiens" or the "booboisee"; when asked why, after all his social criticism, he continued to live in America, Mencken replied, "Why do men go to zoos?"[1]

But beneath the snide remarks and the cynicism, Mencken and his peers held on to each other, to their own world and their own customs, and were terrified to go outside. They rushed to the Algonquin Hotel to sit at the justly celebrated Round Table, traveled from New York to Paris (or, for Mencken, to his beloved Baltimore) without ever daring to stop to see how anyone else lived; the *New Yorker,* one of their finest offspring, openly announced that it was "not for the old lady from Dubuque." Heywood Hale Broun, whose illustrious father used to bring him to the Algonquin Round Table, claimed that for all the panache of that amazing court, although "they are now thought of as a bunch of hard-drinking, loose living aesthetes of jazz-age decadence," he personally remembered them as "jolly innocents, slightly unsophisticated people who loved to play word games and clung together in a mixture of fear and love." Mencken's crew, in other words, had their own *kuklos.*[2]

To win a national election in 1928, a politician needed to appeal to a great many small circles, and Al Smith responded by assembling a team that was mostly familiar players, with some important new faces. On paper, the DNC's campaign apparatus was a loose, clumsy structure. The chair, John Raskob, did not really sit at the top; in the middle was more like it. Every committee, every section, every officer either reported directly to him or to the executive committee he chaired, with no delegation of powers. The secretary, the treasurer, five regional vice chairs, an executive committee, a finance committee, an advisory committee, a women's advisory committee, and a board of counsellors all worked through him, with no other connections to each other, and no sense of hierarchy whatsoever.

That made Raskob look like quite a big shot, which had only a little to do with the truth. Jim Farley said that the job of a campaign manager was to be "a combination political drummer and listening post," but Raskob saw himself as a corporate CEO and as a fund raiser, neither role very surprising given his credentials. Raskob's greatest contribution, in fact, was to establish the DNC as an ongoing entity; in the past it had folded between elections, and in 1926 the women's division had to salvage its records and archives and store them in an attic because there was no other place. Raskob saw to it that the party had a permanent office for the first time, and even hired a publicity director, a move that paid huge dividends a year later when it gave the Democrats full-time capability to attack the Republicans over the Depression.[3]

But while Raskob achieved some long-term strategic goals, he had little to do with the day-to-day business, and staff at all levels tried to either ignore him or dissuade him from pursuing bad ideas. Frances Perkins described him as a "close featured, sharp person. . . . His face came to a point in front," that he had "eyes that sparkled like some animals' do. . . . It was like a mink." She thought he was "an awful crank to deal with . . . fussy . . . and hard to get along with"; Mrs. Moskowitz mostly spent time talking him out of sponsoring Catholic or wet rallies, ideas he seemed constantly to be proposing. Breckinridge Long, a powerful member of the DNC from Missouri, captured Raskob's diminutive role best of all in a note in his diary: Long was at headquarters through most of September and October, but not until October 15 could he write, "Real excitement today. I had a few minutes talk with Raskob—the Chairman!!! My first sight of him."[4]

The *real* flowchart resembled a typical Smith gubernatorial campaign. At the top stood the candidate himself, who made all the important decisions, and these were final. Below this were the triumvirate of Proskauer, Moses, and Moskowitz. Proskauer played the role of *eminence grise*, drafting a few speeches, making policy decisions, the distinguished mind that was Al's alter ego. Moses did writing and all kinds of prep work, collecting arcane data that nobody else could find (his files include documents like "Summary of Receipts of the Government of the United States" or "Appropriations for Partial Cost Only of Construction Projects"), and then turning them into pamphlets, policy reports, or speeches.[5]

But the one who did the most was Belle Moskowitz. Elisabeth Perry asserted that her grandmother was the first woman ever to manage a presidential campaign, and there is plenty of evidence to support that claim.

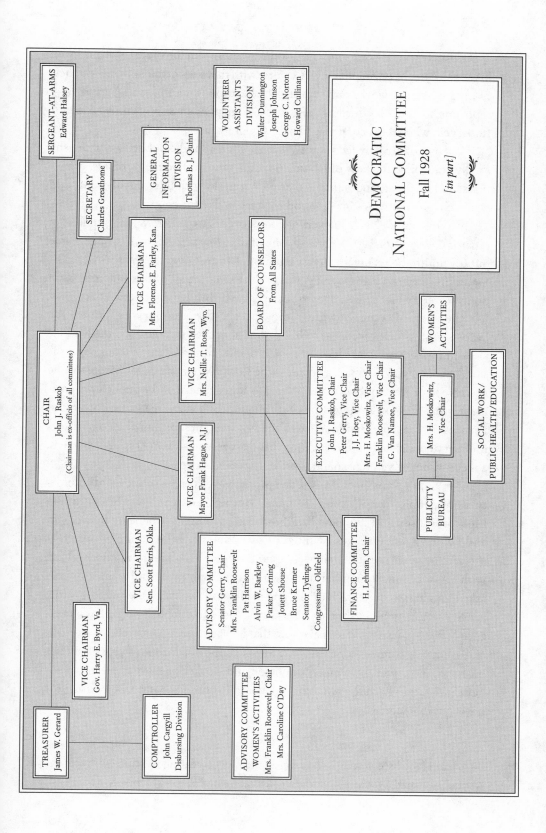

DEMOCRATIC
NATIONAL COMMITTEE

Fall 1928

[in part]

CHAIR
John J. Raskob
(Chairman is ex-officio of all committees)

SERGEANT-AT-ARMS
Edward Halsey

SECRETARY
Charles Greathome

GENERAL INFORMATION DIVISION
Thomas B. J. Quinn

VOLUNTEER ASSISTANTS DIVISION
Walter Dunnington
Joseph Johnson
George C. Norton
Howard Cullinan

VICE CHAIRMAN
Mrs. Florence E. Farley, Kan.

VICE CHAIRMAN
Mrs. Nellie T. Ross, Wyo.

BOARD OF COUNSELLORS
From All States

VICE CHAIRMAN
Mayor Frank Hague, N.J.

VICE CHAIRMAN
Sen. Scott Ferris, Okla.

VICE CHAIRMAN
Gov. Harry E. Byrd, Va.

TREASURER
James W. Gerard

COMPTROLLER
John Cargyill
Disbursing Division

EXECUTIVE COMMITTEE
John J. Raskob, Chair
Peter Gerry, Vice Chair
J.J. Hoey, Vice Chair
Mrs. H. Moskowitz, Vice Chair
Franklin Roosevelt, Vice Chair
G. Van Namee, Vice Chair

WOMEN'S ACTIVITIES

Mrs. H. Moskowitz,
Vice Chair

PUBLICITY BUREAU

SOCIAL WORK/ PUBLIC HEALTH/EDUCATION

ADVISORY COMMITTEE
Senator Gerry, Chair
Mrs. Franklin Roosevelt
Pat Harrison
Alvin W. Barkley
Parker Corning
Jouett Shouse
Bruce Kramer
Senator Tydings
Congressman Oldfield

FINANCE COMMITTEE
H. Lehman, Chair

ADVISORY COMMITTEE WOMEN'S ACTIVITIES
Mrs. Franklin Roosevelt, Chair
Mrs. Caroline O'Day

As usual, Mrs. M's statutory position was minor; on the diagram she is listed in the third tier as one of many vice chairs, with three departments—the publicity bureau, social work/public health/education, and women's activities—reporting to her. The third of these was an independent force, run by Eleanor Roosevelt, while the second played only a minor role.

The basis of Moskowitz's power was her control of the publicity bureau; she totally controlled the flow of information, the flow of statements, of ads, of pictures, and of appearances that had anything to do with the campaign. Mrs. M was in charge of how Al Smith would be presented to the country.

Everyone knew this, and everyone took orders from her. When Republican senator George Norris of Nebraska, one of the great reformers of the age, came out for Smith, he received a letter from the Progressive League for Alfred E. Smith presenting a campaign agenda for the senator; all of this, the organization's secretary made clear, had first been cleared with Belle Moskowitz. Regarding the idea of a nationwide radio speech, the secretary described the process—Mrs. M's power—as follows: "She approved the idea, said the National Committee would take care of it, and that it should be done from her division." Senator Key Pittman, a power in the Rocky Mountain states, wrote that he was able to proceed only because "Mrs. Moskowitz, head of the publicity department, has accepted a suggestion that I made." She also created, according to Frances Perkins, the first modern campaign structure, organizing committees for every conceivable interest group: professors, social workers, labor leaders, college students, veterans, naturalized citizens and more.[6]

After Smith, Proskauer, Moses, and Moskowitz, the next real level of authority were people like Walter Lippmann, Herbert Lehman, and Franklin and Eleanor Roosevelt. Lippmann had direct access to Smith whenever he wanted, and helped draft speeches, while writing articles for the nation's press that praised the governor. Lehman was again treasurer and chief fund raiser (along with Raskob), and a member of the executive committee. Smith, meanwhile, asked Franklin to organize business and professional men for the coming battle, a role FDR, with his customary shrewdness, used to establish himself as a presence at headquarters and to make sure that he had a seat and a voice on the crucial executive committee. Eleanor, a Smith supporter for more years than her husband, took over the women's division and worked as hard as she could for her candidate—harder even than she would for her husband when he ran for governor that same year.

⟿

This team faced some tough challenges, the most daunting of which was that the Republicans had a fabulous candidate, a man named Herbert Hoover.

Herbert Hoover's reputation, our most basic reaction to the sound of his name, will forever be shaped by the story of the Great Depression. From that time on, his image would be sealed as a man who failed to respond to a national tragedy, a leader who would rather see citizens starve than desert his increasingly ineffectual and outdated values.

But for all the solid accuracy of this depiction, it is also important to explain what Hoover's image was *before* the stock market crashed and why he was far and away the strongest opponent Al Smith could have faced in 1928. The truth of the matter was, that year Herbert Hoover was a fantastic candidate.

If in 1920 the census showed that for the first time most Americans lived in cities, this still meant that a majority had been brought up on the farms and small towns of the countryside. And for these people, Herbert Hoover personified the nation and its best beliefs.

Herbert was born in West Branch, Iowa, a small, friendly town in the nation's heartland. It was just a few streets long and wide, and everybody knew each other, so when Herbert's parents died, relatives took in the orphan and saw that he and his siblings were cared for. Out of this came the myth of Hoover as the All-American hero; when Herbert made good, he was not only a small-towner but an orphan as well, one of the great images of American melodramas so prevalent at the time.

And Herbert did *extremely* well. Deciding to become a mining engineer, Hoover arrived at Stanford University with its opening class. After graduation, his first job was in the distant prairie of Australia, where he pioneered new methods of extracting wealth; he then entered the boardrooms of London, becoming a partner in a major overseas firm; and eventually got to China, finding himself caught in the middle of the Boxer rebellion and organizing civilian resistance in Tientsin. By 1914, when he was only thirty years of age, Herbert had become a millionaire (when that still meant something extravagant), and had lived a life of adventure that seemed like a fantasy out of the Arabian nights.

By the time World War I had broken out, Hoover was bored. Living in reasonable splendor in London, he had become a mining capitalist—one who put together and oversaw large projects (and made large amounts of money) but rarely ventured out to the pits anymore. A man of prodigious energy, a man who always had to be doing something, Herbert subconsciously was looking for some new field of endeavor.

He found it by sheer chance. When the conflict of nations erupted, many Americans found themselves stranded. Merchants, panicked by the chaos, would only accept local currency. Thousands of trapped souls crowded the American embassy in panic seeking assistance, with more streaming in from the Continent each day.

In the face of this emergency, the ambassador to the Court of St. James decided to request help from a countryman who had extensive contacts in British banking circles. Hoover accepted the call and set up an apparatus to exchange money, provide relief for stranded parties, and arrange transport home through violent waters. One obstinate old woman demanded a written guarantee that submarines would not sink her ship, and Herbert, ever practical, signed the note figuring that if the worst case occurred, the note would go down with her anyway.[7]

Hoover began to make a name for himself, and soon found his services in greater demand. In the first months of the war, all of Belgium, along with parts of northern France, became trapped behind the German trench lines, and it would remain occupied territory for most of the next four years. No one cared about how these people would survive; the Germans, pressed for supplies, were confiscating local stores for their own needs, while the Allies just ignored the situation as they struggled to survive on the western front. In short order, starvation became a real possibility; Brand Whitlock, the American ambassador in Brussels, noted in his diary how on October 23, 1914, for the first time, "a hungry little girl" had appeared at the embassy gates to plead for food.[8]

The Belgian government now decided that the man to handle this situation was none other than Herbert Hoover. And what a situation it was: Hoover had to negotiate millions of pounds of food and clothing, then get it across war lines, convincing *both* sides that this would be used for humanitarian purposes only. Hundreds of thousands of people—entire nations—held on and survived because Herbert Hoover managed to do the impossible.

In 1917, Woodrow Wilson summoned Herbert back home to serve his country. Wilson asked him to take over as food czar, understanding that American foodstuffs now had to feed not only the civilian population, but a several-million-man American army, the armies of France and Britain, and Europe's hungry civilians as well.

Hoover created a conservation program, and its political, as opposed to humanitarian, significance is still relatively unexplored by historians. To fully appreciate just what he did, one must first understand the assignment: Wilson had asked him to handle what later generations would refer to as a national security matter, to protect a vital war commodity. Hoover had at his command a government publicity apparatus, and the audience seemed obvious: the American people, who had to be convinced to eat less for the war effort. Hoover could have gone at this any number of ways, by asking food corporations to market his ideas to their customers, by appealing to the virility of men, or by using the innocence of schoolchildren.

Instead, he turned to women. Every housewife became a war worker, asked to participate in a national effort run by the U.S. government. Across America, ladies in their kitchens, usually considered second-class citizens—and still not allowed to vote—signed an official document that read, "I pledge myself to use the practical means within my power to aid the Food Administration in its efforts to conserve the food supplies of the country." A "Home Card" listing the now clichéd litany of "Wheatless Wednesdays" and "Meatless Mondays" (there were also "Porkless Saturdays," but this was neither alliterative nor catchy), delivered clear instructions, "Hang this where you will see it every day." No one meant this for the husband or the children; it was momma whom Hoover had enlisted in this struggle. Each woman received, in addition to the pledge card, a button, something they could wear in public to let neighbors know that they were proud, and Herbert Hoover had made them feel that way.[9]

He also enlisted women as workers. The Food Administration used voluntarism, setting up committees to run things at the state, county, and local levels. While many of the people at the top were men, hordes of women got involved, looking for an outlet for their enormous and previously rejected talents. Editor William Allen White, for example, endorsed Linna Bresette to Hoover. She already headed welfare work in Kansas, was in charge of mine inspection, and had won a minimum wage law for women in that state. Quite an impressive record, but Bresette wanted more, to work as men did, in a patriotic campaign; White observed, she "doesn't want a job," she "wants to serve." Herbert appointed her to head the local committee to help win the war.[10]

Hoover did more than appeal to women, of course. He talked to merchants, cajoled producers, and leaned on schoolchildren to persuade their parents. Some of this we look back on now and laugh at: the naiveté of a flier that solemnly proclaimed, "Corn Meal—Our Ally"; the conservation program for schools that told teachers to "Have slogans or pithy sentences repeated"; or a wonderful pamphlet, *Garbage Utilization,* that included this mouth-watering quote from "the health officer of a large New England city": "I believe," he calmly argued, "garbage-fed pork is as wholesome as any that can be obtained. I eat it myself when I can get it, and I wish I could afford more of it." But for millions of women across the nation, the importance of the war years remained unsullied: Herbert Hoover, alone among political leaders and administrators, had asked for their help. Herbert Hoover, and no other, had made them part of the nation.[11]

After the war, Hoover remained a hero by feeding the millions in starving Europe. Richard Hofstadter, one of the most hardnosed of modern American historians, could still be moved to write, "In a time of havoc and hatred the name Hoover came to mean food for the starving and medicine for the sick."[12]

Moving from triumph to triumph, Hoover became the most important man in Washington during the twenties, using his position as secretary of commerce to tackle anything and everything that a succession of lazy administrations ignored. Take radio, for example; Herbert Hoover grabbed it by the throat and set it up for his countrymen, assigning the first series of frequencies and call signs, creating the Federal Communications Commission to enforce these rules. In every home, they could say, "Thank you, Mr. Hoover," as order replaced chaos, and the sounds of music and laughter, adventure and mystery came crisply over the air waves in separate, distinct channels. And if fewer citizens took aeroplanes back then, Herbert organized things for them anyway, establishing the Federal Aviation Administration.

What makes Hoover's candidacy all the more fascinating is that although he got nominated on the first ballot in 1928, Herbert was hardly the consensus choice of his party. Republicans, and many others, perceived Hoover as far and away the most liberal of that party's leaders, a man who had engaged in relief work and other feminine-type activities, and who had said some very dangerous things about free enterprise. In his most famous writing up to that time, a small book with the powerful title, *American Individualism*, Hoover wrote, "We have long since abandoned . . . laissez-faire. . . . We have confirmed its abandonment in terms of legislation, of social and economic justice." The Old Guard of the Republicans, who prayed that Coolidge would change his mind and run again, hated this kind of heresy; Senator Frank Brandegee of Connecticut said simply, "Hoover gives most of us gooseflesh." This would be an interesting nominee, indeed.[13]

Hoover's managers designed a campaign that minimized the use of the real, living candidate, and capitalized on his image. As much as they could, the Republicans talked about prosperity, letting everyone know that they were responsible for it while linking it to Hoover's reputation as a provider. The classic ad read, "A Chicken for Every Pot . . . Vote for Hoover," at a time when fowl remained a delicacy, served only on Sunday in most working-class homes. Workers distributed a copper coin called the "Hoover Lucky Pocket Piece," on which had been inscribed, "Good for four years of prosperity." Negative ads reminded voters of what might happen if Herbert *did not* win, pamphlets with titles like, *Your Job Versus the Spectre of Idleness and Ruin*. Pictures that came with this literature showed a smiling candidate, usually in the company of some warm, all-American prop like a large, friendly dog.[14]

The Republicans knew they had a lot of strengths, not the least of which was that they were the majority party at that time. Yet no one underestimated how formidable an opponent Al Smith would be for their man, one of the members of the Republican National Committee stating at the outset that they had "a serious task," that if they "should go into this great endeavor with a light heart it would be a mistake." One of Hoover's most intimate advisers referred to "the great personal popularity of Governor Smith, even among Republican workers." A reporter quipped that at any other time, Hoover might have made it, but this year he would be lost, "no match for a human cyclone."[15]

This stood in marked contrast to their own man. Herbert was an immensely proper, immensely private individual who did not lend himself to popularization. Reporters noted that there were no funny stories about the candidate—ever—and that unlike Smith, he was "about as gossipy as a multiplication table." For twenty-five years his attire consisted of double-breasted blue suits and nothing else; even the dinner hour required a jacket and tie in the Hoover household. That year, at least, Herbert Hoover was an admirable, but not a likable fellow.[16]

Even worse, before this election, he had never run for public office and had no understanding of what it meant to campaign for a position, nor did he like doing so. Prior to his nomination, Hoover refused to make even a solitary statement that was political, and over the course of the entire race, spoke only seven times. Bert (as his friends called him) told the staff, "I can make only so many speeches. I have just so much to say." To Herbert, this campaign would be no great contest, no magnificent struggle, but a terrible, tedious chore. James Williams, a journalist who had been around since the days of Theodore Roosevelt, noted, "Public sentiment, the public sentiment which Lincoln spoke of when he said, 'Public sentiment is everything . . .' was an absolute stranger to Mr. Hoover."[17]

The Republicans tried hard to overcome this, although sometimes the results were comical. A headline in *Farm Life,* for example, told readers, "That Man Hoover—He's Human." Less successful was the campaign booklet entitled, *Epigrams from Hoover's Acceptance Speech,* not the kind of phrase that grabbed voters.[18]

The candidate did not help, either. Herbert dutifully wrote all his own speeches, and it takes a sense of duty, indeed, to read them. One observer referred to the printed words as "rhetorically cumbersome," while another called it "suggestive of a light fog moving over a gray landscape." His voice, furthermore, could only be complimented by describing it as a monotone; reporter Henry Pringle complained that Hoover did not use even a single gesture during a speech: "He reads—his chin down against his shirt front—rapidly and quite without expression. . . . He can utter a striking phrase in so prosaic, so uninspired and so mumbling a fashion that it is completely lost on nine out of ten of his auditors." During personal interviews, Herbert would give an answer and then stop; no follow through, no smile, no segue, just performing "like a machine that has run down." Even supporters like Agnes Home of Los Angeles, who corresponded with Herbert's wife, felt compelled to "dare to make a suggestion in regard to your husband's delivery of his . . . speeches." "Could he," the genteel Mrs. Home inquired, "possibly put more 'pep' in his delivery?"[19]

∿

Smith could have run strongly against this kind of opponent, maximizing his strengths against Hoover's weaknesses as he stumped vigorously around the country, but his basic campaign strategy was flawed. Al believed in a high-minded, short campaign that would stimulate the voters. He would give a small series of speeches, one every week or so, each focusing on a specific issue he wished to highlight. His model of course, was the gubernatorial contest of 1924, when this strategy had succeeded wonderfully. To Al, this approach treated the people with respect, appealing to their brains and not their instinct for sensationalism, trusting them to listen and think and make a fair decision.[20]

Unfortunately for him, this was not 1924, and the arena was not New York State. Smith needed to put in a lot more appearances to a considerably larger range of audiences and address a much wider set of topics. As governor, for example, Al never had to answer a question on foreign policy; now his view on the League of Nations would become a matter of public record.

Making matters worse, Smith and his advisers deliberately set out to prove that the candidate was no radical, that he believed in a sound business climate. Looking at a booming economy and stock market, this seemed only sensible, a logical way of playing to the era.

But there were also enormous drawbacks to that approach. First, it undercut Al's standing with his most loyal and traditional audience, reformers and progressives. An editorial in the *Nation,* for example, started by branding the Republican candidate as a reactionary, stating, "Mr. Hoover stands in this contest for the old order." But when they looked at Al's record in contrast, they could not see as much to support as they would have liked, which caused them considerable teeth gnashing. They wanted to come out for the New York champion, wanted to so bad you could taste it between the lines, but his pro-business stance stuck in their craw. In the end, the editors had to waffle, telling readers, "The question of whether the voter can this year best contribute . . . by voting for Norman Thomas [Socialist Party candidate] or for Al Smith they leave to the individual conscience of each progressive voter."[21]

There was also another problem that weakened Al's appeal. Smith had every right to run on his record of combining social reform with administrative rigor, but in 1928 that might not have been such a smart move. If he had been up against someone like Coolidge, for example, the contrast would have been striking and successful, but that year his opponent also could claim a record of humanitarianism balanced by superb management skills. So Al dropped that argument, and, by not stressing his long record of getting socially relevant bills through a hostile legislature, failed to highlight significant differences between himself and Hoover.

As a result of all these decisions, when it came to the formal set of issues, the kinds of platform statements that candidates really campaigned on in those days, the Democrats in 1928 sounded too much like the Republicans. One historian said that the two parties' platforms were "as nearly identical as they could be without a mimeograph." Even in 1928, Walter Lippmann complained that he could see no difference between the two documents, except that "the Republican took longer to read."[22]

With no substantial issue to differentiate the parties, the election became a contest between personalities, each representing one image of America. Ernest Abbot, writing in the *Outlook,* summed up what was about to happen when he wrote, "It is becoming more and more clear that the question for debate has been not what you are voting for but for whom."[23]

Both men became symbols. Hoover personified the older America of small towns and villages, whose ancestors had arrived long ago. Smith represented industrial America, living in its cities and its milltowns, families who could still tell you when they first landed, and which relative had taken the citizenship test and which had not. As one writer so aptly explained, "Each candidate carried indelibly the stamp of his beginnings. Never in the history of . . . America did the voters so generally, if unconsciously, apply the natural standard found in the phrase, 'one of our own.'" The 1928 campaign became one of the worst examples of cultural wars in the history of the country.[24]

And Al Smith's greatest achievement, his moment of true and lasting courage, was that he never backed away from *this* fight. If in 1928 he downplayed his progressive heritage, never once did Al do anything but stand proud when it came to his ancestry, his boyhood on the streets, or his parents barely advanced from steerage. By so doing, he became a hero, a leader who stood up when it may not have been wise and repeated instead his message: that these people—his people—were Americans too, just as good, just as valid, just as important as the ones supporting Hoover. As he told a crowd in St. Paul, "Any man who comes to this country, raises a family, educates them in our public schools and, by his labors and toil helps to keep open the channels of trade and commerce, obeys our laws . . . is just as good a citizen of this country as the man or group of men who can point to a long and unbroken line of New England ancestry."[25]

The Democrats had some other telling assets, besides Al's courage. Throughout the modern era of politics, starting with the McKinley-Bryan race in 1896, they had been outspent by the Republicans, usually by ridiculous margins. Bryan, for example, spent only $675,000 compared to McKinley's $3.5 million, and not much had changed by the twenties: in 1920 Republican Warren Harding outspent Democrat James Cox by $5.3 million to $1.3 million, or better than 3:1. Things were so bad that workers showing up at DNC headquarters on Election Day found themselves locked out because the committee had defaulted on its rent; one wag remarked that the only thing working at headquarters was "the revolving electric sign which has the pictures of Cox and Roosevelt on it," adding, "you cannot win an election without money." Four years later, in 1924, the figures were equally dismal, the GOP coughing up $3.1 million for Calvin Coolidge, the Democrats muddling through with $900,000 for John W. Davis.[26]

Raskob made it his business to guarantee that in 1928 the Democrats would not have that problem. Fund raising began early, and by the time the contest ended, the Democrat National Committee had come up with almost $3.2 million, compared to the Republicans' $4.1 million. That year the Democrats were at least in the running, fighting on much more even terms.[27]

Who were these contributors, the unprecedented 90,000 Americans who gave money to the Democrats, the 140,000 who funded the Republicans? Most of it was big money; contributions of $5,000 or more (a greater sum than most Americans made in a year) accounted for 52.7 percent of the DNC total but only 45.8 percent of the RNC funds, indicating that Raskob's efforts among the wealthy had paid off. Bankers and brokers made up 25 percent of Democratic benefactors, just a fraction less than their 28 percent for the Republicans. The Democrats naturally did better among the poorest contributors: 12.5 percent of their money came from donations of less than $100, while only 8.5 percent of the Republican money derived from this source.[28]

At the top of this list of contributors, three men—John Raskob, Herbert Lehman, and William Kenny—deserved the biggest thank-yous, contributing $342,000 between them. Another seventy-three people donated $10,000 or more, including Bernard Baruch and the shipbuilder William Todd; Todd, one of the Tiger Room gang, was a Republican most years, but when asked by a Senate committee how much he would fork over for Al, declared, "I'll give him anything he needs as long as I got anything to give."[29]

All of these funds got spent on the quest for the presidency. Al's personal expenses for the entire campaign, private train and all, came to less than $100,000, while Robinson got just under $40,000. The largest sum—$1.665 million—went to Smith organizations at the state level, but big money got passed to the Agricultural Division ($470,000) and to Moskowitz's publicity apparatus, $844,000, of which $500,000 went for radio time (in 1924 the Democrats spent only $40,000 on this). Franklin Roosevelt's division spent only $38,000. The DNC also maintained a large campaign staff—375 people on the New York payroll alone.[30]

Political campaigning was in a transitional stage at that point, moving from personal, direct contact to the use of mass media. Al came from the old school and dearly preferred the former technique—what Hugh Carey called "the uproarious clambake style . . . with the horns and whistles . . . the mixing with people kinds of campaigns."[31]

Smith traveled around the country in an eleven-car train; the candidate stayed in William Kenny's private coach, a palace regally named the "St. Nicholas." Behind this followed an observation car and three cars for the press, which included newspaper folk, photographers, and even motion picture operators. After that came a diner (open twenty-four hours a day), one car filled with the campaign's own stenographers and mimeograph machines and literature, one car for press conferences with a long mahogany table that also contained a shower and a barber shop, and extra sleeping and storage cars. The total complement of this traveling road show was approximately eighty people, half of them journalists.[32]

When it came time for the candidate to perform, every stop began with a band playing "The Sidewalks of New York." The crowd would wave flags and handkerchiefs, and men and women would stand on chairs they had brought, or hoisted sons and daughters up on their shoulders to see the great man. In towns with a larger Catholic population, places like St. Louis or Boston, they would go wild, people weeping and fainting, holding up babies to be touched.[33]

Al made campaigning look easy, but he was always prepared. He traveled with notes, clippings, briefing books of every kind, and in his memoirs talked about going to bed at 3:00 A.M., "after working over books and papers for four hours," only to find himself "in a station at seven in the morning with the village orator perched on the platform and shouting, 'Come out here Al, and give us a look at you.'"[34]

When Al gave them a look, the audience saw a man about five feet, eight inches tall, though his long body and scrawny neck gave the impression of greater height. There were the first signs of a potbelly, but his skin was pink and clear, with bright blue eyes. He could not appear in public without a brown derby (the train had boxes of them), and though he often wore standard business suits, every so often he would appear in a matching brown outfit, radiant with a raspberry-colored shirt (sometimes with a white collar), this tone picked up by a maroon tie and pocket square.[35]

Smith was at his best in these old-fashioned settings. He could reach out, make eye contact, and engage in verbal byplay. Several years later, he wrote, "No man . . . can deliver a speech to a microphone. It never nods approval. It never stimulates him by expressing dissatisfaction with his statements. It never warms him with a handclap and it never shows its appreciation." Talking to real people was different; for men like Al Smith, it was the essence of true politics.[36]

Wherever he went during those passionate weeks, Al caused a sensation. Traveling to Tennessee, he visited Chattanooga and Nashville, speaking before packed halls. In Philadelphia the *Record* declared for Smith, the first time in thirty years the paper had backed a Democratic candidate. When he went into rib-rock Smith country, the hard land of Massachusetts, the results were epic—thirty thousand turning out when his train stopped in Springfield, the reception in Boston the largest of its kind in the history of the New England states. Forty Harvard professors endorsed Al Smith, while their students organized the Brown Derby Brigade and gave speeches anywhere they could. In the working-class Charlestown district, every house carried a picture of the Democratic standard-bearer; in structures of three or four stories there was often a poster or banner displayed on each floor. Al would stand there and talk to his people, kid with them; when a fan yelled, "I'll vote nine times for you, Al," the candidate roared back, "O.K., pal . . . but don't get caught!"[37]

But the candidate had to use other means to reach the American people. Reams of literature poured from every Smith headquarters in the country; as early as July 30, the New York office had placed orders for 2 million Smith-Robinson pictures, another 2.25 million images of the head of the ticket by himself, and 2.5 million buttons. Over 150 different pamphlets appealed to every taste, pieces like the *Life History of Governor 'Al' Smith in Poetry* (twenty-eight verses), *What Everybody Wants to Know About Alfred E. Smith*, and *Why I Support Alfred E. Smith*, by Henry Morgenthau. The Naturalized Citizens Division produced literature for Carpatho-Ruthenians, Danes, Croats, Armenians, Czechs *and* Slovaks (the campaign wisely understood the difference), Hungarians, Franco-Americans, Greeks, Lithuanians, Puerto Ricans, Norwegians, Serbs, Rumanians, Slovenians, Spaniards, Swedes, and Syrians. All written in the native tongue.[38]

But Smith needed more than volunteers handing out literature to convince the American voter. In an age when *everyone* read a daily newspaper, sometimes two or three, the press was an essential component of any campaign, and Al's relationship with the Fourth Estate was a mirror of the weaknesses and strengths of his entire campaign. As with everything else, his staff was far too heavily weighted toward New Yorkers. For press secretary he and Moskowitz had picked Joe Cohen, a reporter at the tabloid *New York Evening Graphic,* who could not have been more stereotypical. About thirty-five years of age, given to flashy clothes and a braggadocio manner, Cohen personified the Gothamite, and was a Jew to boot; he had little in common with the bulk of journalists covering the governor.[39]

But again, the candidate was always their trump card. Al tried hard, taking reporters everywhere, holding two conferences a day, and by and large it worked. How could anyone resist a guy who began his daily sessions by barking, "Throw in the ball, boys, and I'll kick at it." The contrast with the cold, remote Hoover was too obvious, and colleagues covering the Republican candidate could only grimace in jealousy.[40]

Al, in fact, brought out the best in many of these writers. Bess Furman, eventually one of Washington's premier journalists, in 1928 was a reporter for the *Omaha Bee-News,* assigned to cover Al's upcoming speech in her town. Just before the candidate's train entered the city limits, she hopped aboard, and in a short while had contracted a bad case of Smith fever. Later, when she heard his big talk, this only got worse: "What Mr. Smith was doing to that crowd practically had me mesmerized," she recalled. Afterward, she was so keyed up, she went back "with the boys to the office," just to talk it over and get the excitement out of her system.[41]

But now she had to do justice to that extraordinary experience. After writing a couple of sentences, an idea came to her: she typed, "Al Smith's campaigning was something pretty special, gave a lift, had an effect like the cocktails that our 'best people' went in for in a big way." She described Al as something that had the pizzazz of champagne, but got your attention the way a martini did; efforts to continue the analogy created a problem, however, since, as Furman explained, "Being of a strict Prohibition family myself, I had not the slightest idea of what went into a cocktail." So she called in a more worldly colleague, and they had a ball inventing the right combination of ingredients (vermouth, they solemnly agreed, unquestionably symbolized satire). The final piece opened with a paragraph on all the flimflammery used in campaigns, then segued to the theme— how "without a single superlative, plain-talk Al Smith started politics stirring as gently as he stirs with his brown derby on parade, stirred and stirred and stirred until he could quaff a campaign concoction to his taste." Furman continued: "He had flavored his drink with that mint called humor, added the faintest tang of satiric vermouth, had given it body with logical lime, and had brought it to rosy perfection with the big red maraschino cherry of his own personality." And to

wrap it up, the line, "A connoisseur of that heady vintage called campaigning—
Al Smith."

The biggest problem with this mechanism was that no matter how effective in
person, Al could not extend that humanity, could not project it across any medium that was not upfront and intimate. And 1928 stood out for being the first
presidential election in American history in which electronic media played a
vital role.

The first election broadcasts had been in 1920, as the few radio stations in
existence sent out the news of Harding's election. Even in 1924, this form of
communication was still something of a novelty, and that year Calvin Coolidge
made the first live presidential address over the airwaves.

But by 1928 radio was nationwide. The National Broadcasting Company
(NBC) alone had seventy-five outlets, with the Columbia Broadcasting System
(CBS) close behind with fifty. An audience of 40 million people could listen in to
any big event, and even when Al spoke in Denver, way outside the primary East
Coast and Midwest broadcasting zones, twenty-six stations carried his speech.[42]

Typical were the experiences of Helen Cook, a Hoover supporter in
Louisville, who wrote to the candidate's wife how she had heard Herbert over
the radio, at a friend's house. It happened, like so many other episodes in that
era, when "our friend left the doors of his home open, as the night was warm,
and pretty soon the neighbors began to come to the door, asking if they might be
allowed to 'listen in,' and soon there was quite an audience, listening to, and
'rooting' for Mr. Hoover." What an amazing experience: "Every word of his
speech came home, clear and true. We felt that Mr. Hoover was speaking to each
one of us personally as we sat there enthralled." Even a worldly person like
Frances Perkins, in the cynosure of New York, heard the news from a neighbor's
radio across the airshaft that connected their apartments. Before, the man had
used headphones, but during the summer of '28 he bought a "loudspeaker," and
now Perkins marveled at how she was kept awake in New York "by the noise of
the Democratic convention in Houston."[43]

This new medium, however, was hardly neutral in its impact. Although Al
had used the system back in his gubernatorial days and eventually adjusted
somewhat, he still had pretty much everything against him when it came to
radio.

Take the problem of a speech's length. Carter Glass, U.S. senator from Virginia and a typical politician of his age, once complained, "I have never tried the
experiment of speaking over radio or of making a political speech in thirty minutes. I am sure I could never make one in fifteen minutes." Not once in his life

had Glass ever been timed, and neither had Al. But now, to go on the air, speakers like these two would have to be ratcheted into a limited allotment of minutes, with no overtime allowed. Al's flamboyant style, his greatest asset, was severely curbed.[44]

His showmanship got lost as well. Al used the stage as his friend, dancing across it, arms gesturing, pulling his audience along with him as he unraveled his strange stories of government in action. None of this worked on the radio; no one could see the movement, no one could watch as his body moved and his face got red.

But even worse, any movement at all could ruin one's radio presence. In those days radio stations used what are now referred to as pieplate microphones. They were huge, but by modern standards not very sensitive; in order to be heard, a speaker had to stand right in front and talk plainly, precisely, and directly into the sound system. When Al fidgeted, the result was an annoying presence on the air as the sound of his voice roared and faded unnaturally. In time Smith did much to cure this tendency, standing square and straight where he was supposed to, but he never totally accepted the idea that he had to confine himself in this manner, and the *New York Times* reported that Al forced the medium "to its limit in faithfully recording his utterances."[45]

Finally, there was the issue of his accent. If you saw Al Smith in person, you knew what a great fellow he was, read past the gaudy vernacular. But on the radio there was, for many listeners, nothing but a foreign voice, at minimum one that was coarse and lacking in the language's graces. Andrew White, CBS president, wrote that "radio broadcasting has made pronunciation a factor in a presidential campaign for the first time in history, this year."[46]

Hoover had all the aces in this game; what worked against him on the stump made him a perfect radio speaker. He had no difficulty standing a precise ten inches away from the pieplate and staying there for as long as it took to deliver his speech. If his voice was flat, it also spoke in the tones of the Midwest, without a trace of local coloration, with nothing to offend an audience anywhere in the land. His was the sound of a later generation of newscasters, all of whom would speak in that standardized, generic tongue.

The irony was that another mechanism, in its infancy, would have been much more favorable to Smith. In 1927 Herbert Hoover made a few remarks at a political ceremony that got broadcast in sound *and* picture, but the first real televised political address came in August 1928, when the General Electric Company had its cameras transmit Governor Smith's postconvention acceptance speech from the steps of the state capitol to station WGY in Albany, where it went out over the airwaves. This was a primitive effort: Al had to stand in front of a thousand-watt lamp, and put up with photoelectric cells placed eighteen inches on either side of his head to convert light into electrical current. The result was a barely perceptible image with the now-hard-to-imagine resolution of only forty-eight lines to the inch (even by the next year, they had gotten it up to ninety lines). But for the first time, here was a medium that could catch this man as he really was, with all of his style and personality. It came just a little too late for Al Smith's presidential bid.[47]

Chapter 17

"Politics! Politics!"

OUT ON THE HUSTINGS it was a grand year. The Progressive Era's political reforms were supposed to have done away with the boisterous popular politics that existed in the late nineteenth century; as party organizations lost power to democracy, America gave up its torchlight parades, riots and brawls, and other forms of party-led activism. But 1928 rekindled the old fires, brought campaigning back to life, as Americans engaged in the greatest national debate of their era. All around the country at the local level, people began to get involved in the election in a way that they had not for many, many years. Older folk remembered the two Wilson runs of 1912 and 1916, and maybe when Teddy spoke in 1904. Grandpappy might even be moved to speak with fervor of the great Bryan-McKinley contest of 1896. But for a younger generation—and even for the old-timers—no one had ever seen anything like this.

"Politics! Politics! Everywhere you go, everyone is discussing it," A. J. T. wrote to the *Waco News-Tribune*. He complained that "you can't read any paper without finding it just full of politics. You can't step out on the street without being besieged by politics." Exhausted, he had "reached the stage . . . where I'd like to find a home for the poor worn-out, non politicians." "Please advise me," he pleaded, "what I can do along this line."[1]

It was unlikely he got any relief, for most voters could not have been more excited. Roger Riis, Jacob's son, contacted Franklin Roosevelt to enlist in the cause, making it clear "that I do not want anything whatsoever in the way of reward, or business thrown my way or anything else. I feel violent about this campaign, for the first time since 1912, and I want to work." Rita Mohvay in Auburndale, Massachusetts, had the same feeling, plaintively writing FDR, "I am a shut-in confined to my bed for the past thirty-four months, but I made a special effort to have my Mother take me to register last week so that Al

Smith . . . will have my vote. If I have to go in a wheelchair to cast my vote November 6th I'm going."[2]

So it went, all across the American landscape, with individual passions coalescing into grass-roots organizations. In Minneapolis and St. Louis, German voters rallied to the Smith banner, turning on Hoover, whom they identified with the Wilson administration and the humiliation of their countrymen. Over in Fall River, Massachusetts, their ancestral enemies, organized into the American French League Smith for President Clubs, received a missive from the candidate that told them that he would "serve you as you so generously served our flag during the great World War." Members promptly translated this into French and distributed it widely. In Lansing, Michigan, the Democrats threw a Scandinavian Club banquet, while Frank Walsh organized the "Progressive League for Alfred E. Smith" to pull in the La Follette voters in Wisconsin and other places.[3]

The most complex battleground of all these local scenes was the South, simultaneously the most Democratic *and* the most Fundamentalist Protestant region in the country. The result was at best ambivalence (Cordell Hull, who polled precincts and wards in Tennessee for Smith, wrote about the danger of a large stay-at-home problem for Democrats); at worst, open conflict. In Texas, for example, the governor refused to attend a Smith rally, and the secretary of the State Democratic Committee complained, "We are having a very serious fight on our hands to hold Texas in the Democratic column." Opponents of one state senator who spoke on behalf of the national candidate circulated cartoons that depicted Smith leaving a child, labeled "Eighteenth Amendment," where it could be devoured by the Tammany Tiger. In response, party officials pulled out all the stops to hold their people in line, purging slackers, branding Hoover Democrats as "Republicans, Klansmen, and Bolsheviks." Town after town developed Al Smith grocery stores and Herbert Hoover grocery stores, Smith butchers and Hoover butchers, Smith drugstores and Hoover drugstores.[4]

All of this, in turn, got terribly complicated by the most difficult American social dilemma of them all, the matter of race. At that time, the color line was a real and tangible thing, and it was primarily a southern affair. While the Great Migration of World War I had fostered strong black communities in northern cities like Chicago, New York, and Detroit, in 1928 most Americans still perceived the race question as something southern, to be dealt with by folks who lived below the Mason-Dixon line. But down there, race counted for everything, so the presidential campaign now got mixed into this bitter stew. This would be no simple dish, but a bizarre combination of ingredients, with both sides race-baiting the other.

Since the presidency of Abraham Lincoln, Republicans had held the reputation of being defenders of the Negro, although they had maintained only a mixed record after the end of Reconstruction. In 1928 they tried to have it both ways, organizing black voters in the South, but at the same time recognizing how vulnerable Smith was in that region and thus doing as little as possible in public to alienate white swing voters. Hubert Work, Hoover's campaign manager, told Charles Jonas of North Carolina, "If we make no mistakes nor say any unfortunate things, this campaign will turn the biggest Republican majority in history." One of his assistants observed that they were going to lose the black vote in the North, and "if this knowledge could be used judiciously in the south, it would be helpful to us."[5]

This was sleazy stuff, but they were wading in rotten waters. Democratic senator Coleman Blease of South Carolina gave a speech on the Senate floor, decrying how Secretary of Commerce Hoover had abolished segregation in the Census Bureau, and even forced white girls to use the same bathrooms as their colored sisters. Other southern statesmen picked up the story and began to elaborate on it, making it very clear to their audiences that they were talking about blacks and whites using the *same* soap, the *same* washbowl, the *same* toilet. Even that was not enough for Senator Theodore Bilbo of Mississippi, arguably the worst bigot in the history of the Senate. It was probably biologically impossible for Bilbo to let an election campaign pass without at least some race-baiting, and his contribution that year was the apocryphal claim that Hoover had danced with a black woman while administering flood relief in 1927 down in the Mississippi Delta. Later this was enlarged to the claim that Hoover had tripped the light fantastic with Mary Booze, a black Republican committeewoman; the staid Herbert, of course, was not very likely to be out dancing with anyone, even his wife, let alone a stranger. But a Louisiana paper, just to add spice to things, reported that Hoover planned to appoint two southerners to his cabinet, Ben Davis of Georgia and Perry Howard of Mississippi. Both men, of course, were black.[6]

Democrats campaigning for the governor faced an equally conflicting record. Smith had nothing against African-Americans and looked on them as voters like anyone else (in the best Tammany tradition), but was not about to go out of his way to enlist them either. His campaign did organize a national Smith for President Colored League, and gave the okay to local efforts as well. Negro Democratic organizations sprouted in Richmond and in Norfolk, in Augusta and Savannah, and appeared in Nashville and in Memphis. Down in Texas, the redoubtable "Gooseneck" Bill McDonald put everything he had on the Smith bandwagon.[7]

But the Smith campaign was always worried about losing the white, solid South, and this led them to make some dubious decisions. There was, for example, that terrible accession to the wire cage at the Houston convention; and no one considered that if the choice of a southerner as vice president might woo white voters, it also meant to blacks that a segregationist was only a heartbeat away from the presidency. When Belle Moskowitz arranged through her husband Henry to have Walter White of the NAACP meet with Smith, the result was a statement in which the candidate pledged never to be dominated by "an anti-Negro South." Al initially consented to this document, instinctively telling White that he wanted "to show that the old Democratic party, ruled entirely by the South, is on its way out, and that we Northern Democrats have a totally different approach to the negro." But almost immediately Robinson, Proskauer (who had been raised in Mobile, Alabama), and Senator Pat Harrison prevailed on him not to sign it, claiming it would "too greatly antagonize" whites in that region.[8] Even Eleanor Roosevelt assured an Alabama Democrat, "Governor Smith does not believe in intermarriage. . . . He has a full understanding of conditions as they are in the South. . . . The Democratic Party has always better understood and sympathized with Southern feelings and prejudices than has the Republican."[9]

Republicans in all parts of the country, meanwhile, rebutted with the record and their fantasies, as those in the South claimed that Smith was more favorable to blacks than Hoover, while their northern colleagues told black audiences that running mate Joe Robinson used to "kill a couple of negroes before breakfast" when he was ailing and wanted to feel better about things.

Even that was child's play compared to the infighting within the Democratic ranks. Anti-Smith Democrats in the South figured race was a winning wedge issue in that region, so there was no reason not to use it.[10]

One of their standard images involved Ferdinand Morton, a black politician who founded Colored Democracy, a Harlem organization supporting Smith for president. Morton was a Tammany Hall stalwart, and had been appointed as one of New York City's three civil service commissioners. That appointment, incidentally, could come only from the mayor, making it hard to claim that he was somehow Smith's handpicked choice.

But logic rarely troubles bigots, so the Klan and other anti-Smith Democrats distributed a photo of Morton working with a white secretary. The headline read, "White Supremacy as Practiced by Tammany"; accompanying text explained that Morton was "dictating a letter to Miss Florence Eckstein, a white American-born woman," probably the only time in history the Klan ever applied those terms to a Jewess. Although other fliers would make clear that "The WHITE WOMAN to whom he is dictating is his PRIVATE SECRETARY" and that this was taken in "Morton's private office," the Klan had to observe, "in addition to this beautiful picture of race equality, Morton is one of three, a Roman Catholic, Jew, and Negro, who pass upon the moral, mental and physical qualification" of every person applying for a job there; "no white man or woman can possibly enter the civil service of New York unless this triumvirate approves. What a chance for poor Protestants to ever get their names on any city pay roll." The piece concluded, "MORTON IS A GREAT FRIEND OF GOVERNOR SMITH, CALLING HIM 'AL' WHEN REFERRING TO HIM . . . AL HAS ALWAYS MADE IT HIS BUSINESS TO SPEND AT LEAST ONE NIGHT AMONG THE NEGROES OF HARLEM, WHERE 'KING MORTON' REIGNS AS 'BOSS'."[11]

That little broadside only served as an opening shot in the race war against Smith in the South. If Hoover had danced with a Negro woman, Smith had to have danced with a *naked* Negro woman, and of course he was an advocate of intermarriage. One Alabama politician gave a speech in which he called Smith a "Negro Lover" (that was what was printed), claiming the New Yorker "not only loved negroes but bootlicked 'em and admitted it." Charges flew that Raskob had paid out $100,000 to have a "white slave" charge against the governor dismissed, and "the court records are there to prove it." Some speakers made Al responsible for singlehandedly integrating the New York City public school system, while the *Alabama Christian Advocate* was creative enough to link two obsessions, attacking Smith because "there are ten million Negroes living in the South. To give these . . . negroes free access to liquor—to place this passion-inflamer in the hands of this child race not far removed from their savage haunts in the jungles of Africa—would be to court tragedy unspeakable."[12]

The response to this by pro-Smith Democrats in the South, sadly, was to fight fire with fire, which just meant more appeals to the most blatant racism. They argued that a ballot against Smith was a ballot against white rule, or as the ubiquitous Senator Bilbo put it, "I would swallow the Pope and the whole dern Vatican than vote for Herbert Hoover and negro supremacy in the South."[13]

Again and again they pounded this message home. Y. T. Eggleston of Greenwood felt that "you will find Mississippi in the Smith column alright, in spite of the fact that some of our citizens have lost sight of the fact that when we vote for Hoover we are voting for Rottenness in politics and Negro rule and that means Blood shed in our state for we will not stand for it." One politician told his constituents, "Yes, Smith is a Tammany man, a Catholic, and a wet, but would you rather have him in the White House than a President who compels white men and women to associate with negroes?" A flier in Alabama began with a photo of the integrated state legislature of 1872, under the headline, "What Happened When the Republican Party Was in Power," and concluded, "If you believe in White Supremacy, Vote the Straight Democratic Ticket." The award for succinctness,

however, went to John Sharp Williams, senator from Mississippi, who simply
stated, "The niggers are Republicans and the white men are Democrats."[14]

And what of the target of these calumnies, African-Americans themselves?
These citizens mirrored the national debate in that they too became more
involved in this presidential campaign than in any other recent election, but also
in that their feelings were as sharply divided as the rest of America's.

There was no question that the traditional allegiance to the Republican Party
held many African-Americans to that camp, as did profound fears that Smith,
whatever qualities he may have had, still came from the party of white supremacy. In the North, furthermore, the conflict between poor blacks and recent immigrants over industrial jobs only increased hostility to the Smith camp, a
sentiment exacerbated by ethnic–black fights going back to the terrible riots of
the Civil War era.[15]

Tempering this were a number of other factors that pulled African-Americans to the Smith corner. The Hoover campaign, seeing an opportunity to break
the Democratic hold on the South and win white votes, went out of their way to
ignore and even rebuff black Republicans, alienating what could have been some
of their strongest supporters. Claude Barnett, director of the Associated Negro
Press, constantly sent suggestions to the GOP, but in the end had to complain,
"It is very difficult to get anything through to Mr. Hoover." The Connecticut
League of Independent Negro Voters declared for Smith because its president,
Dr. S. L. Carruthers, explained, "Negroes all over the country are indignant at
the treatment they are receiving from Republican national headquarters . . .
which . . . will not receive negro callers."[16]

More than anything else, however, it was the attacks by the Klan, by the bigots and the hate-mongers, that drew blacks to Al Smith. They understood
implicitly that his enemies were their own, and that by standing against these
forces, he was taking on the people and ideas that oppressed them as well. In
places like Steubenville, Ohio, for the first time a majority of black voters figured
to go Democrat; in Seattle, most of the four thousand registered African-Americans planned to vote for Smith. Among Al's supporters that year was Earl Dickerson, the first of his race to graduate from the University of Chicago Law
School and the person who integrated the Chicago City Council when he joined
their ranks in 1939; Dickerson got his start in electoral politics in 1928 when he
decided to work as an organizer in the Smith campaign.[17]

Black leaders were equally divided. The most *important* black organization
during the twenties was the NAACP, but as a not-for-profit entity, it had to

remain scrupulously nonpartisan. In private, executives had mixed feelings, arguing, "There is very little for the Negro to hope for from either of the major parties. The Republicans have consistently failed to fulfill their campaign promises," while "Alfred E. Smith as Governor of New York has done nothing against the Negro nor has he done anything individually for him." One high official reported, "I for one know of no particular interest shown by Governor Smith in the Negro in New York or anywhere else."[18]

Standing in contrast, the most *popular* black organization in the twenties was the United Negro Improvement Association (UNIA), created by the indefatigable Marcus Garvey. Garvey, a unique combination of determined race activist and brilliant showman, had by then been exiled from the United States following a federal conviction on mail fraud charges, but could still command 4 million followers in this country. In a statement released as he visited Quebec, Canada, Garvey told UNIA members, "A vote . . . for Herbert Hoover is emphatically a vote against the interest of the Negro not only in the United States of America, but throughout the world. . . . A vote for Alfred E. Smith is a vote for human rights and for the extension of human rights and the conservation of the liberty of the Negro throughout the world."[19]

At least as important for these voters as spokespersons, if not more so, was the Negro press. Almost all of these papers were traditionally Republican, and some, like the *New York Age* and the *New York Amsterdam News,* continued to advocate for this party; but many others, including the powerful *Baltimore Afro-American,* the *Boston Guardian,* the *Norfolk Journal and Guide,* and the *Louisville News,* broke ranks to support Governor Smith. The Baltimore paper, when announcing its endorsement, featured a cartoon depicting Hoover as a bird lying atop a nest made up of eggs labeled "race prejudice," "bigotry," and "Ku Klux Klan." The artist portrayed Smith, on the other hand, as someone who tucked in with "religious freedom," "industrial democracy," and "personal liberty."[20]

Almost all of these papers were local, but two of them commanded a national audience. Still powerful in 1928, the *Chicago Defender* remained the most beloved and believed news source for blacks anywhere. Founded by Robert Abbott, the journal was almost recklessly fearless, calling attention to every lynching, every outrage. Abbott refused to kowtow to any convention when it came to pride and dignity, and thus never employed such standard terms as "Negro" or even "African-American" (which had been employed for some time by then). Instead, he referred to his people simply as "The Race," in headlines such as "Southern White Gentlemen Burn Race Boy at Stake," printed in the largest type available in red ink. This forthrightness earned Abbott the largest circulation of any black news source, and the shipping manifest indicated that his paper was bought in such unlikely places as Bibsland, Louisiana; Tunica, Mississippi; and Yoakum, Texas.[21]

As a general rule throughout the twenties, the *Defender* had refrained from commenting on national or, for that matter, even local city politics such as a Chicago mayoral race; everything had to be about The Race. If the paper had any tendency at all, it leaned mildly toward Republicanism.

In 1928, however, the *Defender* came out for Smith, and like everything else Abbott did, it was with a lion's roar. An editorial declared, "What the Democratic party stood for 40 years ago the Republicans stand for today, and what made the Republican party famous two scores ago characterizes the Democratic party of today." Far more important, however, were the constant headlines— "Republicans 'Mouthpiece' Insults Race," or "Citizens Everywhere Rally to Aid Gov. Alfred Smith"—hammering home their message day after day.[22]

Black readers from higher socioeconomic strata (and those who preferred something a tad more subtle) turned to the *Crisis,* put out by the NAACP under the editorial supervision of W. E. B. Du Bois. Du Bois, whom his biographer David Lewis referred to with justification as "the greatest scholar the Negro race had produced," edited a monthly collection of brilliant political writings, powerful examples of advanced culture, and no less than the *Defender,* an important source of pride for the race.[23]

Du Bois felt ambivalent in 1928. In his monthly column, he pressed to have black votes be recognized as an electoral force, but refused to commit to either candidate. "Smith is no enemy to organized wealth," he argued, "and Hoover is no friend to organized labor. It will be hard . . . to choose between the two leaders." "The Republican Party," Du Bois accused, "is playing one of its dirtiest political games" that year, leading him to sarcastically comment, "Let all the northern black voters who are fools vote for Hoover in November." On the other hand, "If the Democratic party was openly and thoughtfully planning to alienate the intelligent Negro vote . . . they . . . were eminently successful. They opened their convention with an atrocious lynching. They segregated their black visitors back of a wire cage. They nominated for Vice-President . . . a typical Arkansas bourbon." As a result, officially, "*The Crisis* is sitting squarely on the fence, naked and unashamed and without apology." In the last issue before the election, however, Du Bois revealed his own choice; in his usual nonpartisan series, where some distinguished citizen would write, "Why I Plan to Vote for," for each candidate, the editor penned the entry on Norman Thomas of the Socialist Party.[24]

One of the pathbreaking aspects of the 1928 race was that women entered presidential politics in huge and enthusiastic numbers. They had had the vote since 1920, but this was the first *exciting* election, the first real contest since then. As Mildred Adams, writing in *Outlook* observed, "The presidential election is the quadrennial circus of America. For years and years the men had all the fun. They played clowns and acrobats . . . rigged the tent and sold the tickets." That was no longer true, since "after two trial appearances, the women are part of the show . . . a vastly important part." And while some played more critical roles, for all of them it was "a way of demonstrating the still debated proposition that women have brains and that they are fit to be trusted with the great gift of political equality which was conferred on them eight years ago. . . . Their ballot is a symbol."[25]

Over and over, the reports came in of women delighting in the very act of politics, the sense of playing a legitimate role for the first time. In one mountain district, a woman walked from house to house to gain new voters, and in another an eighty-year-old signed up every eligible voter in her town save two. Clara Patterson wrote to Lou Hoover, "I am sure that I along with thousands of other women, have *never* been so interested in a presidential election," and Ida Clarke of the *Century* magazine could even voice the unthinkable in that giddy climate, that "a woman presidential candidate is . . . within the range of possibility."[26]

Some of these efforts were nonpartisan, but not many. The League of Women Voters tried hard to keep its members officially neutral, but it was difficult, and many women publicly committed to one or the other of the candidates. Those who remained above the fray stuck to the usual kinds of work: sponsoring study and discussion groups and voters' schools, putting out information booths at shopping areas, holding birthday parties for first-time voters, conducting forums, and generally trying to get women to the polls. They scrupulously advocated only nonpartisan planks: an end to all legal discrimination against women, child protection, and public management of power resources. The League even sponsored weekly radio broadcasts presenting both sides of the important issues.[27]

These kinds of efforts clearly paid off. Women became 49 percent of the electorate, up from 35 percent in 1924 and 30 percent in 1920. In Indiana they added 135,000 names to the polls, while the figures for men stayed the same. And in Kansas City, Missouri, by the time registration had ended that year, 99,494 women voters had signed up, almost gaining electoral equality in a city with only 203,000 registered voters.[28]

The Smith forces attracted women from several different communities. Social reformers knew of his gubernatorial record and became some of his strongest supporters. Lillian Wald wrote Dr. G. E. Sehlbrede, "I have known Governor Smith for thirty years and I think that no one in the presidential chair, with the exception of Abraham Lincoln, has so passionately acted for and understood the needs of humanity." She remarked that it was Smith who continually argued "as only Theodore Roosevelt ever did, that the government is the people's and not the machines'." Other social work colleagues joined in, like the famous Mary K. Simkhovitch, writing a campaign piece entitled, "Al Smith—Able, Honest, Liberal"; or Mary Van Kleck, who felt that any working-class woman who failed to support Smith was "almost guilty of treason," and took over as chair of the national social workers' committee supporting Smith.[29]

A number of women from distinguished families also joined the Smith crusade. Virginia Gildersleeve, a dean at Barnard College, sat at a Tammany rally for the first time in her life and "wondered what these friends of mine would say when they read in the morning that I had spoken there—representing women and the highbrows." Mrs. Casper Whitney chaired the National Women's Committee for Smith, and Mrs. Henry Morgenthau, Jr., did a piece on "Governor Smith and Water Power." Even the genteel ladies of the South and the West rose to the challenge, Mrs. Charles Sharpe of Alabama explaining to her colleagues at an advisory committee meeting what activities had been planned in her state, and suggesting a booklet on "what Catholics and Tammany have done for the people of the South." Anna Struble of South Dakota pointed out that in her area, they had been stressing that "a very large number of the Confederate generals were Catholics."[30]

Although there is still relatively little evidence regarding the voting habits of urban working-class women in 1928, it is fair to assume that Al's role as champion of the immigrant and of the city dweller appealed to them as much as to their husbands. Also, by the mid-twenties political organizations like Tammany had made it a point to recruit women just as fiercely as they had men; one sign of this effort was rising naturalization rates for women. In 1924, the last presidential year before Smith ran, females constituted only 9 percent of all those applying for citizenship, whereas in 1928 they made up 22 percent. Research by historian David Burner, using Boston census reports, turned up a similar pattern, with a sharp increase in voter registration among women in strong Irish and Italian districts. In Chicago, registration for the 1928 election shot up 39.6 percent for men, which women almost matched with a figure of 34.4 percent.[31]

But the person who most personified women's support for the governor was Eleanor Roosevelt. Roosevelt, of course, had backed Smith from 1924 on, playing important roles in two of his gubernatorial campaigns. She believed in him completely.

Eleanor now headed the entire Women's Division, and became a whirlwind of activity, working so hard she had to hire a second secretary. Over and over, she penned articles on various aspects of the platform, on "Governor Smith and Our Foreign Policy" in the *Woman's Journal*, and "Jeffersonian Principles the Issue in 1928" for *Current History*.[32]

Mrs. Roosevelt also took to the podium, notwithstanding a shyness that she was just starting to overcome. Speaking before a gathering of Jewish women, a group she hardly felt comfortable with at that stage in her life, she talked to them about the feelings that had brought her into the Smith campaign, how she and her husband believed that Smith "wanted the welfare of the average man and woman," how a critical issue had to be that "all the people of this country enjoy full privileges of American citizenship." At another setting, she introduced a reluctant Katie Smith with the gentle line, "She will not say a word but at least she will wave her hand," and when even these efforts did not suffice, she took to the campaign trail.[33]

As a result, Eleanor Roosevelt developed into a real power in DNC head-quarters. Long before anyone used the term *turf* for anything besides horse rac-ing, she saw to it that the women's work space matched that of the men, gaining parity in everything from floor space to amenities such as windows and carpet-ing. Mrs. Roosevelt could write with surety to a county boss like Edward Perkins in Poughkeepsie, letting him know "that there ought to be no difficulty . . . to raise the necessary money for the state campaign," and that she had total author-ity to say so.[34]

Eleanor also delivered invaluable service by her recruiting efforts among other women, some of whom would make the transition between the politics of the twenties and what would follow. Molly Dewson, for example, had been active in a number of causes, although she had never engaged in electoral poli-tics. But she was part of that woman's inner circle, so in 1928 got a call from Eleanor, explaining that there was terrible infighting at the Midwestern Head-quarters in St. Louis, and though somebody had to go out, she was bogged down in New York. "Will you go in my place?" Eleanor asked, "I know of only two women whom it would be safe to send and you are one." Dewson sorted things out there and never looked back, eventually delivering radio addresses on "What Campaign Issues Mean to Women." By that time she was hooked and stayed on to work for Franklin Roosevelt, becoming one of his top political operatives, then serving on the Social Security Board during its formative years.[35]

Women like Roosevelt and Dewson tried to stress issues rather than person-alities, thus sidestepping all the baggage Al Smith's name carried. They issued fliers like one that reminded readers, "The women of the country are on trial in this election. . . . Are we able to think clearly and honestly, or are we going to react emotionally? . . . We are not voting for the millennium. . . . We are not going to be swayed by the bug-a-boo of a false religious issue." It was a powerful message that often succeeded, like the time a young girl gave a speech in Carson City, Nevada, that stressed Smith's support for education, how he had dramatically increased state appropriations for the schools, and how salaries of teachers had gone way up during his years as governor; one observer claimed that all this "made a tremendous appeal to the women."[36]

It was not going to be all for Al, however; when it came to women voters, Herbert Hoover was an imposing candidate with an enormous and devoted following. Over and over, commentators echoed the words of a cabdriver talking to Philip Shatts, a Republican: "My wife," the taxi man explained, "said that I might as well be for Mr. Hoover, because the women were going to elect him anyway."[37]

The man who had managed to feed the starving, of course, started on the right foot with women. Lida Robertson of Bessemer, Alabama, wrote that she was "one of his obedients when he 'Hooverized' America to do without the foods which our precious boys over seas needed." When Herbert asked Lida to help starving Europeans after the war, Lida "packed five bags full" of supplies and paid the shipping charges to the New York distribution center out of her own pocket, then went to the public library to look at the stories on the war in the *National Geographic*. She "boohood in tears over the terrible disaster and his picture with the little homeless sufferers" and would now vote accordingly: "I vowed since 1920 when women's suffrage came into a statute that I was old-timey, trained that" it was "men's duty to run politics—and not women." This year, however, "I have marched down and registered for one purpose and that is to cast my very first vote for Mr. Hoover as president of our U.S.A." Campaign literature stressed that "Hoover is the only executive . . . who ever took the women of the United States into his confidence, and who . . . enlisted their aid in a national crisis," and was the only candidate who referred to "men *and* women," to "boys *and* girls." "Did you notice that?" Una Winter asked her radio audience, "Did you realize that for the first time in the history of the world, a man of prominence had thus raised women to a state of equality?"[38]

And it was not just housewives who endorsed Hoover. Feminist leaders supported his humanitarian work, portraying him in nurturing tones, such as the line Jane Addams used on his behalf—that of all the persons associated with the war, Herbert alone had been "distinguished not for his military prowess but for his conservation of tender lives menaced by war's starvation." Even Carrie Chapman Catt, the great philosopher of the women's suffrage movement, came out of retirement to support the Republican candidate in 1928. Among the next generation, this appeal also held; a prenomination poll of college students showed that attendees at women's colleges often gave Hoover his biggest margin, Wellesley choosing him by a stunning ratio of 435 to 68, Connecticut College for Women reporting in figures of 350 to 57, and even Mt. Holyoke, Frances Perkins's beloved alma mater, picking Hoover over Smith in a 570 to 47 landslide.[39]

Hoover's other critical asset, second only to his work with the hungry, was his position on prohibition. The Smith forces always underestimated the gender-based power of the liquor question, ignoring the fact that the crusade against alcohol had been the first modern, national, grass-roots advocacy campaign to be led by women and in which their followers were the majority of participants. Since the late nineteenth century, many women—including Frances Willard, founder of the Women's Christian Temperance Union—had joined the cause, not so much out of hostility to booze, but because it was the only movement that allowed them a place at the table of politics. On the farm and in small towns, women went to meetings, raised their voices and assumed leadership positions, often for the first time.

Some women even backed Hoover because of their support of contraception. Edith Pierce was field secretary for the Birth Control League, and she knew that as much as one-third of the women at many of their clinics were Roman Catholics, in spite of the official church position on this question. This proved "that women are going to seek help in matters that concern their own bodily functions, irrespective of the church laws made by the men of the church who had no such respect for the welfare of women." When it comes to getting laws passed in the secular legislature, furthermore, "the R.C. Church watches every state capital to prevent the passing" of any bills that did not conform to their doctrines. "I was never bigoted," she lamented, "till I had this experience," but it led her to reject Smith's candidacy and support Hoover's. Margaret Sanger, the founder of the modern birth control movement, took this a step further, and according to one correspondent, believed that "Smith is at the bottom of the opposition to her work."[40]

Of course, these women, who opposed Smith because of the Roman Catholic church's position on birth control, represented nothing more or less than the spirit of the twenties. Clearly they do not fit a simple image of reaction; instead, they could just not see how a member of that faith could act independently, could observe the separation of church and state. They understood, in other words, little outside their own circle, their own *kuklos*.

❧

But if women differed in their views of the candidates that year, ethnics had no doubts about their favorite. Jews especially understood deeply what Al Smith stood for, and rallied to his banner in such numbers that the *Jewish Advocate* could crack that, "despite reports to the contrary, all Jews are not going to vote for Smith." Leopold Strauss, an insurance broker in Montgomery, Alabama, replied to a Republican fund-raising appeal by saying that he considered Smith "one of the greatest men in America. He has ability, courage and absolute honesty. . . . Besides he has a great human heart and is a friend of humanity irrespective of race, nationality or social standing." With great emphasis, he added, "If I had a million votes to cast . . . every one would be voted for Smith."[41]

The line about race was particularly important, since the 1928 campaign produced some of the earliest versions of the black-Jewish coalition that operated decades later during the civil rights era. Bayard Rustin, who helped organize the 1963 March on Washington, remembered how a young Jewish friend approached him and asked if he would hand out leaflets and buttons for Al Smith. All guts, the two young men picked an exclusive, all-white, all-gentile country club as the appropriate place to start and, according to Rustin, "were terribly abused." What shocked Rustin, introduced him to anti-Semitism, and shaped him as a lifelong defender of equal rights for everyone, was that "nobody spit at me, or spit on me or called me a bastard, but they did him. That was when I discovered that very often Jews were treated even worse than blacks. And that was in the Al Smith campaign in 1928."[42]

Back at headquarters, the Smith forces were only partially aware of the dynamic forces sweeping the country, and mostly saw splendid, possibly inevitable victory. John W. Davis, 1924 standard-bearer, claimed that he had "never seen a more optimistic spirit" than pervaded Smith's campaign offices, that they were the "cockiest and most confident lot" he had ever experienced. Franklin Roosevelt received reports from fieldworkers "more than surprised at the keen desire to register, especially people who heretofore could never be brought out." Officials felt that they were covering every base, even creating the Democratic Deaf Voters Campaign Committee, prompting one Democratic boss to quip that since "all the blind men are in the Republican party, and as the deaf ones are for us, one offsets the other."[43]

By that point it literally seemed that miracles were occurring, if you were willing to believe some of the news reports. One resident of Lansing, Michigan, wrote that "Al's name seems to be talismanic . . . a shibboleth"—and how about that case of the boy in Rochester who had been speechless for seven years and regained his voice in order to declare for Al Smith? The *New York Times* reported that a doctor innocently asked the lad whom he was going to vote for as a way of coaxing him on, but was nevertheless shocked when the child endorsed Smith in a loud, clear voice. "I'll be jiggered," he told the reporter, "Their candidate is a miracle worker." In Baltimore, Jimmy Buralge, no older than a newsboy, escaped injury when he was slammed by an automobile; but the thick pack of Smith campaign posters he carried under his jacket shielded him from grievous harm.[44]

Staffers in New York were continually awed by the parade of celebrities passing through. As he had in 1924, Irving Berlin volunteered to be Al's songwriter, penning such less-than-immortal ditties as "Good Times with Hoover, Better Times with Al," or reviving "We'll All Go Voting for Al" (which Hugh Carey remembered the nuns teaching him at St. Augustine's parochial school). Kate Smith's shows included a pitchman explaining why "honest and courageous people should vote for Al Smith," and the Broadway Committee to get Al elected included such stars as Fannie Brice, Eddie Cantor, George M. Cohan, George and Ira Gershwin, Helen Hayes, George Jessel, Jerome Kern, Ed Wynn, and Efram Zimbalist. Those less theatrically oriented could still stare in wonderment at intellectuals like John Dewey and lawyers like Clarence Darrow (who criticized Hoover for being an efficiency expert, saying that because of that profession, "one job grows where two bloomed before"). Among the 147 writers who signed onto the Smith for President Literary Committee were H. L. Mencken, Dorothy Parker, Robert Sherwood, Alexander Woollcott, and Edgar Lee Masters.[45]

The Democratic campaign that year even featured some of the first endorsements by professional and amateur athletes in American presidential history. Sports Champions for Al Smith, an official campaign committee with its own letterhead, touted endorsements from Ivy League coaches, plus winners from the fields of golf, swimming, soccer, and even squash tennis, not exactly a mass sport at the time.[46]

Baseball *was* a mass sport, of course, and it was played in the big cities, Al's natural home. John McGraw, manager of the New York Giants, came out for Smith, along with players from the Chicago Cubs, St. Louis Cardinals, Pittsburgh Pirates, Cincinnati Redlegs, and the Philadelphia Athletics. It almost seems superfluous to mention that the New York Yankees backed the governor, but for those in doubt, endorsements came from stars like Lou Gehrig, Tony Lazzeri, and Waite Hoyt.

But the biggest name in sports was also the biggest supporter of Al among the nation's athletes. Maybe it was because Smith and Babe Ruth both came up the hard way, and maybe it was because the Babe, mighty of arm but weaker of brain, was given to whims; either way, he had become a *big* fan of Al Smith since 1924 when Franklin Roosevelt originally called on him to endorse the governor.

The story goes that in 1928 a publicity agent tried to get the Babe to take a picture with Herbert Hoover, and Ruth asked why he would want to meet the man who invented the vacuum cleaner. In fact, he did turn down the meeting with the comment, "Nothing doing, I'm for Al Smith."[47]

Ruth turned the trip home from that year's World Series (the Yankees won) into a campaign trip for Smith, a mixed blessing to put it mildly. Possibly worried that he might starve to death on the way back from St. Louis, Ruth had made sure that the victory train was stocked with a full load of beer, pickles, rye bread, four bushels of spare ribs, and other comestibles. As they passed through the little towns of America, the locomotive would grind to a halt, and Babe would come out on the platform of the last car, sometimes clad in an undershirt and holding a hamhock in one hand and a pitcher of lager in the other. He would offer a few words of pearly wisdom about American sport, and finally discuss why Al Smith should be elected president, although no one, unfortunately, ever recorded the Babe's bon mots. Sometimes the crowd would cheer these remarks, sometimes it would clam up in hostility; on those occasions, the great Bambino would holler, "If that's the way you feel, to hell with you," and go back inside.[48]

The high point of Babe's political career came when he gave a radio speech for Smith, which included heartfelt homilies like, "I'm not in politics, I'm in baseball. . . . Governor Smith is the type of man who appeals not only to the baseball fan, but to all red-blooded lovers of American sport." Enthusiastic as ever, Ruth then departed from the prepared text and gave a five-minute lecture on why Sunday baseball was a great idea, giving the party honchos a fit.[49]

Irregardless of the Babe's heroics, things overall seemed to be going extremely well, a sense that the trends were all running their way. Senior official Pat Harrison wrote that he did not think "there is any doubt that the situation is improving in sections," and most fantastic of all, added, "Take for instance the south—there is a trend toward us."[50]

About this time Al received the most stirring tribute of them all, that is, if you came from the Fourth Ward. It was a magnificent leatherbound book, with silk insides. The volume was thin, but the first page, printed elaborately in four colors of radiant ink, told everything that ever needed to be said to Al Smith about politics. It read, simply, "We the undersigned first voters of your old home district . . . do hereby pledge our first votes, our initial political activities, our every endeavor to you, our ideal of American manhood, as the Democratic candidate for the highest office within the gifts of the citizens of this great Republic." The printing was beautiful, in the style of an illuminated manuscript, but what followed was most precious of all: fourteen pages full of signatures. With support like this, what could possibly go wrong?

Chapter 18

And the Pope Will Move to Washington

IN RETROSPECT, IT IS hard to grasp just how bad a situation Al Smith faced in 1928, but that year's presidential race remains arguably the strangest and sickest in American history. For if the general climate then could be described as a fear of modernism, this took a variety of virulent forms: bigotry against cities, immigrants, anyone who was outside the *kuklos*. Above all, the vision that gripped the nation was the spectre of a Roman Catholic in the White House, playing off deep-rooted American traditions.

Catholics had been demonized since the founding of an initially Protestant nation, but at certain times they attracted special attention. During the 1830s and 1840s, for example, as immigration and industrialization surged, a vogue of fantastic, horrific accounts purported to tell what really went on behind the mysterious walls of Catholic convents. The pioneering work in this genre, *The Awful Disclosures of Maria Monk*, presented a sickening account of rape and beatings, plus the grim execution of infants resulting from illicit couplings between priests and nuns; the fact that this was actually written by the Reverend J. J. Slocum did little to deter readers, who turned it into a best-seller with more than 300,000 copies sold prior to the Civil War. Plenty of imitations followed, with titles like *Secrets of Female Convents Exposed*, *The School Girl in France or the Snares of Popery*, and *Thrilling Mysteries of a Convent Revealed*. Guy Fitch Phelps authored *The Moan of the Tiber*, whose advertisement included a drawing of a nun whipping a young blonde-haired woman, and the promise that "every touch of human agony and despair suffered by this girl victim decoyed from a Protestant home into the charnel house of popery is woven into the account."[1]

From then on, the "lurid nun's story" served as a common vehicle for bigots' rantings. Tom Watson, former Populist champion turned race baiter, filled his numerous publications in the early 1900s with articles like "The Roman Catholic Hierarchy: The Deadliest Menace to Our Liberties and Our Civilization," "The

Murder of Babes," "One of the Priests Who Raped a Catholic Woman in a Catholic Church," along with the inevitable, "What Happens in Convents." Watson was even able to mix racial and religious hates in "The Sinister Portent of Negro Priests."[2]

But by then, several other movements were keeping this prejudice alive. The campaign for prohibition, for example, always carried with it an anti-immigrant, anti-Catholic taint. Bishop James Cannon, one of the stalwarts of the Anti-Saloon League, declared in the *Christian Advocate* (a publication he owned and edited) that the Catholic church must be regarded as the "Mother of ignorance, superstition, intolerance and vice."[3]

Far more noxious, however, was the Ku Klux Klan. Only in later years would the Klan acquire its image as a chiefly racist organization that oppressed blacks. When William Simmons resurrected it in 1915 at Stone Mountain, Georgia, his chief concern was the rising population of the cities that threatened to engulf America: not blacks (who had already been put in their place by the Jim Crow laws), but the new immigrants. The KKK's first and most emphasized targets in the twentieth century therefore were foreigners, Jews, and, above all, Roman Catholics.[4]

One of the Klan's best orators, for example, was Helen Jackson, another of those supposedly former nuns. Jackson toured the country, and her lectures would have won the award for being the most sickening example of this genre if such an honor had ever been bestowed. Her stock in trade was to describe forced abortions conducted by the priests who had fathered the children; for her grand finale she brought out a series of small leather pouches which she claimed had been used to dispose of aborted fetuses and the infant corpses. If that did not rivet the audience, however, she could always resort to her lurid description of the time priests burned a cross on her back.[5]

Despite such images, however, the Klan in the twenties was no hillbilly organization. Members usually came from the lower middle class, people fearing displacement by all the forces affecting American life. Studies of Klan records indicate that the majority of hooded knights held white-collar positions or were small businessmen, its blue-collar workers usually coming from the better-off skilled trades. All these groups feared an erosion of their income and status from new people and a newly urbanized and large-scale economy. In terms of religion, their affiliations covered the full range of Protestant denominations, but Northern Methodists and Disciples of Christ were particularly likely to join the order.[6]

Estimates of total membership at its height in 1923 range from 2 to 4 million, and the distribution was far more national than it would be in later years. The state with the largest number of Kluxers was Indiana, where between one-quarter and one-third of all native-born white males belonged to the Invisible Empire. Klansmen controlled the state governments there and in Colorado, elected the mayors of a number of cities, and even got the Oregon legislature to pass a law requiring all Catholic children to attend public schools. Chicago had at least forty thousand members, and important chapters existed in Ohio and Pennsylvania. In small towns, Klansmen would display their power by descending on a presumably friendly church unannounced, entering abruptly, then marching down the aisle in full regalia to interrupt the minister and hand him an envelope with money. They would then either leave just as dramatically, or offer a brief talk on the evils facing America.[7]

Their power even extended to Smith's home state. The Albany metropolitan area produced eleven thousand Klan members, with seven thousand more in Buffalo, and as many as sixteen thousand in the New York–Yonkers–New Rochelle region, the most urbanized in the nation. In Syracuse hate-mongers called themselves the Guardians of Loyalty; and Hugh Carey remembered KKK parades in Hicksville, and how scared he was of the place because "there was a real anti-Catholic sentiment."[8]

Al Smith had seen all of this, of course—the prejudices the Klan both reflected and invigorated. As governor he had confronted, for example, bigotry against Jews, when he had to discipline state police and municipal officials in Massena for arresting a rabbi on the high holy days on charges that he had murdered a child as part of his rituals. Smith also saw a copy of a letter sent to Joseph Proskauer, claiming that the judge's record proved "Ford's contention that Jews favor their own race 'Crooked or straight;'" as payback Proskauer was "going to be removed by Maxim silencer Gun poison," or in plain English, a poisoned slug from a quiet pistol.[9]

Throughout Al's years as governor, it had always been easy to dismiss sick fanatics like that anonymous letter writer, and that was exactly what Smith and those around him did. They just could not conceive that bigots had any influence on the American mainstream, so when the Klan marched in Queens, Al's secretary responded to pleas for action by explaining, "the governor is giving no heed" to that organization, since "it is not believed that fair-minded people are taking them at all seriously." Smith felt that people would dismiss such rantings, that as far as he was concerned, he would "allow them to say anything they like," since "they don't help their cause any by it." He referred to hate mail as "crackpot letters," telling friends that episodes like the Klan were something the country went through every thirty years or so, with no lasting impact.[10]

Because Al believed that groups like this were marginal, his normally acute political instincts sometimes shut down, leading him to make innocent but dubious judgments that affected the pending presidential campaign. In 1926, for example, the Roman Catholic church staged a Eucharistic Congress in Chicago, a gathering that brought together thirteen cardinals, five hundred bishops, and thousands of priests and nuns. The guest of honor was papal legate Giovanni Cardinal Bonzano, and after landing in New York, His Eminence agreed to appear for a photo session on the steps of city hall with his entire entourage and the local Catholic hierarchy. Mayor Jimmy Walker was there, of course. But Al also attended, genuflecting before the church official and kissing his ring. From a standpoint of naiveté, of course, he was right; any American has the right to practice the religion of his choice in public. But in terms of realpolitik, Al knew that he was a leading contender for the presidential nomination two years hence, and had been rudely informed plenty of times that Catholicism might be an issue. He now appeared in every press photo in a sea of red velvet cardinals, leading to questions like the one asked by the *Baptist Advance,* "How would you like to have a thing like that staged in the White House or the Capital?" Smith even traveled to Chicago and attended the giant rally in person, telling reporters that this was the final proof that "there is no religious bigotry in this great country."[11]

The first anti-Catholic challenge that the Smith campaign took seriously came in April 1927, when the *Atlantic Monthly* published an article by Charles C. Marshall entitled, "An Open Letter to the Honorable Alfred E. Smith." Marshall, a graduate of Columbia University Law School and an expert on canon law, had spoken and written on the issue of Catholics' holding political and judicial positions in this country, claiming that they should be barred from both because of their dual allegiance to the pope and to U.S. law. A flier enunciating his views came to the attention of Ellery Sedgewick, editor of the *Atlantic,* and Sedgewick invited Marshall to write a longer piece, focusing on Smith and his potential candidacy.[12]

It is hard to understand, so many decades later, why this particular article caused such a fuss. Marshall's work raised no new issues and was anything but flamboyant, as he employed a style that could only mercifully be described as dull and pedantic. His primary argument was the traditional one that a Catholic's loyalty to Rome should preclude him from high office, but Marshall couched it in daunting scholarship, quoting encyclicals and works like the *Catholic Encyclopedia* whenever possible. Many of his sentences ran between ten and twenty lines apiece.[13]

But this piece was the first time that the leading contender for a presidential nomination of a major party had ever had his religion questioned—not in private, not in a dining room or over the back fence, but in one of the nation's most prestigious publications. It became front-page news, with every paper in the country carrying the story; even the foreign press picked it up. Sedgewick, meanwhile, had provided advance knowledge of Marshall's piece to Franklin Roosevelt and had suggested that Smith reply at length. Roosevelt asked Sedgewick not to publish the work at all, that the debate over this "fool article" would not bring out anything good in American political life, but FDR knew that no matter what he said, the *Atlantic* was going to proceed anyway. He passed the proofs along to Belle Moskowitz, who alerted Al and the senior staff.[14]

Most accounts indicate that Joe Proskauer first talked to Al about the article, and that the candidate was dumbfounded. Al's Catholicism did nothing to prepare him for this assault; he was a simple but true believer who knew nothing of papal bulls or any other of the church's legal documents. Proskauer claimed the governor told him, "To tell you the truth, I've read it, but I don't know what the words mean." Smith tried to avoid the subject, grumbling, "I'm not going to answer the damn thing," and did not change his mind until the judge, and especially Moskowitz, leaned heavily on him and he finally authorized a response.[15]

The capable pair of advisers immediately took over. Mrs. M called the *Atlantic*'s editors and asked them to hold space for a reply in their next issue, while Joe agreed to write a draft. Proskauer had originally declined "the contract" (as Al referred to it), but then accepted, savoring the irony: "A Protestant lawyer charges a Catholic candidate for the Presidency . . . and you want it answered by a Jewish judge." He asked for only one form of assistance, a senior Catholic priest to aid him in preparing arguments. Proskauer wound up working with the famous Father Francis Duffy, chaplain to the 165th Regiment of World War I fame, and for whom Duffy Square in Manhattan would later be named.[16]

Their essay (which Proskauer felt was "the perfect answer") appeared in the May issue as "Catholic and Patriot: Governor Smith Replies," taking up eight pages. Over and over, quoting almost as many religious works as Marshall had, it hammered home the theme that Roman Catholics could be loyal American citizens. In the end, it had Smith agreeing to "summarize my creed as an American Catholic." While remaining faithful to his religion, he insisted, "no power in the institutions of my Church" could ever "interfere with the operations of the Constitution of the United States" in any Smith administration, past, present, or future. He endorsed separation of church and state, the public school system, and "freedom of conscience for all men." The last line of the piece read simply, "I join with fellow Americans of all creeds in a fervent prayer that never again in this land will any public servant be challenged because of the faith in which he has tried to walk humbly with his God."[17]

Smith's reply became a public sensation. It was the lead story on the front page of the *New York Times* and got carried everywhere, with editorials and commentaries appearing in Madrid's *El Sol* and *El Debate,* among other European papers. Sales for the *Atlantic,* which normally hovered around thirty thousand, shot up to fifty-four thousand for the issue in which Marshall's letter ran, and then peaked at seventy-two thousand when Al's piece came out. Marshall, meanwhile, the least combative of souls, never recovered from the fight he had blundered into, writing endless angry letters to Sedgewick over the fact that he had not been provided an opportunity to offer the last word, bitterly complaining that the abuse he had suffered from Catholics over this affair had destroyed the favorable opinions he felt he had had of them when it started.[18]

Marshall's article, however, raised the two substantive issues that would haunt Smith in 1928, even if they had no more substance than the stories of convent rapes and abductions. First, many Americans believed that Catholics take an oath of allegiance to a foreign monarch, so that their first loyalty is, and always will be, to the pope in Rome. After that came the claim that because the church was hierarchical, because it tried to enforce total loyalty to papal views, Roman Catholics were more like serfs than citizens; they did not understand, could never practice American democracy. Both of these, of course, ignored how freethinking American Catholics were, how they could easily maintain dual identities just like other Americans, how they had no problems voting, serving in Congress, dying in wars, or winning the Medal of Honor. Logic and evidence, however, rarely impress bigots.

But Marshall's article was just the opening salvo, the prelude to future combat. By the fall of 1928, ideas like these had become solidified into rigid doctrine for many Americans. Making matters even worse, presidential campaigns in those days were short, dramatic affairs of only 8–10 weeks length, condensed, potentially feverish episodes where every cheap taunt could become a major event, with little time to rebut. As the campaign officially opened in September, Al Smith now confronted, for the first time in his life, a nation obsessed with, and basing judgments on, fantasies and hate.

Robert Schuler, for example, a Los Angeles minister,* wrote a pamphlet entitled *Al Smith: A Vigorous Study,* in which he told readers, "Al Smith is distinctly Rome's candidacy. It has been fostered by Tammany, for years recognized as an active ally of Rome. It is headed by Rome's active chamberlain to the Pope. . . . If America desires a President born and raised in a foreign atmosphere, politically

---

*This Schuler has no relation to his Crystal Cathedral namesake.

trained and promoted by a foreign political machine . . . that man may be had by electing Al Smith." Schuler went on to warn Americans that if Smith was elected, the public school system would be destroyed and civil marriages would no longer be recognized. He also reported that Lincoln, Garfield, and McKinley had all been killed by Romanists.[19]

Ridiculous claims now started to appear across the nation. Mrs. J. L. Swint wrote Franklin Roosevelt that her neighbor told her that "if Gov. Smith is elected President, the *Pope's son* will be his secretary." Mrs. Caroline Bond wrote John Roach Straton, a minister who took on the holy duty of following Smith around the campaign trail to denounce his depravity, that she had discovered the keys to the secret of Roman Catholicism. They had been revealed to her three times: first, by the wife of a man who had turned from Catholicism to Methodism; second by a Presbyterian member of the Klan; and third by a Jewish woman "whose husband read it out of the book of the secret order of the rules of the Knights of Columbus—found by her husband on the way home," where they assumed it had been dropped by a workman. That "book of sacred rules of the Catholic Church," Mrs. Bond explained, contained the following dictum: "When opportunity offers itself in a time or place under cover—it is the will of the Almighty God as a Roman Catholic to tear out the womb of any Protestant Woman—For by so doing you abolish the perpetuity of that Satanic following." J. H. Fletcher, "Kligrapp" or secretary of the Bay Shore, Long Island, chapter of the Klan, also wrote Straton, telling him, "This fight is not only a battle against Rome, but against all the evil forces in America, cutthroats, thugs, the scum from the cesspools of Europe."[20]

But that was just the beginning, and now the Republicans would also have to decide what to do with this; eventually they would make their own contributions to the rhetoric of hate. Officially, Herbert Hoover reiterated over and over that he would have nothing to do with any attacks on Governor Smith's religion; Hubert Work, his campaign manager, announced, "All such activities are vicious and beyond the pale of decent political campaigning." Hoover, a shy and proper man with no experience of political roughhousing, truly felt shocked at the bigotry that year, and it is hard not to believe that his fundamental sense of right and wrong was not offended by groups like the KKK.[21]

His immediate circle, however, shared no such reticence, especially Herbert's wife, his closest companion and adviser. Lou Hoover was a witty, worldly, charming woman, with plenty of moxie and lots of character. Much like Katie Smith, however, she was also devoted to her husband, and exquisitely sensitive to any attacks on him. This defensiveness soon overwhelmed both her cosmopolitan edge and any charitable feelings she may have entertained toward the Democratic candidate.

Thus, Lou's private comments during the campaign became twisted and malicious. She considered Smith a sham and a liar because he spoke out against smears directed at himself, but did not defend Herbert against the far fewer personal attacks aimed his way, like that the Hoovers were really Brits and tools of the empire; or that because he was a Quaker, Herbert had to be a coward. At one point she complained, "The cry from Smith himself and from many of his . . . cohorts against the whispering campaign is such a travesty!"[22]

Even worse, Lou Hoover soon joined the ranks of those who claimed they despised bigotry, but found nothing wrong with denigrating Catholicism. She argued that Smith's religion "should not be whispered against," but also believed that "there are many people of intense Protestant faith to whom Catholicism is a grievous sin. And they have as much right to vote against a man for public office because of that belief" as anyone else; "that is not persecution."[23]

Because of these beliefs, she could even descend to underhanded tactics. In one letter, Mrs. Hoover wrote that it would be impossible for Smith to have a "clean administration" because of his Tammany background. On another occasion, her secretary responded to a Smith denunciation of charges that he was drunk in public with a snide private letter that if Al really wanted to put an end to these rumors, all he had to do was to declare that he had never broken the law since the inception of the Eighteenth Amendment in any way, shape or form. Lou Hoover then took this document and sent it along to a friend with a note that she "could not resist . . . a bit of impudence. . . . While of course it could not come out of our camp, and is too undignified for you personally, you may know someone else who would like to use it, or you might like paraphrasing it."[24]

Adding to this character assassination were members of Herbert's campaign. Hoover, for all his organizational genius, had no background in elective politics, and Hubert Work, his campaign manager, was relatively ineffective (Herbert felt that Work was doing a poor job but just did not know of anyone better). Their staff control, therefore, was particularly weak, even in an era of decentralized campaigns; Stanley Washburn, a Republican worker who quit because he could not take the anti-Catholicism that darkened the campaign, said that "Hoover officially denounced" the bigotry, "but he never stepped on it."[25]

This weakness became particularly apparent in the state and local campaigns. Despite the candidate's denunciations of bigotry, the Republican Committee of Louisville and Jefferson County sent a solicitation letter that declared: "The American theory of government is threatened. . . . Our immigration laws are attacked. American institutions are at stake." Anonymous Republicans used the slogan, "A Christian in the White House"; while the New Jersey Klan billed its rallies as being "in conjunction with the National Republican Committee," and in truth, the Virginia party chairman turned out to be co-owner of the *Fellowship Forum*. R. W. Patterson, reporting from Florida, noted that he had to "soft peddle . . . some of the local Republican papers that have featured . . . the religious issue," but confessed that it was "dynamite," and was "the one thing that is turning thousands of votes to the Chief." And when a reporter for the *New York World*, acting undercover, went to the Washington, D.C., Republican headquarters to ask for information, an aide suggested that she stop instead at the KKK office nearby, and even offered to drive her there himself.[26]

The worst example of this lack of control involved a complex Republican official. Mabel Walker Willebrandt was, in more ways than one, a pioneer. Born on the Kansas prairie, marriage and family eventually brought her to the Golden State, where she received bachelor's and master's of law degrees from the University of Southern California. After passing the bar exam Willebrandt became active in local politics; and in 1921, the Harding administration, in a bid for women's votes, appointed her assistant attorney general in charge of prohibition enforcement, the highest position a female would hold in national law enforcement for many years. She became a source of pride for women everywhere, the *Ladies' Home Journal* beaming as it reported how the nation's top female official "sits in a big many-windowed room on the seventh floor of the Department of Justice" and "commands a little army" of forty-two attorneys and countless clerks and stenographers. All this, and not yet forty years of age.[27]

But Willebrandt was a product of the old America. In her autobiography she referred to Abraham Lincoln as "the greatest Anglo-Saxon"; her position in prohibition enforcement, furthermore, meant her views would bitterly clash with Governor Smith's.[28]

On September 7, 1928, campaigning for fellow Republican Herbert Hoover, Willebrandt crossed the line that separated legitimate advocacy from indecent partisanship, even demagoguery. Using her title as a cabinet official conspicuously, she addressed a meeting of twenty-five hundred Methodist ministers at Springfield, Ohio, in an openly political speech. After praising her candidate, Mrs. Willebrandt turned to Smith, claiming that "Tammany had reared him; gave him his power"; and that he "was the one Governor in all the American states who, notwithstanding his oath to support the Constitution of the United States, pulled down one of the . . . pillars the people had erected for its support." That was fair politics, but she then urged the ministers to embark on a holy crusade, pointing out that "there are two thousand pastors here. You have in your churches more than six hundred thousand members . . . in Ohio alone. That is enough to swing the election." And these six hundred thousand had friends in other states. "Write to them," she beseeched, work from the pulpit tirelessly, since "every day and every ounce of your energy" were needed.[29]

Willebrandt's talk made national headlines, and they were not complimentary. The *Chicago Tribune,* one of the most Republican papers in the country, called the speech "an act for which an official should be removed from office. . . . The administration has permitted one of its conspicuous officials to promote a church war in a Presidential campaign, an instance of pernicious political activity which it would be hard to equal." The national magazine *Independent* editorialized, "No event . . . has been more fatuous or less in keeping with fair play than the proselytizing of Mabel Walker Willebrandt"; and Robert Taft quietly wrote the head of the Republican Speakers' Bureau that "continued speeches by her are the only thing which can possibly defeat Mr. Hoover."[30] (After the election, ironically, Willebrandt resigned her prohibition job at the Justice Department to become counsel to the Vine-Glo Company, a California firm that sold liquid grape concentrates available in flavors like sherry, port, muscatel, and burgundy. Although these beverages were nonalcoholic, one could, however, add water and sugar, let the mixture stand for sixty days, and end up with a beverage of 24 proof.)[31]

But by then Mrs. Willebrandt was being shoved aside by far larger forces, by a blitzkrieg of hate that was gathering strength and speed. Along the byways of towns and villages, roadside signs—small, handwritten notices—appeared, reading, "For Hoover and America, or For Smith and Rome. Which? Think It Over Americans." In Atlanta, ministers issued a statement, "You cannot nail us to a Roman cross and submerge us in a sea of rum"; while that city's *Wesleyan Christian Advocate* took to calling the Republicans the party of the "upperworld," that a vote for the GOP was a vote for "the kingdom of God." The Knights of Luther, who noted with scholarly pride that all their material came from the "Washington Bureau of Statistics," informed readers that every Catholic priest, bishop, and cardinal had to "make and repeat the following statements: "The public schools are nurseries of vice. They are Godless, and unless suppressed will prove the damnation of this country." J. C. Hale, pastor of the Baptist church at Ralls, Texas, argued that the Catholic church was not Christian, a pretty serious charge given that he felt that "this is a Christian nation. The law of the Federal Constitution was founded on the Christian Bible." In Muncie, Indiana, some folks believed that Catholics were engaged in a conspiracy with blacks; the Romanists had invented a powder that would bleach the skins of black men so they could go out and marry white women, the chief goal of the race. But the real spirit of that year's election was summed up by a voter whose name is lost to the ages, an honest man or woman who admitted "that in all reason we ought to put Smith in the White House for the ability that he has shown. . . . But I suppose at my mother's knees I acquired a prejudice against Catholics and I cannot really forget it."[32]

Violence—imagined and real—now began to crop up everywhere. Robert John Cunningham, Organizer and Chief of the United Protestant Secret Service for United States, and Prohibition, took his exalted title very, very seriously. He let Republican Ogden Mills know that "we have current information that Catholics have been killing Protestants. I also have seen this, and they tried to murder me." Wisely, Cunningham marked the letter, "Personal and Confidential." Laughable, perhaps; but when the Smith campaign train pulled into Billings, Montana, a cross burned on Rim Rock, just north of the business district, and several charges of dynamite went off.[33]

The best example of all the ignorance that year was a conversation that took place when Arthur Rhorer, a lawyer, interviewed two workers in a tanning factory in Middlesboro, Kentucky. Rhorer asked how most of the men down at the works were going to vote; the vast majority favored Hoover, only a few supported Al Smith. When queried if this meant that "you men are satisfied with conditions and think we are having good times . . . under the Republicans," the interviewees answered, "No, times are rotten." Rhorer asked what the problem was with Smith and got told, "Well, they say he's a Catholic." He then inquired, "What is a Catholic?" and the first man calmly replied, "DamifIno."[34]

And then there was the pope. In 1928, a great many Americans honestly believed that if Al Smith became president, the pope would come over and rule America. The *American Standard* headlined, "Rome Suggests That Pope May Move Here," and in North Manchester, Indiana, a Klan lecturer warned his audience what to watch for, to beware the imminent arrival of the pope. "He may even be on the Northbound train tomorrow!" the Klansman exhorted. "He may! He may! Be warned! Prepare! America is for Americans! Search everywhere for hidden enemies, vipers at the heart's blood of our scared Republic! Watch the trains!"[35]

A lot of people went even further, claiming that the preparations for the pope's arrival were already underway. One source held that plans had been drawn up, so that the minute the election was over, the president-elect could send a battleship to Rome to bring the pope to the United States (intellectuals in New York joked that the day Al Smith lost the election, the pope received a one-word telegram: "Unpack."). According to this account, Smith would install the pontiff in a fortress in the Georgetown section of Washington, a citadel already built and guarded by rows of artillery. Other pundits were not so sure, claiming that the chosen site was in Lafayette Square, across from the White House. Smith's opponents distributed photos nationwide showing the construction of New York's Holland Tunnel, claiming this was the secret passageway being built to bring the pope all the way from Rome (the candidate tried to argue that tunnels cost $25 million a mile, that Vatican City was thirty-five hundred miles away, but what was the use?). Others feared the worst—that he was here now, in an underground lair beneath a Franciscan monastery in the District of Columbia; some people had even seen the facilities down there. At one time or another, someone, somewhere, also accused the pontiff of taking over just about every federal department, or at least plotting to do so. Lillie Case of Charlottesville, Virginia, reminded Lou Hoover that "the Pope wanted a navy and an army and an outlet to the sea," and that was why he had created the Smith candidacy—to take these from America—while the Klan's organ, *Fellowship Forum*, ran the headline, "Pope Tries to Run U.S. Post Office."[36]

Now the horrible truth had become apparent: contrary to Al Smith's deepest beliefs about America, anti-Catholicism had moved to center stage in the election of 1928. National magazines wrote how "in no political campaign since the Civil War have the churches played so prominent a part in political discussions," and compared it to a religious conflict. One survey found that out of eighty-five hundred Southern Methodist preachers, a grand total of four supported Smith, a situation paralleled in the ranks of Northern Methodists, Southern Baptists, and the Disciples of Christ; even the moderator of the Presbyterian church announced, "The plain duty of every churchman is to work and pray for the election of Herbert Hoover." Senator Matthew Neely of West Virginia felt that he lost sixty thousand votes that year because he spoke on behalf of the Democratic candidate; one voter wrote him about the 65 million dead martyrs the Roman Catholics had produced, and how he "would much sooner and with far more honor vote for Satan than such a man as Smith." In Kansas, a little girl came home to ask, "Mama, why don't they kill that bad man . . . that bad man Smith that they told us about in Sunday school?"[37]

Leading this campaign was often the Klan. By 1928 the KKK had been in significant decline since a series of mid-decade revelations of their violence and sickness, the most famous of which was when D. C. Stephenson, head of the all-powerful Indiana organization, was convicted of raping and maiming a secretary. But the Smith candidacy revived their fortunes magnificently, and they went all out in a national effort, distributing millions of pamphlets, newspapers, and images. America was blanketed with material from their national organ, the

Fellowship Forum; one piece, a flier for a book that exposed the evils of Catholicism, asked, "Will It Come to This?" over images of a priest throwing a baby into a fire; torture that appears to include vivisection; a priest whipping a woman as she is burned at the stake; and the hanging of numerous Protestants from a single tree. The *Tocsin,* the KKK's vehicle in Garden City, Kansas, announced that an "Alien Army is Now Marching on Washington. . . . Al Smith Stalking Horse of Jesuits. . . . Murderous 'Society of Jesus' Under the 'Black Pope'. . . . He had agenda for years plotting downfall of nation." "The alien hordes of the Roman Catholic political machine," they pointed out, "led and driven by Jesuits, have invaded America. Already they have captured many large cities." Franklin Roosevelt estimated that the printing and postage bills of the *Fellowship Forum* alone ran between $2 and $5 million, and told how even in small towns like his beloved Hyde Park, from July onward, "practically all" the families received a steady flow of material from sources like this. The *Forum* was now an enterprise with fifteen people in the editorial department and a total staff of 125.[38]

Complicating things even further, many people who opposed Smith on religious grounds, sometimes quite coarsely, did not feel that they were bigots, and resented anyone addressing them as such, lumping them with thugs like the Ku Klux Klan. In 1928 middle-class Americans could sincerely believe that they were free from prejudice, but still make outrageous, hurtful statements.

Thus, an editorial in the *Presbyterian* told readers, "If the Protestants hesitate to vote for Catholics, because Catholics hold and teach their children a political creed which is unAmerican and . . . opposed to liberty of conscience . . . of worship . . . of speech . . . and . . . of the press, it is neither just nor honest to accuse Protestants of religious intolerance." Charles Hillman Fountain, writing in *Current History,* argued vehemently that he had no prejudice, that his followers would never keep Smith out of the White House "on account of religious grounds," but only "because the Catholic Church is opposed to the principles of democracy." Because of that, however, they had decided that "not only should no Catholic be made President, but no Catholic should be elected to any political office."[39]

The foremost example of this dubious self-righteousness appeared in October, when the country's leading Protestant magazine, *Christian Century*—a publication that epitomized respectability—came out against Al Smith's candidacy because the editors could not "look with unconcern upon the seating of a representative of an alien culture, of a medieval Latin mentality, of an undemocratic hierarchy and of a foreign potentate in the great office of President of the United States." They believed that the reasonable voter would agree, and "it is not because he is a religious bigot. It is not because he does not like the Roman Catholic religion or does not like its ways of worship." Simply, it is because there exists "a real issue between Catholicism and American institutions." How, the Smith camp must have asked, does one ever respond to that kind of logic?[40]

But there was more, much more, for Al Smith symbolized the challenges of modernism in so many ways. It was Smith's misfortune, for example, to run during the era of prohibition; for many Americans, it was the issue of alcohol, more than any other, that had dominated their political thinking throughout the twenties, and they were not likely to abandon it during this presidential season. One Baptist paper explained, "We base our opposition to Governor Smith entirely on the fact that he has been the implacable foe of Prohibition. The Roman Catholic papers insist on lugging in the religious issue." The *Waterloo* (Iowa) *Evening Courier* began its coverage of Smith's acceptance speech, a long and complex document, with the headline, "Democratic Nominee Outlines Stand on Prohibition."[41]

This meant big problems for the Smith campaign. Many Americans could not discuss prohibition calmly, since for them, it meant the fate of civilization. Kate Penney, for example, mailed Lou Hoover a piece called, "I Wonder!" a series of homilies the lady had written that included the line, "I wonder if the 'Wets' realize the full significance of their sobriquet? 'Wet' with beer and whisky, drenched in the tears of women and children, soaked with the blood of drunkards and criminals." The Midland Baptist Association declared that they would "take their stand against the enemy of the souls of . . . children," while one ward heeler in Nashville told a reporter, "I shall never forget to my dying day the look on the face of my dear old mother when I told her that the great Democratic Party . . . was in favor of likker. I had to wait a week before I told that sainted lady that he was a Catholic too."[42]

But in 1928, the discussions of prohibition shifted focus dramatically, to direct attacks on Al Smith. In every account he appeared as a drunkard; the tale repeated over and over in every small town was that someone had personally seen him, up close, too drunk to even talk or walk. In Kansas City the story circulated that when Smith attended a dinner at a yacht club he and his party "showed signs of having been drinking strong liquor"; and in Wilmore, Kentucky, gossips told how Al showed up at the New York State Fair to give a talk, but was so sloshed they had to shut him down after ten minutes. When Smith gave his acceptance speech he was bombed, they said, and when he delivered his first talk over the radio two men had to hold him up. The *Western Christian Advocate* believed "the Al Smith smile will break forth in maniacal glee should he ever have the opportunity to sign a document of nullification," and the rumor raged that he was sure to appoint a bootlegger as secretary of the treasury. Nasty little sayings appeared, like Bishop Cannon of the Anti-Saloon League's "Shall Dry America

Elect a Cocktail President?" William Hamilton Anderson, one of the heads of the prohibition movement, bragged to interviewers that he "had a lot of fun in that campaign" on his weekly radio show; he gleefully explained, "I went after Al Smith and even took up the question of his personal drinking habits. . . . I had a lot of fun, very carefully avoiding any complication with the libel law." Anderson's parent organization, the Anti-Saloon League, spent $1.5 million to influence the election that year.[43]

And this confluence of dryness with anti-Catholic bigotry created a terrible problem for the Smith camp. How could they tell when attacks from the prohibition camp were real, and when they were simply a mask for anti-Catholic bigotry? Hugh Evans of Macon, Georgia, for example, told the Democrats, "The Real reason . . . many people are opposing the governor is on account of his religion, although they maintain that their opposition to him is based on his declaration on the Eighteenth Amendment"; while Marvin Jones of Texas referred to this use of the liquor issue as an alibi for other, less polite sentiments.[44]

This evolved into a diabolical trap: trying to defend himself, Smith attacked all bigots, many of whom hid behind these false facades. Yet by attacking all of them with the same vehemence, tarring with a broad brush, his campaign ran the risk of alienating large numbers of voters who felt that they were being unjustly accused of prejudice. William Gibbs McAdoo wrote that he knew "thousands of sincere men and women . . . who intensely believe that the prohibition policy ought to be maintained and whose opposition to Governor Smith is based solely on that ground. I think it is a grave mistake . . . for Governor Smith's friends to charge all who oppose him with bigotry, intolerance, and prejudice against him because of his religion." It was a terrible position to be in, and severely limited the Democrats' ability to respond.[45]

But by then it hardly mattered. The election had become a visceral declaration of war, not just on Al Smith, but on foreigners and cities, on the Irish and on Tammany, a hurricane attempting to remove everyone and everything the candidate had ever stood for. In Clarkesville, Tennessee, the president of the Kiwanis Club explained that "in the last thirty years the tide of immigration has undergone a decided and alarming change. Prior to that time the overwhelming majority of entrants were of a racial stock akin to our own and therefore easily assimilable." But now, "the inflow has been of a distinctly different and decidedly inferior character, Italians, southern Slovenes, Magyars . . . the very antithesis of the Anglo-Saxons." No match was possible, no assimilation attemptable for these peoples, since "among them the most revolting diseases are more prevalent. . . . They are unable to appreciate our conceptions of political liberty. Their ideas of right and wrong are so diametrically opposed to our own that no reconciliation . . . is possible." Baptist minister A. J. Barton felt "the greatest issue in this campaign" was "whether we shall continue our American civilization or lower it to the standards" of this untamed mob; and Bishop Alma White of the KKK spoke for many when she remarked, "I am 100 per cent Anglo-Saxon. . . . We are the keepers of the Constitution, of the flag and of American citizenship."[46]

Many Americans felt this way in 1928. Lillie Case begged Lou Hoover to "think of the large number of immigrants . . . being admitted by this friend of Rome! If we fail this time, how can we ever hope to win again?" In Tennessee Ned Carmack editorialized that the Democratic Party "had its birth in the very veins of our Anglo-Saxon ancestors," and it would be sacrilege to "let a tumultuous horde of the scum of Southeastern Europe inundate the land"; that was why he would vote for Hoover. Even in New York, Judge David Edelstein remembered, "You can't imagine the bigotry that existed in this very city" that year; it was horrible . . . vicious . . . horrible slurs against Jews, against Italians, against Irish."[47]

And these foreigners, of course, lived in cities, places John Roach Straton referred to as nothing more than a nest of "saloons and cabarets." According to Bishop Cannon, Al Smith could never be president—never—because he stemmed from the "sneering, ridiculing, nullifying . . . foreign-populated city of New York." Speakers presented an image of the Tammany Tiger gobbling up innocents, asked listeners to consider that "if Tammany stole millions when it had charge of New York City, what will it do when it has the whole nation to feed on?" The rotten joke made the rounds that Al—the immigrant, ignorant governor of New York—went on a trip and forgot his gun (ignore the fact that he never carried one in his life), then phoned home to have it sent to him. The connection was poor, so he had to recite: "I want my gun. G-U-N. G for Jesus; U for Europe; N for Pneumonia."[48]

⌘

It got so personal, so sickeningly bitter, that even poor Katie Smith became an issue. If Al was cheap, she had to be cheaper; gossips referred to her as vulgar, unkempt, overweight, a drunkard, someone who did her own housework (and did it poorly), someone, in other words, totally unsuitable as first lady. Stories made the rounds that when complimented on her gown by an ambassador's wife, Katie replied, "You said a mouthful," as critics painted images of a White House smelling of "corned beef, cabbage, and home brew," a scene from Jiggs and Maggie. Annie Hugillmof of Seattle wrote John W. Davis, complaining, "Aside from Smith's weak face and uncertain manners . . . who would want to see such a looking woman as his wife . . . as the First Lady of the Land?" One man suggested that the Republicans take pictures of Hoover and his family, and Smith and his family, then put them side by side under the caption, "Let Your Conscience Be Your Guide"; while Thomas Robins wrote Franklin Roosevelt that "one of the most intelligent women" he knew was committed to a Republican victory, strictly to "help keep Mrs. Smith" out of the White House. Throughout the land it swept, one member of Eleanor Roosevelt's advisory committee remarking, "The kind of stupid talk that is circulating around tea-tables and dinner-tables is positively disgusting."[49]

Even the public versions were only slightly muted. In Alabama speakers suggested politely that poor Katie's "social training had been inadequate" for the role she aspired to. The Republicans slyly alluded to the issue when they issued a pamphlet entitled, *Mrs. Herbert Hoover: "American Through and Through,"* although Florence Griswold, Republican national committeewoman from Texas, felt this hardly sufficed and openly raised the question, "Can you imagine Mrs. Smith in the White House?" Most brazen of all, Massachusetts senator Frederick Gillett teased his audience one night with the line, "I cannot say very much of Mrs. Smith, but if the contest were between Mrs. Hoover and Mrs. Smith . . . ," then left the rest of his obvious contempt unspoken. When the *New York Times* called this "execrable taste," Senator Gillett claimed that he had "neither conceived nor uttered" any such statement as reported, only to have the pressman who broke the story reply that his account was "accurate and fair," and that he still had his notes, if the senator was interested. The *Christian Century* reported that the "Katie issue" had become "the most widespread whispering campaign of all."[50]

The Smith people were stunned. No one had ever dreamed in his wildest imagination that Katie would become a target, let alone planned for this contingency. For Al, this was something he could never have conceived was possible in America, and according to Frances Perkins, "it almost killed him . . . he could stand anything but that."[51]

The attacks broke his heart, and not surprisingly, caused the only outburst he ever permitted himself during that long, hard season of hate. The photographer's request seemed innocuous enough; before he took Mrs. Smith's picture, would she mind removing some of her jewelry? Did he ask this because she looked garish, or because the gems reflected light into his lens? Now Al exploded in front of the press, finally letting out the anger, snarling, yelling, "Leave Katie alone!"[52]

❦

But even Katie Smith was small pickings; as Election Day neared, the contest emerged as nothing less than a war over the nation's destiny, over who had the right to be called "American" and to choose its values. Bishop Alma White, author of *Heroes of the Fiery Cross,* explained, "Who are the enemies of the Klan? They are the bootleggers, law-breakers, corrupt politicians, weak-kneed Protestant church members, white slavers, toe-kissers, wafer-worshippers, and every spineless character who takes the path of least resistance." While she referred to Smith as "the papal Governor of New York," she also pointed out that "among the forces threatening America are the great Hebrew syndicates that have acquired a monopoly of the motion-picture industry. These conscienceless, money-mad producers have no worthy ideals, either of dramatic art or virtue. Playing with sex themes, they are so depraved as to give the public any thrills they dare, for profit. They are destroying the moral standards of America and educating our youths in vice." Elaborating on this theme, Bishop White told how, "Great numbers of young women are employed in foreign-controlled theaters and the motion picture industries, which are ... completely under the domination of the Hebrew producers and white slavers." She recalled how on one railroad trip she overheard a young woman in a theatrical troupe explaining to a companion what her boss forced her to wear when she danced the "shimmy"; regarding that unusual term, Bishop White noted, "I am not sufficiently familiar with the language of the vaudeville to know what she meant, but I understood enough to know that she was the slave of her Hebrew master."[53]

That fall, lots of ministers used Al Smith as a vehicle to attack the horrors of modern culture. Things like the Sunday newspaper (a defiler of the Sabbath!), gambling, the mixed bathing pool, and especially dancing. One minister listed the evils: "bunny hug, turkey trot, hesitation, tango, texas tommy, hug-me-tight (this one just *sounded* sinful), foxtrot, shimmy-dance, sea-gull, swoop, camel-walk, and the unforgettable skunk-waltz."[54]

To John Roach Straton, Al Smith represented "card playing, cocktail drinking, poodle dogs, divorces, novels, stuffy rooms, dancing, evolution, Clarence Darrow, overeating, nude art, prize fighting, actors, greyhound racing, and modernism." Clearly he got that last one right, but poodle dogs? This was the year, however, that the Klan drove readers to action by warning, this man would get the Catholic and the wet vote, "the Jew and negro vote. ... He will get the vote of the Jew-Jesuit movie gang who want sex films and Sunday shows to coin millions through the corruption of youth. ... He will get the vote of the vice trust, the gamblers, the red-light and the dope-ring vote."[55]

As Election Day appeared on the horizon, the 1928 presidential campaign had become something far more than just another episode in a strange era. That year, the American people reached into the muck at the bottom of the well, pulling up primordial hate from those murky places we hope never see light, turning a man's bid for the White House into one of the most revolting spectacles in the nation's history.

Every commentator stood stunned. Lillian Wald wrote a friend about "the organized bigotry, the like of which I have never seen. I feel as if some poison gas had spread over us, and that our democracy will suffer from this for many years to come." Frances Perkins, campaigning in Maryland, the oldest Catholic settlement in America, encountered what she described as "some of the most terrible fantastic prejudices and dreadful yarns that I ever heard. . . . I had pointed out to me . . . the estate which had been purchased for the Pope and where the Pope was coming as soon as Smith was elected. . . . It was pointed out to us. They knew it for a fact." Marvin Jones, a Texas Democrat, went into a drugstore in his home town of Amarillo and was asked if he was going to vote for Smith. Jones, a good party man and a liberal to boot, said that, yes, he was most definitely going to vote for Smith. The proprietor sneered, "We've been fighting that bunch for 2,000 years. Do you think I'm going to turn the government over to them?" John W. Davis, the Wall Street lawyer who had been the party's candidate in 1924, gave a radio address supporting Smith; he got a letter telling him, "Your talk went over big with Micks but rotten with the most intelligent minds of America." It was signed, "a 100% American."[56]

Judge Simon Rifkind was, in 1994, one of the last people still alive to have actually been on the Smith campaign train. He explained that "having been brought up in New York, with plenty of Catholics around me [Rifkind was Jewish], I had not been aware of the intense anti-Catholic feeling that prevailed in this country." But "when I came to mid-America . . . it hit you in the face. . . . There were some times when nobody showed up at the platform. . . . He would be boycotted because he was a Catholic." Above all, Rifkind explained, "It was a terrible coming of age for me, losing my innocence on that subject. . . . It startled me." Judge Rifkind was not the only one to lose his innocence during that terrible season of hate.[57]

Chapter 19
_____

The Decision

ON THE EVE of an election, signals flood the senses like a switchboard on the verge of collapse. The Republicans had used the Whaley-Eaton Service as their private intelligence source, and that agency's last, confidential report, delivered just before the big day, said there was "a *possibility* that the result of the election might be very close." The soothsayers still believed that "the *probabilities* . . . strongly favor Mr. Hoover," although as members of their craft have always done, they hedged their bets: explanations covered which state may go which way, although it was clear that Al would carry the cities by a huge margin. Finally, they admitted that "the introduction . . . of issues, previously unemphasized but now determinative . . . has made analysis very difficult." It had reached the point, indeed, that "many astute political leaders . . . do not themselves know how their own precincts are going," which was "unprecedented."[1]

The Democrats, meanwhile, felt good, facing what they saw as a flurry of positive omens. When voter registration closed in mid-October, the figures in New York City set a stunning new record, climbing to 2,026,000 from a 1924 high of only 1,500,000. On October 31, the *New Republic* headlined an article by Felix Frankfurter, "Why I Am for Smith," a major endorsement. The last campaign trips had been triumphant, and after seeing, feeling the crowd in St. Louis, Smith told Frances Perkins, "I know politics and I know political crowds. I know political loyalties. I have never seen anything like this." Determined, he argued, "I've run for election before and this is not just an ordinary election. This is something. This can't mean anything else."[2]

Yet the anti-Smith forces were also active. Hoover supporters, Protestant fundamentalists, prohibitionists—anyone and everyone who hated Al, and cities, and modernism, and poodle dogs—printed and distributed 1 million sample ballots to show voters how to vote a split ticket. They sent 400,000 of them to addresses on the rural free delivery routes, and papers like the *Dallas Advance* carried samples as well. Ominously, even in New York State, Jim Farley, boss of Rockland County, found that Democrats who did not depend on patronage for their jobs were sporting Hoover stickers on their cars.[3]

Only a few Democrats expressed their fears. Frances Perkins tried to reason with her friend, Belle Moskowitz, explaining how "some parts of the country are terrible. I don't know whether we've really got them or not. In the places I've been the feeling was so deep seated that I'm alarmed"; but Moskowitz loyally argued back, "You're absolutely wrong! You're absolutely wrong! . . . We have intimate reports that we're all right. The Governor feels absolutely sure." The day of the presidential ballot would be Katie's birthday, and the first lady of New York had told the press, "The election is the only present I want from the Governor. And I'm going to get it, too."[4]

Election morning dawned with the country in a feverish mood. In Texas, Smith haters had held an all-night prayer vigil, and then en masse voted against their Satan before going home to get some sleep. Fifteen thousand Philadelphians and their guests, spectators at a championship football match, swarmed on the field at half-time to argue the merits of Hoover and Smith. In Cynthiana, Kentucky, a Hoover follower shot and killed a Smith supporter; and in Jesup, Georgia, deputy sheriff C. W. Madray objected when Judge R. Thomas called him an "Al Smith man." Words flew, and in the finest Southern traditions of honor and violence, someone eventually called someone a liar, a scuffle started, Judge Thomas pulled a knife and slashed the deputy, who then proceeded to pull a revolver and put His Honor away with two shots to the abdomen. Four New Englanders expired from heart attacks. It was that kind of day.[5]

Al Smith played the role of presidential candidate to a tee. By 1928 he and Katie had taken up residence in the Biltmore Hotel, so when it came time to vote, their polling place was in a stationery store just off Madison Avenue. Crowds jammed the entryway—"almost uncontrollable," according to the *New York Times*—but Smith made his way in, where the clerks presented Katie with a bouquet of roses. Al gingerly removed brown kid gloves (explaining, "The hands are kind of swollen after all the handshaking"), and then slowly doffed his coat, another exercise in pantomime; the old showman, who never missed the opportunity for a line, mock-complained, "This is a lot of work for one vote." The clerk then handed him ballot 473, and Smith stepped into the booth, while friends and supporters shouted encouragement and instructions on how to use the new-fangled gadget introduced that year, a mechanical voting machine.[6]

But after finishing this ritual, Al Smith did something different, something nobody expected, the kind of thing that is so personal, so private, you do not even tell your wife until after you have finished. Just before leaving his hotel, the governor had told reporters, "I would like to be alone for a little while. That is the big thing with me—to be left alone for a while, although I am not really tired and I feel well."[7]

So after casting his vote, Al Smith dismissed his police escort, eluded reporters, got into his limo, and went down to the Fourth Ward. Without any fanfare, in a moment of extreme privacy, he walked into the Downtown Tammany Club, 59 Madison Street, to sit for half an hour. Over his head hung a portrait of Tom Foley, the man who had done so much for the budding politician; the only other picture in the place was a photo of Smith himself, not as governor or presidential candidate, but as a smiling young assemblyman starting his career. Smith just sat and talked, a wonderful luxury for any candidate at the end of a harsh trail of speeches and promises, but especially that year. And then the neighbors heard the news and came flooding in. Al stepped out, the streets packed now, every tenement fire escape filled with men and women, cheering, yelling, waving whatever they could get their hands on, women with shirts snatched from the ironing board, plenty of people showing brooms, the age-old symbol of the clean sweep. He looked about and waved, said hello to Mrs. Morris Sunshine, who had laundered his shirts for twenty years at the shop she ran with her husband at 30 Oliver Street; and to Steve Roberto, the bootblack who had shined Al Smith's shoes. In the end, Al had gone home.[8]

But that could not last, and as night fell, the country turned from all other activities to tensely await the pending decision. In Pittsburgh, Eddie Cantor was appearing in the show *Whoopee;* in one scene he got captured by Indians, and they explained how Pocahontas had saved John Smith. Cantor ad-libbed, "Why couldn't they have done anything for his brother Al," and brought down the house. North in Albany, in the home of Mildred Graves Ryan, her father sat down his Smith-loyalist children and told them he thought the governor "just can't do it." As had happened so many times these tense months, a fight broke out, and in quieting compromise, they all went down to Democratic Party headquarters to watch the returns come in. At the offices of the *New York World,* publisher Herbert Swope, who had never touched a drink on the job for thirty years, threw down some hard liquor, the excitement finally getting to him.[9]

And then at last it was time to face the reality of America in 1928. Political news was still a spectacle in those days, and all kinds of mechanisms were employed to keep the public abreast of the latest developments. In the center of New York, the Times Tower, in its eponymous square, rigged up an astoundingly complicated set of signals to let people know what was happening. If the flagpole in front flashed a circle of white lights, it meant that Smith was leading; if the lights glowed red, Hoover had surged ahead. Next to this was a searchlight, which, if it swung in a semicircle to the north, meant that Smith had finally clinched it; but if the semicircle went south, Hoover's ship had arrived.[10]

The Democratic National Committee had rented New York's Sixty-Ninth Street Armory, and set out accommodations for six or seven thousand persons. When Al showed up he took a seat in the second row, stuck a large, unlit cigar in his mouth, and then proceeded to churn it from side to side. Frances Perkins, meanwhile, felt uneasy. She thought Smith had "a glassy look in his eye" and that his face was set "in kind of a permanent smile. It wasn't natural," she believed, for a man who normally had "a very mobile face which never was set."[11]

The preliminary returns gave hope. Al might have taken heart if he could have seen the earliest edition of the *San Francisco Call* (the one that featured "First Smith Voting Telephoto"); it showed Smith and Hoover running neck and neck, with the Democrats ahead in Massachusetts, the Republicans in Texas. Edgar Rickard, one of Hoover's closest confidants, noted in his diary that the early figures, from where he sat, seemed to favor Smith.[12]

Just after that, however, the tide broke. Hoover started to sweep state after state, even gobbling up Virginia, North Carolina, Florida; for the first time since before the Civil War, the solid Democratic South had cracked wide open.[13]

Somewhere between 9:30 and 9:40 came the most crushing blow of all. Back in June at the Republican convention, Herbert Swope, the *World*'s publisher, offered to bet anyone twenty-five thousand dollars at even money that Hoover could not take New York against *any* Democratic candidate. With Al Smith the likely nominee, no one took his marker.[14]

But now it was happening. The Empire State went for Hoover by over 110,000 votes. With that news, the *Times* reported, "the cigar ceased to shift and remained still."[15]

It was a night of sad memories. Al had tried to be jovial in the armory, talking about the party for his wife's birthday, but Herbert Lehman remembered that there were only a few hundred people there, in a room that seated thousands: "There he sat . . . surrounded by not much more than a corporal's guard of his friends and associates and admirers, listening to these reports, and one was worse than the other." Lehman said that by 9:00 "it was perfectly hopeless. . . . And he stayed there—he stayed there for a long time," while John W. Davis wrote that the governor, "was really surprised . . . by the defeat—or its magnitude."[16]

The family left shortly after 10:00 P.M. to go back to the hotel. Despite Al's forced conviviality, Katie could not hide her tears, and Al consoled her, told her they would still have that birthday party and he would cut her piece of cake himself. Around midnight he sent a telegram of congratulations to his opponent, which was not released until 12:50 A.M.[17]

Hoover, in fact, had chosen to remain at home with a few close friends that night, and at 7:30 Pacific Time, his scorecard tallied victory, and Herbert broke *his* traditions and grinned. The president-elect then retired to the solitude of his study, while his guests viewed films of his campaign speeches.[18]

The next morning revealed the full story: the election had been a disaster for the Democratic Party. Hoover knocked Al for a loop in the popular vote, 21,391,993 to 15,016,169, or 58.2 percent to 40.9 percent, practically an historic landslide. Smith carried only eight out of forty-eight states in the Electoral College, bringing him 87 votes to Hoover's 444, a greater margin than the Harding triumph of 1920. In the solid South, Arkansas, Louisiana, Mississippi, Alabama, Georgia, and South Carolina all stuck with Smith, although often by the thinnest of margins; 7,000 votes would have swung Alabama to the Republican banner, 13,000 in Arkansas, 15,000 in Georgia. But the rest—Virginia, North Carolina, Kentucky, Tennessee, Florida, Oklahoma, and Texas—deserted the Democrats; some of these states had voted Democratic since before Reconstruction. Smith lost *every* western state; *every* midwestern industrial state (even liberal bastions like Wisconsin); and in his homeland, the great, populous Northeast, he took just Massachusetts and Rhode Island. In New York State, outside the city, Al carried only four counties; even here, voters could not accept the vision of this kind of man in the White House, despite his record as their governor.[19]

From the time of the election itself, the traditional explanation of these results has been that prosperity beat Al Smith; no Democrat—no matter what his background—could have won that year. As early as November 21, two weeks after the polls closed, *Outlook* ran an article that concluded, "The voters had a choice between economics and politics and they chose economics. . . . Prosperity elected Hoover." Republicans most assuredly felt this way, and liked this analysis: Charles Hilles of the RNC congratulated Herbert on "winning by adhering to . . . economic doctrines in a year in which other issues . . . were expected to be determinative." Hoover himself agreed, claiming in his memoirs that Smith lost because of "general prosperity" and that, "in fact, the religious issue had no weight in the final result." And in 1960, the great historian Richard Hofstadter ruled that "there was not a Democrat alive, Protestant or Catholic, who could have beaten Hoover in 1928. . . . Religion proves nothing."[20]

More recent analysis, however, casts doubt on this argument. Allan Lichtman, in his 1979 book, *Prejudice and the Old Politics,* used a battery of statistical analysis to conclude that religion counted more than anything else that year. Controlling for every possible factor he could manage, Lichtman flatly stated, "Statistical analysis distinguishes religious divisions of the electorate from those founded on ethnic background, prohibition, or urban-rural residence." Of all of these, "Differences between Catholics and Protestants best explain the unique shape of electoral politics" that year. Even more, he pointed out, "Protestant opposition to Smith's religion was remarkably widespread, extending to all regions of the country, to city and country, to church members of unaffiliated Protestants." Indeed, "of all possible explanations for the distinctive political alignment of 1928, religion is the best."[21]

The anecdotal evidence to support this thesis is even more overwhelming. In letter after letter, diary after diary, men and women across the nation all made the same observation. John Ward of Columbus, Ohio, knew that "if Governor Smith had not been born a Catholic he would have been elected. The religious issue . . . surmounted all others." Carl Ristine of Lexington, Missouri, wrote, "If the religion feature had been eliminated . . . Smith would have been elected." One woman in Little Rock complained, "The Democratic defeat was . . . caused . . . by the absolute, medieval religious prejudice existing in many parts of our country . . ."; but James Kiernan of Providence, Rhode Island, reached the most terrible conclusion: "I am a Catholic and am satisfied that a Catholic need not apply for President of the United States during this generation."[22]

Political leaders shared this verdict as well. Herbert Lehman said religion was "dominant"; George Norris, the great progressive from Nebraska, wrote, "Smith was defeated because of his religion," and Henry Agar Wallace said, "Religion beat Smith in 1928." When FDR polled hundreds of Democratic leaders around the country after the election, 55.5 percent attributed Smith's defeat to his religion, compared to only 33.0 percent for prohibition; only 2.4 percent believed prosperity did Al in. Ross Lillard of Oklahoma City understood what had happened: "They wiped us off the face of the earth down here because of religion, do not let anybody tell you different—that is what did it, and this question has to be settled some day . . . or the nation cannot stand."[23]

Another powerful means of analysis buttresses this conclusion. In 1928 Al Smith never challenged business-based prosperity, and even though he did have a history of regulating business, he consciously decided not to use that approach during his presidential bid. No less a magnate than Henry Ford predicted, just before the election, that "so far as the economic doctrines of political parties are concerned, the country's prosperity is as safe with one as with the other."[24]

But one other man did fight this battle in the twenties. In 1924 Wisconsin progressive Robert La Follette organized a third party to launch a progressive crusade. More than any other candidate of the decade, La Follette did advocate an alternative to business as usual, campaigning on a platform that called for government ownership of the railroads, trust busting, a federal corporation to market farm goods, and, in general, a radical revision of American society away from the business interests and back to farmers and laborers. His support came from agrarian and socialist nonpartisan leagues, the still strong Socialist Party, and from every major labor union in the country. Republicans denounced his plans to reorganize the Supreme Court as an attempt to overthrow the basic principles of government, and branded him as un-American. And not, by the way, because he had much to say about immigrants, but because he had *a lot* to say about business. If fear of losing prosperity really was the great issue of the twenties, the one that would get people upset and make them turn to the polls in droves, 1924 was when this would have happened.[25]

Big deal. Or at least so the American people felt, compared to what happened in 1928. In 1924, with three parties running (which increases turnout), only 48.9 percent of the American people voted, the lowest until 1988 and the Bush-Dukakis race; in 1928, by comparison, the corresponding figure was 56.9 percent. Of forty-eight states, forty-five experienced increases in turnout between 1924 and 1928, and in eleven of them it was by more than 10 percent. Counting the two major parties in 1928 and the three in 1924, nearly 8 million more Americans voted for Smith or Hoover, a 28 percent jump.[26]

Money figures, another way people express their interest in a race, also reinforce this finding. In 1928 the Republicans spent $4.1 million and the Democrats $3.2 million. This represents only the budgets for the national committees, however; if one includes spending by the state committees and by independent supporters of each party, expenditures reach $7.1 million for the Dems and $9.4 million for the Reps, or a total of $16.5 million. Add in local and county party fund raisers, and it is possible that the nation spent $20 million during the 1928 presidential race. But this was nearly *four times* greater than the tallies in 1924, when instead a paltry $4.2 million was spent by three organizations.[27]

Every indicator, every form of analysis, thus points to the same conclusion. If Al Smith had not been a Catholic, a wet, a representative of immigrants, a New Yorker, 1928 *might have been* a referendum on prosperity, and the Democrats *may* have lost anyway. But we will never know, because Al Smith was, in fact, all of the above, and the election hinged on those issues. Al Smith lost in 1928 because of his religion, and because of the people he stood up for.[28]

If the mainstream historians were wrong in analyzing why Al Smith lost the election, they have been entirely accurate in assessing its importance. Social scientists from various disciplines have spent reams of paper arguing about "realigning elections," using 1932 as the paradigm. In that year, FDR captured blue-collar, immigrant, urban, and black voters, in both the North and the South, and the Democrats became the dominant party in America for decades to come.

All of this discussion centered on Franklin Roosevelt, until 1951, when an academic named Samuel Lubell produced a bombshell. During the twenties, he observed, cities in the United States had grown by an enormous amount: 6.5 million people left the farms to move to the nation's urban centers—4.5 million just to New York, Chicago, Detroit, and Los Angeles. By the mid-twenties, in fact, almost 70 percent of the nation's population growth was occurring in cities.[29]

On the basis of these numbers, Lubell concluded that the big political shift had actually happened four years before Franklin Roosevelt ever became president. Looking at the nation's twelve largest cities, in 1920 the Republicans carried these places by a cumulative margin of 1.64 million votes. But in 1928 Al reversed these figures, bringing metropolitan centers into the Democratic column with the slim but satisfying margin of 38,000 votes. The political scientist claimed that "the Republican hold on the cities was broken not by Roosevelt but by Alfred E. Smith," creating a Democratic hegemony that would last for at least four decades. Smith, not Roosevelt, became the pioneer of realignment, or as Lubell put it in his memorable phrase, "Before there was a Roosevelt Revolution there was an Al Smith Revolution."[30]

Over time, Lubell and others would expand on this thesis. If Smith had split the solid Democratic South, he had also fractured the solid Republican North: Hoover carried 200 southern counties for the first time in the history of his party, but Smith captured 122 northern counties from the GOP, 57 of which stayed with the Democrats in every election from 1928 to 1948. Democrats also carried Massachusetts, the first time they had done this since Woodrow Wilson slipped in the year the Republicans split in 1912; there too, the effect would last. Before there was the Kennedy revolution, in other words, Al Smith had had to run for president.[31]

Throughout the country, in cities small and large, results tallied true to this analysis. In Boston, 93 percent of all eligible voters went to the polls, an increase of 40 percent; the Jewish-Italian Third Ward rewarded Al with 81 percent, and in Irish Charlestown, Smith took 90 percent of the ballots, and God, and the Democratic ward boss, meted justice to the rest. Chicago's Poles and Czechs gave the Democrats only 40 percent in 1924, but Al won them over by a stunning 70 percent margin; in the Stockyards neighborhood, the Democratic vote in the core Fourteenth Ward jumped from 5,185 to 12,253, a 236 percent increase.[32]

Jews in every city went for Smith. In Chicago, Jewish wards where the Democrats had failed in 1924 gave Al majorities as high as 75 percent. Poor Hebrew districts on the Lower East Side of New York turned in higher figures than even the Irish wards in Hell's Kitchen. Even in Richmond, Kentucky, Democratic scouts reported that when it came to Al Smith, "most of the negroes seem to be for him, and all Jews are."[33]

These figures point the way to an even more sophisticated understanding of what happened in 1928. The most important corollary to Lubell's thesis came in Gerald Gamm's 1989 study of Boston's politics. In *The Making of New Deal Democrats*, Gamm looked, not just at the final polling results, but also at Democratic registration in critical immigrant wards. In these stacks of figures, he discovered that while city dwellers voted for Al in 1928, they did not change their party affiliation until 1932—that it was Roosevelt and the New Deal that actually turned them into Democrats. Gamm showed that "Al Smith had no lasting impact on registration figures."[34]

Then what did 1928 mean? Gamm saw it as a "deviating" election, but still recognized Smith's enormous hold on the voters, concluding that what occurred that year "was merely a testament to the popularity . . . of Al Smith."[35]

That of course, was the key. The election of 1928 was only in part the great realignment scholars spoke of. More than anything, it was a testimonial to Al Smith, a moment when the immigrants and their children, the people of the cities, paid homage to the man who had always been their champion. They adored him, and would now give him their votes, which seemed like so little to do by way of returning the years of pride he had offered them. And they were even happier to do so that year, when the hatemongers had gone wild, assaulting Smith and, by proxy, them as well. Party registration would have to wait.

But the pain from that election ran deep, and would linger. Will Bell of Washington, D.C., a Protestant and seven-degree Mason, found that his Methodist brother and sister had voted for Hoover. "I have served notice on them," he wrote John Raskob, "that I shall never darken the door of a Methodist church again so long as I live—not even to attend one of their funerals and by the grace of God I shall live up to that promise." Joseph Hughes of Detroit asked incoming governor Franklin Roosevelt to "resign, immediately after taking the oath, as a protest to the ingratitude and disloyalty of New York State towards Governor Smith." The White House head cook told Lou Hoover she was an Irishwoman, a Democrat, and had voted for Al Smith, and if that meant she would be fired, she was still proud; Lou kept her on anyway. As late as 1950, the author Henry Morton Robinson was still so incensed about the election that when he wrote his best-seller, *The Cardinal*, he included a long dissertation—using Department of Commerce statistics, hardly the typical literary device—on what a great governor and statesman Al Smith had been after all.[36]

Citizens of goodwill felt the country had gone too far this year, that the kind of bigotry that emerged should be fought by more than one man. Ministers, priests, and rabbis, laypersons and clerics, gathered in New York, took a nascent

organization and invigorated it, thus creating the force for tolerance and pluralism that became the National Conference of Christians and Jews.

And on October 16, 1997, Brother Philip O'Brien sat in a room in Manhattan
College in the Bronx and recalled the morning after an election almost sixty-
nine years prior. He had grown up in a "Catholic ghetto" in New York, where
everybody was for Al. When he got up and heard the news he felt shocked and
terribly disillusioned. Though he was only seven years old back then, and many,
many years had passed, sitting in that cold archive room, Brother O'Brien could
still vividly remember his emotions, they had been so devastating.[37]

In 1928 Al returned to Albany, telling reporters, "I . . . do not expect to run
for . . . office again. I have had all I can stand of it." A huge crowd met him at the
station and filled the streets, the people calling out, "We love you." Al lifted his
brown derby but could not manage, for the first time in a very, very long political career, a smile for the crowd; it was all he could do to keep his lips clamped
shut, they were trembling so hard. Katie, ensconced on his arm as ever, felt and
looked the same.[38]

In the mansion, they tried to make sense of things, not an easy task, as all the
servants were crying. As the days passed, they began to pack, not very quickly,
and not very well. At Christmastime, they received more presents than ever
before, and on December 25 gave the servants special tokens, each one handpicked by Al and Katie. That night, however, the family dined in private, not
even permitting friends to join them. For generations to come, as Al's granddaughter Helen McManus remembered, at least one part of that ritual remained
the same; generally speaking, the family did not talk about the 1928 election.[39]

If there was one loss that broke his heart during those long, lame-duck
months, it was not the bags appearing in the hall or the knowledge that the campaign headquarters furniture was being sold off for a pittance; Tammany bought
two walnut desks and three other pieces for only $137.40.[40]

But now Al had to give up his animals. He knew the monkeys would have to
go (he kept one), and what apartment in New York would permit an elk, a deer,
or a baby fawn? Hardest of all were the seven dogs. As late as December 6, news
accounts claimed that he would keep six of them, but by the end of the month
only one was left in the Smith household. Worst was the loss of Jeff, the giant
great dane that Al had gotten as a pup in 1923, and who had puzzled, frightened,
and entertained visitors every since. When it came time to drop the dog off at a
farm, Al told the press that he "never felt so bad about anything . . . in all my life,"
and Jeff reciprocated: "That dog knew all day long that there was something
wrong. He wouldn't leave my side at the mansion." At last, the governor turned

the job over to Al, Jr., but Jeff refused to come, so Smith had to pack him into the car and make the trip himself. When they arrived, the dog reared up and put his paws on Al's shoulders, "as if he was pleading with me not to leave him."[41]

On Al Smith's last day in the governor's office, correspondents who had seen 'em come and seen 'em go shook his hand and said good-bye in a shaky voice. Stenographers tried to hold back the tears, but when Al told them whenever he came to Albany he would run in and see them, they wept. His last official act, fittingly enough, was to commute the sentence of an Italian immigrant sentenced for murder. When Franklin and Eleanor Roosevelt arrived to take up residence, most of the Smiths' possessions had not been packed.[42]

For Al Smith, the election of 1928 was the pivotal event of his career; everything in the past was the buildup, everything after that would represent decline. An obituary in *Commonweal,* written in 1944, made the observation, "His defeat was a blow from which he never fully recovered." In a 1931 article, journalist Charles Stewart noted that Smith looked "older and more subdued than when I met him . . . a few months before his nomination . . . older out of proportion to the amount of time that has elapsed since then." Alfred E. Smith IV described his great-grandfather in the period after 1928 as "a broken man," and Frances Perkins remarked, "He was a lost soul after that. . . . There was great sadness over Al."[43]

Al had never felt his victory was a sure thing in 1928, but he most definitely did believe that it would be a fair fight—that when all was said and done, voters would look at "the record." But that year, Al Smith found out that America was *not* like the Fourth Ward, that it could, for all its honor and decency, still have a spasm of intense cruelty. A year later, the stock market crashed, and the twenties, the era that Al Smith was so fundamentally a part of, ended for good.

PART IV

FINALE

Chapter 20

Up to Now

AFTER THE 1928 ELECTION, Al Smith sought new outlets for his energies. He had every reason to expect that as a result of these efforts, he would enjoy the status of an elder statesman and the income of a top executive. But like so many others, he did not foresee the Depression that was about to begin, or the havoc it would wreak on his life.

At first, following November's electoral tragedy, things seemed to go Al's way. The Smith family had moved uptown, literally and figuratively, first taking an apartment at Fifth Avenue and Twelfth Street, then moving up to more regal quarters on the same boulevard, all the way north to Sixty-Third Street, across from Central Park; the palatial residence cost an astounding ten thousand dollars a year to rent. The Governor (as he would be referred to for the rest of his life) also maintained an office in the Prudence Building at Forty-Third and Madison, and rode around town in limos with the license plates "4" or "5" (only the sitting governor could have plate "1").[1]

These months before the crash were good ones for Al. On May 14, 1929, he attended a testimonial dinner on his behalf at the Union Club in Boston, sponsored by local Democrats and a gathering of professors from Harvard University. Law school professor Felix Frankfurter sat to his left, and at the end of the table was William Thompson, who had represented Sacco and Vanzetti. At the end of the evening, Smith rose to give a half-hour speech on the meaning and function of American government, and so captivated the learned audience that they were ready to offer him an appointment in the Political Science Department. His calendar was constantly full, as he danced back and forth from a meeting of the board of Syracuse University to becoming a director of the Henry Street Settlement, down the block from where Al grew up.[2]

That last item was typical, in that, whatever else was going on in his busy life, Al Smith continued to like helping people. His correspondence files bulged with the letters he sent on behalf of so many local citizens who were in trouble, and just happened to know someone named Alfred E. Smith. One missive to a General Motors executive sought employment, for example, for a young woman who, besides other legitimate qualifications, "lives down in my neighborhood." In another instance he got involved in an immigration case: a brother had sent money overseas to bring his siblings from Ireland, but one of the sisters had difficulties obtaining a visa. The little girl had been raised in a convent and never ventured outside its walls until she was ushered before the U.S. consul and a formal application inquiry; flustered, she flunked the exam. Al's only connection may have been that the girl's American brother happened to be "the elevator runner in the office building where I am located," but now he was writing top Democratic officials in Washington because, "I want to be sure that this gets into the hands of somebody that understands what to do."

If children came into the picture, Al really lit up. On Christmas 1929, the governor showed up at the children's ward of the Beekman Street Hospital, a facility catering to the poor of his beloved old neighborhood, to play the role of Santa. Handing out presents right and left, he came upon Gertrude Aquina, a black-eyed beauty of two (the hospital chart read, "occupation—infant") with a broken leg. Only Al could know the right thing to say and do, and instinctively asked her name *in Italian*. No slacker, Gertrude cut to the chase and said "Dolls," pointing a baby-sized finger at her goal. Al gently placed two flaxen-haired dolls in her arms and moved on to the next charmer.[3]

But bills were not paid with good deeds. Right after the election, Al earned his income in a variety of ways. He received from New York's Employees' Retirement Service an annual stipend of $6,100.51, or $508.38 a month, a long way from paying the rent. Far more important were the profits from investments John Raskob set up for him; one series of stock transactions, which took place between June 14 and September 12, 1929, netted Al $39,304.58, a massive sum in such a short time, and one of many deals Al participated in during those heady days of the bull market. He was also not above selling his name, and his picture began to grace ads for Simmons mattresses above the caption, "My day's program is determined by the amount of sleep I get."[4]

Above all, Al Smith now made a living as a writer. As early as 1927, word got out that the governor had been thinking of doing some magazine articles after he left politics, and by December he was solicited by George Bye, a literary agent. Al agreed to the arrangement, and by 1929 the two came up with the idea that he would write his autobiography. Publishers flocked to pick up the rights, G. P.

Putnam's Sons, The Viking Press, Simon & Schuster, and Harper's all offering a $10,000 advance.[5]

On May 29, Al finally signed with The Viking Press, receiving the expected $10,000 up front. What made this offer stand out, however, were the royalty terms: instead of the usual ascending scale where an author got a larger percentage later on, as sales of the book increased, Al started with the maximum figure of 20 percent on the first twenty-five thousand copies sold, dropping to 15 percent after that, which guaranteed that he got the maximum return no matter how the book did. Bye also sold the serial rights to the *Saturday Evening Post;* they would publish excerpts in a series of installments, in exchange for which Smith received an additional $55,000.[6]

By June Al was busy at the job of author, spending two hours a day exclusively on the book, dictating five thousand to eight thousand words a session. After transcription, the manuscript went to Belle Moskowitz for cleanup, and then the governor took a last look and made final revisions before they sent it on to the publisher. Someone also chose a hopeful, upbeat title, *Up to Now,* which implied there might be more news to come when it came to Al Smith. Early leaks to the press by Harold Guinzberg, Viking's president, promised that the book would contain facts "that will probably surprise even his close friends," a modest piece of hype.[7]

The book appeared in fall 1929, priced at five dollars. No literary masterpiece, Al's natural exuberance and Mrs. M's careful editing turned his story into a reasonably charming tale. That, combined with the natural popularity of Smith's story in New York, ensured that the book would be successful and reviews positive. Henry Pringle, writing in the *New York Times Book Review,* claimed the work was marked by "the discreet caution of the politician," but even he had to admit it was "fascinating to read." The *Evening World* called it "packed with . . . precious detail," while *The Nation*'s Harold Kellock complimented its "many excellent points," but had to add the crack, "Former Governor Smith is probably one of the few grade-A politicians in this land who could write a full-sized autobiography without creating in the intelligent reader a mood of acute depression." John Owens, editor of the *Baltimore Sun,* wrote to tell Al that his paper's review, "which finds similarity in your style to that of the famous Mr. Hemingway, was not written by a political expert, but by a literary critic."[8]

In retrospect, only two things stand out about *Up to Now* as being of lasting importance. First, because of the primacy of its source, it contains some details not found anywhere else. Second, it reveals just how angry Smith still was. While no stemwinder of a text, the one compelling section is the book's finale, in which Al discussed recent political events. A polished, polite segment, beneath the surface the reader confronts bottled rage, a barely controlled fury about what had happened during the election. Both these points—the detail and the anger—came through best of all in a comment from Al's old friend, Abram Elkus; after reading parts of the text, Elkus wrote Smith that the manuscript "was *you* all over."[9]

There were other Smith literary ventures as well. Al penned a piece called "Safeguarding Our Assets—The Children" for the *Ladies' Home Journal* and collected $5,000, which along with his royalties from the autobiography meant that he earned $63,500 as a writer in 1929, even after deducting his agent's commission. In 1931 he wrote another article, this time for the *Saturday Evening Post*, on campaign methods old and new (another $5,000), and started writing columns that year for the McNaught Syndicate, which also handled Will Rogers. This continued through to late 1932, and Al's work soon appeared in seventy-eight papers nationwide.[10]

Some of the plans did not work out, often for good reason. One syndicate promised Smith $100,000 a year if he wrote editorials for them, but because of his contract with McNaught, they got no reply. Al even came up with the idea that he could write a movie script, and sent his proposal along to Fox Studios. The story involved "a young man . . . and the great city of New York . . . waiting for him with open arms." Our hero suffers trials and tribulations, eventually meets "the girl" (who lives, significantly, on Madison Street down in the Fourth Ward), and eventually perseveres till he becomes a success. In the end he stands in a window surrounded by young people, looks out at Gotham, and declares, "This grew up in my lifetime and I grew up with it." Al at least had the good taste not to recommend that he star in the film as well.[11]

If that project sounded goofy, however, it was still not the strangest undertaking involving the Governor. For when Al was not writing books, he could sometimes wind up the subject of them.

In 1929 Al received some publicity—minor, dubious, and unsolicited—in Floyd Gibbons's *The Red Napoleon*. Written in the style of pulp fiction crossed with political commentary, the novel depicts the rise of a communist, mongol conqueror who proceeds to overpower all of Europe and Asia, and then invades the United States.[12]

Gibbons, unfortunately both for the plot and for his audience, was obsessed with race. Karakhan, the villain of the piece, is a rancid stereotype, the brilliant, rapacious oriental whose goal is to destroy the white race. To achieve this end he lures all of the world's colored races to his banner, just after he has taken over the

Soviet Union (following the assassination of Stalin in 1932). He leads them with the slogan "Conquer and Breed," a cry to commit miscegenation all over the world.

But when Karakhan invades the United States, he confronts an amazing array of public leaders. According to Gibbons, in 1932 the Republicans would split badly over the issue of prohibition, and through that gaping hole Al Smith would gain the presidency. Rallying the nation in time of war, the new president appoints Herbert Hoover to head the War Industries Board, turning the United States into a military-industrial juggernaut; John Raskob, not surprisingly, becomes secretary of the treasury.

Below this level, other public celebrities (and their thinly disguised counterparts) appeared as well. In the fighting for New York City, Al Jolson and Flo Ziegfield are killed when a building collapses on them. Jimmy Walker, on the other hand, is just wounded badly. Gorkus Marvey, meanwhile, head of the Amalgamated Ethiopian Order of the Black Plume, is arrested on charges of inciting revolt among his fellow African-Americans.

In the end, President Smith, down in Washington, moves his headquarters from the bombed and endangered capital to the safety of St. Louis; the enemy is cut off; the peoples of the world see the light of reason; and right and order are restored to the world.

There is no indication of what Al Smith—the real Al Smith—thought of this novel.

⤙

But despite all the money and acclaim Smith reaped from his writing, he still needed a job. A real job, the kind that you went to every morning, and provided a secure salary. Public speculation ranged from his return to the U.S. Trucking Company (he actually did receive an offer, but turned it down), to running a real estate firm, to taking a job as president of a powerful bank. It got to the point, he told the press, that he could have sworn he read somewhere that he was about to become a ballplayer for the New York Giants. When the big announcement really came, however, it turned out to be a doozy.[13]

There is still some mystery as to where the idea for the Empire State Building came from, and how Al Smith got involved. Some accounts claim it was the brainchild of John Raskob, the Du Pont financial wizard who was now becoming a very, very close friend of the governor. According to this version, Raskob, always on the lookout for business trends, spotted the building boom of the twenties and decided, as he usually did, not only to join in but to lead the pack. The figures were powerful—from 1920 to 1930, the amount of office space in New York went from 74 million to 112 million square feet, an increase of 51 percent—

but really, all he had to do was look out his window at the business-driven, man-made forest. In 1929, in an age that defined skyscrapers as buildings with ten or more stories, Chicago had 449 of these cloud-grabbers, Los Angeles 135, New York City 2,479. Raskob heard that the 40 Wall Street Corporation and Chrysler Company were both contemplating seventy-story structures. Figuring the race—and the business—went to the swift and the tall, he planned a building of eighty or more stories, to go up right away.[14]

Under this version, there are several variations as to how Raskob broached the idea to Smith. One account has Raskob bringing Al on board over a golf game at Palm Beach. The showman Eddie Dowling, on the other hand, claimed that he and the governor were attending to business at adjoining urinals in the Lotus Club, when Smith started to complain that he was in such a bad way financially, he could just cry. By this time Raskob had walked in and taken the facility on Al's other flank, and the little man now piped up to reveal that a giant project was in the works, and that Al would become president.[15]

Other reports tell it a whole different way; they place Smith, not Raskob, in the driver's seat. Empire State Building chronicler John Tauranac argues that because Al held a seat on the board of Metropolitan Life, the giant insurance firm that invested heavily in real estate, it was he who had spotted building trends and could plan financing. Smith came up with the idea for the world's tallest building as a way of creating a job for himself, and then convinced Raskob and others to go along.[16]

Historians debate issues like these, but pedestrians marvel at the physical structure before them. Regardless of who originated the idea, in a short while, a financial team led by John Raskob and Pierre Du Pont began to put together a package to buy the land under the old Waldorf-Astoria Hotel on Thirty-Fourth Street and Fifth Avenue and build a structure so gigantic, it would become the tallest and most famous building in the nation.

From the first, everything about the Empire State seemed larger than usual, even in a city not shy of extravagance. The land alone cost $16 million, the equivalent of $200 per square foot. Overall the planners estimated that before the job got done they would need to acquire financing in the neighborhood of $50 million.[17]

That was a pretty high-priced neighborhood, even for the flush twenties, but the money came from a limited number of sources. The biggest chunk was put up by Metropolitan Life, which offered one of the largest first mortgages in its history, for $27.5 million; this also made them holder of the first lien if trouble occurred. Another $12 million resulted from a transaction with the Chatham Phenix Allied Corporation; they would offer $13.5 million in Empire State bonds and debentures, on the basis of a written guarantee that Raskob and Du

Pont would buy half of this, at 90 percent of face value. Besides these two arrangements, the planners also expected to sell another $10 million worth of common and preferred stock.[18]

If the amounts seemed considerable, the backers *knew* that this was a money-maker. The building would be the greatest showcase in a city filled with them, and tenants would line up in order to print "Empire State Building" on their letterhead. Transportation, they argued, was unparalleled: subways flanked the site on both the East and West sides, while buses and streetcars traversed every major avenue and key cross-streets like Thirty-fourth, with Penn Station just two streets away and Grand Central not far either.* Diagonally opposite, B. Altman (where Katie liked to shop) brought in crowds of customers, and up Fifth Avenue people flocked to emporiums like Lord & Taylor, Tiffany, Arnold Constable, and Best & Co. One block over on Sixth Avenue sat the most mammoth mess of all, Herald Square, featuring the world's largest department store (Macy's); one of the city's most complex subway stations (trains from four IRT lines, and eventually from the IND and BMT as well); and the most congested traffic in the world. Planners for the Empire State Building figured on a 10 percent rate of return from rentals and other sources, convinced that they were right.[19]

On August 29, 1929, Al made the big announcement, projecting a rosy future for the edifice and for himself. The building would be the tallest in the world, capable of holding sixty thousand people—more, Al proudly pointed out, than could be found in half the counties of New York State. He would become the president of the Empire State Building Corporation, and his salary would be $50,000 a year; in financial terms, he was set.

Everything about this project stunned the mind. The structure weighed an incredible 600 million pounds. Construction required 58,000 tons of steel, the largest order ever placed, and too big for any one company to fill; that much metal, for example, was enough to build a double-track railroad from New York City to Baltimore. Each of the central columns weighed 12 tons, and were then encased in huge concrete forms for added strength—not surprising, given that several of these had to bear a weight of 10 million pounds apiece. Total interior volume was thirty-seven million cubic feet, with 2.1 million square feet of rentable space, which seemed to the backers to ensure a profit as solid as the building itself.[20]

---

*Actually, transportation was poor. The building was near a number of subway lines but not on any of them, placing it outside the predominant flow of pedestrians.

Figures piled up. Windows, 6,400 of them, would let light in, and other things as well. Because the building was so high and the offices were not air-conditioned, workers on the upper floors saw "little wisps of clouds" come in through the apertures. The building's lights and other appliances consumed 3,500 kilowatts of electricity, roughly the amount used by the entire city of Albany. Workers installed sixty *miles* of water pipe, 6,700 radiators, 17 million feet of telephone cable, and a ventilation system that drew 1 million cubic feet of fresh air into the building every minute. Most astounding—and frightening—of all were the sixty-two express elevators put in by the Otis Company. Prior to this time, New York City limited elevator speed to 700 feet per second, but a new law changed this to the rocket pace of 1,200 feet per second; the Empire State's became the fastest passenger elevators ever constructed, traveling at what experts considered the limit of what the human ear could stand. Even the sedate *Scientific American* gushed, "Empire State statistics are staggering in their magnitude"; but then, dismayed by this emotional outburst, added, "and it will be interesting to read some of them."[21]

And to everyone, it was Al Smith's building. Headline writers launched columns full of newsprint with titles like "Al Smith Building to Be World's Tallest" or "Smith Shows Off His Skyscraper." They called it "The House That Al Built," and wags commented that "if Al can't rise in the world one way, he certainly can in another." Will Rogers talked about "Al Smith's skyscraper, the tallest building in the world, the one he built so he could look down on the Republicans," then added, "It's big enough to hold all the Democrats and give 'em each a different room so that they can't meet and disagree." One journalist joked, "I tell you a 102 story building seems impossible. If it was being put up by just a regular politician and not Al Smith, wouldn't any of us believe it. We would demand a recount."[22]

Al took these remarks to heart, and did, in fact, make it his building. When the New York State Assembly installed new seats and desks and sold off the old ones, Al bought his, number 44, and had it brought to his office at the Empire State. He had his own private elevator there, and saw to it that everyone in the Smith family got in for free. Long after the founding member had passed from the scene, Smith descendants echoed the newspapers and called it "the House That Al Built."[23]

On May 1, 1931, Smith took every step possible to make opening day a roaring success, even swallowing his pride and writing Herbert Hoover to say, "Nothing would give us greater pleasure than to have you as a guest speaker at a luncheon on the eighty-sixth floor that afternoon." If the man who had beaten Al for the nation's highest office could not arrange that kind of time, would he at least agree to press a button connected by telegraph wire to New York and thus symbolically start up the building's lights? Herbert could not say no to this towering accomplishment of order and commerce, so even the president of the United States joined the celebration.[24]

When the momentous day arrived, crowds jammed the streets in front of the building. Two hundred invitations had been sent out for the luncheon, but 350 people showed up, as many individuals brought spouses, relatives, friends, all wanting to get a peek inside this fabled tower. Add to that sightseers lured by the publicity din, the usual curiosity seekers, and any and all New Yorkers who just happened to be walking by, and the result was a decent-sized spectacle.[25]

Al showed up serious but dapper, outfitted in a black double-breasted suit with matching derby. He also brought with him two surprise scene stealers, his grandchildren Arthur and Mary. At 11:15 grandpa took his two darlings—Arthur in a blue suit with knickers, Mary decked out in apple green—and marched them to the front entrance, where they would cut the big red, white, and blue ribbon and officially open the building. The word came down from on high ("All right kids, get to it"), but little hands do not manage big scissors very well, so finally, after repeated failures, Al stepped in and tore the sash from its moorings, opening the doors. Decades later, Arthur, by then a retired priest, claimed that he remembered nothing of the event, and when asked what came to mind when he looked at historic photos, could only reply, "I need a haircut."[26]

In 1931, people poured into the lobby, gaping at the pink marble lining the walls, at the gleaming steel art deco trim. After a few moments, however, they had to pause, for at 11:30, down in Washington, President Hoover walked out of a cabinet meeting to push a button. Up on Fifth Avenue, the building seemed to glow, as the lights came on in fixtures up and down the lobby. Al shouted that the best was yet to come, and he started to pull people into the elevators, to take them to the observatory on the eighty-sixth floor.[27]

He knew what he was talking about, too. Cynics made fun of the Empire State—bon vivants called it "Al Smith's biggest erection," and Jimmy Walker cracked it looked like the kind of joint "some public official might like to come and hide" out in—but the truth was, that view from the observation deck stole the senses. Even decades later, time has not outdated the Empire State Building; the vista is no less impressive than when the observation platform first opened. But back then, it was astonishing. Relatively few people had ever been in an airplane, and this was possibly the highest they would ever go up in the air. And unlike today, when visitors are protected by extremely high guard rails, there was nothing but a waist-high stone parapet to keep one from falling. For someone like Al, who had never risen above the earth in a propeller-driven craft, this had to be something out of a strange novel; Walter Smith recalled that to his grandfather, "it was sort of like a miracle . . . to be able to stand that far up on a building."

Even more, it may have helped Al realize how far he had come. The Brooklyn Bridge, symbol of monumental scale of his youth, was a dim, thin image now, far in the distance of the vast city's landscape, blocked by the newer Manhattan and Williamsburg bridges, its towers barely visible. And the Statue of Liberty, emblem of Al's constituency, commemorating their entry and titanic struggle, looked small and far away. Walter Trumbell, a New York columnist, wrote, "No matter how many times I pass it, I can't get used to the Empire State Building," and William Lamb, one of the architects who had conceived this structure, telegraphed Smith triumphantly from on board an ocean liner, "One day out and I can still see the building!"[28]

It was good that these fellows shared that kind of giddiness, because the reality was, the Empire State Building had become a financial disaster and was turning Al's life into a nightmare. This magnificent structure had been conceived in prosperity but opened in Depression. When Al announced, for example, on August 29, 1929, that the Empire State Building project had begun, it was exactly two months to the day before Black Tuesday and the stock market crash.

This spelled disaster. As the historian Carol Willis pointed out, the initial plans for the building had all been financial, not architectural. Raskob's initial notes discussed real estate formulas, number of stories, cubic feet, rate of profit; nothing about beauty or art. This was a building designed to make money.[29]

And that was the one thing it did not do. The original plans called for a yearly rental income of $7,961,580, enough money to pay off the various notes and allow a profit for investors. Indeed, Met Life's loan had been granted because of the strength of this figure, although by 1930, considering the fact that the owners now predicted a 10 percent vacancy rate, they had scaled this down to $6,863,114.[30]

Instead, when the building opened in 1931, the vacancy rate was an unbelievable 75 percent. While technically the building could rent space as high as the eighty-fifth floor, everything from the forty-first floor up was totally vacant (because rents increased the higher one went), and there were few enough tenants on the lower floors as well. As late as 1938, rental income was still only $1,843,790, or 27 percent of the 1930, downward-revised estimate. The only thing making money was the observation deck, such an immense draw that it could charge a dollar admission at the height of the Depression and still bring in over $1 million a year.[31]

The building was bankrupt. At one point Raskob tried to sell it, but got no takers. Metropolitan Life had originally signed a contract agreeing to solid rates on its $27 million mortgage loan: 5½ percent interest for the first five years, then 5 percent after that. But Empire State could not pay that, so the insurance company dropped the rate to 3 percent, then 2½ percent, and finally, in December 1937, Al signed an agreement that his firm would promise to pay 2 percent "upon condition that no default . . . shall occur." The only reason Met Life did not foreclose was the knowledge that they could not manage this disaster—one columnist called it "the most gigantic of the skyscraper flops"—any better than Smith and Raskob could.[32]

For Alfred E. Smith, Empire State had become an ordeal. The job of president was supposed to have been a sinecure; Al would enjoy a huge salary, and have little to do—the world's tallest building would sell itself. This aging politician might sit back and enjoy semi-retirement, or plan his return to the spotlight.

Instead, he became a joke. *Judge* magazine ran a cartoon of a man and woman passing a figure with a derby and a cigar, obviously Smith. The woman says, "There goes Al Smith—all alone." The man replies, "Since he built the Empire State he's used to being all alone." In 1933, at the New York political writers' dinner, one skit had a figure dressed as Smith approach another dolled up as Franklin Roosevelt, by then the president-elect. Al is assigned the task of settling the British debt problem and comes back to tell Roosevelt it is all taken care of, that he had "agreed on behalf of the United States to cancel the whole British debt." When Franklin asks, "Yes, but what did they agree to?" Al replies, "They agreed to take six floors in the Empire State Building."[33]

But that was not the worst of it. Al had faced ridicule far worse in 1928 without flinching, and could laugh at himself if he thought the joke was funny. The real tragedy was much deeper and broader than that.

For Al Smith remained a fundamentally decent man. The building project may have gone sour, may not have turned out the way anybody expected, but it still paid his salary, and he would do the best he could, even if the job had changed dramatically.

Now, however, with the New York rental market in ruins, all Al had were the observation deck admissions, and any publicity he could perform to get the crowds up there. This meant gimmicks and guffaws, making Empire State a spectacle instead of a showcase. So Alfred E. Smith, former governor and presidential candidate, now had to become a shill, a carney broker, to get the rubes to his show.[34]

No stunt was too far-fetched. Someone came up with the idea to celebrate the *New York Journal*'s thirty-fifth anniversary by having a blimp deliver that day's papers to the Empire State Building's newsstands. The news racks were down on the ground floor, but the airship arrived near the mooring mast, 103 stories up. Al ignored the fact that the *Journal* was a Hearst paper—something he could never have overlooked in days past—and not only showed up for the event but brought John Raskob with him as well. When the blimp arrived, dangling a one-hundred-foot line with a bundle of papers, chief rigger Andrew Kelley of the ground crew leaned over so far, pen knife in hand, that he had to ask somebody to hold his legs, "in case I get pulled." Raskob magnanimously assented to this frightening task, till Kelley snagged the package and pulled it in. Al accepted the papers gracefully, and then went down to make a speech for the newsreel cameras.[35]

Every celebrity visiting New York had to visit Smith's building so the publicity machine could crank out another story. Winston Churchill showed up, as did Premier Pierre Laval of France. Al wrote Joe Kennedy to ask if the king and queen of England could make it, and wound up imploring their social secretary (the Hon. Sir Ronald Lindsey, P.C., G.C.M.C, K.C.B., C.V.O.): "I realize how brief will be the time at their disposal," but promised that "they will be richly rewarded for the half hour they spend on the Empire State Tower." Over the years, Smith appeared with Crown Prince Olaf and Princess Martha of Norway; Premier Loukas Roufas of Greece; Prince Chichibu of Japan (Emperor Hirohito's brother); and escorted King Zog of Albania's three unmarried sisters, Ruhjie, Myzejen, and Maxhide: the princesses spoke no English, but Al still welcomed them with a loud, "Hello, girls!" When the dapper, impeccably attired King Prajadhipok of Siam showed up, His Highness remarked that he had things like this in his own country, referring blandly to the fabled building Al headed. Dumbfounded, Smith asked what he was talking about, and the king replied that, indeed, there were white elephants in Siam.[36]

Movie stars showed up. Mary Pickford released hundreds of balloons from the top of the Empire State Building; the gimmick was that two of them contained tickets to the circus, down at Madison Square Garden. Josef Israels II, Belle Moskowitz's son and Al's public relations consultant, used personal contacts at Paramount to have their star Lenny Ross sing tunes from his upcoming feature, *Melody in Spring*, on the observation deck. And Fay Wray admitted that she had never actually visited the Empire State Building, even though she had starred in *King Kong*, as she was not comfortable in high places.[37]

But when the celebrities departed, all that was left was the garish. Al welcomed cowboys from the Ozarks, chorus girls from Times Square, and spelling bee champions from New Hampshire. He awaited the arrival of King Taylor of Churchill River, Canada, who drove his dog sled team three thousand miles to get to New York. When the rodeo came to town, Eileen Caldwell, billed as "a Texas beauty," gave Al a ten-gallon hat, while he offered her his brown derby. The world's largest miniature railroad appeared in the lobby, and when Robert

Wadlow, the circus' eight foot, seven inch tallest man in the world, stopped by, the former governor of New York hammed it up and kneeled in front of him with a telescope from the observatory.[38]

⤝

In this era of Al Smith's life, the hard blows came again and again. The Depression, for example, had done a lot more than undo his job; it also decimated his plans for financial security, making him scared of the future and hurt by the present.

There are no precise records of how much money Smith lost in the crash, but it was sizable. John Raskob saw what was coming—in December 1928 he wrote an official at the DNC, "Personally I think the stock market is very high and I am keeping in very liquid condition myself . . . "—but also kept this news to himself, buoyantly expounding on the glories of the market in an interview in the August 1929 *Ladies' Home Journal* titled "Everybody Ought to Be Rich."[39]

Instead, men like Al took the hit. By 1932 he wrote a friend, "I simply have not got money to buy anything with. . . . During the last six months I have scratched and scraped everything I had to margin up loans, collateral to which are high grade stocks and would be sold at a time like this at great sacrifice. Were it not for my salary, it would be difficult for me to get along." In another letter, the governor revealed that he had lost $48,000 on Warner Brothers stock alone, and he had also owned shares of the National Surety Company, which went under in 1933. As early as 1931, Smith was sufficiently embittered that Robert Moses felt confident in forwarding a tearsheet with the headline, "Wall Street's Greatest Crime," including descriptions of how stocks were watered and trades manipulated. Moses underlined in red the line, "The stock markets are actually artificial, manufactured 'Games' which methodically inflict ruin and misery on our People."[40]

Al was hurting, badly. He had to cancel his membership in the Chamber of Commerce, a decision that required him to write and apologize for his actions. By 1934 the New York County Democratic Party had to remind him that he had not forwarded his usual contribution; there is no record that Smith replied. That same year he had to cancel an order to buy forty shares of General Motors at a low price, killing what was possibly a tiny, sad effort to recoup. When Al told Bronx boss Ed Flynn, "Financially I am in an extremely bad position," he spoke the truth.[41]

But as bad as his financial situation was, as the Depression worsened, it caused Al Smith grief in ways he could never have predicted or imagined. James Riordan was one of Al's best buddies, founder of the U.S. Trucking Company, charter member of the Tiger Club, and a leading contributor to the 1928 campaign. In 1926 Riordan started a new venture, the County Trust Company, a bank on the corner of Eighth Avenue and Fourteenth Street. Most of the original board were Irish-American businessmen, and the firm, with a modest capital of $1 million, sought business from the meat and poultry firms that clustered in nearby Gansevoort Market.[42]

Al helped his friend with this business in a number of ways. He was there to make the first deposit on opening day, and arranged to have John Raskob become a director in 1927. In January 1929, after he had stepped down as governor, Al joined the board himself.[43]

This had seemed like a grand idea at the time. By May 1, 1929, total assets of the County Trust Company were listed as $36 million, up from $29.5 million in January. Earnings within the first three years jumped from $10 to $41 a share. And the best indication of success, the stock price took off, from an initial price of $100 to as high as $500 or even $1,000 a share.[44]

But like other stocks of that era, it died in the crash. The price started to drop, hitting $400 and still moving south. Riordan tried to do what he could to convince investors to stay with his institution, to no avail. Deposits dwindled while, at the same time, his personal finances were also being battered; two days after Black Tuesday Riordan paid up $200,000 in a single margin call, and had little in the way of liquid assets left after that for any other creditors.[45]

On Friday, November 8, James Riordan left his house on Twelfth Street at about 10:00 A.M. and went up to the bank. He worked for about an hour, then left to go home, having handled only some minor details; one of those was to remove from a cashier's drawer the revolver stored there for protection against robbers, a small .38 caliber Colt. Upon arrival back at his residence, Riordan went upstairs to the office he maintained in a corner of his bedroom, sat in the overstuffed chair in front of the commercial desk he used, took the gun in his right hand, put it to his temple, and pulled the trigger. He was forty-seven years old.[46]

Alfred E. Smith and William Kenny arrived soon after the police and the medical examiner that Friday. Both men were close friends of the deceased and also directors of the company he had founded; the New York Times began its article with the lines, "James J. Riordan, president of the County Trust Company and intimate friend of former Governor Alfred E. Smith, committed suicide." Smith stood there stunned and wept, as did Kenny. Four days later at the funeral, Al, as honorary pallbearer, led the procession, crying as he walked. This loss, this shock had been too much for him.[47]

The business, however, had to be protected, especially in what was developing into an era of bank panics. Raskob immediately took the reins, issuing a statement that County Trust was "tremendously strong," flush with assets, and better off than any ten banks in the city. While he also had himself named temporary chairman of the board, by the end of the month he came up with a better idea, and Al Smith assumed that post, soon taking on the duties of president as well. The *New York Times* editorialized about the virtues he brought to the job, noting, "If the respect and confidence of the community, familiarity with large affairs and the ability to see through a financial statement and make it clear to others are qualifications for a banking career, then Alfred E. Smith should have a very successful one."[48]

But from the first, the Riordan suicide involved Smith in controversies. For one, the form of death was problematic because suicide is a mortal sin in the Roman Catholic religion, and it took some doing to even arrange a funeral. Then there was the timing of Riordan's demise: Dr. Charles Norris, chief medical examiner for the City of New York, told the press that Smith and Kenny had asked him to withhold the news for twenty-four hours—until after the bank closed following its Saturday half-business day—to prevent a panic. Norris claimed he agreed even though it "broke all the rules and regulations," arguing to the press, "it helped everybody and hurt nobody . . ."; not until 11:30 Saturday morning did he turn in his report to the police commissioner. Both of the two directors denied the charge—and the implication that County Trust was in trouble—but the timing was suspect, since those extra hours had enabled the board to meet, appoint Riordan's replacement, and conduct an audit. As a result, when the news broke in Sunday's press, they could issue an accurate and reassuring public statement based on fact.[49]

The worst was yet to come, however; an old sin would now come back to haunt Al and test his beliefs about friendship and honor. In October, during the last days of Al's 1928 campaign, Raskob, the campaign manager, projected a $1 million shortfall in donations, the funds he felt he needed to win the election. In order to make up this amount, he and Riordan conceived the idea of having County Trust donate the money, knowing, as they did in those heady days, that the money would be paid off once Al won and funds poured into the coffers of a winning DNC.

The problem was the bank could not make such a donation and stay within the law. To skirt such formalities, the two financiers suggested the bank only make a loan to the Democratic Party, backed by promissory notes signed by various of Al's friends—notes that stated they would underwrite a portion of the loan and guarantee its repayment in case of default. By the time the governor made it to the White House, they were told, the principal would all be repaid, and they could sign knowing full well they would never actually be responsible for the face amount of their individual notes. Above all, they could ignore the line that said, "Each and every of the underwriters agrees . . . that he will on demand pay the amount set opposite his signature."[50]

The sums involved were prodigious, eventually totalling $1,127,500. Herbert

Lehman and Raskob both gave markers for $150,000 each, followed by Michael Meehan for $100,000, while Riordan, Bernard Baruch, and Thomas Fortune Ryan agreed to $50,000 apiece. Pierre Du Pont and August Hecksher weighed in for $25,000, and all the lesser lights of the Tiger Club participated as best they could, most in the $10,000 to $50,000 range.[51]

Raskob fittingly was in charge of contacting his peers, the big money men who took out the larger amounts. If the project did fail, they could afford the loss—not necessarily gracefully—and Smith's campaign manager did nothing to indicate anything other than the full responsibility they were accepting.[52]

Riordan, however, contacted the "good sports," the other members of the Tiger Club who loved Al so dearly, but were nowhere near as secure financially. In order to get them to sign, however, he changed the rules, explaining that this was just a formality, that even if Al lost, they would never actually be asked to ante up. Patrick Kenny (no relation to William), a Yonkers plumbing contractor, recalled that when Riordan asked him to underwrite $25,000 of the loan, he responded, "Jim, I can't sign a note for any such sum as that"; Riordan countered, "Don't be a sap. . . . This is the baloney. You never will have to pay," and Kenny's name went on the list. In some cases Riordan lied even further, telling George Van Namee, for example, that he was acting on Raskob's orders, and that the financier had approved all the conditions of his plan fully and completely.[53]

The sad fact was, Raskob did manage to raise another $3 million for the campaign, but he also spent it and more, leaving a $1.4 million debt. By late 1929, the financier began to call in the notes, but even then, Riordan still told the boys, on the side, to ignore the summonses, that they did not have to pay. When the crash occurred, things just got worse; Riordan had to deal with his own payment, and even put up some of the money for the others to try and protect his friends from the bad investment he had lured them into. But there was never enough cash in those terrible days, and when the notes came due, they would have to be collected by the County Trust Company, eventually headed by Alfred E. Smith.[54]

As early as April 24, 1929, things had started to get ugly. Raskob wrote to everyone concerning the DNC deficit, explaining how, "After discussing several ways of meeting our requirements, the best plan developed seems to be that of calling on the Underwriters for the full amount of their subscriptions" and asking that they send a check out right away. William Kenny, Herbert Lehman, and Pierre Du Pont all paid within two days, Michael Meehan by the thirtieth.[55]

For others it was not so easy. Men like T. J. Mara, who owed $50,000, or Patrick Keeney, who signed for twenty-five grand, simply could not afford it. Raskob agreed, instead, on Riordan's urging, to roll the notes over, asking only that the promissees sign a renewal notice every six months, requiring them to pay the interest. But by 1930 Riordan was gone, and conditions had gotten so bad that seven of them refused to even sign that kind of note; they simply told Raskob he would have to cover their sums in full, to forget about any further payment of any kind. By November Raskob was sending out notarized letters calling on them to honor their debts.[56]

In December 1930, Smith got word of what was happening. He had not even known about the deal and was now finding out in the worst way possible and at the worst time. Raskob, who had tried to keep the full story from this increasingly sad man, now had to confess the whole sordid tale in detail. Some of this was terribly painful; George Van Namee, Al's personal secretary back in the golden days in Albany and later Smith's manager at the 1928 convention, had backed out of a note for $10,000. Raskob wrote at the bottom of a grim three-page statement to the governor, "I would not write this letter were it not for the fact that you took the matter up with me by telephone and asked me to hold things in abeyance till you could see me"; then added, "I do not quite see why you should be drawn into the matter because it must be quite embarrassing to you."

Soon things got even worse. By July 1931, Raskob had to write Van Namee and the others a nasty note, telling them, "I cannot understand this sort of conduct," that if "you won't pay or renew the notes, then it will be necessary for me to instruct the County Trust Company to sue for collection." In another piece to Patrick Kenny, the leader of the holdouts, Raskob struck back at men who had once been Smith's closest friends and allies; the financier complained of the bitter words Kenny and others had directed against him, then scolded, "It is most contemptible that men should resort to the kind of gossip that one usually hears from a lot of irresponsible, brainless women." Van Namee had to admit, in print, that "$10,000 is a sum which I, under no circumstances, would have subscribed to the campaign . . ."; a confession that must have embarrassed Al enormously. In November 1931 County Trust—and Smith—sued Kenny and Mara, but the story did not hit the press till March 1932, when it became a media circus, with the two defendants publicly accusing Raskob and Smith of fraud and illegal campaign financing. Raskob denied the charges, even sending the head of the Scripps-Howard papers a fact sheet in order to try and get his story onto the front pages. Finally, on October 20, 1933, former governor and presidential candidate, now beleaguered bank president Alfred E. Smith testified in open court that as chairman of the board, he had had to advise the two men that they must pay the notes, even though they had acquired the debt in order to help pay for his own aspirations. Eventually, John Raskob accepted that he could not get money from businessmen all but bankrupt, and quietly wrote off the bills, taking a tax loss. But Al had been terribly, terribly hurt.[57]

Like so many other Americans, Alfred E. Smith had never planned on the Depression, but like them, he had to handle its repercussions. He struggled with finances, fighting to make ends meet at a point in his life when he should have had a secure income. Because he believed in putting in an honest day's work for his pay, he became a front man for a failed building. And because he believed you took the lumps with the bouquets, making the hard decisions when they were required, he sued friends of long standing because they owed money to his bank. Al Smith was still Al Smith, but the smile was becoming strained, the laughter less boisterous, as his anguish and turmoil grew. And soon, one man would personify this pain, and become the almost singular focus of Al Smith's resentments.

Chapter 21

The Little Boy

FRANKLIN DELANO ROOSEVELT, more than any other person, would shape the last part of Al Smith's life. The two men had first met around 1910, when Smith was rising in the New York State Assembly and Roosevelt had joined the state senate.[1] There was no close rapport; Smith was the quintessential city man, speaking with a New York twang and championing the interests of tenement dwellers, while Roosevelt was a patrician squire from a rural upstate district. The latter's comments on the strike that preceded the Triangle Shirtwaist Fire, for example, showed little understanding of labor conditions or bargaining tactics, and after the conflagration he did little to support the safety codes Robert Wagner and Smith pushed through the legislature. Most of Roosevelt's comments on New York City politics at this time, instead, consisted of the usual attacks on political corruption and Tammany Hall.[2]

Within a few years, however, FDR was trying to mend fences and expand the scope of his contacts. Louis Howe, his political sage, suggested, "Now is the time to show you don't hate all Tammany," so in 1915 he gave a speech in Greenwich Village, praising Tammany's candidate for sheriff of New York County, Alfred E. Smith. When Smith ran for governor in 1918, Roosevelt again offered strong support, releasing a letter that talked about how Smith was "the best equipped" man for the office in light of his long legislative career. Grateful, the candidate wrote back, "Your letter of endorsement made quite a hit with all the men around me. It will certainly help," then added, "I will thank you for it in person. I can't do it well enough by letter." By this time, in other words, Smith was beginning to look on the young man with some considerable appreciation, even fondness. Nevertheless, young Franklin was still not considered one of the inner circle, was not invited to join the regulars at the Tiger Club.[3]

Smith won that race in 1918, and by 1920 the relationship was sufficiently close that he had Roosevelt second his name at the Democratic National Convention in San Francisco. Frances Perkins claimed that it was this event that cemented the friendship between the two, that they "were on good, chummy terms" after that. Emily Warner also recalled how she first met FDR at this outing; Roosevelt was still serving as assistant secretary of the navy, and there was a battleship in the harbor, so he invited the entire New York delegation to join him on board for tea. Emily went along; "it was the first time I had ever seen him," and she noted that "he was very good looking."[4]

Smith did not get the nomination, but Roosevelt did, as vice president, in a campaign that Thomas Chadbourne, a Wall Street lawyer and Democratic Party stalwart, claimed was "doomed to disaster from the start." Nevertheless, Smith spoke on behalf of the national ticket and called Franklin "a young man, democratic and able, who should have the support of forward looking citizens." On November 8, 1920, after the Democrats lost the election, Al wrote "My dear Franklin" an intimate letter, revealing, "I do not know what I would be able to accomplish here in the next two years standing alone by myself," a rather personal admission given Al's natural reticence.[5]

More and more, events brought the men into closer contact. In 1922, the "Al and Frank" exchange (the series of letters that persuaded Al to run for governor again) initiated Smith's return to power. Two years later, Smith forces again turned to Roosevelt, naming him chair of Citizens for Al Smith, FDR's first serious political work since the onset of polio had seemed to finish his career. At the convention, Franklin's famous "Happy Warrior" address stayed with many Democrats over the next four years, including Smith; the photograph files at the Roosevelt Library, for example, include a picture of Al standing in front of the Roosevelt mansion in 1925.[6]

By the time of the 1928 election, their relationship was among the most solid in politics. Smith had handpicked Roosevelt to succeed him as governor, as well as once again delivering the nominating speech at the national convention. Throughout the campaign, furthermore, Franklin seemed to be far more concerned about speaking up for Al Smith than promoting his own candidacy for governor, and even tackled the religious question. At first he did this with the usual Rooseveltian brio; when confronted with the claim that Smith's election would nullify all Protestant marriages and make their children illegitimate, Franklin simply threw back that wonderful profile and laughed. Even though he was a resident of the state in which Al Smith presided as governor, he told the audience, he still believed he was safely married, and concerning his "five pretty husky kids . . . I have every reason to believe that they are legitimate."[7]

But even FDR's goodwill could stand only so much. More and more, he found himself confronting the bigots, becoming increasingly brittle, till on October 17 at Binghamton, he lost control and in an impromptu speech thundered, "Persons responsible for literature against Governor Smith on religious grounds" should be literally banished. He railed about how "circulars are being distributed . . . that you persons would be ashamed to have in your homes," documents "so unfit for publication that the people who wrote them and printed them and paid for them ought not to be put in jail, but ought to be put on the first ship and sent away from the United States."[8]

An uproar ensued, and word came down from Democratic headquarters, "Tell the candidate that he is not running for President but for Governor; and tell him to stick to state issues." Even Moskowitz let it be known that religion should be "dropped" from the Roosevelt campaign, but Al must have felt warmed that someone—and someone close by—understood his feelings and his values, and was saying the things that he as a candidate cried over but could never utter.[9]

But beneath this pleasant story, Smith's feelings toward Roosevelt had developed into a much more complex mix of emotions. The governor early on recognized some of the political potential of this young man: the patrician Franklin, as few Democrats could, carried classically Republican upstate districts, and as the nephew of Theodore, was the holder of one of the most magical names in American politics. There was also affection. Smith liked the dapper, charming upstater, enjoyed his remarkable joie de vivre, reveled in training the young man, and in sharing cocktails with him. Eleanor maintained even closer ties with Smith, long after her involvement in his campaigns had passed, so that her connection would weather the storms that eventually sank the Smith-Roosevelt friendship. In the good years, she would invite Katie Smith to Hyde Park, including the older woman in her amazing circle of friends. After Franklin won the 1928 gubernatorial nomination, Emily Warner wrote Eleanor, "Your husband is a wonderful friend. . . . It is a foregone conclusion that you will live here, and I can't tell you how happy I am about it."[10]

Tempering this was Al's sense that Franklin was young, immature, and flighty. This was not surprising, given that Smith had worked his way up the ladder the hard way, with guts and brains, while Roosevelt had been born with a silver spoon and a silver name. Joseph Proskauer said that in 1920 "none of us took him seriously," and Robert Moses referred to Roosevelt, whom he detested, as "window dressing." Frank Freidel, the FDR biographer, observed, "Smith and his advisers underestimated Roosevelt, regarding him as . . . rather superficial." Colonel Edwin House, Woodrow Wilson's personal adviser, felt that "Smith looks on Roosevelt as sort of a Boy Scout . . . doesn't really think of him as an equal."[11]

In all fairness to Al and his crew, however, many people shared this perception. Even as a young man, Franklin had been considered a lightweight, the girls in his circle gossiping that "F.D." stood for "feather duster." Marvin Jones, a Texas farm Democrat who later served in the New Deal, said, "At first I thought Roosevelt was a bit breezy," while Felix Frankfurter felt that there was a "lack of an incisive intellect." Walter Lippmann called him an "amiable boy scout," and as late as 1932 wrote, "Franklin Roosevelt . . . is a pleasant man who without any important qualifications for the office would very much like to be President."[12]

There was also one other factor that exacerbated this belief terribly. Al Smith was a totally dedicated public servant, who gave his all in service to the state. He perceived the job as a consuming task, near impossible to accomplish, and horribly destructive of one's health. Despite Smith's robust physique, he was constantly ill, constantly exhausted.

Evidence of this dedication, and of the toll it took on the public servant, abounds in Smith's correspondence, studded with accounts of frequent minor illness brought on by exhaustion. In 1924 he wrote Eleanor, "I am going out next week to French Lick Springs to get a little rest. I am pretty well worn out"; at the same time he wrote Joe Tumulty, "I am going away for a week or two. . . . I need it very badly." He told a correspondent that "every minute of my time is consumed in Albany with the business that I have on my desk. It is getting larger in volume every week"; and by 1927, his secretary was forced to write Norman Mack—the political leader of Buffalo and Erie County, a dear friend, and one of Smith's top statewide campaign advisers—that the governor was "very tired after the arduous work of the Legislative Session . . . and felt the need of a short vacation. I can do no more than to place your letter on his desk awaiting his return."[13]

As a result, Smith conceived of his job as a killer, as one that only an individual possessed of remarkable strength and stamina could stand up to. Years later, Al told politico George Van Schaick "that he didn't see how Governor Lehman,[14] being as conscientious as he was, could ever live through the grueling work of the Executive Office. . . . He said, 'He is going to kill himself.'"[15]

What then, in an age far less enlightened as to the abilities of those with disabilities, did Al think of a man who wrote to Bob Moses in 1924, "I fear I cannot get to your office as it is so difficult to manage on crutches"? The story of the 1924 Democratic Convention is that of the triumphant return of Franklin to national politics, with the "Happy Warrior" speech. But did Al notice the effort it took, notice how difficult the task, and how ineffectual and cumbersome were the braces? After the convention, Franklin wrote to his doctor, "I have tried the new braces, and I fear they will not be successful. The trouble seems to be that I cannot make one foot move more than three and a half inches beyond the other and the progress is therefore so slow that it would take me ten minutes to walk across the room!" In 1925 he told Al, in a personal note from Warm Springs, how, with time and a lot more therapy, "I would be able to get around without crutches."[16]

The cumulative result of all these factors was that Smith took a paternal attitude toward the man from Hyde Park. He felt sincere and deep affection for Roosevelt, but considered him far less than an equal, at best a prized student in the art of politics that Smith had long ago mastered. Franklin, in other words, was perceived by Al as a child: loved and cared for, played with and sometimes indulged, but always subordinate. Louis Howe, with remarkable insight, stated simply, "Smith considered Franklin a little boy."[17]

Roosevelt, of course, was never as shallow or as weak as the Smith camp assumed. He was smart and ambitious, and while his feelings for Al were deep, real, and affectionate, his main goal was to advance his own political career. After 1924 FDR became a figure with national stature, and he quickly and successfully set out to build on this. He saw himself as being perfectly capable of independent action, in July 1924 writing a mutual friend about the kind of advice that he was going to give Smith about whether or not to run for governor again.[18]

This unique relationship came to light only once, albeit with excruciating clarity, in an angry exchange of letters between the two in 1927 and 1928. Franklin had been asked by Smith to head the Taconic Park Commission; this brought him into direct conflict with Robert Moses, parks commissioner, who hated FDR. Moses did everything in his power to make the job miserable, from cutting budgets to denying Louis Howe's salary. Eventually Roosevelt had taken all he could stand; on December 14, 1927, he finally wrote Smith, "I only took this job at your request and because it was you." He was proud of his own record and the commission's: "The work accomplished during the past year . . . has been carried on in an economical manner and the Commission has nothing to apologize for." But enough was enough: "I know all about the need of cutting appropriations. Try just for once making the cut on somebody else—I decline the honor." Finally, on January 30, 1928, he sent "Dear Al" a letter that began, "This is wholly personal and confidential; the enclosed is the official letter of the Commission." Having clarified his intentions, Roosevelt wrote, "When all is said and done, I wasn't born yesterday. You see I have been in the game so long that I now realize the mistake I made with this Taconic State Park Commission was in not playing the kind of politics that our friend Bob Moses has used." Roosevelt eventually added, "Just one other point. You and I have not got a 'meeting of the minds' on what the . . . Commission exists for."[19]

Smith responded on February 3, 1928, addressing his letter to "Dear Frank," then began with an intensely personal statement: "I know of no man I have met in my public career who I have any stronger affection for than for yourself. Therefore, you can find as much fault with me as you like. I will not get into a fight with you for anything or anybody." Notwithstanding this sentiment, the governor pressed on: "But that does not prevent me from giving you a little tip and the tip is don't be so sure about things that you have not the personal handling of yourself. I have lived, ate, and slept with this park question for three-and-one-half years. I know all about it and I know the attitude of the legislative leaders to the whole thing. I fought and battled with them in the regular session. . . . When I told you . . . that the legislative leaders would not stand for these appropriations, I was telling you what I knew to be a fact and you were guessing at it." He then proceeded to explain the situation, and his position, in some detail.[20]

The letters are remarkable for their passion; nothing else even remotely like them exists in the files. Roosevelt is asking to be treated with honesty and openness—in other words, like an adult. When he is not, he is justifiably angry.

But Smith will have none of this characterization. His letter is a lecture to a child, moving from affection to sternness. Franklin was clearly the object of deep and real tenderness, but at the same time, Al felt that the young man "had milk on his chin."[21] Franklin Roosevelt, the man he had brought out of obscurity and then nurtured, would be consoled and advised, helped along on the road to maturity, but put down with a reprimand when he got cocky about matters he did not understand.

Smith's perceptions of FDR had a powerful impact on the 1928 Democratic nomination for governor of New York State. For some time FDR had declared that he was not a candidate: on July 4, 1928, he wrote, "I, myself, am very certain that I cannot be a candidate for the governorship this year"; on July 26, "I fear it is absolutely impossible for me to undertake the run this year." At one point he wrote a friend to explain that he was "ducking both the national chairmanship and the nomination for governor this fall. It is far more interesting to be an elder statesman with flowing white locks and lots of sage advice to hand out." Smith also accepted Franklin's protestations, and a *New York Times* article on August 26, 1928, mentioned Herbert Lehman, James Foley, and Jesse Straus, but did not include Franklin Roosevelt as a possible nominee. As late as September 14, the *Times* headlined, "Smith Forces Seek New York City Man for Governor."[22]

By the time of the state convention in Syracuse, Roosevelt had retired to Warm Springs. On one occasion he had actually taken a few steps without the use of canes (albeit with braces); that was exhilarating, and he believed that another year or two down there might restore the use of his legs. In addition, he had just invested a good chunk of his fortune in the Georgia resort—over $200,000—and needed to stay, supervise, and ensure its success. Roosevelt was waiting, thinking more about the 1930 or 1932 nominations than the one that year.[23]

Party leaders, however, led by Smith, needed the upstate patrician with the famous moniker. Roosevelt refused to take their calls, so they turned to Eleanor, who was present at the gathering, and asked her to contact her husband and persuade him to run. She refused, saying that she would not, as Bronx boss Ed Flynn remembered, "interfere in his decision. She would not urge him either to run or not to run." Finally they got her to agree to at least place the phone call to her husband. He was out, making a speech, and did not return until after midnight. When she at last got him on the line, she recalled, Franklin "told me with evident glee that he had been keeping out of reach all day and would not have answered the phone if I had not been calling." There was "just time enough to tell him that I had called because Mr. Raskob and Governor Smith begged me to, and that I was leaving him to Governor Smith to catch the train [to New York City]. Then I ran. I can still hear Governor Smith's voice saying: 'Hello Frank.'"[24]

Smith picked up the phone and explained that Roosevelt was the only man who could carry the state; he would balance the ticket, playing a powerful upstate card against Smith's strong identification with New York City. John Raskob spoke next, and he agreed to help finance Warm Springs, promising $50,000 of his own money;[25] Al then promised that Herbert Lehman would be Roosevelt's running mate as lieutenant governor. Most accounts claim that at one point Smith played off their friendship, saying, "Frank, I told you I wasn't going to put this on a personal basis, but I've got to." When Al asked FDR what he would do if the convention nominated him the next day, Franklin, in typical fashion, equivocated but did not decline; Smith took that for a "yes" and proceeded accordingly.[26]

After the event everyone seemed happy. Eleanor telegraphed her husband, "Regret that you had to accept but know that you felt it obligatory; good luck, much love." Breckinridge Long commented on "the present tribute of confidence in you. . . . It makes New York State a cinch." Franklin himself was swell-headed, writing his Uncle Frederic Delano a few days later, "There is no question that at the time the convention was in a hopeless quandary—there was no one else to satisfy all parts of the State."[27]

Franklin should not have been so self-confident. While this account is totally accurate and depicts the public record as it exists in all historical works, it leaves out the details of some other, crucial meetings. In the Private Files of the Jim Farley Papers at the Library of Congress, there is a memo recounting an earlier series of conferences "when we met to take up the name of the man to be nominated to succeed Smith."[28]

In his notes on these sessions, Farley told how "all agreed that inasmuch as Smith was a Catholic that a non-Catholic be named." His choice was Franklin Roosevelt, and he presented it to the group.

Smith's reaction to this suggestion was focused and intense: he "threw it out on the theory that it was a mistake to attempt to nominate a man in his physical condition. He stressed the great amount of work attached to the Governorship and said Roosevelt could not be expected to do it." According to Farley, "It was apparent that Smith wanted Lehman."

Following this parlay there were two other meetings to discuss candidates. By the third one Smith was still supporting Lehman, while others pushed Wagner. Al seemed to be looking for a candidate, any candidate but the inevitable: when George Olvany, reigning head of Tammany Hall, "insisted that Wagner would not run . . . Smith replied that he would not take no for an answer until he had talked to him." "Considerable discussion of candidates" followed, with Smith holding out for Lehman. Finally, after "all recommendations were thrown out," Farley "made a motion that we communicate with Roosevelt and ascertain whether or not he would accept the nomination and the motion was unanimously carried." The final line of the memo reads simply, "Smith had to accept it." Years later, when Ruth Proskauer Smith asked her father why, if he hated FDR so much, they had nominated him for governor and put him on the path to the White House, he replied that it was a "purely political deal."[29]

Thus, as the 1928 campaign began, Smith was running with a man he cared about but did not respect; Eleanor Roosevelt wrote, "In many ways Governor Smith did not know my husband." Al still woefully underestimated Franklin's abilities and skills, regardless of any evidence to the contrary, despite his very real affection for the man.[30]

In the end, of course, it was the voters of New York State who let Al Smith know how wrong he was. During the campaign, Smith's people ignored Franklin, treating him, according to the president's memory a decade later, as "one of those pieces of window-dressing that had to be borne with because of a certain political value in non–New York City areas." But FDR was already showing himself to be a superb campaigner; while Al stuck to his strategy of few cities and big speeches, Franklin pulled into the small towns and villages of New York in his special car, snapped his braces into position, stood up in the back seat and talked about Al, farming, whatever FDR's research and instincts told him was important to the people of that area. In the end, there was usually that joyous, triumphant, rhetorical question, "Not Bad, For A Sick Man?"[31]

It was great theater—not quite Al's style, but winning nevertheless—and people took to it. When it was all over in 1928, the citizens of New York State had started Roosevelt on the way to greater triumphs, while leaving Smith hurt and humiliated. If Al had lost the state by over 103,000 votes, Franklin carried it by 25,000. This was a narrow margin, closer than in any of Al's gubernatorial victories, but that year it was in striking contrast to how the national ticket had done.[32]

In the lame-duck period, things seemed to go well. Roosevelt made every effort to consult Smith, writing him for advice and then meeting with the governor in Albany to go over the state of the state in a mammoth four-hour session. On the night before the inauguration, the new first family showed up to look around, and Al greeted them at the door, saying, "God bless and keep you, Frank. . . . A thousand welcomes. We've got the home fires burning." Some of the Roosevelt luggage had already arrived, and Smith christened it with champagne. "Now Frank," he explained, "if you want a drink, you will know where to find it." In his inauguration speech Franklin graciously observed, "This day is notable not so much for the inauguration of a new Governor as that it marks the close of the term of a Governor who has been our Chief Executive for eight years." His self-appointed mission was simply to carry on the same policies, the traditions of his predecessor. Al spoke extemporaneously as usual, congratulating Frank, telling the crowd, "I hope you will be able to devote that intelligent mind of yours to the problems of the state."[33]

⁂

But differences had already started to crop up. At first, it was just little things: Al had failed to dismantle his huge menagerie, leaving it to Eleanor and Franklin. The newcomers also found, when they moved in, that some of the Smiths' suitcases, clothing, and other items were still there; they seemed reluctant to move out.[34]

More pressing were the difficulties regarding inaugural arrangements. Franklin wanted an outdoor ceremony, notwithstanding that it was winter in Albany, snow covered the ground and made walking difficult, and there was the possibility of a blizzard. Ted Morgan, a Roosevelt biographer, felt that "it would be a display of his stamina and good health and would symbolize the qualities he hoped to bring to his administration—open for all to see, with the spaciousness of a progressive program."[35]

But Al Smith did not see it that way. Frederick Stuart Greene, the head of public works for the state, telegraphed Roosevelt that he and the governor had inspected the Assembly Chamber regarding the ceremony. Smith "strongly urges that it be held indoors," because of both the cold and Franklin's infirmity: "You can enter chamber from Speaker's room having only one low step," Greene informed FDR.[36]

The next day, the governor-to-be wrote back, "I am a very obstinate cuss." He assumed that in all likelihood the event would have to be indoors, but he hoped for better weather, "and if that is the case, I do want the ceremonies held on the steps." Cheerily, he added, "Faint heart ne'er won fair lady!"[37]

The inauguration was, in fact, held outside, but the incident revealed what would become a familiar pattern: Smith feeling Roosevelt was not up to the job, and Roosevelt determined to be his own man.

Tensions blossomed after Roosevelt took office. Lonely and desperate for something to do in public life, Al Smith wanted to still be governor, still enjoy what had been the golden era of his career, and continued to treat Franklin as a pupil to be guided and managed.

Franklin tried to be attentive and positive. On February 8, 1929, he wrote Al, "There are many things I would like to talk to you about," and to let him know when he was in town. A year later he asked for Al's advice on both legislation and some appointments regarding the Port Authority, then queried, "Which do you think is best?" regarding nominees for the Water Power Commission. As late as 1931 Roosevelt was still writing that the first version of the new budget was about to be announced, and asking Smith if he wanted to "talk with me about it."[38]

This was not just politeness; it also reflected the legitimate fondness the two men felt toward each other, something that would never entirely disappear. In September 1929 Al sent Eleanor a chatty letter about how he was at the seashore with Emily and her baby, and how, "I hope Frank is enjoying Warm Springs." By 1930 the two men were still sufficiently comfortable to engage in what otherwise might have been a dangerous jest. Franklin wrote Al a thank-you card for a birthday message, but added the friendly jibe: "By the way did I tell you that it is high time for you to return to Albany? A few weeks ago, when my granddaughter was here, your granddaughter came to the house to spend the afternoon and five minutes after I had joined the party [she] was calling me 'Ganpa.'" Roosevelt added that, "I feel highly honored and have certainly cut you out." Al replied, playful and unfazed, from a vacation hotel in Palm Beach, "I will be up to Albany when I return. . . . I will be glad to see you and will take that little girl away."[39]

But Smith was having difficulty adjusting to Frank's new status and power. In a December 30, 1928, letter to a third party, Al wrote, "When the governor-elect arrives I am going to have a talk with him." He then presented a detailed discussion of the state's finances, beginning, "If any readjustment of the estimated income of the state for the next fiscal year can be arrived at, it is possible to get something started, but the present set-up is devoted almost entirely to projects that are half completed," and continued on for several pages. A year later he would still be writing the governor, "Before you make any appointment for the vacancy in the New York State Bridge and Tunnel Commission, I would like to talk to you."[40]

Then there were the terrible decisions to fire Al's trusted lieutenants. Robert Moses and Franklin were bitter enemies, and only Al's Pollyanna-like view of his immediate world allowed him to overlook the obvious conflict. When Roosevelt inevitably dismissed Moses, it was Al, and only Al, who was surprised and, even worse, took it as a personal affront.

Even worse was the situation with Belle Moskowitz. She loved Smith with all her heart, was devoted to him, and could not conceive of anyone else in the governor's chair. Moskowitz told Frances Perkins that "Franklin Roosevelt can never run that show. Somebody's got to help him," and she "needled" Smith about his successor. Just before Christmas 1928, Al stopped by Roosevelt's office and said that Moskowitz was writing a draft for both his inaugural address and the message to the legislature. In notes dictated a decade later, Franklin recalled, "Honestly I think he did this in complete good faith. . . . But at the same time with the rather definite thought that he himself would continue to run the Governorship. His first bad shock came when I told him that I had already prepared my . . . Address and that my Message . . . was nearly finished." By this time Eleanor was warning her husband, "Don't let Mrs. Moskowitz get draped around you for she means to be and it will always be one for you and two for Al!"[41]

And Smith was getting worse. He had discovered a new position for himself: the power behind the throne. He told Franklin not to worry, to spend most of his time down in Warm Springs recovering, while Al and Lieutenant Governor Herbert Lehman ran things; in fact, FDR need not even return to Albany until the end of the legislative session. Frances Perkins remembered Smith's telling her how helpful he wanted to be to the new governor: "I'd come up every week if he wanted me to. I'd come up and spend days. . . . I could see people for him. . . . I would deal with them. . . . I could help with a lot of things. . . . I could keep track of things and be around all the time." Eleanor Roosevelt commented of this period, "It became evident that he thought he was going to retain a behind-the-scenes leadership in the state." "It would not work," she concluded, "and he soon discovered that it would not work."[42]

Franklin had to set things straight, had to declare his independence and establish his own political career, even if it meant hurting Al's feelings. Herbert Lehman said, "I think he was sensitive to any implication that he was not in fact the governor of the state. I think it was on that account, more than any other, that he decided to put in people of his own choosing, who he felt would be exclusively loyal to him." Lehman added, "I certainly do not think he did it with the idea of hurting Smith. He remained very fond of Smith, even though he had sometimes great reason for a different attitude. But he made his mind up he was going to be governor, and he *was* the governor." Significantly, Perkins observed at this time that FDR "didn't like being father's oldest son"; he told her, "I've got to be Governor of the State of New York and I have got to be it MYSELF. . . . I'm awfully sorry if it hurts anybody, particularly Al."[43]

So now, Roosevelt had to do more than just remove Smith's aides, he had to break with Al himself, refusing to invite the old governor to Albany for advice, knowing that Smith would misinterpret such queries and become way too involved. At the same time FDR knew that he was replacing Al on the national scene, noticed when *The Nation* exclaimed that the Democratic Party had a new leader, and that he came from Hyde Park, New York. He had to make sure no one shoved that spotlight aside, even if it meant wounding Smith.[44]

For all these reasons, Al came to resent, to break with Franklin Roosevelt "a lot sooner than people think," according to the governor's great-grandson, Alfred E. Smith IV. He began not only to notice, but to complain bitterly about how his successor had frozen him out; friends reported outbursts of Smith's grumbling, "Do you know, by God, that he has never consulted me about a damn thing since he has been Governor? . . . He has ignored me." Later on, when a reporter asked why he split with the man who would become president, Al replied, "Frank Roosevelt just threw me out the window."[45]

The 1930 gubernatorial campaign revealed both the strengths and strains of this tortured relationship. Roosevelt began with an affable yet shrewd gesture, given Smith's continued, if not increased, popularity with the people of New York. Al had moved recently, and his new ward leader had inadvertently passed him over when it came time to issue delegates' credentials to the state's nominating convention. Several delegations offered to let him attend as a proxy member, but Louis Howe heard about the situation, and cabled FDR that they should arrange for a vacancy in the Hyde Park contingent that could then be turned over to Smith, making him a full-fledged delegate. Al turned this down (eventually he attended the convention illegally, without credentials, but who was going to challenge him?), but it was a nice move at the start of FDR's bid for reelection.[46]

Smith reciprocated with equal goodwill, agreeing to deliver the speech that would place Roosevelt's name before the floor. The *New York Times* took this as a good sign, noting that while many had tried to "sow misunderstanding and dissension between the two men," statesmanship and the reality that both "have a generous and candid temper" had brought them to the same cause, as it had so many times in the past.[47]

Al's speech in Syracuse, however, revealed a lot more about himself, his emotions, and beliefs in 1930 than it did about the candidate he was ostensibly supporting. The opening line, for example, read, "I appear this morning in an entirely new role for me; for the last twelve years I have been so busy getting nominated myself." After that, he spoke long enough to fill five and three-quarters columns in the next day's *Times,* but only in the last half-column's material did he mention the man he had ostensibly come there to honor.[48]

Not that the rest extolled Al Smith; quite the contrary. Instead, it dealt with all the old wounds, consisting mostly of attacks on Republicans, on prohibitionists, on all those who had lied to the American people, all those who had hurt him so badly. Two years had gone by, and he had let go of so little.

In all fairness, when he did get to Franklin, the words were moving and sincere: the event had brought out the old feelings, the warmth he had always felt toward FDR. Smith asked the crowd to consider how "there is something about Frank . . . that draws people to him," and answering his own question, replied, "First he has a clear brain, and second, he has a big heart."

But even here there were echoes of the old hesitations, the prejudices and the suspicions. Even though he spoke glowingly of Roosevelt's accomplishments, Smith nevertheless let slip the fears that should have been left unsaid. "All through his administration," Al asserted, "you can find . . . that milk of human kindness that comes from a big heart, a heart that thinks for the cripple, for the sick, for the poor, for the weak and for the afflicted." The list was generous, the order was not.

Smith now performed an extensive speaking tour on FDR's behalf. At every place he went, the governor packed them in, pulling a crowd of fifty-five hundred in Buffalo, for example, double what FDR had managed just a short time before. Throughout it all, the note never changed. The speeches were about Al's pain, his resentments, not about the candidates. In Troy he shot bolts at the hypocrisy of prohibition, the old issue he had blundered into and then cost him so badly. When the DNC sent the headliner to campaign in Boston, the rawness of his wounds rose to the surface when he angrily, if wishfully, thundered that "the American people . . . will not again be fooled by false propaganda, by misleading statements and by the promotion of what are really not issues and should have no place in American political campaigns."[49]

Al's efforts helped, but so did the year-old Depression and, above all, the solid record Franklin had built in his first term as governor. It was no great trick to predict that FDR would win in 1930, but no one gauged how dramatic a victory it would become.

When the speeches ended and the registrars tallied the votes, the results were astounding. Roosevelt took the state with a margin of 725,001 votes; by way of comparison, the previous record had been set by Smith in his 1922 romp, with 386,000. Upstate, Roosevelt accomplished what no Democrat had been able to do for a century, defeating the Republican candidate; in forty-one of fifty-seven of the counties north of the Bronx, Roosevelt triumphed, picking up a lead of 167,000 votes, something Al could never have dreamed of. Even down in New York City, Roosevelt's margin came in at 552,000, or 40,000 more than Smith had ever been able to manage in his hometown.[50]

Al went up to Albany for the inauguration, journeying to the governor's mansion to congratulate the winner, but chose not to stay for the afternoon and evening receptions. Belle Moskowitz did not go at all, feeling, according to Frances Perkins, "very hurt" by the whole situation. In all likelihood, she was not alone in these emotions by then.[51]

Chapter 22

Mr. Smith Does Not Go to Washington

By 1932, Al Smith had still not gotten used to the idea of Franklin Roosevelt as headliner, and soon a much bigger issue exacerbated these feelings. Despite initial protests to the contrary, Smith decided to pursue the 1932 Democratic nomination for president—largely as a way to still his personal demons—only to be thwarted by a man he still believed was inferior to him.

⤞

Although Smith had announced right after the election he would never run for office again, it was an immediate and hasty remark. By December 1928 he was telling reporters, "I will never be out of politics as long as I live," and soon after reminded Norman Mack, "Like myself . . . you will never be able to stay away" from the grandest game of all.[1]

Now, the most important victory was in sight. A lot had happened since Al lost the 1928 election, all of it bad for the Republicans. The stock market crash had been succeeded by what was turning out to be the worst economic catastrophe in the nation's history; bankruptcies mounted, financial institutions shut their doors, most of the nation's housing was in foreclosure. Unemployment rose to stratospheric levels, the dull numbers hiding a human despair that no one seemed able to fix. For the first time, not just workers and farmers, but middle-class urbanites began to actually feel the very real pain that hunger caused. More than just a few people died from lack of the human basics, from starvation and exposure, and all Herbert Hoover could promise was, "Prosperity is just around the corner."

Some of this must have been bitter irony for Smith. During the 1928 elections, Republicans had branded him an enemy of business prosperity and warned of calamities if he was elected. Now a joke appeared about an alien applying for citizenship: as part of the exam the judge repeatedly asked the name of the president of the United States, and each time the applicant replied, "Al Smith." Finally, His Honor asked the man why he kept repeating this, and the fellow replied, "Well, in the campaign the Republicans kept on saying that if Al was elected we'd have a stock market crash, unemployment, bread lines. . . . We've had them all, so I know Al must be president." According to the *New York Times,* their source was Smith himself, joyously repeating that story to everyone he knew.[2]

So by 1932, Al Smith knew, both intuitively and from a lot of different sources, it would be a good year to be a Democratic presidential candidate. Harold Ickes, at that time a GOP stalwart, wrote Belle Moskowitz that "not one Republican voter in ten wants President Hoover renominated and hardly anyone believes he can be reelected." A Missouri lawyer told Raskob that the nation's slogan should be "HOOVER, HELL, AND HARD TIMES."[3]

But as the horses began to line up for the race, the frontrunner was obviously Franklin Roosevelt, especially after his resounding victory in the 1930 gubernatorial contest. Even way back in November 1928, the *Nation* referred to FDR as the leader among "the heirs and assigns of the party machinery"; as Louis Howe, FDR's mentor, told Democratic publicity head Charlie Michaelson, Al "has lost the state and Franklin has carried it, and the country is not going to forget that when 1932 comes around."[4]

Roosevelt had also reached that status because of shrewd planning and hard work. All through the twenties, he had maintained an amazing correspondence with party leaders at every level above that of the precincts. After both the 1924 and 1928 defeats, he had conducted a unique political poll, writing every Democratic official down to the county commissioners, asking what each of them thought should be done to change their party's track record. The three thousand letters he sent out produced several hundred replies, and these provided unparalleled political intelligence; at the same time, they also made the name Franklin Roosevelt a presence in every district in the United States.[5]

Out of this data, and by sheer observation and analysis, Roosevelt and his crew developed a strategy that would win where Smith lost. FDR figured he could count on the votes of the northern cities, the people Al had brought into the Democratic Party. He would add to this the South that Smith could not carry, and the West as well; his Warm Springs resort gave him bragging rights to a Georgia residency and as a man who knew the soil, roles he played to the hilt. When Hollins Randolph of Atlanta visited Franklin down there—one of a parade of guests—the two men talked for hours about farm relief, covering so many ideas that Randolph's follow-up letter went on for three single-spaced, typed pages.[6]

Unspoken, of course, was one other asset, that the patrician, WASP Roosevelt would encounter none of the prejudices Al Smith had faced. James Farley, a Roosevelt manager, found on one of his scouting trips that friends of Al now said, "For God's sake, don't let us have another religious war as we had in 1928." Senator Burton K. Wheeler of Montana similarly remembered he had been for Smith in 1928 and "did everything I could for him," but bigotry "was raised so badly at that time that I didn't want to see it raised again, and I thought the best way to do this was to be for Roosevelt."[7]

And unlike Smith, Roosevelt deliberately sidestepped prohibition. John Raskob, who stayed on as head of the Democratic Party, had become obsessed with the Eighteenth Amendment, and believed that winning its repeal was the key to victory in 1932. He used all his influence and considerable power to get this to become the dominant issue that year, arguing to FDR, "There is one thing I shall insist and demand, with all the force of the office of Chairman, and that is that the Democratic platform treat honestly, fairly and squarely with the prohibition question." This was madness; whatever the merits of restoring the saloon may have been, adopting it as a strategy in 1932 was both criminal and stupid. As the *Christian Century* pointed out, unemployed Americans were demanding bread; Raskob offered them beer.[8]

Franklin Roosevelt recognized this, and he fought the concept, choosing to focus instead on economics and hunger. It was honorable and obvious, but also smart. Southern dry leaders now quietly accepted FDR, knowing that he would not push repeal as his foremost campaign issue, in contrast to Raskob's good friend Al Smith.[9]

Smith started to respond to Roosevelt's prominence, and by March 1931, replied to a reporter's query, "Then you are not out of politics?" with a smiling, "Well, not altogether." The Governor might have known of the letters Raskob was starting to receive, like the one from the vicar general of the Cleveland archdiocese, how Clarence Darrow had come by and was "begging me to do everything to have Al run again." Bruce Barton, one of America's founding public relations practitioners, also corresponded; referring to FDR, he argued, "I do hope the Democratic Party is not going to come before the American people with its weakest candidate," and offered his support for a Smith nomination instead. Sylvester Andriano of San Francisco simply wrote of Al, "My love and enthusiasm for him has never abated and consequently I refused to tie up with any other candidate until I ascertained his attitude."[10]

So on February 8, 1932, Smith took the plunge—sort of. His official statement began with the line, "I feel I owe it to my friends and to the millions of men and women who supported me so loyally in 1928 to make my position clear," but what followed was anything but. Instead, the key section read, "If the Democratic National Convention after careful consideration should decide that it wants me to lead, I will make the fight; but I will not make a pre-convention campaign to secure the support of the delegates." This was an artwork of ambivalence, with an "if," a "should," and a "will not." Only one thing came through clear: Smith declared, "I am the leader of my party in the nation. With a full sense of the responsibility . . . imposed, I shall not . . . either support or oppose the candidacy of any aspirant for the nomination."[11]

But why did Al take this jump, hesitant as it was, exposing himself once again to cold political fortune? Part of it was clearly lack of respect for Franklin Roosevelt; Al still believed that FDR was a lightweight, hardly the figure to take over in this time of crisis. Belle Moskowitz told Felix Frankfurter, "Many of us feel that the party needs a well-equipped candidate, able to lead, courageous and willing to take responsibility. We do not think the record of the candidate who . . . was leading the field as we knew him intimately gave that kind of promise." Joseph Proskauer went even further, referring to Roosevelt as "a mucker and a liar," the strongest language he would ever use at home.[12]

But Proskauer protested any role in Smith's statement, claiming, "Smith's decision to go into the fight in 1932 was motivated entirely by him," and the judge was right. The truth was, Al Smith, above all, entered the race in 1932 because he thought he could win, thus ending the pain and restoring his faith in America. Later, after the campaign ended in November, Herbert Bayard Swope wrote his dear friend about what the country had lost: "Your election would have marked the greatest flowering of democracy that the world had ever seen. Up from Fulton Street and over the hurdles of religious bigotry! Why History would have rung with the achievement." This was what Al Smith really wanted—the chance to redeem himself, to finally overcome the hate-mongers of 1928 who had hurt him so deeply.[13]

Al's motivation, however human, still posed a terrible threat to Franklin's chances. If Smith took the urban centers, then FDR's whole strategy might fall apart, and Roosevelt knew just how good his old mentor really was, lamenting, "Al Smith knows these city people better. He can move them. I can't." Under these circumstances, the nomination would blow wide open, or as the *New York Times* argued, "what promised . . . to be a rather tame contest . . . will hereafter be bristling with excitement. When one of the contestants is named 'Al' Smith, none of the others can afford for an instant to be off their guard."[14]

Roosevelt came out of the chutes solid at first, taking the delegates at early party conferences held in North Dakota, Washington, and Wisconsin. On March 8 he triumphed in the New Hampshire primary, beating Smith 14,500 to 9,000 and carrying eight of the state's eleven cities, supposedly Smith's most fertile hunting grounds.[15]

But then things soured for the Roosevelt forces. On April 26, Massachusetts voted; FDR should have known that this was practically Smith's adopted state and refused to enter the lists there. Back in 1931, however, he had encountered James Michael Curley, the cantankerous and charismatic mayor of Boston, who pledged his support to FDR and convinced him to try for the Bay State's delegates.

The Boston politico had his own reasons for this, but for FDR it was a very bad move. The contest quickly turned into a Curley-Smith choice, with the mayor's primary contribution being one of the best wisecracks about how the Republicans had mishandled the Depression: "If we have another era of Hoover," Curley quipped, "Gandhi would be the best-dressed man in America." Beyond that he had little to offer, and the state came in overwhelmingly for Al. The low man on Smith's Walsh-Ely slate received more than 134,000 votes, while Curley, who ran the best of any of the Roosevelt-pledged delegates, drew only 56,500. Roosevelt lost every one of the thirty-six districts that sent a member apiece to the national convention, and it looked like even Mayor Curley would not be able to attend, although anyone who totally counted him out was a fool. In Curley's home ward, workers handing out Roosevelt slips watched as voters tore them into scraps and stamped on the pieces, enraged at this treachery against the champion of Catholics and immigrants.[16]

After that came other setbacks. Pennsylvania voted the same day as Massachusetts did and produced a clouded result, with few delegates pledged to either of the candidates, instead of the clear victory Roosevelt sought. Rhode Island and Connecticut entered the Smith column shortly after that. Even more frightening, California—covered by a unit rule that dictated all forty-four delegates going to the winner—chose Texas's John Nance Garner, opening the possibility of a totally fragmented Democratic convention. In San Francisco, Smith supporters told voters, "If you are Wet, vote for Smith—if you are Dry, vote for Garner—if you don't know what you are, vote for Roosevelt."[17]

This spate of losses, however, only disguised the fact that Roosevelt soon began piling up delegates in the caucuses and by courting the party's hierarchy. He developed a commanding lead as states like Colorado, Iowa, Kansas, Minnesota, and Michigan, then Maine and Vermont and Oregon joined up, along with the solid South. The limited successes of the Smith camp were exactly that; as Jack Beatty, Curley's biographer, wrote, "Al Smith was yesterday's candidate, his victory in Massachusetts a last hurrah."[18]

Smith ignored this reality, fooling himself, gazing instead at the letter signed by the mayors of Hartford, New Haven, Waterbury, and three other Connecticut cities that began, "We recognize you as the leader of the Democratic party," and spoke of his "fearless . . . leadership." Phillip Meighen of Minneapolis wrote that when Al spoke in the Twin Cities, no one could "get within half a mile of the auditorium," but when Roosevelt appeared, Meighen and his wife arrived late and still got a seat at the head table. Al and Moskowitz and Proskauer knew that in Massachusetts they had spent only $3,000 against Roosevelt's $150,000, and won every delegate there was to be had. Most pressing of all, they could all see that because of the Depression, 1932 would be a Democratic year just about regardless of who the candidate was. It *must* be Smith's year.[19]

And that meant toppling Frank Roosevelt. Josef Israels wrote a correspondent in Texas that Smith "is out to stop Roosevelt and he is sincere about it. He knows it is going to be a very very long shot at the nomination for himself, but is willing to go a long way to stop the other man."[20]

Soon this would mean arguing against FDR's words and ideas. On April 7, 1932, Franklin Roosevelt delivered a ten-minute speech over national radio, during the *Lucky Strike Hour*. He described the Depression in strong language, as a greater emergency than World War I had been. Roosevelt spoke not to the generals, but to "the infantry of our economic army," attacking Hoover's Reconstruction Finance Authority for granting loans to big business, insisting it should have dealt instead with the wave of foreclosures among homeowners. (Ray Moley, FDR's brain trust adviser, said that Hoover's policy was like trying to fertilize soil by putting manure in the trees.) Above all, in what became the tag line of the speech, FDR spoke on behalf of "the forgotten man at the bottom of the economic pyramid."[21]

Smith was furious, but not because he disagreed with Roosevelt on how to handle the crisis. Like Franklin, Al recognized that the enormity of the situation required massive government intervention, and merely stressed that this should be financed by a huge federal bond issue, rather than by deficit spending; always he remained the administrative reformer.

His anger was, instead, personal, so as a result the answer came out angry and emotional, and with no other place to turn, quite conservative in its emphasis. Speaking at the Jefferson Day Dinner, Smith looked like a man possessed, his voice hoarse and face red as he proclaimed, "This is no time for demagogues." In times of widespread poverty there would always be efforts to start class warfare, to "stir up the . . . rich against the poor and . . . the poor against the rich." Against such efforts, Smith stood "uncompromisingly," ready to "take off my coat and fight to the end any candidate who persists in . . . appeals to the masses of working people of this country to destroy themselves." A *New Republic* columnist observed, Smith's "hostility goes beyond reason and debate; it is one of those . . . poisons which so often burrow in the flesh of a man accustomed to action and power, who happens for the time being to be confined to inaction, to be a spectator to the deeds of another."[22]

Wounds and grievances rarely make for good politics, however. To pundits, the Happy Warrior had been corrupted by his big business friendships; one columnist mocked his fears that Roosevelt's pleas "would disturb the perfect equanimity of our political life and throw the apple of discord into what is now a harmonious family scene," and wound up denouncing Smith's "political knavery." Smith's speech also alienated the millions of farmers in desperate circumstances in the West and the South, regions he needed to win at the convention. Now more than ever, Democrats in those states had to turn to FDR as the only candidate who addressed their problems.[23]

As the convention approached, Roosevelt was strong, but hardly a sure thing. Various estimates gave him between 485 and 600 delegates, with 770 needed to clinch the top spot. Smith came in a distant second, with only 94 votes. Nevertheless, there remained the nagging fear—not just from Smith—that the glib young man was somehow not up to a job of this magnitude. H. L. Mencken perceived what he called the "burden" of Franklin's "own limitations. He is one of the most charming of men, but like many another charming man he leaves . . . the impression that he is also somewhat shallow and futile." Walter Lippmann claimed that "among the national Democrats . . . the belief is widespread and strong that the election of Franklin D. Roosevelt would bring to the office of the President a man of only moderate capacity," that he "just doesn't . . . have a very good mind. . . . He has never thought much, or understood much, about the great subjects which must concern the next president."[24]

Al Smith, meanwhile, remained a potent force. He could say anything, do anything, and the urban masses would stick with him, love him to the end. He could block FDR from acquiring the two-thirds vote needed to get the nomination, resulting in another dark horse candidate, and Smith was willing to be a spoiler that year.

It may not have been not Al's first choice, but he was prepared to take that role now. George Van Schaick, a party wheelhorse, noted the growing gap between the reality of Smith's complaints and the depths of his emotions. "Every grievance that he had," Van Schaick recalled, "it seemed to be so petty. . . . Al Smith was groping for little things to build up his sense of grievances. . . . They didn't amount to *anything* much . . . but they all lead up to this thing. He almost lost control of himself as he related his grievances." Later, after the Democratic convention, Clark Howell of the *Atlanta Constitution* experienced the same thing when he approached Smith to ask him to support FDR's bid for the presidency.

Howell told Smith that the nation expected him to back the ticket, that he could not say no to such a request. Smith blurted out, "The hell I can't," and when the newspaperman asked, "Is there any ground for personal hostility on your part against Roosevelt?" Smith said at first that they were friends, that Franklin had "always been kind to me and my family." Then, however, the pot boiled over; Al yelled, "Do you know by God, that he has never consulted me about a damn thing since he has been Governor? He has taken bad advice and from sources not friendly to me. He has ignored me." At various times during the tirade that followed, Smith stamped his foot and banged his fist on the table.[25]

As Al traveled to the convention, he stood and shaved with a straight razor, singing the *Pater Noster,* while the train rocked back and forth; it was not the only risk he would take. Thousands of people greeted Smith at the station when he arrived in Chicago, but when he got to his hotel, he displayed, for the first time, some of that new-found brittleness, his inability to accept or suffer the campaign demands that had once been so comfortable to him. When reporters asked for pictures, for example, he now bristled; a Chippewa chief presented him with a freshly caught bass, a typical publicity stunt, but Smith refused to take part, telling photographers, "I've been posing for nine hours. . . . Take one of the other pictures and paint a fish on it." Other bitternesses remained as well: when a reporter asked Smith if he had talked at all with Governor Franklin Roosevelt, still back home, Al snarled, "No, I know that number well. It didn't call me."[26]

Smith's people figured their man had a fighting chance. On June 10 the powerful Scripps-Howard papers delivered a ringing endorsement. He already had four states—Connecticut, Massachusetts, New Jersey, and Rhode Island—and a plan for victory. Belle Moskowitz (who was still telling reporters, "I'm just sort of a secretary to the governor") estimated that Roosevelt had at most six hundred votes, and that many would break to Smith once things deadlocked. James Farley, FDR's campaign manager, had been making "too many claims," or so wrote Moskowitz's husband Henry to another Smith stalwart, and in the end they would prevail: Roosevelt "may have the arithmetic but he has not the psychology." The tide would turn.[27]

The convention began on June 27, 1932, another great American political spectacle. The keynote speech by Alben Barkley of Kentucky took a full two hours to deliver, prompting one wag to comment, how, "As a history of the United States in modern times it left little untold." Somehow, the Boston boss James Michael Curley had now made it to the floor of the convention, improbably as the chairman of the Puerto Rican delegation. The show would go on.[28]

Smith had the spotlight only twice. The first time came when the Resolutions Committee collapsed in conflict over what kind of prohibition plank they should report to the full convention. Roosevelt's people advocated a new constitutional amendment that would give each state the right to decide individually on alcohol, but generally wished to avoid the issue. Smith's forces—and many others who had reached the end of their patience with the "noble experiment"—pushed for a full platform of repeal. His supporters won the argument, and their statement got sent to the floor.[29]

Smith smelled blood now, and asked to speak on behalf of this plank. He delivered a short talk, attacking not just the prohibitionists in the party but all those who would not stand squarely against the Anti-Saloon League, all the bigots who had struck at him four years prior. It was notable only because it sparked one of the largest demonstrations of the entire event—twenty thousand people standing and cheering for him over and over. It was a small conquest, but it made Al feel good.

The victory, however, was even less than Smith realized. Roosevelt, understanding the effort to box him in, easily countered by reversing tack and endorsing the repeal statement. When it passed by a huge margin, he had escaped the trap and, if anything, forced Smith to appear as the unbending partisan who refused to take anyone else's views into account. This would set the pattern for future conflicts: Smith, blinded by his bitterness, taking rigid and unpolitic positions; Roosevelt always managing the smart gesture.

The second opportunity to cheer Alfred E. Smith came during the nominations. Norman Mack delivered a dull speech on Roosevelt's behalf, no great piece of rousing oratory. When Governor Joseph Ely of Massachusetts placed Al's name in the ring with a neat stemwinder, however, the pandemonium continued for a full hour.

When the applause stopped, it was time to vote. Everyone figured Roosevelt would do fine on the first ballot, coming in first but well short of the two-thirds he needed, and then the deal making would begin.

So it went. After every state and territory had counted in, the tally read: Roosevelt, 666¼; Smith, 201¾, with the rest going to a variety of native sons, the most important of them John Nance Garner of Texas, with 90¼. Roosevelt had done a little better than expected, Smith a lot better.[30]

Over the next two ballots, nothing broke; the lines stayed pretty much the same, Roosevelt gaining a few votes (682.79 on the third ballot), Smith losing a few (190¼ at the same point). Garner also gained, up to 101¼. By now, however, dawn's sunshine was filtering into the arena, and everyone decided to get some sleep before the next round.

In the back rooms, however, in the candidates' suites, everyone began scrambling to make deals, with the biggest prize Garner and his bloc of votes. Jim Farley,

Roosevelt's floor manager, made the first move, contacting Sam Rayburn, a member of Garner's inner circle. Farley talked Rayburn into supporting Roosevelt, the best plan, he claimed, to finally get a Democrat in the White House, and Sam agreed to call up Garner.[31]

But Rayburn could not get through to him. Neither could Judge Proskauer, the man delegated by Smith to approach the Texan. Neither could Belle Moskowitz, who got an angry hotel manager to yell at her, "You may tell Governor Smith from me . . . that Speaker Garner is here. The reason you can't get him is that he refuses to answer the phone." Garner would not talk to anyone—with one exception.[32]

At this point, Al's long career in American politics came round to bite him, a danger all senior figures run, and that relative newcomers—like Franklin Roosevelt, for example—have yet to worry about. John Nance Garner had another longtime and very serious supporter besides Rayburn; his name was William Randolph Hearst. Hearst could reach Garner, and the publisher had, at that moment, a lot of good reasons to do so.

As Hearst followed events from his San Simeon castle, the results in Chicago all looked bad, and were getting worse. He did not want Al Smith to win, of course. But his advisers—including Joe Kennedy, a strong Roosevelt supporter—pointed out that if FDR lost and the whole convention went to hell, the most likely winner would instead be Newton D. Baker. Among other attributes, Baker had been Woodrow Wilson's secretary of war, and was the leading living advocate of that president's internationalism. Hearst, on the other hand, was the country's foremost isolationist, a man who hated internationalists more than anything or anyone. Add to that Kennedy's and then Farley's entreaties that Roosevelt was really a decent candidate, and Hearst agreed to pick up the phone. He called Garner and added his powerful voice to the others urging a Roosevelt nomination.

Hearst had influence, but men still make their own decisions, especially men like John Nance Garner, outspoken and independent, also Speaker of the House of Representatives and thus one of the most powerful men in the United States. And Garner understood what he had to do in this situation.

So when Farley finally got in touch with him, offering the second spot on the ticket, Garner accepted. Not that he wanted the job; he later observed that the vice presidency was worth less than "a bucket of warm piss." But on that day, he wanted his party to win and knew that a broken convention would not help the Democrats do that. So accept he did, and agreed to release his delegates to Roosevelt.

That night the lines broke early. When California's turn came, William Gibbs McAdoo took the rostrum and with a sense of vengeful triumph announced that his state "did not come here to deadlock this convention, or engage in another desolating contest like that of 1924," and endorsed FDR. Al Smith was not the only one who had arrived with baggage, and as H. L. Mencken wickedly put it, "If revenge is really sweet," McAdoo "was sucking a colossal sugar teat."[33]

It was over. Roosevelt swept to 945 votes on the fourth ballot, way over the 770 he needed even under the two-thirds rule, and Smith supporters in the galleries started a brief but violent little riot, with some bloody noses. James Gerard, DNC treasurer, asked Mrs. Charles Dana Gibson to go up to Smith and suggest he do the generous thing: go down to the floor and request that the convention make the nomination unanimous. Mrs. Gibson made the appeal, but she said Al just sat there, his arms folded in front of him. All he could say, over and over again, was, "I won't do it. I won't do it. I won't do it."[34]

Instead, Al Smith walked out, missing the chance to see Franklin Roosevelt break precedent by appearing in person before the convention, to hear FDR's pledge to give the American people a New Deal. Roosevelt was so concerned by Smith's act, he delegated one of his entourage—Dorothy Rosenman, wife of speechwriter Sam Rosenman—to get in touch promptly with some friend of Al who would calm him down, intercept him before he got back to New York and the press. Dorothy contacted Judge Bernard Sheintag, who went way back with Smith, and the intervention succeeded; when the train arrived, Al just mumbled, "I have absolutely nothing to say to newspaper men. . . . I am tired and I want to get a rest."[35]

In time Smith came around, though not well and not gracefully. He waited five days before even endorsing the party, and then fell silent all through July, August, and September. FDR, on the other hand—ever buoyant—wrote a friend on September 13 how he felt confident that "at his own time and in his own way, Governor Smith will openly support the ticket."[36]

He should not have been so confident; Al's emotions were torn. The governor felt a mixture of jealousy, anger, pride, and affection toward the younger man who had won the nomination instead of him. But on October 4, at the New York State Democratic Convention, the positive emotions, the very real fondness he felt, got the better of Smith.

Al was supposed to nominate his old friend Herbert Lehman for the gubernatorial slot, and as he walked across the platform, shook hands with each dignitary he came to. When he reached Franklin Roosevelt, Smith stopped. Both men, each on their own, stretched out his right hand, Frank seated, Al standing, and shook the other's vigorously and warmly. The band blared as they did this, so only those close around them heard the words they spoke, but James Farley later reported what happened. Roosevelt simply and movingly said, "Al, this is from the heart," and Smith replied, "Frank, that goes with me," and grinned. The press photo showed that smile, and it stretched from ear to ear, sincere, a moment of real friendship that would not last. Later, they worked out a deal for Al to campaign in the places where his popularity would count: Massachusetts, Connecticut, Rhode Island, and New Jersey, plus the big cities of New York State, including, but not limited, to the wilds of Tammanytown itself.[37]

But by the time Al appeared on the stump, that moment of joy had passed; each time he stood up to speak, he was hit with the fact that he was appearing on behalf of someone else, that someone else would win the position that had eluded him four years before in so terrible a way. As a result, his speeches again concentrated on past events—with all the bitterness and recrimination this involved for Al Smith—while the governor neglected to mention the national ticket except in passing.

On the 1932 campaign stump, Al Smith was not supporting FDR, he was refighting 1928. In Newark, Al attacked Republicans for their earlier duplicity, and how time had proved them so wrong and him so right. He battled, once more, the bigots of that era, slashing out at Mabel Walker Willebrandt, long since gone from the national scene. He discussed prohibition, not because it was important to the nation, but because it had cost Al Smith so dearly. And in the end, finally, the merest of mentions, "The best way to bring back prosperity is the election of Roosevelt, Garner and the entire Democratic ticket." Four lines in the *New York Times,* in other words, at the end of a speech that filled several columns, his only reference to FDR that entire night. After another one of these talks, an article in the *Christian Century* headlined, "Governor Smith Comes Out for Smith."[38]

It was the pattern all that season. Three days later, in Boston, he delivered a speech whose text ran seventeen typed pages, only eight lines of which mentioned the men running for president and vice president. Any concerns for them had been replaced by pure, unadulterated rage, as Al described how his enemies "were absolutely wrong in 1928. They forgot the principles upon which this country was established, and because of them she has flourished." For Al Smith, that was what the election was all about, always would be about.[39]

Franklin won and Herbert lost, and that made Al Smith happy. On election night, he was among the first to congratulate the president elect. Smith marched proudly in the inaugural parade, saluting Roosevelt as he passed and getting a pleasant wave in return. Other tributes and moments of joy followed: the pen Franklin used to sign the formal oath of office as president was the same one

Smith employed when he began his gubernatorial career back in 1919. When President Roosevelt came to New York in 1933 for the first time since taking office, giving a speech at a dinner for the National Conference of Catholic Charities, he stopped off at Smith's table for a bit of old-fashioned gabbing. Farley was not there to record this one, but observers saw FDR lean over and whisper something to Al, some lines that made the governor break into another broad grin; Smith replied, and in an unconscious but implausible gesture, whacked Franklin generously on the back. The image was awkward, but it was innocent as well. Such good times would not last.[40]

Chapter 23

Nadir

By 1932 Al Smith had many other things on his mind—the repeal of prohibition, his building's continued financial woes, the death of an old friend, and his ongoing career as a writer—but nothing could shake his anger at Franklin Roosevelt. The low point of his public career, however—when he would turn not just on his friends but on his own ideals—was still before him.

Not at first. If World War I had been the final straw that enabled prohibitionists to enact the Eighteenth Amendment, then the unemployment rolls of the Great Depression ensured its repeal. The nation soon ratified the Twenty-First Amendment, a much more fun-loving proposition than its dry predecessor, and on April 7, 1933, beer could be sold legally in America for the first time in years. Whistles blew in St. Louis, while in Milwaukee crowds stood atop autos and sang "Sweet Adeline." Al Smith had been offered a job as the first chair of New York's State Beer Control Board, but turned it down.[1]

He was content, instead, to revel in the removal of a measure that he had fought so hard against. On this fabled day, brewer Jacob Ruppert took the first two cases that came off his reinvigorated production line, pasted "Al Smith" on instead of the brand name, and shipped them off to the governor. Augie Busch went even further, personally writing Smith's name on two cases of Budweiser, then having them flown from the Midwest to New York City at a time when flying resembled space travel in the public's imagination. The precious potables were then conveyed to the doorstep of the Empire State Building in a loaded, five-ton beer wagon drawn through the streets of Manhattan by "six butter-fat" Clydesdales. As a crowd of over a thousand watched, Al accepted the bounty (unfortunately only a twelve-bottle case, prompting the appeal, " . . . sort of small, isn't it?"), and hoped that such production would "deplete the ranks of the unemployed." He also noted how he had "seen many amusing, interesting and imposing sights" on the streets of New York, "but nothing has thrilled me as much as . . . these six big horses pulling a wagonload of beer . . . to the door of the Empire State Building." His only regret: "that the wagonload was not all mine."[2]

But the end of prohibition was one of the few highlights in what was otherwise the bleakest period of Al Smith's life. The towering skyscraper he ran, for example, was still floundering. On March 8, 1935, he wrote Raskob that the business "outlook . . . is so poor"; and a month later reported, "the year as a whole remained exceedingly disappointing," with total rental of only 51,635 square feet (out of 2.1 million) for a paltry $145,681.[3]

Personal tragedy made the pain of Al's business failure all the more acute. On January 2, 1933, Belle Moskowitz passed away, a devastating loss to Smith both personally and professionally. He had been up in Albany, attending Herbert Lehman's inauguration, when the call came, and Al just stood and cried. Composing himself, he rushed back to New York to take care of her family. Some people, understanding the extent of the loss, sent condolence letters to Al as well.[4]

But there were other ramifications besides grief. Oswald Garrison Villard referred to Moskowitz as Smith's "most devoted and loyal friend." "Nobody has been found," he observed two years later, "to take her place. His mail is not always being well taken care of; invitations go unacknowledged." Al had lost "his mentor, his secretary, his publicity agent, and . . . at times his conscience." As the columnist noted, Belle Moskowitz "could not wholly have saved" Smith from debacles like the 1932 Democratic convention, but she had made a difference in his life. All along, she had been his anchor, keeping him steady, steered in the right direction as much as possible. Now she was gone.[5]

By 1933, fortunately, Al had plenty to keep him busy. His writing career was in full swing, especially since October 1932, when he decided to become editor of *New Outlook* magazine. This had once been a reasonably important journal of politics and opinions (under the title *The Outlook*), but like so many other periodicals, it fell on bad times with the rise of radio and the decline caused by the Depression. Publisher Frank Tichenor bought up the rights for little more than a song—$12,500 at a bankruptcy sale—added *New* to the title, and hired a former presidential candidate for a nice, fat $10,000 salary.[6]

Al's job was not only to select content, but to write a series of brief editorials for the front matter, usually four to six pieces that took up a few pages of double-column type. Topics ran the usual gamut of issues, from "War Debts" (January 1933), to "American Housing" in February 1934, and "Child Labor" the month after. Often he enlisted the aid of Robert Moses, who did background research, provided ideas, edited some works, and even ghost-wrote them on occasion.[7]

The job at *New Outlook* lasted less than a year and a half, Al's final columns appearing in March 1934, but other writing projects kept him going. He constantly cranked out articles, the mawkish "I Have 7,000,000 Neighbors" in *American Magazine,* a call for a "Sane Fourth" in *Parent's Magazine,* and a piece on "Leisure Time Facilities" in *Recreation.*[8]

None of these were exactly literary triumphs, but they helped bring in income. The same was also true of his next book, *The Citizen and His Government,* which appeared in 1935. More of a textbook than a polemic, it explained and critiqued the current state of politics. In what the *New York Times Book Review* described as "that brief, ice-clear style of his," Smith laid out his positions on every political issue—some general, many technical. Early comments from the editors at Harper & Brothers highlighted the lack of entertaining anecdotes, their concern that "the reader will be disappointed unless the book strikes a personal note constantly." But the book sold decently, particularly given the times. On June 27, 1935, the governor wrote his agent, "I am very pleased with the result; under all the circumstances, I think it has been a hit."[9]

Soon, however, Al had another topic to discuss, far more important than the need for housing or parks, one that would shape much of his last years in public life. By then, Al Smith was facing the rise of the New Deal, and he did not like what he saw at all.

The first editorial Al Smith wrote on this subject for *New Outlook* was positive; right after the inaugural, he felt, "The new national administration, led by the president, has made a good beginning." Soon, however—very soon—other sentiments began to creep into his writing.[10]

Al began raising objections to various aspects of Roosevelt's approach to dealing with the Depression, sometimes attacking general concepts, sometimes specific programs. In the July 1933 issue, he claimed that the New Deal was too theoretical and unrealistic, too much the work of "the academic planner . . . the man who has been sitting in the library, writing books and lecturing to students, and who now for the first time has a great big public laboratory for experiment." By December Smith began to worry about the fiscal soundness of FDR's policies, releasing for publication a letter he had sent to the Chamber of Commerce of New York State; "What we need in this country," he wrote, "is absolute dependability in our money standards. . . . The latest fiscal moves of the Administration have undermined public confidence." Beyond his views there was a nastiness to this note, like the line, "I am for gold dollars as against baloney dollars," or, "I am for experience as against experiment." Criticizing the Civil Works Administration (CWA), he said that although it looked like "one of the absent minded professors had played anagrams with the alphabet soup," the truth was, this new set of letters had been created just "to hide the failure of another existing agency," in this case the Public Works Administration (PWA), which "had broken down." Inside sources meanwhile offered Roosevelt an early copy of Smith's open letter; the handwritten note chronicling his response read, "President saw—had nothing to say—no comments."[11]

Then things got worse. Smith began to find fundamental conflicts between his own values and what was being done by the New Deal, not just differences over specific programs. In powerful language he wrote, "All this is a long way from the traditional role of the Democratic Party, which has been since the days of Jefferson the party opposed to highly centralized Federal control." He began to get a lot more upset about what was happening in Washington, having every issue of a syndicated feature called "Today's Boon-Doggle"—that revealed the latest excess or folly of the New Deal—clipped and pasted into a scrapbook for reference.[12]

Al became vicious, always refusing, however, to direct his jabs at Franklin himself. Cheap lines flew, instead, at those around the president—cabinet members and brain-trusters—as Al made cracks like, "Who is Ickes, who is Wallace, who is Hopkins, and in the name of all that is good and holy, who is Tugwell, and where did he blow from?" The last of these became one of Smith's favorite pin cushions, so that by 1936 the governor would suggest, "Let Tugwell get one of those raccoon coats that the college boys wear at a football game and let him go to Russia, sit on a cake of ice and plan all he wants. Let him buy six or seven more one-way tickets and take the rest of the brain trust with him." It felt as if, according to one politician, Smith was "presenting Roosevelt with the sidewalks of New York one brick at a time."[13]

By this time Al was not alone in his attacks. His emotions roiling, he set aside his heritage and joined up with an organization remembered most of all for its wealth and for its blind, ineffective reactionaryism: the American Liberty League.

The League's origin was typical of its later role in public life. R. R. M. Carpenter, a retired Du Pont executive, started having problems with the hired help, a fact he blamed on those new-fangled federal programs. "Five negroes on my place in South Carolina refused work this spring . . . saying they had jobs with the government," Mr. Carpenter complained to his friend John Raskob; to make matters worse, the cook he employed on his Florida houseboat also quit, because he could now make a dollar an hour as a painter on a national project. Carpenter asked his friend if there was something Raskob could do, given his ties to the Democratic Party, about FDR's radical initiatives.[14]

Raskob was in no position to influence the Roosevelt administration, having drifted far afield; instead he came up with another idea. This one had probably been germinating since the first time the financier got a look at the Hundred Days, an event that prompted him to remark, "Never in my whole life have I been so mistaken about a man . . . as I was about Franklin Roosevelt."[15]

The financier decided to form an organization "to protect society from the sufferings which it is bound to endure if we allow communist elements to lead the people to believe that all businessmen are crooks." Correspondence flew back and forth between executives of Du Pont and its subsidiary, General Motors. S. M. DuBrul of GM, for example, agreed with the idea, which was probably sincere, since he honestly believed that if the "present trends continue, it seems to me that representative government will become mob government and not only will property rights be repudiated, but . . . all of our other constitutional guarantees will be lost" as well.[16]

Even more, the search for a suitable title provides a window into how these men perceived their great mission. Alfred M. Sloan told Raskob that their slogan should be "Rights of Property is the Foundation of All Social Order," and that they should adopt the name, Association Asserting the Rights of Property. That was at least better than Raskob's original idea—Union Asserting the Integrity of Persons and Property—but still terribly clunky (even if it was honest). Someone else then shortened it to the National Property League, a shorter, catchier phrase that still captured the basic point of what they believed in. Only at the last minute did John W. Davis come up with the American Liberty League. This one sounded patriotic, and thus hid the fact that it was really about rich men protecting their interests, so naturally they adopted it, becoming the official title of the organization when it took out papers in Washington, D.C., on August 22, 1934.[17]

The Liberty League was a nonpartisan organization with two fundamental tenets. First was how desperately the rights of property had to be preserved. Their initial handbook, with the rat-ta-tat title, *The American Liberty League: What It Is. What It Stands For. What It Proposes to Do,* discussed "the protection of property," safeguarding capital's right to a proper return, and the inequity of a tax system that forced some people to pay a larger share than others.[18]

Their other major point was that the Roosevelt administration seemed to be a giant plot of some sort. In official pamphlets, the League called the programs of the thirties "hare-brained," and likely to "retard social and economic progress." But in private, men like Irénée Du Pont believed that "if something is not done shortly, this country is going the way of . . . Italy, Germany . . . or Russia, and it is high time we did something." Haywood Scott, a lawyer in Joplin, Missouri, liked to talk about "King Franklin I . . . Defender of the Faith of All Socialists and other professors in political experiments, unrestricted by . . . constitutional limitations." Of course, these were the same people who had complained bitterly that, "to finance these ever-increasing disbursements, Congress is now planning huge additional taxes to be paid for out of the shrunken income of . . . industry and individuals," during the *Hoover administration*.[19]

At its height, the League's membership actually did hit 75,000, but still drew its support from only a tiny portion of society's upper stratum. All initiatives stemmed from a small board of very wealthy individuals, most of them corporate executives, many with the last name Du Pont. They saw to it that the League had an income in 1935 of $483,000—$76,000 more than the Republican Party that year—and enjoyed a thirty-one-room headquarters suite. Edward F. Hutton of Wall Street fame, Sloan of General Motors, and Montgomery Ward's Sewell Avery sat on the League's advisory board; during World War II the last of these told the attorney general, "To hell with the U.S. Government," and got arrested for refusing to obey federal laws regarding union contracts.[20]

Now Al Smith had become a charter member of this crowd, even serving on the Liberty League's executive committee. They would meet at his offices in the Empire State Building, and by October 1935 Raskob informed Walter Chrysler, "Governor Smith is giving a great deal of his valuable time . . . to the League and its work and I think is much enthused by the progress it is making." Al even got Joseph Proskauer to join, although Robert Moses refused, believing, as one historian put it, the whole thing was "God's gift to Franklin Roosevelt."[21]

All this meant that Alfred E. Smith was on board as the League began its work to make America safe for the rich; in fact he was one of four members of the special committee set up to create their educational campaign. He became instrumental in approving all the pamphlets sent out—5 million copies of titles like *Economic Planning—Mistaken But Not New; Legislation—By Coercion or Constitution;* and *The Imperilment of Democracy.* Al was also there when the Liberty League organized a committee of fifty-six conservative lawyers to review New Deal legislation, a body that reported back how the Wagner Act (which created the National Labor Relations Board and is still on the books) was unconstitutional, and that employers should refuse to obey it.[22]

Al must have known what people thought of his new affiliation, how politicians like James Farley joked that it should be called "the American Cellophane League" because, "first, it's a DuPont product and second, you can see right through it." Harry Hopkins figured it was "so far to the right that no one will ever find it," and Stuart Chase in the *Nation* referred to "the loud-speaker of what Veblen used to call the kept classes." When John Raskob sent out a membership appeal to 156,000 Americans, one man answered, "I still have the poor man's point of view" and "am still with my gang, while you and your friend, Governor Smith, have run out on yours." The playwright Elmer Rice replied, "To the hungry, the maimed, the disinherited of this land of ours, your phrases about liberty and freedom must seem as empty as the Empire State Building."[23]

So why did Al join, and why did he stay? Why did Alfred Emanuel Smith, child of the Brooklyn Bridge and hero of the Triangle Shirtwaist Fire, become part of a group that did not know a socialist from a Bolivian (the kind of line Al would have used, by the way, back in his days in the legislature), a clique so utterly alien to both his origins and his politics?

The easy answer was that he had gotten rich and sold out his past, that Fifth Avenue had made him forget Oliver Street; his friends were now captains of industry, not of fire battalions. John Raskob was inviting Smith for golf games, and could send a letter to the Smith residence at a Long Island inn, "I find that I left my evening clothes in your locked closet." H. L. Mencken felt that Smith was "ruined by associating with rich men—a thing far more dangerous to politicians than even booze or the sound of their own voices."[24]

But there are other answers, far more important. One piece of the puzzle, often overlooked, was that Al Smith and Franklin Roosevelt actually did have ideological differences, that Smith really did object to an expansion of the federal government. Joseph Proskauer later told interviewers that Smith's "inherent opposition" to the New Deal stemmed from his belief in the primacy of state and local government, and that the governor sincerely feared "a tremendous concentration" of federal power, a force, "reaching its tentacles into every kind of social and political question on the lower level." Smith himself wrote that the Democratic Party had been, "since the days of Jefferson the party opposed to highly centralized Federal control, the party of individualism" and "state's rights."[25]

Al Smith held these views, furthermore, not because of any innate reactionaryism, but because of his own political experiences; he was a product, in other words, of the twenties, not the thirties. During his years as governor, the federal government had been a conservative force, led by business-oriented presidents, Congresses, and courts. After the 1928 election, for example, Breckinridge Long, a Democratic Party wheelhorse, wrote in his diary about returning to the nation's capital, "Back again—in this Republican town."[26]

So when the governor thought of federal intervention in social affairs, two images came to mind. The first was prohibition; if Al Smith ever had a model of what expansive federal power meant, this was it. A government run by bigots and small towners would come in and ignore the rights of local minorities, people they did not understand, and did not really like either.

His other example was water power. In the twenties, Governor Smith of New York State had fought to control the electricity rights to giant dams and rivers for the good of the people, and he always did this in opposition to federal officials, who tried to turn those same rights over to private sector monopolists. Smith equated doing good for the common folk with the state level of politics, a notion that must have been reinforced as he saw progressive state governments like the La Follette administration in Wisconsin, fighting against the Harding and Coolidge and Hoover administrations.[27]

Smith's belief in a strong state presence was also reinforced by his close association with Joseph Proskauer, a product of the Deep South and staunch advocate of states' rights. Proskauer often agreed with the idea behind a Rooseveltian initiative, but bitterly denounced it because he considered the move a violation of the separation of powers. As his grandson pointed out—and as Smith must have heard constantly—Proskauer was a devotee of the Tenth Amendment to the Constitution—that any powers not relegated to the federal government must and should revert back to state control.[28]

Smith and Proskauer, furthermore, were not alone in their opinions; many other progressives shared these views. Otis Graham, in *An Encore for Reform*, studied the responses of 168 liberals to the rise of the New Deal and found, after removing those who took no position or for whom there was insufficient data, that forty of his participants supported Roosevelt's reforms, but sixty opposed them as being unwise extensions of federal authority. Even William Greene, head of the American Federation of Labor, originally fought the idea of social security because he did not want workers' pensions handled by a national government he associated with reactionaries.[29]

Finally, Al Smith always considered one of his greatest accomplishments administrative reform—taking the state government and putting it on a rational basis, one that emphasized sound, precise accounting. He reacted with horror to the casualness of the New Deal, the cornucopia of approaches that answered Roosevelt's call for dynamic action in the face of a national crisis. As early as April 1932, campaigning for the Democratic nomination, Smith had demanded "a vigorous and forceful effort to reduce the cost of this government; to cut out useless activities, to consolidate necessary ones and so to reorganize the various departments as to eliminate overhead." The kind of steps, in other words, that had brought him victory back in the twenties, and that may—or may not—have been applicable in the thirties. Historian Richard Magurno wrote that "Al Smith did not become a reactionary after 1928; he simply stood still and let the times pass him by."[30]

These arguments are accurate, but still not sufficient to completely explain Smith's unprecedented turnabout, a drama of monstrous psychological proportions. Much deeper causes are required.

If Al Smith had been hurt deeply by Franklin Roosevelt, he had been even more wounded by the American people. Walking into the 1928 election, Smith carried with him a fundamental, rock-solid belief that they were decent, that they worked hard and respected others, that they followed the social code of the Fourth Ward, and that in the long run, they always did the right thing.

In 1928, however, the American people did none of these things. They had been vile, and they had made the wrong decision in the worst possible way. On the most primeval of levels, the people had betrayed him.

Once in a while Smith and those around him expressed this sentiment, sometimes in an obvious way, but usually in a more oblique fashion. Emily Warner, Al's daughter, claimed that he told her, after the split with Roosevelt, "I sometimes think that the American people get just about the government they deserve"; while Rexford Tugwell observed that Al's road to the Liberty League began, not when Franklin became a governor and an independent, "but because the American people had refused Al their votes in 1928."[31]

The most telling outburst came by accident. On May 1, 1929, the Waldorf-Astoria held a lavish ball to celebrate its demise, its destruction to occur immediately after to make way for the Empire State Building which would rise on the same site. Shortly after, workers started to tear the place down, and Al stopped off to get a souvenir of the main ballroom where he had spoken so many times, enjoyed so many moments when the public had worshipped and honored him.

This time was different. Claude Bowers, keynoter in 1928, accompanied Smith and recorded in his diary the governor's feelings. "In the banquet room where I've spoken so many times," Bowers recalled Smith saying, "it was pathetic. Those great gold and brass moldings and decorations . . . that I supposed were really costly—nothing but gilded plaster. And the chandeliers! They looked magnificent hanging, but on the floor—just junk." Angrily, he concluded, "I went thinking I might pick up something for my apartment, but there was nothing there worth having. It was pathetic."[32]

This was Al Smith's new vision of America: a shallow facade of glitter covering a reality of "pathetic junk." A facade, moreover, that had cruelly deceived and hurt him. Al Smith would need a symbol for his new concept of America, and he would find it in the subsequent career of Franklin Delano Roosevelt.

Thus, Al Smith's break with Franklin Roosevelt was caused, above all else, by the simple fact that FDR became Smith's symbolic scapegoat for heartbreak. Smith had been a politician for too long, had mouthed the homilies too many times, to denounce the voters openly, the body politic he had loved and then had scorned him. So instead, he picked the perfect proxy. Just as he now envisioned the American people, Smith had always seen Franklin as worthy of affection, but lacking in substance; as Heywood Broun put it, Smith viewed Roosevelt with "a fondness . . . mixed with a slight measure of contempt. He didn't think the Harvard boy really had very much on the ball." And after 1932, young Franklin, just like the American people, had taken something dear—the nation's highest political prize and the chance for redemption—away from Al Smith.[33]

In January 1936 Al Smith's rage peaked. The Liberty League decided to hold a gala dinner; Smith would deliver the keynote speech, a resounding thumper of a talk that would signal the start of their assault on Franklin Roosevelt in this presidential season.

The event would be held at the Mayflower Hotel in Washington; originally the idea was to have twelve hundred attendees, but six thousand rich men and women asked for tickets, and even after weeding out some riffraff, the League's leaders still had to accept two thousand of these applications, making it the largest event in the hotel's history. James Farley, surveying the guest list, recognized that, "ninety-five percent of the people at the dinner did not vote for Smith in 1928 and said many unkind things about the Governor and Mrs. Smith." But now Al was attacking FDR, and they could support him wholeheartedly.[34]

For months the League's publicists had worked effectively, so press and radio coverage was complete. Even Roosevelt stalwart Harold Ickes recalled in his diary the "wonderful build-up for this meeting," how it "had been widely commented upon in all the newspapers of the country these last two weeks." The whole nation would turn out to hear this one, listening in as the CBS radio network carried Al's words to so many households.[35]

And they expected blood. The Liberty League had made it clear Smith would be delivering a blistering assessment of the Roosevelt administration. On the day after the speech, the *New York Times* would write, "Not since the break between Theodore Roosevelt and William H. Taft in 1912 has there been a comparable rupture in the friendship of two public men."[36]

In the midst of these preparations, however, a strange episode occurred that revealed the complexity of the Smith-Roosevelt relationship. Al had always been closer to Eleanor than to Franklin, since she received all the affection Smith felt toward that family, but incited none of the anger and jealousy that her husband did. Where FDR had failed Smith, Eleanor had always stood by the governor, always believed in him, to the point that she refused to celebrate Franklin's victory in 1928 because Al Smith had lost; that November, it was Eleanor who told the press, "No, I'm not excited about my husband's election. I don't care. What difference can it make to me?"[37]

So as 1935 came to an end, with Smith's speech being trumpeted on the front pages, that old and strong friendship still compelled her to invite Al to stay in the White House, when he came down to Washington to speak at the Mayflower. On December 18, 1935, she wrote Smith a missive that captured her own good nature, as well as the real affection she felt for the man about to attack the president, her husband. "I see by the papers that you will be down here to speak on the 25th of January," Eleanor gently noted. "Franklin and I hope very much that you and any of your family will stay with us at least for the night. You can feel as free as you wish to come and go."[38]

It was the epitome of grace, but Al could never have accepted, given the circumstances. He thanked her for the invitation, stating, "It is a matter of regret that I will be unable to avail myself of it." After that, however, he added, "No member of my family is to accompany me and I have made arrangements with a party of men and it looks like I will have to stay with them," a nice way of saying that on this trip he had to stay with a Raskob, not a Roosevelt.

Smith's letter went out on December 26, 1935, and right after, the *New York Times* printed the exchange, and the story became Al's supposed negligence, how, despite the fact that the Roosevelts had invited him over every year that they had been in the White House, he had always turned them down. Stung, Al told reporters, "We might as well have the record straight," that few such invitations had ever appeared.

This hurt Eleanor, so she wrote the governor. She began with care, remarking on how "The newspapers seem to have managed to involve us in a rather foolish and extremely disagreeable controversy." Like him, she knew "only too well how untrue quotes often are," and instead reminded Al of the time, the summer past, when they had invited the Smiths to stay but Katie had injured her arm, and how solicitous Eleanor had been to that lady's pursuit of good health. Above all, she told Al, "I feel sure that you have the same desire that I have, not to let political differences injure a personal relationship. I have never felt anything but friendship for you and your family." Then, in closing, "I think it is a great pity for people who have had respect and admiration for each other to be prodded into antagonistic personal feelings, and so, in this new year, I wish to assure you and all your family of our good wishes for the future, and that always . . . our home is open to you, with or without an invitation."

Eleanor's tender letter raised difficult emotions for Al. In his January 5, 1936, answer—marked *"Personal and Confidential"*—he told her, "Like you, it would be a great pity if political differences were permitted to grow into personal animosities and I deprecate the efforts being made to that end. . . . Throughout my political life I have had honest differences with many men but have never allowed them to interfere with personal friendship." Then came his confusion, his deeply felt ambivalence toward these Roosevelts. Without any preamble, Smith wrote the single sentence, "I earnestly supported Frank in 1928, 1930 and 1932 and if I take issue now with some of the policies of the administration it is not with any personal animosity towards him or you." Plaintive and melancholy, he concluded, "Please accept the assurance of my regard for you both and my best wishes for the new year."

But now it was too late to indulge these feelings, as Smith turned to the business at hand. Twenty days after the end of the Al and Eleanor exchange, on January 25, 1936, the Mayflower banquet began promptly at 7:00 P.M. Everything moved smoothly, or as one guest remarked, "The food was delicious, the service prompt and the speeches went off like clockwork." Five men stood up to speak; the last of these was Alfred E. Smith.[39]

It would become one of the great tragedies of twentieth-century American politics. Al Smith—a child of Tammany Hall, protégé of Tom Foley and then Charles Francis Murphy, four-term Democratic governor of New York State and the party's 1928 presidential candidate—launching vicious, hate-filled attacks on the most popular Democratic president ever, Franklin Delano Roosevelt, at a Liberty League banquet.

This oration, one of the most famous denunciations of Franklin Roosevelt and the New Deal of the era, accused the new administration of having given in to extreme left-wing elements: "Just get the platform of the Democratic Party, and get the platform of the Socialist party, and lay them down on your dining-room table, side by side . . . get a heavy lead pencil, and scratch out the word 'Democrat' and scratch out the word 'Socialist' and let the two platforms lay there."[40]

To Smith, the results would be obvious, as was the problem: "This country was organized on the principles of a representative democracy, and you can't mix socialism or communism with that" (parenthetically, he added that "that is the reason why the United States Supreme Court is working overtime throwing the alphabet out the window three letters at a time"). "They are like oil and water. They refuse to mix."

By this time his anger could not be contained, despite the fact that he was reading from a prepared speech, and he started to bellow: "It is all right with me.

It is all right with me if they want to disguise themselves as Norman Thomas or Karl Marx, or Lenin, or any of the rest of that bunch, but what I won't stand for is allowing them to march under the banner of Jefferson, Jackson or Cleveland."

His voice rising in volume as he moved to his finale, Smith delivered a "solemn warning." His audience, whether they be the bejeweled guests in the Mayflower Hotel ballroom, or denim-clad workers and their families, must realize that "there can be only one capital—Washington or Moscow." Even more, now: "There can be only one atmosphere of government, the clear, pure, fresh air of free America or the foul breath of communistic Russia. There can be only one flag, the Stars and Stripes, or the red flag of the godless union of the Soviet."

Afterward, Americans felt outraged. J. M. Burnett of New York City telegraphed his president, "Just listened to the silly warrior. His inane discourse was pathetic." Farris Mitchell told Roosevelt that "my wife and I just turned off our radio. We will not listen to a talk from a traitor against you." Three residents of Alameda, California, wrote, "Our joint reaction is one of rage mingled with pity." Vern Fox cabled, "Judas gained hundreds of thousands of votes for you tonight"; and Herbert Houston said that his greatest wish was to attend Al Smith's funeral. In Grand Coulee Dam, Washington, one hundred men burned an effigy of Alfred E. Smith.[41]

Columnists shared the sense of fury. One writer for the *Nation* declared, "The Al Smith all of us knew died in 1928." Paul Ward, in the same journal, observed how that night, Al Smith "did more than read himself out of the Democratic Party. He read himself out of the respect and affections of all men of good faith." Back in 1935, when Al had joined the Liberty League, Oswald Garrison Villard wrote in the *American Mercury* that this political shift, "makes his friends weep."[42]

⌒

The questions of before fester now: how can the split between Smith and Roosevelt, the incredible anger, be explained? What caused Smith to turn so forcefully on his heritage in 1936?

After the election in which he lost the presidency, Smith appeared to others as a changed man. Marvin Jones said that Al's spirit was "broken," and Lorena Hickok remarked that he had become "a lonely, embittered man. The warmth of his greeting . . . was almost pathetic." James Michael Curley, the Boston boss, told friends, "Smith had changed since 1928. He had lost the common touch." But Al's soul had not changed; rather, he had lost his joie de vivre, lost his innocence and spontaneity and spunk, as he had lost his vision of America.[43]

And the ultimate target of that frustration, that anger, that sadness, was Franklin Delano Roosevelt. Simon Rifkind said that "Al Smith wanted to run for president. Even after Mr. Roosevelt had been president one or two terms. Al Smith very much wanted to be president." He wanted this as revenge on old enemies, but above all as a way of restoring his faith; if the American people reversed their decision, rejected the bigotry and the falseness of 1928, he could believe in them again. And this had been denied by FDR, whom he considered a lesser man, really, in fact, no more than a child.[44]

In 1932 Franklin Roosevelt achieved the goal Al Smith never attained: inauguration as president of the United States. Within a little more than one hundred days, he was not just the president but a national hero. Hugh Carey commented, "If Smith was Barnum, Roosevelt was Ziegfield. Roosevelt put on a bigger show, a better show." Even in public appearances, according to Carey, Smith could not keep up; on radio, for example, "Roosevelt owned every set. . . . You can't depict Al Smith giving a fireside chat."[45]

To Al Smith, it was a final, unforgivable insult. The American people had rejected him for an adolescent, a cripple, a fop who had never had to work a day in his life. And by 1936 even Smith's people, the urban immigrants, were lining up to support Roosevelt in record numbers. This became the ultimate symbol of the fraud that was the American spirit, the supreme manifestation of the shallowness that had destroyed his life. It was only fitting and appropriate that it would be the greatest target of his rage as well.

Chapter 24

Elder Statesman

ONLY ONE MAN could bring Al Smith and Franklin Roosevelt together again, and that turned out to be Adolf Hitler. Smith, like Roosevelt and Winston Churchill, immediately recognized the fundamental evil of nazism, although in his case it also represented an attack on everybody and everything he had ever championed. So finally, late in life, Smith returned to the fold, to the defense of the people he had fought for back during the Triangle investigation, as governor, and above all in 1928. It was Al Smith's opposition to the greatest scourge of the twentieth century that would bring him onto Franklin Roosevelt's team at last, enabling him to enjoy his last years.

The roots of Al's antifascism predated even the Smith-Roosevelt feud. Smith had wasted no time in decrying events in Germany, first speaking out in March 1933, a few months after Adolf Hitler became chancellor of a new Reich. At a rally in Madison Square Garden on March 27, Al observed that much pressure had been brought on him to back away from this appearance; instead he told the crowd that nothing gave him more pleasure than showing up at a meeting to denounce the thugs who persecuted Jews, part of a regime that suppressed freedom of speech and freedom of the press as well. The only way to deal with nazism, Smith argued, was "to drag it out into the same sunlight and give it the same treatment that we gave the Klan. . . . It doesn't make any difference to me whether it is a brown shirt or a night shirt." In 1937 Rabbi Stephen Wise, who had denounced Al's attack on Roosevelt, remembered the Madison Square Garden speech and thanked Smith for being "the first great American publicly to make known your condemnation of Hitler as a menace to world civilization."[1]

That speech began a crusade that lasted as long as swastikas embodied the German nation. Three months later, Smith turned to the columns of *New Outlook* and declared, "The spirit and the letter of every provision of our bill of rights has been violated by the Hitler government." Then, voicing views that only later would become commonplace, he asserted, "The greatest indictment which can be brought against the German people is that to date they have proved themselves incapable of living under a democratic government." In later speeches he referred to the Hitler regime as "stupid," as "boneheaded," and as one that had returned the "Germanic state to cave-man law."[2]

Now at last, Smith could once again speak from his heart. In his best speech, he made it clear that "those of us who believe in democracy and love liberty find it impossible to remain silent in the face of this desperate challenge." The defense of immigrants, of religious minorities, was not something new, but stemmed from the best in the American vision; the ideals of Jefferson were still valid. Al exhorted audiences, "This is not merely a Jewish question, a Catholic question, a Protestant question, a political question or a labor question." Instead, "It is one . . . that goes to the foundations on which we have erected the America that has stood all during our political life for the preservation of . . . civilization."[3]

Far more remarkable, Smith also took the bold step of linking concern over the Nazis in Germany to the treatment of African-Americans in the United States. Al's daughter Emily remembered how, after hearing Hitler on the radio for the first time, her father said that, although it would be an immense task, America would handle that group in the long run, but "the big issue this country is going to face in the future . . . is the question of the Negroes." Speaking at Lincoln University, he used words astonishingly similar to those of W. E. B. Du Bois when he explained that "what we call the Negro problem is a white problem," that it was not people of color who were engaging in discriminatory acts, but whites. Smith echoed what black spokespersons had been saying for years, applauding political consciousness and that "the Negro race wants its own leaders." And when four New York City African-Americans won the local championship for best barber shop quartet and the national organization banned their participation in its finals, Al and Bob Moses promptly and publicly resigned their vice presidencies in that group, a move that the *New York Times* covered on its front page.[4]

The rise of totalitarianism in Europe would unite Al and Franklin Roosevelt as the New Deal could not, when they—as opposed to Al's Liberty League friends—responded to the crisis with intelligence and courage. By 1938, after Kristallnacht, Smith not only declared that Germany had returned to the dark ages, he also added, referring to the White House's statement on this tragedy, "The president spoke for the whole nation." They were the first warm words Al had had for Franklin's policies in a long time.[5]

Even stronger language followed. In October 1939, Roosevelt asked for a change in the Neutrality Act that would allow other nations to buy American war goods, as long as they transported them in their own vessels; quickly this became known as "cash and carry," and it clearly represented FDR's attempt to support the nations now at war with Germany.

As he had done in the past, Smith got on the radio, this time to "stand solidly" behind the president, proclaiming, "Mr. Roosevelt is so clearly right, so obviously on the side of common sense and of sound judgement and of patriotism," that no right-thinking American could oppose him. In 1936 Roosevelt had refused to reply directly to Smith's Liberty League speech (he got Senate minority leader Joseph Robinson—Al's running mate in 1928—to do so for him), but now he sent a telegram reading, "Very many thanks. You were grand," to which Smith replied, "Thanks for the kind telegram. I am sure you are going to win."[6]

Now, at last, with this issue, Smith had broken past his pain, and could return to the visions that had always been at the core of his political faith. He supported aid to England, urging every "red-blooded American" to stand behind his president, at the same time that Irenée Du Pont was writing his bother Pierre, "Mr. Roosevelt is capable of trying to embroil this country in war for the purpose of having himself made dictator by force." Smith turned from this and came back to his roots, telling the Anti-Nazi League, "A great many years of my life have been given over to fighting against the very things Hitler exalts. If his teachings prevail, then I and millions who, like me, have fought for spiritual and political freedom, have fought in vain."[7]

So despite the horrors overseas, the last years of the thirties and into the forties became good ones in Al Smith's life, a time to enjoy senior status, to forget and to let the years be a salve for the pain.

There was so much to enjoy now. Al and Katie lived at 820 Fifth Avenue, between Sixty-third and Sixty-fourth streets. This was a palatial, twelve-story apartment building with an exterior of gray granite, fronted by an awning that extended all the way to the street, a residence befitting Al's position as an elder statesman.

Grandson Walter called the Smith residence, "the grandest apartment I ever saw," and his cousin, Father Arthur Smith remembered it being "enormously large." Guests came up in an elevator that reeked of mahogany, then entered through a vestibule flanked by small tables. There were tall ceilings, vast oriental rugs, and a balcony that overlooked Central Park, the only one of its kind in the building. The living room included a fireplace, and there was a library, plus a huge dining room. After that came a large kitchen and pantry, with a passageway leading from there to the bedrooms; it was down this hallway that the Smiths kept the world's nastiest parrot, a bird that cried, "Hi Al, Hi Al," and loved the governor (naturally), but bit everyone else.[8]

It would have been a lot of space for two people, but Al and Katie were rarely alone. This was the time of grandchildren, hordes of tykes that flooded through on a regular basis, and if they did not show, the old folks went to them. The youngsters called Katie "Auntie 'Em," while Al was usually "Pappa." Some of them, however, called him "Umpa," since Al used to smoke luxurious H. Uppmann stogies from Cuba; eventually, of course, the kids forgot the origins of the nickname, and came to believe that the cigar had been named for their favorite relative.[9]

The moppets came screaming over on lots of different occasions, but especially after ten o'clock Mass on Sundays. Al would sing or do magic for them, or they would entertain themselves with a trick savings bank, a wooden box that would stick out a tongue and take the money. At times they just got wild; Walter Smith referred to his siblings and cousins as "hellions," and described how they used to skid back and forth on the carpet, build up static electricity, and then shock each other. With eight or more "yelling and screaming all at once," the din could get unbearable, and then, Walter recalled, the governor "would come out and basically say, 'THAT'S IT,' and you could hear this tremendous voice, still booming in quality." But if Al had not lost the knack of commanding an audience, he rarely had to employ this skill; the children's visits were friendly and frequent, so much so that the cousins became more like brothers and sisters, "that was how much we saw each other."[10]

Of course, if the grandkids did not show up, Al and Katie went to them instead. They would smell the cigar before they saw Al, and there was always a basket of fruit; every grandchild remembered these displays. "Pappa" made an immense production out of his gifts, slowly unwrapping the package, then prolonging the agony with sleight of hand when suddenly a grape or a quarter appeared behind the ear of one of the younger children.[11]

There were lots of family events in those years. Al and Katie maintained their own tabernacle in the apartment and said daily prayers there, but sometimes they took some of the children up to St. Patrick's Cathedral for Sunday services. At Christmas, every grandchild wrote a letter to Santa Claus, but these all wound up at the Empire State Building instead of the North Pole; the elves in the world's tallest structure saw to it that each of the letter writers got a package from FAO Schwarz with just what he or she wanted. The biggest surprise of all came the year granddaughter Anne actually went to the Empire State on her birthday, "a real treat" for her. There waiting beside the governor was an adorable taffy-colored puppy, a mutt which promptly urinated all over Al's office.[12]

☙

There were animals for Al too. The governor had left behind his precious zoo and lost the great dane, but for Smith's last days, the animals of his youth returned.

The gentle touch behind much of this came from Robert Moses, by now parks commissioner. Moses saw to it that the old Central Park menagerie was completely rehabbed, turning it into a first-rate zoo. It was just off Fifth Avenue at 64th Street, right across from 820 Fifth.[13]

On December 2, 1934, Moses threw an opening-day party, but it really was a thinly disguised celebration for his governor, an act of true respect and deep affection. He told Al to show up, but gave no hint of what would await him, implying that Smith should merely take a seat in the reviewing stand.

But that morning, when Al walked out of the building to the street, three hundred schoolchildren—from the Fourth Ward, no less—stood there cheering and waving balloons, his official escort across Fifth Avenue and to the zoo.

There, his seat was right up front, next to the mayor himself; before the governor got comfortable, however, a voice called him to the podium. Before Al could get a word in, Earle Andrews, standing in for the parks commissioner, officially appointed Smith "Honorary Night Superintendent of the Central Park Zoo."

This was Moses's finest act, because while the title sounded phony, its benefits were real. Al received, not just a fulsome medal, but a working key to the zoo—one that actually opened the doors to the entrance and to all the animal cages, day or night. For the first time since he had left Albany, Al Smith again had his own menagerie. As tributes go, this one was a gem.

Al quickly made use of his new position. It became part of the mythology of Fifth Avenue—an accurate part, in this case—of how Governor Smith would walk across the street in a business suit to spend hours in the cages with his beloved animals; or even how he would go out at night, sometimes in a nightshirt, to comfort a roaring beast.[14]

Al became involved with every one of the creatures. Robert Moses wrote Smith on a major state matter on February 15, 1935, when he reported, "I thought you should know about the end of Caliph." Caliph, naturally enough, was a deceased hippopotamus, but soon after Smith began to tell anyone who listened, "I've got a new girlfriend. She lives right near me. Her name is Rosie." Rosie, of course, was Caliph's replacement.[15]

This, of course, made for magical moments with the grandchildren, as Al would lead them after dinner to his private domain. Some of them got something special, like the time he took little Anne out "in the dead of night" to feed the animals. Her cousin Walter remembered Joey, a cute little gorilla who spit on everybody who came near him. The big game (if you were, say, ten years old) was "To get out of the arc so he wouldn't be able to reach you." None of this was necessary, by the way, if you were the one-and-only, the incomparable Grandpa Al, whom Joey always let in the cage unmolested. Of course.[16]

But Joey did not make for the best zoo story; that one went to the tiger. In September 1934, the Parks Department held a contest for schoolchildren, "Name Our Animals," in which youngsters submitted names for the zoo's various critters. Presiding judge would be His Honor, the night superintendent of the Central Park Zoo.[17]

The city's children ate it up, submitting 43,282 suggestions, and Al chose judiciously, but was not above going outside the ballot box in his search for the perfect moniker. When faced with the task of christening two African water bucks, for example, the subject of prohibition came up, and officials bandied about names like Volstead, WCTU, and William Jennings Bryan; Al settled for "Bucket" and Spring," a lovely show of moderation on his part.

No such restraint occurred, however, when it came the turn of the zoo's tiger. Al arbitrarily dubbed it "Tammany," "a name that apparently had not occurred to any of the youngsters," as the *Times* gently commented.

What placed Tammany—the tiger, not the Hall—in the folklore of New York City, however, was a stunt the governor rigged up. There are several versions as to how Al managed this, one claiming that he spent long hours training the cat, the other that he used crabapples to excite him, but the end result was a classic piece of New York political theater. Whenever Smith showed visitors around, he would be sure to stop at Tammany's cage. Facing the symbol of the ultimate urban machine, the governor would go up to the bars and yell out the name of the Hall's greatest foe: "La Guardia." Tammany would then jump up and roar, baring his fangs to everyone's fear and amazement.[18]

In his later years the old Al reappeared, the leader who could still feel deeply the pain of an average New Yorker and would go to great lengths to cure this.

One of his best moments began when an unusual letter arrived at the Empire State Building; it was addressed, like so many others, to "Mr. 'Al' Smith, c/o Empire State Building, New York City, New York." What made this one unique, however, were the beautiful hand-inked cartoons that graced both the envelope and the pages inside. The first thing you saw, therefore, even before you opened it, were two newsboys amid a typical East Side street scene. One of them, eyes wide with disbelief, complains, "How In Der Sam Hills Are Yer Gonner Prove It After All Dese Years?" His companion, clearly the leader of the two, aggressively gestures and replies, "Well Dots Easy. Our Pal Mr. 'Al' Smith Was Once Der Gov-ner For New York—An' Such News 'Al' Smith Kin Never Ferget, See!!"[19]

Inside the mystery was revealed. The artist, Otto Eppers, grew up in Smith's old neighborhood, and in 1910 got the brilliant idea to "earn some money by taking a real brodie from the new Manhattan Bridge." For the uninitiated, that meant taking a dive off the aforementioned span as a publicity stunt. But someone squealed and the cops blocked that little trick, so Otto turned instead to the first of its kind, Al's beloved Brooklyn Bridge, and took the appropriate header off its noble walkway. Somehow he managed to survive, but after being suitably arrested and booked, Otto "opened the summer season in Coney Island" on the strength of his exploit.

This took four pages to tell, but the first was a doozy. Covering most of the sheet was a remarkable ink drawing: in the background was the Brooklyn Bridge, with a splash in the water representing where Eppers had concluded his illustrious jump. Dominating the scene, however, was the foreground section: on a pier, back to the observer but watching the action, stood a man with a derby, arm wrapped around the largest, fluffiest striped cat imaginable.

But if the art seemed festive, the letter was sad. Eppers had retired and was living in Clearfield, Pennsylvania. Still a churchgoer, he told his story to the local priest, but Father Leo Anderton first "showed signs of doubt," and then just laughed out loud. An old man had been humiliated.

Though a lot of years, miles, and bodies had passed under the bridge, Eppers still believed only one man could or would help him; he asked Al Smith to obtain the court record of his arraignment and then send it with a personal letter to Father Anderton, because "this . . . will surely open their eyes." Eppers ended with all he could give: "I hope I didn't bore you any," he pleaded, "And should you ever need a favor that I could grant—upon request—I would fulfill it even at the cost of my own life."

No matter how moving the appeal, it is important to stop and think about what Eppers had requested, and whom he had requested it from. Obtaining any kind of evidence of this obscure event, whether it be a court document or a press clipping (let alone both), would be a long and painstaking process. And Al Smith was fighting for the Empire State Building, rebuilding his own finances, and figuring out what to do with Franklin Roosevelt. He was a little busy, in other words, to be handling that kind of solicitation from a total stranger.

But on May 2, 1935, Father Leo Anderton received a letter from Mary Carr,

Smith's secretary, who enclosed "a photostatic copy of a newspaper clipping as well as the copy of a report from the Police Department."[20]

And in time, Al would even reconcile with Frank Roosevelt, the boy he had cared for, the man who had spurned him. Even in the worst of times, there were signs of Al's ambivalence, of the conflict between affection and jealousy that racked his relationship with the president. If Smith refrained from mentioning Roosevelt in his attacks, this was partially a refusal to recognize Roosevelt's presidency, but subconsciously, by not getting personal, it also left the door open for a future rapprochement. Even in private conversations, Smith would avoid vituperation, telling Jim Farley, for example, "he had no feeling against Roosevelt personally," just his policies; or writing Walter Lippmann as late as May 1936 that "confidentially . . . I have the opinion that the President started out to make good the 1932 platform." Roosevelt's people also took pains to avoid political retribution, making sure, for example, that Smith's name did not appear in the DNC's attack pamphlet, *Who's Who in the American Liberty League.*[21]

People like Farley helped keep the door open, but none did more than Frances Perkins. She maintained a regular correspondence with Smith, even after he had broken with the New Deal. Al wrote back, but he would always address her as, "Dear Commissioner," even after she had become secretary of labor; that was the time and the role he remembered most fondly, so he continued to honor it, and she understood and sympathized. Roosevelt also delighted in this conduit, frequently asking Perkins, "How's the old governor?"[22]

This connection finally bore ripe fruit in 1941. Smith had decided to accompany a friend, Daniel Moody, to the graduation of Moody's son at Georgetown University. Some time before he left, however, he had enjoyed a social visit with "the Commissioner," and after that Frances Perkins mentioned Al's trip to FDR.[23]

On most occasions Roosevelt offered some polite message, but this time he got thoughtful; "You're very good, aren't you?" he asked, "You keep up the friendship." "I'm fond of him," Perkins replied. "I don't like him to feel he's got no friends of the old crowd." Too much time had passed to be angry now, and Franklin knew the moment when it was time to stop fighting and remember what counted. "Tell Al," he instructed Perkins, "that I think a lot of him and am grateful to him. I wish he would come down and see me. I honestly mean that."

Al was no easy sell; his pain really was the greater of the two. He grumbled and harumphed, needling Perkins, "You think he really means it?" She did.

Smith agreed to consider a visit, but once he got to Washington, he remained cautious. He called FDR's secretary, Grace Tully, telling her, "I'm in town for a short while and I'm simply calling to pay my respects to the President. I don't want a thing from him and I don't want to bother him. Just give him my best wishes."

You could hear the gruffness over the phone, feel the desperate need to be reached out to. Grace Tully did not become one of the most famous presidential secretaries for nothing, and before Al could erase his embarrassment by hanging up, she demanded, "Governor, where are you? I know the president will want very much to see you." Al told her he was at the Mayflower Hotel, but again insisted he "didn't want to bother the President," still torn between his need to restore the friendship and the fear of being hurt one more time.

But seconds after Tully got off the phone, Roosevelt rolled by in his wheelchair. When she told him about the conversation, FDR told her to get Smith on the phone "and tell him to come over." When she asked when to squeeze in the meeting, Roosevelt said, "Any time that's convenient for him"; and when she asked how much time to pencil in, the president replied, "Oh, as long as he wants—several hours."

So on June 9, 1941, for the first time since Franklin Roosevelt had become president, Al Smith stopped by with no congratulations on an inaugural, no appeal or message, just to talk. It did not last hours, but for these two men it meant reconciliation after many years.

And finally, by the end, he achieved peace with Franklin Roosevelt, the man and not the child. On August 4, 1944, months before his death, Al Smith was sitting on the porch of his friend John Coleman's summer house. Coleman's wife asked what should have been the most deadly question imaginable, "Governor what do you think of Roosevelt?" As their son, John, Jr., remembered it, this was a terrible indiscretion; "My father," he said, "could have killed her."[24]

But this was 1944, not 1928 or 1936. Smith took a puff on his cigar, waited—he had lost none of his timing—and replied, "He was the kindest man who ever lived, but don't get in his way." It was Al Smith at his best: funny, fair, and politically savvy.

⁂

The linchpin for all these changes was always Katie. She may not have been bold or brilliant, but she gave Al what he needed, security and love. Grandchildren used to spot the two of them walking on Fifth Avenue, and would giggle and gasp as Al reached out to take his bride's hand and stroll up the avenue with her; in later years they referred to the relationship as an "old-fashioned love affair."[25]

In late March 1944 Catherine Dunn Smith got sick and entered St. Vincent's Hospital. The official story was pneumonia, but the diagnosis, kept from Al, was cancer. Eventually he found out the horrible truth, and had to live through crises like the operation to try and save her by removing a tumor from beneath her windpipe. She survived that trial, but such strength could not last long. On May 4, after five weeks of care, Katie suffered a blood clot that took her life at 5:42 A.M. Two days later would have been the forty-fourth anniversary of their marriage.[26]

Al tried hard to deal with it, but could not. The night before he had stopped by at 5:00 P.M. as always to see her, and she looked fine ("coming along slow but sure" was how Smith's secretary described that visit), so the news the next morning devastated him. During the wake he remained secluded in the bedroom, his children carefully screening visitors. Marion Dickerman was one of those who saw him, and as often happens in grief, he remembered the small, special moments, like how when Katie took the Fifth Avenue buses, reaching the strap was difficult for this short, matronly woman. Al put his arms around Dickerman and cried, "Oh Marion—I want to thank you for giving her the seat on the bus." When they took the body out, grandson Arthur Smith, by then a young serviceman home on leave, remembered hearing Al in the other room, calling, "Katie, Katie. . . . Where are they taking Katie?"[27]

The Mass took place at St. Patrick's Cathedral, celebrated by Archbishop Francis Spellman, with five thousand in attendance and three thousand more outside on the streets. Even though Al sat with his offspring, grandson Walter remembered him being "slumped over all by himself," isolated by grief. When the governor walked down the steps of the cathedral, he moved in a trance, "like a shriveled old man." Grandson Arthur recalled that the only time he ever "really felt angry" regarding his grandfather's life and career (he was too young to remember 1928) was "the photographers rushing up to take pictures . . . when he looked so beat, just an old man, a tired man, grieving for his wife." After the burial service, Archbishop Spellman walked over and softly took his arm, saying, "Al, let's go home. It's time to go home."[28]

Al went back to the Empire State Building after that, attempting to handle the flood of letters and telegrams, a task eventually taken over by the Catholic Charities. Some of them were special, however, and had to be handled personally. Eleanor wrote of "her deepest sympathy," and added, "It must be a consolation to know that you always made her happy."[29]

But by this time the letter that mattered was the one from the president of the United States. Franklin Roosevelt telegraphed feelingly, "I am thinking about you in your great loss and wish it were in my power to do something to lighten a grief so overwhelming." He offered his sympathy and prayed, "May God bless and keep you." Two and a half weeks later Al replied, still writing, "Dear Frank," thanking him for the "kind telegram," and graciously noting that the president had "returned to good health again," and "I hope God will keep you that way." Even the grandchildren remembered that FDR's note was "beautiful" and that Al seemed "greatly touched by it."[30]

The *New York Times* editorialized, "The presses swarm with novels and romances. In none can be found anything half as pleasant and as touching as the game of cards that Mr. and Mrs. Smith played every night before bedtime." In marriages like that, neither partner can exist without the other. Al could not bear his loss, even asking his friend John Coleman if he could move in with that family. Coleman had to refuse, promising instead he could be over in five minutes, to "just call me anytime, day or night."[31]

On August 10, Al Smith became ill and entered St. Vincent's Hospital, under the care of Dr. Raymond Sullivan. His bedroom became a meeting ground for the business elite as John Raskob, Bernard Baruch, Pierre Du Pont, and John D. Rockefeller III all visited. On the night table, however, sat the regular telegrams Al received from Frank Roosevelt. From the Quebec conference, which opened the negotiations over how to divide postwar Germany, the president telegraphed that Al should "follow the doctor's orders," and sent along his "affectionate regards"; Roosevelt then ending with the line, "Winston is with me and joins heartily in good wishes."[32]

But Al Smith was a very sick man; the final cause of death would be an acute heart condition and lung congestion. John Rockefeller suggested to Emily Warner that they transfer her father to his Rockefeller Institute, where Smith could receive the most advanced care in the world. This occurred on September 25, but Rockefeller's doctors made no difference. On Saturday, September 30, Al Smith's situation became critical, and Bishop Francis McIntyre administered the last rites. Still, the governor held on, but when Arthur received another in a series of passes to come visit, his grandfather was already in a coma. "Umpah," Arthur gently called, "It's me." Emily tried to explain, "Father, this is Arthur. Arthur's come all the way from Fort Dix." But Al could not hear either of them; Arthur remembered that he leaned over and then, "I kissed him. . . . I don't think he knew I was there."[33]

Early in the morning on October 4, 1944, Emily, who had moved into 820 Fifth Avenue, got the call that her father was fading quickly. She rushed to the hospital, but arrived too late. At 6:20 A.M., by himself, Alfred Emanuel Smith died, less than three months short of his seventy-first birthday.[34]

Archbishop Spellman placed himself personally in charge of the funeral. He permitted the governor a rare honor, to lie in state in the center aisle at St. Patrick's overnight; Al was only the second layman to be allowed this distinction, the first having been the statesman Ignace Paderewski. From midafternoon the day before the funeral to opening ceremony the next morning, in dismal drizzling rain, 200,000 of the people Al Smith had been part of and had fought for, filed past his coffin. The next morning 7,000 mourners squeezed into the cathedral, with 35,000 more outside; all flags in the state stood at half-mast and would remain so for thirty days, by order of Governor Thomas Dewey. At 10:45 the family arrived, and took their places.

What followed, then, however grand the setting, was still a Mass, a ceremony Al Smith practiced all his life, one that comforted him. Once again, now over his body, came the sounds of *Kyrie Eleison,* of the epistle, the gradual, the offertory, the sanctus, and finally the consecration. In the end, there was still religion, but also, so much more.[35]

On the day Al Smith died, President Franklin Roosevelt released a statement that spoke of "the qualities of heart and mind and soul which . . . made him the idol of the multitude." "To the populace," the president explained, "he was a hero. Frank, friendly and warmhearted, honest as the noonday sun, he had the courage of his convictions, even when his espousal of unpopular causes invited the enmity of powerful adversaries."[36]

And this cost him. During Smith's "tenure as Governor of the great State of New York, he attracted national attention by his skill as an administrator. It was a natural sequence that he should become the candidate of his party for the highest office in the land. In a bitter campaign, in which his opponent won, Al Smith made no compromise with honor, honesty or integrity. In his passing the country loses a true patriot."

The Smith children loved that statement, but other tributes flooded in. By the end of 1944, the legislature in Albany passed a bill renaming the State Office Building for Alfred E. Smith. Then, in 1948 a housing project in the governor's old neighborhood, twelve seventeen-story apartment buildings that replaced slums, became the Alfred E. Smith Homes. Robert Moses started a campaign to build a memorial for his old boss there, and after the funds arrived, saw to the construction of an appropriate monument. The base of the site's flagpole, for example, had sculptures of birds and bears and deer, the creatures Al had loved since the days when he adopted his first monkey off the New York docks. In the center of the plaza stood a statue of the governor, proud and happy, derby in hand; on the altar to his side, the inscription read, "The greatest privilege that can come to any man is to give himself to the nation which reared him."[37]

The Diocese of New York also formed the Alfred E. Smith Foundation to support the Catholic Charities, whose leading fundraiser is the Al Smith Dinner each fall. In 1960, the man who would finally close the debt America owed Al Smith, stood up, and in those rich Hyannisport tones, proclaimed, "The bitter memory of 1928 will fade, and all that will remain will be the figure of Al Smith, large against the horizon." John Kennedy went on from there to the presidency, and to his own tragedy as well.[38]

Roosevelt's and Moses's and Kennedy's words were all noble, but Al Smith's appeal was always in part personal. Frances Perkins remembered how, during the gubernatorial campaigns, the behavior of the crowds at first surprised her, no matter how much she thought she knew about politics. "I recognized their liking him," she explained, "but they cried." Folks would rush out when Al Smith appeared, run to see him, and just cry, "tears rolling down the cheeks of many people." They did this for many reasons, but above all, because Al Smith had stood up and told everyone who could hear that honker of a voice, that these people—his people—had the right to be called Americans.[39]

Guide to Sources Used in Notes

AESOP   Alfred E. Smith Official Papers, New York State Archives, Albany, New York

AESPP   Alfred E. Smith Private Papers, New York State Library, Albany, New York

ASPNY   Al Smith Papers, Museum of the City of New York

CMP   Charles Marshall Papers, Library of Congress

CUOHC   Columbia University Oral History Collection, Columbia University

CUP   Citizens Union Papers, Columbia University

EKC   Edwin Kilroe Collection, Columbia University

ESBP   Empire State Building Collection, Drawings and Archives, Avery Architectural and Fine Arts Library, Columbia University

EWP   Emily Warner Papers, Georgetown University

FDR24   Franklin D. Roosevelt Papers—1924 Campaign Files, Franklin D. Roosevelt Presidential Library, Hyde Park, New York

FDR28   Franklin D. Roosevelt Papers—1928 Campaign Files, Franklin D. Roosevelt Presidential Library, Hyde Park, New York

FDRB   Franklin D. Roosevelt Papers—Business, Family and Personal Files, Franklin D. Roosevelt Presidential Library, Hyde Park, New York

GVNP   George Van Namee Papers, Diocese of Fresno

HHCT   Herbert Hoover Campaign and Transition Files, Herbert Hoover Presidential Library, West Branch, Iowa

JFP   James Farley Papers, Library of Congress

JRP   John Raskob Papers, Hagley Museum, Wilmington, Delaware

JWDP   John W. Davis Papers, Sterling Memorial Library, Yale University

JWP   James Wadsworth, Jr., Papers, Library of Congress

NMP   Norman Mack Papers, Buffalo and Erie County Historical Society

PDP   Pierre Du Pont Papers, Hagley Museum, Wilmington, Delaware

WLP   Walter Lippmann Papers, Sterling Memorial Library, Yale University

Notes

PROLOGUE

1. Michael Williams, *The Shadow of the Pope* (New York: McGraw-Hill, 1932), pp. 198, 215, 227; see also Materials in Box 57, JWDP.

2. Frances Perkins interview, Book 2, p. 686, CUOHC; Mr. and Mrs. Edmund Ford to Franklin Roosevelt, October 18, 1928, Box 11, FDR28; Opal Kunz to Pierre DuPont, August 10, 1928, Series A, File 1023-46, PDP; Box 58, JWDP.

3. *Baltimore Sun*, September 18, 1928, Box 12, CMP; Hugh Dorsey, "The Presidential Campaign of 1928 in Alabama," Ph.D. diss., University of Texas, 1961, pp. 212–13; Martin Feldman, "The Political Thought of Alfred E. Smith," Ph.D. diss., New York University, 1963, p. 125; John Buenker, *Urban Liberalism and Progressive Reform* (New York: Charles Scribner's Sons, 1973), p. 228; Spencer Murray, "The Role of Major Protestant Denominations in the 1928 Presidential Campaign of Alfred E. Smith," Ph.D. diss., Vanderbilt University, 1971, pp. 100, 108.

4. Charles Alexander, *The Ku Klux Klan in the Southwest* (Norman: University of Oklahoma Press, 1995), pp. 105, 199; Kenneth Jackson, *The Ku Klux Klan in the City* (Chicago: Ivan Dee, 1967), pp. 84, 237; David Chalmers, *Hooded Americanism* (Chicago: Quadrangle Books, 1965), p. 50.

5. Alexander, *Klan in the Southwest*, pp. 60, 66.

6. Edmund Moore, *A Catholic Runs for President* (New York: Ronald Press, 1956), p. 180; see materials in Folder 6, Box 19, Henry Johnson Papers, University of Oklahoma.

7. Wade Loofbourrow to James Tolbert, March 16, 1928, Folder 1, Box 36, James Tolbert Papers, University of Oklahoma; Williams, *Shadow of the Pope*, pp. 208–209.

8. Belle Moskowitz to James Tolbert, March 19, 1928, Folder 1, Box 36, Tolbert Papers.

9. The letter is in the archives of the Museum of the City of New York.

10. *New York Times*, September 21, 1928; Robert Wagner interview, p. 215, CUOHC.

11. Matthew Josephson and Hannah Josephson, *Al Smith* (Boston: Houghton Mifflin, 1969), p. 383; Alfred E. Smith, *Up to Now* (New York: Viking Press, 1929), p. 396; Charles Michaelson, *The Ghost Talks* (New York: Putnam, 1944), p. 155.

12. *Daily Oklahoman*, September 20, 1928; William Smith, "Alfred E. Smith and John F. Kennedy: The Religious Issue During the Presidential Campaigns of 1928 and 1960," Ph.D.

diss., Southern Illinois University, 1964, p. 208. One of the original tickets can be found in Box 11, John Roach Straton Papers, American Baptist Historical Society, Rochester, New York.

13. *Daily Oklahoman,* September 20, 1928; Smith, "Smith and Kennedy," p. 208; Smith, Smith and Kennedy, pp. 210–211; Elton Wallace, "Alfred E. Smith, the Religious Issue: Oklahoma City, September 20, 1928," Ph.D. diss, Michigan State University, 1965, p. 24.

14. There are several versions of the speech Al Smith made at Oklahoma City on September 20, 1928. I used the verbatim transcript that was recorded by a *New York Times* reporter and appeared in that paper on September 22, 1928. A more refined, cleaned-up version is in *Campaign Addresses of Governor Alfred E. Smith* (Washington, D.C.: Democratic National Committee, 1929), pp. 43–59. The version released to the press on September 21 is in Folder 311, Box 13, AESPP. In the account of Smith's speech, I also made use of Smith, "Smith and Kennedy," pp. 210–223; Wallace, "Smith, The Religious Issue," p. 24; Herbert Lehman interview, pp. 232–233, CUOHC; interviews with Anne Smith Cadigan, June 21, 1996, and Father Arthur Smith, June 28, 1996; and Michaelson, *Ghost Talks,* p. 155.

CHAPTER 1. THE SIDEWALKS OF NEW YORK

1. Data on population from Ira Rosenwaike, The *Population History of New York City* (Syracuse: Syracuse University Press, 1972), pp. 63, 67, 72.

2. James McCabe, Jr., *Lights and Shadows of New York Life* (Philadelphia: National Publishing Company, 1872), p. 683. See also the illustration on p. 20 of Kenneth Scherzer, *The Unbounded Community* (Durham, N.C.: Duke University Press, 1992).

3. McCabe, *Lights and Shadows,* p. 685; Robert Ernst, *Immigrant Life in New York City* (Syracuse: Syracuse University Press edition, 1994), p. 197; Stephen Crane, *Stories and Tales* (New York: Vintage Books, 1952), pp. 42–44; Alfred E. Smith, *Up to Now* (New York: Viking Press, 1929), p. 273; interview with Helen Graff, January 21, 1993.

4. Alvin Harlow, *Old Bowery Days* (New York: D. Appleton and Company, 1931), p. 354; Frank Oppel, ed., *Gaslight New York Revisited* (Secaucus, N.J.: Castle, 1989), p. 299; McCabe, *Lights and Shadows,* p. 699.

5. McCabe, *Lights and Shadows,* p. 191.

6. Harlow, *Old Bowery Days,* pp. 387, 403; Bill Harris, *Black and White New York* (Charlottesville, Va.: Thomasson-Grant, 1994), p. 24.

7. Harlow, *Old Bowery Days,* pp. 447–448.

8. Ibid., pp. 473–475; Smith, *Up to Now,* p. 49.

9. Gene Fowler, Beau James (New York; Viking Press, 1949), p. 42; Harlow, *Old Bowery Days,* p. 483.

10. Leslie Shaw, "The Seaport City in 1883," *Seaport* 17 (Summer 1983): 14.

11. Steven Jaffe, "A Trader in 'Brown Gold,'" *Seaport* 27 (Summer 1994): 44; Smith, *Up to Now,* pp. 23–24.

12. Alfred E. Smith, "Recollections of My Childhood," *Recreation* 33 (December 1939): 512; Emily Warner, *The Happy Warrior* (Garden City, N.Y.: Doubleday, 1956), p. 25.

13. Oscar Israelowitz, *Guide to the Lower East Side* (New York: Israelowitz Publishing, 1988), pp. 11–12.

14. Richard Stott, *Workers in the Metropolis* (Ithaca, N.Y.: Cornell University Press, 1990), pp. 71, 73; Hasia Diner, "Overview: 'The Most Irish City in the Union,'" in Ronald Bayor and Timothy Meagher, *The New York Irish* (Baltimore: Johns Hopkins University Press, 1996),

p. 92; Norman Hapgood and Henry Moskowitz, *Up from the City Streets* (New York: Grosset & Dunlap, 1927), p. 45.

15. "Appendix," p. 552 and John Ridge, "Irish County Societies in New York," p. 276, in Bayor and Meagher, *The New York Irish.*

16. Stott, *Workers*, p. 287; Ernst, *Immigrant Life*, pp. 194–196.

17. Charlie Chin, "Chinatown," in Kenneth Jackson, *The Encyclopedia of New York City* (New Haven, Conn.: Yale University Press, 1995), p. 215.

18. Unnamed, undated article in Box 1, EWP.

19. William McAdoo, *Guarding a Great City* (New York: Harper Brothers, 1906), pp. 145–146, 167–168.

20. Donn Neal, *The World Beyond the Hudson* (New York: Garland Publishing, 1983), p. 6.

21. Ibid., Smith, *Up to Now*, pp. 3, 4; Emily Smith Warner interview, p. 118a, CUOHC; George Van Namee Papers, Diocese of Fresno.

22. *Addresses of Alfred E. Smith* (New York: Friendly Sons of St. Patrick, 1945), p. 84; *New York Times*, September 2, 1928.

23. Depending on whether you trust the 1855 census or his death certificate.

24. All material on Alfred E. Smith's ancestry, unless otherwise noted, comes from the Alfred E. Smith Genealogical Material, Single Accession, New York State Library.

25. Joseph Marc Di Leo, "The Italian Connection," in Francis Femminella, *Italians and Irish in America* (Staten Island: American Italian Historical Association, 1985), p. 251.

26. Smith Genealogical Material, Single Accession; Di Leo, "Italian Connection, p. 249; Scherzer, *Unbounded Community*, p. 200.

27. Stott, *Workers*, p. 93; Graham Hodges, *New York City Cartmen* (New York: New York University Press, 1986), p. 6.

28. Hodges, *New York City Cartmen*, p. 179; Josephson and Josephson, *Al Smith*, p. 11; James Farley and James Conniff, *Governor Al Smith* (New York: Farrar, Straus & Cudahy, 1959), p. 41; Henry Pringle, *Governor Alfred E. Smith* (New York: Macy-Masius, 1927), p. 92.

29. Frank Graham, *Al Smith—American* (New York: Putnam, 1945), p. 7; Hapgood and Moskowitz, *Up from the City Streets*, p. 55; Josephson and Josephson, *Al Smith*, p. 25; *New York Evening World*, October 17, 1922.

30. Smith Genealogical Material, Single Accession.

31. Ibid.; Di Leo, "Italian Connection," p. 248; James Walsh, "Governor Alfred E. Smith," *Studies* 17 (June 1928): 198; Josephson and Josephson, *Al Smith*, p. 10.

32. Di Leo, "Italian Connection," pp. 248–249.

33. Josephson and Josephson, *Al Smith*, p. 9; Smith, *Up to Now*, p. 3; Richard O'Connor, *The First Hurrah* (New York: Putnam, 1970), p. 13.

34. Josephson and Josephson, *Al Smith*, pp. 10–11; Di Leo, "Italian Connection," p. 249; Warner, *Happy Warrior*, p. 25.

35. Frances Perkins interview, Book 1, p. 95, and Book 2, pp. 218, 216–217, CUOHC.

36. Ibid., Book 1, p. 95, and Book 2, pp. 218, 216–217, and Emily Warner interview, p. 3, both in the CUOHC; Joseph Proskauer, *A Segment of My Times* (New York: Farrar, Straus, 1950), p. 44; William Shannon, *The American Irish* (Amherst: University of Massachusetts Press, 1963), p. 153; Henry Moskowitz, *Alfred E. Smith* (New York: Thomas Seltzer, 1924), p. 23; Jerry Costello, *The Life of Al Smith* (New York: Avon Books, 1928), p. 26.

37. Stott, *Workers*, p. 92; Josephson and Josephson, *Al Smith* pp. 12, 13; Genealogical Mate-

rial, Single Accession; David Colburn, "Alfred E. Smith: The First Fifty Years, 1873–1924," Ph.D., diss., University of North Carolina at Chapel Hill, 1971, p. 20.

38. Interview with Father Arthur Smith, June 28, 1996; Di Leo, "Italian Connection," p. 245.

39. William Griffin, *The Book of Irish Americans* (New York: Random House, 1990), p. 271.

CHAPTER 2. NEIGHBORHOOD

1. Mary Shapiro, *A Picture History of the Brooklyn Bridge* (New York: Dover Publications, 1983), p. v.

2. *New York Evening World*, October 16, 1922; Alfred E. Smith, *Up to Now* (New York: Viking Press, 1929), p. 22; *New York Times*, May 26, 1933. For a picture that captures the relationship of the bridge to surrounding tenements, see Brendan Gill, "Seaport Neighbors," *Seaport* 17 (Summer 1983): 41.

3. Matthew Josephson and Hannah Josephson, *Al Smith* (Boston: Houghton Mifflin, 1969), pp. 23–24.

4. Robert Moses, "Al Smith—A Friend 'Looks at the Record,'" *New York Times Magazine*, January 21, 1945, p. 18.

5. "Passing of Tom Lee, Mayor of Chinatown," *Literary Digest*, February 9, 1918, pp. 78–81; *New York Times*, September 13, 1926; William McAdoo, *Guarding a Great City* (New York: Harper and Brothers, 1906), p. 171; John Tchen, "Quimbo Appo's Fear of Fenians," in Ronald Bayor and Timothy Meagher, eds., *The New York Irish* (Baltimore: Johns Hopkins University Press, 1996), pp. 126–27, 134–35.

6. Daniel Czitrom, "The Wickedest Ward in New York," *Seaport* 20: (Winter 1986–1987), 20–26; Charles Stelzle, *A Son of the Bowery* (New York: George H. Doran, 1926), p. 13.

7. Irving Allen, *Mean Streets* (New York: Oxford University Press, 1993), pp. 155, 157, 158; Steve Gilbert, "Tattoo," *Seaport* 29 (Summer 1995): p. 12.

8. Alvin Harlow, *Old Bowery Days* (New York: D. Appleton, 1931), pp. 398–399, 454; Elmer Bendiner, *The Bowery Man* (New York: Thomas Nelson, 1961), pp. 81–82; Allen, *Mean Streets*, p. 148.

9. See material in Committee of Fourteen Papers, Box 28, New York Public Library.

10. Material on prostitution, including quotations, from Timothy Gilfoyle, *City of Eros* (New York: Norton, 1992); Peter Gammie, "The Bards of Chatham Street," *Seaport* 27: (Spring 1993): 36.

11. *New York Times*, August 2, 1908.

12. Account of Sportsman's Hall from Martin Kaufman and Herbert Kaufman, "Henry Bergh, Kit Burns, and the Sportsmen of New York," *New York Folklore Quarterly* 28 (March 1972): 15–29.

13. Jimmy Durante and Jack Kofoed, *Night Clubs* (New York: Knopf, 1931), pp. 51, 89, 92.

14. George Chauncey, *Gay New York* (New York: HarperCollins, 1994), pp. 33, 90, 136, 162, 179, 198; Durante and Kofoed, *Night Clubs*, p. 50.

15. Interviews with Bernard Pisani, June 28, 1994; Helen Graff, January 21, 1993; and Hugh Carey, June 21, 1994.

16. Smith, *Up to Now*, pp. 25, 85; Robert Murray, *The 103rd Ballot* New York: Harper and Row, 1976), p. 58.

17. For a full discussion of these stages, see Chapters 5 and 6 of Slayton, *Back of the Yards* (Chicago: University of Chicago Press, 1986).

18. Arthur Bonner, *Alas? What Brought Thee Hither?* (Madison, N.J.: Fairleigh Dickinson University Press, 1997), pp. 17–18, 48.

19. In 1908 Smith moved his family to 25 Oliver Street, where he lived most of the rest of his life, raising his children there. It is now a National Historic Site.

20. Interviews with Bernard Pisani June 28, 1994, and Helen Graff, January 21, 1993.

21. C. W. Seaton, *Census of the State of New York, 1875* (Albany: Weed, Parsons and Company, 1877), pp. 38–39; John Billings, *Vital Statistics of New York City and Brooklyn* (Washington, D.C.: Department of the Interior, 1894), pp. 230–231.

22. Walter Laidlaw, *Population of the City of New York, 1890–1930* (New York: Cities Census Committee, 1932), p. 255.

23. *New York Evening World*, October 19, 1922; Frances Perkins interview, Book 3, pp. 344, 352, 356–357, and John O'Brien interview, p. 197, both in CUOHC.

24. *New York Herald*, September 3, 6, 1836; *New York Evening Star*, September 1, 1836.

25. The account of the founding of the American branch of the Ancient Order of Hibernians is surrounded by mystery and controversy, in part because there is so little documentation of early events. The standard source is John Dea, *History of the Ancient Order of Hibernians and Ladies' Auxiliary* (Philadelphia: National Board of the AOH, 1923), 2: 884–886. This was supplemented by material provided to me by the Ancient Order of Hibernians. The 1986 anecdote appears on a plaque on the front of St. James.

26. St. James Parish, *One-Hundred-Fiftieth Anniversary Book* (New York: Park Publishing, 1977), pp. 9, 11; John Shea, *The Catholic Churches of New York City* (New York: L. G. Goulding, 1878), pp. 390–404; Rev. Msgr. Florence Cohalan, *A Popular History of the Archdiocese of New York* (Yonkers, N.Y.: United States Catholic Historical Society, 1983), p. 60.

27. St. James, *Anniversary Book*, p. 11.

28. Shea, *Catholic Churches*, pp. 39–404; St. James, *Anniversary Book*, p. 12.

29. Emily Warner, *The Happy Warrior* (Garden City, N.Y.: Doubleday, 1956), pp. 13–14.

30. A picture of Father Kean appears in the St. James Union's *Silver Jubilee Celebration*, June 10, 1896, in the Wells Fargo Scrapbook, Item 6474, ASPNY; Frank Graham, *Al Smith–American* (New York: Putnam, 1945), p. 12; Hasia Diner, *Erin's Daughters in America* (Baltimore: Johns Hopkins University Press, 1983), p. 114; Richard O'Connor, *The First Hurrah* (New York: Putnam, 1970), pp. 19–20.

31. Shea, *Catholic Churches*, pp. 400–403; O'Connor, *First Hurrah*, pp. 19–20; Smith, *Up to Now*, p. 41; Colleen McDannell, "Going to the Ladies' Fair," in Bayor and Meagher, *New York Irish*, p. 238.

32. Shea, *Catholic Churches*, pp. 390–404; St. James, *Anniversary Book*, pp. 12, 17; Donn Neal, *The World Beyond the Hudson* (New York: Garland Press, 1983), pp. 87–88; interview with Helen Graff, January 21, 1993.

33. Pictures of the building appear in St. James, *Anniversary Book*, p. 15. Other observations are based on a personal tour I took one summer.

34. St. James, *Anniversary Book*, p. 12; Josephson and Josephson, *Al Smith*, p. 35; Al Smith, "The Song of the Shirt," *New Outlook* 161 (March 1933): 11.

35. New York's Catholic school system was highly decentralized at this time, with all pur-

chases made at the parish level. No records exist at St. James that would help us discover what books were bought and when.

36. William Swinton, *First Lessons in Our Country's History* (New York: Ivison, Blake and Company, 1872), pp. 103–104, 105, 106.

37. James Farley and James Coniff, *Governor Al Smith* (New York: Farrar, Straus & Cudahy, 1959), pp. 86–87.

38. *The Life and Battles of John L. Sullivan* (New York: Richard Fox, 1883), pp. 5, 6, 22.

39. Quoted in Richard White, "Frederick Jackson Turner and Buffalo," in James Grossman, ed., *The Frontier in American Culture* (Berkeley: University of California Press, 1994), pp. 11–12.

40. *New York Evening World,* October 17, 1922; Richard Lynch, *Alfred E. Smith—An Anthology* (New York: Vantage Press, 1966), p. 9; Walter Lippmann, *Men of Destiny* (New York: Macmillan, 1928), p. 4; Will Rogers, "The Illiterate Digest," February 8, 1931, clipping in the Empire State Building Scrapbooks, ESBP.

41. *New York Evening World,* October 20, 1922.

42. For a fuller discussion of the development of segmented communities, see Chapter 5 of Slayton, *Back of the Yards;* Emily Smith Warner interview, p. 5, CUOHC.

43. *Campaign Addresses of Governor Alfred E. Smith* (Washington, D.C.: Democratic National Committee, 1929), p. 121.

CHAPTER 3. THE F.F.M. MAN

1. Matthew Josephson and Hannnah Josephson, *Al Smith* (Boston: Houghton Mifflin, 1969), p. 47; Norman Hapgood and Henry Moskowitz, *Up from the City Streets* (New York: Grosset & Dunlap, 1927), p. 23.

2. Josephson and Josephson, *Al Smith,* p. 36; Alfred E. Smith, *Up to Now* (New York: Viking Press, 1929), pp. 39–40; Hapgood and Moskowitz, *City Streets,* p. 21; David Colburn, "Alfred E. Smith: The First Fifty Years, 1873–1924," Ph.D. diss., University of North Carolina at Chapel Hill, 1971, pp. 27–28.

3. Josephson and Josephson, *Al Smith,* p. 34; Robert Ernst, *Immigrant Life in New York City* (Syracuse: Syracuse University Press edition, 1994), p. 136; Tape 16, November 22, 1957, Frances Perkins Papers, School of Industrial Relations, Cornell University; interviews with Walter Smith, December 17, 1996, and Father Arthur Smith, June 28, 1996.

4. Smith, *Up to Now,* p. 40.

5. Material on pets and Smith's childhood comes from Volume 3 of the Empire State Building Scrapbooks, ESBP; Smith, *Up to Now,* pp. 19–20; James Farley and James Conniff, *Governor Al Smith* (New York: Farrar, Straus & Cudahy, 1959), p. 67; Josephson and Josephson, *Al Smith,* p. 23.

6. Hapgood and Moskowitz, *City Streets,* p. 20; Farley and Conniff, *Governor Al Smith,* p. 36.

7. Colburn, "Alfred E. Smith", pp. 21–22; Henry Pringle, *Alfred E. Smith* (New York: Macy-Masius, 1927), p. 87.

8. Colburn, "Alfred E. Smith," p. 26; *New York Evening World,* October 18, 1922.

9. *New York Evening World,* October 18, 1922.

10. Josephson and Josephson, *Al Smith,* pp. 41–42; Richard O'Connor, *The First Hurrah*

(New York: Putnam, 1970), p. 23; James Walsh, "Governor Alfred E. Smith," *Studies* 17 (June 1928): 198.

11. Josephson and Josephson, *Al Smith,* pp. 42–43.

12. Josephson and Josephson, *Al Smith,* p. 43; O'Connor, *First Hurrah,* p. 23; Robert Caro, *The Power Broker* (New York: Random House, 1974), p. 115; Smith, *Up to Now,* p. 7.

13. Smith, *Up to Now,* pp. 7–8; Josephson and Josephson, *Al Smith,* p. 43; O'Connor, *First Hurrah,* pp. 23–24.

14. Smith, *Up to Now,* p. 8; Josephson and Josephson, *Al Smith,* p. 43; Richard Stott, *Workers in the Metropolis* (Ithaca, N.Y.: Cornell University Press, 1990), p. 30.

15. Smith, *Up to Now,* p. 8; Josephson and Josephson, *Al Smith,* pp. 43–44.

16. The account of the blizzard of 1888 is drawn from John Maxim, "The Jim-Dandy Blizzard of 1888," *Seaport* 21 (Winter 1987–1988): 14–21, and Marsha Ackerman, "Buried Alive! New York City in the Blizzard of 1888," *New York History* 74 (July 1993): 253–276.

17. Farley and Conniff, *Governor Al Smith,* pp. 67–77.

18. Smith, *Up to Now,* p. 10; Emily Warner, *The Happy Warrior* (Garden City, N.Y.: Doubleday, 1956), pp. 28–29.

19. Frances Perkins interview, Book 2, pp. 216–217, CUOHC.

20. Leona Becker, "Alfred E. Smith: A Personality Study of a Political Leader," M.A. thesis, University of Chicago, 1938, p. 32.

21. Josephson and Josephson, *Al Smith,* pp. 40–41; Elisabeth Perry, *Belle Moskowitz* (New York: Oxford University Press, 1987), p. 219; Smith, *Up to Now,* p. 14.

22. Smith, *Up to Now,* p. 14; Jerry Costello, *The Life of Al Smith* (New York: Avon Books, 1928), p. 15.

23. Smith, *Up to Now,* p. 14; O'Connor, *First Hurrah,* pp. 26–27.

24. Material on the Fulton Fish Market comes from Leslie Shaw, "The Seaport City in 1883," *Seaport* 17 (Summer 1983): 15; Bruce Beck, *The Official Fulton Fish Market Cookbook* (New York: Dutton, 1989), pp. 3–29; interview with Richard Lord, June 22, 1991.

25. George Goode, *The Fisheries and Fishing Industry of the United States,* (Washington, D.C.: U.S. Commission of Fish and Fisheries, 1887), sec. 2, pp. vi–vii; Norman Browuer, "The Port of New York," *Seaport* 23 (Winter–Spring 1990): 14; Ellen Rosebrock, "The Old Fulton Markets," *Seaport* 14 (Winter 1981): 8–14.

26. Frank Graham, *Al Smith-American* (New York: Putnam, 1945), p. 20.

27. Interview with Richard Lord, June 22, 1991.

28. Farley and Conniff, *Governor Al Smith,* pp. 88–90.

29. Graham, *Al Smith,* p. 20; Smith, *Up to Now,* pp. 14–16; Warner, *Happy Warrior,* p. 30.

30. Graham, *Al Smith,* p. 20; Smith, *Up to Now,* pp. 14–16; Warner, *Happy Warrior,* p. 30; Robert Duffus, "Al Smith: An East Side Portrait," *Harper's* (February 1926): 321–322.

31. Pictures of Al Smith from this period can be found in the Museum of the City of New York, Portrait Archives Photos, image numbers 45.117.143 and 45.117.269, and *New York Evening World,* October 17, 1922; O'Connor, *First Hurrah,* p. 29.

32. Smith, *Up to Now,* pp. 36–37.

33. Ibid., pp. 37–38; Farley and Conniff, *Governor Al Smith,* pp. 91–93; Henry Moskowitz, *Alfred E. Smith* (New York: Thomas Seltzer, 1924), p. 246 (picture opposite page).

34. Oscar Handlin, *Al Smith and His America* (Boston: Little, Brown, 1958), p. 13.

35. St. James Parish, *One-Hundred Fiftieth Anniversary Book* (New York: Park Publishing Co., 1977), p. 17.

36. Hapgood and Moskowitz, *City Streets*, p. 26; Smith, *Up to Now*, pp. 42–43; Josephson and Josephson, *Al Smith*, p. 50.

37. Josephson and Josephson, *Al Smith*, pp. 48–49; Warner, *Happy Warrior*, p. 36.

38. Stories about the theater come from Smith, *Up to Now*, pp. 44–45.

39. Warner, *Happy Warrior*, p. 37.

40. Benjamin Woolf, *The Mighty Dollar*, n.d., pp. I—17, II—26, in the University of Texas at Austin library.

41. David Krause, ed., *The Dolmen Boucicault* (London: Dolmen Press, 1964), pp. 9, 10; Peter Thomson, ed., *Plays by Dion Boucicault* (Cambridge: Cambridge University Press, 1984), p. 6.

42. Krause, *Dolmen Boucicault*, p. 46; Michael Booth, ed., *English Plays of the Nineteenth Century* (London: Oxford University Press), 2: 165; Thomson, *Plays*, p. 19.

43. Smith, *Up to Now*, p. 43.

44. All data on Smith's theatrical career come from the Wells Fargo Scrapbook, Object 6474, ASPNY.

45. Josephson and Josephson, *Al Smith*, p. 53.

46. Warner, *Happy Warrior*, pp. 31–32; Graham, *Al Smith*, p. 20.

47. Details on the courtship come from Smith, *Up to Now*, pp. 62–63; Graham, *Al Smith*, p. 22; William Schofield, *Sidewalk Statesman* (New York: P. J. Kennedy & Sons, 1958), pp. 49–69; Hapgood and Moskowitz, *City Streets*, pp. 33–37.

48. Information on Katie's parents comes from her death certificate; *New York Times Magazine*, June 3, 1928, p. 3; *New York Evening World*, October 17, 1922.

49. The photo is number 45.117.152, Portrait Archives Photos.

50. For Katie's reticence about her first reactions, see *New York Times Magazine*, June 3, 1928, p. 3. Regarding Al's dating record, see Josephson and Josephson, *Al Smith*, p. 64.

51. Gene Fowler, *Beau James* (New York: Viking Press, 1949), p. 12; Edward Flynn, *You're the Boss* (New York: Collier Books, 1947), pp. 17–18; Ira Rosenwaike, *Population History of New York City* (Syracuse: Syracuse University Press, 1972), p. 58.

52. Hapgood and Moskowitz, *City Streets*, pp. 34–37.

53. Smith, *Up to Now*, pp. 62–63.

54. Colleen McDannell, "Going to the Ladies Fair," in Ronald Bayor and Timothy Meagher, *The New York Irish* (Baltimore: Johns Hopkins University Press), p. 243; records provided by St. Augustine's Church.

55. Josephson and Josephson, *Al Smith*, p. 66.

56. Warner, *Happy Warrior*, p. 41.

CHAPTER 4. "THE HALL"

1. The history of Tammany is drawn from the following sources, unless otherwise noted: Oliver Allen, *The Tiger* (Reading, Mass.: Addison-Wesley, 1993), pp. 2–50; Alfred Connable and Edward Silberfarb, *Tigers of Tammany* (New York: Holt, Rinehart, & Winston, 1967), pp. 21–25; M. R. Werner, *Tammany Hall* (Westport, Conn.: Greenwood Press, 1968), p. 1; George Olvany, "Tammany as a Patriotic Society," *Current History* 29 (November 1928): 252–264;

Edwin Kilroe, "The Early History of the New York Tammany Society," lecture given April 13, 1928, Box 14, pp. 1–30, 40–42, EKC.

2. Roy Peel, *The Political Clubs of New York City* (New York: Putnam, 1935), p. 32.

3. Allen, *The Tiger*, pp. 5–6; Connable and Silberfarb, *Tigers of Tammany*, photo section; *Political News* (May, 1926): 2; Don Seitz, "Tammany Hall," *Outlook*, June 2, 1926, p. 183.

4. Allen, *The Tiger*, p. 145.

5. David Hammack, *Power and Society* (New York: Columbia University Press, 1982), p. 100; Joseph McGoldrick, "The New Tammany," *American Mercury* 15 (September 1928): 3.

6. Luc Sante, *Low Life* (New York: Farrar, Straus, & Giroux, 1991), p. 265.

7. Peel, *Political Clubs*, p. 165; interview with Helen Graff, January 21, 1993.

8. Nathan Glazer and Daniel Patrick Moynihan, *Beyond the Melting Pot* (Cambridge: MIT Press, 1963), p. 228; Harry Roskolenko, *The Time That Was Then* (New York: Dial Press, 1971), pp. 195–196.

9. Peel, *Political Clubs*, pp. 320–321; Alfred E. Smith, *The Citizen and His Government* (New York: Harper & Brothers, 1935), p. 4; interview with Helen Graff.

10. Arthur Gorenstein, "A Portrait of Ethnic Politics," *American Jewish Historical Society* 1 (1961): 227. The Hooey quotation appears in Thomas Henderson, "Tammany Hall and the New Immigrants," Ph.D. diss., University of Virginia, 1973, pp. 237–238.

11. Thomas Henderson, *Tammany Hall and the New Immigrants* (New York: Arno Press, 1976), pp. 10, 166; *Tammany Times*, September 2, 1911.

12. Hartley Davis, "The Most Perfect Political Organization in the World," *Munsey's Magazine* 24 (October 1900): 67.

13. Werner, *Tammany Hall*, p. 504; Alvin Harlow, *Old Bowery Days* (New York: D. Appleton, 1931), p. 488.

14. Harlow, *Bowery Days*, pp. 512, 513; Sante, *Low Life*, p. 270; Daniel Czitrom, "Underworlds and Underdogs: Big Tim Sullivan and Metropolitan Politics in New York, 1889–1913," *Journal of American History* 78 (September 1991): 536. A picture of one of Big Tim's banquets, showing the enormous size of the event, appears on p. 87 of Susan Kismaric, *American Politicians* (New York: Museum of Modern Art, 1994).

15. Sante, *Low Life*, p. 268; Werner, *Tammany Hall*, pp. 504–505; Henderson, *Tammany Hall*, pp. 6–7; George Walsh, *Gentleman Jimmy Walker* (New York: Praeger, 1974), p. 24.

16. Sante, *Low Life*, pp. 270–271; Werner, *Tammany Hall*, pp. 506–507; Harlow, *Bowery Days*, pp. 518–520; Elmer Bendiner, *The Bowery Man* (New York: Thomas Nelson, 1961), pp. 76–77.

17. Sante, *Low Life*, pp. 272–273.

18. William Schofield, *Sidewalk Statesman* (New York: P. J. Kenedy & Sons, 1958), p. 23; "Foley, Last of the Old-Time Tammany Bosses," *Literary Digest*, January 31, 1925, p. 42; "Thousands Mourn the Passing of Thomas F. Foley," *Political News* (February 1925): 3–4.

19. "Thousands Mourn," pp. 3–4; Harlow, *Bowery Days*, pp. 503–504.

20. Interviews with Bernard Pisani, June 28, 1994, and Helen Graff, January 21, 1993.

21. *Tammany Times*, September 2, 1911; *New York Evening Telegram* article, n.d., EWP.

22. "Thousands Mourn," p. 4; "Foley," p. 44.

23. *New York Times*, January 17, 1942; Frank Graham, *Al Smith-American* (New York: Putnam, 1945), p. 29; Robert Duffus, "Al Smith: an East Side Portrait," *Harper's Magazine* 152

(February 1926): 322; Norman Hapgood and Henry Moskowitz, *Up from the City Streets* (New York: Grosset and Dunlap, 1927), pp. 40–41, 44–47; Henry Moskowitz, *Al Smith* (New York: Thomas Seltzer, 1924), p. 26.

24. Alfred E. Smith, *Up to Now* (New York: Viking Press, 1929), p. 50; Harlow, *Old Bowery Days*, p. 369; James Farley and James Conniff, *Governor Al Smith* (New York: Farrar, Straus & Cudahy, 1959), pp. 63–65.

25. Smith, *Up to Now*, pp. 50, 53; Graham, *Al Smith*, p. 174.

26. Smith, *Up to Now*, p. 59; Matthew Josephson and Hannah Josephson, *Al Smith* (Boston: Houghton Mifflin, 1969), p. 57.

27. Josephson and Josephson, *Al Smith*, p. 26; Smith, *Up to Now*, p. 55; George MacAdam, "Governor Smith of New York," *World's Work* 39 (January 1920): 237–238; item 6474, Wells Fargo Scrapbook, ASPNY.

28. Smith, *Up to Now*, p. 54; S. J. Woolf, "Al Smith at 60 Recalls Old New York," *New York Times Magazine*, December 31, 1933, p. 7; Louis Silveri, "The Political Education of Alfred E. Smith: The Assembly Years, 1904–1915," Ph.D. diss., St. Johns University, 1963, pp. 12–13.

29. Smith, *Up to Now*, p. 54; Silveri, "Political Education," p. 13.

30. Smith, *Up to Now*, pp. 54–55.

31. Ibid., p. 55; Silveri, "Political Education," pp. 13–14; Josephson and Josephson, *Al Smith*, p. 59.

32. The Wells Fargo Scrapbook is at location 6474; the *Incog* program is item 45.117.41 at location 6588, both in ASPNY.

33. Al Smith to Bessie Foley, January 24, 1925, and Bessie Foley to Al Smith, n.d., both in Box 22, George Graves Papers, New York State Archives, Albany, New York; *New York Times*, January 16, 17, 18, 1925.

34. Smith, *Up to Now*, pp. 56–57; Josephson and Josephson, *Al Smith*, pp. 62–63; Emily Warner, *The Happy Warrior* (Garden City, N.Y.: Doubleday, 1956), p. 40; Richard O'Connor, *The First Hurrah* (New York: Putnam, 1970), pp. 38–39.

35. Location 6474, Wells Fargo Scrapbook, ASPNY; Silveri, "Political Education," p. 16; *New York Evening World*, October 17, 1922.

36. Warner, *Happy Warrior*, p. 46.

37. Ibid., pp. 46–47.

38. Smith, *Up to Now*, pp. 65–66; MacAdam, "Governor Smith," p. 238.

39. Smith, *Up to Now*, p. 67; Warner, *Happy Warrior*, p. 47.

40. Smith, *Up to Now*, p. 66; MacAdam, "Governor Smith," p. 238.

41. Smith, *Up to Now*, p. 67; undated, unattributed article in the Walter Smith Personal Clippings Collection, McLean, Va.; Silveri, "Political Education," p. 19.

42. Eddie Cantor, *Take My Life* (Garden City, N.Y.: Doubleday, 1957), pp. 187–188.

43. Smith, *Up to Now*, pp. 67–68.

44. *New York Times*, November 5, 1903; Smith, *Up to Now*, p. 68.

CHAPTER 5. ALBANY

1. John McEneny, *Albany* (Woodland Hills, Calif.: Windsor Publications, 1981), p. 138; Cecil Roseberry, *Capitol Story* (Albany: State of New York, 1964), p. 82; William Kennedy, "The Capitol: A Quest for Grace and Glory," in *Capitol in Albany* (New York: Aperture Foun-

dation, 1986), p. 6; Matthew Josephson and Hannah Josephson, *Al Smith* (Boston: Houghton Mifflin, 1969), p. 70.

2. Roseberry, *Capitol Story*, pp. 74–75.

3. Ibid., pp. 24, 73, 100–110; McEneny, *Albany*, p. 139.

4. Ehrenkrantz Group, *New York State Capitol: Historic Structure Report* (Albany: Temporary State Commission on the Restoration of the Capitol, 1982), pp. 8–9; Roseberry, *Capitol*, p. 83.

5. Temporary Commission on the Restoration of the Capitol, *The Master Plan for the New York State Capitol* (Albany: Temporary Commission on the Restoration of the Capitol, 1982), p. 75; Roseberry, *Capitol Story*, p. 46.

6. Stuart Witt, "Modernizing the Legislature," in Robert Connery and Gerald Benjamin, eds., *Governing New York State* (New York: Academy of Political Science, 1974), p. 45; John Buenker, *Urban Liberalism and Progressive Reform* (New York: Charles Scribner's Sons, 1973), p. 18.

7. Material on the New York State legislature comes from Harold Gosnell, *Boss Platt and His New York Machine* (Chicago: University of Chicago Press, 1924), pp. 47–53, 125, 151–153.

8. Warren Moscow, *Politics in the Empire State* (New York: Knopf, 1948), pp. 53, 166–167. Data on the Assembly seats come from *Manual for the Use of the Legislature of the State of New York* (Albany: State of New York).

9. "Autobiography," handwritten document in Box 15, JWP.

10. Gosnell, *Boss Platt*, pp. 156–157.

11. Ibid., pp. 157–158, 262; Alden Hatch, *The Wadsworths of the Genesee* (New York: Coward-McCann, 1959), p. 164.

12. Richard O'Connor, *The First Hurrah* (New York: Putnam, 1970), p. 53; George Martin, *Madame Secretary* (Boston: Houghton Mifflin, 1976), p. 80.

13. *Journal of the Assembly of the State of New York, 1904* (Albany: J. B. Lyon, 1904), pp. 26–44, 51; Alfred E. Smith, *Up to Now* (New York: Viking Press, 1929), pp. 74–75.

14. Louis Silveri, "The Political Education of Alfred E. Smith: The Assembly Years, 1904–1915," Ph.D., diss., St. Johns University, 1963, p. 20; *New York Evening World*, October 17, 1922; O'Connor, *First Hurrah*, p. 55; Josephson and Josephson, *Al Smith*, p. 72.

15. Josephson and Josephson, *Al Smith*, pp. 76–77; State of New York, *Public Papers of Alfred E. Smith, Fourth Term, 1927* (Albany: J. B. Lyon, 1937), p. 466; Lawrence Veiller interview, p. 210, CUOHC; interview with Hugh Carey, June 21, 1994.

16. Milton Rakove, *Don't Make No Waves, Don't Back No Losers* (Bloomington: Indiana University Press, 1975), pp. 6–7.

17. Edmund Terry, "How Murphy Works," *Harpers' Weekly*, October 18, 1913, p. 22; Henry Pringle, *Alfred E. Smith* (New York: Macy-Masius, 1927), p. 133. Bryce is quoted in Thomas Schick, "The New York State Constitutional Convention of 1915 and the Modern State Governor," Ph.D., diss., New York University, 1976, pp. 35–36.

18. Smith, *Up to Now*, p. 76; Silveri, "Political Education," p. 32; material on total number of Assembly votes provided by the New York State Library; Ray Tucker, "The Story of Al Smith," *American Review of Reviews* 77 (February 1928): 156.

19. Alfred E. Smith, "Electioneering, Old and New," *Saturday Evening Post*, August 30, 1930, p. 10.

20. Alfred E. Smith, "Spellbinding," *Saturday Evening Post,* May 24, 1930, p. 3; Samuel Dickstein interview, p. 10, CUOHC; Smith, "Electioneering," p. 10; interview with Bernard Pisani, June 28, 1994.

21. Figures on elections come from a chart in the appendix of Leona Becker, "Alfred E. Smith: A Personality Study of a Political Leader," M.A. thesis, University of Chicago, 1938.

22. Pringle, *Alfred E. Smith,* p. 142; Silveri, "Political Education," p. 34.

23. Roseberry, *Capitol Story,* p. 3; Smith, *Up to Now,* p. 72; interview with Emily Smith Warner, p. 13, CUOHC.

24. Ray Tucker, "The Story of Al Smith," *American Review of Reviews* 77 (February 1928): 156.

25. Smith, *Up to Now,* p. 75.

26. Pictures of the old New York State Library, destroyed by a fire in 1911, appear in Roseberry, *Capitol Story,* p. 54, and Temporary State Commission on the Restoration of the Capitol, *Proceedings of the New York State Capitol Symposium* (Albany: Temporary State Commission on the Restoration of the Capitol, 1983), p. 169; Robert Caro, *The Power Broker* (New York: Random House, 1974), p. 120; Norman Hapgood and Henry Moskowitz, *Up from the City Streets* (New York: Grosset and Dunlap, 1927), pp. 58–59; Emily Warner, *The Happy Warrior* (Garden City, N.Y.; Doubleday, 1956), p. 52; O'Connor, *First Hurrah,* p. 59; Pringle, *Alfred E. Smith,* p. 150; Smith, *Up to Now,* p. 345.

27. Pringle, *Alfred E. Smith,* pp. 141–142.

28. Material on James Wadsworth, Jr., is compiled from Martin Fausold, *James W. Wadsworth, Jr.: The Gentleman from New York* (Syracuse: Syracuse University Press, 1975); Henry Holthusen, *James W. Wadsworth,* Jr. (New York: Putnam, 1926); and Hatch, *The Wadsworths.*

29. Holthusen, *Wadsworth,* pp. 179–180.

30. Interview with Emily Smith Warner, p. 12, CUOHC.

31. "Autobiography," p. 127, Box 15, JWP.

32. Ibid., pp. 142–143.

33. Ibid., pp. 138, 139.

34. Ibid., p. 140.

35. Ibid., pp. 139–140; James W. Wadsworth, Jr., interview, pp. 66–68, CUOHC.

36. Silveri, "Political Education," pp. 34–38; Josephson and Josephson, *Al Smith,* pp. 83–84.

37. Josephson and Josephson, *Al Smith,* p. 84; Silveri, "Political Education," p. 38.

38. Pringle, *Alfred E. Smith,* pp. 150–151; see materials in box A-35, CUP; *New York Times,* February 23, 1906.

39. Silveri, "Political Education," pp. 47–48; Murlin, *The New York Red Book* 1907 ed. (Albany: J. B. Lyon, 1907), p. 15.

40. Silveri, "Political Education," pp. 53–54; David Colburn, "Alfred E. Smith: The First Fifty Years, 1873–1924," Ph.D. diss., University of North Carolina at Chapel Hill, 1971, p. 63; see materials in box A-35, CUP.

41. Silveri, "Political Education," pp. 54–55.

42. The account of the state library fire comes from Roseberry, *Capitol Story,* pp. 120–122; Smith, *Up to Now,* pp. 99–100.

43. *New York Herald,* no other date than 1911, Walter Smith Personal Clippings Collection, McLean, Va.; *New York Evening World,* October 18, 1922.

44. Smith, *Up to Now*, pp. 110–111.

45. J. Joseph Huthmacher, *Massachusetts People and Politics* (New York: Atheneum, 1959), p. 168; Emily Warner interview, p. 15, CUOHC.

46. *New York Herald*, no other date than 1911, Walter Smith Personal Clippings Collection; Harry Roskolenko, *The Time That Was Then* (New York: Dial Press, 1971), pp. 196–197, 199–200; Alfred E. Smith to Citizens Union, November 12, 1910, box A-35, CUP.

47. Warner, *Happy Warrior*, pp. 18–19.

48. Interviews with Helen Graff January 21, 1993, and Bernard Pisani, June 28, 1994; telephone interview with Joseph Hopkins, June 30, 1994.

49. Warner, *Happy Warrior*, p. 14; Smith, *Up to Now*, p. 84.

50. *New York Times*, March 31, 1909; Silveri, "Political Education," p. 62; interview with Hugh Carey, June 21, 1994; Colburn, "Alfred E. Smith," p. 90.

51. James Farley, *Behind the Ballots* (New York: Harcourt, Brace, 1938), p. 39; interview with Hugh Carey; Henry Moskowitz, *Alfred E. Smith* (New York: Thomas Seltzer, 1924), p. 33; Jonah Goldstein interview, p. 18, CUOHC.

52. Material on the Allds scandal comes from Colburn, "Alfred E. Smith," p. 65.

53. Colburn, "Alfred E. Smith," p. 68; Silveri, "Political Education," pp. 74–75.

54. Silveri, "Political Education," pp. 75–76; Warner, *Happy Warrior*, p. 61.

55. Colburn, "Alfred E. Smith," p. 74.

56. Franklin Roosevelt, *The Happy Warrior* (Boston: Houghton Mifflin, 1928), pp. 4–5.

57. Christian Gauss, "How Governor Smith Educated Himself," *Saturday Evening Post*, February 27, 1932, p. 109.

58. Josephson and Josephson, *Al Smith*, pp. 97–98; Silveri, "Political Education," p. 70; Price Fishback and Shawn Kantor, "The Adoption of Workers' Compensation in the United States, 1900–1930," working paper 5840, National Bureau of Economic Research, 1996, pp. 2, 49.

59. Frederick Binder and David Reimers, *All the Nations Under Heaven* (New York: Columbia University Press, 1995), p. 104.

60. Josephson and Josephson, *Al Smith*, pp. 1–3.

61. Citizens Union, *The Searchlight*, May 16, 1911, box A-35, CUP.

62. The account of Murphy comes from Nancy Weiss, *Charles Francis Murphy* (Northampton, Mass.: Smith College Press, 1968).

63. Alfred Connable and Edward Silberfarb, *Tigers of Tammany* (New York: Holt, Rinehart, Winston, 1967), p. 236.

64. M. R. Werner, *Tammany Hall* (Westport, Conn.: Greenwood Press, 1968), pp. 486–487.

65. "Peep into Murphy's Brain," *Literary Digest*, March 7, 1914, p. 517; Weiss, *Murphy*, p. 30; William Shannon, *The American Irish* (Amherst: University of Massachusetts Press, 1963), p. 82.

66. Hapgood and Moskowitz, *Up from the City Streets*, pp. 82–83; David Burner, *The Politics of Provincialism* (New York: Knopf, 1968), pp. 24–25; Robert Binkerd interview, p. 32, and John Lord O'Brian interview, p. 192, CUOHC; interview with Hugh Carey, June 21, 1994.

67. Edward Flynn, *You're the Boss* (New York: Collier Books, 1947), p. 21.

68. Edwin Levinson, *John Purroy Mitchel* (New York: Astra Books, 1965), p. 48; Isabel Paterson, "Murphy," *American Mercury* 14 (July 1928): 350.

69. David Hammack, *Power and Society* (New York: Columbia University Press, 1982), pp.

170–171. Thomas Henderson, "Tammany Hall and the New Immigrants," Ph.D. diss., University of Virginia, 1973.

70. Paterson, "Murphy," pp. 349–350.

71. J. Joseph Huthmacher, "Charles Evans Hughes and Charles Francis Murphy," *New York History* 46 (January 1965): 31–32, 38.

CHAPTER 6. THE TRIANGLE SHIRTWAIST FIRE

1. Nancy Green, "Sweatshop Migrations," in David Ward and Olivier Zunz, eds., *The Landscape of Modernity* (New York: Russell Sage Foundation, 1992), pp. 214, 218; "Triangle Shirtwaist Fire," *WNYF* (With New York Firemen) 2 (July 1941): p. 12.

2. Details on the Triangle Shirtwaist Fire come from Leon Stein, *The Triangle Fire* (Philadelphia: Lippincott, 1962), and Corinne Naden, *The Triangle Shirtwaist Fire, March 25, 1911* (New York: Franklin Watts, 1971).

3. Stein, *Triangle Fire*, p. 48; Naden, *Shirtwaist Fire*, p. 5; *New York Times*, March 26, 1911.

4. *New York Times*, March 26, 1911; *Los Angeles Times*, September 28, 1999.

5. *New York Herald*, March 27, 1911; Bruce St. John, ed., *John Sloan's New York Scene* (New York: Harper & Row, 1965), p. 520. The Sloan drawing can be found in the picture section of Stein, *Triangle Fire*.

6. Matthew Josephson and Hannah Josephson, *Al Smith* (Boston: Houghton Mifflin, 1969), pp. 124–125; Stein, *Triangle Fire*, pp. 207–208.

7. The account of this meeting comes from Stein, *Triangle Fire*, pp. 141–145,

8. The meeting between Al Smith and the Committee on Safety is described in George Martin, *Madame Secretary* (Boston: Houghton Mifflin, 1976), pp. 88–89.

9. Thomas Kerr IV, "New York Factory Investigating Commission and the Progressives," D.S.S. diss., Syracuse University, 1965, p. 22.

10. State of New York, *Preliminary Report of the Factory Investigating Commission, 1912* (Albany: Argus Company, 1912), 1: 13–16; J. William Gillette, "Welfare State Trail Blazer; New York State Factory Investigating Commission, 1911–1915," M.A. thesis, Columbia University, p. 18; Kerr, "Factory Investigating Commission," p. 22; Martin, *Madame Secretary*, pp. 110–111.

11. J. Joseph Huthmacher, *Senator Robert D. Wagner and the Rise of Urban Liberalism* (New York: Atheneum, 1968), p. 5; State of New York, *Report of Commission*, 1: 22–23, 2:5; Kerr, "Factory Investigating Commission," pp. 77–78.

12. David Colburn, "Alfred E. Smith: The First Fifty Years, 1873–1924," Ph.D. diss., University of North Carolina at Chapel Hill, 1971, pp. 32–33.

13. Kerr, "Factory Investigating Commission," p. 142.

14. Ibid., p. 147.

15. Ibid., p. 192; Martin, *Madame Secretary*, pp. 114–115.

16. Mary Chamberlain, "Children in Bondage," *Good Housekeeping* 56 (May 1913): 623, 624; Kerr, "Factory Investigating Commission," p. 197.

17. Kerr, "Factory Investigating Commission," pp. 165, 198.

18. Ibid., pp. 149–150; State of New York, *Report of Commission*, p. 24; Frederick Taylor to H. B. Woolston, October 1, 1913, Records of the New York State Factory Investigating Commission, New York State Archives. Taylor's response, incidentally, was pedantic, neurotic, and overly complicated.

19. Martin, *Madame Secretary,* p. 106.

20. Ibid., p. 109.

21. Letters between Smith and reform leaders are in the Records of the New York State Factory Investigating Commission. State of New York, *Public Papers of Alfred E. Smith, 1927* (Albany: J. B. Lyon, 1937), p. 459; Martin, *Madame Secretary,* p. 108.

22. Josephson and Josephson, *Al Smith,* pp. 130–131.

23. Frances Perkins interview, Book 1, p. 143, CUOHC. There are several versions of the story about Al Smith and the woman who worked at night. This one is drawn from Martin, *Madame Secretary,* pp. 119–120.

24. Louis Silveri, "The Political Education of Alfred E. Smith," Ph.D., diss., St. Johns University, 1963, pp. 97–98; Abram Elkus, unpublished ms., pp. III-37–38, 40–41, 43; Nancy Weiss, *Charles Francis Murphy* (Northampton, Mass.: Smith College Press, 1968), p. 82.

25. Abram Elkus, "Social Investigation and Social Legislation," *Annals of the American Academy of Political and Social Science* 48 (July 1913): 60; Hugh Clevely, *Famous Fires* (New York: John Day, 1957), p. 52; Frances Perkins, "Industrial Work: The Factory Inspector," in Catherine Filene, *Careers for Women* (Boston: Houghton Mifflin, 1920), p. 260; Colburn, "Alfred E. Smith," p. 17.

26. There are several versions of the actual text of his comments. This one comes from *Let's Look at the Record* (New York: Thistle Press, 1962), p. 7.

27. *New York Legislative Index, 1912,* "Assembly Bill Introductory #1582, p. 4; State of New York, *Second Report of the Factory Investigating Commission,* January 15, 1913, p. 333.

28. Fire Department of the City of New York, *Annual Report, 1912,* pp. 5, 9–10.

29. Assembly Members' Books, New York State Archives.

CHAPTER 7. LEADERSHIP

1. Committee of Fourteen to Alfred E. Smith, November 7, 1912, Folder 232, Box 10, AESPP.

2. Upstate Democrats protested the choice of Smith as Speaker and fought to have a person from their territory installed as majority leader. Instead they settled for a seat on the Ways and Means Committee. *New York Times,* January 1, 1913.

3. Alfred Smith, *Up to Now* (New York: Viking Press, 1929), p. 124; Emily Warner, *The Happy Warrior* (Garden City, N.Y.: Doubleday, 1956), p. 69.

4. *Journal of the Assembly of the State of New York, 1913* (Albany: J. B. Lyon, 1913), pp. 9–10.

5. Ibid., p. 2406. Both quotations come from Richard O'Connor, *The First Hurrah* (New York: Putnam, 1970), pp. 74–75.

6. Committee of Fourteen to Alfred E. Smith, April 19, 1913, Folder 232, Box 10, AESPP; Lawrence Veiller interview, pp. 101–104, CUOHC.

7. Material on the Sulzer fight comes from Jacob Friedman, *The Impeachment of Governor William Sulzer* (New York: Columbia University Press, 1939).

8. Ibid., pp. 84, 88–89.

9. Thomas Kerr IV, "New York Factory Investigating Commission and the Progressives," D.S.S. diss., Syracuse University, 1965, p. 103; Allen Nevins, *Herbert Lehman and His Era* (New York: Charles Scribners, 1963), p. 82; *New York Times,* June 30, 1913; Smith, *Up to Now,* p. 130.

10. Matthew Josephson and Hannah Josephson, *Al Smith* (Boston: Houghton Mifflin, 1969), p. 151.

11. Friedman, *Impeachment,* p. 167; Louis Silveri, "The Political Education of Alfred E. Smith: The Assembly Years, 1904–1915," Ph.D. diss., St. Johns University, 1963, p. 118.

12. Josephson and Josephson, *Al Smith,* pp. 152–153.

13. *New York Times,* April 1, 1915.

14. *New York Evening World,* October 16, 1922.

15. Thomas Schick, "The New York State Constitutional Convention of 1915 and the Modern State Governor," Ph.D. diss., New York University, 1976, pp. 66–69.

16. Pictures of delegates appear in Burton Hendrick, "Making Over New York's Constitution," *World's Work* 30 (September 1915), 545–558.

17. Philip Jessup, *Elihu Root* (New York: Archon Books, 1964), 2: 297.

18. Citizens Union, "Preliminary Report on Delegates," Box H-5, and *Searchlight,* October 30, 1914, Box A-35, both in CUP; David Colburn, "Alfred E. Smith: The First Fifty Years, 1873–1914," Ph.D. diss., University of North Carolina at Chapel Hill, 1971, p. 228.

19. Jonah Goldstein interview, pp. 19–20, CUOHC.

20. *Revised Record of the Constitutional Convention of the State of New York, 1915* (Albany: J. B. Lyon, 1916), pp. 345, 428; Louis Zuccarello, "The Political Thought of Alfred E. Smith," Ph.D. diss., Fordham University, 1970, p. 34.

21. *Revised Record,* pp. 3048–3050.

22. Robert Duffus, "Al Smith: An East Side Portrait," *Harper's Magazine* 152 (February 1926): p. 324; Josephson and Josephson, *Al Smith,* pp. 163–164.

23. Hendrick, "New York's Constitution," p. 556.

24. "Progress and Reaction at Albany," *Outlook,* August 25, 1915, pp. 949–950; Samuel Lindsay, "Constitution Making in New York: Industrial Relations, Conservation, Education," *Survey,* September 11, 1915, pp. 538–539; John Buenker, *Urban Liberalism and Urban Reform* (New York: Charles Scribners, 1973), p. 51.

25. Josephson and Josephson, *Al Smith,* pp. 167–169; Frederick Collins, *Our American Kings* (New York: Century Company, 1924), p. 14.

26. *Revised Record,* p. 2975.

27. Ibid., pp. 2974–2975.

28. "Outcome of the Constitutional Convention in New York," *Outlook,* September 15, 1915, p. 119; "The End of the Constitutional Convention," *Outlook,* September 22, 1915, p. 179; *Revised Record,* pp. 4324–4325; State of New York, *Public Papers of Alfred E. Smith, 1926* (Albany: J. B. Lyon, 1929), p. 881.

29. Frank Moore, "Constitutional Conventions in New York State," *New York History* 38 (January 1957): 14; Godfrey Hodgson, *The Colonel* (New York: Knopf, 1990), p. 80; "Insiders and Outsiders," *New Republic,* November 13, 1915, p. 35.

30. Geoffrey Ward, *A First-Class Temperament* (New York: HarperCollins, 1989), p. 506; Lawrence Tanzer interview, p. 46, CUOHC; Colburn, "Alfred E. Smith," p. 61.

31. Frank Graham, *Al Smith, American* (New York: Putnam, 1845), p. 69; Henry Moskowitz, *Al Smith* (New York: Thomas Seltzer, 1924), p. 42; James Cox, *Journey Through My Years* (New York: Simon & Schuster, 1946), pp. 332–333; Thomas Chamberlain interview, p. 129, CUOHC; William Schiefflin, executive secretary, Citizens Union, to Elihu Root, August 12, 1915, Elihu Root Papers, Box 134, Library of Congress; Jessup, *Root,* 2: 299, 304; New York, *Public Papers of Alfred E. Smith,* p. 883.

32. New York, *Public Papers of Alfred E. Smith,* pp. 879–880.

33. Henry Pringle, *Alfred E. Smith* (New York: Macy-Masius, 1927), p. 227.

34. Edward Flynn, *You're the Boss* (New York: Collier Books, 1947), p. 31.

35. *New York Times,* August 11, 13, September 2, 1915; Colburn, "Alfred E. Smith," pp. 99–101.

36. Box A–35, CUP.

37. All material from Boxes A-35 and W-56, CUP.

38. Eddie Cantor, *Take My Life* (Garden City, N.Y.: Doubleday, 1957), p. 188; Colburn, "Alfred E. Smith," p. 102; *New York Times,* October 23, 25, 1915.

39. *New York Times,* October 27, 28, November 4, 1915; Leona Becker, "Alfred E. Smith: A Personality Study of a Political Leader," M.A. thesis, University of Chicago, 1938, p. 186; Thomas Henderson, "Tammany Hall and the New Immigrants," Ph.D. diss., University of Virginia, 1973, pp. 261–268.

40. James Farley and James Conniff, *Governor Al Smith* (New York: Farrar, Straus, 1959), p. 141.

41. *New York Times,* December 29, 1915; Box 1, Emily Warner Papers; Alfred Connable and Edward Silberfarb, *Tigers of Tammany* (New York: Holt, Rinehart and Winston, 1967), p. 273; Alfred E. Smith to the Citizens Union, October 1, 1917, and Office of the Sheriff of the County of New York, "A Comparative Statement of Expenditures," both in Box A-35, CUP; Jonah Goldstein interview, pp. 586–588, CUOHC; Smith, *Up to Now,* pp. 42–43.

42. Al Smith to Harold Stokes, November 9, 1915, Folder 96, Box 3, Harold Stokes Papers, Sterling Memorial Library, Yale University; Colburn, "Alfred E. Smith," pp. 103–104; *New York Times,* March 31, 1913.

43. *New York Sun,* June 29, 1915; A large number of clippings and other materials from this period appears in Folder 740, Box 24, AESPP.

44. *New York Times,* June 13, 1915, November 22, 1916, January 21, 1917, July 20, 1917.

45. *Political News,* November 1, 1926, p. 4; Clifton Hood, *722 Miles* (New York: Simon & Schuster, 1993), pp. 187–188; Henderson, "Tammany Hall," pp. 166–168; *New York Times,* August 15, 16, 1917.

46. *New York Times,* October 20, 1917.

47. Ibid., November 7, 1917, August 6, 1928; Smith, *Up to Now,* pp. 159–160.

48. William Anderson interview, pp. 34–35, CUOHC; Alfred E. Smith speech, 1918, n.d., Folder 151, Box 6, AESPP.

49. *New York Times,* May 8, September 14, 1918.

50. Becker, "Alfred E. Smith," p. 70; Colburn, "Alfred E. Smith," p. 113; *New York Times,* October 24, 25, 1918.

51. *New York Times,* August 19, September 12, 13, October 4, 8, November 2, 1918; Paula Eldot, *Governor Smith* (New York: Garland Press, 1983), p. 15.

52. My thanks to Elisabeth Perry for clarifying the precise manner in which Belle Moskowitz joined the Smith campaign of 1928.

53. Rev. William Karg, "A Short Life of Mrs. Henry Moskowitz and Her Influence upon Governor Alfred E. Smith," M.A. thesis, St. Bonaventure University, 1960, p. 15.

54. Elisabeth Perry, *Belle Moskowitz* (New York: Oxford University Press, 1987), pp. 118–199.

55. Hood, *722 Miles,* pp. 190–192.

56. Ibid., pp. 192–193.

57. Josephson and Josephson, *Al Smith*, pp. 206–207.

58. Smith, *Up to Now*, pp. 164–165; Emily Warner, *The Happy Warrior* (Garden City, N.Y.: Doubleday, 1956), p. 96.

59. Warner, *Happy Warrior*, pp. 97–99.

60. Robert Wesser, *A Response to Progressivism* (New York: New York University Press, 1986), p. 237; George Martin, *Madame Secretary* (Boston: Houghton Mifflin, 1976), p. 141; Timothy Henderson, *Tammany Hall and the New Immigrants* (New York: Arno Press, 1976), p. 237; Jackson, "Prohibition as State Issue," p. 137.

61. Wesser, *Response*, p. 232; Thomas Foley to James Farley, December 2, 1918, Box 1, JFP.

CHAPTER 8. THE NEW GOVERNOR

1. Richard O'Connor, *The First Hurrah* (New York: Putnam, 1970, p. 103.

2. The story of the Smith's arrival in Albany comes from Emily Warner, *The Happy Warrior* (Garden City, N.Y.: Doubleday, 1956), pp. 100–101.

3. *New York Times*, December 31, 1918, January 2, 1919; *Albany Knickerbocker Press*, December 30, 1918. The inaugural address appears in State of New York, *Public Papers of Alfred E. Smith, 1919* (Albany: J. B. Lyon, 1920), pp. 7–8.

4. State of New York, *Public Papers of Alfred E. Smith, 1920* (Albany: J. B. Lyon, 1921), p. 642.

5. Joseph Proskauer, *A Segment of My Times* (New York: Farrar, Straus, Giroux, 1950), p. viii.

6. Louis Hacker and Mark Hirsch, *Proskauer* (University, Ala.: University of Alabama Press, 1978), p. 16.

7. Ibid., p. 14.

8. Proskauer, *Segment*, pp. 18–19.

9. Ibid., pp. 30–33, 120; Hacker and Hirsch, *Proskauer*, p. 23.

10. Interviews with Ruth Proskauer Smith July 27, 1995, Judge David Edelstein, October 16, 1996 and Anthony Smith, July 23, 1995.

11. Hacker and Hirsch, *Proskauer*, p. 25.

12. Interview with Anthony Smith, July 29, 1995.

13. Interviews with Ruth Proskauer Smith, July 27, 1995, and Anthony Smith, July 23, 1995; Joseph Proskauer interview, p. 16, CUOHC.

14. Material on Belle Moskowitz comes from Elisabeth Perry, *Belle Moskowitz* (New York: Oxford University Press, 1987).

15. Interview with Judge David Edelstein, October 16, 1996.

16. Geoffrey Perrett, *America in the Twenties* (New York: Simon & Schuster, 1982), p. 309.

17. Belle Moskowitz to James Farley, November 16, 1927, Box 1, JFP; Denis Lynch, "Friends of the Governor," *North American Review* 226 (October 1928): 421.

18. Joseph Proskauer interview, p. 107, CUOHC; Frank Graham, *Al Smith—American* (New York: Putnam, 1945), pp. 209, 220; Henry Moskowitz to Oswald Garrison Villard, January 9, 1933, Oswald Garrison Villard Papers, Houghton Library, Harvard University; Alfred E. Smith to Walter Lippmann, January 6, 1932, Series III, Box 102, Folder 1960, WLP.

19. Material on Robert Moses comes from Robert Caro, *The Power Broker* (New York: Random House, 1974).

20. Robert Moses to Joseph Wilson, July 27, 1927, and Joseph Wilson to Robert Moses, August 1, 1927, both in Folder 200–42, AESOP.

21. Interview with Hugh Carey, June 21, 1994.

22. Robert Moses, "Al Smith's America," *Atlantic Monthly* (April 1958): 74; Robert Moses interview, p. 14, CUOHC; Robert Moses, *A Tribute to Governor Smith* (New York: Simon & Schuster, 1962), p. 17.

23. Frances Perkins interview, p. 208, Book II, CUOHC; Perry, *Moskowitz*, pp. 120–121; Ellis Hawley, *The Great War and the Search for a Modern Order* (New York: St. Martin's Press, 1992), p. 37.

24. Perry, *Moskowitz*, pp. 120–121.

25. *Knickerbocker Press*, January 21, 1919, in Box 66, George Foster Peabody Papers, Library of Congress; State of New York, *Public Papers of Smith, 1919*, pp. 52–53.

26. State of New York, *Public Papers of Smith, 1920*, pp. 569–570.

27. "Report of Reconstruction Commission on Americanization," in State of New York, *Public Papers of Smith, 1919*, pp. 627–629. For the postwar repression, see Robert Murray, *Red Scare* (Minneapolis: University of Minnesota Press, 1955).

28. Alfred Smith, *Up to Now* (New York: Viking Press, 1929), pp. 172–173; Matthew Josephson and Hannah Josephson, *Al Smith* (Boston: Houghton Mifflin, 1969), p. 212.

29. George Martin, *Madame Secretary* (Boston: Houghton Mifflin, 1976), pp. 141–142.

30. George Chandler interview, pp. 70–72, CUOHC; George Chandler to Arthur Pierson, December 18, 1920, Folder 260–79, AESOP.

31. State Archives and Records Administration, New York State, "The Lusk Committee: A Guide to the Records of the Joint Legislative Committee to Investigate Seditious Activities," pp. 5–6.

32. *New York Times*, May 8, June 21, 1919.

33. Paula Eldot, *Governor Alfred E. Smith* (New York: Garland Press, 1983), pp. 316–317; Louisa Lasker, "Back in the Districts," *Survey*, March 20, 1920, p. 768; Murray, *Red Scare*, pp. 236–237.

34. State of New York, *Public Papers of Smith, 1920*, p. 581.

35. Eldot, *Governor Smith*, pp. 319–320; Proskauer, *Segment*, p. 168; E. J. Kahn, Jr., *The World of Swope* (New York: Simon & Schuster, 1965), p. 239.

36. Edward Murlin, *The New York Red Book*, 1920 ed. (Albany: J. B. Lyon), pp. 20–21; Eldot, *Governor Smith*, pp. 320–321.

37. Eldot, *Governor Smith*, pp. 321–322.

38. Rev. William Karg, "A Short Life of Mrs. Henry Moskowitz and Her Influence upon Governor Alfred E. Smith," M.A. thesis, St. Bonaventure University, 1960, pp. 34–35.

39. Ibid., p. 35; Eldot, *Governor Smith*, p. 322; State of New York, *Public Papers of Smith, 1920*, p. 582; Kahn, *World of Swope*, p. 239.

40. Eldot, *Governor Smith*, pp. 322–325.

41. Smith, *Up to Now*, pp. 204–205.

42. Ibid., pp. 205–206.

43. *New York Times*, February 24, 1920.

44. State of New York, *Public Papers of Smith, 1920*, p. 31.

45. Eldot, *Governor Smith*, p. 330.

46. State of New York, *Public Papers of Smith, 1919* p. 715; State of New York, *Public Papers of Smith, 1920*, p. 580.

CHAPTER 9. PICKING FIGHTS

1. Julie Miller, "To Stop the Slaughter of Babies," *New York History* 74 (April 1993): 160.

2. Ibid., pp. 160, 184.

3. "Report of the Fair Price Milk Committee of the City of New York," in State of New York, *Public Papers of Alfred E. Smith, 1920* (Albany: J. B. Lyon, 1921), pp. 77, 85, 87.

4. "Statement to the Legislature," April 7, 1919; "Preliminary Report of Commissioner Battle," October 9, 1919; Alfred E. Smith to the Council of Farms and Markets, October 9, 1919; all in Folder 260–148, AESOP.

5. Paula Eldot, *Governor Alfred E. Smith* (New York: Garland Press, 1983), p. 278; message from Alfred E. Smith to the legislature, January, 1919, Folder 260–148, AESOP.

6. State of New York, *Public Papers of Alfred E. Smith, 1919* (Albany: J. B. Lyon, 1920), pp. 36–37; Governor Smith in the Milk Problem, c. January 1919, Folder 260–148, AESOP.

7. Message to the Legislature, January 1919; Alfred E. Smith to the Department of Farms and Markets, January 16, 1919; Governor Smith on the Milk Problem, c. January, 1919; message to the legislature, April 7, 1919; press release on the Fair Price Milk Committee, August 27, 1919; Alfred E. Smith to the Council of Farms and Markets, October 9, 1919; George Gordon Battle, "Final Report," December 12, 1919; Alfred E. Smith to George Perkins, November 11, 1919, all in Folder 260–148, AESOP; *New York Times* January 17, 1919.

8. Raymond Potter, "Royal Samuel Copeland, 1868–1938: A Physician in Politics," Ph.D. diss., Western Reserve University, 1967, p. 251; W. A. Swanberg, *Citizen Hearst* (New York: Bantam Books, 1961), pp. 365–366, 375–376; Richard O'Connor, *The First Hurrah* (New York: Putnam, 1970), p. 108.

9. O'Connor, *First Hurrah*, pp. 108–109; Emily Smith Warner interview, pp. 18–19, CUOHC.

10. Geoffrey Perrett, *America in the Twenties* (New York: Simon & Schuster, 1982), p. 310

11. The cartoons from the March 19, 1920, *New York World* and from the August 12, 1919, *New York American* appear in Folder 260–148, AESOP, as does Alfred E. Smith to A. Berg, August 2, 1919; O'Connor, *First Hurrah*, p. 110; Emily Warner interview, p. 19, CUOHC; Eldot, *Governor Smith*, pp. 280–281.

12. Letters appear in Box 20, AESPP.

13. *New York Times*, October 19, 1919.

14. Ibid., October 27, 28, 1919; Swanberg, *Citizen Hearst*, p. 390; O'Connor, *First Hurrah*, p. 111.

15. Henry Pringle, *Alfred E. Smith* (New York: Macy-Masius, 1917), p. 29.

16. The official version of the Carnegie Hall speech appears in State of New York, *Public Papers of Smith, 1919*, pp. 776–785; *New York Times*, October 30, 1919.

17. State of New York, *Public Papers of Smith, 1919*, p. 777; Pringle, *Alfred E. Smith*, pp. 29–31; Matthew Josephson and Hannah Josephson, *Al Smith* (Boston: Houghton Mifflin, 1969), p. 250; *New York Times*, October 30, 1919.

18. *New York Times*, June 16, 1920.

19. Memo regarding Belle Moskowitz, 1920, Box 453, Edward Bernays Papers, Library of Congress.

20. Ibid., pp. 73, 79.

21. Emily Warner, *The Happy Warrior* (Garden City, N.Y.: Doubleday, 1956), p. 124; David Colburn, "Alfred E. Smith: The First Fifty Years, 1873–1924", Ph.D. diss., University of North Carolina 1971, p. 153.

22. Henry Moskowitz, *Alfred E. Smith* (New York: Thomas Seltzer, 1924), pp. 306–307.

23. Alfred E. Smith, *Up to Now* (New York: Viking Press, 1929), p. 210.

24. "How 'The Sidewalks' Became Smith's Song," *Literary Digest*, June 2, 1934, p. 9; *Addresses of Alfred E. Smith* (New York: Society of the Friendly Sons of St. Patrick, 1945), pp. 56–57; William Manchester, *Disturber of the Peace* (New York: Harper and Brothers), p. 147; Moskowitz, *Smith*, pp. 307–308; Geoffrey Ward, *A First-Class Temperament* (New York: HarperCollins, 1989), p. 508.

25. Society of St. Patrick, *Addresses*, p. 57; Smith, *Up to Now*, p. 210.

26. *New York Times*, July 1, 1920; Smith, *Up to Now*, p. 209.

27. Eldot, *Governor Smith*, p. 16; Colburn, "Alfred E. Smith," p. 159.

28. "Address by Governor Alfred E. Smith Accepting Renomination as Governor," September 24, 1920, p. 14, Box 11, Folder 255, AESPP.

29. Donn Neal, *The World Beyond the Hudson* (New York: Garland Press, 1983), p. 103; Pringle, *Alfred E. Smith*, p. 249; Josephson and Josephson, *Al Smith*, p. 257.

30. Joseph Proskauer, *A Segment of My Times* (New York: Farrar Straus, 1950), p. 43; Josephson and Josephson, *Al Smith*, pp. 257–258. See also the correspondence between Proskauer and George McClellan, Jr., Box 5, George McClellan, Jr., Papers, Library of Congress.

31. Eldot, *Governor Smith*, pp. 15, 287–288; *New York Times*, October 28, 1920.

32. Robert Caro, *The Power Broker* (New York: Random House, 1974), p. 111; Leona Becker, "Alfred E. Smith," M.A. thesis, University of Chicago, 1938, p. 188; Thomas Henderson, *Tammany Hall and the New Immigrants* (New York: Arno Press, 1976), p. 248.

33. Robert Lansing to Alfred E. Smith, November 4, 1920, in the personal possession of Anne Cadigan; Smith, *Up to Now*, p. 220; Bourke Cockran to Alfred E. Smith, December 9, 1920, Box 2, William Bourke Cockran Papers, New York Public Library.

34. *New York Times*, December 13, 1920; *Moody's Analyses of Investments* (New York: Moody's Investors Service, 1921), p. 1378.

35. O'Connor, *First Hurrah*, pp. 127–129.

36. *New York Times*, December 13, 1920. See also the picture of Smith at the helm of a U.S. Trucking Company vehicle, photo 45.117.181, Portrait Archives—Photos, Museum of the City of New York.

37. *New York Times*, December 13, 1920; Smith, *Up to Now*, p. 223; *Moody's Analyses of Investments* (New York: Moody's Investors Services, 1923), p. 1438.

38. *New York Times*, May 11, 1928; Dennis Lynch, "Friends of the Governor," *North American Review* (October 1928): 428; Oscar Handlin, *Al Smith and His America* (Boston: Little, Brown, 1958), pp. 87–88; Josephson and Josephson, *Al Smith*, p. 261.

39. John Tauranac, *The Empire State Building* (New York: Scribners, 1995), p. 91. There is a picture of the Tiger Room cronies on p. 8 of the April 1928 edition of *Political News*, a Tammany organ. Details of the Tiger Room are drawn from personal observation of the facilities.

40. Smith, *Up to Now*, pp. 223–225; Robert Moses, "Al Smith's America," *Atlantic Monthly* (April 1958): 73; Alfred Smith to James Farley, January 11, 1921, Box 1, JFP; *New York Times*,

January 4, October 31, 1921, January 11, July 21, 1922; Alfred E. Smith to Marion Dickerman, January 17, 1922, Folder 2, Box 6, Marion Dickerman Papers, Franklin D. Roosevelt Presidential Library.

41. Pringle, *Smith*, pp. 44–45.

42. Warner, *Happy Warrior*, p. 132; *New York Times*, April 7, 1922.

43. Pringle, *Smith*, p. 45; *New York World*, September 30, 1922.

44. Warner, *Happy Warrior*, p. 132; Smith, *Up to Now*, p. 229.

45. The "Al" and "Frank" letters are on pp. 230–232 of Smith, *Up to Now*.

46. The account of the Cockran meeting comes from James Farley, *Behind the Ballots* (New York: Harcourt, Brace, 1938), pp. 36–37 and from a memo in the Private Files, Box 37, JFP.

47. Warner, *Happy Warrior*, pp. 136–137; memo in the Private Files, Box 37, JFP; *New York Times*, October 1, 1922.

48. *New York Times*, October 10, 1922.

49. Colburn, "Smith," p. 169; "Two Significant Political Conventions" *Outlook*, October 11, 1922, p. 229; Smith, *Up to Now*, pp. 236–237; J. Stanley Lemons, *The Woman Citizen* (Urbana: University of Illinois Press, 1973), pp. 98–99.

50. Walter Arndt to Alfred E. Smith, October 3, 1922, Box A-35, CUP; Warner, *Happy Warrior*, p. 138.

51. *New York Times*, November 1, 1922.

52. Ibid., October 31, November 6, 1922.

53. Becker, "Smith," p. 188; State of New York, *Public Papers of Alfred E. Smith, 1924* (Albany: J. B. Lyon, 1926), p. 534; *Political News* (November, 1922): 22.

54. Henderson, *Tammany Hall*, p. 265.

55. *Political News* (December 1923): p. 14.

56. *New York World*, September 30, 1922, *New York Times*, November 8, 1922.

CHAPTER 10. WINNING ADMINISTRATIVE REFORM

1. Account of Al's arrival and the inauguration comes from *New York Times*, December 17, 29, 1922, January 2, 1923; "Governor Smith and His Programme," *Outlook*, January 17, 1923, p. 120; Kolin Hagar interview, p. 8, CUOHC.

2. State of New York, *Public Papers of Alfred E. Smith, 1923* (Albany: J. B. Lyon, 1924), pp. 9–11.

3. Material on New York State comes from Robert Wesser, *A Response to Progressivism* (New York: New York University Press, 1986), pp. 2–3; State of New York Handbook to Delegates to the 1928 Democratic Convention, pp. 3–4, in GVNP; Lillian Symes, "Such Things Can Be," *Survey*, April 15, 1927, p. 93.

4. Paula Eldot, *Governor Alfred E. Smith* (New York: Garland Publishing, 1983), pp. 27–76.

5. Material on the history of New York State government comes from David Ellis, et al., *A Short History of New York State* (Ithaca: Cornell University Press, 1957), pp. 351–353.

6. Oscar Handlin, *Al Smith and His America* (Boston: Little, Brown, 1958), p. 95.

7. *Speeches of Hon. Alfred E. Smith and Hon. Charles Evans Hughes at the City Club of New York*, December 8, 1919, p. 8, in the collection of the New York Public Library.

8. State of New York, *Public Papers of Alfred E. Smith, 1920* (Albany: J. B. Lyon, 1921), p. 617; "Speech of Governor Smith Before the New York League of Women Voters," January 16, 1923, pp. 3, 4, Folder 260, Box 11, AESPP.

9. State of New York, *Public Papers of Alfred E. Smith, 1924* (Albany: J. B. Lyon, 1926), p. 600.

10. State of New York, *Public Papers of Alfred E. Smith, 1919* (Albany: J. B. Lyon, 1920), p. 105.

11. Frances Perkins, "Al Smith As I Knew Him," November 22, 1957, p. 3, Tape 16, Frances Perkins Papers, School of Industrial Relations, Cornell University.

12. Eldot, *Governor Smith*, pp. 75, 76, 78, 99; speech in Schenectady, April 28, 1923, Folder 272, Box 11, AESPP; Elton Wallace, "Alfred E. Smith, the Religious Issue: Oklahoma City, September 20, 1928," Ph.D. diss., Michigan State University, 1965, p. 126; Alfred E. Smith, *Up to Now* (New York: Viking Press, 1929, p. 352; *The New York Red Book*, 1924 ed. (Albany: J. B. Lyon, 1924), p. 55.

13. Henry Moskowitz, *Alfred E. Smith* (New York: Thomas Seltzer, 1924), pp. 145–147. The Dewey quote comes from James Crown, "The Development of Democratic Government in the State of New York Through the Growth of the Power of the Executive Since 1920," Ph.D. diss., New York University, 1955, p. 131.

14. Discussion of how administrative reform got passed comes from Ellis et al., *Short History of New York*, pp. 400–401, and from "Reorganization," Folder 167, Box 7, AESPP.

15. "Speech Before the New York League of Women Voters," p. 6.

16. *New York State Women's Democratic News* (September 1925) 1, vertical file, Franklin D. Roosevelt Presidential Library; John Buenker, *Urban Liberalism and Progressive Reform* (New York: Charles Scribner's Sons, 1973), pp. 14–125.

17. Eldot, Governor Smith, pp. 52–53.

18. Ibid., pp. 43, 53.

19. Kenneth Davis, *FDR: The New York Years* (New York: Random House, 1979), p. 80; "Governors as State Bosses," *New Republic*, March 17, 1926, p. 85; Warren Moscow, *Politics in the Empire State* (New York: Knopf, 1948), p. 11.

20. "'Al' Smith, Hypnotist," *Nation*, April 8, 1925, p. 372.

21. *New York Times*, December 30, 1922, August 3, 1927.

22. Claude Bower, *My Life* (New York: Simon & Schuster, 1962), p. 175; State of New York, *Public Papers of Smith, 1920*, p. 619; David Colburn, "Alfred E. Smith: The First Fifty Years, 1873–1924," Ph.D. diss., University of North Carolina, 1971, p. 197.

23. State of New York, *Public Papers of Alfred E. Smith, 1925*, (Albany: J. B. Lyon, 198), p. 732.

24. George Martin, *Madame Secretary* (Boston: Houghton Mifflin, 1976), p. 185; State of New York, *Public Papers of Alfred E. Smith, 1926* (Albany: J. B. Lyon, 1929), pp. 644–645.

25. Donn Neal, *The World Beyond the Hudson* (New York: Garland Press, 1983), p. 44.

26. Leona Becker, "Alfred E. Smith: A Personality Study of a Political Leader," M.A. thesis, University of Chicago, 1938, pp. 136–137; Norman Hapgood and Henry Moskowitz, *Up from the City Streets* (New York: Harcourt, Brace, 1927), p. 70; Henry Pringle, *Alfred E. Smith* (New York: Macy–Masius, 1927), p. 211; Martin, *Madame Secretary*, p. 92; William White, *Masks in a Pageant* (New York: Macmillan, 1928), pp. 463–464; interview with Judge David Edelstein October 16, 1996; *New York Times*, June 25, 1928; Lithgow Osbourne interview, p. 164, CUOHC.

27. Hapgood and Moskowitz, *Up from the City Streets*, p. 217; Becker, "Smith," p. 54; Pringle, *Smith*, p. 29; James Jones, "An Analysis of Alfred E. Smith's Speaking Using Aristo-

tle's and Toumlin's Systems of Argument," M.A. thesis, Cornell University, 1965, p. 46; interview with Ruth Proskauer Smith, July 27, 1995.

28. Interview with Hugh Carey, July 10, 1994; Raymond Moley, *27 Masters of Politics* (New York: Funk and Wagnalls, 1949), p. 59; Smith, *Up to Now*, p. 142.

29. *New York Post*, November 6, 1915, Box 1, EWP; Joseph Van Raalte, "Al Smith and His Hard–Boiled Hat," *New York World*, November 1, 1922; Gene Fowler, *Beau James* (New York: Viking Press, 1949), p. 38.

30. William Shannon, *The American Irish* (Amherst: University of Massachusetts Press, 1963), p. 155; *New York Post* article, November 6, 1915, and *Knickerbocker Press* article, January 19, 1913, both in Box 1, EWP; Robert Moses, *A Tribute to Governor Smith* (New York: Simon & Schuster, 1962), pp. 13–14.

31. Interview with Judge Simon Rifkind June 27, 1994; Clinton Rossiter and James Lare, eds., *The Essential Lippmann* (New York: Random House, 1963), p. 493.

32. Pringle, *Smith*, pp. 184–185, 208–209; Hapgood and Moskowitz, *Up from the City Streets*, pp. 202–203; Frank Graham, *Al Smith—American* (New York: Putnam, 1945), pp. 142–143; Frances Stoddard interview, p. 108, CUOHC; Becker, "Smith," p. 95.

33. "Smith as an Administrator," *American Review of Reviews* 78 (October 1928): 384; Becker, "Smith," p. 101; Lillian Wald to Mary McDowell, September 27, 1928, Box 5, Lillian Wald Papers, New York Public Library.

34. Allan Nevins, *Herbert Lehman and His Era* (New York: Scribner's, 1963), p. 156; Colburn, "Alfred E. Smith," pp. 121–122; Cleveland Rogers, *Robert Moses* (New York: Henry Holt, 1952), pp. 60–61; Shannon, *American Irish*, p. 164; Hapgood and Moskowitz, *Up from the City Streets*, p. 176.

35. Jonah Goldstein interview, p. 18, CUOHC.

36. Frank Kent, "A Good Look at Al Smith," *Collier's*, March 3, 1928, p. 9; Alfred E. Smith to Herbert Bayard Swope, February 4, 1937, Single Accession, New York State Library, Albany, New York; Christian Gauss, "How Governor Smith Educated Himself," *Saturday Evening Post*, February 27, 1932, p. 22.

37. Kent, "Look at Smith," p. 9; Edward Flynn, *You're the Boss* (New York: Collier Books, 1947), p. 228.

38. *New York Evening World*, October 20, 1922; Alfred E. Smith to Dr. Newton Campbell, September 10, 1924, File 2112, JRP; Alfred E. Smith to Joseph Tumulty, October 6, 1927, Box 74, Joseph Tumulty Papers, Library of Congress.

39. Warner, *Happy Warrior*, p. 173.

40. Ronald Steel, *Walter Lippmann and the American Century* (Boston: Little, Brown, 1980), p. 246; *Let's Look at the Record* (New York: Thistle Press, 1962), p. 25.

CHAPTER 11. FORGING A NEW AMERICA

1. State of New York, *Public Papers of Alfred E. Smith, 1927* (Albany: J. B. Lyon, 1929), pp. 29–30; State of New York, *Public Papers of Alfred E. Smith, 1923* (Albany: J. B. Lyon, 1924), p. 67; Norman Thomas interview, Pt. II, p. 22, CUOHC.

2. Alfred E. Smith, *Up to Now* (New York: Viking Press, 1929), pp. 276–277.

3. State of New York, *Public Papers of Alfred E. Smith, 1928* (Albany: J. B. Lyon, 1938), pp. 46, 47; *School and Society*, January 21, 1928, p. 83; W. C. Bagley, "Alfred E. Smith's Record in the Promotion of Public Education," *School and Society*, October 14, 1944, p. 243.

4. David Colburn, "Alfred E. Smith: The First Fifty Years, 1873–1924," Ph.D. diss., University of North Carolina at Chapel Hill, 1971, pp. 178–180.

5. Smith, *Up to Now*, p. 323.

6. "How the Facts Did It," *Survey*, (December 15, 1923), pp. 336–337.

7. State of New York, *Public Papers of Alfred E. Smith, 1925* (Albany: J. B. Lyon, 1927), pp. 195, 196, 198; State of New York, *Public Papers of Alfred E. Smith, 1924* (Albany: J. B. Lyon, 1926), p. 81; Colburn, "Smith," p. 131. The definition of how vacancy rates affect the housing market was provided by the National Low Income Housing Coalition.

8. Alfred E. Smith, "To Stimulate Low-Cost Housing," *American City Magazine* 34 (February 1926): 127; Paula Eldot, *Governor Alfred E. Smith* (New York: Garland Publishing, 1983), p. 187.

9. "Governor Smith's Plan to End New York City Slums," *Literary Digest*, March 13, 1926, p. 5; Martin Feldman, "The Political Thought of Alfred E. Smith," Ph.D. diss., New York University, 1963, pp. 91–92; "What Everybody Wants to Know About Alfred E. Smith," pp. 17–18, Box 5, FDRB; Robert Ingalls, *Herbert H. Lehman and New York's Little New Deal* (New York: New York University Press, 1975), p. 187; press release, April 26, 1923, p. 5, Folder 200–251, AESOP.

10. Ingalls, *Lehman*, p. 187; Clarke Chambers, *Seedtime of Reform* (Ann Arbor: University of Michigan Press, 1963), p. 136; "Smith's Plan," p. 5. As late as 1929, the New York State legislature refused to pass changes in the housing code that would have required a separate toilet for each family in tenements, removal of all outside toilets, and an end to cellar dwellings by 1935— hardly "revolutionary demands," as Lillian Wald commented.

11. Robert Moses, "Alfred Emmanuel Smith," *Recreation* 38 (December 1944): p. 451.

12. "Smith as an Administrator," *America Review of Reviews* 78 (October 1928: 384; Emily Warner, *The Happy Warrior* (Garden City, N.Y.: Doubleday, 1956), p. 167; Frank Graham, *Al Smith—American* (New York: Putnam, 1945), p. 140; Robert Caro, *The Power Broker* (New York: Random House, 1974), pp. 187–188.

13. Lynn Dumenil, *Modern Temper* (New York: Hill and Wang, 1995), pp. 58–59, 127–128; Ellis Hawley, *The Great War and the Search for a Modern Order* (New York: St. Martin's Press, 1992), p. 71; William Leuchtenberg, *The Perils of Prosperity* (Chicago: University of Chicago Press, 1958), p. 190; David Shannon, *Between the Wars* (Boston: Houghton Mifflin, 1965), p. 88; Michael Parrish, *Anxious Decades* (New York: Norton, 1992), p. 37.

14. State of New York, *Public Papers of Smith, 1924*, p. 40.

15. Press release, April 9, 1924, Folder 200–78, AESOP; Colburn, "Smith," p. 190.

16. State of New York, *Public Papers of Smith, 1924*, pp. 65, 151.

17. *The New York Red Book*, 1923 (Albany: J. B. Lyon, 1923), p. 31; "Motor Vehicle Law," Folder 134, Box 5, AESPP; *Political News* (February 1924): 27; "What Everybody Wants to Know About Alfred E. Smith," pp. 20–21, Box 5, FDRB.

18. Norman Hapgood and Henry Moskowitz, *Up from the City Streets* (New York: Grosset and Dunlap, 1927), p. 141; Louis Silveri, "The Political Education of Alfred E. Smith: The Assembly Years, 1904–1915," Ph.D. diss., St. John's University, 1963, p. 149; State of New York, *Public Papers of Smith, 1925*, p. 537.

19. Samuel Lubell, *The Future of American Politics* (Garden City, N.Y.: Doubleday, 1951), p. 39; Nathan Glazer and Daniel Moynihan, *Beyond the Melting Pot* (Cambridge: MIT Press, 1963), p. 246.

20. Undated article and *Jewish Daily News,* January 27, 1915, both in Box 1, EWP; Irving Howe, *World of Our Fathers* (New York: Harcourt Brace Jovanovich, 1976), pp. 385–386.

21. Interview with Hugh Carey, June 21, 1994.

22. *New York Times,* July 5, 1919, January 22, 1920, January 7, March 5, 1921; Matthew Josephson and Hannah Josephson, *Al Smith* (Boston: Houghton Mifflin, 1969), pp. 235–236; Smith, *Up to Now,* pp. 316–317.

23. See Jack Beatty, *The Rascal King* (Reading, Mass.: Addison-Wesley, 1992), for a masterful biography of James Michael Curley. George Van Namee to George Foster Peabody, July 18, 1919, Box 66, George Foster Peabody Papers, Library of Congress.

24. Records of the American Irish Historical Society, including Alfred E. Smith's application form; Richard Lynch, *Alfred E. Smith* (New York: Vantage Press, 1966), p. 80; interview with Paul O'Dwyer, January 19, 1993.

25. Edwin Lewinson, *Black Politics in New York City* (New York: Twayne Publishers, 1974), pp. 40–46; Jervis Anderson, *This Was Harlem* (New York: Farrar, Straus, Giroux, 1981), p. 111.

26. Gilbert Osofsky, *Harlem: The Making of a Ghetto* (New York: Harper and Row, 1983), pp. 169–170; Warren Moscow, *What Have You Done for Me Lately?* (Englewood Cliffs, N.J.: Prentice Hall, 1967), p. 134; Lewinson, *Black Politics,* pp. 59–61; Jason McGoldrick, "New Tammany," *American Mercury* 15 (September 1928): 8.

27. Lewinson, *Black Politics,* pp. 59–60.

28. Josephson and Josephson, *Smith,* pp. 16–17.

29. Smith, *Up to Now,* pp. 47–48; Robert Moses, "Al Smith: A Friend Looks at the Record," *New York Times Magazine,* January 21, 1945, p. 26.

30. William Jackson, "Prohibition as an Issue in New York State Politics, 1836–1933," Ed.D. diss., Columbia University, 1974, pp. 191–192.

31. Jervis Anderson, *This Was Harlem* (New York: Noonday Press, 1981).

32. Colburn, "Smith," pp. 207–209; Eldot, *Governor Alfred E. Smith,* pp. 388–389.

33. Thomas Coffey, *The Long Thirst* (New York: Dell, 1975), pp. 270–271.

34. State of New York, *Public Papers of Smith, 1924,* p. 551.

35. State of New York, *Public Papers of Smith, 1927,* p. 53.

36. Eldot, *Governor Smith,* pp. 202–203.

37. Telegrams from Smith to the manufacturers' association and Barondess to Smith are in Folder 260–202, letter from Belle Moskowitz to Alfred E. Smith, February 12, 1920, Folder 260–213, AESOC.

38. State of New York, *Public Papers of Alfred E. Smith, 1926* (Albany: J. B. Lyon, 1928), p. 680.

39. Book 1, p. 431, Frances Perkins interview, CUOHC; telephone interviews with Alice Cook, October 28, 1996, and Maurice Neufield, September 27, 1996.

40. Alfred E. Smith to Frances Perkins, November 14, 1918, Single Accession, New York State Library, Albany, New York; State Archives and Records Administration, "Guide to Records in the New York State Archives," p. 253; Lillian Mohr, *Frances Perkins* (Croton-on-Hudson, N.Y.: North River Press, 1979), p. 63.

41. The account of the Rome strike comes from George Martin, *Madame Secretary* (Boston: Houghton Mifflin, 1976), pp. 151–162. Al became very angry when she later told him about the dynamite.

42. Frances Perkins, "The Factory Inspector," in Catherine Filene, ed., *Careers for Women* (Boston: Houghton Mifflin, 1920), p. 260.

43. Minutes of the meeting of the Governor's cabinet, February 23, 1927, Box 7, Robert Moses Papers, New York Public Library.

44. *New York Morning Telegraph*, November 1, 1915, Box W-56; "New York State Federation of Labor Bulletin," September 29, 1928, p. 1, Box A-35, both in CUP.

45. Hasia Diner, *Erin's Daughters in America* (Baltimore: Johns Hopkins University Press, 1983).

46. Susan Ware, *Partner and I* (New Haven: Yale University Press, 1987), p. 150; Leona Becker, "Alfred E. Smith: A Personality Study of a Political Leader," M.A. thesis, University of Chicago, 1938, p. 101; Frances Perkins interview, Book 1, p. 636, CUOHC.

47. Frances Perkins interview, Book 1, p. 98, CUOHC.

48. Ibid., Book 2, p. 215, CUOHC.

49. The line about "taking care" is in an e-mail from Jo Freeman to me, November 25, 1994; Elisabeth Israels Perry, *Belle Moskowitz* (New York: Oxford University Press, 1987), pp. 151, 220.

50. All of the 1924 letters dealing with Perkins and the position of industrial commissioner are in Folder 103, Box 16, Governor's Appointment Correspondence, New York State Archives, Albany, New York; Joseph Lash, *Eleanor and Franklin* (New York: Norton, 1971), p. 324.

51. Nancy Cott, *The Grounding of Modern Feminism* (New Haven: Yale University Press, 1987), pp. 4–5, 278.

52. *New York Times*, May 13, 1919, May 14, 1920; *Let's Look at the Record* (New York: Thistle Press, 1962), p. 31; Silveri, "Political Education of Smith," p. 145.

53. Cott, *Modern Feminism*, pp. 128, 138.

54. Eldot, *Governor Smith*, p. 393.

55. State of New York, *Public Papers of Smith, 1924*, p. 369; Moskowitz, *Smith*, p. 82.

56. Interview with Hugh Carey, June 21, 1994.

57. Smith, *Up to Now*, p. 164; Emily Smith Warner interview, p. 47, CUOHC.

58. Hapgood and Moskowitz, *City Streets*, p. 90; Smith, *Up to Now*, p. 57.

59. Elinor Lerner, "Immigrant and Working Class Involvement in the New York City Woman Suffrage Movement, 1905–1917," Ph.D. diss., University of California, Berkeley, 1981, p. 285.

60. Ibid., pp. 213–217.

61. Ibid., pp. 229, 237, 241.

62. Ibid., p. 8; Paula Baker, *The Moral Frameworks of Public Life* (New York: Oxford University Press, 1991), pp. 44–46; Ware, *Partner and I*, p. 76; *New York Times*, June 11, 1919; John Buenker, *Urban Liberalism and Progressive Reform* (New York: Charles Scribners, 1973), p. 158; State of New York, *Public Papers of Alfred E. Smith, 1919* (Albany: J. B. Lyon, 1920), pp. 18–19; Ellis et al., *Short History*, p. 392.

CHAPTER 12. PROHIBITION

1. Thomas Pegram, *Battling Demon Rum* (Chicago: Ivan R. Dee), p. 45.

2. *New York Times*, December 27, 1922.

3. Joseph Gusfield, *Symbolic Crusade* (Urbana: University of Illinois Press, 1972), pp. 80–81, 130; Pegram, *Demon Rum*, p. 114.

4. Norman Dohn, "The History of the Anti-Saloon League," Ph.D. diss., Ohio State University, 1959, pp. 34, 94, 95, 127–129.

5. Ibid., p. 73.

6. Ibid., pp. 96, 97.

7. All of these quotations appear on p. 45 of Andrew Sinclair, *Era of Excess* (New York: Harper & Row, 1964).

8. Dohn, "Anti-Saloon League," pp. 38–39.

9. Gusfield, *Symbolic Crusade*, pp. 99, 100, 106, 108–110.

10. Jimmy Breslin, *Damon Runyon* (New York: Dell Publishing, 1991), p. 300.

11. Sinclair, *Excess*, pp. 158–163; Dohn, "Anti-Saloon League," pp. 203–204.

12. Material on beer in early New York comes from Richard Stott, *Workers in the Metropolis* (Ithaca: Cornell University Press, 1990), pp. 219–220; William Jackson, "Prohibition as an Issue in New York State Politics," Ph.D. diss., Columbia University, 1974, p. 145; John Buenker, *Urban Liberalism and Progressive Reform* (New York: Charles Scribner's Sons, 1973), p. 191.

13. Paula Eldot, *Governor Alfred E. Smith* (New York: Garland Publishing), p. 375.

14. Emily Smith Warner interview, p. 42, and Herbert Lehman interview, p. 572, both in CUOHC; Matthew Josephson and Hannah Josephson, *Al Smith* (Boston: Houghton Mifflin, 1969), p. 348; Emily Warner, *The Happy Warrior* (Garden City, N.Y.: Doubleday, 1956), pp. 208–209.

15. Interview with Ruth Proskauer Smith, July 27, 1995; *Political News* (April 1924): 42.

16. Differing accounts of what exactly Smith said appear in Josephson and Josephson, *Smith*, p. 293, and Richard O'Connor, *The First Hurrah* (New York: Putnam, 1970), p. 168. Smith's letter does not restate his comment. State of New York, *Public Papers of Alfred E. Smith, 1923* (Albany: J. B. Lyon, 1924), pp. 536–537.

17. Oswald Villard, "Presidential Possibilities: Alfred E. Smith," *Nation* November 30, 1927, p. 596.

18. Ibid., p. 595.

19. Villard, for example, was one of the founders of the NAACP.

20. Oswald Villard to Mr. McNeely, October 12, 1928, Oswald Garrison Villard Papers, Houghton Library, Harvard University. See also Lillian Wald to Henry Farnum, October 22, 1928, Box 5, Lillian Wald Papers, New York Public Library. Christopher Finan, "Fallen Hero," Ph.D. diss., Columbia University, 1992, p. 29.

21. Alfred Smith to D. Robertson Browne, June 24, 1924, Box 6, Folder 153, AESPP; Alfred Smith to Caroline Slade, February 1, 1924, Box 1, League of Women Voters of the City of New York Papers, Columbia University.

22. Alfred E. Smith, *Up to Now* (New York: Viking Press, 1929), p. 120; Emily Smith Warner interview, p. 41, CUOHC.

23. Anonymous letter to Governor Smith, January 25, 1920, Folder 260–205, AESOP.

24. William Anderson to Alfred Smith, September 8, September 21, 1920, Folder 260–205, AESOP; *New York Times*, May 6, 1920, October 26, 1922.

25. Louis Hacker and Mark Hirsch, *Proskauer* (University, Ala.: University of Alabama Press, 1978), p. 60; Sinclair, *Excess*, p. 193.

26. Hacker and Hirsch, *Proskauer,* p. 60; Henry Pringle, *Alfred E. Smith* (New York: Macy-Masius, 1927), p. 328; Jackson, "Prohibition," pp. 169–171; Thomas Coffey, *The Long Thirst* (New York: Dell Books, 1975), p. 126.

27. Pringle, *Smith,* p. 329; Mabel Willebrandt, *The Inside of Prohibition* (Indianapolis: Bobbs-Merrill, 1929), pp. 185–186.

28. Edward Flynn, *You're the Boss* (New York: Collier, 1947), p. 55; Coffey, *Long Thirst,* p. 127; Warren Moscow, *What Have You Done for Me Lately?* (Englewood Cliffs, N.J.: Prentice Hall, 1967), p. 71.

29. Coffey, *Long Thirst,* p. 126; Richard Magurno, "Franklin D. Roosevelt and Alfred E. Smith: Their Alliance and Their Feud," M.A. thesis, University of Wisconsin, 1965, pp. 23–24.

30. Jackson, "Prohibition as an Issue," p. 163; chart in Folder 137, Box 5, AESPP.

31. Jackson, "Prohibition as an Issue," p. 173; Eldot, *Governor Smith,* p. 363.

32. Eldot, *Governor Smith,* pp. 364–365; Hacker and Hirsch, *Proskauer,* p. 61; Emily Smith Warner interview, p. 89, CUOHC.

33. The text of this statement is on pp. 293–303 of State of New York, *Public Papers of Smith, 1923.*

34. See, e.g., his statement of p. 179 of his later work, *The Citizen and His Government,* Alfred E. Smith (New York: Harper and Brothers, 1935).

35. Smith, *Up to Now,* p. 268; Warner, *Happy Warrior,* p. 147.

36. *New York Times,* June 3, 1923; "New York's Secession from the Dry Column," *Literary Digest,* May 19, 1923, p. 5; Shawn Lay, *Hooded Knights on the Niagara* (New York: New York University Press, 1995), p. 59.

37. *New York Times,* June 2, 1923.

38. Letters to Alfred E. Smith from Harry Hartwell, June 7, 1923; Frank Fletcher, June 16, 1923; R. E. Corkins, June 2, 1923; George Bradshaw, June 2, 1923, all in Folder 200-4, AESOP; "Governor Smith Burns His Bridges," *Outlook* June 13, 1925, p. 164.

39. Louis Zuccarello, "The Political Thought of Alfred E. Smith," Ph.D. diss., Fordham University, 1970, p. 43.

40. *New York Times,* June 10, 1923.

41. Ibid., June 11, 1923.

42. James Farley, *Behind the Ballots* (New York: Harcourt, Brace, 1938), p. 41; Warner, *Happy Warrior,* p. 147; Douglas Craig, *After Wilson* (Chapel Hill: University of North Carolina Press, 1992), p. 49.

43. Felix Frankfurter to Henry Moskowitz, May 22, 1923, Reel 52, Felix Frankfurter Papers, Josephus Daniels to H. C. Thomas, July 21, 1928, Reel 29, Josephus Daniels Papers, both in the Library of Congress.

CHAPTER 13. THE SOUND OF THE SIREN

1. "Governor Alfred E. Smith and the Presidency," *World's Work* 45 (March 1923): 463.

2. Louis Knox to Al Smith, June 2, 1923, Folder 200-4, AESOC; James Farley to Al Smith, June 23, 1923, Box 1, JFP; *New York Times,* July 10, 1923.

3. Material in this paragraph comes from David Burner, *The Politics of Provincialism* (New York: Knopf, 1968), pp. 88–89; and Robert Murray, *The 103rd Ballot* (New York: Harper and Row, 1976), p. 88.

4. The account of this meeting is in the December 17, 1923, edition of the *New York Times*.

5. H. L. Mencken, *A Carnival of Buncombe*, ed. Malcolm Moos (Baltimore: Johns Hopkins University Press, 1956), p. 71; Emily Warner, *The Happy Warrior* (Garden City, N.Y.: Doubleday, 1956), p. 156.

6. State of New York, *Public Papers of Alfred E. Smith, 1924* (Albany: J. B. Lyon, 1926), p. 609.

7. Murray, *Ballot*, pp. 95–96; *Political News* (December 1923): 20.

8. *New York Times*, April 26, 1924; statement released by the governor's office, April 26, 1924, Reel 10, James Farley Scrapbooks, Library of Congress.

9. Frances Perkins interview, Book 2, p. 84, CUOHC.

10. *F.D.R.: His Personal Letters*, vol. 2: *1928–1945*, ed. Elliott Roosevelt (New York: Duell, Sloan and Pearce, 1950), pp. 1089–1090; Kenneth Davis, *FDR: The Beckoning of Destiny* (New York: Putnam, 1971), pp. 733–735.

11. Davis, *FDR*, p. 735; Geoffrey Ward, *A First-Class Temperament* (New York: HarperCollins, 1989), p. 690; Elisabeth Perry, *Belle Moskowitz* (New York: Oxford University Press, 1987), p. 185; outline of 1924 Citizens for Smith Committee, Folder 1, Box 5, FDR24; *Political News* (May 1924): 12. *New York Times*, May 1, June 17, 1924; Alfred Rollins, Jr., *Roosevelt and Howe* (New York: Knopf, 1962), pp. 210–215; Donn Neal, *The World Beyond the Hudson* (New York: Garland Press, 1983), p. 142.

12. "What Everybody Wants to Know About Alfred E. Smith," Folder 9, Box 13, and Irving Berlin to Franklin Roosevelt, June 19, 1924, Folder 10, Box 2, both in FDR24; *New York Times*, May 7, 1924. The complete text of "We'll Al Go Voting for Al" appears in Box 25, EKC.

13. Frederick Greene to Franklin Roosevelt, April 30, 1924, Folder 5, Box 10, and Babe Ruth to Franklin Roosevelt, May 9, 1924, Folder 6, Box 13, both in FDR24.

14. *New York Times*, June 28, 1924; Vincent Offner to Al Smith, June 8, 1924, Folder 5, Box 2, FDR24; S. R. Williams to Alfred Smith, June 10, 1924, Folder 701, Box 23, AESPP.

15. Herbert Lehman to Franklin Roosevelt, May 2, 1924, Folder 6, Box 11, and George Van Namee to Anna Germain, June 14, 1924, Folder 5, Box 1, both in FDR24; Norman Mack to Charles Evans Hughes, May 31, 1924, Box 1, NMP.

16. Warner, *Happy Warrior*, p. 156; *New York Times*, June 22, 1924; Norman Mack to James Fleming, May 5, 1924, Box 1, NMP; Murray, *103rd Ballot*, p. 70; John Maley to Franklin Roosevelt, June 9, 1924, Folder 7, Box 7, An American-Democrat to F. D. Roosevelt, May 27, 1924, Folder 14, Box 14, KKK to F. D. Roosevelt, May 26, 1924, Folder 14, Box 14, all in FDR24.

17. Arthur Levy to James Hooey, June 18, 1924, Folder 7, Box 3, FDR24; Murray, *Ballot*, p. 109; *New York Times*, June 24, 1924.

18. Douglas Craig, *After Wilson* (Chapel Hill: University of North Carolina Press, 1992), pp. 32–35; William McAdoo, *Crowded Years* (Boston: Houghton Mifflin, 1931), p. 240.

19. Ralph Goldman, *The National Party Chairmen and Their Committees* (New York: M. E. Sharpe, 1990), p. 308; George Foster Peabody to Nellie Hall Root, July 14, 1924, Box 20, George Foster Peabody Papers, Library of Congress.

20. *Political News* (February 1924): 21.

21. William Harbaugh, *Lawyer's Lawyer* (New York: Oxford University Press, 1973), p. 209.

22. Joseph Proskauer interview, p. 5, CUOHC.

23. The only source for these meetings is, unfortunately, Joseph Proskauer, who went on to

hate FDR. The accounts used here are those in the CUOHC (Joseph Proskauer interview, pp. 4–7), and in Robert Caro, *The Power Broker* (New York: Random House, 1974), p. 286. Caro stated that he based his description on interviews with Proskauer, Emily Smith Warner, and two other Smith intimates. Anthony Smith, Proskauer's grandson, told me that Caro's account was totally faithful to Proskauer's memory of the event, that it was "the description that is my grandfather's." Ruth Proskauer Smith, Proskauer's daughter, also told me that Roosevelt's refusal to acknowledge Proskauer's authorship of the "Happy Warrior" speech was one of the reasons that Proskauer hated FDR so deeply.

24. Murray, *Ballot*, p. 128.

25. Lela Stiles, *The Man Behind Roosevelt* (New York: World Publishing Company, 1954), p. 92.

26. The account of Roosevelt's walk to the podium comes from George Martin, *Madame Secretary* (Boston: Houghton Mifflin, 1976), p. 184; Stiles, *Man Behind*, pp. 3, 92–93; Ward, *Temperament*, pp. 694–696; Davis, *FDR*, pp. 755–756. I thank Irwin Gellman for sharing with me the fruits of his many conversations with his friend James Roosevelt.

27. Roosevelt's speech appears in the *New York Times*, June 27, 1924.

28. Murray, *Ballot*, pp. 130–131.

29. Frances Perkins interview, Book 2, p. 328 and Marion Dickerman interview, p. 22, both in CUOHC; Walter Lippmann to Franklin Roosevelt, June 27, 1924, Folder 7, Box 11, FDR24.

30. Kenneth Jackson, *The Ku Klux Klan in the City* (New York: Oxford University Press, 1967), pp. 237, 239.

31. Joseph Proskauer interview, p. 28, CUOHC; David Chalmers, *Hooded Americanism* (Chicago: Quadrangle, 1965), p. 206.

32. Murray, *Ballot*, pp. 150–151.

33. Ibid., pp. 154–156; Dorothy Wayman, *David I. Walsh* (Milwaukee: Bruce Publishing Company, 1952), p. 149.

34. The account of the debate on the Klan comes from Murray, *Ballot*, pp. 153–161, unless otherwise cited.

35. The account of the balloting, unless otherwise noted, is from ibid., pp. 166–207.

36. Woman voter to William Jennings Bryan, July 3, 1924, Box 40, William Jennings Bryan Papers, Library of Congress; siren man letter is in Folder 2, Box 17, FDR24.

37. Oscar Handlin, *Al Smith and His America* (Boston: Little, Brown, 1958), p. 123; letters to Bryan are in Box 40, William Jennings Bryan Papers, Library of Congress.

38. Untitled manuscript in the Elizabeth Tilton Papers, Schlesinger Library, Radcliffe Institute.

39. William Leuchtenburg, *The Perils of Prosperity* (Chicago: University of Chicago Press, 1958), p. 133; Harbaugh, *Lawyer*, p. 212; H. L. Mencken, *Making a President* (New York: Knopf, 1932), p. 5; Arthur Brisbane to William Jennings Bryan, July 3, 1924, Box 40, William Jennings Bryan Papers, Library of Congress; David Colburn, "Alfred E. Smith," Ph.D. diss., University of North Carolina at Chapel Hill, 1971, p. 233.

40. Harbaugh, *Lawyer*, p. 215; Farley's notes are in Box 37, Private Files, JFP.

41. James Kearney, "A Personal Portrait of Governor Al Smith," *Scribner's Magazine* 80 (September 1926): 245.

42. Text of the speech is in State of New York, *Public Papers of Smith, 1924*, pp. 617–620.

43. Mary Dreier to Governor Smith, July 10, 1924, Box 18, George Graves Papers, New York State Archives.

CHAPTER 14. BUSINESS AS USUAL

1. Alfred E. Smith, *Up to Now* (New York: Viking Press, 1929), p. 291.

2. Ibid., p. 292.

3. Robert Ingalls, *Herbert H. Lehman and New York's Little New Deal* (New York: New York University Press, 1975), p. 8; Belle Moskowitz to George Graves, November 17, 1924, Folder 200–30, AESOP; James Riordan to Bernard Baruch, November 8, 1924, Unit VI, Vol. 12, Bernard Baruch Papers, Princeton University.

4. Alfred E. Smith, *The Citizen and His Government* (New York: Harper and Brothers, 1935), p. 73.

5. Lawrence Madras, "The Public Career of Theodore Roosevelt, Jr.," Ph.D. diss., New York University, 1964, pp. 221, 222; Lawrence Madras, "Theodore Roosevelt, Jr. Versus Al Smith," *New York History* 47 (October 1966): 372–375.

6. David Colburn, "Alfred E. Smith: The First Fifty Years, 1873–1924," Ph.D. diss., University of North Carolina at Chapel Hill, 1971, p. 241; Norman Hapgood and Henry Moskowitz, *Up from the City Streets* (New York: Grosset and Dunlap, 1927), p. 216.

7. Colburn, "Smith," p. 243.

8. Elisabeth Perry, *Belle Moskowitz* (New York: Oxford University Press, 1987), p. 80.

9. Eleanor Roosevelt to William Culliton, February 25, 1925, William Culliton Papers, Buffalo and Erie County Historical Society; Joseph Lash, *Eleanor and Franklin* (New York: Norton, 1971), p. 291; Geoffrey Ward, *A First-Class Temperament* (New York: HarperCollins, 1989), p. 688.

10. Eleanor Roosevelt, *This I Remember* (New York: Harper and Brothers, 1949), p. 31; Ward, *Temperament*, pp. 700–701; *New York Times*, October 18, 1924; Emily Smith Warner interview, p. 31, CUOHC.

11. Lenora Becker, "Alfred E. Smith: A Personality Study of Political Leadership," M.A. thesis, University of Chicago, 1938, p. 58; Edward Murlin, *The New York Redbook* (Albany: J. B. Lyon, 1928), p. 377.

12. Data on longevity of New York governors in office were provided by James Folts of the New York State Archives; Madras, "Roosevelt," p. 241; *New York Times*, January 2, 1925, November 5, 1928.

13. Herbert Hoover, *The Memoirs of Herbert Hoover: The Cabinet and the Presidency, 1920–1933* (New York: Macmillan, 1952), p. 199; *New York Times*, May 9, 1922.

14. Warren Moscow, *Politics in the Empire State* (New York: Knopf, 1948), p. 95.

15. Thomas Kessner, *Fiorello LaGuardia* (New York: Penguin Books, 1989), p. 157; Jimmy Breslin, *Damon Runyon* (New York: Dell, 1991), pp. 103–104.

16. Paul Sann, *The Lawless Decade* (New York: DaCapo Press, 1957), p. 216; Gene Fowler, *Beau James* (New York: Viking Press, 1949), pp. 70–71; interview with Father Arthur Smith, June 28, 1996.

17. Smith, *Up to Now*, p. 60; Frank Graham, *Al Smith—American* (New York: Putnam, 1945), p. 55; Emily Smith Warner interview, p. 14, CUOHC; Richard O'Connor, *The First Hurrah* (New York: Putnam, 1970), p. 121.

18. Joseph Proskauer interview, p. 23, CUOHC; Robert Caro, *The Power Broker* (New York: Random House, 1974), p. 201.

19. Frances Perkins interview, Book 3, pp. 410–411, CUOHC; interview with Father Arthur Smith, June 28, 1996.

20. Most of this account comes from O'Connor, *Hurrah*, pp. 159–160. See also Joseph Proskauer interview, pp. 23–24, CUOHC.

21. Hearst, and thus Hylan, had supported McAdoo, widely perceived as the Klan's candidate. *New York Times*, August 25, 1925; State of New York, *Public Papers of Alfred E. Smith, 1925* (Albany: J. B. Lyon, 1927), pp. 774–779.

22. *New York Times*, August 25, 29, 30, September 2, 1925; Breslin, *Runyon*, p. 252.

23. *New York Times*, September 3, 5, 1925; William Randolph Hearst to Arthur Brisbane, February 21, 1925, and Joseph Moore to Hearst, February 19, 1925, both in Box 1, William Randolph Hearst Papers, Bancroft Library, University of California, Berkeley; Breslin, *Runyon*, p. 253.

24. Gustavus Meyers, "The New Tammany," *Century Magazine* 112 (August 1926): 394; Fowler, *Beau James*, p. 148.

25. *New York Times*, November 5, 1925; "Smith's Triumph over Hylan and Hearst," *Literary Digest*, September 26, 1925, p. 8.

26. Interview with Mildred Graves Ryan, July 17, 1994.

27. Allan Nevins, *Herbert Lehman and His Era* (New York: Charles Scribner's Sons, 1963), p. 151; interview with Mildred Graves Ryan, July 17, 1994; Anne Herendeen, "A Pen Portrait of Mrs. Smith," *New York Times Magazine*, June 3, 1928, p. 20; Frederick Collins, *Our American Kings* (New York: Century Co., 1924), p. 21.

28. Interview with Judge David Edelstein, October 16, 1996.

29. Undated article in GVNP; Frederick Collins, "What Sort of Man Is Smith?" *Women's Home Companion* 55 (October 1928): 100; Henry Moskowitz, "Alfred E. Smith," *Bookman* 68 (October 1928): 147.

30. "The Candidates As They Really Are," *New York Times Magazine*, October 14, 1928, p. 8; Collins, "Smith," p. 100. Regarding cigars, see letters from Smith to John Bowman, May 20, 1927, Box 6, to Joseph Back, November 6, 1925, and August 21, 1923, both in Box 3, and letters to Smith from Back, January 2, 1923, Box 4, and from Howard Cullman, Box 15, George Graves Papers, New York State Archives.

31. Frances Perkins interview, Book 2, p. 268, CUOHC; article in Book 5.1, Empire State Building Scrapbooks, ESBP; interview with Father Arthur Smith, June 28, 1996; Frank Graham, *Al Smith—American* (New York: Putnam, 1945), p. 125.

32. Collins, *American Kings*, p. 16; interview with Alfred E. Smith IV, August 3, 1994.

33. Interviews with John Dunn Murphy and John Coleman, Jr., July 12, 1993; *New York World* article, November 4, 1915, Box 1 of EWP.

34. Emily Smith Warner interview, pp. 60, 92, CUOHC; interviews with Father Arthur Smith, June 28, 1996, and Mildred Graves Ryan, July 17, 1994.

35. Interviews with Hugh Carey, June 21, 1994, and Alfred E. Smith IV, August 3, 1994; *New York Times*, April 17, 1925.

36. Emily Smith Warner interview, p. 6, and Frances Perkins interview, Book 2, pp. 270–272, both in CUOHC; interviews with Helen McManus, November 15, 1996, Father Arthur Smith, June 28, 1996, and Walter Smith, December 17, 1996.

37. *New York Times*, May 14, 24, 26, 1926; George Martin, *Madame Secretary* (Boston: Houghton Mifflin, 1976), p. 190.

38. Interviews with Walter Smith, December 17, 1996, and Father Arthur Smith, June 28, 1996. See the photo of Arthur Smith playing golf in GVNP.

39. Interviews with John Dunn Murphy, Joseph Sano, and Josephine Sano. The story of Walter and the police was originally described to me in my interview with Walter Smith. The details appear in the *New York Times*, August 5, 1925.

40. Interviews with Bernard Pisani and Helen Graff; Eugene Weare, "When Al Smith Went to the University," *Extension Magazine* (October 1928), in Alfred E. Smith Papers, Manhattan College; *New York Times*, October 17, December 5, 1924.

41. Smith, *Up to Now*, pp. 249–251; undated article in Book 5.1 of the Empire State Building Scrapbooks, ESBP; Perry, *Belle Moskowitz*, p. 219; *New York Times*, July 16, 21, 1924, January 4, 1926; Collins, *American Kings*, p. 17; *New York Evening World*, October 23, 1922.

42. The delightful bear story appears in James Farley and James Conniff, *Governor Al Smith* (New York: Farrar, Straus & Cudahy, 1959), pp. 149–150. I choose to believe it; who wouldn't?

43. The author grew up in the Bronx; you figure it out.

44. Ray Robinson and Christopher Jennison, *Yankee Stadium* (New York: Penguin, 1998), p. 13.

45. This figure may have been a publicity stunt by Yankee management to exaggerate the scale of their new stadium. No one really knows the true figure. See ibid., p. 17.

46. The account of this game comes from the *New York Times*, April 19, 1923, April 17, 1992, April 19, 1998.

47. In 1998 Ruth's home run ball, discovered in an attic in New Jersey, sold for $126,500 at auction. *New York Times*, November 14, 1998. Robinson and Jennison, *Yankee Stadium*, p. 17; Frederick Lieb, "74,200 Fans See Yankees' Opening," in Miro Weinberger and Dan Riley, eds., *The Yankees Reader* (Boston: Houghton Mifflin, 1991), pp. 43, 44, 46; *New York Times*, April 19, 1923.

48. *New York Times*, October 20, 1925, January 15, August 15, 1926; Felix Ray, "Milk Punch," *New Republic*, November 3, 1926, p. 294; cartoon is in GVNP.

49. Herbert Lehman interview, CUOHC; for the campaign organization, see, e.g., the letterhead of Herbert Lehman to James Walker, October 1, 1926, Box 104, James Walker Papers, New York City Municipal Archives; Folder 699, Box 23, AESPP.

50. Hapgood and Moskowitz, *Up from the City Streets*, p. 215; Smith, *Up to Now*, p. 358.

51. Mills's speeches appear in Boxes 132 and 133, Ogden Mills Papers, Library of Congress; George Walsh, *Gentleman Jimmy Walker* (New York: Praeger, 1974), pp. 93–94.

52. State of New York, *Public Papers of Alfred E. Smith, 1926* (Albany: J. B. Lyon, 1929), p. 807; Henry Pringle, *Alfred E. Smith* (New York: Macy-Masius, 1974), pp. 275–276.

53. State of New York, *Public Papers of Smith, 1926*, pp. 827, 837–841.

54. Box 4, Odgen Mills Papers, Library of Congress; Lash, *Eleanor and Franklin*, p. 312; Eleanor Roosevelt to George Graves, December 17, 1926, George Graves Papers, Franklin Roosevelt Presidential Library, Hyde Park, New York.

55. Chris McNickle, *To Be Mayor of New York* (New York: Columbia University Press, 1993), p. 30.

56. Timothy Henderson, "Tammany Hall and the New Immigrants, 1910–1921," Ph.D. diss., University of Virginia, 1973, pp. 261–270.

CHAPTER 15. OPENING ROUNDS

1. Edward Woodhouse, "The South Studies Governor Smith," *Independent* January 9, 1926, pp. 45–46; "Governor Smith's Victory," *Nation*, November 18, 1925, p. 562; *New York Times*, January 10, 1925.

2. Joe Tumulty to Governor Smith, November 19, December 14, 1925, and E. L. Scharf to Joe Tumulty, May 20, 1927, all in Box 74, Joe Tumulty Papers, Library of Congress; Franklin Roosevelt to Norman Mack, March 10, 1927, Box 1, NMP.

3. *New York Times,* June 13, 1925; "Al Smith's Sun Rising in the West," *Literary Digest,* October 8, 1927, p. 7; clipping from the *San Francisco Bulletin,* December 2, 1927, Folder 200–333, and Tadao Wikawa to Alfred Smith, March 6, 1926, Folder 200–241, both in AESOP.

4. Don Seitz, "'Al' Smith and the Nation," *Outlook,* December 15, 1926, p. 495; *New York Times,* September 22, 1927; James Smallwood, ed., *Will Rogers' Daily Telegrams,* Vol. 1, *The Coolidge Years: 1926–1929,* by Will Rogers (Stillwater: Oklahoma State University Press, 1978), p. 243; "Democrats Before the Battle," *Independent,* October 1, 1927, p. 325.

5. Pierre Crabites, "The American Presidential Election," *Fortnightly Review* 130 (August 1928): 181; Nicholas Butler to Claude Bowers, October 3, 1927, Claude Bowers Papers, Indiana University.

6. Colonel Edward House to Alfred Smith, November 5, 1928, Folder 3574, Box 104, Colonel Edward House Papers, Sterling Memorial Library, Yale University; Marion Fox, "A Forecast," *Atlantic Monthly* 140 (September, 1927): 384.

7. *New York Times,* February 22, 1928.

8. George Milton, "Smith's Southern 'Gains,'" *Outlook,* July 27, 1927, p. 405; Dixon Merritt, "Al Smith and the Doubtful Seaboard," *Outlook,* November 30, 1927, p. 398; Dixon Merritt, "Al Smith and the Solid South," *Outlook,* October 26, 1927, p. 236.

9. "Keeping Prohibition Out of Party Platforms," *Literary Digest,* September 10, 1927, p. 12; Carter Glass, "Could Smith Get Elected?" *American Review of Reviews* 75 (May 1927): 477; "Will the Democrats Make Prohibition the Issue?" *Literary Digest,* October 15, 1927, pp. 7–8.

10. "'Selling' Tammany to the South," *Literary Digest,* November 21, 1925, p. 8; Milton, "Smith's Southern 'Gains,'" p. 405.

11. Donald Day, *Will Rogers* (New York: David McKay Company, 1962), p. 178; Walter Lippmann to Belle Moskowitz, October 14, 1927, Folder 845, Box 21, Series I, WLP.

12. "Coolidge's Renunciation," *Outlook,* August 17, 1927, p. 495.

13. Norman Brown, *Hood, Bonnet, and Little Brown Jug* (College Station: Texas A&M University Press, 1984), p. 375; "Mr. McAdoo Also Chooses Not to Run," *Literary Digest,* October 1, 1927, p. 95.

14. Norman Mack to Alfred Smith, April 19, 1927, and Norman Mack to Franklin Roosevelt, April 8, 1927, both in Box 1, NMP.

15. *New York Times,* December 31, 1927.

16. Rev. William Karg, "A Short Life of Mrs. Henry Moskowitz and Her Influence upon Governor Alfred E. Smith," M.A. thesis, St. Bonaventure University, 1960, p. 43; Vaughan Bornet, *Labor Politics in a Democratic Republic* (Washington, D.C.: Spartan Books, 1964), p. 59; "Governor Smith the Nominee," *Nation,* July 11, 1928, p. 30.

17. Address of James Tolbert, February 25, 1928, Folder 2, Box 36, James Tolbert Papers, University of Oklahoma; "Presidential Chances," *Collier's,* January 14, 1928, p. 50; Douglas Craig, *After Wilson* (Chapel Hill: University of North Carolina Press, 1992), p. 103.

18. "How Delegates to National Conventions Are Chosen," *Congressional Digest* 7 (August 1928): 221; Roy Peel and Thomas Donnelly, *The 1928 Campaign* (New York: Richard Smith, 1931), p. 13.

19. *New York Times,* March 14, 1928.

20. Ibid., April 4, 15, 1928.

21. "The Rumbling of Al Smith's Band-Wagon," *Literary Digest,* April 28, 1928, p. 10.

22. Belle Moskowitz, "Reminiscences of the Movement to Nominate Governor Alfred E. Smith for the Presidency of the Democratic Ticket," undated ms., p. 48, Belle Moskowitz Papers, Connecticut College; George Van Namee to Franklin Roosevelt, March 23, 1928, Box 10, FDR28.

23. Data on the California primary come from the *New York Times,* May 2, 1928.

24. James Cox to Alfred Smith, May 2, 1928, Box 37, James Cox Papers, Wright State University; Hugh Reagan, "The Presidential Campaign in Alabama," Ph.D. diss., University of Texas, 1961, p. 140.

25. Donn Neal, *The World Beyond the Hudson* (New York: Garland Publishing, 1983), p. 241.

26. "National Conventions in Action," *Congressional Digest* 7 (August 1928): 225.

27. Reagan, "Presidential Campaign," p. 75. Most accounts cite a $200,000 figure, although Owen White claims it was $250,000. Reagan, "Presidential Campaign," p. 45; Owen White, "A Tale of Two Cities," *Collier's,* June 16, 1928, p. 20; Dixon Merritt, "Harmony of Jackson Day," *Outlook,* January 25, 1928, p. 142.

28. White, "Tale," p. 20; Peel and Donnelly, *1928 Campaign,* p. 30.

29. Merritt, "Harmony," p. 142; *Official Report of the Proceedings of the Democratic National Convention Held at Houston, Texas* (Indianapolis: Bookwalter-Ball-Greathouse Printing Company, 1928), p. 323.

30. Peel and Donnelly, *1928 Campaign,* p. 30; Clark Howell, "Houston—1928," *North American Review* 225 (June 1928): 641.

31. "Lesser Half," *Collier's,* June 23, 1928, p. 36.

32. "The Republican and Democratic Candidates—1928," *Congressional Digest* 7 (August 1928): 231.

33. The statement by Heflin appears in *The Culture of the Twenties,* ed. Loren Baritz (Indianapolis: Bobbs-Merrill Educational Publishing, 1970), pp. 55–65.

34. *New York Times,* July 21, 1927; Michael Williams, *The Shadow of the Pope* (New York: Whittlesey House, 1932), pp. 174–175; Arnold Rice, *The Ku Klux Klan in American Politics* (Washington, D.C.: Public Affairs Press, 1962), p. 137. Heflin also shot a black man in broad daylight, claiming in a later flier, "The failure to have separate street cars for whites and Negroes in Washington caused him to inflict severe punishment upon a drunken Negro who had insulted a white woman." J. Mills Thornton III, "Alabama Politics, J. Thomas Heflin and the Expulsion Movement of 1929," *Alabama Review* 22 (April 1968): 95.

35. It was remarks like this that made Heflin such a pariah. To this day, he remains an embarrassment to the family, which is why former Senator Howell Heflin refused me access to his late uncle's papers, claiming that the country was still not ready to deal with such hatred. Thomas Heflin's Senate remarks came from Cecil Weller, Jr., "Always a Loyal Democrat: The Life of Senate Majority Leader Joseph Taylor Robinson," Ph.D. diss., Texas Christian University, 1993, pp. 231–232; William Smith, "Alfred E. Smith and John F. Kennedy: The Religious Issue During the Presidential Campaigns of 1928 and 1960," Ph.D. diss., Southern Illinois University, 1964, pp. 63–64; and from the *New York Times,* January 19, 1928.

36. *New York Times,* January 19, 1928; Weller, "Loyal Democrat," p. 232.

37. W. G. Lewis to Joseph Robinson, January 21, 1928, Folder 3, Box 36, Joseph Robinson Papers, University of Arkansas at Fayetteville; Weller, Loyal Democrat," pp. 233–234; *New York Times,* January 20, 1928; Smallwood, ed., *Rogers' Daily Telegrams,* p. 172.

38. Weller, "Loyal Democrat," p. 236; Claude Bowers interview, p. 80, CUOHC; Key Pittman to Joseph Robinson, July 24, 1928, Folder 3, Box 32, Joseph Robinson Papers.

39. Weller, "Loyal Democrat," p. 237; *New York Times*, June 24, 1928.

40. Article from June 1928 in the GVNP; unattributed newspaper article, 1928, Walter Smith Personal Clippings Collection.

41. White, "Tale," p. 51.

42. James Phelan to Thomas Walsh, January 13, 1928, Box 182, Thomas Walsh Papers, Library of Congress; Allan Nevins, *Herbert H. Lehman and His Era* (New York: Charles Scribner's Sons, 1963), p. 97; W. R. Hollister to Breckinridge Long, January 28, 1928, Box 89, Breckinridge Long Papers, Library of Congress; David Lawrence, "Choosing the Candidates," *Ladies' Home Journal* 45 (June 1928): p. 10; Claude Bowers, *My Life* (New York: Simon & Schuster, 1962), p. 193.

43. *New York Times*, June 26, 29, 1928; Sherwin Cook, *Torchlight Parade* (New York: Minton, Balch and Company, 1929), p. 282; Frances Keyes, "The American Woman and the Democratic Party," *Delineator* 113 (November 1928): 17.

44. *New York Times*, June 21, 23, 1928.

45. Reagan, "Presidential Campaign," pp. 151–152; *New York Times*, May 23, 1928; Henry Pringle, "Barbecues in Politics," *World's Work* 56 (August 1928): 356.

46. *New York Times*, June 23, 1928.

47. Reagan, "Presidential Campaign," pp. 150–151; Irwin Kurtz to Ogden Mills, July 11, 1928, Box 6, Ogden Mills Papers, Library of Congress.

48. A complete diagram of the convention floor appears in Box 15; and George Peabody to Franklin Roosevelt, Box 11, both in FDR28; *Chicago Defender*, July 7, 1928.

49. "The National Conventions in Action," *Congressional Digest* 7 (August 1928): 225; Peel and Donnelly, *1928 Campaign*, p. 31.

50. Smallwood, ed., *Rogers' Daily Telegrams*, p. 227; Bowers, *My Life*, p. 186.

51. The account of this meeting comes from the Bowers interview, pp. 79–80, CUOHC.

52. Bowers, *My Life*, p. 194.

53. Ibid.; Bowers's speech appears in *Official Proceedings . . . Democratic Convention*, pp. 8–21.

54. Page Smith, *Redeeming the Time* (New York: Penguin Books, 1987), p. 270; Lewis Gannett, "Big Show at Houston," *Nation*, July 11, 1928, p. 34.

55. Lewis Gannett, "It's All Al Smith," *Nation*, July 4, 1928, p. 8.

56. *New York Times*, June 28, 1928; unattributed newspaper article, 1928, the Walter Smith Personal Clippings Collection.

57. Gannett, "All Al," p. 8; William Smith, "Smith and Kennedy," p. 70.

58. Peel and Donnelly, *1928 Campaign*, p. 31; Smallwood, ed., *Rogers' Daily Telegrams*, p. 228.

59. Bornet, *Labor Politics*, p. 125; Kenneth Davis, *FDR: The Beckoning of Destiny* (New York: Putnam, 1971), p. 821; Franklin Roosevelt to W. Brandebury, June 5, 1928, Box 7, FDR28.

60. Roosevelt's speech was published as *The Happy Warrior* (Boston: Houghton Mifflin, 1928).

61. Peel and Donnelly, *1928 Campaign*, p. 32; Austin Hoover, "The Presidential Campaign of 1928 in Texas," M.A. thesis, University of Texas at El Paso, 1967, pp. 131–132.

62. Davis, *FDR*, p. 822; "East Side, West Side, All Around Houston," *Literary Digest*, July 21, 1928, p. 35.

63. The text of the platform is in Peel and Donnelly, *1928 Campaign*, pp. 152–169. See also Dixon Merritt, "The Party of Governor Smith," *Outlook*, July 4, 1928, p. 373; Joseph Proskauer interview, p. 128, CUOHC; Louis Hacker and Mark Hirsch, *Proskauer* (University: University of Alabama Press, 1978), pp. 92–93; "Democratic Convention," *Current History* 28 (August 1928): 708.

64. Allan Lichtman, *Prejudice and the Old Politics* (Chapel Hill: University of North Carolina Press, 1979), pp. 80–81.

65. Peel and Donnelly, *1928 Campaign*, p. 165.

66. Bowers, *My Life*, p. 190; Emily Warner, *The Happy Warrior* (Garden City, N.Y.: Doubleday, 1956), p. 201.

67. *New York Times*, June 12, 1928; Thomas Coffey, *The Long Thirst* (New York: Dell Books, 1975), p. 262.

68. Ernest Lindley, "Captains Courageous," *Newsweek*, October 14, 1944, p. 38. It is interesting that Lindley refused to publish his account of Smith's gaffe until after the governor had died. Al really did have the loyalty of the press.

69. Coffey, *Long Thirst*, p. 262.

70. "Democratic Convention," p. 708; Coffey, *Long Thirst*, p. 263; Peel and Donnelly, *1928 Campaign*, pp. 33–34.

71. Coffey, *Long Thirst*, p. 263; *New York Times*, June 29, 1928; Collins, "Sort of Man," p. 98.

72. Isabel Ross, *Ladies of the Press* (New York: Arno, 1936), p. 125; *New York Times*, June 29, 1928. Al could not resist putting Sam in the front of the reception line when he accepted the nomination, later giving him freedom of the grounds, where the donkey "chewed Albany grass to his heart's content and frolicked with the dogs and other animals." Sam could not take the northern winters, however, and contracted pneumonia and died. Smith, *Up to Now*, p. 381.

73. The analysis is based on figures in Peel and Donnelly, *1928 Campaign*, pp. 212–217; Robert Murray, *The 103rd Ballot* (New York: Harper and Row, 1976), p. 273; Brown, *Hood, Bonnett*, p. 9.

74. Pringle, "Harmony," p. 412. The telegram is reprinted on pp. 258–259 of the *Official Proceedings . . . Democratic National Convention.*

75. Bowers, *My Life*, p. 228.

76. Coffey, *Long Thirst*, pp. 263–264; Alice David, "Brass Rails or Church Spires?" Folder 6, Box 19, Henry Johnson Papers, University of Oklahoma.

77. Bowers, *My Life*, p. 228; *F.D.R.: His Personal Letters*, ed. Elliott Roosevelt (New York: Duell, Sloan and Pearce, 1950), pp. 109–110; Walter Lippmann to Belle Moskowitz, June 25, 1928, Folder 845, Box 21, Series I, WLP.

78. *New York Times*, June 28, 1928.

79. James Young, "Raskob of General Motors," *World's Work* 56 (September 1928): p. 488; John Riggs, *A Guide to Manuscripts in the Eleutherian Mills Historical Library* (Greenville, Del.: Eleutherian Mills Historical Society, 1970), p. 916; Edmund Moore, *A Catholic Runs for President* (New York: Ronald Press, 1956), p. 122.

80. Young, "Raskob," p. 488.

81. Ibid., pp. 488–489; Riggs, *Guide*, pp. 917–918.

82. Young, "Raskob," p. 489; Henry Pringle, "John J. Raskob," *Outlook*, August 22, 1928,

p. 648; Geoffrey Perrett, *America in the Twenties* (New York: Simon & Schuster, 1982), pp. 353–354; Riggs, *Guide*, p. 919.

83. Young, "Raskob," pp. 490, 492; Pringle, "Raskob," pp. 645, 678; David Burner, "The Brown Derby Campaign," *New York History* 46 (October 1965): 368.

84. Eddie Dowling interview, pp. 104–107, and Frances Perkins interview, Book 2, pp. 524–525, both in CUOHC; Edward Flynn, *You're the Boss* (New York: Collier Books, 1947), pp. 78–79; Richard O'Connor, *The First Hurrah* (New York: Putnam, 1970), p. 163; Frank Graham, *Al Smith—American* (New York: Putnam, 1945), p. 186.

85. See John Raskob to Alfred Smith, March 9, 1928, and Smith to Raskob, February 18, 1928, File 2112, JRP.

86. Raskob's copy of the speech is in File 602, Box 1, JRP: See also "Democratic Campaign Manager," *American Review of Reviews* 78 (August 1928): 125.

87. Willmoore Kendall to Franklin Roosevelt, August 9, 1928, Box 13, FDR28; Reagan, "Campaign of 1928," p. 249; George Davis to John Raskob, July 19, 1928, File 602, Box 1, JRP; Bornet, *Labor Politics*, pp. 76–77; Michael Williams, *The Shadow of the Pope* (New York: Whittlesey, 1932), p. 194; David Burner, *The Politics of Provincialism* (New York: Knopf, 1968), p. 199; Carter Glass to Josephus Daniels, July 16, 1928, Reel 51, Josephus Daniels Papers, Library of Congress.

88. Bernard Baruch to Alfred Smith, July 3, 1928, Vol. 21, Unit VI, Bernard Baruch Papers, Princeton University; Pringle, "Raskob," p. 646; Davis, *FDR*, pp. 823–824; Franklin Roosevelt to Josephus Daniels, July 20, 1928, Box 94, Josephus Daniels Papers, Library of Congress.

89. Sean Cashman, *Prohibition* (New York: Free Press, 1981), p. 190; "Washington Notes," *New Republic*, July 25, 1928, p. 249.

90. Collins, "Kind of Man," pp. 10, 97.

91. Stewart Bach, "Democracy's Happy Warrior Tells the World," *Independent*, September 1, 1928, p. 214; Ralph Casey, "Party Campaign Propaganda," *Annals of the American Academy of Political and Social Science* 179 (May 1935): 101; "Smith Accepts," *Outlook*, September 5, 1928, p. 732; *Official Proceedings . . . Democratic National Convention*, pp. 263–286. A picture of Smith at the podium appears on p. 5 of the September 1, 1928, edition of *Literary Digest*.

CHAPTER 16. TAKING ON AMERICA

1. Frederick Allen, *Only Yesterday* (New York: Harper & Row, 1931), pp. 191–198. The social critic who posed that question was Mencken's absolute favorite writer, himself, in the pages of the Fifth Series of his omnibus *Prejudices*.

2. Ibid., p. 196; *New York Times*, November 20, 1994, Arts and Leisure Section, p. 22.

3. Marie Chatham, "The Role of the National Party Leader from Hanna to Farley," Ph.D., diss., University of Maryland, 1936, pp. 96, 248–249; David Burner, *The Politics of Provincialism* (New York: Knopf, 1968), p. 148.

4. Frances Perkins interview, Book 2, pp. 526–527, 528, CUOHC; the diary is in Box 4, Breckinridge Long Papers, Library of Congress.

5. See material in Box 4, Robert Moses Papers, New York Public Library.

6. Frederick Howe to George Norris, September 28, 1928, Box 4, George Norris Papers, Library of Congress; Key Pittman to Harold Hale, July 30, 1928, Box 14, Key Pittman Papers, Library of Congress; Frances Perkins interview, Book 3, p. 139, CUOHC.

7. Herbert Hoover, *The Memoirs of Herbert Hoover: Years of Adventure* (New York: Macmillan, 1951), pp. 139–147.

8. The diary, marked "Journal," is in Box 1, Brand Whitlock Papers, Library of Congress.

9. Boxes 7 and 9, U.S. Food Administration Documents, Herbert Hoover Presidential Library, West Branch, Iowa.

10. William Allen White to Herbert Hoover, July 20, 1917, Box 42, Series C, William Allen White Papers, Library of Congress.

11. Box 8, U.S. Food Administration Documents, Herbert Hoover Presidential Library.

12. Richard Hofstadter, *The American Political Tradition* (New York: Random House, 1948), p. 285.

13. Herbert Hoover, *American Individualism* (Garden City, N.Y.: Doubleday, Page, 1922), p. 10; Robert Murray, "Herbert Hoover and the Harding Cabinet," in Ellis Hawley, ed., *Herbert Hoover as Secretary of Commerce* (Iowa City: University of Iowa Press, 1981), p. 19.

14. Boxes 174 and 178, HHCT; Box 606, Gifford Pinchot Papers, Library of Congress; Geoffrey Perrett, *America in the Twenties* (New York: Simon & Schuster, 1982), p. 315.

15. Republican Party Papers, Reel 3, p. 22, Library of Congress; undated memo in Lewis Straus Papers, Name and Subject File, Box 14, Herbert Hoover Presidential Library; Felix Ray, "The Somewhat Happy Warrior," *New Republic,* September 12, 1928, p. 94.

16. Alan Lichtman, *Prejudice and the Old Politics* (Chapel Hill: University of North Carolina Press, 1979), p. 6; "Washington Notes," *New Republic,* April 6, 1927, p. 199; "Studies in Temperament," *Atlantic Monthly* 142 (October 1928): 544.

17. Hoover, *Memoirs,* p. 198; Lichtman, *Prejudice,* p. 8; Craig Lloyd, *Aggressive Introvert* (Columbus: Ohio State University Press, 1972), p. 85; Joan Wilson, *Herbert Hoover* (Boston: Little, Brown, 1975), p. 127; Ray Tucker, "The Personalities Have It," *Outlook,* November 7, 1928, p. 1123; James Williams interview, pp. 722–723, CUOHC.

18. Both documents are in Box 178, HHCT.

19. Dorothy Brown, *Mabel Walker Willebrandt* (Knoxville: University of Tennessee Press, 1984), p. 155; Robert Miller, *American Protestantism and Social Issues* (Chapel Hill: University of North Carolina Press, 1958), p. 48; Wilson, *Hoover,* pp. 28–29; Agnes Home to Lou Hoover, September 20, 1928, Box 18, Subject Files, Lou Hoover Papers, Herbert Hoover Presidential Library.

20. Leona Becker, "Alfred E. Smith: A Personality Study of a Political Leader," M.A. thesis, University of Chicago, 1938, p. 52.

21. "Should Liberals Vote for Smith?" *Nation,* September 26, 1928, pp. 284–285.

22. William Klingaman, *1929* (New York: Harper & Row, 1989), p. 20; Robert Murray, *The 103rd Ballot* (New York: Harper & Row, 1976), p. 276.

23. Ernest Abbott, "What the Country Is Thinking," *Outlook,* October 24, 1928, p. 1013.

24. Sherwin Cook, *Torchlight Parade* (New York: Minton, Balch and Company, 1929), p. 291.

25. *Campaign Address of Governor Alfred E. Smith* (Washington, D.C.: Democratic National Committee, 1929), pp. 102–103.

26. Special Senate Committee Investigating Presidential Campaign Expenditures, *Presidential Campaign Expenditures,* 70th Cong. 1st sess., 1928, p. 5; Douglas Craig, *After Wilson* (Chapel Hill: University of North Carolina Press, 1992), p. 25.

27. Louise Overacker, *Presidential Campaign Funds* (Boston: Boston University Press, 1946), p. 34.

28. Ibid., pp. 14–15; Louise Overacker, "Trends in Party Campaign Funds," in Leonard White, ed., *The Future of Government in the United States* (Chicago: University of Chicago Press, 1942), p. 134; Special Senate Committee, *Campaign Expenditures*, p. 6.

29. Overacker, *Campaign Funds*, pp. 14–15; Overacker, "Trends in Party Campaign Funds," p. 134; Special Senate Committee, *Campaign Expenditures*, p. 6; Matthew Josephson and Hannah Josephson, *Al Smith* (Boston: Houghton Mifflin, 1969), p. 355.

30. Raskob's account statement for the Democratic campaign of 1928 is in File 602, Box 1, JRP. See also Ralph Casey, "Party Campaign Propaganda," *Annals of the American Academy of Political and Social Science* 179 (May 1935): 101.

31. Interview with Hugh Carey, June 21, 1994.

32. *New York Times*, September 19, 1928; Bruce Bliven, "Trouping with Al Smith," *New Republic*, October 10, 1928, p. 200; Alfred E. Smith, "Common Sense in Conventions and Campaigning," *Saturday Evening Post*, July 11, 1932, p. 89.

33. *Chicago Daily Journal*, October 1, 1928; George Martin, *Madame Secretary* (Boston: Houghton Mifflin, 1976), p. 199.

34. Alfred E. Smith, *Up to Now* (New York: Viking Press, 1929), p. 395.

35. Becker, "Smith," p. 126; Martin, *Madame Secretary*, p. 92; Henry Pringle, *Alfred E. Smith* (New York: Macy-Masius, 1927), p. 211; *Chicago Daily Journal*, September 14, 1928.

36. Alfred E. Smith, "Electioneering, Old and New," *Saturday Evening Post*, August 30, 1930, p. 66.

37. Frank Graham, *Al Smith—American* (New York: Putnam, 1945), p. 204; Leslie Gower, "The Election of 1928 in Tennessee," M.A. thesis, Vanderbilt University, 1959, p. 138; J. David Stern interview, p. 45, CUOHC; Dorothy Wayman, *David I. Walsh* (Milwaukee: Bruce Publishing, 1952), p. 171; J. Joseph Huthmacher, *Massachusetts People and Politics* (New York: Atheneum, 1959), p. 175; letters to Franklin Roosevelt from Charles Cole, March 28, 1928, and John McBean, September 11, 1928, both in Box 5, FDR28; Herbert Mitgang, *Once Upon a Time in New York* (New York: The Free Press, 2000), p. 69.

38. Memorandum from George Van Namee, July 30, 1928, GVNP; Casey, "Party Propaganda," p. 102. Many of the Smith pamphlets are in the vertical file at the Franklin Roosevelt Presidential Library. The most complete collection of foreign language pamphlets is in GVNP.

39. David Burner, "The Brown Derby Campaign," *New York History* 46 (October 1965): 374; Becker, "Smith," pp. 96–97.

40. Becker, "Smith," pp. 97–98; "Happy Warrior," *Time*, October 16, 1944, p. 26.

41. The story of the Bess Furman article appears in Bess Furman, *Washington By-Line* (New York: Knopf, 1949), pp. 11–17.

42. Louis Liebovich, *Bylines in Despair* (Westport, Conn.: Praeger, 1994), p. 52; *Chicago Daily Journal*, September 22, 1928; "Radio Debunking the Campaigns," *Literary Digest*, December 1, 1928, p. 13.

43. Helen Cook to Lou Hoover, October 16, 1928, Box 17, Subject Files, Lou Hoover Papers, Herbert Hoover Presidential Library; Martin, *Madame Secretary*, p. 196.

44. Carter Glass to Harry Byrd, October 1, 1928, Box 250, Carter Glass Papers, University of Virginia.

45. R. L. Duffus, "Our Radio Battle for the Presidency," *New York Times,* July 8, October 28, 1928.

46. Andrew White, "Hoover vs. Smith as Radio Orators," n.d. but circa 1928, Box 2, EWP.

47. Susan Kismaric, *American Politicians* (New York: Museum of Modern Art, 1994), pp. 204–205; clipping from the *Albany Evening News* in the Personal Clippings File of John Dunn Murphy, Albany, New York; Irvin Weir interview, p. 20, CUOHC; *New York Times,* December 2, 1996.

CHAPTER 17. "POLITICS! POLITICS!"

1. Tony Talbert, "The Actions and Reactions of Waco and McLennan County Voters to the 1928 Presidential Candidacy of Alfred E. Smith," M.A. thesis, Baylor University, 1991, p. 106.

2. All to Franklin Roosevelt: Roger Riis, August 15, 1928, Box 9; Rita Mohvay, October 13, 1928, Box 5, FDR28.

3. L. C. Barnett to Franklin Roosevelt, October 22, 1928, Box 6, FDR28; *Chicago Daily Journal,* August 20, 1928; press release, October 25, 1928, Archives of the College of the Holy Cross, Worcester, Mass.; Ralph Watkins to William Comstock, October 18, 1928, Box 7, William Comstock Papers, Bentley Historical Library, University of Michigan; Broadside by Frank Walsh, September 1928, Box 16, Frank Walsh Papers, New York Public Library.

4. Cordell Hull to Tom Henderson, September 19, 1928, Reel 6, Cordell Hull Papers, Library of Congress; Joseph Myers to William McAdoo, October 3, 1928, Box 340, William McAdoo Papers, Library of Congress; Albert Johnson to Henry T. Allen, September 29, 1928, Box 24, Henry T. Allen Papers, Library of Congress; *New York World,* September 11, 1928; Herbert Doherty, Jr., "Florida and the Presidential Election of 1928," *Florida Historical Society Quarterly* 26 (1947): 175; William Carleton, "The Popish Plot of 1928," *Forum* 112 (September 1949): 141–142; Mo Stokes to James Cox, August 30, 1928, Box 4, James Cox Papers, Wright State University.

5. Donald Lisio, *Hoover, Blacks, and Lily-Whites* (Chapel Hill: University of North Carolina Press, 1985), p. 82; Henry J. Allen to Herbert Hoover, August 28, 1928, Henry J. Allen File, HHCT.

6. *New York Times,* April 10, 1928; John Meloan to Alben Barkeley, undated but c. 1928, Alben Barkley Papers, University of Kentucky; Glenda Morrison, "Women's Participation in the 1928 Presidential Campaign," Ph.D. diss., University of Kansas, 1978, p. 83; Joan Wilson, *Herbert Hoover* (Boston: Little, Brown, 1975), p. 129; Steven Zink, "Cultural Conflict and the 1928 Presidential Campaign in Louisiana," *Southern Studies* (December 1978): 180.

7. *New York Telegram,* September 7, 1928; Paul Lewinson, *Race, Class, and Party* (New York; Russell & Russell, 1963), p. 158.

8. Belle Moskowitz later told Walter White that in retrospect, they had been wrong; Smith should have gone all out for the black vote. Of course, by then she knew that they had lost the white South anyway.

9. Irwin Kurtz to Ogden Mills, July 11, 1928, Box 6, Ogden Mills Papers, Library of Congress; Elisabeth Perry, *Belle Moskowitz* (New York: Oxford University Press, 1987), pp. 203–204; Hugh Reagan, "The Presidential Campaign of 1928 in Alabama," Ph.D. diss., University of Texas, 1961, p. 441; Arthur Schlesinger, Jr., *The Politics of Upheaval* (Boston: Houghton Mifflin, 1960), pp. 426–427; Joseph Lash, *Eleanor and Franklin* (New York: Norton, 1971), p. 319.

10. Jule Felton to Franklin Roosevelt, September 22, 1928, Box 2, FDR28; Cecil Weller, Jr., "Always a Loyal Democrat: The Life of Senate Majority Leader Joseph Taylor Robinson," Ph.D. diss., Texas Christian University, 1993, p. 247.

11. A copy of this appears in Box 2, FDR28

12. *F.D.R.: His Personal Letters,* ed. Elliott Roosevelt (New York: Duell, Sloan and Pearce, 1950), p. 29; Reagan, "Presidential Campaign," pp. 302, 308–309, 317; Ethel Smith to Eleanor Roosevelt, July 23, 1928, Folder 4, Box 6, Eleanor Roosevelt Papers, Franklin Roosevelt Presidential Library.

13. Leslie Gower, "The Election of 1928 in Tennessee," M.A. thesis, Vanderbilt University, 1959, p. 204.

14. Y. T. Eggleston to Franklin Roosevelt, October 10, 1928, Box 6, and the flier with the picture of the Alabama Legislature, Box 1, both in FDR28; Lisio, *Hoover,* p. 31; I. Newby, *Jim Crow's Defense* (Baton Rouge: Louisiana State University Press, 1965), p. 164.

15. Monroe Work, *Negro Year Book: An Annual Encyclopedia of the Negro, 1931–1932* (Tuskegee, Ala.: Negro Year Book Publishing Company, 1931), pp. 89–91.

16. Claude Barnett to George Baker, October 8, 1928, George Baker Papers, Hoover Institute Collection, Herbert Hoover Presidential Library.

17. Britton Johnson, October 24, 1928, Box 12, and Henry Volkmar, October 25, 1928, Box 14, both to Franklin Roosevelt in FDR28. Obituaries of Earl Dickerson appeared in the *Chicago Tribune,* September 4, 1986, and the *Chicago Sun-Times,* September 3, 1986.

18. Assistant Secretary of the NAACP to Hester Greene, September 19, 1928, Box C-190, Group I, NAACP Papers, Library of Congress.

19. A copy of Garvey's complete statement in the *Negro Age* appears in Box 168 of the Furnifold Simmons Papers at Duke University; *New York Times,* October 29, 1928.

20. *New York Amsterdam News,* October 24, 1928; Henry Moon, *Balance of Power* (Garden City, N.Y.: Doubleday, 1948), p. 106.

21. James Grossman, *Land of Hope* (Chicago: University of Chicago Press, 1989), pp. 74–85.

22. *Chicago Defender,* October 20, 1928.

23. David Lewis, *W. E. B. Du Bois* (New York: Henry Holt, 1993), p. 10.

24. *Crisis* (August 1928): 275, (September 1928): 312, (November 1928): 368, 381, 386.

25. Mildred Adams, "A Woman Voter Thinks," *Outlook,* October 24, 1928, p. 1012.

26. Clara Patterson to Lou Hoover, October 17, 1928, Box 20, Subject Files, Lou Hoover Papers, Herbert Hoover Presidential Library; Ida Clarke, "A Woman in the White House," *Century* 113 (March 1927): 590.

27. Glenda Morrison, "Women's Participation in the 1928 Presidential Campaign," Ph.D. diss., University of Kansas, 1978, pp. 213–214; "Planks Proposed by the National League of Women Voters for Inclusion in the Platforms to Be Adopted by the Political Parties, 1928," Reel 17, Part III, League of Women Voters Papers, Library of Congress; Kristi Anderson, *After Suffrage* (Chicago: University of Chicago Press, 1996), p. 71.

28. Kristi Anderson, "Women and Citizenship in the 1920s," in Louise Tilly and Patricia Guerin, eds., *Women, Politics, and Change* (New York: Russell Sage Foundation, 1990), p. 194; Mandel Sener to Henry J. Allen, October 1, 1928, Henry J. Allen File, HHCT.

29. Lillian Wald to Dr. G. E. Selbrede, November 14, 1928, and to Mary McDowell, September 27, 1928, both in the Lillian Wald Papers, New York Public Library; Mary Simkhovitch, "Al Smith—Able, Honest, Liberal," *Nation,* July 4, 1928, p. 10.

30. Victoria Gildersleeve, *Many a Good Crusade* (New York: Macmillan, 1954), p. 218; press release by the National League of Women Voters, October 10, 1928, Box 539, Series III, League of Women Voters Papers, Library of Congress; Mrs. Henry Morgenthau, Jr., "Governor Smith and Water Power," *Woman's Journal* 13 (November 1928): 20; minutes of the Advisory Committee meeting of August 12, 1928, Box 44, Lillian Wald Papers, New York Public Library.

31. Anderson, "Women"; *New York Times,* October 1, 1928.

32. Kenneth Davis, *FDR: The Beckoning of Destiny* (New York: Putnam, 1971), p. 827; Eleanor Roosevelt, "Governor Smith and Our Foreign Policy," *Woman's Journal* 13 (October 1928): 21; Eleanor Roosevelt, "Jeffersonian Principles the Issue in 1928," *Current History* (June 1928): 354–357.

33. Eleanor Roosevelt, *This I Remember* (New York: Harper & Brothers, 1949), pp. 38, 43; *New York Times,* October 17, 1928; *New York Herald-Tribune,* August 24, 1928.

34. Blanche Cook, *Eleanor Roosevelt* (New York: Penguin Books, 1992), p. 366; Eleanor Roosevelt to Edward Perkins, August 1, 1928, Edward Perkins Papers, Franklin D. Roosevelt Presidential Library.

35. Susan Ware, *Partner and I* (New Haven: Yale University Press, 1987), p. 146; "What Campaign Issues Mean to Women," Box 4, Molly Dewson Papers, Franklin D. Roosevelt Presidential Library.

36. Ware, *Partner,* p. xii; "For Women to Think About" appears in the 1928 Campaign-Democratic File in the Vertical File, Franklin Roosevelt Presidential Library; Key Pittman to Joseph Robinson, October 3, 1928, Folder 2, Box 34, Joseph Robinson Papers, University of Arkansas at Fayetteville.

37. Philip Shatts radio speech, October 2, 1928, Box 22, Subject Files, Lou Hoover Papers.

38. Lida Robertson to Lou Hoover, January 31, 1928, Box 21, and Una Winter, "Talk Over Radio Station KGFJ," November 1, 1928, Box 24, both in Subject Files, Lou Hoover Papers; Kathleen Norris," "A Woman's View of Herbert Hoover," Box 178, HHCT.

39. Jane Addams's statement is in Box 1, HHCT, Herbert Hoover Papers; "The Students Elect a President," *Independent,* April 7, 1928, pp. 324–325.

40. Edith Pierce to Charles Marshall, April 26, 1927, Box 2, CMP; J. G. Sims, Jr., to James Talbert, June 5, 1928, Box 36, James Talbert Papers, University of Oklahoma.

41. J. Joseph Huthmacher, *Massachusetts People and Politics* (New York: Atheneum, 1959), p. 173; Leopold Strauss to Henry Rosenfelt, October 20, 1928, Box 13, Name and Subject File, Lewis Straus Papers, Herbert Hoover Presidential Library.

42. Bayard Rustin interview, pp. 22–23, CUOHC.

43. John W. Davis to Claude Meeker, September 6, 1928, and to "Lad," September 11, 1928, both in Box 57, JWDP; Margaret Behan to Franklin Roosevelt, n.d., Box 7, and Franklin Roosevelt to James Hooey, April 17, 1928, and James Hooey to Franklin Roosevelt, May 1, 1928, both in Box 8, all in FDR28.

44. Resident of Lansing, Michigan (signature illegible) to William Comstock, July 7, 1928, Box 7, William Comstock Papers, Bentley Historical Library, University of Michigan; *New York Times,* October 14, 27, November 4, 1928.

45. Emily Smith Warner interview, p. 73, CUOHC; Sean Cashman, *Prohibition* (New York: Free Press, 1981), p. 193; interview with Hugh Carey, June 21, 1994; Eddie Dowling to Alfred Smith, September 5, 1928, Box 18, George Graves Papers, New York State Archives, Albany,

New York; John Dewey, "Why I Am for Smith," *New Republic*, November 7, 1928, pp. 320–321; *New York Times*, September 26, October 25, 1928; *Democratic Campaign News*, GVNP.

46. A copy of the letterhead of Sports Champions for Al Smith is in Box 148, James Walker Papers, New York Municipal Archives.

47. Ibid., p. 378.

48. Ibid., p. 385.

49. *New York Times*, October 20, 1928; handwritten diary of Breckinridge Long, October 19, 1928, Box 4, Breckinridge Long Papers, Library of Congress.

50. Pat Harrison to Alben Barkley, September 21, 1928, Alben Barkley Papers, University of Kentucky.

CHAPTER 18. AND THE POPE WILL MOVE TO WASHINGTON

1. Roberta Rosen, "A Roman Catholic Runs for President," M.A. thesis, Smith College, 1961, p. 14; Michael Williams, *The Shadow of the Pope* (New York: Whittlesley House, 1932), pp. 68–72, 124; e-mail from Victor Greene on H-Ethnic, October, 6, 1999; Jody Roy, *Rhetorical Campaigns of the 19th Century Anti-Catholics and Catholics in America* (Lewiston, ME: Edwin Mellen Press, 2000), p. 25.

2. C. Vann Woodward, *Tom Watson* (New York: Oxford University Press, 1938), pp. 419–421.

3. Thomas Coffey, *The Long Thirst* (New York: Dell Books, 1975), p. 161.

4. David Chalmers, *Hooded Americanism* (Chicago: Quadrangle Books, 1965), p. 33; David Goldberg, "Unmasking the Ku Klux Klan," *Journal of American Ethnic History* 15 (Summer 1996): 33.

5. Kathleen Blee, *Women of the Klan* (Berkeley: University of California Press, 1991), p. 89.

6. Stanley Coben, *Rebellion Against Victorianism* (New York: Oxford University Press, 1991), pp. 141–142.

7. Kenneth Jackson, *The Ku Klux Klan in the City* (Chicago: Ivan Dee, 1967), pp. 125, 237; John Barry, *Rising Tide* (New York: Simon & Schuster, 1997), p. 142; Arnold Rice, *The Ku Klux Klan in American Politics* (Washington, D.C.: Public Affairs Press, 1962), p. 12; William Smith, "Alfred E. Smith and John F. Kennedy: The Religious Issue During the Presidential Campaigns of 1928 and 1960," Ph.D. diss., Southern Illinois University, 1964, p. 37; Charles Alexander, *The Ku Klux Klan in the Southwest* (Norman: University of Oklahoma Press, 1995), p. 87.

8. Jackson, *Klan in the City*, p. 239; John Beadles, "The Syracuse Irish, 1812–1928," Ph.D. diss., Syracuse University, 1974, pp. 371–372; Chalmers, *Hooded Americanism*, pp. 242–246; interview with Hugh Carey, June 21, 1994.

9. Material on the Massena incident appears in Folder 200-18, and Vigilantes to Judge Proskauer, December 20, 1926, Folder 200-17, both in AESOP.

10. Letters from George Graves to Patrick McGovern, December 19, 1923, and to C. C. McCarty, June 11, 1923, both in Folder 200-341, and Alfred E. Smith to Thomas Hanley, September 8, 1926, Folder 200-517, all in AESOP; Emily Smith Warner interview, p. 76, CUOHC; David Colburn, "Alfred E. Smith: The First Fifty Years, 1873–1924," Ph.D. diss., University of North Carolina at Chapel Hill, 1971, p. 21.

11. Charles Morris, *An American Church* (New York: Times Books, 1997), pp. 135–138; *New York Times*, June 16, 22, 1926; Cashman, *Prohibition*, pp. 196–197.

12. Edmund Moore, *A Catholic Runs for President* (New York: Ronald Press, 1956), p. 67.

13. Charles Marshall, "Open Letter to the Honorable Alfred E. Smith," *Atlantic Monthly* 139 (April 1927): 540–549.

14. Ellery Sedgewick to Franklin Roosevelt, March 3, 1927, and Roosevelt to Sedgewick, March 19, 1927, both in Box 5, FDR28; Kenneth Davis, *FDR: The New York Years* (New York: Random House, 1979), p. 814.

15. Joseph Proskauer, *A Segment of My Times* (New York: Farrar, Straus, 1950), pp. 55–56; Elisabeth Perry, *Belle Moskowitz* (New York: Oxford University Press, 1987), pp. 188–189.

16. Perry, *Moskowitz*, pp. 188–189; Joseph Proskauer interview, pp. 29–32, CUOHC; Emily Smith Warner, *The Happy Warrior* (Garden City, N.Y.: Doubleday, 1956), p. 184; interview with Anthony Smith, July 23, 1995.

17. Interview with Ruth Proskauer Smith, July 10, 1995; Alfred E. Smith, "Catholic and Patriot: Governor Smith Replies," *Atlantic Monthly* 139 (May 1927): 721–728.

18. *New York Times*, April 18, 1927; "Al Smith's Letter in Spain," *Living Age*, June 15, 1927, pp. 1046–1047; Moore, *Catholic Runs*, p. 67. The correspondence between Sedgewick and Marshall over a possible reply appears in Box 2, CMP.

19. Robert Schuler, *Al Smith, a Vigorous Study* (Los Angeles: J. R. Spencer, 1928), frontpiece, pp. 54–58, unnumbered pages.

20. Mrs. J. L. Swint to Franklin Roosevelt, n.d., Box 4, Democratic National Committee Papers, FDRL; Caroline Bond to John Roach Straton, August 20, 1928, and J. H. Fletcher to John Roach Straton, August 20, 1928, all in Box 12, John Roach Straton Papers, American Baptist Historical Society.

21. Alfred Kirchhofer interview, p. 8, and Edward Anthony interview, p. 5, both in the Herbert Hoover Presidential Library; Marie Chatham, "The Role of the National Party Leader from Hanna to Farley," Ph.D. diss., University of Maryland, 1953, pp. 171–172.

22. Lou Hoover to Edgar Rickard, October 4, 1928, Box 21, Personal Correspondence Files, Lou Hoover Papers.

23. Ibid.

24. Lou Hoover to Mrs. C. A. Broaddus, October 29, 1928, Box 16, and to Mrs. Peabody, October 11, 1928, Box 17, both in Subject Files, Lou Hoover Papers.

25. Edgar Rickard Diaries, August 15, 1928, Herbert Hoover Presidential Library; Stanley Washburn interview, pp. 187–188, CUOHC.

26. Letter from Henry Stites to "My Fellow Republicans," October 29, 1928, Alben Barkley Papers, University of Kentucky; campaign slogans used in the 1928 and 1932 campaigns, Herbert Hoover Presidential Library; Klan notices and clippings in GVNP; Chalmers, *Hooded Americanism*, p. 234; R. W. Patterson to Lewis Straus, Jr., August 22, 1928, Box 13, Name and Subject File, Lewis Straus Papers, Herbert Hoover Presidential Library.

27. Winifred Mallon, "Mrs. Willebrandt and Her Job," *Woman's Journal* 13 (October 1928): 18; Alice Winter, "The First Lady in Law," *Ladies' Home Journal* 42 (June 1925): 39.

28. Mabel Willebrandt, *The Inside of Prohibition* (Indianapolis: Bobbs-Merrill, 1929), p. 344.

29. The version of this speech used was the one printed in ibid., pp. 303–317.

30. Clippings in GVNP; "Mrs. Willebrandt Runs Amuck," *Independent*, September 22, 1928, p. 269; Robert Taft to Walter Newton, September 27, 1928, Box 1287, Robert Taft Papers, Library of Congress.

31. Frank Buckley to Alfred E. Smith, October 25, 1932, Folder 235, Box 10, AESPP; Coffey, *Long Thirst*, pp. 291–294.

32. Donald Heath, "The Presidential Election of 1928: Protestants' Opposition to Alfred E. Smith as Reflected in Denominational Journals," Ph.D. diss., Vanderbilt University, 1973, p. 7; Tract No. 1 appears in the Alben Barkley Papers, University of Kentucky; Austin Hoover, "The Presidential Campaign of 1928 in Texas," M.A. thesis, University of Texas at El Paso, 1967, pp. 224, 231–232; Blee, *Women of the Klan*, p. 86; Rembert Smith, *Politics in a Protestant Church* (Atlanta: Ruralist Press, 1930), p. 98; Lillian Wald to Mary McDowell, September 27, 1928, Box 5, Lillian Wald Papers, New York Public Library.

33. Robert Cunningham to Ogden Mills, n.d., Box 6, Ogden Mills Papers, Library of Congress; clipping in Box 2, EWP.

34. Rhorer affidavit appears in the Alben Barkley Papers, University of Kentucky.

35. Chalmers, *Hooded Americanism*, p. 162; *The American Standard* is in the "Book of Horrors" in the Rare Book Room, Columbia University.

36. Undated clipping in GVNP; Marion Fox, "A Forecast," *Atlantic Monthly* 140 (September 1927): 388; Heath, "Presidential Campaign," pp. 172–173; James Farley and James Cardiff, *Governor Al Smith* (New York: Farrar, Straus & Cudahy, 1959), pp. 159–160; John Beadles, "The Syracuse Irish, 1812–1928," Ph.D. diss, Syracuse University, 1974, p. 385; *Fellowship Forum* appears in Box 884 of the Franklin Roosevelt Papers; Leslie Case to Lou Hoover, October 6, 1928, Box 21, Subject Files, Lou Hoover Papers. The display at the Herbert Hoover Library, West Branch, Iowa, includes a photo of the tunnel construction that was used to attack Smith, although the caption refers to it erroneously as the Lincoln Tunnel.

37. "Churches Mixing in the Political Fray," *Literary Digest*, September 15, 1928, p. 8; Virginius Dabney, *Dry Messiah* (New York: Knopf, 1949), p. 181; Robert Miller, *American Protestantism and Social Issues* (Chapel Hill: University of North Carolina Press, 1958), p. 53; Heath, "Presidential Campaign," pp. 25, 109; Matthew Neely to Franklin Roosevelt, November 23, 1928, Box 6, FDR28; Henry Allen to Joseph Robinson, November 7, 1928, Folder 2, Box 37, Joseph Robinson Papers, University of Arkansas at Fayetteville.

38. *Fellowship Forum* and *Tocsin* are in the "Book of Horrors," Columbia University Rare Book Room; Davis, *FDR*, p. 67; Alan Lichtman, *Prejudice and the Old Politics* (Chapel Hill: University of North Carolina Press, 1979), p. 59; Regina Benson to Franklin Roosevelt, October 18, 1928, Box 2, FDR28; Williams, *Shadow*, p. 241.

39. Heath, "Campaign of 1928," p. 163; Charles Fountain, "The Case for the Opposition to a Catholic President," *Current History* 27 (March 1928): 767, 778.

40. John Ryan, "A Catholic View of the Election," *Current History* 29 (December 1928): 379; Miller, *American Protestantism*, p. 61.

41. Miller, *American Protestantism*, p. 55; *Waterloo Evening Courier*, October 22, 1928, Box 36, Subject Files, Lou Hoover Papers.

42. Kate Penney's piece is in Box 20, Subject Files, Lou Hoover Papers; Spencer Murray, "The Role of Major Tennessee Denominations in the 1928 Presidential campaign of Alfred E. Smith," Ph.D. diss., Vanderbilt University, 1971, p. 177; Walter Davenport, "Tennessee for Hoover, Missouri for Smith," *Collier's*, September 29, 1982, p. 8.

43. Thomas Garvey to George MacNamee, August 11, 1928, File 602, Box 1, JRP; Ben Smith to Democratic National Committee, September 24, 1928, Alben Barkley Papers, Univer-

sity of Kentucky; *New York Times*, October 6, 1928; Jacob Dickinson to John Davis, October 15, 1928, Box 57, JWDP; *Journal of the Thirteenth Delegated General Conference of the Methodist Episcopal Church* (New York: Methodist Book Concern, 1928), p. 1733; Leslie Gower, "The Election of 1928 in Tennessee," M.A. thesis, Vanderbilt University, 1959, pp. 190, 200; William Anderson interview, p. 71, CUOHC; Louise Overacker, *Presidential Campaign Funds* (Boston: Boston University Press, 1946), p. 6.

44. Hugh Evans to Robert Moses, September 22, 1928, Box 4, Robert Moses Papers, NYPL; Marvin Jones interview, pp. 384–385, CUOHC.

45. William McAdoo to Joseph O'Neill, October 19, 1928, Box 340, William McAdoo Papers, Library of Congress.

46. David Burner, *The Politics of Provincialism* (New York: Knopf, 1968), p. 75; Hugh Reagan, "The Presidential Campaign of 1928 in Alabama," Ph.D. thesis, University of Texas, 1961, p. 213; Ruth Silva, *Rum, Religion, and Votes* (University Park: Pennsylvania University Press, 1962), p. 16.

47. Lillie Case to Lou Hoover, October 6, 1928, Box 21, Subject file, Lou Hoover Papers; Gower, "Election of 1928," pp. 108–109; interview with Judge David Edelstein, October 16, 1996.

48. Austin Hoover, "The Presidential Campaign of 1928 in Texas," Ph.D. diss., University of Texas at El Paso, 1967, pp. 233, 238; Coffey, *Long Thirst*, p. 155; Reagan, "Presidential Campaign," p. 55; Edgar Rickard to Hugh Gibson, September 11, 1928, Hugh Gibson Papers, Hoover Institute Collection, Herbert Hoover Presidential Library.

49. David Burner, "Brown Derby Campaign," *New York History* 46 (October 1965): 376–377; Richard O'Connor, *The First Hurrah* (New York: Putnam, 1970), p. 210; Annie Hugillmof to John Davis, October 11, 1928, Box 57, JWDP; Eleanor Fox to Lou Hoover, August 3, 1928, Box 17, Subject Files, Lou Hoover Papers; Thomas Robins to Franklin Roosevelt, October 9, 1928, Box 9, FDR28; Cecelia Casserly to Key Pittman, October 16, 1928, Box 11, Key Pittman Papers, Library of Congress.

50. Reagan, "Presidential Campaign," p. 326; pamphlet on Mrs. Hoover is in Box 6, Ogden Mills Papers, Library of Congress; Moore, *Catholic Runs for President*, pp. 158–159; *New York Times*, July 13, 17, 19, 1928; "The Whispering Campaign," *Christian Century*, September 20, 1928, pp. 1120–1121.

51. Frances Perkins interview, Book 2, p. 692, CUOHC.

52. Oscar Handlin, *Al Smith and His America* (Boston: Little, Brown, 1958), p. 130.

53. Alma White, *Heroes of the Fiery Cross* (Zarepath, N.J.: Good Citizen, 1928), pp. 10, 19, 21, 34.

54. Murray, "Role of Tennessee Denominations," pp. 112, 182.

55. Marc Gold, "From State House to White House," *Seaport* 22 (Fall 1988): 19; Gustavus Myers, *History of Bigotry in the United States* (New York: Random House, 1943), p. 324.

56. Lillian Wald to Henry Farnum, October 22, 1928, Box 5, Lillian Wald Papers, New York Public Library; Frances Perkins interview, Book 2, pp. 579–80, and Marvin Jones interview, pp. 375–76, CUOHC; the letter to Davis appears in Box 57, JWDP.

57. Interview with Judge Simon Rifkind, June 27, 1994.

CHAPTER 19. THE DECISION

1. Letter from Whaley-Eaton Service, November 3, 1928, Box 15, Name and Subject Files, Lewis Straus Papers, Herbert Hoover Presidential Library.

2. *New York Times*, October 14, 1928; Felix Frankfurter, "Why I Am for Smith," *New*

Republic, October 31, 1928, pp. 292–295; Jack Beatty, *The Rascal King* (Reading, Mass.: Addison-Wesley, 1992), pp. 256–258; Frances Perkins interview, Book 2, pp. 643–645, CUOHC.

3. Austin Hoover, "The Presidential Campaign of 1928 in Texas," M.A. thesis, University of Texas at El Paso, 1967, p. 241; James Farley interview, pp. 147–148, CUOHC.

4. Frances Perkins interview, Book 2, p. 689, CUOHC; *New York Times,* November 6, 1928.

5. James Gerard interview, p. 80, CUOHC; William Klingaman, *1929* (New York: Harper & Row, 1989), p. 26; *New York Times,* November 5, 6, 1928.

6. *New York Times,* November 7, 1928.

7. Ibid.

8. Ibid.

9. Ibid., November 7, 1928; Eddie Cantor, *Take My Life* (Garden City, N.Y.: Doubleday, 1957), p. 189; interview with Mildred Graves Ryan, July 17, 1994; E. J. Kahn, Jr., *The World of Swope* (New York: Simon & Schuster, 1965), p. 287.

10. *New York Times,* November 7, 1928.

11. Ibid., November 7, 1928; Frances Perkins interview, Book 2, p. 691, CUOHC.

12. The *San Francisco Call* is in Box 35 of the Subject Files, Lou Hoover Papers; Edgar Rickard Diaries, November 6, 1928, Herbert Hoover Presidential Library.

13. Kahn, *Swope,* p. 288.

14. Ibid.

15. *New York Times,* November 8, 1928.

16. Bernard Bellush, *Roosevelt as Governor* (New York: Columbia University Press, 1955), p. 26; Herbert Lehman interview, p. 229, and Frances Perkins interview, Book 2, p. 694, both in CUOHC; John W. Davis to Emma Davis, November 8, 1928, Box 58, JWDP.

17. James Farley, *Jim Farley's Story* (New York: McGraw-Hill, 1948), p. 5; Joseph Lash, *Eleanor and Franklin* (New York: Norton, 1971), p. 319.

18. *New York Times,* November 8, 1928; Allan Lichtman, *Prejudice and the Old Politics* (Chapel Hill: University of North Carolina Press, 1979), p. 3.

19. "Concerning the Democratic Party," *American Review of Reviews* 78 (December 1928): 474; James Sweeney, "Rum, Romanism, and Virginia Democrats," *Virginia Magazine of History and Biography* 90 (October 1982): 403; Roy Peel and Thomas Donnelly, *The 1928 Campaign* (New York: Richard Smith, 1931), map opposite p. 106.

20. Ernest Abbott, "The Press and the Poll," *Outlook,* November 21, 1928, p. 1196; Charles Hilles to Herbert Hoover, November 6, 1928, Folder 1421, Box 118, Charles Hilles Papers, Sterling Memorial Library, Yale University; Herbert Hoover, *The Memoirs of Herbert Hoover: The Cabinet and the Presidency* (New York: Macmillan, 1952), pp. 208–209; Hofstadter's article appeared in the March 17, 1960, issue of *Reporter.*

21. Lichtman, *Prejudice,* pp. 42–43, 47–48, 56–57, 71, 76, 213.

22. Letters to Franklin Roosevelt: John Ward, December 7, 1928, Box 584; Carl Ristine, December 5, 1928, Box 327; Jeanne (last name not clear), December 7, 1928, Box 20; and James Kiernan, January 16, 1929, Box 702, all in Democratic National Committee Papers, Franklin D. Roosevelt Presidential Library.

23. Herbert Lehman interview, p. 238, and Henry Wallace interview, p. 195, both in CUOHC; George Norris to L. B. Lilliedoll, November 15, 1928, Boxes 4–5, George Norris Papers, Library of Congress; Lichtman, *Prejudice,* pp. 52–53; Ross Lillard to Henry T. Allen, November 12, 1928, Box 25, Henry T. Allen Papers, Library of Congress.

24. "Smith, Hoover, and Prosperity," *Forum* 80 (November 1928): 748.

25. J. Joseph Huthmacher, *Massachusetts Politics and People* (New York: Atheneum, 1959), pp. 99–100; Stanley Coben, *Rebellion Against Victorianism* (New York: Oxford University Press, 1991), pp. 112–135; James Shideler, "The LaFollette Progressive Party Campaign of 1924," *Wisconsin Magazine of History* 33 (June 1950): 456.

26. Bureau of the Census, *Historical Statistics of the United States,* part 2 (Washington, D.C.: Department of Commerce, 1975), pp. 1067–1072.

27. Ibid., pp. 12, 34.

28. Fabian Franklin, "Analyzing the Election Results," *Current History* 29 (December 1928): 370.

29. Samuel Lubell, *The Future of American Politics* (Garden City, N.Y.: Doubleday, 1951), p. 32; Robert Murray, *The 103rd Ballot* (New York: Harper and Row, 1976), p. 23.

30. Lubell, *American Politics,* pp. 36–37; Samuel Eldersveld, "The Influence of Metropolitan Party Pluralities in Presidential Elections Since 1920," *American Political Science Review* 43 (December 1949): 1194.

31. Lubell, *American Politics,* pp. 36–37; Kenneth Davis, *FDR: The New York Years* (New York: Random House, 1979), p. 48.

32. Huthmacher, *Massachusetts Politics,* p. 184; Beatty, *Rascal King,* p. 259; Stephen Erie, *Rainbow's End* (Berkeley: University of California Press, 1988), p. 119; Paul Street, "Clearing a Path Through the Jungle," ms. provided to the author, p. 330.

33. Lawrence Fuchs, *The Political Behavior of American Jews* (Glencoe, Ill.: Free Press, 1956), pp. 66–67; "Survey of the Election of 1928. New York State," Box 15, Name and Subject File, Lewis Straus Papers, Herbert Hoover Presidential Library; J. A. Sullivan to Alben Barkley, August 22, 1928, Alben Barkley Papers, University of Kentucky.

34. Gerald Gamm, *The Making of New Deal Democrats* (Chicago: University of Chicago Press, 1989), p. 130.

35. Ibid., p. 67.

36. Will Bell to John Raskob, November 9, 1928, File 602, Box 1, JRP; Joseph Hughes to Franklin Roosevelt, November 8, 1928, Box 6, FDR28; Henry Robinson, *The Cardinal* (New York: Simon & Schuster, 1950), pp. 398–399.

37. Interview with Brother Philip O'Brien, October 16, 1997.

38. *New York Times,* November 8, 1928; clipping in GVNP.

39. *New York Times,* December 11, 25, 26, 1928; interview with Helen McManus, November 15, 1996.

40. Memorandum from M. M. Moran to Mr. Seer, December 12, 1928, Folder 602, Box 1, JRP.

41. *New York Times,* December 6, 30, 1928, January 1, 1929.

42. Ibid., January 1, 1929.

43. "Al Smith and Wendell Willkie," *Commonweal,* October 20, 1944, p. 4; article by Charles Stewart, October 24, 1931, Volume 2, Empire State Building Scrapbooks, ESBP; interview with Alfred E. Smith IV, August 13, 1994; Frances Perkins interview, Book 3, p. 35, and Book 2, p. 698, CUOHC; Richard O'Connor, *The First Hurrah* (New York: Putnam, 1970), p. 237.

CHAPTER 20. *UP TO NOW*

1. Christopher Finan, "Fallen Hero," Ph.D. diss., Columbia University, 1992, p. 107; *New York Times,* January 5, 1929; document with Governor Smith's business address is in Box 74,

Joseph Tumulty Papers, Library of Congress; E. J. Kahn, Jr., *The World of Swope* (New York: Simon & Schuster, 1965), p. 46.

2. The actual account of the Boston dinner is in *New York Times,* May 15, 1929. The legend that developed is faithfully told in J. M. Gillis, "Al Smith as Statesman," *Catholic World* 160 (November 1944): 101, and James Farley and James Coniff, *Governor Al Smith* (New York: Farrar, Straus & Cudahy, 1959), p. 167. The reality, as depicted in the *Times,* was that only two of Harvard's academic departments were not represented at the dinner, ethics and the science of government, thus undermining at least some elements of the story as told by devout Smith supporters. References to Smith's busy schedule can be found in Frances Perkins interview, Book 3, P. 300, CUOHC; letters from Smith to Newton Baker, November 8, 1929, and to Edward Robert, November 7, 1929, both in Box 209, Newton Baker Papers, Library of Congress; and in the *New York Times,* January 13, 1929.

3. Alfred Smith to H. G. Seer, January 31, 1931, File 2112, JRP; Alfred Smith to Joseph Tumulty, June 20, September 25, 1929, Box 74, Joseph Tumulty Papers, Library of Congress; *New York Times,* October 24, 1929.

4. *New York Times,* February 9, 1929; John Raskob to Alfred Smith, January 18, 1929, File 2112, JRP; the Simmons ad, dated August 19, 1929, is in File 197, Box 8, AESPP.

5. George Bye to Alfred Smith, December 1, 1929, Box 9, George Graves Papers, New York State Archives; George Bye to Belle Moskowitz, May 24, 1929, Folder 513, Box 17, and George Bye to Belle Moskowitz, May 16, 1929, Folder 511, Box 17, both in AESPP; *New York Times,* June 11, 1929.

6. The contract is in Folder 513, Box 17, AESPP; George Bye to Belle Moskowitz, April 13, 1929, and Belle Moskowitz to George Bye, June 20, 1929, both in Folder 511, Box 17, AESPP; George Bye to Alfred Smith, July 17, 1929, James O. Brown Papers, Columbia University.

7. *New York Times,* June 11, 1929.

8. Henry Pringle, "Al Smith and His New York," *New York Times Book Review,* October 6, 1929, p. 1; *New York Evening World* editorial, July 26, 1929, Folder 509, Box 17, AESPP; Harold Kellock, "Up from the City Streets," *Nation,* November 27, 1929, p. 629; John Owens to Alfred E. Smith, July 26, 1929, Alfred E. Smith Papers, Manhattan College.

9. Abram Elkus to Alfred E. Smith, July 27, 1929, Alfred E. Smith Papers, Manhattan College.

10. George Bye to Alfred E. Smith, August 9, 1929, Folder 548, and January 18, 1930, and February 6, 1931, both in Folder 539, all in Box 18; ad for the McNaught Syndicate in Folder 518, Box 17; Charles McAdam to Belle Moskowitz, January 20, 1932, Folder 518, Box 18; Frank Murphy to Alfred E. Smith, October 21, 1932, Folder 540, Box 18, all in AESPP; Alfred E. Smith, "Safeguarding Our Assets," *Ladies' Home Journal* 46 (October 1929): 3–4, 75, 78.

11. William McMasters to Alfred E. Smith, June 16, 1931, Folder 544, Box 18, AESPP. The treatment for the movie is in Folder 542 of the same box.

12. Floyd Gibbons, *The Red Napoleon* (New York: J. Cape and H. Smith, 1929).

13. Finan, "Fallen Hero," pp. 111–112; *New York Times,* January 3, 1929.

14. Carol Willis, "Form Follows Finance: The Empire State Building," in David Ward and Olivier Zunz, eds., *The Landscape of Modernity* (New York: Russell Sage Foundation, 1992), p. 166; John Tauranac, *The Empire State Building* (New York: Scribner's, 1995), p. 42; undated, handwritten memo by John Raskob describing the origins of the Empire State Building, File 743, JRP.

15. William Klingaman, *1929* (New York: Harper & Row, 1989), pp. 107–108; Tauranac, *Empire State*, p. 96; Eddie Dowling interview, p. 111, CUOHC.

16. Tauranac, *Empire State*, pp. 96–97.

17. Douglas Haskell, "A Temple of Jehu," *Nation*, May 27, 1931, p. 589; Willis, "Form," p. 170.

18. Details of the financing come from a memo of understanding between Empire State, Inc. and respectively, Chatham Phenix Allied Corporation, Pierre S. Du Pont, and John J. Raskob, February 18, 1930, File 743 of JRP.

19. Tauranac, *Empire State*, pp. 123–124; Willis, "Form," p. 170.

20. "Our Tallest Sky-Piercing Pinnacle," *Literary Digest*, May 16, 1931, p. 11; Empire State, Inc., *The Empire State Building* (New York: Select Printing Company, 1931), p. 63; Andrew Eken, "The Ultimate in Skyscrapers?" *Scientific American* 144 (May 1931): 318–319; "Man's Mightiest Monument," *Popular Mechanics* 54 (December 1930): 920–921.

21. "Mightiest Monument," p. 922; *New York Times*, July 28, 1995; Eken, "Ultimate," p. 320; Jonathan Goldman, *The Empire State Building* (New York: St. Martin's Press, 1980), p. 38; Kenneth Swezey, "Robot Elevators to Serve 85,000 in Greatest Building," *Popular Science* 118 (April 1931): 151.

22. Clippings from Vols. 1, 2, and 6, Empire State Building Scrapbooks, ESBP.

23. Interviews with Helen McManus, November 15, 1996, and Walter Smith, December 17, 1996; Vol. 12, Empire State Building Scrapbooks, ESBP.

24. Alfred E. Smith to Herbert Hoover, March 30, 1931, and telegram from Hoover to Smith, April 29, 1931, both in Empire State Building File, Box 110, President's Personal File, Herbert Hoover Papers, Herbert Hoover Presidential Library.

25. Empire State, Inc., *Empire State*, p. 93.

26. Scrapbook 5.2, Empire State Building Scrapbooks, ESBP; Empire State, Inc., *Empire State*, pp. 93–94; interview with Father Arthur Smith, June 28, 1996.

27. Empire State, Inc., *Empire State*, p. 95.

28. Geoffrey Perrett, *America in the Twenties* (New York: Simon & Schuster, 1982), p. 422; Richard O'Connor, *The First Hurrah* (New York: Putnam, 1970), p. 238; interview with Walter Smith, December 17, 1996; Vol. 3, Empire State Building Scrapbooks, ESBP; "Tallest Pinnacle," p. 11.

29. Willis, "Form," p. 171.

30. Leonard Moore to John Raskob, August 31, 1939; memo from George R. Read & Co., April 8, 1930, both in File 743, JRP.

31. Vols. 5.2 and 12, Empire State Building Scrapbooks, ESBP; Edmund Wilson, "Progress and Poverty," *New Republic*, May 20, 1931, p. 13; memo from Patterson and Ridgeway to John Raskob, December 15, 1937, File 743, JRP.

32. Handwritten memo by John Raskob, Leonard Moore to John Raskob, August 31, 1939, Alfred E. Smith to Frederick Ecker, December 22, 1937, all in File 743, JRP; Vols. 12 and 17, Empire State Building Scrapbooks, ESBP.

33. Vol. 14, Empire State Building Scrapbooks, ESBP.

34. Willis, "Form," pp. 180–181.

35. *New York Times*, September 30, 1931; Vol. 11, Empire State Building Scrapbooks, ESBP.

36. Vols. 5.2, 12, 13, 14, 16, 19, 17, 20, Empire State Building Scrapbooks, ESBP; *New York*

Times, October 27, 1931, February 10, 1932; Alfred E. Smith to Joseph Kennedy, November 10, 1938, and to the Hon. Sir Ronald Lindsey, December 2, 1938; Joseph Kennedy, November 25, 1938, and Ronald Lindsey, December 3, 1938, to Alfred E. Smith, all in the Personal Files of Anne and John Cadigan.

37. Vol. 14, Empire State Building Scrapbooks, ESBP.

38. Vols. 15, 16, 17, 19, Empire State Building Scrapbooks, ESBP.

39. John Raskob to Henry T. Allen, December 4, 1928, Box 25, Henry T. Allen Papers, Library of Congress; "Everybody Ought to Be Rich," *Ladies' Home Journal* 46 (August 1929); p. 9.

40. The Alfred E. Smith Private Papers Collection at the New York State Library includes the following: Alfred E. Smith to Fred French, February 29, 1932, and Smith to William Kelly, March 9, 1932, both in Folder 242, Box 11; Alfred E. Smith to J. P. Evers, February 8, 1934, Folder 245, Box 11; Robert Moses to Alfred E. Smith, January 19, 1931, Folder 26, Box 1.

41. The Alfred E. Smith Private Papers includes: Smith to Junius Morgan, January 16, 1932, Folder 243, Box 11; Phillip Donohue to Smith, October 19, 1934, Folder 244, Box 11; Smith to A. O. Slaughter, Folder 246, Box 11. Gene Smith, *The Shattered Dream* (New York: Morrow, 1970), p. 91.

42. Finan, "Fallen Hero," pp. 114–115.

43. *New York Times,* January 18, 1929; John Broderick, February 15, 1927, and James Riordan, February 23, 1927 to John Raskob, File 500, Box 1, JRP.

44. *New York Times,* January 18, 1929; data on the assets of the County Trust Company are in File 500, Box 1, JRP; Finan, "Fallen Hero," p. 117.

45. Finan, "Fallen Hero," pp. 117–118; *New York Times,* November 10, 1929.

46. *New York Times,* November 10, 1929; clippings in GVNP.

47. *New York Times,* November 10, 13, 1929.

48. Ibid., November 10, 30, December 2, 1929.

49. Ibid., November 10, 1929; clippings in GVNP; Finan, "Fallen Hero," p. 119.

50. The underwriting agreement is in File 602, Box 17, JRP.

51. The list of participants, with amounts, is in File 602, Box 17, JRP.

52. See for example, Raskob to Thomas Fortune Ryan, October 17, 1928, File 602, Box 1, JRP.

53. *New York Times,* March 21, 1932. See also John Raskob to T. J. Mara, July 28, 1931, File 500, Box 2, and George Van Namee to John Raskob, August 3, 1931, Folder 602, Box 15, JRP.

54. See John Raskob to P. J. Kenny, August 1, 1931, File 500, Box 2, JRP.

55. All of these letters are in File 602, Box 17, JRP.

56. John Raskob to Alfred E. Smith, December 2, 1930, and legal notice to T. J. Mara, November 24, 1930, both in File 602, Box 17, JRP.

57. Orie Kelly to John Raskob, July 22, 1931, Raskob to George Van Namee, July 23, 1931, and Alfred E. Smith, July 23, 1931, George Van Namee to John Raskob, August 3, 1931, and Raskob to Roy Howard, March 23, 1932, all in File 602, Box 15; and Raskob to P. J. Kenny, August 1, 1931, White & Case (law firm) to Orie Kelly, November 25, 1935, and to John Raskob, April 13 and November 28, 1936, Ernst, Cane & Bender to Orie Kelly, October 3, 1936, and Orie Kelly to John Raskob, December 2, 1936, all in File 500, Box 2, JRP; *New York Times,* March 22, 24, 1932, October 21, 1933; Finan, "Fallen Hero," p. 152.

CHAPTER 21. THE LITTLE BOY

1. James Farley states that the two met in 1910, but also cites that this was the year that Smith was Speaker of the Assembly, a position he did not attain until 1913. It is likely that the two met somewhere around this period as part of the regular schedule of meetings dealing with either the state's legislative business or party affairs. James Farley and James Coniff, *Governor Al Smith* (New York: Farrar, Straus and Cudahy, 1959), p. 153.

2. Ted Morgan, *FDR* (New York: Simon & Schuster, 1985), p. 144; Geoffrey Ward, *A First-Class Temperament* (New York: HarperCollins, 1989), p. 165.

3. Lela Stiles, *The Man Behind Roosevelt* (Cleveland: World Publishing Company, 1954), p. 63; *New York Times*, October 21, 1918; Alfred Smith to Franklin Roosevelt, October 19, 1918, Box 5, FDRB; James MacGregor Burns, *Roosevelt: The Lion and the Fox* (New York: Harcourt, Brace & World, 1956), p. 98.

4. Frances Perkins, *The Roosevelt I Knew* (New York: Viking Press, 1946), p. 27; Frances Perkins interview, Book 2, p. 83, and Emily Smith Warner interview, p. 32, both in CUOHC.

5. Thomas Chadbourne, *The Autobiography of Thomas Chadbourne*, ed. Charles Goetsch and Margaret Shivers (New York: Oceana Publications, 1985), p. 165; Franklin Roosevelt to Al Smith, July 30, September 4, 1920, Box 10, Franklin D. Roosevelt Papers, 1920 Campaign, Franklin D. Roosevelt Library; speech by Governor Smith, October 29, 1920, Box 22, Folder 255, AESPP; Al Smith to Franklin Roosevelt, November 8, 1920, Box 5, FDRB.

6. Robert Murray, *The 103rd Ballot* (New York: Harper and Row, 1976), pp. 68–70; *Political News* (May 1924): 12; photograph NPx78-129, Franklin D. Roosevelt Presidential Library.

7. Ward, *Temperament*, p. 767; Eleanor Roosevelt, *This I Remember* (New York: Harper & Brothers, 1949), pp. 39–40.

8. *New York Times*, October 18, 1928.

9. Samuel Rosenman, *Working with Roosevelt* (New York: Harper & Brothers, 1952), pp. 16–17; telegram from Louis Howe to Franklin Roosevelt, October 18, 1928, Louis Howe Papers, Box 40, Folder 3, Franklin D. Roosevelt Presidential Library.

10. See photo NPx65-312, Eleanor Roosevelt photo file, Franklin D. Roosevelt Presidential Library. This shows Katie Smith at Hyde Park, with, among others, Marion Dickerman, Caroline O'Day, and Anna Roosevelt. Emily Smith Warner to Eleanor Roosevelt, October 3, 1928, Folder 4, Box 6, Eleanor Roosevelt Papers, Franklin D. Roosevelt Presidential Library.

11. Joseph Proskauer interview, p. 23, CUOHC; Joseph Lash, *Eleanor and Franklin* (New York: Norton, 1971), pp. 322–23; Frank Freidel, *Franklin D. Roosevelt: A Rendezvous with Destiny* (Boston: Little, Brown, 1990), p. 51; Page Smith, *Redeeming the Time* (New York: Penguin Books, 1987), p. 319.

12. Blanche Cook, *Eleanor Roosevelt* (New York: Penguin Books, 1992), 1: 148; Marvin Jones interview, p. 450, CUOHC; Jordan Schwartz, *The New Dealers* (New York: Random House, 1993), p. 126; David Kennedy, *Freedom from Fear* (New York: Oxford University Press, 1999), p. 101.

13. Alfred E. Smith to Mrs. Franklin D. Roosevelt, November 8, 1924, Eleanor Roosevelt Papers, Folder 16, Box 3, Franklin D. Roosevelt Presidential Library; Alfred E. Smith to Joe Tumulty, November 8, 1924, Box 74, Joe Tumulty Papers, Library of Congress; George Graves to Silas Bent, Box 4, George Graves Papers, New York State Archives, Albany, New York; George Graves to Norman Mack, Box 1, NMP.

14. Herbert Lehman, FDR's successor as governor of New York State.

15. Allan Nevins, *Herbert Lehman and His Era* (New York: Charles Scribner's, 1963), p. 392.

16. Franklin Roosevelt to Robert Moses, July 20, 1925, Robert Moses Papers, New York Public Library; Franklin Roosevelt to Dr. Byron Stookey, August 12, 1924, Folder 1, Box 14, FDR24.

17. Quoted in Murray, *103rd Ballot*, p. 287.

18. Franklin Roosevelt to Abram Elkus, July 18, 1924, Folder 1, Box 10, FDR24.

19. Louis Howe to Joseph Wilson, October 19, 1926, Franklin Roosevelt to George Graves, c. November 1926, George Graves to Franklin Roosevelt, November 30, 1926, Franklin Roosevelt to Alfred E. Smith, December 30, 1927, Alfred E. Smith to Franklin Roosevelt, January 23, 1928, Folder, Franklin Roosevelt to Alfred E. Smith, January 30, 1928, Franklin Roosevelt to Alfred E. Smith (private correspondence), January 30, 1928, all in Folder 200–276, and Franklin Roosevelt to Alfred E. Smith, December 14, 1927, Folder 200–42, AESOP.

20. Alfred E. Smith to Franklin Roosevelt, February 3, 1928, Folder 200–276, AESOP.

21. This was the phrase my father always used when I was talking about things that I knew nothing about.

22. Franklin Roosevelt to Paul Sheehan, July 4, 1928, Box 9, Franklin D. Roosevelt to Charles Treman, Box 11, Franklin D. Roosevelt to J. Lionberger Davis, July 7, 1928, Box 6, FDR28; *New York Times*, August 26, September 14, 1928.

23. Burns, *Lion and Fox*, pp. 99–100; Roosevelt, *This I Remember*, p. 44.

24. Ed Flynn, *You're the Boss* (New York: Collier Books, 1947), pp. 82–83; Roosevelt, *This I Remember*, pp. 45–46.

25. FDR wryly noted later in life that while Raskob made good on $37,500 of that pledge, he still owed the president $12,500. James Farley, *Jim Farley's Story* (New York: McGraw-Hill, 1948), pp. 59–60.

26. Smith, *Redeeming the Time*, p. 272; Alfred Rollins, *Roosevelt and Howe* (New York: Knopf, 1962), pp. 233–235; Morgan, *FDR*, p. 290; Davis, *FDR: The New York Years*, p. 24; Nevins, *Herbert Lehman*, pp. 103–104.

27. Telegram from Eleanor Roosevelt to Franklin Roosevelt, October 2, 1928, Box 9, and Franklin Roosevelt to Frederic Delano, October 8, 1928, Box 10, FDR28; telegram from Breckinridge Long to Franklin Roosevelt, Box 89, Breckinridge Long Papers, Library of Congress.

28. The Farley memo is in Box 37, Private Files, JFP.

29. Interview with Ruth Proskauer Smith, July 10, 1995.

30. Roosevelt, *This I Remember*, p. 51.

31. *F.D.R.: His Personal Letters*, ed. Elliott Roosevelt (New York: Duell, Sloan and Pearce, 1950), 2:772; Freidel, *Franklin D. Roosevelt*, p. 52.

32. Sean Savage, *Roosevelt* (Lexington: University Press of Kentucky, 1991), p. 8.

33. Franklin Roosevelt to Alfred E. Smith, November 17, 1928, Folder 14, Box 24, Franklin D. Roosevelt Papers, Family Papers Donated by the Children, Franklin D. Roosevelt Presidential Library; *New York Times*, December 15, 1999; William Klingaman, *1929* (New York: Harper and Row, 1989), p. 45; Sean Cashman, *Prohibition* (New York: Macmillan, 1981), p. 200; Paula Eldot, *Governor Alfred E. Smith* (New York: Garland Press, 1983), p. 25; Davis, *FDR*, p. 65.

34. Lash, *Eleanor and Franklin*, p. 321; Frances Perkins interview, Book 3, p. 9, CUOHC.

35. Bernard Bellush, *Roosevelt as Governor* (New York: Columbia University Press, 1955), p. 3; Morgan, *FDR*, p. 297.

36. Telegram from Frederick Stuart Greene to Franklin Roosevelt, December 7, 1928, Franklin Greene Papers, Franklin D. Roosevelt Presidential Library.

37. Franklin Roosevelt to Frederick Stuart Greene, December 8, 1928, Frederick Stuart Greene Papers, Franklin D. Roosevelt Presidential Library.

38. Franklin Roosevelt to Al Smith, February 8, 1929, April 12, 1930, and June 18, 1920, all in Box 75, Franklin D. Roosevelt Papers, Governor of New York State Papers, Franklin D. Roosevelt Presidential Library; Franklin Roosevelt to Al Smith, November 10, 1931, Folder 9, Box 1, AESPP.

39. Al Smith to Eleanor Roosevelt, September 30, 1929, Folder 177, Box 7, AESPP; Franklin Roosevelt to Al Smith, February 4, 1929, and Al Smith to Franklin Roosevelt, undated, both in Box 75, Franklin D. Roosevelt Papers, Governor of New York State Papers, Franklin D. Roosevelt Presidential Library.

40. Alfred E. Smith to Douglas Robinson, December 30, 1928, Folder 200–455, AESOP; Alfred E. Smith to Franklin Roosevelt, September 11, 1929, Folder 14, Box 24, Roosevelt Family Papers, Donated by the Children, Franklin D. Roosevelt Presidential Library.

41. Frances Perkins interview, Book 3, pp. 33, 331, CUOHC; *New York Post*, February 1, 1936; Freidel, *Franklin D. Roosevelt*, p. 56; Cook, *Eleanor Roosevelt*, p. 387.

42. Freidel, *Franklin D. Roosevelt*, p. 56; Frances Perkins interview, Book 3, pp. 27, 63, and Book 2, pp. 718–719, CUOHC; Roosevelt, *This I Remember*, p. 50.

43. Nevins, *Lehman*, p. 107; Frances Perkins interview, Book 2, p. 720, CUOHC; Lash, *Eleanor and Franklin*, p. 325.

44. "What of the Democracy?" *Nation*, November 21, 1928, p. 536.

45. Interview with Alfred E. Smith IV; Robert Caro, *The Power Broker* (New York: Random House, 1974), p. 320; Julius Cohen, *They Builded Better Than They Knew* (New York: Julian Messner, 1946), p. 127.

46. Stiles, *The Man Behind Roosevelt*, pp. 126–127; Sister James Vlaun, "Alfred E. Smith and His Relationship With Franklin D. Roosevelt," M.A. thesis, St. Bonaventure University, 1968, p. 64.

47. Christopher Finan, "Fallen Hero," Ph.D. diss., Columbia University, 1992, p. 190.

48. The transcript of this speech appears in the *New York Times*, October 1, 1930.

49. Material on the 1932 campaign tour comes from Finan, "Fallen Hero," pp. 196–201.

50. George Martin, *Madame Secretary* (Boston: Houghton Mifflin, 1976), p. 217; Rosenman, *Working with Roosevelt*, p. 46; Finan, "Fallen Hero," p. 206.

51. Frances Perkins interview, Book 3, pp. 293–294, CUOHC.

CHAPTER 22. MR. SMITH DOES NOT GO TO WASHINGTON

1. *New York Times*, December 30, 1928; Alfred E. Smith to Norman Mack, May 27, 1929, Box 1, NMP.

2. *New York Times*, March 19, 1930.

3. Harold Ickes to Belle Moskowitz, March 15, 1932, Folder 562, Box 18, AESPP; Joseph Lasson to John Raskob, June 21, 1932, File 602, Box 12, JRP.

4. "What of the Democracy?" *Nation*, November 21, 1928, p. 536; Charles Michaelson, *The Ghost Talks* (New York: Putnam, 1944), pp. 133–134.

5. Earland Carlson, "Franklin D. Roosevelt's Post-Mortem of the 1928 Election," *Midwest Journal of Political Science* 8 (August 1964): 299–301.

6. Hollins Randolph to John W. Davis, October 5, 1928, Box 57, JWDP; Sean Savage, *Roosevelt* (Lexington: University Press of Kentucky, 1991), p. 104.

7. Memo in Box 37, Private Files, JFP; Burton Wheeler interview, p. 27, CUOHC.

8. "The New Raskobian Uproar," *Literary Digest,* April 25, 1931, p. 12; memo from John Raskob to Franklin Roosevelt, File 1989, JRP; "Mr. Raskob Proposes Chaos and Hypocrisy," *Christian Century,* December 2, 1931, p. 1511.

9. Wayne Williams, "What Will the Dry Democrats Do?" *Christian Century,* March 16, 1932, p. 354.

10. *New York Times,* March 4, 1931; Joseph Smith to John Raskob, December 6, 1928, Box 1, File 602, and Bruce Barton to John Raskob, April 14, 1932, File 602, Box 11, both in JRP; Sylvester Andriano to Francis Mancuso, April 9, 1932, Belle Moskowitz Papers, Connecticut College.

11. Press release, February 8, 1932, Folder 361, Box 14, AESPP.

12. Belle Moskowitz to Felix Frankfurter, Folder 567, Box 18, AESPP; interview with Anthony Smith, July 29, 1995.

13. Joseph Proskauer interview, p. 131, CUOHC; Herbert Swope to Alfred E. Smith, November 9, 1932, Folder 243, Box 11, AESPP.

14. Raymond Moley, *The First New Deal* (New York: Harcourt, Brace & World, 1966), p. 9; Kenneth Davis, *FDR: The New York Years* (New York: Random House, 1979), p. 261.

15. Table of preferential primaries, Box 37, Private Files, JFP; Frank Freidel, *Franklin D. Roosevelt* (Boston: Little, Brown, 1956), p. 281; Christopher Finan, "Fallen Hero," Ph.D. diss., Columbia University, 1992, p. 326.

16. Jack Beatty, *The Rascal King* (Reading, Mass.: Addison-Wesley, 1992), pp. 306–307; J. Joseph Huthmacher, *Massachusetts People and Politics* (New York: Atheneum, 1959), p. 237.

17. Freidel, *Roosevelt,* pp. 283, 287; Alfred Rollins, Jr., *Roosevelt and Howe* (New York: Knopf, 1962), p. 328.

18. Table of preferential primaries, Box 37, Private Files, JFP; Beatty, *King,* p. 308.

19. Mayors of Connecticut Cities to Alfred E. Smith, April 4, 1932, File 558, Box 18, Phillip Meighen to Smith, June 23, 1932, Folder 570, Box 18, letter from James Vance of the *Fellowship Forum,* February 1932, Folder 640, Box 21, Charles Dollie to Orie Kelly, May 16, 1932, Folder 242, Box 11, and telegram from Frank Donahue to P. M. Abbott, April 27, 1932, Folder 567, Box 18, all in AESPP.

20. Josef Israels to Alvin Romansky, April 22, 1932, Folder 585, Box 19, AESPP.

21. Material on Roosevelt's speech comes from Freidel, *FDR,* pp. 267–268, and Davis, *FDR,* pp. 272–273.

22. *New York Times,* January 9, 1932; "The Angry Warrior's Blast," *Literary Digest,* April 23, 1932, p. 11; Finan, "Fallen Hero," p. 367; "Demagogues and Plutagogues," *New Republic,* April 27, 1932, pp. 285–286.

23. "Mr. Smith and Mr. Roosevelt," *World Tomorrow* 15 (May 1932), 133; Freidel, *FDR,* p. 271.

24. H. L. Mencken, *Making a President* (New York: Knopf, 1932), p. 170; Walter Lippmann, *Interpretations,* ed. Allan Nevins (New York: Macmillan, 1932), pp. 272–275; Page Smith, *Redeeming the Tide* (New York: Penguin Books, 1987), p. 326.

25. George Van Schaick interview, pp. 26–27, CUOHC; Freidel, *FDR*, p. 237.

26. Interviews with Father Arthur Smith, June 28, 1996, and Walter Smith, December 17, 1996; Finan, "Fallen Hero," p. 404; *New York Times*, June 24, 1932; "Interview with Governor Alfred E. Smith, June 23, 1932," Folder 664, Box 22, AESPP.

27. *New York World-Telegram*, June 10, 1932; Freidel, *FDR*, p. 289; Empire State Building Scrapbooks, Vol. 14, ESBP; Henry Moskowitz to Norman Hapgood, June 20, 1932, Box 9, Norman and Elizabeth Hapgood Papers, Library of Congress.

28. Most of the details of the convention, including the quote on Barkley's speech, come from Morgan, *FDR* (New York: Simon and Schuster, 1985), p. 348. On Curley, see Beatty, *Rascal King*, p. 312.

29. Davis, *FDR*, p. 319; Freidel, *FDR*, pp. 302–303.

30. Tables on the first three ballots come from Freidel, *FDR*, p. 306.

31. The story of how Roosevelt secured Garner's support, the deals and events of that day, is among the most complex in the annals of American politics, and is still mildly shrouded in mystery because no one exactly took notes at some of these conversations. This account drew primarily on Freidel's and Davis's work, along with: Frank Freidel, *Franklin D. Roosevelt: A Rendezvous with Destiny* (Boston: Little, Brown, 1990), pp. 70–73; Michael Parrish, Anxious Decades (New York: Norton, 1992), p. 284; Robert McElvaine, *The Great Depression* (New York: Times Books, 1984), pp. 128–130; Emily Warner, *The Happy Warrior* (Garden City, N.Y.: Doubleday, 1956), p. 261.

32. Warner, *Happy Warrior*, p. 261.

33. Sean Cashman, *Prohibition* (New York: Free Press, 1981), p. 232; Mencken, *Making a President*, p. 163.

34. The riot is on display in footage provided to me by the A&E Network. James Gerard interview, pp. 85–86, CUOHC.

35. Samuel Rosenman, *Working with Roosevelt* (New York: Harper & Brothers, 1952), p. 75; Dorothy Rosenman interview, pp. 48–49, CUOHC; *New York Times*, July 4, 1932.

36. Finan, "Fallen Hero," p. 453; *F.D.R.: His Personal Letters*, ed. Elliott Roosevelt (New York: Duell, Sloan and Pearce, 1950), 1: 300.

37. The account of this meeting comes from the *New York Times*, October 5, 8, 1932, and James Farley, *Jim Farley's Story* (New York: McGraw-Hill, 1948), p. 29.

38. *New York Times*, October 25, 1928; speeches in Folder 354, Box 14, AESPP; "Governor Smith Comes Out for Smith," *Christian Century*, November 2, 1932, p. 1324.

39. Speeches in Folder 354, Box 14, AESPP.

40. James Farley, *Behind the Ballots* (New York: Harcourt, Brace, 1938), p. 186; Bess Furman, *Washington By-Line* (New York: Knopf, 1949), p. 148; *New York Times*, October 5, 1933, February 22, 1945.

CHAPTER 23. NADIR

1. William Leuchtenberg, *Franklin D. Roosevelt and the New Deal* (New York: Harper & Row, 1963), pp. 46–47; Empire State Building Scrapbooks, Vol. 14, ESBP.

2. *New York Times*, April 8, 1933; Empire State Building Scrapbooks, Vol. 14, ESBP.

3. Smith to John Raskob, March 8, April 9, 1935, Folder 249, Box 11, AESPP.

4. Elisabeth Perry, *Belle Moskowitz* (New York: Oxford University Press, 1987), pp. 215–216.

5. Oswald Garrison Villard, "Al Smith—Latest Phase," *American Mercury* 34 (February 1935): 145.

6. Frances Kunstling, "A Study in Defeat: Alfred E. Smith After 1928," M.A. thesis, University of North Carolina at Chapel Hill, 1968, pp. 101–103; "Al Smith Breaks with a Critic of Roosevelt," *Newsweek,* March 31, 1934, p. 28; Oswald Villard, "Al Smith—Latest Phase," *American Mercury* 34 (February 1935): 152; statement by Publisher Frank Tichenor in the October 1932 issue of *New Outlook.*

7. See the list of all of Smith's published works, including the *New Outlook* editorials, in Folder 620, Box 19, AESPP. In the Robert Moses Papers, New York Public Library, see Moses to Smith, July 9, 1931, Box 9, June 20, 1933, Box 134, and November 9, 1932, Box 191.

8. Press release, March 22, 1934, Folder 522, Box 18, AESPP. Smith wrote the following works: "I Have 7,000,000 Neighbors," *American Magazine* 116 (August 1933): 36–38, 90–92; "Work for a Sane Fourth," *Parent's Magazine* 10 (July 1935): 13; "Publicizing Leisure Time Facilities," *Recreation* 27 (January 1934): 451, 485–486.

9. Charles Thompson, "Al Smith's View of Government," *New York Times Book Review,* May 19, 1935, pp. 1, 14; memo from unnamed editor at Harper & Brothers, May 2, 1934, Folder 193, Box 7, and Smith to George Bye, June 27, 1935, Folder 247, Box 11, AESPP; Alfred E. Smith, *The Citizen and His Government* (New York: Harper & Brothers, 1935).

10. "The Right Turn," *New Outlook* 161 (April 1933): 9.

11. "Business Control," *New Outlook* 162 (July 1933): 9–10; "Sound Money" and "Civil Works," *New Outlook* 162 (December 1933): 9–11; telegram from Early to McIntyre, November 24, 1933, File 676, President's Personal File, Franklin D. Roosevelt Papers, Franklin D. Roosevelt Presidential Library.

12. "Business Control," *New Outlook* 162 (July 1933): 10; the scrapbook is in Folder 611, Box 20, AESPP.

13. Leona Becker, "Alfred E. Smith: A Personality Study of a Political Leader," M.A. thesis, University of Chicago, 1938, p. 180; Arthur Schlesinger, Jr., *The Politics of Upheaval* (Boston: Houghton Mifflin, 1960), p. 625; Jordan Schwarz, "Al Smith in the Thirties," *New York History* 45 (October 1964): 319.

14. Frederick Rudolph, "The American Liberty League, 1934–1940," *American Historical Review* 196 (1950): 19.

15. Quoted in Douglas Craig, *After Wilson* (Chapel Hill: University of North Carolina Press, 1992), p. 279.

16. Martin Fausold, *James J. Wadsworth, Jr.* (Syracuse: Syracuse University Press, 1975), p. 248; S. M. DuBrul to Donaldson Brown, June 19, 1934, File 61, Box 10, JRP.

17. John Raskob's original proposal, plus letters from Alfred M. Sloan, July 24, 1934, Jouett Shouse, July 25, 1934, and John W. Davis, August 8, 1934, are all in File 61, Box 10, JRP; *New York Times,* August 23, 1934.

18. The certificate of formation of the American Liberty League is in File 61, Box 10, JRP. The draft of the Liberty League pamphlet is in Folder 7, Box 9, Jouett Shouse Papers, University of Kentucky.

19. "Why You Should Join the Liberty League," and Haywood Scott to John Raskob, February 1, 1936, both in File 61, Box 11, JRP; Irénée Du Pont to G. D'Andelot Belin, September 8, 1934, Series A, Box 109, Irénée Du Pont Papers, Hagley Museum; President of E. I. Du Pont de Nemours to stockholders, April 8, 1932, Folder 45, Box 2, AESPP.

20. Fausold, *Wadsworth*, p. 249; "Big Businessmen Helped Pack Liberty League's War Chest," *Newsweek*, January 11, 1936, p. 13; Craig, *After Wilson*, p. 281; Democratic National Committee, "Who's Who in the American Liberty League," Folder 8, Box 9, Jouett Shouse Papers, University of Kentucky; Frank Freidel, *Roosevelt* (Boston: Little, Brown, 1990), p. 519.

21. William Stayton to Irénée Du Pont, December 31, 1935, Series J, Box 112, Irénée Du Pont Papers; John Raskob to Walter Chrysler, October 25, 1935, File 61, Box 11, JRP; interview with Ruth Proskauer Smith, July 27, 1995; Sister James Augustine Vlaun, "Alfred E. Smith and His Relationship with Franklin D. Roosevelt," M.A. thesis, St. Bonaventure University, 1968, p. 93.

22. "Report to the Executive Committee of the American Liberty League," Folder 8, Box 9, Jouett Shouse Papers, University of Kentucky; William Harbaugh, *Lawyer's Lawyer* (New York: Oxford University Press, 1973), p. 345; pamphlet titles come from the back of "Facts About the American Liberty League," File 61, Box 12, JRP; "56 Unofficial Judges," *Literary Digest*, August 31, 1935, p. 9; George Soule, "Liberty League Liberty," *New Republic*, September 9, 1936, p. 122.

23. Craig, *After Wilson*, p. 285; Robert Bendiner, *Just Around the Corner* (New York: Dutton, 1967), p. 60; Stuart Chase, "Ode to the Liberty League," *Nation*, November 27, 1935, p. 613; Sherman Minton, February 3, 1936, and Elmer Rice, February 4, 1936, to John Raskob, both in File 61, Box 11, JRP.

24. Mary Carr to John Raskob, July 18, 1931, and John Raskob to Alfred E. Smith, August 4, 1930, File 2112, JRP. Mencken is quoted in Richard O'Connor, *The First Hurrah* (New York: Putnam, 1970), p. 175.

25. Joseph Proskauer interview, p. 8, CUOHC; "Business Control," p. 10.

26. Breckenridge Long, handwritten diary, November 8, 1932, Box 4, Breckenridge Long Papers, Library of Congress.

27. For material on Smith's opposition to federal control of New York State water power, see Alfred E. Smith, "The Stake of the Public," *Survey*, March 1, 1924, pp. 574–576, and Julius Cohen, *They Builded Better Than They Knew* (New York: Julian Messner, 1946), pp. 330–332.

28. Interviews with Anthony Smith, July 29, 1995, Ruth Proskauer Smith, July 27, 1995, and Father Arthur Smith, June 28, 1996; Joseph Proskauer, *A Segment of My Times* (New York: Farrar, Straus, 1950), p. 70.

29. Otis Graham, *An Encore for Reform* (New York: Oxford University Press, 1967), pp. 192–193.

30. Speech by Alfred E. Smith, April 13, 1932, Folder 352, Box 14, AESPP; Richard Magurno, "Franklin D. Roosevelt and Alfred E. Smith: Their Alliance and Their Feud," M.A. thesis, University of Wisconsin, 1965, p. 123.

31. Emily Warner, *The Happy Warrior* (Garden City, N.Y.: Doubleday, 1956), p. 286; Tugwell is quoted in Kunstling, "A Study in Defeat," pp. 64–65.

32. Claude Bowers, *My Life* (New York: Simon & Schuster, 1962), pp. 206–207.

33. Heywood Broun, "Broun's Page," *Nation*, October 10, 1936, p. 421.

34. *New York Times*, January 5, 26, 1936; Christopher Finan, "Fallen Hero," Ph.D. diss., Columbia University, 1992, pp. 5, 411; James Farley to Claude Bowers, March 16, 1936, Claude Bowers Papers, Indiana University.

35. Harold Ickes, *The Secret Diary of Harold L. Ickes* (New York: Simon & Schuster, 1954), pp. 516, 525, 526.

36. *New York Times,* January 24, 27, 1936.

37. Joseph Lash, *Eleanor and Franklin* (New York: Norton, 1971), p. 320.

38. The exchange of letters between Eleanor Roosevelt and Alfred E. Smith between December 18, 1935, and January 5, 1936, is in Box 1404, Eleanor Roosevelt Papers, Franklin D. Roosevelt Presidential Library. See also George Wolfskill, *The Revolt of the Conservatives* (Boston: Houghton Mifflin, 1962), p. 143, and Vlaun, "Smith," pp. 87–88.

39. Frederick Harvey to Jouett Shouse, February 4, 1936, Folder 11, Box 3, Jouett Shouse Papers, University of Kentucky. There is a copy of the program, which lists the dinner speakers, in Folder 8, Box 9 of the same collection; and the place card announcing time, place, and menu is in Series J, Box 112 of the Irénée Du Pont Papers, Hagley Museum.

40. Alfred E. Smith, *The Facts in the Case* (Washington, D.C.: American Liberty League, January 25, 1936), pp. 13, 14, 18–19.

41. All popular responses to the speech are from File 1925, Franklin D. Roosevelt Papers, President's Official File, Franklin D. Roosevelt Presidential Library; see also *New York Times,* February 7, 1936.

42. "Al Smith's Ghost," p. 144, and Paul Ward, "Washington Weekly," p. 153, both in *Nation,* February 5, 1936; Villard, "Al Smith—Latest Phase," p. 149.

43. Marvin Jones interview, p. 444, CUOHC; Blanche Cook, *Eleanor Roosevelt* (New York: Penguin Books, 1991), pp. 448–449; James Michael Curley, *I'd Do It Again* (Englewood Cliffs, N.J.: Prentice-Hall, 1957), p. 231.

44. Interview with Simon Rifkind, June 27, 1994; Herbert Swope to Alfred E. Smith, November 9, 1932, Folder 243, Box 11, AESPP.

45. Interview with Governor Hugh Carey, June 21, 1994.

CHAPTER 24. ELDER STATESMAN

1. *New York Times,* March 28, 1933; telegram from Rabbi Stephen Wise to Alfred Smith, July 17, 1937, Anne and John Cadigan Papers.

2. Alfred E. Smith, "Hitler and the Constitution," *New Outlook* 161 (June 1933): 9–10; *New York Times,* September 11, 1933, March 8, 1934; Alfred E. Smith, "Speech to the Friendly Sons of St. Patrick," March 17, 1939, Folder 454, Box 15, AESPP.

3. This section of the speech was transcribed from "Perspective on Greatness: The Man from Oliver Street," Hearst Metrotone Production, made available by the A&E Network.

4. Emily Smith Warner interview, p. 110, CUOHC; the Lincoln University speech is in Folder 438, Box 15, AESPP; *New York Times,* July 13, 1941.

5. The speech on Kristallnacht is in Folder 716, Box 23, AESPP.

6. *New York Times,* October 2, 1939; Martin Feldman, "The Political Thought of Alfred E. Smith," Ph.D. diss., New York University, 1963, p. 225; telegram from Franklin Roosevelt to Alfred E. Smith, October 1, 1939, File 676, Franklin D. Roosevelt Papers, President's Personal File, Franklin D. Roosevelt Presidential Library; *F.D.R.: His Personal Papers,* ed. Elliott Roosevelt (New York: Duell, Sloan and Pearce, 1950), 2: 932.

7. *New York Times,* January 11, 1941; Irénée Du Pont to Pierre Du Pont, January 25, 1940, Box 113, Series A, Irénée Du Pont Papers, Hagley Museum; speech to the Anti-Nazi League, November 11, 1938, Folder 202, Box 8, AESPP.

8. Interviews with Walter Smith, December 17, 1996, Father Arthur Smith, June 28, 1996, and Alfred E. Smith IV, August 3, 1994.

9. Interviews with Walter Smith, December 17, 1996, John Coleman, Jr., August 4, 1993, and Alfred E. Smith IV, August 3, 1994.

10. Interviews with Father Arthur Smith, June 28, 1996, and Walter Smith, December 17, 1996.

11. Interviews with Anne Smith Cadigan, June 21, 1996, and Father Arthur Smith, June 28, 1996.

12. Interviews with Father Arthur Smith, June 28, 1996, and Anne Smith Cadigan, June 21, 1996.

13. The account of the Central Park Zoo comes from Robert Caro, *The Power Broker* (New York: Random House, 1974), pp. 380–383; Thomas Kessner, *Fiorello H. LaGuardia and the Making of Modern New York* (New York: Penguin Books, 1989), pp. 318–319; *New York Times*, December 3, 1934.

14. Caro, *Power Broker*, pp. 382–383; Richard O'Connor, *The First Hurrah* (New York: Putnam, 1970), p. 287.

15. Robert Moses to Alfred E. Smith, February 15, 1935, Folder 249, Box 11, AESPP; Frank Graham, *Al Smith—American* (New York: Putnam, 1945), p. 226; Caro, *Power Broker*, p. 382.

16. Interviews with Anne Smith Cadigan, June 21, 1996, Walter Smith, December 17, 1996, and Alfred E. Smith IV, August 3, 1994.

17. *New York Times*, September 28, 1934.

18. Caro, *Power Broker*, p. 383; interview with John Coleman, Jr., August 4, 1993.

19. The letter appears in Folder 247, Box 11, AESPP.

20. Mary Carr to Father Leo Anderton, May 2, 1935, Folder 247, Box 11, AESPP.

21. "Warrior to War," *Time*, February 3, 1936, p. 14; James Farley, *Jim Farley's Story* (New York: McGraw-Hill, 1948), p. 148; Alfred E. Smith to Walter Lippmann, May 13, 1936, Series A, Folder 1960, Box 102, WLP; "Who's Who in the American Liberty League," Folder 8, Box 9, Jouett Shouse Papers, University of Kentucky.

22. Interview with Father Arthur Smith, June 28, 1996.

23. The account of the Smith-Roosevelt meeting is drawn from *New York Times*, June 10, 1941; George Martin, *Madame Secretary* (Boston: Houghton Mifflin, 1976), p. 397; Grace Tully, *F.D.R.: My Boss* (New York: Scribner's, 1949), pp. 58–59.

24. This story was related to me in an interview with John Coleman, Jr., August 4, 1993. The date is pinpointed in Smith's 1944 calendar, Item 45.117.107, ASPNY.

25. Interview with Father Arthur Smith, June 28, 1996.

26. Details on Katie Smith's death come from *New York Times*, May 5, 1944; Catherine Smith death certificate; Mary Carr to Joseph Israels, May 3, and 9, 1944, Belle Moskowitz Papers, Connecticut College; interview with Father Arthur Smith, June 28, 1996.

27. Mary Carr to Josef Israels, May 3, 1944, Belle Moskowitz Papers, Connecticut College; Marion Dickerman interview, pp. 281–282, CUOHC; interview with Father Arthur Smith, June 28, 1996.

28. *New York Times*, May 9, 1944; interviews with Walter Smith, December 17, 1996, and Father Arthur Smith, June 28, 1996.

29. Eleanor Roosevelt to Al Smith, May 5, 1944, Anne and John Cadigan Papers.

30. Telegram from Franklin Roosevelt to Alfred E. Smith, May 4, 1944, and Smith to Roosevelt, May 22, 1944, both in File 676, President's Personal File, Franklin D. Roosevelt Papers, Franklin D. Roosevelt Presidential Library; interview with Father Arthur Smith, June 28, 1996.

31. *New York Times*, May 5, 1944; interview with John Coleman, Jr., August 4, 1993.

32. Sister Marie De Lourdes Walsh, *With a Great Heart* (New York: St. Vincent's Hospital, 1965), p. 121; telegram from Franklin Roosevelt to Alfred E. Smith, September 13, 1944, File 676, President's Personal File, Franklin D. Roosevelt Papers, Franklin D. Roosevelt Presidential Library.

33. Interviews with John Coleman, Jr., August 4, 1993, and Father Arthur Smith, June 28, 1996; *New York Times*, October 4, 5, 1944; Oscar Handlin, *Al Smith and His America* (Boston: Little, Brown, 1958), p. 185.

34. *New York Times*, October 4, 1944; interview with Father Arthur Smith, June 28, 1996.

35. *New York Times*, October 5, 7, 8, 1944; interview with Father Arthur Smith, June 28, 1996. "The Happy Warrior," *Time*, October 16, 1944, pp. 25–26.

36. "Statement by the President," October 4, 1944, File 676, President's Personal File, Franklin D. Roosevelt Papers, Franklin D. Roosevelt Presidential Library.

37. Emily Warner to Franklin Roosevelt, December 20, 1944, File 676, President's Personal File, Franklin D. Roosevelt Papers, Franklin D. Roosevelt Presidential Library; *New York Times*, November 11, 1944; St. James Parish, *One-Hundred Fiftieth Anniversary Book* (New York: Park Publishing, 1977), p. 24; documents on the Alfred E. Smith Memorial are in Box 57, JFP, and in the Nicholas Murray Butler Papers at Columbia University.

38. Kennedy is quoted in Robert Wagner, Jr.'s speech at the 1964 Al Smith Dinner, which is in the Robert Wagner, Jr., Papers, Wagner-LaGuardia College.

39. Frances Perkins interview, Book 2, p. 643, CUOHC.

Acknowledgments

DOING A BIOGRAPHY of a New York politician while teaching in California is easy; all it takes is lots of time and money. These were provided by a number of sources, to whom I am most grateful; truly, this work could not have been accomplished without their support.

Foremost of these is Chapman University. The school awarded me a number of grants, as well as a semester-long sabbatical to finish up research. In particular, I thank President James Doti, Provost Harry Hamilton, and Vice Provost Barbara Mulch, administrators who backed this project throughout and did it, not only with words and smiles, but with real financial help.

In addition, I received the Arnold L. and Lois S. Graves Award for 1991–1993, and a timely grant from the American Philosophical Society.

But doing a biography of Al Smith takes even more. Robert Moses, who loved Smith, once wrote that "it is too bad . . . that Al Smith was not more of a writer." Moses explained that the governor he served so faithfully had a remarkable memory and a great gift for argument and debate, but he "left little in the way of letters other than official documents." He concluded, "You cannot reconstruct and animate the man from such thin records. The personality somehow evades the pen, the brush, the chisel."

Moses was accurate as well as insightful in his comments; Smith left a meager paper trail, with no vast collection of letters such as that which surrounds, for example, Franklin or Eleanor Roosevelt. And for all his flamboyance, Al Smith remained a reticent man when it came to matters of the heart, to the ideas, the feelings, the visions that moved him.

As a result, any historian tackling this subject needs a lot of other kinds of help as he tries to tease out the elements of his story, as he attempts to shape a portrait. I have benefited from the assistance of a legion of librarians, the custodians of hundreds of manuscript collections all over the United States. These experts saved me countless hours of work, simply by sharing their knowledge and by pointing me in the right direction. I can honestly say that I met at least one such individual at every library I worked at.

Nevertheless, certain persons, both in research institutions and in other walks of life, stand out as having provided something more. The largest collections of materials by and related to Alfred E. Smith are in the New York State Library and the New York State Archives in Albany. The staff at both these places have been amazingly helpful, showing me new and undiscovered sources, providing answers, and then replying to countless questions via telephone, mail, and e-mail for too many years. At the library I worked with Billie Aul, Paul Mercer, and James Corsaro; and at the archives there were James Folts, Roger Ritzmann, and William Gorman.

I would also like to acknowledge the following librarians and archivists: Bruce Abrams, archivist, New York County Clerk, Division of Old Records; Andrea Cantrell, Special Collections, University of Arkansas, Fayetteville; Michael Kelly, Special Collections, Wichita State University; Carol Lockman and Roger Horowitz of the Hagley Museum and Library; David Ment and Bette Weneck, Special Collections, Teachers College Library, Columbia University; Dale Meyer, Dwight Miller, Wade Slinde, and Pat Wildenberg, Herbert Hoover Presidential Library; Stephen Saks, New York Public Library Map Room; and Richard Strassberg, School of Industrial Relations, Cornell University.

Others who provided special help include Father Perry Kavookjian of the Diocese of Fresno, Ed Muehl, and Emily Wray at the St. James Rectory. Christopher Elkus was kind enough to provide sections of his grandfather's unpublished manuscript; Richard Lord took me on a wonderful tour of the Fulton Fish Market; and there was also my cousin, Stan Rogosin, and his wife, Eileen, who became lifesavers when my car broke down three thousand miles from home. Dave and Sue Gordon put me up in Boston, and Chair Leland Estes and the inimitable Sharon Gregg saw to it that the Chapman University Social Sciences Division provided solid backing for this project. A number of individuals graciously consented to being interviewed for this book, providing wonderful knowledge unavailable anywhere else.

I also received another invaluable kind of assistance, as the following individuals all read parts of this manuscript, always making it a better work: Jay Dolan, Paula Eldot, Irwin Gellman, James Grossman, Dominic Pacyga, Elisabeth Perry, and Rita Slayton. Charles Morris was particularly giving of his time, and helped to shape this book in countless ways.

I gained enormously, as well, from being a member of the Los Angeles Social History Study Group, one of the smartest but also most congenial groups of scholars in the nation; my thanks go to Hal Barron, Clark Davis, Nancy Fitch, John Laslett, Frank Stricker, Tom Zakim, and Leila Zenderland. Above all, it is hard to express my appreciation to Steven Ross, who tackled the bulk of an enormous manuscript and delivered nothing but sound advice.

Finally, there are some individuals whose contribution has been so extraordinary, it is difficult to sum up my thanks in a brief statement. The few words that follow are, for me, small acknowledgment for all that they have done.

To be blunt, this work would never have been published by a commercial press if not for two people. My agent, Susan Rabiner, and my editor, Bruce Nichols, saw something in the story of Al Smith that others missed, and singlehandedly made sure that this book would appear in its current form. It is extremely hard for me to express my gratitude for their vision and their confidence in me; this appreciation must inadequately perform that task. Bruce Nichols also did a brilliant job of editing, assisted throughout by the talented Daniel Freedberg. Edith Lewis carefully and gracefully made sure the copyediting was successful.

Chapman University has a minuscule library; it was able to function primarily because of the talents and skills of an exceptional individual who served as its director while I researched this book, Mary Sellen. To say that Mary supported this project is sheer understatement; what I needed she got for me, because she believed in this book with her heart and her head. In part, what she did was hire and turn loose Gina Wilkinson, the best InterLibrary Loan specialist around; Gina has not only filed *a lot* of ILL requests (in the four figures range), but she has managed to track down the most obscure items in the most hidden parts of the library system of the United States.

In Washington, D.C., Phyllis Dobin and Alan Luehrmann, friends old and new, were always there for me. They put me up, weathered crises with me, and just made my life better.

Alfred E. Smith IV never even thought to look at the manuscript; he just asked how he could help. Another set of Smith descendants, John and Connie Cadigan, also provided endless amounts of assistance and support.

James Nau has been my dearest friend for close to a third of a century. He provided my New York base, putting me up for weeks, and even months, at a time, disregarding the realities of a small studio apartment. Between 1991 and 1996 I spent the equivalent of a full year camped out on his floor. And he was always glad to have me. It is a relationship that still astonishes me, a friendship that I supremely treasure.

And there was one other. Maybe because of the fact that I work in and teach history, I am aware of how time's passage can affect all of us. I have been married to Rita LaVerde Slayton for many years, through rain and Chicago snow, in smog and in Orange County sunshine. When I think back on who I was, who she was, on our wedding day, I realize how much time has meant, and that I love her more than ever.

Index